Ageing, Gender and Family Law

This book explores the intersecting issues relating the phenomenon of ageing to gender and family law. The latter has tended to focus mainly on family life in young and middle age; and, indeed, the issues of childhood and parenting are key in many family law texts. Family life for older members has, then, been largely neglected; addressing this neglect, the current volume explores how the issues which might be important for younger people are not necessarily the same as those for older people. The significance of family, the nature of family life, and the understanding of self in terms of one's relationships, tend to change over the life course. For example, the state may play an increasing role in the lives of older people – as access to services, involvement in work and the community, the ability to live independently, and to form or maintain caring relationships, are all impacted by law and policy. This collection therefore challenges the standard models of family life and family law that have been developed within a child/parent-centred paradigm, and which may require rethinking in the turn to family life in old age. Interdisciplinary in its scope and orientation, this book will appeal not just to academic family lawyers and students interested in issues around family law, ageing, gender, and care; but also to sociologists and ethicists working in these areas.

Beverley Clough is a Lecturer in Law at the University of Leeds, UK.

Jonathan Herring is Professor of Law at the University of Oxford, UK.

Contents

Ageing, Gender and Family Law

Edited by
Beverley Clough and Jonathan Herring

Routledge
Taylor & Francis Group
LONDON AND NEW YORK

First published 2018
by Routledge

2 Park Square, Milton Park, Abingdon, Oxfordshire OX14 4RN
52 Vanderbilt Avenue, New York, NY 10017

A GlassHouse book

Routledge is an imprint of the Taylor & Francis Group, an informa business

First issued in paperback 2019

British Library Cataloguing in Publication Data
A catalogue record for this book is available from the British Library

Library of Congress Cataloging in Publication Data
Names: Clough, Beverley, editor. | Herring, Jonathan, editor.
Title: Ageing, gender and family law / edited by Beverley Clough, Jonathan Herring.
Description: New York, NY : Routledge, 2018. | Includes bibliographical references and index.
Identifiers: LCCN 2017048423 | ISBN 9781138744943 (hbk)
Subjects: LCSH: Older people--Legal status, laws, etc.--Great Britain. | Women--Legal status, laws, etc.--Great Britain. | Domestic relations--Great Britain.
Classification: LCC KD665.A43 A34 2018 | DDC 346.4101/5--dc23
LC record available at https://lccn.loc.gov/2017048423

ISBN: 978-1-138-74494-3 (hbk)
ISBN: 978-0-367-40443-7 (pbk)

Typeset in Galliard
by Taylor & Francis Books

Contributors

Daniel Bedford is a Senior Lecturer in Law at University of Portsmouth. His research is largely focused on the theory and practice of human rights and engages with judicial use of human dignity as an argument in enhancing the protection of the human rights of the vulnerable subject. He is currently exploring the connection between dignity and care, especially in relation to implications for social care law.

Alison Brammer is Head of School at The School of Law, Keele University. Her primary research interests relate to the interplay between law and social work practice – a theme which is fully explored in her books (*Critical Issues in Social Work Law* (Palgrave Macmillan, 2017; ed. with J. Boylan); *Social Work Law*, 5th Edition (2015, Pearson) and *Safeguarding Adults* (Palgrave Macmillan, 2014)). She is interested in two particular aspects of that interplay, the law relating to child care law and practice and the law relating to adult safeguarding, as well as the comparisons between both areas of practice. She has a longstanding interest in the application of law to the relatively recently recognised phenomena of adult abuse, whether this is located in a private or institutional setting.

Beverley Clough is a Lecturer in Law & Social Justice at the University of Leeds. Her research focuses on mental capacity law, social care and healthcare law, engaging with feminist legal theory, care ethics, and critical disability studies.

Jennifer Collins is Lecturer in Law at the University of Bristol. Her research interests include criminal law, criminal justice, human rights law, and labour standards. She has written on property offences, defences, and the state's obligations to protect the vulnerable using criminal law. Jennifer's current research focuses on the implications of criminalisation in the labour market.

Pip Coore is a PhD candidate at the University of Oxford and was awarded the Oxford Law Faculty's Family Law Scholarship. Pip's research interests are mainly in the field of elder law, family law, and succession law, particularly within England and Australia. Pip worked as a Senior Associate to the Honourable Justice Edelman in the High Court of Australia.

Susan Easton is Professor of Law at Brunel Law School, a barrister and the editor of the *International Journal of Discrimination and the Law*. She specialises in prisoners' rights and is the author of *Prisoners' Rights: Principles and Practice* and *The Politics of the Prison and the Prisoner: Zoon Politikon*, also to be published by Routledge in 2018, and co-author of *Sentencing and Punishment: The Quest for Justice*.

Jonathan Herring is a Professor of Law at the University of Oxford. His research spans medical law, family law, criminal law, and law relating to care. His current research focuses on relationality, personhood, and vulnerability, particularly in the context of care and older people.

Felicity Kaganas is a Professor of Law at Brunel University. She teaches Family Law and Children and the Law and has published widely in these fields. She is joint author, with Alison Diduck, of *Family Law, Gender and the State* (Hart Publishing), now in its Third Edition.

Liz Lloyd is Professor of Social Gerontology in the School for Policy Studies at the University of Bristol and a Senior Research Fellow at the NIHR School for Social Care Research. Liz's research and publications have focused on health and social care policies and practices related to ageing as well as on older people's experiences of support and care. She continues to pursue a long-standing interest in developing the links between gerontological theory and feminist perspectives on care.

Daniel Monk is Professor of Law at Birkbeck, University of London. Adopting a variety of socio-legal methods his research has examined a wide range of issues about children, families, education, and sexuality.

Christine Piper is an Emeritus Professor in Brunel Law School and a Fellow of the Academy of Social Sciences. Her research interests have focused on family law, sentencing and, more recently, eighteenth-century rural industries. Her books include *Investing in Children* (2008, Routledge) (with S. Easton), *Sentencing and Punishment: The Quest for Justice*, 4th Edition (2016, OUP) and (with M. King) *How the Law Thinks About Children*, 2nd Edition (1995, Ashgate).

Laura Pritchard-Jones is a Lecturer in Law at Keele University. Her research interests lie in both the doctrinal and theoretical aspects to social welfare, adult safeguarding, and mental disability law, and particularly how they operate in relation to older people.

Ann Stewart is Professor of Law at University of Warwick Law School and specialises in the area of gender and the law, particularly in the context of international development with a focus on southern and eastern Africa and in South Asia. Areas of particular interest are caring, care/body work in relation to older people within the UK and within East Africa.

Rachel Taylor is Associate Professor of Law at the University of Oxford and Fellow of Law at Exeter College Oxford. She has written widely on issues around children's rights, with a particular interest in issues concerning religion.

Sue Westwood is a socio-legal and social gerontology scholar. Her research interests cohere around ageing, diversity, and equality, particularly in health and social care contexts, and in relation to the regulation of the end of life. She is currently working on a new edited collection, *Ageing, Diversity & Equality*, also to be published by Routledge in 2018.

Introduction

Family law textbooks present one image of typical family life: partnership; parenthood; divorce. The cases discussed are those of couples wanting to create a child; disputing the upbringing of their children; or seeking a division of their assets. Those walking the streets of family law textbooks are children, young adults and the middle aged. Older people rarely appear, save perhaps in a small section on grandparents. For them much of what appears in the standard textbooks is irrelevant. Even when an attempt is made to include a chapter on older people the themes presented are bound by stereotypes of old age: it's all about inheritance; loss of capacity; and the need for care.[1] The day-to-day lives of older people seems to escape family law.

This book seeks to explore family law for older people. We believe this is not simply a matter of discovering 'older family law'. Rather an understanding of what family life is about for older people throws considerable light on what family life should be about for everyone. Gender plays a major theme in this book. Feminism has historically rather overlooked older people and focused attention on issues impacting younger women. Recently this has been an upsurge in interest among feminists in old age and we welcome this and seek to use this in this collection. Again, the issue is not simply one of discovering 'feminist gerontology' but exploring how feminist insights into old age reveal much about the lives of women and the impact of patriarchy generally.

Old age

Many regard ageing as one of the great issues of the day. The media are keen to report considerable concern at the 'surge' in the number of older people.[2] However, there is little agreement about who these dangerous 'older people' are. One possibility is to select a particular age at which one becomes an 'older people'. For example, the World Health Organisation uses the age of 60 (Brandl and Meuer 2001). Opponents of such an approach object that setting a particular age at which a person becomes old, would be arbitrary. Among people of any given age there will be a huge variation in health, lifestyle, appearance etc. For example, in 2008 Omkari Panwar, a 70-year-old woman, in India gave birth (Rees et al 2010).

It would be difficult to say anything that would be true for all those of a particular age, except something about their birthdays. More importantly Helen Small notes 'The age we feel is not necessarily the same as our calendrical age, nor is it the same as how we are perceived, or how we register ourselves being perceived by others' (Small 2007, 3). So our chronological age is only one aspect of what it is to experience age personally and in our society.

Supporters of an age-based definition of old age might reply that inevitably the law has to use generalisations, even if that means that some people are unfairly categorised. We do this with children for example. Children under 17 are not allowed to drive, even though there may well be some under-17s who would have the necessary skills (Herring 2003). But this raises the issue of why it is we want to use the category of older people in the law. Is it to mark out a category of people who are particularly vulnerable, or upon whom it is justifiable to place certain obligations? While generally speaking those under 16 are not able to make complex competent decisions, it is not clear whether we could make any generalisation of any kind about older people (Fries 1980).

Another alternative would be to define 'older people' as those who have reached the age when a state pension becomes payable. This would be the age at which the state would have indicated that they could be expected to stop work and undertake retirement. The benefits of this approach would be that there would be a clear definition of the category. Further it would link the definition of old age to being a pensioner which itself is linked with the problems of poverty, vulnerability, and social exclusion. These are the very reasons why the category of older people might be of interest to politicians, lawyers, and academics. The difficulty with this definition is that it is increasingly outdated. The notion of retirement is undergoing a major rethink. Indeed, it is become increasingly rare for there to be a particular point in time when a person stops full time work and starts retirement.

A third approach would be to argue that someone is an 'older people' if they are perceived to be an older person by society. This would capture the argument that old age is essentially a social construct and while there is no consistency in the actual characteristics of older people, there is among those they are thought to have based on ageist assumptions. The disadvantage of this approach is that it does not provide a very clear cut definition of old age for older purposes. However, the concept is not unknown to the law as the Employment Equality (Age) Regulations 2006 protects people from being discriminated against on the basis of the age or 'apparent age' Rees et al 2010).

It may be that all three of these approaches to defining old age have something to be said for them, depending on the purpose to which the term is being put. If we are seeking to combat or explore ageism it seems sensible to rely on the perception approach. If we are looking at issues around poverty and intergenerational economic equality, the retirement age may be more sensible. There may be medical purposes for which the biological age is most appropriate. And so forth.

Whichever approach is taken it is important to understand ageing as a narrative (Baars 2012). An older person is not a static entity. Their ageing take place in the context of a life course, which will have a central impact on their current state. That is a major theme in this book. Old age is not a static entity either from the perspective of the individual, nor from society. Indeed, Simon Biggs (2005) describes 'a climate of considerable cultural confusion' on age as life course categories become indistinct (Featherstone and Hepworth, 1995). One response is to increase our divisions of age categories to introduce a 'fourth age' of ageing.

These arguments are played out in debates over whether or not there should be a field of study called 'elder law' or some similar title. It is notable that in other jurisdictions, in particular the USA, elder law is a well acknowledged area of academic study, with courses and textbooks in the area. Indeed, there is even a 'Nutshells in Elder Law' (Frolik and Kaplan 2014) the ultimate indica that a subject has entered the legal academy!

The case against studying 'elder law' is that doing so will perpetuate, rather than redress ageism (Kapp 2005). Indeed the fact that as studied in the States it commonly covers issues around 'estate planning', nursing care, and medical costs may be seen to perpetuate the idea older people are frail and facing imminent death. Age, it might be said, is an utterly arbitrary factor to use as category of legal study (Brandl and Meuer 2001). Mike Brogdon and Preeti Nijhar (2000, 151) argue that 'There are few collective characteristics that clearly mark out elderly people from younger people'. Indeed it might be thought that there are greater differences among those over 70 that any other age group (Settersten 2005, 8). It would make far more sense to consider the law and people lacking in competence; or the law and those living in institutional settings, rather than the law and older people.

The law can reflect and reinforce, both directly and indirectly ageist attitudes (Kohli 2005, 427). Robert Butler claims that ageism is manifested through:

> stereotypes and myths, outright disdain and dislike, or simply subtle avoidance of contact; discriminatory practices in housing, employment and services of all kinds; epithets, cartoons and jokes. At times ageism becomes an expedient method by which society promotes viewpoints about the aged in order to relieve itself from the responsibility towards them, and at other times ageism serves a highly personal objective, protecting younger (usually middle-aged) individuals – often at high emotional cost – from thinking about things they fear (aging, illness and death).
> (1995)

The response to ageism is carried. Some seek to challenge the assumptions about old age and argue that older people can be 'as young' as older people. Others argue that old age should be celebrated. Molly Andrews (1999) is concerned that promoting agelessness would deprive older people of one of the 'hard earned resources: their age'. Betty Friedan has written:

> How long, and how well, can we really live by trying to pass as young? By the fourth face-lift (or third?) we begin to look grotesque, no longer human. Obsessed with stopping age, passing as young … Seeing age only as decline

> from youth, we make age itself the problem and never face the real problems that keep us from evolving and leading continually useful, vital, and productive lives. Accepting that dire mystique of age for others, even as we deny it for ourselves, we ultimately create or reinforce the conditions of our own dependence, powerlessness, isolation, even senility.
>
> (1993, 25–6)

Molly Andrews argues that old age should be regarded as like any other stage of life. It has real challenges and difficulties which should be acknowledged. But it carries benefits too and these would be lost if the 'agelessness' model were lost. Old age should not be regarded as the absence of youth abut rather as she sees it 'the project of a lifetime'.

Others emphasise the importance of acknowledging the bodily impact of age. Toni Calasanti and Kathleen Slevin write:

> Age categories have real consequences, and bodies – old bodies – matter. They have a material reality along with their social interpretation. Old people are not, in fact, just like middle-aged persons but only older. They are different. And as is the case with other forms of oppression, we must acknowledge and accept these differences, even seen them as valuable.
>
> (2006, 3)

The argument is that although there are prejudices about old age and unfair assumptions are made; that should not be used to disguise the fact that for most people old age is different from other stages in life. These differences must be recognised and treasured.

The intersection of age and race and sex

It is crucial, when discussing ageism to consider it in the context of sex and race (Walker and Northmore 2006) and indeed other forms of power within society (Ward and Bytheway 2008), such as discrimination on the basis of sexual orientation (Kimmel et al 2006; Heaphy et al 2004) or disability (Sargenat 2005). It is often said, for example, that a woman's attractiveness is judged against an extremely youthful ideal (Sontag 1978). While men are commonly said to be attractive even while showing signs of ageing a woman's attractiveness requires removal of visible signs of ageing. Lynda Aitken and Gabriele Griffin write of attitudes towards older women:

> They have outlived their status as sex objects and their usefulness as child-bearers, and are to some extent freer from direct male control than younger women in whom males still have vested interests. One might argue that the patronizing attitudes frequently displayed towards older women are one means of social control of these women's behaviour, exerted because they have this greater degree of freedom.
>
> (1996, 63)

The impact of aging on masculinities raises interesting issues too:

> The men pictured in the anti-aging advertisements drive themselves into expensive and strenuous fun, translating the achievement orientation of the labor market into those of recreational consumption. Banned from the competition for salaries and promotions, they struggle for status by spending the wealth and strength they have to play as young men do in their attempts to appear as vigorous as possible.
>
> (Calasanti and Slevin 2006, 4)[3]

Older people in family law

As already mentioned, family law seems dominated by the young and the middle aged. Apart from a section on grandparents, older people play little role. Family life is centred around the production and raising of children. Interestingly debates about marriage seem to focus on the claims around the need to produce a stable structure for a relationships or a device to enable courts to regulate the end of the relationship; the role and nature of intimate relationships towards the end of life gets little look in.

In part the issue is a more general focus in family law on conjugal couples, biological relationships, which leave friendship and close relationships outside the scope of regulation. Yet more generally in life, and perhaps particularly in old age, close friends play a key role (Westwood 2013).

With these issues in mind – the difficulties with categorising old age, and the intersecting subject positions that impact upon experience of ageing – it is important to note that the collection does not seek to reinforce or define the category. The collection seeks instead to highlight and open up the centrality of ageing in family law in order to enable a rethinking of the central tenets and boundaries of the field through this.

Care vulnerability and age

Daniel Bedford's chapter explores the assumptions that older people are particularly vulnerable. As they note this is normally regarded as a failing, which successful ageing avoids or at least postpones. Vulnerability is seen as a mark of weakness and a harm. Daniel argues the opposite: we should recognise the positive in vulnerability. He notes that the perception vulnerability is something to be avoided creates a fear of it and a wish to ignore or deny it. He argues that it 'enables positive affectability and makes possible positive forms of connection, engagement and functioning. It is the basis of change and transformation'. (p. 116) Looking at cases in the Court of Protection, he explores how understanding the positive potentials of the vulnerable state can transform the way courts respond to cases involving older people.

Pip Coore explores the use of family agreements for the care of older people. She brings out the fact that care in old age can be a source of financial loss and vulnerability for both the older person and family member in a caring relationship with them. A family contract, supporters claim, offers a way that both the older person and family member can find a degree of security: the family member being guaranteed some compensation for their care; and the older person being able to rely on the contracted levels of care. As Pip points out these contracts are no panacea. The nature of care which might otherwise be given altruistically becomes commercialised through the contract. The informal nature of it may become more structured. Further, there are considerable difficulties for those drafting these contracts in predicting future care needs.

Liz Lloyd's chapter also explores the significance of care, drawing on an ethic of care. As Liz notes old age can be a time of increased need for care. However, this can bring challenges in terms of human rights. Increased appreciation of the need for care and the desire to protect rights can be connected to increased regulation and commodification of care. As she notes increased statutory regulation of care creates a tension, promoting well-being and protecting rights on the one hand; and cutting the costs of welfare on the other. Care, which has traditionally been seen as a private matter is now regularly seen as a public matter. A crucial aspect she raises is that caring is now commonly performed by people who are older themselves. This makes the balance between protecting human rights and promoting care all the more complex in old age.

Jennifer Collins in her chapter explores the issue of financial exploitation of older people. She argues that there are considerable difficulties in formulating a specific response to the issue. One lies in difficulties of formulating an offence which satisfies the requirements of legal certainty in criminal law. The concept of exploitation, which most naturally could be used in this context is imprecise and ambiguous. Another difficulty is that the creation of a specific offence could 'entrench the vulnerability of older persons'. It might, for example, make people wary of dealing with older people or restrict which products they can choose. This might, in turn, impact on the autonomy of older people. In the seminar in which we discussed the chapters of the book, we were told of an older person who wanted to make a Christmas gift to some carers in her home, was distressed after she was told she could not due to regulations designed to prevent financial abuse. Jen sees more potential in using the current offences of abuse of position to protect older people. She sees these as avoiding the portrayal of older people as necessarily financially vulnerable, while taking seriously cases where older people have been dishonestly deprived of money. This chapter offers a fine example of the tensions between recognising the reality that older people are often the victim of financial abuse and protecting them from that, while not reinforcing an image of older people being particularly vulnerable. These issues are, of course, familiar in other contexts, such as sex and race.

This chapter contributes to the theme of 'Ageing, Gender and Family Law' by examining the limits and potential of the criminal law in regulating the financial abuse of older persons, especially but not exclusively, by family members. Two inter-connected arguments about the limits of the criminal law in penalising this form of wrongdoing are put forward. First, it is argued that it is far from clear that the creation of new criminal law measures to target financial abuse of older persons specifically can be justified, given the significant challenges this type of wrongdoing poses for legal certainty. The notion suffers from deep imprecision and ambiguity, which cannot easily be resolved. Secondly, another limitation consists of the dangers of using the criminal law to legislate in an older person-protective mode; increasing the risk, it will be argued, of entrenching vulnerability of older persons and of driving these practices further beneath the radar of public policy. The final part of the chapter turns to consider the latent potential of the criminal law in protecting older persons from financial abuse. It argues that there is scope to interpret an existing property offence in a vulnerable person-protective mode.

Alison Brammer picks up these themes in her chapter, which reflects upon the potential in the Care Act 2014 in relation to safeguarding and abuse. The chapter provides important reflections from the perspective of gender and older women to offer new insights into the way in which the law in this area may navigate the paradoxes involved in recognising and responding to vulnerability and abuse. This provides an interesting lens through which to question how we conceptualise inter-personal elder abuse – as an issue for adult safeguarding, or as domestic violence – and respond to it through different pathways. Recognising the issues arising for older women in these situations reveals the consequences of responding through these different channels and services, and the particularised impact of these. The promises and pitfalls of the Care Act, alongside *Making Safeguarding Personal*, enable a more nuanced appreciation of both the conceptual and the pragmatic challenges faced by older people who are facing inter-personal abuse.

Rights and state institutions

As seen in the previous section, the concept of vulnerability has provoked interesting and novel approaches to our understanding of ageing and care. The chapters in the section 'Rights and State Institutions' continue this theme of reconsidering care and vulnerability in this way, but shift the focus to the role of state. This reflects the call from care ethicists such as Joan Tronto (1993) for a political ethic of care, and from vulnerability theorists such as Martha Fineman (2015) for a focus on the 'responsive state'. In essence, such scholars emphasise the need to look at the broader structures and institutions that create and perpetuate disadvantage, dis-empowerment, and inequality, and the ways in which the state responds to this. As Fineman has argued, reflecting on the inadequacies of approaches to equality that are facially neutral:

> An approach that considers vulnerability would make forms of societally-produced differences a predominant focus because they provide the foundation for the assertion that we need a responsive state – one with a clear duty to effectively ensure realistic equality of access and opportunity to society's resource-generating institutions for everyone regardless of their individual

> characteristics. Instead, what equality of treatment has provided is the passive toleration of inequality and complicity in the conferral of often unwarranted privilege on the few.
>
> (2015, 20)

The chapter by Beverley Clough picks up this call for a focus on the responsive state and explores the ways in which the state and its institutions (including the courts) respond or, conversely, fail to respond in the context of adult social care. The chapter argues that despite the valuable rights contained in the European Convention on Human Rights and their potential utility in the context of adult social care, the way in which access to these is structured, and in particular the way in which courts have responded through judicial review, prevents very real barriers to enjoyment of these.

Laura Pritchard-Jones's chapter develops this thread of thinking about the role of human rights here, and provides an important contribution in the context of calls for a UN Convention on the Rights of Older People (p. 116). There has been increasing interest in such a convention, and there is the potential to model any change on the UN Convention on the Rights of Persons with Disabilities (2006) which has been widely welcomed as ushering in a 'paradigm shift' in disability rights. At the same time, however, human rights have faced sustained criticism, particularly from feminist legal scholars who highlight the gendered underpinnings and effects of rights. Laura considers the critical insights to be heeded by drafters of a convention, with a particular focus on the 'subject' of rights and on the public/private divide that pervades this context.

Ann Stewart's chapter similarly reflects upon the way in which those least able to accumulate assets over their life course – primarily women – are most affected by the vagaries of the market and the way this impacts our social care system. Like the other chapters in this section, the chapter picks up on the way in which the state is responding here, through the provision of social care and also through the regulation of it through the Care Quality Commission. In exploring this often overlooked interaction, Ann argues that the form of regulation here is not adequate to respond to the problems created by a market which is both dependent on and influenced by large private equity financed providers. This raises broader questions about the role of the state here, the interaction between the different structures and institutions and the productive effects of these interactions. Alongside Clough's chapter, the discussion adds an additional call for a focus on the responsive state.

The chapter by Sue Easton turns to the increasingly important issues raised by an ageing prison population. In particular, the chapter highlights the marginalisation of older people – and particularly older women – through policies which have specifically been designed with a younger, male prison population in mind. There are a number of age and gender related effects which stem from this policy design, including a lack of access to appropriate healthcare, difficulties in meeting the pace of prison routines, and loneliness and isolation. The difficulties in maintaining family relationships or building relationships is particularly important here. A critical dimension here is that the way these issues are responded to, and indeed the broader policy question of whether incarceration is appropriate for elderly offenders, is necessarily going to be constrained by contemporary criminal justice goals and political will. An interesting theme which comes from this chapter is the way in which existing inequalities outside of the prison can be reinforced or exacerbated inside the prison. This again raises questions as to the role of the state and how it ought to respond to socio-economic inequality.

Relationships in old age

The chapter by Jonathan Herring provides an interesting provocation in light of ongoing debates about ageing, vulnerability, identity, and relationality. The chapter engages with the ways in which negative traits of ageing are historically emphasised, and the way in which cosmetic surgery and the marketisation of particular life-styles can reinforce this 'masking' of age. Controversially, Jonathan exposes the way in which the very traits that are disavowed through this discourse – such as dependence, mental and physical exposure to others – are realities that we all face. Instead, we need to recognise that dependence and vulnerability is the essence of human nature. Such an approach could have widespread implications for how we conceptualise family law, particularly in the context of ageing. One such area which Jonathan focuses on here from this perspective is that of relationships, sexuality, and identity in old age – something that the literature traditionally has overlooked or viewed through a more 'youthful' lens.

Sue Westwood's chapter follows on from this and engages with ageing lesbian, gay, bisexual, trans*, and/or queer (LGBT*Q) family forms. Echoing Herring's chapter, Sue highlights how such family forms are often the focus of socio-legal debates in terms of parenting and partnership recognition, and indeed how the term 'family' itself has been seen as problematic with heteronormative undertones. However, the particularised family law issues for ageing LGBT*Q 'families', such as the 'constellations of biological family, friends, lovers, ex-lovers, partners, ex-partners, and various connections with children via those relationships' have been overlooked here. Sue highlights a range of legal contexts in which non-normative relations are marginalised – in particular, focusing on pensions, tax, inheritance, tenancy rights, and informal carers. This is an important intervention here which argues for increased legal recognition of non-normative families in order to redress exclusions and inequalities in later life.

Daniel Monk carries the questions surrounding the social and economic context, and ideas about care and relationships, into the often-overlooked issue of inheritance law. Given the recent reforms to this area of law with the Inheritance and Trustees' Powers Act 2014, and the increase in property ownership in the second half of the twentieth century, this is a key issue for socio-legal scholars and this chapter provides an important overview of relevant debates. One of the central themes in this collection, that of the public/private divide, emerges again here. As the chapter demonstrates, seeing will-making as a 'private' and 'responsible' act can individualise the process and implications. However, this masks the important interactions between care, family, and the state, and the way in which testamentary freedom can reinforce the inequality and disadvantage that the wider socio-political context may foster.

The following chapter by Felicity Kaganas and Christine Piper is an important contribution which explores trends in grandparental care. As they highlight, grandparental care is often seen as a relatively new phenomenon, with grandparents perceived to be increasingly taking up caring responsibilities. After exploring the evidence and literature on this, they move on to consider grandparent care for children who would otherwise be in the care of the state. Important issues arise here in terms of access to resources to facilitate this care, and the discretionary nature of the powers of Local Authorities to respond in this context. We see again the issues of the social and political economy context, and the ways in which this structures responses to care and dependency, and social reproduction. The chapter further raises the issues of choice and autonomy which feature in many of the chapters in this collection, reinforcing the idea that choice is inevitably shaped and constrained by our social situatedness and networks of relations – not just at the interpersonal level but also with the state.

Rachel Taylor picks up the theme of grandparental care and considers the way that legal rights safeguard (or fail to safeguard) relationships between children and grandparents. However, rather than arguing for stronger legal rights for grandparents in this area, Taylor suggests that a flexible legal approach is preferable here and allows for a sustained focus on the welfare of the child. Whilst this may initially seem to sit at odds with some of the chapters in this collection, through engaging with recent case law in this context Taylor reveals the way in which a focus on biological relation has distorted litigation. This does not always work in beneficial ways for grandparents. The issue of resources in a social and political context of austerity again features here, with a particular focus on the ways in which in terms of the resourcing of family justice, grandparents are often placed under considerable burdens by the privatising (through the use of private orders) of what would otherwise be public cases. This has important implications for access to quality legal advice and representation here – an issue similarly highlighted by Kaganas and Piper.

Notes

1 E.g., unfortunately, Herring (2017), Chapter 12.
2 www.telegraph.co.uk/news/health/news/11005945/No-rise-in-numbers-in-care-homes-despite-surge-in-elderly-population.html
3 See also Dougherty et al (2016).

References

Aitken, L. and Griffin, G. (1999) *Gender Issues in Elder Abuse*. London: Sage.

Andrews, M. (1999) 'The Seductiveness of Agelessness' *Ageing and Society* 19, 301.

Baars, J. (2012) 'Critical Turns of Aging, Narrative and Time' *International Journal of Ageing and Later Life* 7(2), 143.

Biggs, S. (2005) 'Beyond Appearances: Perspectives on Identity in Later Life and Some Implications for Method' *The Journals of Gerontology: Series B* 60(3), S118.

Brandl, B. and Meuer, T. (2001) 'Domestic Abuse In Later Life' *Elder Law Journal* 8, 297.

Brogdon, M. and Nijhar, P. (2000) *Crime, Abuse and the Elderly.* Cullompton: Willan Publishing.

Butler, R. (1995) 'Ageism' in G. Maddox (ed.) *The Encyclopaedia of Aging.* New York: Springer.

Calasanti, T. and Slevin, K. (2006) *Age Matters.* Abingdon: Routledge.

Dougherty, E. N., Dorr, N. and Pulice, R. T. (2016) 'Assisting Older Women in Combatting Ageist Stereotypes and Improving Attitudes Toward Aging' *Women & Therapy* 39(1–2), 12.

Featherstone, M. and Hepworth, M. (1995) 'Images of Positive Ageing' in M. Featherstone and A. Wernick (eds) *Images of Ageing.* London: Routledge.

Fineman, M. A. (2015) 'Equality and Difference – The Restrained State' *Alabama Law Review* 66(3), 609.

Friedan, B. (1993) *The Fountain of Age.* London: Jonathan Cape.

Fries, J. (1980) 'Aging, Natural Death and Compression of Morbidity' *New England Journal of Medicine* 303, 134.

Frolik, L. and Kaplan, R. (2014) *Elder Law in a Nutshell* (6th edn) Saint Paul, MN: West Publishing.

Heaphy, B., Yip, A. and Thompson, D. (2004) 'Ageing in a Non-Heterosexual Context' *Ageing and Society* 24, 881.

Herring, J. (2003). 'Children's Rights for Grown-Ups' in S. Fredman and S. Spencer (eds) *Age as an Equality Issue.* Oxford: Hart.

Herring, J. (2017) *Family Law.* Harlow: Pearson.

Kapp, M. (2005) 'Aging and the Law' in R. Binstock and L. George (eds) *Handbook of Aging and the Social Sciences.* Cambridge, MA: Academic Press.

Kimmel, D., Rose, T. and David, S. (2006) *Lesbian, Gay, Bisexual, and Transgender Aging.* New York: Columbia University Press.

Kohli, M. (2005) 'Aging and Justice' in R. Binstock and L. George (eds) *Handbook of Aging and the Social Sciences.* Cambridge, MA: Academic Press.

Jones, I. R. and Higgs, P. F. (2010) 'The Natural, the Normal and the Normative: Contested Terrains in Ageing and Old Age' *Social Science & Medicine* 71(8) 1513.

Sargenat, M. (2005) 'Disability and Age – Multiple Potential for Discrimination' *International Journal of the Sociology of Law* 33, 17.

Settersten, R. (2005) 'Aging and the Life Course' in R. Binstock and L. George (eds) *Handbook of Aging and the Social Sciences.* Cambridge, MA: Academic Press.

Small, H. (2007) *The Long Life.* Oxford: Oxford University Press.

Sontag, S. (1978) 'The Double Standard of Ageing' in V. Carver and P. Liddiard (eds) *An Ageing Population.* Sevenoaks: Open University Press.

Tronto, J. (1993) *Moral Boundaries: A Political Argument for an Ethic of Care.* New York: Routledge.

Walker, A. and Northmore, S. (eds) *Growing Older in a Black and Minority Ethnic Group.* London: Age Concern.

Ward, R. and Bytheway, B. (2008) *Researching Age and Multiple Discrimination.* London: Central Books.

Westwood, S. (2013) '"My Friends are my Family": An Argument about the Limitations of Contemporary Law's Recognition of Relationships in Later Life' *Journal of Social Welfare and Family Law* 35(3), 347.

Part 1

Care, vulnerability and age

Chapter 1

Embracing vulnerability in ageing

Our route to flourishing

Daniel Bedford

Old age is often perceived as a time of vulnerability. It is time that apparently marks the ageing body as weaker, sicker, and less dependable, in decline and frail (Bergoffen 2014). A body more exposed to harm and suffering, and less capable of safeguarding its needs and interests. This image of vulnerability in old age has been observed as exerting a powerful influence on social care practice (Fenge 2010). It has been suggested, for instance, that a culture of risk aversion in decisions affecting older people, and those with age-related impairments, has arisen due to an unhealthy focus on vulnerability, and the associated need to control and manage that vulnerability (Faulkner 2012, Bailey et al 2013).

It is an image that has also seemingly come to influence the case law on the exercise of the inherent jurisdiction of the High Court. It is not difficult to find examples of cases where vulnerability appears to be related to the fact that a person is 'old', 'frail', and 'incapacitous' (*London Borough of Redbridge* v *G* [2014] EWCOP 17 at para. 12), 'elderly' and 'infirm' (*LLBC* v *TG, JG and KR* at para. 40), 'weak', and 'helpless', exposed to 'risk', and less capable of 'coping' (*Re MM (an adult)* [2007] EWHC 2003 at para. 118, 120). Indeed, in *DL*, it was recognised that safeguarding of the 'elderly' was one of the strongest justifications for the survival of the inherent jurisdiction to protect vulnerable adults (*DL v A Local Authority* [2012] EWCA Civ 253 at para. 63). A number of judicial decisions appear therefore to have tied old age, as an inherent characteristic, with vulnerability, which is in turn related to notions of harm, weakness, frailty, and incapacity (Pritchard-Jones 2016). Linking old age to vulnerability in this manner has been said to contribute to a 'negative paradigm' of ageing, rendering it an unwelcome process to be resisted and feared (Lloyd-Sherlock 2004).

It is precisely for the reason that vulnerability has been equated with weakness and passivity that is has been resisted as a guide for policy and for law relating to ageing (Hall 2008). Martha Fineman (2012) has explored the ways in which the stigma attached to vulnerability, and its disempowering implications, has led some jurisdictions to reject vulnerability as a useful concept in elder law. Similar concerns led the UK Law Commission to reject the term 'vulnerable adult' in its review of adult social care legislation (2011). This follows earlier criticisms of the 'patronising and disempowering' connotations of the use of the term in the *No*

Secrets (DH 2009) guidance, which had linked age as a characteristic to weakness and harm.

Alternative paradigms of ageing have emerged that reject the stereotype that older people are necessarily vulnerable or dependent. These paradigms perpetuate the idea that older people are capable of conforming to the myth of the liberal subject – independent, autonomous, and self-reliant. Paradigms of 'successful', 'healthy', and 'active' ageing, which have become important international and national policy tools, suggest in various ways that such an ideal is both achievable and desirable for older people (WHO 2002, DH 2005). These paradigms have all been closely linked to the Western cultural emphasis on independence, liberal autonomy, and personal responsibility, as well as the societal preference for youth (Harper 1997, Holstein and Minkler 2003, Ranzijn 2010). They encourage the myth that the changes associated with ageing are within our control, and that vulnerability and dependence are undesirable qualities that can be avoided through the exercise of personal choice, so long as the right opportunities have been made available (Boudiny 2013).

The so-called positive paradigms of ageing, as with the negative paradigms, also have the potential to be oppressive through the construction of an ideal of ageing that is unrealistic and obtainable for many older adults (Lloyd-Sherlock 2004). An ideal of an '"elderly elite" … [who] are robust individuals who remain physically, mentally and socially active and who are determined to remain independent and control their future' (Gattuso 2003). This denies that ageing means change, and suggests that success in ageing be measured in terms of extent to which one is youthful. The inability to obtain such an ideal, due to disability, or frailty, can come to signify failure. These 'vulnerable elderly' thus become a distinct sub-group of the ageing community who are stigmatised as less than ideal, and deviant. Indeed, in light of the (false) suggestion that avoidance of dependence in old age is in our control, it is even possible to blame older adults for their failure to achieve success in ageing. This can only add to, and reinforce, a diminished sense of self-worth for those who deviate from the ideal.

The 'negative' and 'positive' paradigms of ageing appear to share in common a particular understanding of vulnerability and dependence. Both paradigms treat these conditions as negative and group-based. The 'negative' paradigm associates vulnerability with weakness, and treats it as a characteristic of ageing. At least on some accounts, 'positive' paradigms treat vulnerability and dependence as a sign of less than ideal ageing. Moreover, both models implicitly assume that vulnerability is opposed to strength, activity, and flourishing. A narrative is constructed that 'tells us that autonomy is to be respected and promoted while vulnerability is to be pitied, remedied or alleviated' (Diduck 2013). In such a dualistic framework, any possibility of experiencing and embracing vulnerability as vital to human flourishing, and as a source of positive meaning and strength, is already foreclosed.

This chapter seeks to draw attention to the (often neglected) positive aspects of vulnerability and the possibilities and implications for the law relating to older adults of treating that condition as vital to flourishing. The first section addresses the reasons for moving beyond an understanding of vulnerability that reduces it to harm and weakness. It highlights how oppressive practices relating to older adults are linked to the disavowal of vulnerability as a purely negative condition and the pursuit of invulnerability as the ideal. The second section proceeds to discuss how vulnerability can be conceptualised in a more positive manner. It outlines an expanded account of vulnerability as openness, affectability, and changeability. The third and fourth sections discuss the manner in which vulnerability – understood as openness – can be a source of connection, strength, and personal development in old age. The final section then turns to consider the implications of the expanded account of vulnerability for the law relating to older adults.

Pursuing invulnerability and oppressing older adults

The underlying assumption that vulnerability is a defect to be remedied, as stated above, has led to the view that it is a negative condition. This has contributed to the oppression and social exclusion of older adults. This is because, seen solely as a negative condition, vulnerability gives rise to fear and anxiety, which informs our desire to suppress, ignore, deny, and avoid it. A number of strategies are developed to eliminate that fear that negatively impacts on the treatment of older adults. First, and foremost, is the strategy of isolating older adults. This entails distancing ourselves from those older adults whose leaky, open, unbounded, and deteriorating bodies are an acute reminder of our own vulnerable and mortal condition (Shildrick 2002, Wendell 2008, Howarth 2014). Such bodies threaten to unsettle the illusion of invulnerability – a mask-like abstraction – that assuages our fears, and enables us to mistakenly think that we can escape the dangers of being vulnerable (Bergoffen 2014).

One particular mechanism by which to reinforce the illusion of invulnerability is sequestration. A number of studies have, in this regard, highlighted how having an 'unbounded' ageing body has been associated with a loss of personhood and a trigger for admission of an older adult to certain institutional settings, or segregation within those settings (Lawton 1998, Howarth 2014). These spaces, it has been suggested, do not always serve to improve the quality of care, but, in reality, act as a way of concealing the visible signs of vulnerability, at the same time as symbolically reinforcing the bounded, sealed, and self-contained body (Lawton 1998).

Second, seeing vulnerability as a deficiency that leads to suffering can result in a refusal on the part of a care-worker to experience vulnerability, which, in turn, can lead to the dehumanisation of older adults. As has been recognised in the nursing literature, fear of vulnerability can result in a care-worker adopting a self-protective attitude that entails detachment and emotional disengagement. This attitude has been linked to the pursuit of invulnerability (security, strength, control), and has been observed as leading to 'hardness and coldness, a lack of closeness and feelings' (Stenbock-Hult and Sarvimäki 2011, see also Michaels and Moffett 2008, Bouchal 2007). Pursuit of invulnerability can numb the care worker to their personal feelings and the feelings of a patient, and result in a lack of receptiveness, sensitivity, and involvement. In this regard, those who are incapable of being vulnerable with themselves and others can lack empathy – unable to engage in fellow-feeling and perceive the pain of others. Worse still, it is through being immune to the feelings of others that care workers can fail to see how they create hurt, and can go on to inflict harm (Jordan 2008, Stenbock-Hult and Sarvimäki 2011). As Daniel (1998) summarises: 'if we deny the opportunity to participate in vulnerability, we deny the opportunity to participate in humanness, which then permits us to practice dehumanising acts'.

Third, in a cultural environment that treats vulnerability as indignity and deficient agency, it may be difficult to acknowledge dependence and accept help. To do so risks the older adult being seen by society as weak or passive, and the older adult feeling that they have become a burden on others. In order not to feel diminished, an older adult may seek to conceal their need for care and present themselves as in-control. But, as Sally Gadow (1987) argues, this means presenting an inauthentic facade or mask that can obstruct a 'true relation between [the] self and world' in a way that actually reinforces a sense of isolation. If it is no longer possible to maintain this facade, an older adult may then choose to disassociate from others in order not to experience indignity. Gadow gives as an example the elderly person who, out of their own disgust at their vulnerable bodies, refuses to be in the company of others whilst eating. Their inability to present their body as in-control and self-possessed means that they feared being humiliated before others.

Families can also ignore the vulnerability of an older adult and decline to offer certain forms of care so as not to damage a sense of self-esteem that is attached to being independent. They may try to avoid shaming and patronising an older adult by declining to bring attention to vulnerability, or pretending that there has been no deterioration in functioning. However, as a study conducted by Motenko and Greenberg (1995) found, collective denial of vulnerability in late-life can ultimately be damaging to the family unit and, in some cases, result in neglect. In fact, it can deprive an older adult of those forms of support and relationships that are actually vital to maintaining a continued sense of competence and self-esteem.

Fourth, and finally, splitting society into those who are 'strong' and 'capable' actors, and those who are 'weak' and 'helpless' passive recipients, can support forms of intervention that are objectionably paternalistic. In such a society, the vulnerability of the liberal subject is denied, and the decision-making capacity of the independent autonomous subject is emphasised. In contrast, those who are deemed vulnerable are seen suffering from a deficiency that needs, as far as possible, to be remedied or overcome (Diduck 2013). The liberal subject is then in a superior position. He is capable of intervening into the lives of those deemed vulnerable to 'make good the perceived lack' (Shildrick 2002). This may be pursued without regard to the personal wishes and values of an older adult who is incapable of being an agent so long as vulnerability remains. Their life may be reduced to a set of objectively assessed risk factors. Focus may be on control, creating certainty, and the foregrounding of an age-related impairment, rather than meaningful engagement with the particular older adult. Such attitudes, some scholars have noted, are reflected in risk-averse practices relating to the care of dementia patients (Clarke et al 2010, Sabat et al 2011). Some of these sorts of concerns have also been directed at the way in which the vulnerable adult has been constructed in law (Dunn et al 2008).

The linking of oppression to the societal aim of suppressing the fear of vulnerability, and pursuing the comforting illusion of invulnerability, provides us with good reason to reassess the assumption that vulnerability is negative. Indeed, as long as vulnerability is conceptualised as a defect, which is intrinsically linked to old age, ageing will continue to be perceived as a mark of shame and diminished dignity. In this light, reconceiving vulnerability has the potential to unlock more constructive forms of engagement and complicate the possible range of responses to a fundamental feature of the human condition. Envisioning vulnerability as a potential site of flourishing, rather than just harm, means that it need no longer be reduced to an inherent defect in the human condition or something to fear. It might instead become something to be embraced and supported.

Reconceiving vulnerability: openness, affectability, and changeability

The possibility that vulnerability might have positive dimensions has been given limited attention in legal scholarship. It is only recently that scholars have begun to explore understandings of vulnerability that seek to move it beyond mere suffering and harm (Grear 2010, Grear 2013, Fineman, 2012, Bergoffen, 2011, Herring, 2016). These theorists have argued that vulnerability has positive dimensions and is a source of multiple forms of well-being. They have further suggested that vulnerability is generative of a range of basic goods and is an aspect of empathy, joy, desire, intimacy, social-connectedness, and creativity. But the precise manner in which vulnerability can give rise to these positive phenomena is not always clear or self-evident. In this section, I draw on the work of Anna Grear, Erinn Gilson, and Henk ten Have in order to explore how vulnerability can be a gate to flourishing.

The common thread that unites these scholars is the idea that vulnerability should be understood as a *universal* condition of openness to affectation and change in our connection to the world and others. They all draw on the phenomenological account of the lived body developed by Merleau-Ponty in order to re-theorise vulnerability as a condition of world-openness. Our bodies are, on this account, unique openings on to the world – a receptive interface with a world in which we are embedded, and from which we are incapable of being extracted. It is through our open bodies that we exist as a 'living, sensory circuit with the world [that] form[s] the dynamic, living bond through which we co-relate with and in the world' (Grear 2013). This is a world which we share with others, to whom we already connected, and with whom we are engaged and exposed. As such, our openness guarantees that we are always already in a dynamic inter-relationship with the world and others, which precedes our self-development. As openings on to the world, and as beings that are connected to others, we are also affectable – impressionable, perceiving, sensitive, yielding, feeling, and responsive. In this respect, we are capable of being shaped through our relationships to the world and others that can both sustain or diminish us, and can help or hinder flourishing. This affectability necessarily renders us dynamic beings. To be capable of being affected is to be exposed to the unchosen and unknown, and also susceptible to changes and transitions that one cannot fully predict or control.

There are four qualities that combine on this account to make us vulnerable – openness, affectability, alteration, and lack of full control. We are vulnerable because we are open to being affected in ways that bring about alterations that are incapable of being fully controlled or predicted. This represents a *common* or *primary* vulnerability that we all share, whether we are young or old. It is an aspect of the human condition that is not a limitation or debased condition, but a 'condition of potential' that enables the experience of positive forms of affectability. This means that vulnerability, as Gilson (2013) argues, is an 'open-ended condition that makes possible learning, love, affection, and self-transformation just as much as it makes possible suffering and harm'. It is an enabling condition, which makes room for self-development, and provides possibilities for change and growth.

Moreover, and unlike accounts that reduce vulnerability to passivity or powerlessness, it is a condition that can facilitate activity. Being open and receptive to the world and others, which calls and invites us to respond, can be a prompt for our engagement and participation. Affectability is not then limited to the condition of being acted upon from the outside. It is also a condition of being alive to a world that solicits our involvement to which we creatively respond. This amounts to an intertwining of passivity and activity in the form of a dynamic receptivity. As Judith Butler (2009) puts it, our vulnerable bodies are not 'a mere surface upon which social meanings are inscribed' but they are 'that which suffers, enjoys, and responds to the exteriority of the world, an exteriority that defines its disposition, its passivity and activity'.

As a condition of potentiality, our common or primary vulnerability is a condition that makes possible flourishing and activity. But, of course, it also makes possible harm. One can be negatively affected in ways that lead to suffering. This relates to the ambiguous nature of vulnerability as a condition of potential that entails both negative and positive possibilities for life. On this account, suffering and harm, as well as well-being and joy, are 'potentialities' that arise from the 'same basic corporeal openness' (Gilson 2013). As ten Have (2016) puts it:

> [V]ulnerability is ambiguous; it may lead to care and compassion but also to abuse and violence, it may produce transformation or devastation, healing or suffering. Human beings are capable of harming others but also of offering care to them.

Our bodies are thus open and exposed to others with whom we are inter-related and are capable of undergoing something that is outside of our control. This is a condition of *potential* that can be *realised* and *experienced* in diverse ways in the social world. It enables and invites friendship, intimacy, care, and joy. But, in light of being ambiguous, can also be exploited in ways that transform it into a site of humiliation, suffering, anguish, and shame. This relates to the reality that, although a *universal* condition of openness to affectability, our experience of vulnerability is *particular* and *varied*. This is because we are differently embodied and situated, exposed to particular social contexts that affect the ways in which we can experience and live our vulnerable openness.

Our individual experiences of vulnerability are thus formed from within concrete relationships and are contingent on the social contexts to which we are exposed. Some individuals, for instance, may be trapped in exploitative relationships in which their experience of vulnerability is reduced to its negative manifestations (open only to being affected by harm and suffering), which serves the narrow purposes and interests of those in a position to dominate and control (passively acted upon).Their experience of life is no longer open or fluid, but is frozen and trapped in a state of humiliation and suffering (Gilson 2013). As discussed in the first section, such patterns of exploitation can be supported through the pursuit of invulnerability.

An oppressor establishes themselves as invulnerable to the power of another by allowing those under their control to exist only as passive objects in their world, unable to affect their situation. It is in refusing to experience vulnerability – closed to allowing the other to affect the conditions of the relationship, and indifferent to the harm and pain they inflict – that a person can go on to abuse, exerting 'power over' the other. Such 'power over' relationships can be a way of affirming a sense of personal security, for it is in dominating the other that we gain control over the ways which the other might disrupt us, and we are protected from being affected in ways that we did not plan or will. In order not to be threatened by the experience of vulnerability, a person may seek to control those situations and relationships that evoke anxiety, and become impermeable to the experiences of those that they affect. This can be contrasted with 'power with' relationships in which there is mutual vulnerability, with all parties open to being impacted and changed through the relationship (Jordan 2008). All involved are susceptible to being affected, and no person exercises exclusive control over the relationship.

The focus is then on re-working social, political, and economic structures that limit and reduce the experience of vulnerability to its predominantly negative manifestations. The aim is not to (re-)establish certainty, absolute security, masterful control, and immutability (hallmarks of invulnerability). Invulnerability equates to closure to being affected in ways that are incapable of being controlled or predicted (Gilson 2013). Invulnerability means being 'untouchable, unexposed, not open or sensitive, and also self-contained and not sociable' (ten Have 2016). Nor is the aim to remedy vulnerability as a perceived defect, which is not present in the autonomous subject. As Gilson argues, the aim is to address the 'exploitation of vulnerability that renders it a wholly negative condition' whilst 'preserving the ambiguity and indeterminacy of vulnerability'. It is about, it is suggested here, ensuring that a person is not alienated from the positive possibilities that their vulnerable openness entails. This includes transforming the experience of being vulnerable, so that it is no longer *exclusively* a site of suffering and abuse, but also a site of *potential* flourishing and connection. This ultimately entails expanding the *potential* range of affectability. Ensuring that the world and others can elicit interest and engagement, rather than being experienced as hostile, and things from which to withdraw and disengage.

Embracing vulnerability: connection, strength, and development

The preceding section has discussed how vulnerability means openness to alteration and is a constitutive condition of our humanity. There is no doubting, in this regard, that ageing is one of the most manifest ways in which we are confronted with our vulnerable condition. We face being affected and changed in ways that are outside of our control. As noted in the second section, we may be inauthentic in relation to that condition and engage in self-deception by ignoring the ways in which we are vulnerable, whilst clinging to the comforting illusion of being invulnerable. Some 'positive paradigms' of ageing, for instance, ignore the ways in which changes in ageing are many and real, all in a vain attempt to counter ageism. But such changes are not so easily ignored, even if we wilfully ignore the ways in which we are vulnerable over the life-course.

In ageing, our bodies can come into the foreground of our attention. Studies point to how the (outer) body can be experienced as obstructing the (inner youthful) self, as certain tasks and activities become more difficult to perform (Gadow 1987, Bullington 2006). We may experience disruption to our functioning and life-plans, alterations in our social roles, and an inability to engage in once valued activities. Such changes also mean that our experiences of the world, which we live through our bodies, can be transformed. Our world, and the ways in which it affects us, can centre on frustration and pain, and be felt as cumbersome and unwelcoming (Toombs 2006). Such transitions can be experienced as threats to flourishing. But, as is argued in this section, it is not in adopting an inauthentic attitude, and repudiating vulnerability, that we can address this threat and continue to flourish.

In order to continue to flourish an older adult may adopt an authentic attitude and embrace vulnerability. That means assuming a posture of tender openness to the world and others. This is possible when vulnerability is not seen as just a place of terror, but is part of what it means to be human, and can enable flourishing. This does not mean that all experiences of vulnerability should be unequivocally embraced, but it does mean the rejection of invulnerability as the ideal. An authentic attitude to life is thus characterised by acceptance that one must, in certain circumstances, be open and exposed, even though that leaves one susceptible to some hurt. In particular, it is suggested here that embracing vulnerability is crucial to enabling genuine connection, strength and self-development in old age (and at all stages of life). This will again require us to move beyond negative conceptualisations of vulnerability that equate it with isolation, weakness, and decline.

In terms of genuine connection, it is through being open to being affected, and transparent in our neediness, that healing and growth-enhancing forms of relationship can be developed. As Carse (2006) puts it, it is 'in taking our vulnerability to heart – in embracing rather than fearing or denying it – that vital forms of human connections, crucial to our flourishing, are made possible'. She goes on to say that:

> While our flourishing can be imperiled by our vulnerability, it also requires us to be vulnerable – that is, our flourishing is in crucial ways constituted by vulnerability. Being open, receptive, flexible and tender, being emotionally invested in relationships or committed to undertakings, being capable of nurturing and being nurtured, of loving and growing are necessary to realizing some of the most profound goods of human life.

This requires us to have the courage to move beyond certainty and control. We must give ourselves over to another in trust, and, in so doing, dare to relax control and be exposed, allowing ourselves to be changed in unforeseen and unexpected ways. It is through such openness that authentic relationships can be cultivated that nourish and strengthen, enabling growth, development and transformation. Kay Toombs (2006) provides, in this regard, a useful discussion of how her experience of multiple sclerosis was transformed in a social setting where each person embraced vulnerability. In that social setting, each person was 'dedicated to *opening* themselves to one another without masks or defensive images, [without] fear that [the] others [would] … use [their] … weakness and *openness* to their own advantage – *opening* themselves up in return – in the spirit of love'. This *transformed* an otherwise negative life-circumstance into an opportunity to develop intense forms of affection, adoration, and appreciation, which she explained she had not experienced before. Her initial experience of isolation and unrelenting pain in affliction was displaced. She was brought into true connection, which made her feel valued, and provided her with a supportive environment in which to explore her changed life-world. Like Toombs, other scholars have pointed to the fact that *better and more authentic* relationships can be cultivated by embracing vulnerability, with illness and old age providing a context within which such relationships can flourish (Motenko and Greenberg 1995, Hoffmaster 2006, Carel, 2009). Such relationships can even, as Kittay (2011) argues, transform difficult intimate tasks into times of trust that are 'dignifying to both the caregiver and the recipient of care'.

The capacity to be open to one another without fear that such openness will be exploited is crucial to at least two forms of growth-enhancing human connection that are vital to flourishing. These are care and love. As Nussbaum (2001) has argued, such relational goods require 'openness towards the world and its possibilities … a yielding and receptive character of soul that is not compatible with an undue emphasis on self-protection'. To be cared for depends, for instance, on our willingness to be open in our need for others, allowing them to impact us, and to trust that the other will respond with appropriate tenderness. A person calls out for support in their unprotected openness. In turn, if we are to honour and respect that vulnerability, and respond with genuine care, we must be open to being affected by the call, and situation of the one in need, who demands my attention.

To care for others also requires the capacity to be vulnerable to what the other is feeling – requiring 'receptiveness' and 'openness' (Noddings 1984, Noddings 2010, Kittay 2001), and 'sensitivity' and 'empathy' (Noddings 2010, Stenbock-Hult and Sarvimäki 2011). This can give the carer some insight into the experiences of the one in need. It also means they are capable of being 'moved' or 'unsettled' by those in need, and are susceptible to being impacted and changed. This can be vital to enhancing self-esteem by communicating to the person in need that they do matter, can make a difference, and are able to evoke a response (Jordan 2008). The receptiveness of those who care can then enable the development of a 'power with' relationship, whereby the active agency of those in need is promoted, as they are capable of affecting the relationship, and soliciting a response. Of course, those who care also make themselves vulnerable by investing in the well-being of another human being, which leaves them exposed to strains and stresses, and tragedy and loss. At the same time, such concern and dedication also enables us to take delight in the flourishing of those that they care about (Stenbock-Hult and Sarvimäki 2011).

Love is another relational good that depends on and demands that we are vulnerable. As Gilson (2013) puts it, love entails an 'exceptional openness that characterises the relationship and, indeed, the expectation that one will change in unforeseen ways in relation to the loved one'. It is an openness to being affected by another, in which the 'unpredictability and uncontrollability of other beings has a heightened effect on the self, one is more vulnerable because one is more open to this other'. This is connected to the idea that our identities are co-created through a loving relationship. The identity of the self is thus negotiated and developed through a relationship with an intimate other. A person is thus 'made, and unmade and remade, only in virtue of its permeability and is interwoven with the selves of others' (Gilson 2013). This entails a dynamic conception of the self that constructs its meanings in close relationship with others (Curk 2016). Our intimate relationships, on this account, constitute who we are. Thus, when we feel we lose the one we love, we not only 'mourn the loss', but we lose those 'ties or bonds that compose us' (Butler 2006). But it is not just loss that indicates the ways in which we undergo transformation. Desire too points to how, through a relationship with an intimate other, we do not 'stay intact … despite one's best efforts; one is undone, in the face of the other, by the touch, by the scent, by the feel, by the prospect of the touch, by the memory of the feel' (Butler 2006). These alterations are hardly negative, but they are not something we can fully plan or control.

Both love and care are *states of vulnerability*. They require us to be vulnerable. Contrary to the negative accounts of vulnerability, such relational goods are not mere sources of weakness; they are important sources of strength. This relates to the second point, mentioned above, that embracing vulnerability is what can make us strong and resilient. It is some of our most central relationships of care and love that help to sustain us during challenging life-circumstances. It is by caring for others and being cared for, and loving others and being loved, that one can sustain an interest in life during difficult circumstances. At the very same time, these relationships also open us up to strain and devastation. We can lose those that we love and care about. As George Harris (1997) argues, such relationships leave us both *weak* and *strong*. It is by remaining open to caring and loving relationships that one is best able to cope with the devastation of losing someone that we cared about and loved, even though it was such openness that made the devastation possible in the first place. Strength is thus enhanced through the development of a rich tapestry of caring and loving relationships; a 'cloth woven from different strands' which is 'individually and collectively vulnerable to integral stress, but nonetheless collectively very strong'. This means that one of the resources that we can draw upon to ameliorate the negative consequences of vulnerability are themselves states of vulnerability.

It is within a loving and caring environment that accepts and embraces mutual vulnerability that a person can also learn to adapt to the changes that might accompany ageing. This concerns the third point that embracing vulnerability can support personal development and growth. As noted above, ageing persons can face the challenges of an obstructive body that no longer complies, and a world that is difficult to navigate. They can find that their bodies stand in the way of their goals, life plans, and projects. The self has a choice as to how to respond. The (inner youthful) self can, for instance, engage in battle with the (outer ageing) body as an enemy, and fight against those changes. This is all so an older adult can continue to participate in a social world that prefers qualities associated with youth – productivity, creativity, and virility. Or the (ageless, unchanging) self can renounce the body as a failed object, refusing to be affected by (and identified with) its deterioration, at the same time as withdrawing from a now hostile world (Gadow 1987). Both entail the cultivation of a felt sense of contradiction between self and body, and loss of an authentic connection to the world. As some studies have found, and as alluded to in the second section, these responses to ageing can contribute to the lived experience of suffering and isolation (Bullington 2006).

A third option for the self is to respond by accepting vulnerability and transforming it into a resource for personal development. It will be recalled that vulnerability is the condition of affectability and openness to alteration. In ageing we can be vividly confronted with our vulnerable condition – our bodies and our interactions with the world can alter markedly. We face alterations that we did not choose, and we undergo changes that are neither willed nor planned. We can respond at the level of the self by fighting or repudiating those alterations, but we can also allow those 'alteration[s] to go all the way down, to *affect* what one does (the practices that shape self-identity), how one things about and defines one*self*' (Bluhm 2012). This means acknowledging our openness to being changed, and allowing our*selves* to be vulnerable (open to being affected) by those changes. This can entail recreating the self to accommodate ageing by revising goals, life plans, social roles, and projects (Carel 2009, Bluhm 2012). In this way, we participate in self-formation in relation to a process that we did not instigate.

This is an ambiguous experience of vulnerability; it can be perceived as loss, but it can also be perceived as an opportunity to promote personal development. As Bluhm (2012) puts it, although a person may 'no longer be able to attain all of their previous goals, in responding to (being vulnerable to) health problems, they [can] grow, change, and develop new priorities'. To be vulnerable in this way, according to Bluhm, can be crucial to maintaining a sense of well-being in illness through the reconciliation of personal goals and abilities, and the fostering of a conscious integrity of self-body-world. It is also a creative challenge for it requires us to be open to transforming our ways of engaging and relating with the world and others, as well as our existing ways of thinking and feeling, in relation to changing life-circumstances. This entails moving into unfamiliar territory, and muddling about in experience as we explore different ways of realising our*selves.*

A good example of how embracing vulnerability can facilitate self-development can be found in the study conducted by Motenko and Greenberg (1995) referred to above. In that study, it was discovered that development and growth in all generations was promoted in those family networks that adjusted to the changing needs of older family members. This required the capacity on the part of an older adult to acknowledge their mutability, to be open to receive, and to relinquish control over certain responsibilities. It was through such openness that mutually enhancing relationships were developed that enabled the older family member to maintain competence at new levels of functioning. It freed them to take on new roles and to give in new ways, which enabled a renewed sense of competence and self-esteem. It was openness to change that enabled the older adult to adapt and flourish in the context of ageing. Other studies have also highlighted how older adults can come to describe their experiences of vulnerability as providing an opportunity for further learning and growth (Sarvimäki and Stenbock-Hult 2016).

Vulnerability in law: beyond deficiency and weakness

The possibility that embracing vulnerability can contribute to flourishing through facilitating connection, strength, and personal development, has not been *explicitly* addressed in judicial engagement with the concept. There is little appreciation of the ways in which vulnerability is a condition of potential that can be differently experienced in the social world. In fact, as discussed at the outset, judicial constructions of vulnerability tend to reinforce the view that it is a limitation associated with weakness, passivity, and harm. It is a designation that has usually been applied to specific groups, including older adults and those with age-related impairments, who are deemed to have defective agency and lack power or competence. As Alison Diduck (2013) summarises, vulnerability is seen as 'afflicting the [vulnerable] subject with almost a kind of disability that requires repair'. This is a disability that does not afflict those who are deemed autonomous – competent, strong, in-control, and independent. To treat vulnerability as a deficiency in this way invariably limits the repertoire of responses available to law in addressing that condition. It centres focus squarely on making good the perceived deficiency by either restoring autonomy or establishing basic security for those who are weak and helpless.

Of course, and to be clear, any imperative to protect the vulnerable by establishing basic security may need to be balanced against other considerations. In *Re MM* ([2007] EWHC 2003), for instance, Munby J made it clear that protection of the weak and helpless, from exposure to an objective risk of harm, was a good that needed to be balanced against some other 'vital good', such as happiness and dignity. But even here vulnerability appears to be coded as negative (equated with passivity and susceptibility to harm), and is treated as something only to be 'tolerated' or 'managed'. Vulnerability can't be positively embraced as an aspect of flourishing. Law needs, however, to find ways to acknowledge, support, and encourage some experiences of vulnerability critical to flourishing, whilst discouraging others. It must to do so in order to avoid the pitfalls of viewing vulnerability as a homogenous experience (harm, weakness, loss) that is always the problem that requires a solution. Take, for instance, decisions relating to whether it would be in the best interests of an older adult to be removed from their home and placed in public care. There are various ways in which vulnerability in a positive sense can figure as an important consideration in identifying what is an aspect of an older adults 'vital good'.

The first is in the assessment of the relative quality of care. An important aspect of any best interest assessment, for instance, will be the quality of any caring relationship that exists in the home environment (*Re MM*). Part of what will impact the quality of that relationship is the presence or absence of mutual vulnerability. As noted above, relationships of mutual openness and affectability are essential to good care, enabling a 'power with' relationship. All involved are susceptible to being affected, and neither party exercises exclusive power or control over the relationship. Such relationships can transform difficult life-circumstances into times of trust and devotion, dignifying to both parties. They can provide a source of strength and enhance agency. This requires attention to be paid to the ways in which a person may experience being vulnerable as positive within a particular social and relational context. There is a danger that this can be ignored when vulnerability is assessed in terms only of an objective set of risk factors. The result can be actions that seek to eliminate or reduce risk, even though it deprives a person of those relationships of mutual vulnerability that enable them to remain strong and engaged.

Perhaps, more importantly, it means that insufficient attention can be paid to the meaning ascribed to certain actions for the persons within a relational context based on mutual openness and receptiveness. A decision, for instance, of a husband to use a sling to help support a wife to sit in an armchair can be seen exclusively in terms of a professionally assessed risk of pressure sores (see *A London Local*

Authority v JH ([2011] EWHC 2420 (COP))). Or, it can be understood as an example of the way in which a husband was acutely sensitive and receptive to what caused his wife pain and discomfort (per Eldergill DJ in *JH*). The husband, for instance, may have learnt that the use of the sling eased the pain and discomfort, and encouraged participation and engagement of the wife. The wife, in turn, may be more receptive and open to the care of her husband who she trusts to be sensitive to her needs. In a relationship of mutual receptiveness, such an action may be an example of the deep devotion and affection that exists between the persons, rather than abuse. Assessed separately from this relational context, there is a danger that the meaning of such an act can be misconstrued. To further seek to prevent that act can entail the adoption of a posture of invulnerability and a lack of open responsiveness to the particular feelings or concerns of an older adult. It can mean indifference to what causes them pain and discomfort, resulting in a 'power over' relationship in which an older adult is unable to affect their situation and is reduced to a passive object of concern.

The second is in terms of the connection between the vital good of an older adult and those to whom they are related. As Herring (2013) has argued, there is a tendency in law to look at the interests of a person in isolation. The emphasis is on the competing interests of detached and separate individuals. The result can be that the interests of those in a loving and caring relationship are ignored or excluded in decision-making. This is not possible when vulnerability is recognised as a vital aspect of good caring and loving relationships. In such relationships, the flourishing of one person becomes susceptible to, and is an aspect of, the flourishing of another. Through an intimate connection each person makes him/herself vulnerable in the person of another. On this account, a decision to remove an older adult from the home environment must take into consideration the impact of the measure on the interests of all those in the caring and loving relationship. A decision might need to be reached, for instance, which enables a wife to continue to live in the home with her husband on the basis that her happiness is contingent on the happiness of her husband to whom she is devoted (see *JH*).

Vulnerability is not then just a matter of the risk faced by one person alone, who is passive, and in need of protection. It is rather the condition that connects the flourishing of an older adult to the flourishing of another, with each person making their flourishing dependent on that connection. There is a necessary corollary of this, of course. Where a person has hitherto refused to make themselves vulnerable in the person of another, there is less reason to consider their interests as intertwined. The ability of the law to then identify the presence of mutual vulnerability becomes a crucial factor in determining the importance of the interests of those to whom an older adult may be related.

The third concerns the need to support relationships based on mutual vulnerability so that they remain sources of co-flourishing. It is part of good caring relationships that a person has the qualities of receptiveness and responsiveness, leaving them vulnerable to the demands and needs of another person. At the same time, as Diemut Bubeck (2003) notes, these qualities also leave the person who cares particularly susceptible to being burdened. They are more likely to take on the strains and stresses of attending to the needs of another, and are, as a result, less able to address their own needs. If these strains and stresses are not to become overwhelming experiences, suffocating the potential for devotion and affection, those burdens must be shared across the community. Law can have a role to play in this regard in requiring forms of social support that enable the burden to be shared.

Crucially, this does not mean removing the qualities associated with vulnerable openness – receptiveness and responsiveness – as this would be detrimental to the standard of care. It means supporting the vulnerability, ensuring that those who care can remain open and sensitive, without that resulting invariably in suffering. In order for that burden to be shared, however, what is requiring is a more caring community; where more people are receptive and responsive, and are vulnerable to the demands of those in need, sharing in the strains and stresses of care; a community in which each person also acknowledges their dependence on caring relationships, and the ways in which they have been shaped and formed within those relationships.

The fourth is in identifying and informing our response to certain forms of oppression and abuse. As mentioned above, it is clear that the focus of law tends to be on the vulnerability of a person as a deficiency that afflicts them. Vulnerability becomes the cause of the problem that requires a solution. The unfortunate consequence is that the law subscribes to the ideology that actually makes possible the oppression of older adults in the first place, and, as such, may be unable to afford an effective response. As argued above, it is the pursuit of invulnerability and relationships of non-mutual vulnerability that often facilitate patterns of oppression and abuse. A daughter, for instance, who is charged with the care of her elderly mother, but who remains insensitive and unaffected by her plight, and who is impervious to the mother's pain and cries for help, becomes the problem (see *IIBCC v LG* [2010] EWHC 1527). Her hardness and coldness denies the mother the ability to impact the relationship, or change the distressing and dangerous situation to which she is exposed. As such, it is the refusal of the daughter to respect the vulnerability of the mother, through in turn being vulnerable, which requires a response.

The appropriate legal response is not then the elimination of vulnerability. It is enabling a person to live their vulnerability with those who are also willing to be vulnerable in a 'power with' relationship. This can mean seeking to transform the experience of vulnerability – narrowly restricted to harm, isolation, pain, and distress in the home – into a basis for possible connection, trust, and affection. Affording a social and relational context in which the older adult is more open (and susceptible) to being positively affected by the world and others, which can elicit interest and engagement, calling for participation and response. In a different context, an older adult may also be better able to engage in personal development. As noted in the previous section, it is possible for a positive life-transition to occur when an older adult renders them*selves* vulnerable to the changes of ageing. This can include, for instance, making positive adjustments to changing needs, accepting dependence and support, and exploring new ways of giving and relating.

Clearly, the ability to move forward in development is contingent on broader forms of social support. In particular, an older adult must be enabled to meet new needs and manage certain tasks, whilst being afforded opportunities to give and relate in new ways. A great deal of social policy and law, however, is directed at avoiding or reducing dependence, due in part to the perception that dependence is a sign of decline and deterioration. Any move to dependence is perceived as unwelcome. This is mistaken. Our social support mechanisms need to be structured around the idea that acceptance of dependence, and the transitions that accompany it, can contribute to ongoing development and growth, competence and self-esteem.

Conclusion

Perceiving vulnerability as a potential source of connection, strength, and personal development in old age raises profound questions about how law should respond to that condition. It casts doubt on the prevailing reductionist narrative that focuses on protection, and restricts vulnerability to weakness and suffering, which, as it turns out, can be integral to the oppression and exploitation of older adults. It calls, in particular, for further consideration of how law might be instrumental to facilitating oppression and exploitation, or incapable of providing an adequate response, by largely subscribing to that narrative. It also requires us to consider how exploring vulnerability as a positive value can enable a richer set of possibilities for the law relating to older adults, and what those possibilities are.

This chapter has begun to sketch out some of the ways vulnerability may figure as more than a consideration related to basic security. It has challenged the perception that vulnerability (capacity to be affected) is incapable of coexisting with, or is a perpetual threat to, agency (capacity to affect). Vulnerability, it has been argued, can contribute in a positive sense to the identification of what enhances flourishing and agency in decisions concerning the living arrangements of older adults. In terms of protective interventions, it has further been suggested that the refusal of a person charged with care to participate in vulnerability is what can precipitate the dehumanisation of older adults. An appropriate response will be directed at transforming the experience of vulnerability, so that it can be experienced as a potential site of co-flourishing. These are only some of the myriad possibilities that a differently theorised notion of vulnerability poses for the law relating to older adults. Other possibilities may be more far-reaching still. It is hoped that by bringing greater attention to the positive dimensions of vulnerability, this chapter will prompt further consideration of the transformative implications of that concept.

References

Bailey, C. et al (2013) 'Risky and Resilient Life with Dementia: Review of and Reflections on the Literature' *Health, Risk & Society* 15(5), 390–401.

Bergoffen, D. (2011) *Contesting the Politics of Genocidal Rape: Affirming the Dignity of the Vulnerable Body*. New York: Routledge.

Bergoffen, D. (2014) 'The Dignity of Finitude' in S. Stoller (ed.) *Simone de Beauvoir's Philosophy of Age: Gender, Ethics, and Time*. Berlin: Walter de Gruyter, 127–143.

Bluhm, R. (2012) 'Vulnerability, Health, and Illness' *International Journal of Feminist Approaches to Bioethics* 5(2), 147–161.

Bouchal, S. (2007) 'Moral Meanings of Caring for the Dying' in N. Johnston and A. Scholler-Jaquish (eds) *Meaning in Suffering: Caring Practices in the Health Professions*. Madison, WI: University of Wisconsin Press, 232–275

Boudiny, K. (2013) '"Active Ageing": From Empty Rhetoric to Effective Policy Tool' *Ageing Society* 33(6), 1077–1098.

Bubeck, D. (2003) 'Justice and the Labour of Care' in F. E. Kittay and E. K. Feder (eds) *The Subject of Care: Feminist Perspectives on Dependency*. Lanham: Rowman & Littlefield, 160–185.

Bullington, J. (2006) 'Body and Self: A Phenomenological Study on the Ageing Body and Identity' *Medical Humanities* 32, 25–31.

Butler, J. (2006) *Precarious Life: The Powers of Mourning and Violence*. London: Verso.

Butler, J. (2009) *Frames of War: When is Life Grievable?* London: Verso.

Carel, H. (2009) 'A Reply to "Towards an Understanding of Nursing as a Response to Human Vulnerability" by Derek Sellman: Vulnerability and Illness' *Nursing Philosophy* 21(3), 214–219.

Carse, A. L. (2006) 'Vulnerability, Agency, and Human Flourishing' in C. Taylor and R. Dell'Oro (eds) *Health and Human Flourishing: Religion, Medicine, and Moral Anthropology*. Washington, D.C., MD: Georgetown University Press.

Clarke, C. et al (2010) 'Dementia and Risk: Contested Territories of Everyday Life' *Journal of Nursing and Healthcare of Chronic Illness* 2(2), 102–112.

Curk, P. (2016) 'Passions, Dependencies, Selves: A Theoretical Psychoanalytic Account of Relational Responsibilities' in H. Keating (ed.) *Taking Responsibility, Law and the Changing Family*. Abingdon: Routledge.

Daniel, L. (1998) 'Vulnerability as a Key to Authenticity' *Journal of Nursing Scholarship* 30(2), 191–192.

Diduck, A. (2013) 'Autonomy and Vulnerability in Family Law: The Missing Link' in J. Wallbank and J. Herring (eds) *Vulnerabilities, Care and Family Law*. Abingdon: Routledge, 95–114.

Department of Health (DH) (2005) *Independence, Well-Being and Choice. Our Vision for the Future of Social Care in England, Cm 6499*. London: DH.

DH (2009) *Safeguarding Adults: Report on the Consultation on the Review of No Secrets*. London: DH.

Dunn, M. et al (2008) 'To Empower or to Protect? Constructing the "Vulnerable Adult" in English Law and Public Policy' *Legal Studies* 28, 234–253.

Faulkner, A. (2012) *The Right to Take Risks: Service Users' Views of Risk in Adult Social Care* (Joseph Rowntree Foundation Programme Paper: Risk, Trust and Relationships in an Ageing Society). York: Joseph Rowntree.

Fenge, L.-A. (2010) 'Promoting Inclusiveness: Developing Empowering Practice with Minority Groups of Older People' in K. Brown (ed.) *Vulnerable Adults and Community Care*. London: Sage, 90–96.

Fineman, M. A. (2012) '"Elderly" as Vulnerable: Rethinking the Nature of Individual and Social Responsibility' *The Elder Law Journal* 20(1), 101–112.

Gadow, S. (1987) 'Frailty and Strength: The Dialectic of Ageing' in T. Cole and S. Gadow (eds) *What Does It Mean to Grow Old?: Reflections from the Humanities*. Durham, NC: Duke University Press, 235–243.

Gadow, S. (1980) 'Body and Self: A Dialectic' *The Journal of Medicine and Philosophy* 5(3), 172–185.

Gattuso, S. (2003) 'Becoming a Wise Old Woman: Resilience and Wellness in Later Life' *Health Sociology Review* 12, 171–177.

Gilson, E. (2013) *The Ethics of Vulnerability: A Feminist Analysis of Social Life and Practice*. New York: Routledge.

Grear, A. (2010) *Redirecting Human Rights: Facing the Challenge of Corporate Legal Humanity*. Basingstoke: Palgrave.

Grear, A. (2013) 'Vulnerability, Advanced Global Capitalism and Co-Symptomatic Injustice: Locating the Vulnerable Subject' in M. Fineman and A. Grear (eds) *Vulnerability: Reflections on a New Ethical Foundation for Law and Politics*. Farnham: Ashgate, 41–60.

Hall, M. I. (2008) 'Equity Theory: Responding to the Material Exploitation of the Vulnerable but Capable' in I. Doron (ed.) *Theories on Law and Ageing: The Jurisprudence of Elder Law*. Berlin: Springer, 107–119.

Harper, S. (1997) 'Constructing Later Life/constructing the Body: Some Thoughts from Feminist Theory' in A. Jamieson, S. Harper and C. Victor (eds) *Critical Approaches to Ageing and Later Life*. Buckingham: Open University Press, 160–172.

Harris, G. (1997) *Human Dignity and Vulnerability: Strength and Quality of Character*. Oakland, CA: University of California Press.

Herring, J. (2013) *Caring and the Law*. Oxford: Hart Publishing.

Herring, J. (2016) *Vulnerable Adults and the Law*. Oxford: Oxford University Press.

Hoffmaster, B. (2006) *What Does Vulnerability Mean?* Hastings Center Report, 36, 38–45.

Holstein, M. and Minkler, M. (2003) 'Self, Society and the "New Gerontology"' *Gerontologist* 43(6), 787–796.

Howarth, C. (2014) 'Encountering the Ageing Body in Modernity: Fear, Vulnerability and "Contamination"' *Journal for Cultural Research* 18(3), 233–248.

Jordan, J. (2008) 'Valuing Vulnerability: New Definitions of Courage' *Women & Therapy* 31(2), 209–233.

Kittay, E. F. (2001) 'When Caring Is Just and Justice Is Caring: Justice and Mental Retardation' *Public Culture* 13(3), 557–579.

Kittay, E. F. (2011) 'The Ethics of Care, Dependence, and Disability' *Ratio Juris* 24, 49–58.

Law Commission (2011) *Adult Social Care Law Com No 326*. London: Law Commission.

Lawton, J. (1998) 'Contemporary Hospice Care: the Sequestration of the Unbounded Body and "Dirty Dying"' *Sociology of Health and Illness* 20(2), 121–143.

Lloyd-Sherlock, P. (2004) 'Ageing, Development and Social Protection: Generalizations, Myths and Stereotypes' in P. Lloyd-Sherlock (ed.) *Living Longer: Ageing, Development and Social Protection*. London: UNRISD and Zed Books, 1–20.

Michaels, C. and Moffett, C. (2008) 'Rethinking Vulnerability' in M. de Chesney and B. Anderson (eds) *Caring for the Vulnerable: Perspectives in Nursing Theory, Practice, and Research*. London: Jones and Bartlett Learning, 15–24.

Motenko, A. and Greenberg, S. (1995) 'Reframing Dependence in Old Age: A Positive Transition for Families' *Social Work* 40(3), 382–390.

Noddings, N. (1984) *Caring, a Feminine Approach to Ethics & Moral Education*. Berkeley, CA: University of California Press.

Noddings, N. (2010) 'Complexity in Caring and Empathy' *Abstracta* 6(2), 6–12.
Nussbaum, M. (2001) *The Fragility of Goodness: Luck and Ethics in Greek Tragedy and Philosophy*. Cambridge: Cambridge University Press.
Pritchard-Jones, L. (2016) 'The Good, the Bad, and the "Vulnerable Older Adult"' *Journal of Social Welfare and Family Law* 38(1), 51–72.
Ranzijn, R. (2010) 'Active Ageing – Another Way to Oppress Marginalized and Disadvantaged Elders? Aboriginal Elders as a Case Study' *Journal of Health Psychology* 15(5), 716–723.
Sabat, S. et al (2011) 'The "Demented Other" or Simply "A Person"? Extending the Philosophical Discourse of Naue and Kroll Through the Situated Self' *Nursing Philosophy* 12(4), 282–292.
Sarvimäki, A. and Stenbock-Hult, B. (2016) 'The Meaning of Vulnerability to Older Persons' *Nursing Ethics* 23(4), 372–383.
Shildrick, M. (2002) *Embodying the Monster: Encounters with the Vulnerable Self*. London: Sage.
Stenbock-Hult, B. and Sarvimäki, A. (2011) 'The Meaning of Vulnerability to Nurses Caring for Older People' *Nursing Ethics* 18(1), 31–41.
ten Have, H. (2016) *Vulnerability: Challenging Bioethics*. Abingdon: Routledge.
Toombs, K. (2006) 'Vulnerability and the Meaning of Illness: Reflections on Lived Experience' in C. Taylor and R. Dell'Oro (eds) *Health and Human Flourishing*. Washington, D.C., MD: Georgetown University Press, 119–140.
Wendell, S. (2008) 'Towards a Feminist Theory of Disability' in A. Bailey and C. Cuomo (eds) *The Feminist Philosophy Reader*. New York: McGraw Hill, 826–841.
World Health Organization (WHO) (2002) *Active Ageing: A Policy Framework*. Geneva: WHO.

Cases

A London Local Authority v JH [2011] *EWHC* 2420 (COP)
DL v A Local Authority [2012] *EWCA Civ* 253
HBCC v LG [2010] *EWHC* 1527
LLBC v TG, JG and KR
London Borough of Redbridge v G [2014] *EWCOP* 17
Re MM (an adult) [2007] *EWHC* 2003

Chapter 2

The contractualisation of care in an ageing world

Pip Coore

Introduction

We will all, at some point in our lives, care for an ill or disabled loved one, or need care ourselves (Herring 2013, Carers UK 2014). As the global population ages, the number of people affected by age-related illnesses requiring on-going, extended care will dramatically increase (Alzheimer's Australia 2006). Currently, limited places in aged care facilities, coupled with governments encouraging people to remain in the community as they age, puts new pressures on families to care for their older relatives (Herd 2002b). This is creating a situation where life comes 'full circle'; where the older parent becomes the dependent and the adult child becomes the carer (Herd 2002a, 73). With new pressures on families to care for their older relatives, family agreements are increasingly being entered into (Herd 2002a). Family agreements are, as Herd (2002b, 24) explains, arrangements in which an older parent transfers property, or pays compensation, to their adult child during their lifetime in return for the promise that their adult child will care for them 'for life ('Family Agreements').

Although Family Agreements are intended to safeguard older people from harmful outcomes, there is currently no legislation governing or regulating them (Committee Report 2007), there is little written about them, and there is limited information available to guide families wishing to enter into Family Agreements (Alzheimer's Australia 2006). In an attempt to shed some light on this 'shadowland of family caring' (Herd 2002a, 73), this chapter seeks to consider some of the advantages and disadvantages associated with Family Agreements. Due to the limited literature on Family Agreements in England, this chapter draws on useful research from countries with comparable health and aged care systems, particularly Australia and British Columbia Canada.

Although many people create their own circle of members they consider 'family' (BCLI 2002, 4), this chapter largely deals with the relationship of care between an older parent and their adult child. Given there is no legal age at which a person becomes 'old', the use of the generic phrase 'older person' is accepted in the academic world of gerontology to describe persons over the age of 65 (Brammer and Biggs 1998). Therefore, for the purposes of this chapter, 'older person' and 'older parent' will be used to describe persons over the age of 65.

This chapter will start by setting out why it is that older people are turning to Family Agreements to create a formal legal basis for their care. It will then examine the current legal response to these agreements. It will conclude by exploring how the law ought to respond to Family Agreements.

An ageing world

In life one thing is certain, we all age. Due to decreased mortality and declining fertility (UN 2013), the world is ageing at a rate 'without parallel in the history of humanity' (UN 2001, xxviii). Today, there are over 11.6 million older people living in the United Kingdom ('UK') (ONS 2016a, 2). The Office for National Statistics ('ONS') (2015 cited in Age UK 2017) predicts that by 2030 this number will surpass 20 million and by 2040, it is expected that nearly one in four people in the UK will be aged 65 or over. In addition to societal population ageing, life expectancy at an individual level has also increased (ONS 2016b). The ONS (2016b) observed that a woman aged 65 today can expect to live another 21.1 years, while a man can expect to live for another 18.7 years.

Although, for most people, 'living for longer is to be celebrated' (House of Lords 2013, 8), and despite arguments that ageing is not an automatic proxy for a decline in health (Grimley-Evans 2003), increased life expectancy means 'longer stretches of frailty, disability, and dependence' (Kulik et al 2014, 930). The dramatic shift in the age structure of the population presents significant challenges for governments, particularly in relation to the provision of 'both present needs and future demand' of long-term healthcare for disabled older people (House of Lords 2013, 14). Alarmingly, the House of Lords (2013, 7) concluded that the Government is 'woefully underprepared' for the rapidly ageing population, noting (p. 14) that '[n]othing like enough is being done to face up to these challenges.' Moreover, the House of Lords (2013, 14) commented that '[p]ublicly funded care alone has never met all the needs of older people who are frail, vulnerable, ill or isolated.' As Clough discusses in this collection (Chapter 6), due to the rationing of subsidised aged care and cuts to local authority budgets, disabled older people have difficulty accessing appropriate services and support. The King's Fund (Humphries et al 2016, 3) found that the current social care system is 'struggling to meet the needs of older people.' Carers UK (2014, 128) concluded that due to diminishing support from Government, there is an 'increasingly divergent picture' of families providing unpaid care for their older relatives that aged care services cannot meet. Therefore, the demand for unpaid long-term care for older people by family members, particularly adult children, will 'increase substantially' (Pickard 2015, 96 citing Colombo et al 2011a).

The certainty of family care

It is well understood that families are the main source of care and support for older people (Carers UK 2014, Pickard et al 2007, Pickard 2015). As Herring

(2013, 187) argues, '[c]are is at the centre of family life.' Despite previous care literature (Pickard et al 2007, 354 citing Parker 1990 and Henz 2004) suggesting that spouses are 'the most important group of carers' for older people, recent research (Pickard 2015, 110) predicts that adult children, particularly daughters, will be the most 'important source of care for older people with disabilities in future.' Yet, the literature, and the law, pays very little attention to the caring relationship between an adult child and their older parent or the position of older people in families (Herring 2013).

As dependence on families to care for their older parent increases, Alzheimer's Australia (2006, 20) argue that there is an urgent need for 'guidelines within a legal framework to support the many families who choose to care for their elderly relative within the family.' Further, Holzhausen (2015) argued that supporting families to care is 'not only a moral goal, but also an economic one', observing that without family carers the health and social care systems would 'collapse.' Currently, there is an estimated 6.8 million people providing unpaid care in the UK, which saves the 'public purse' £15.1 million per hour and has an economic value of £132 billion per year (Buckner and Yeandle 2015, 4). Carers UK (2014) have estimated that by 2037, nine million people will be caring for an older or disabled loved one. As many older people wish to remain in a familial and familiar environment (Herd 2002a), much of the care provided by family members takes place in the context of co-residence of the disabled older parent with their adult child (Pezzin et al 2007). It is therefore evident that an older person's choice about their living arrangement is influenced by their care needs (ABS 2013).

Living arrangements of older people

Unlike many cultures, co-residence of older parents with their adult children is not traditionally common in England (Herring 2013). Although evidence suggests that older people in Britain are 'fiercely independent' (Izuhara 2004, 661), the need for older people to co-reside with their family members is increasing (Postigo and Honrubia 2010), which is challenging the traditional concepts of living arrangements of families. Monro (2002) observed that a decline in health, the death of a spouse, and loneliness are all circumstances that may precipitate an older person's decision to co-reside with their adult child. The Australian Bureau of Statistics ('ABS') (2013) reported that out of the 8.2% of older people living with relatives other than their spouse or partner, 6.9% were living with their adult child. Further, the ABS (2013) reported that older people living with an adult child are most likely to need assistance with one or more of the core everyday activities of self-care, mobility, and communication. Moon (1983 cited in Pezzin et al 2007, 71) observed that older people 'cared for in the home of a family member have better health outcomes than those in similar health who were cared for in an institution.'

The genesis of the Family Agreement

The phenomenon of families caring for their older relatives is not a new concept (Herd 2002a). Traditionally, societies supported older people via a system of 'intergenerational reciprocity', whereby adults provided for their young children, and, when those children grew up, they cared for their older parents (Kulik et al 2014, 929). Today, however, many adult children have significant personal debts with little savings to afford to reduce their working hours to care for their older parent (Herd 2002a, 73). An increasing number of adult children, particularly women, are forced to reduce their paid working hours to provide unpaid care for their older parent(s). Burns (2005, 301–302) commented that unless the older parent assumes responsibility for some of the financial liabilities incurred by the adult child in relation to their care, this dependency is likely to be 'an intolerable financial burden on younger generations.' In recognition of this, it is argued that uncompensated caring is unrealistic and will therefore be replaced with the notion of compensated caring (BCLI 2002, Herd 2002a, Grootegoed et al 2010). This is what Herd (2002b, 24) describes as 'the genesis of the family agreement', which is 'the transformation of a cultural duty into a compensatable, contractual obligation of care.'

Family Agreements

What are Family Agreements?

In 2006, the Australian House of Representatives Standing Committee on Legal and Constitutional Affairs ('the Committee') investigated whether Australian legal regimes adequately addressed the legal needs of older people. In 2007, the Committee tabled its report to the Parliament of Australia ('Committee Report') and the Australian Government's response to the Committee Report was tabled in 2009. The Committee received a total of 157 submissions and 43 supplementary submissions and the Committee Report (2007) made a total of 48 recommendations with a particular focus on Family Agreements. The Committee described Family Agreements as:

> an arrangement between an older person and another party or parties (usually family members or carers) whereby the older person provides a benefit to the other party in exchange for continuing (or lifelong) care. The benefit can take various forms, for example a transfer of property or a compensatory payment.
> (2007, 135)

Typically, Family Agreements are made between an older parent and their adult child (Lewis 2004) and usually involve a transfer of the older person's home to their adult child in exchange for a promise of 'care for life' (Herd 2002b, Hall 2003). Given the transfer of property from an older parent to their adult child under a Family Agreement is 'made by one living person to another', it is characterised as a 'gift inter vivos' (Greenberg 2015, 1076).

Due to their 'private nature' the prevalence of Family Agreements is difficult to quantify (Monro 2002, 68). Consequently, there is little statistical or empirical evidence of families systematically formalising or documenting Family Agreements (Herd 2002a). However, anecdotal evidence suggests that an increasing number of families are entering into Family Agreements, albeit on an informal or oral basis (Alzheimer's Australia 2006, Herd 2002a, Hall 2003). Herd (2002b, 25) has identified a number of reasons why Family Agreements are gaining popularity:

- our general aversion to 'institutional' residential aged care;
- the lack of such facilities or, at least, of any more sympathetic and empathetic alternatives;
- people are living longer and as a result, living longer with disabilities;
- our fixation in later life to preserve assets for succeeding generations; and
- our consequent reluctance to dissipate assets (especially the family home) to pay any premium for assisted care, such as an accommodation bond in a hostel.

Advantages of Family Agreements

Although documenting a loving, caring, and supportive personal relationship may seem abhorrent to many, English law has already challenged the 'cultural aversion' of contracting with family members with the acknowledgment of, and legislative support for, cohabitation agreements and prenuptial agreements (Herd 2002b, 23). In the context of cohabitation agreements, it is commented (Reece 2014, 119 citing Advice Services Alliance 2004) that '[m]aking a [living together] agreement prompts you to discuss how your living together will work in practice and what your expectations of each other are.' Similarly, in the context of Family Agreements, Carers Queensland (2006, 5) have argued that the 'most beneficial' feature of Family Agreements is 'that they provide an avenue for people to discuss and consider their, often previously unstated, expectations and assumptions regarding the provision and receipt of future care for older people.'

Another advantage of Family Agreements is that they allow older people to exercise choice and control over how, and by whom, care is provided (Herd 2002b), which Glendinning (2008) observed is crucially important in helping redress the vulnerabilities and inequalities that exist within the caring relationship. As Vernon and Qureshi (2000 cited in Glendinning 2008, 461) observed, '[t]he capacity to exercise choice and control over daily life is a social care outcome that is commonly desired by older people.'

Carers Queensland (2006 cited in Committee Report 2007, 140) observed that Family Agreements can also function to compensate the caregiving family member for 'income lost, career prospects foregone and expenses incurred as a result of caring for the older person.' Grootegoed et al (2010, 478) commented that compensation for care can 'restore a balance in the give-and-take' associated with long-term care, which is 'crucial for the material wellbeing of the care-giver.' A study by Izuhara (2004) on long-term care and inheritance found that although one child did most of the care, older parents tended to split the inheritance equally among their children. Although no strong link between property transfer and long-term care responsibilities was found, Izuhara (2004, 659–660) observed that older parents are willing to compensate their caregiving adult child 'on the spot rather than let them accumulate any advantage and pass it on to them at death.' Family Agreements are therefore challenging the 'cultural aversion' (Herd 2002b, 23) against 'cash-for-care schemes' (Grootegoed et al 2010, 468) and altering preconceived ideas of property transfer within the family (Izuhara 2005, Monk, this volume).

Disadvantages of Family Agreements

Although Family Agreements are intended to 'safeguard older people' from harmful outcomes, they are 'fraught with difficulties' (Office of the Public Advocate and Queensland Law Society 2010, 8). One common derivative of Family Agreements is the 'granny flat scenario', which involves an older parent using their life savings, or the settlement proceeds from the sale of their previous home, to build a self-contained residence on their adult child's property (Committee Report 2007, 136–137). In 'the ubiquitous granny flat' scenario, Field (2005, 104) observed that it is common for the title of the property to remain in the name of the adult child and rightly noted that '[t]he problems associated with the transfer of money, without an associated transfer of title, are all too obvious.' Field (2005, 103) commented that, in many instances, 'the family home constitutes the majority of, if not the entire, asset of the older person.' Therefore, the transfer of an older person's property to their adult child without the simultaneous transfer of title leaves the older person vulnerable to financial exploitation. State Trustees (2006, 12) argued that Family Agreements 'are an area of considerable risk to older people' as they can 'result in significant depletion of the older person's assets for minimal tangible benefit.'

Due to the inherent belief that 'family relationships should be preserved at any cost' (Monro 2002, 71), many older people are reluctant to seek legal advice when they experience financial exploitation so as to 'maintain a family relationship' (Kyle 2013, 2). As a consequence, instances of financial exploitation are likely to be discovered after the older person's assets have been squandered, with virtually no practical avenue for redress (Committee Report 2007). The Australian Institute of Criminology (2006 cited in Committee Report 2007, 12) noted that the impact of such financial exploitation on an older person can be 'severe', particularly because 'they may not have the time or the opportunity for financial recovery.' Further, '[a] blow to financial security is often a permanent and life-threatening setback, characterised by fear, lack of trust, and is often the onset of acute and chronic anxiety' (Committee Report 2007, 12 citing the Australian Institute of Criminology 2006).

It is a distressing irony that the majority of perpetrators of financial exploitation are family members, particularly the older person's son or daughter (Bagshaw et al

2013). In order to understand more about this threat posed to older people, the Association of Chief Police Officers (2011) commissioned an assessment of financial crime against vulnerable adults. Although the majority of family carers act with 'probity and integrity' (Carers Queensland 2006, 1), this assessment (City of London Police 2011, 8) revealed that the most frequent perpetrator of financial abuse is 'a person acting in a trusted capacity', such as a family carer. Given the majority of care for an older person is provided by a 'trusted' family member, there is a concern that abuse within the caring relationship will increase as the usage rates of Family Agreements increase. In the absence of specific legislation to govern and regulate Family Agreements, the Committee (2007) recommended that a review of the law is necessary to adequately protect the rights of older people wishing to enter into Family Agreements.

Despite being 'best intention agreements' (Field 2005, 104), anecdotal and case law evidence suggests that the majority of Family Agreements fail due to relationship breakdowns (Herd 2002a, Monro 2002, Hall 2003). As Bryson J (*Bennett v Horgan*, unreported, Supreme Court of New South Wales, 3 June 1994 cited in Cockburn 2008, 41) observed, '[i]t is a sadly recurring judicial experience to see that family relationships do deteriorate and become intolerable, and that the persons involved did not foresee that this might happen.' In the event that the caring relationship breaks down, particularly within the granny flat scenario, the older parent is likely to lose their entire savings with the subsequent breakdown of the relationship with their adult child being 'inevitably irretrievable' (Field 2005, p 104). In recognition of this, the Australian Law Reform Commission ('ALRC') (2016a, 31) recently concluded that the current legal regime is inadequately protecting the rights of older people where the caring relationship under a Family Agreement breaks down.

Ironically, despite the considerable risk of financial exploitation associated with Family Agreements, the Office of the Public Advocate (2006, 8) argued that Family Agreements 'are an important safeguard for older people who may have invested their life saving into the building of a granny flat of a family member's home in exchange for services to be provided by the family.' Contrastingly, the Committee (2007, 146) concluded '[t]he potentially disastrous consequences that can be suffered by parties to Family Agreements due to uncertainty, dispute or abuse warrant some form of regulation, particularly if the use of Family Agreements increases in the future.'

Legal status and enforcement of Family Agreements

The contractualisation of care is 'anathema to many' (Herd 2002b, 23). The Office of the Public Advocate (2006, 8) observed, '[f]or many families there is a psychological barrier to formalising care arrangements in a legally binding contract', particularly 'where trust is thought to be sufficient.' Due to the reluctance of families to formalise intimate relationships in a written contract (BCLI 2002), the majority of Family Agreements are being made informally and on an oral basis (Committee Report 2007). Hall (2003) commented that a significant problem with Family Agreements is that they tend to be nothing more than a very general and vague promise of the adult child to take care of their older parent for the rest of their life. In recognition of this, the Victorian Government (2006, 29) commented that the informal and familial nature of Family Agreements 'may make it difficult for the law to recognise and/or enforce them as contracts, and common law presumptions may assume that the transfer of property is a gift with no obligations attached.' This is inevitably leading to 'ambiguous arrangements' (Monro 2002, 69) that are breaking down 'behind closed family doors' (Herd 2002a, 77).

Although the legal status of Family Agreements is 'unclear' (NSW Ministerial Advisory Committee on Ageing 2006, 5), many argue there is no legal reason why Family Agreements cannot form valid written contracts if all of the requirements of a contract are satisfied (Alzheimer's Australia 2006, Herd 2002a, Hall 2003). Furmston et al noted that in order to establish an enforceable contract:

> the parties, through a process of offer and acceptance, must enter into an agreement, whose terms are sufficiently certain to allow for legal enforcement, with the intention that the agreement be legally binding; the agreement must be supported by consideration; and the agreement must comply with any formal requirements laid down by law.
>
> (2015, [2.1])

This 'schematic analysis' of the elements of a contract established in the late nineteenth and early twentieth centuries is said to be 'artificial because it bears little relation to the way in which, whether as a result of the formal negotiation of a written document, or as a result of oral haggling, contracts are 'formed' in real life situations' (Furmston et al 2015, [2.2]). In the context of Family Agreements, Alzheimer's Australia (2006, 22) commented '[t]he common law of contract still has the perception that the "family" is based on early twentieth century notions of a family when there were much clearer expectations of the role of each member with no expectation of compensation.' In recognition of this, Skousgaard argued (2006 cited in Alzheimer's Australia 2006, 22) that the 'way to move forward is for the common law of contract to become responsive to current needs and practices.' Keyes and Burns (2002, 578) critically scrutinised contract law's treatment of Family Agreements arguing that 'it no longer reflects social conditions and is inconsistent with other areas of law', 'namely estoppel and family law' (p. 595). Further, the British Columbia Law Institute (2002, 11) commented that the common law is 'neither clear nor consistent' in its treatment of Family Agreements.

The confusion regarding the legal status of Family Agreements has arguably arisen due to the well-established presumption of fact that agreements between spouses (*Balfour v Balfour* [1919] 2 KB 571) and agreements between close relatives, such as parent and child (*Jones v Padavatton* [1969] 1 WLR 328), are not contractual in character nor are they intended to create legal relations. Atkin LJ in *Balfour* outlined the rationale for this presumption:

> It is quite common, and it is the natural and inevitable result of the relationship of husband and wife, that the two spouses should make arrangements between themselves (…). To my mind those agreements, or many of them, do not result in contracts at all, and they do not result in contracts even though there may be what as between other parties would constitute consideration for the agreement.
>
> (…)
>
> Nevertheless they are **not** contracts, and they are **not** contracts because the parties did not intend that they should be attended by legal consequences. To my mind it would be of the worst possible example to hold that agreements such as this resulted in legal obligations which could be enforced in the Courts.
>
> (578–579, emphasis added)

Although *Balfour* was a case regarding husband and wife, the same principles have unanimously been held to apply to dealings between an adult child and their older parent (*Jones*). While courts are sceptical regarding the contractual intention of Family Agreements, Salmon LJ (*Jones*, 333) commented, 'this presumption, like all other presumptions of fact, can be rebutted.' In order to rebut this presumption, the older parent and/or the adult child would need to adduce evidence proving that, in such circumstances, there was an intention to create a legally binding agreement (*Balfour, Jones*).

In *Ermogenous v Greek Orthodox Community of SA Inc* ((2002) 209 CLR 95), the High Court of Australia affirmed that an intention to create a contractual relationship is an essential precondition to contractual liability (Keyes and Burns 2002). When considering this issue, the majority (Gaudron, McHugh, Hayne, and Callinan JJ, 105) were sceptical of the ability to formulate rules that were 'intended to prescribe the kinds of cases in which an intention to create contractual relations should, or should not, be found to exist', noting that '"intention to create contractual relations" requires an objective assessment of the state of affairs between the parties' rather than searching for the 'uncommunicated subjective motives or intentions of the parties' (p. 106). In the context of Family Agreements, their Honours (p. 106) doubted the 'utility of using the language of presumptions' as '[r]eference to presumptions may serve only to distract attention from that more basic and important proposition.'

If the requisite intention to create legal relations under a Family Agreement is found, and if a term of the contract is not performed, the aggrieved party may commence civil litigation for breach of contract (BCLI 2002, Queensland Attorney-General 2006). However, due to the reluctance of older people to seek legal advice before entering into Family Agreements (Monro 2002), they are rarely being prepared and executed as full legal contracts (Committee Report 2007), which is 'fatal' to their enforcement (Monro 2002, 70). Therefore, under the current law, Family Agreements are likely to be 'merely one of those family or domestic arrangements where the parties at the time had no thought or intention of invoking the assistance of the courts should the arrangement not be honoured' (*Jones*, 336 per Fenton Atkinson LJ) or be 'far too vague and uncertain to be itself enforceable as a contract' (*Jones*, 337 per Fenton Atkinson LJ). Herring (2016, 297) commented that Family Agreements are likely to be far too vague because such agreements are 'impossible to draft', noting that care, especially for disabled older people, 'is not a matter of nine to five, with four weeks' holiday' and is therefore 'not reducible to the black and white of print.' Similarly, the ALRC (2016b, 145) commented '[i]t may be difficult to establish that a contract was intended, and what its terms were.' Accordingly, contractual remedies will not be available (Committee Report 2007, Cockburn 2008).

Post-death Family Agreement feuds

Given a gift inter vivos strips the older person of their property during their lifetime (*Craig v Lamoureux* [1920] AC 349, 356), the inter vivos transfer(s) made under a Family Agreement is likely to largely deplete the older parent's estate. Due to the natural reluctance of an older parent to sue their adult child, Hamilton and Cockburn (2014) observed that equitable claims alleging undue influence and/or unconscionable conduct are increasingly being made post-death by children of the deceased to set aside inter vivos transactions, generally to enlarge the available estate for the benefit of the beneficiaries or an applicant of a family provision application ('FPA').

In *Gill v Woodall* ([2011] 3 WLR 85, 91), a probate case, Lord Neuberger of Abbotsbury MR made comments that can arguably be applied to Family Agreement feuds between siblings following the death of their older parent:

> Wills frequently give rise to feelings of disappointment or worse on the part of relatives and other would-be beneficiaries. Human nature being what it is, such people will often be able to find evidence, or to persuade themselves that evidence exists, which shows that the will did not, could not, or was unlikely to, represent the intention of the testatrix, or that the testatrix was in some way mentally affected so as to cast doubt on the will. If judges were too ready to accept such contentions, it would risk undermining what may be regarded as a fundamental principle of English law, namely that people should in general be free to leave their property as they choose, and it would run the danger of encouraging people to contest wills, which could result in many estates being diminished by substantial legal costs.
>
> Further, such disputes will almost always arise when the desires, personality and state of mind of the central character, namely the testatrix herself [or himself], cannot be examined other than in a second hand way, and where much of the useful potential second hand evidence will often be partisan, and will be unavailable or far less reliable due to the passage of time. As Scarman J put it graphically in *In the Estate of Fuld, deceased (No 3)* [1968] P 675, 714E: 'When all is dark, it is dangerous for a court to claim that it can see the light.' That observation applies with almost equal force when all is murky and uncertain.

Due to the strongly held belief that parents should treat children equally (Izuhara 2005), the inter vivos transfer(s) made by the older parent to the caregiving adult child under a Family Agreement will undoubtedly give rise to 'feelings of disappointment or worse' (*Gill v Woodall*, 91 per Lord Neuberger of Abbotsbury MR) on the part of the sibling(s) who did not equally benefit.

Under English law, if a will or intestacy laws fail to make adequate provision for the proper maintenance and support of the deceased's person's spouse, child or dependant, the court may, in its discretion, order provision to be made out of the estate for such person under the Inheritance (Provision for Family and Dependants) Act 1975 ('the 1975 Act'). An Australian study by Tilse et al (2014) found that 'family provision claims were the most frequent category of will contestation across all States' (p. 5), and '[c]laims by biological children of the deceased were the largest category of persons instigating disputes' (p. 7). Although a family provision claim by an adult child with earning capacity is 'unlikely to succeed' (Sloan 2013, 192), Matthews (2009; cited in Sloan 2013, 192) observed that there has been a recent increase in successful claims by 'ostensibly able-bodied' adult children under the 1975 Act. Yet, ironically, the law fails to adequately recognise the value of care work provided by an adult child prior to the death of the testator (Sloan 2013, 192). Consequently, a caregiving adult child may, after defending an equitable claim by their siblings, be stripped from the benefit of the inter vivos transfer and subsequently may not receive adequate provision under family provision laws for care work they performed in the past.

This chapter has demonstrated that an inter vivos transfer made between an older parent and their adult child under a Family Agreement leaves the caregiving adult child vulnerable to post-mortem claims challenging the validity of the transaction. In these circumstances, the deceased's intentions can only be examined in a second hand way and much of the evidence will often be partisan. In the event that the inter vivos transfer is set aside, the caregiving adult child is eligible to bring a FPA however, given unpaid carers 'fall outside the protection of the legislation' (Herring 2016, 298), their care is given 'no recognition' (Sloan 2013, 194). It is therefore argued (Sloan 2013, 138) that the law needs to better recognise the value of care work so as to encourage family caring and 'to reward them justly for their efforts.'

Family Agreements: the way forward?

Family Agreements, like cohabitation agreements, are said to force family members 'into the future' (Reece 2014, 126 citing Beck-Gernsheim 2002). Given care is 'unbounded' and 'unpredictable', Herring (2016, 297) commented that it is often difficult to foresee now what care will be needed in the future. It is perhaps arguable that a more suitable time to determine the value, and thus the reward, of care performed by an adult child is at the time the caring ends, which, in most cases, will be upon death of the older parent. It is commented that '[t]he resolving of payment for care ex post facto, post-death carries many benefits' (Herring 2016, 298 citing Gallanis and Gittler 2012). Similarly, Monk, in this collection (p. 193, citing Westwood 2013), argues 'a post-mortem attempt to recognise care within inheritance law would include this as a ground for challenging wills and intestacy.' If this argument is accepted, consideration of the courts' power to redistribute property upon the breakdown of the caring relationship or the death of the older parent requires further attention. Herring (2016, 297) believes that an adult child who provided care to the deceased has the 'strongest' family provision claim and argues (p. 302) that the use of legislation, such as the 1975 Act, 'is an effective tool to encourage the care of older people and the best way of ensuring compensation for the costs of that care.'

Although, in theory, Family Agreements have the potential to safeguard older people and compensate the caregiving adult child, the informal and familial nature of Family Agreements is creating significant potential for 'problems and disputes' (Committee Report 2007, 140), which may have 'harsh and unfair consequences' for both the older person and the caregiving adult child (BCLI 2002, 24). In the absence of specific legislation to govern and regulate Family Agreements, families are too readily entering into agreements that 'exist beneath both the legal and the law maker's radar' (Herd 2002a, 74). Although the implementation of legislative safeguards has resulted in positive changes to guardianship laws, the current law is inadequate in protecting the rights of older people and their caregiving adult child who have entered into a Family Agreement. It is commented that legislation allowing the courts to dissolve Family Agreements, restore property, and compensate the caregiving adult child would be useful (BCLI 2002, Committee Report 2007). Therefore, lawmakers need to consider regulating family care relationships so as to ensure the rights of older people, and their caregiving family members, are protected from harmful outcomes.

Bibliography

Age UK (2017) *Later Life in the United Kingdom*. Available at: www.ageuk.org.uk/Documents/EN-GB/Factsheets/Later_Life_UK_factsheet.pdf?dtrk=true

Alzheimer's Australia (2006) *Submission No. 55 to the House of Representatives Standing Committee on Legal and Constitutional Affairs*. Available at: www.aph.gov.au/parliamentary_business/committees/house_of_representatives_committees?url=/laca/olderpeople/subs.htm

Australian Bureau of Statistics (2013) *Where and How do Australia's Older People Live? Reflecting a Nation: Stories from the 2011 Census*. Available at: www.abs.gov.au/ausstats/abs@.nsf/Lookup/2071.0main+features602012–602013

Australian Law Reform Commission (ALRC), Australian Government (2016a) *Elder Abuse: Issues Paper*. (IP 47). Available at: www.alrc.gov.au/publications/elder-abuse

ALRC (2016b) *Elder Abuse: Discussion Paper*. (DP 83). Available at: www.alrc.gov.au/publications/elder-abuse-dp83

Bagshaw, D., Wendt, S., Zannettino, L. and Adams, V. (2013) 'Financial Abuse of Older People by Family Members: Views and Experiences of Older Australians and their Family Members' *Australian Social Work* 66(1), 86.

Brammer, A. and Biggs, S. (1998) 'Defining Elder Abuse' *Journal of Social Welfare and Family Law* 20(3), 285.

British Columbia Law Institute (BCLI), Committee on Legal Issues Affecting Seniors (2002) *Private Care Agreements Between Older Adults and Friends of Family Members*. BCLI Report No 18. Available at: www.bcli.org/sites/default/files/Private_Care_Agreements_Between_Older_Adults_and_Friends_or_Family_Members.pdf

Buckner, L. and Yeandle, S. (2015) 'Valuing Carers 2015: The Rising Value of Carers' Support', CarersUK. Available at: www.carersuk.org/for-professionals/policy/policy-library/valuing-carers-2015

Burns, F. R. (2005) 'Protecting Elders: Regulating Intergenerationally Transmitted Debt in Australia' *International Journal of Law and Psychiatry* 28, 300.

Carers Queensland (2006) *Submission No. 81 to the House of Representatives Standing Committee on Legal and Constitutional Affairs*. Available at: www.aph.gov.au/parliamentary_business/committees/house_of_representatives_committees?url=/laca/olderpeople/subs.htm

Carers UK (2014) *Caring and Family Finances Inquiry: UK Report*. Available at: www.carersuk.org/for-professionals/policy/policy-library/caring-family-finances-inquiry

City of London Police (2011) 'Assessment: Financial Crime Against Vulnerable Adults', Social Care Institute for Excellence. Available at: www.scie.org.uk/

Cockburn, T. (2008) 'Equitable Relief to Enforce Family Agreements' *Precedent* 86, 41.

Field, S. (2005) 'Issues Facing Older Australians: Legal, Financial and Societal' *Journal of International Aging, Law & Policy* 1, 101.

Furmston, M., Mik, E. and Tolhurst, G. J. (2015) 'Formation of Contracts' in M. Furmston (ed.) *Common Law Series: The Law of Contract*, 5th edn. London: LexisNexis.

Glendinning, C. (2008) 'Increasing Choice and Control for Older and Disabled People: A Critical Review of New Developments in England' *Social Policy & Administration* 42(5), 451.

Greenberg, D. (ed.) (2015) *Jowitt's Dictionary of English Law*, 4th edn. London: Sweet & Maxwell.

Grimley-Evans, J. (2003) 'Age Discrimination: Implications of the Ageing Process' in S. Fredman and S. Spencer (eds) *Age Discrimination: Implications of the Ageing Process*. Oxford: Hart.

Grootegoed, E., Knijn, T. and Da Roit, B. (2010) 'Relatives as Paid Care-givers: How Family Carers Experience Payments for Care' *Ageing and Society* 30, 467.

Hall, M. I. (2003) 'Care for Life: Private Care Agreements Between Older Adults and Friends or Family Members' *Elder Law Review* 2, 1.

Hamilton, B. J. and Cockburn, T. L. C. (2014) 'Equity in Australian Estate Litigation' *Trusts & Trustees* 20(5), 437.

Herd, B. (2002a) 'The Family Agreement: Legal Good Sense or Social Bad Taste for the Aged?' *Alternative Law Journal* 27, 72.

Herd, B. (2002b) 'The Family Agreement – A Collision between Love and the Law?' *Reform* 81, 23.

Herring, J. (2013) *Caring and the Law*. Oxford: Hart.

Herring, J. (2016) 'Will-substitutes and the Claims of Family Members and Carers' in A. Braun and A. Rothel (eds) *Passing Wealth on Death: Will-Substitutes in Comparative Perspective*. Oxford: Hart.

Holzhausen, E. (2015) 'Without carers, health and social systems would collapse', NHS England, London. Available at: www.england.nhs.uk/blog/emily-holzhausen/

House of Lords, Select Committee on Public Service and Demographic Change (2013) 'Ready for Ageing?', Report of Session 2012–2013. Available at: www.cpahq.org/cpahq/cpadocs/UK%20Parliament%20HOL%20Ready%20for%20the%20Ageing.pdf

House of Representatives Standing Committee on Legal and Constitutional Affairs, the Parliament of the Commonwealth of Australia (2007) *Older People and the Law*. Available at: www.aph.gov.au/Parliamentary_Business/Committees/House_of_Representatives_Committees?url=laca/olderpeople/report.htm

Humphries, R., Thorlby, R., Holder, H., Hall, P. and Charles, A. (2016) *Social Care for Older People: Home Truths*. London: The King's Fund.

Izuhara, M. (2004) 'Negotiating Family Support? The "Generational Contract" between Long-term Care and Inheritance' *Journal of Social Policy* 33(4), 649.

Izuhara, M. (2005) 'Residential Property, Cultural Practices and the "Generational Contract" in England and Japan' *International Journal of Urban and Regional Research* 29(2), 327.

Keyes, M. and Burns, K. (2002) 'Contract and the Family: Whither Intention?' *Melbourne University Law Review* 26(3), 577.

Kulik, C., Ryan, S., Harper, S. and George, G. (2014) 'Aging Populations and Management: From the Editors' *Academy of Management Journal* 57(4), 929.

Kyle, L. (2013) 'Out of the Shadows – A Discussion on Law Reform for the Prevention of Financial Abuse of Older People' *Elder Law Review* 7(4), 1.

Lewis, R. (2004) *Elder Law in Australia*. Chatswood: LexisNexis Butterworths.

Monro, R. (2002) 'Family Agreements: All with the Best of Intentions' *Alternative Law Journal* 27(2), 68.

New South Wales Ministerial Advisory Committee on Ageing (2006) *Submission No. 103 to the House of Representatives Standing Committee on Legal and Constitutional Affairs*. Available at: www.aph.gov.au/parliamentary_business/committees/house_of_representatives_committees?url=/laca/olderpeople/subs.htm

Office for National Statistics (ONS) (2016a) *Population Estimates for the UK, England and Wales, Scotland and Northern Ireland: Mid-2015*. Available at: www.ons.gov.uk/peoplepopulationandcommunity/populationandmigration/populationestimates/bulletins/annualmidyearpopulationestimates/mid2015

ONS (2016b) *Health State Life Expectancies, UK: 2013 to 2015*. Available at: www.ons.gov.uk/peoplepopulationandcommunity/healthandsocialcare/healthandlifeexpectancies/bulletins/healthstatelifeexpectanciesuk/2013to2015

Office of the Public Advocate, Queensland Government (2006) *Submission No. 76 to the House of Representatives Standing Committee on Legal and Constitutional Affairs*. Available at: www.aph.gov.au/parliamentary_business/committees/house_of_representatives_committees?url=/laca/olderpeople/subs.htm

Office of the Public Advocate, Queensland Government and Queensland Law Society (2010) *Elder Abuse: How well does the law in Queensland cope?* Available at: www.justice.qld.gov.au/__data/assets/pdf_file/0007/54691/elder-abuse_issues-paper.pdf

Pezzin, L. E., Pollak, R. A. and Schone, B. S. (2007) 'Efficiency in Family Bargaining: Living Arrangements and Caregiving Decisions of Adult Children and Disabled Elderly Parents' *CESifo Economic Studies* 53(1), 69.

Pickard, L., Wittenberg, R., Comas-Herrera, A., King, D. and Malley, J. (2007) 'Care by Spouses, Care by Children: Projections of Informal Care for Older People in England to 2031' *Social Policy & Society* 6(3), 353.

Pickard, L. (2015) 'A Growing Care Gap? The Supple of Unpaid Care for Older People by Their Adult Children in England to 2032' *Ageing and Society* 35(1), 96.

Postigo, J. M. L. and Honrubia, R. L. (2010) 'The Co-Residence of Elderly People with Their Children and Grandchildren' *Educational Gerontology* 36(4), 330.

Queensland Attorney-General (2006) *Submission No. 107 to the House of Representatives Standing Committee on Legal and Constitutional Affairs*. Available at: www.aph.gov.au/parliamentary_business/committees/house_of_representatives_committees?url=/laca/olderpeople/subs.htm

Reece, H. (2014) 'Leaping Without Looking' in R. Leckey (ed.) *After Legal Equality: Family, Sex, Kinship*. Abingdon: Routledge.

Sloan, B. (2013) *Informal Carers and Private Law*. Oxford, Hart.

State Trustees Limited (2006) *Submission No. 88 to the House of Representatives Standing Committee on Legal and Constitutional Affairs*. Available at: www.aph.gov.au/parliamentary_business/committees/house_of_representatives_committees?url=/laca/olderpeople/subs.htm

Tilse, C., Wilson, J., White, B., Rosenman, L. and Feeney, R. (2014) 'Families and generational asset transfers: making and challenging wills in contemporary Australia'. Available at: www.uq.edu.au/swahs/Review%20of%20Public%20Trustee%20files.pdf

United Nations (UN) (2001) *World Population Ageing: 1950–2050*. Available at: www.un.org/esa/population/publications/worldageing19502050/pdf/62executivesummary_english.pdf

UN (2013) *World Population Ageing 2013*. Available at: www.un.org/en/development/desa/population/publications/pdf/ageing/WorldPopulationAgeing2013.pdf

Victorian Government (2006) *Submission No. 121 to the House of Representatives Standing Committee on Legal and Constitutional Affairs*. Available at: www.aph.gov.au/parliamentary_business/committees/house_of_representatives_committees?url=/laca/olderpeople/subs.htm

Cases

Balfour v Balfour [1919] 2 *KB* 571

Craig v Lamoureux [1920] *AC* 349

Ermogenous v Greek Orthodox Community of SA Inc (2002) 209 *CLR* 95; [2002] HCA 8

Gill v Woodall and others [2011] 3 *WLR* 85; [2010] EWCA Civ 1430

Jones v Padavatton [1969] 1 *WLR* 328

Legislation

Inheritance (Provision for Family and Dependants) Act 1975

Chapter 3

Ageing, vulnerability and care

A view from social gerontology

Liz Lloyd

Introduction

In this chapter the focus is on the relationship between ageing and care in order to examine what is distinctive about needs in later life at this point in time and to discuss the range of factors that shape need and perceptions of need in old age. It is argued that the risks and limitations associated with later life are not only intrinsic to the individual but also constituted by prevailing cultural values, expressed in practices of care. Of itself, age categorisation, an enduring feature of British welfare services, plays a part in shaping perceptions of old age and older people's moral claims for care. Old age has a long established association with vulnerability, but the nature of this varies (see Clough and Herring, this volume). At this point in time, reliance on publicly funded services in later life produces particular forms of precariousness.

In the UK as elsewhere, societal ageing is associated with a number of different trends, including reductions in fertility and mortality rates as well as extended life expectancy. The perception that an ageing society represents a burden is well entrenched in policy-making, although there are competing narratives concerning the best way to respond. Based on simple extrapolation from current service utilisation by people aged 65 and over, predictions of future needs for care present an alarming picture concerning the affordability of health and social care services. Policy-makers' attention is focused on ways to *reduce demand* and *cut costs*. At the same time, older people's organisations call for attention to those who, despite their evident needs, receive no support and to those within the care system whose rights have been seriously undermined (e.g. Age UK 2017). These different perspectives raise deep moral and ethical questions about the way in which a society supports its people when they are in need. In this chapter the focus is primarily on the social care system, which at the time of writing is in a state of crisis that has stimulated controversy over intergenerational relations and raised questions about the allocation of responsibility for the care of older people. Discussion of these questions inevitably involves revisiting the debates concerning the relationship between public and private realms of care (see in a different context Taylor, this volume).

Longer life, changing needs

Increasing life expectancy at all ages has been a dramatic feature of the past century. Life expectancy at birth is now double what it was in the middle of the nineteenth century and there is a similarly dramatic trend in life expectancy at older ages. At age 65, men can now expect to live for a further 18.8 years and women for a further 21.2 years, approximately double the expectancy of the early twentieth century. Socioeconomic inequalities in life expectancy are stark, with men in Kensington and Chelsea having a life expectancy at age 65 of 21.6 years compared with 15.9 in Manchester. For women at age 65, life expectancy was highest in Camden (24.6 years) and lowest in Manchester (18.8 years) (Office for National Statistics 2015).

There is a related trend in age at death. In 2013, the majority of all deaths in the UK were of people aged 80 and over (46% men and 63% women), while deaths below the age of 60 accounted for only 14% of all male deaths and 9% of all female deaths. These figures compare vividly with those at the turn of the twentieth century, when deaths over the age of 60 accounted for approximately a quarter of all deaths. At this point in history, therefore, old age is more strongly linked to death than at any time in human history, a linkage that has significant social and cultural consequences. The expectation of a long life is now deeply embedded in cultural norms and premature deaths are widely regarded as unnatural, unfair, and requiring explanation.

The added years of life are not an unqualified benefit, however. Typically they are spent with long-term illnesses, some of which affect people's mobility and thus their everyday life and activities. Current figures (Office for National Statistics 2014) for England show a difference of 15.7 years between men's average life expectancy of 79.2 years and healthy life expectancy of 63.5 years, while the equivalent for women is 18.2 years difference between average life expectancy of 83 years and healthy life expectancy of 64.8 years (thus 18.2 years spent 'not in good health'). Long-term illnesses are not always disabling and evidence suggests that a high proportion of older people remain independent to a very old age (Newcastle University 2017). There are, however, growing numbers of older people whose health conditions are disabling. The 2001 UK census revealed that over 50 per cent of the population aged 75 and over had at least one limiting long-standing illness. Figures for disabling illness in later life reflect a sharp socioeconomic gradient. Figures for England published in 2016 show a five-fold difference between the local authority areas with the lowest and the highest disability free life expectancy after the age of 65 (Office for National Statistics 2016). These socioeconomic differences in later life have usually accumulated over the life course. Health in later life thus reflects a complex mix of causal factors.

Action to replace the discourse of illness and decline with a more positive and active view of ageing has been supported by the World Health Organization (WHO) and reflected in diverse strategies developed by governments around the world. In the words of the WHO these strategies are about 'adding life to years, not merely years to life'. They are many and diverse and encompass the promotion of healthy lifestyles in later life as well as engagement in social and community life and continuation of paid employment past retirement age. In policy terms, active ageing strategies have also provided a focus for delaying age-related illness and maximizing people's capacity for independent living, as evident in this extract from a UK government policy paper (Department for Work and Pensions 2015):

> We see retirement as an increasingly active phase of life where people:
>
> - have opportunities to continue contributing to society by working longer or volunteering in their communities
> - take personal responsibility for their own wellbeing by working, saving and looking after their health

Ideas about 'active ageing' have been influential within gerontology, also. In 1987 Peter Laslett (1987) published 'The Emergence of the Third Age', in which he argued that the post retirement years should be seen not as the beginning of a period of decline but as a period of activity and opportunity in which new forms of leisure and personal-growth become possible, when individuals with occupational pensions are freed from the shackles of work. The concept of the third age unsettled traditional ideas about ageing (e.g. Minichiello and Coulson 2005), although critiques have subsequently been developed which point to its limitations. The quotation above from a British government policy paper demonstrates how the ideal of active ageing can be adapted by policy makers to emphasise values that are consistent with a wider political agenda – in this case the promotion of individual responsibility above pooled risk in welfare. Moreover, as Julia Twigg (2006) has argued, it is only possible to have a third age by projecting into a 'fourth age' all the problems and difficulties associated with ageing. A binary distinction between the active, healthy, and zestful old on the one hand and the frail, unhealthy, and dependent old on the other runs the risk of marginalising the latter group. Evidence suggests that, in retrospect, some older people can identify a time, almost invariably coinciding with bereavement and/or significant changes in health, when their lives changed and they began to 'become old'. Others experience a more gradual and change and perceive themselves as 'slowing down' (Lloyd et al 2014). The influence of wider sociocultural values must also be taken into account when considering subjective interpretations of ageing (Grenier 2012), how older people adjust to their changing physiological state and make decisions about whether or not to seek assistance with everyday tasks. True, old age is not all about decline and illness, but decline and illness are an inevitable part of old age. There are therefore good reasons to perceive support as a social rather than an individual social responsibility. Otherwise, those with limiting health conditions run the risk of being perceived as having failed when they seek social support.

Dependency and the need for care in later life

The complexity of older people's experiences of long-term illness is exemplified in studies of frailty (e.g. Grenier 2007). There are different perspectives on the causes and definitions of frailty but currently, the emphasis is on refining medical knowledge and improving practitioners' recognition of the signs or indicators. This improved knowledge is seen as essential for better decision-making about the efficacy of medical interventions as well as the efficient targeting of public resources. In practice, identification of frailty has been problematic. Higgs and Gilleard (2015), for example, argue that whatever the methods and advantages of improved assessment and diagnosis, frailty has come to signify 'personal marginality and vulnerability'. The concept of frailty emphasises the deficits in a person's health – a 'diagnosis' depends on an accumulation of deficits – and comes to mean all there is to know about a person (Nicholson, Gordon and Tinker 2016). It means that health and social care professionals know only what an individual *cannot* do rather than what they *can* do and bears the risk that the individual will be seen as beyond help. Older people resist being labelled frail for this reason and because it they see it as a sign that an individual has given up the struggle to maintain health. There is, therefore, a deeply moral dimension to frailty in old age, the significance of which is not widely recognised in policy-making or professional practice.

Dementia carries particular risks, especially in the advanced stages when people's personhood is called into question. The loss of citizen rights becomes more all the more likely in these circumstances, because the individual is regarded as beyond redemption or restoration to 'normal' independent life. Indeed, it has been argued that when an individual's ability to articulate their needs and preferences has diminished because of dementia, professionals are released from responsibility for understanding what these are (Kontos 2005, Adams and Gardiner 2005). Jaworska (1999), for example, points to evidence that people with dementia continue to have a *capacity to value* and that this should be distinguished from their loss of cognitive capacity. Such a distinction would improve understanding of people's preferences and well-being and could transform their experience of dementia. She also argues that better recognition of the capacity to value could change perceptions of dementia more widely. A related point is the distinction between cognitive and practical knowledge (Lloyd 2015). For example, care home residents with dementia can often continue to do the things they are accustomed to doing, such as peel vegetables with sharp knives or boil water to make tea. The priority given to safety and protection in care systems, however, frequently overrides their ability to do things regarded as risky. Given contemporary legal and insurance contexts this is understandable but the effect is to diminish the quality of life of people with dementia and to exacerbate their dependency.

The ethics of care perspective (Barnes 2012, Tronto 1993) provides a useful framework for understanding the complex picture of health, illness, and the need for support in later life. A fundamental tenet of this is that dependency should be understood as integral to human life at all ages but that it varies at different points in the life course. At the present time in the UK, it is in *old* age that the ultimate vulnerability of the human being – our mortality – is usually manifested. For the majority, it is in old age that our greatest need for support and care is most likely to occur – usually in the months and years preceding death. The ethics of care perspective places vulnerability in later life in the context of a whole life course and into the social and historical contexts that shape the conditions of vulnerability.

Joan Tronto (1993) describes her four-stage model for an ethic of care – attentiveness, responsibility, competence, and responsiveness – as *political.* She points to the false dichotomy between the moral and political domains to argue that moral claims, such as the right to be cared for when in need, cannot be separated from the political processes through which rights are realised in practice. She highlights the link between resources and competence in care – an extremely pertinent point in the current context of health and social care in the UK, when concerns are raised about diminishing standards of services concurrent with cuts in expenditure. Nevertheless, a critique of the feminist ethics of care is that it lends itself more easily to analyses of policies and practices of care than to the broader social and political determinants of vulnerability that contribute to the need for care. Grenier, Lloyd and Phillipson (2017), drew on Judith Butler's analysis of the precarious life in their examination of dementia (Butler 2006). Like Tronto, Butler argues that all human life should be understood as precarious but her focus is on the ways in which life is rendered *more* precarious for particular groups and populations whose lives are perceived as low value. These include refugees, migrants, low-waged workers, and welfare recipients of all ages. From this perspective it is possible to discern what vulnerable people of different ages share in terms of their devalued social status, to distinguish more clearly between existential and contingent factors that influence ageing and how particular historical locations shape conditions of precariousness.

The next section of this chapter looks in greater depth at the ways in which policies designed to support older people can have the effect of exacerbating their precarious position. It draws together evidence on the contingent limitations of ageing and the particular conditions that exist today, which blur the boundaries between the private and public spheres of care.

Crisis in the market for care

A century ago, according to Lloyd George, old age was one of the 'spectres' that haunted the poor and a core aim of social policies ever since his 1908 Old Age Pensions Act has been to banish this spectre. A report by the Fiscal Studies Institute (2017) estimated that the median income of pensioners is now £9 per week higher than the median income of the working aged population. Rather than being hailed as a policy success story, however, the relative wealth of older age cohorts is frequently framed in terms of the potentially damaging effect of this kind of intergenerational inequality. For the old to be relatively well-off goes against the grain of long-standing perceptions of old age, as a time of relative poverty. A twist to this perception is that the old have improved their position at the expense of the young. Thus, David Willetts (2010) argued that 'the baby boomers have concentrated wealth in the hands of their own generation'. In the space of a century, the 'needy old' have become the 'greedy old'. The circulation of such ideas in the context of policy-making plays an important part in shaping public perceptions of ageing and contributing to a new form of negative stereotype of later life. The 'needy old' have not disappeared from the picture. The Joseph Rowntree Foundation (2017) estimates that 1 in 6 pensioners live below the poverty line (that is, an income below 60 per cent of the contemporary median household income).

An underpinning theme of the contemporary policy context is that increasing numbers of older people represent an economic burden and that health and social care will become unaffordable (The Economist 2014). Dependency ratios, which reflect the proportion of a population of working age to those above or below that age, provide a rough and ready measure of the relationship between income tax revenue and welfare expenditure. They are open to criticism because they overlook tax revenues on pensions as well as continued economic activity beyond retirement age and because they fail to acknowledge the productivity of unpaid work, such as volunteering and unpaid care. A European study, for example, revealed that over 40 per cent of grandparents provided child care that enabled parents to work (Glaser et al 2013). Nevertheless, the perception of increasing numbers of older people as burdensome is well entrenched. The current overarching policy context of austerity has had particular impacts on the market system of care services for older people and generated new forms of risk and precariousness.

The market model that has dominated social care services since the 1990s has redefined care as a commodity to be commissioned by local authorities, or purchased by individual consumers, from a range of independent providers in the form of measurable tasks and time slots. Over the same time, need has become strongly linked to the loss of functional health, the ability to get in and out of bed, get dressed, wash, eat, and use the lavatory are identifiable as need. The process of needs assessment produces an account of an individual's 'eligible' needs, which in turn becomes the basis of a transaction and a contract. The market system, coupled with the bureaucratic process of assessment, has produced an impoverished understanding of need and care to the aspects that can be measured. The current context of austerity and the associated squeeze on eligibility impoverishes this understanding yet further by redefining specific needs as 'non-essential'. An example from experience is where an individual who can stand at a basin and wash is not considered to need help to have a bath. In 2011, the Equalities and Human Rights Commission (EHRC 2011) Inquiry into Home Care concluded that the cuts in care services for people in their own homes had amounted to neglect. Six more years of austerity budgets have deepened the crisis, generating more cuts to services affecting more people and calling into question the potential effectiveness of the 2014 Care Act. The Association of Directors of Adult Social Services (ADASS) recently reported that funding for social care simply does not match growing needs for and costs of care and that the effects of this mismatch (referred to as the 'social care gap') is being felt by increasing numbers of people. The effects of crisis in social care have spread to healthcare ('bed-blocking' by older people in hospitals because of no suitable alternative places of care) and to families, who have been obliged to take on yet more responsibilities for caring for older relatives. The neglect of older people within the British care system exemplifies the point above that political practices cannot be separated from the moral agenda of rights. The theoretical right of vulnerable people not to be neglected has been, in some localities, almost totally eclipsed by the political priority of cutting the cost of welfare.

A question that arises from the above discussion concerns the extent to which the social care gap is the consequence of demographic trends. The answer is complex and multi-factorial and draws attention to the supply side as well as demand side. This is not to suggest that demographic trends have no impact on demand but to consider the bigger picture. For example, the Local Government Association's Adult Social Care Funding: 2016 State of the Nation Report, points to cost pressures arising from general inflation and increases in core costs, such as national insurance, the national living wage, and pension contributions, all of which have arisen in the context of a 40 per cent reduction in real terms in their core government grant. There is also a wide range of influences on demand (Appleby 2013). These include the health status of older people, their income, the suitability and accessibility of services, as well as technological developments. Another set of factors relates to age at mortality. Evidence suggests that it is not age *per se* but proximity to death that increases the individual's need for health care (Seshamani and Gray 2004). Current policies encourage care homes to provide for residents to die *in situ* rather than being transferred to hospital to die, which has an impact on social care spending. A deeper related question is why older people's need for social care is framed in terms of its affordability. Currently, expenditure on social care for all adults (of which older people's services amount to just over one half) amounts to less than 2 per cent of GDP (The Audit Commission 2010). Equally importantly, according to the Audit Commission, around 15 per cent of older people use social care services, while carers over the age of 60 provide care worth twice public spending on care.

The crisis in social care affects not only service users but also providers. In the 2016 ADASS budget report cited above it is claimed that the continuity of the care market is currently under threat because of the increased risk of provider failure. Currently, local authorities are grappling with the effects of closures of independent home care agencies and care homes. Providers point to central and local government policies as the reasons behind these closures – most particularly, the introduction of the living wage by central government and the stagnation of local authority payments for commissioned services. These policies have created tensions in the relationships between the state and commercial providers. Reluctant to impose heavier regulations on providers, the government has instructed local authorities to be alert to the possibility of service provider failure (regarded by them as a normal and acceptable aspect of any market) and to be ready to act to protect service users if it should occur. The network of relationships between central and local government, service providers, older people, and their families has become entangled, as the policy aims of reduction of the cost of social care services and the promotion of care markets have collided. The crisis has shown in stark relief the weaknesses of a market model and the precarious conditions it generates for older people, care workers, and family carers.

For example, the continuing emphasis on the provision of services in people's own homes carries particular risks related to the protection of their rights. The 2014 Care Act (section 73) has extended the rights of people who receive domiciliary services from private care providers under contract with the local authority. Independent care providers are now regarded as exercising 'functions of a public nature' and must respect ECHR rights, such as those associated with Article 8 ECHR (respect for private and family life). This extension does not, however, cover the increasing numbers of people who purchase personal care services independently. A related point is that the 2014 Care Act secured greater recognition for carers and parity of esteem with the people they care for, entitling them to assessments of need and access to support services. There is greater recognition of the value of the work carers do, which in monetary terms, according to Carers UK, is £132 billion a year. Under the 2014 Care Act local authorities are encouraged to provide free support to carers on the understanding that there is a sound economic rationale for doing so (DH et al 2014). Yet, under conditions of austerity, support provided to carers has been calculated in terms of what it *costs* the public purse rather than what it saves. Some local authorities have concluded that because of the severe constraints on their resources they must introduce charges for carer support or relabel support for carers (free) as support for the cared-for person (chargeable). Thus carers are faced with a 'double whammy': paying from their own resources in order to save public resources through their unpaid care.

The current crisis in social care has raised deep questions about responsibility for care. In a recent representation to the government, the ADASS urged the government to engage in a 'radical reconsideration of how to incentivise family and other informal carers' and to revisit 'the roles of the individual, family, community and the state' to consider all funding options. The Minister for Communities, Health and Care, David Mowat, argued that people should 'start thinking about how we look after our parents', a phrase that reveals a lot about how older people are regarded as passive recipients who have nothing to contribute to the debate about who cares for them.

The public/private divide of care: blurred boundaries

The boundary between the public (formal) and private (family) realms of care has never been crystal clear but contemporary conditions have caused it to be blurred in new ways. As budgets for care become more stretched and there is a reduction of provision, the pressure is felt by families and by front line care workers to take on more caring tasks, including more complex tasks. At the same time, there are increased demands for emotional labour from paid care workers. Arlie Hochschild (1983) has commented that since her seminal work *The Managed Heart* was published in 1983, new types of service role in the care sector have merged in the realm between home and work, which she has termed 'marketized private life'. This description applies aptly to the situation of personal assistants employed by older people to provide personal support. For those who can afford it, employing a live-in carer offers a positive alternative to moving to a care home. Live-in carers are expected to provide not only personal care but also companionship and sensitivity to the older person's wishes. The website of one employing organisation described it as follows:

> It takes a special kind of person to be a live-in carer. A good carer is someone who truly cares about others and is not just earning a living. This is a special job, and it needs special people to do it.

There are no reliable data on the numbers of people employed in this way, the terms and conditions under which they are employed, nor how many of them are migrant workers. In this private, home-based sphere there is little regulation of employment practices and, as discussed above, the ECHR protections applied to people whose care is organised through the local authority do not apply to those who make their own arrangements.

Tensions concerning the regulation of care provided in people's own homes are reflected also in the use of observational technologies, which affect older people and paid care workers. Some technologies have facilitated ever more intrusive monitoring of older people's private lives, extending into the areas of the home that would previously have been considered the most private – the bedroom and the bathroom. Mortensen and Sixsmith (2015) discuss how the use of technologies has been hailed as a means of deploying scarce resources in the most efficient way possible. Technologies for safety, security, and the reduction of risks associated with falls are justified on the grounds that they can reduce hospital and nursing home admissions. Technologies can be a boon if they enable someone to remain at home but also raise questions about the individual's right to privacy and the intrusion into their homes by publicly sponsored agents. Similar debates surround the use of technological surveillance of home care workers by their employers. The use of hand-held devices and other technologies enable employers to measure the exact amount of time each care worker spends with an individual service user. These monitoring measures provide the basis for calculating care workers' wages, the time in between appointments sometimes being judged as non-work time, or might be used to discipline them if they overstay their time at one appointment and are late for the next. They also reinforce the definition of care as a set of tasks that take a set amount of time rather than as a relationship between the care worker and the person they care for.

Conclusion

Hochschild's observation about marketised private life highlights the particularities of precariousness at this point in history in the context of social care, which has become hyper-marketised. As Michael Sandel (2012) commented, markets are now not something we *have* but something we, as a society have *become.* Although it is an intensely private activity, the personal care of older people has become the subject of intense public debate, raising questions about the private, 'hidden' nature of care. It is noteworthy, however, that much of this public debate is focused on cost and on responsibility for payment. Policies are effectively distanced from actual practices of care and the commodification of care in a market system reinforces this separation. A balance sheet that portrays the hours spent on specific care tasks can be used to demonstrate efficiency in service delivery but reflects nothing of the complexity of relationships between the carer and the older person being cared for, it provides no indication of the difference that care has made to the individual's life and well-being and it tells us nothing about the physical and emotional effort made by individuals in the care relationship. Indeed, the highly technical and managerial approaches now firmly established in care agencies are geared towards overlooking the relational nature of care to focus on what can be measured, counted, and accounted for.

The current crisis in social care is a watershed moment not only for the organisation but for the fundamental principles of care concerning mutuality, pooled risks, and shared responsibility. The current crisis raises questions about who should provide care, who should pay for it, and who should monitor and control the conditions under which care is provided? An important argument in critical gerontology is that societal ageing has provided a means of legitimating the cuts to welfare spending that were essential to the neo-liberal economic agenda that has dominated policy-making since the 1980s (Baars 2006). Through this agenda welfare in general has become characterised as an *impediment to* rather than a *beneficial outcome of* prosperity. Cuts to public resources for social care are, from this perspective, a necessary political strategy, whatever the age profile or level of need in the population. A long life has come to be the norm but, as argued above, the cultural norms and values that underpin contemporary policy-making have generated risks and vulnerabilities within the social care system. The alternative perspective argued here stresses the social nature of ageing and the need for policies and practices that maximise the quality of life through the process of ageing to the end of life.

Bibliography

Adams, T. and Gardiner, P. (2005) 'Communication and Interaction within Dementia Care Triads: Developing a Theory for Relationship-centred Care' *Dementia* 4(2), 185.

Age UK (2017) *The Health and Care of Older People in England.* London: Age UK.

Appleby, J. (2013) *Spending on Health and Social Care over the Next 50 Years: Why Think Long Term?* London: The King's Fund.
Audit Commission (2010) *Under Pressure: Tackling the Financial Challenge for Councils of an Ageing Population: Local Government Report.* London: The Audit Commission.
Baars, J. (2006) 'Beyond Neomodernism, Antimodernism and Postmodernism: Basic Categories for Contemporary Critical Gerontology' in J. Baars et al (eds) *Ageing, Globalization and Inequality: The New Critical Gerontology.* New York: Baywood.
Barnes, M. (2012) *Care in Everyday Life: An Ethic of Care in Practice.* Bristol: The Policy Press.
Butler, J. (2006) *Precarious Life: The Powers of Mourning and Violence.* London: Verso.
Department of Health (DH) et al (2014) *The Care Act 2014: A Guide to Efficient and Effective Interventions for Implementing the Care Act 2014 as it Applies to Carers.* Available at: www.local.gov.uk/documents
Department of Work and Pensions (DWP) (2015) *2010–2015 Government Policy: Older People.* London: DWP.
The Economist (2014) 'Age Invaders' 24 June.
Equalities and Human Rights Commission (EHRC) (2011) *Close to Home: Inquiry into Older People and Human Rights in Home Care.* London: ECHR.
Glaser, K. et al (2013) *Grandparenting in Europe: Family Policy and Grandparents' Role in Providing Childcare.* London: Grandparents Plus.
Grenier, A. (2007) 'Constructions of Frailty in the English Language, Care Practice and the Lived Experience' *Ageing and Society* 27(3), 425.
Grenier, A. (2012) *Transitions and the Lifecourse: Challenging the Constructions of 'Growing Old'.* Bristol: The Policy Press.
Grenier, A., Lloyd, L. and Phillipson, C. (2017) 'Precarity in Late Life: Rethinking Dementia as a "Frailed" Old Age' *Sociology of Health and Illness* 39(2), 318.
Higgs, P. and Gilleard, C. (2015) *Rethinking Old Age.* Basingstoke: Palgrave.
Hochschild, A. (1983) *The Managed Heart.* Berkeley, CA: University of California Press.
Institute for Fiscal Studies (IFS) (2017) *The Distribution of Wealth in the UK.* London: IFS.
Jaworska, A. (1999) 'Respecting the Margins of Agency: Alzheimer's Patients and the Capacity to Value' *Philosophy and Public Affairs* 28(2), 105.
Joseph Rowntree Foundation (2017) *Data.* Available at: www.jrf.org.uk/data
Kontos, P. (2005) 'Embodied Selfhood in Alzheimer's Disease: Rethinking Person-centred Care' *Dementia* 4, 533.
Laslett, P. (1987) 'The Emergence of the Third Age' *Ageing and Society* 7, 133.
Lloyd, L. et al (2014) 'Identity in the Fourth Age: Perseverance, Adaptation and Maintaining Dignity' *Ageing and Society* 34(1), 1.
Lloyd, L. (2015) 'Understanding the Fourth Age' in J. Twigg and W. Martin (eds) *The Routledge Handbook of Cultural Gerontology.* Abingdon: Routledge.
Minichiello, V. and Coulson, I. (eds) (2005) *Contemporary Issues in Gerontology: Promoting Positive Ageing.* Abingdon: Routledge.
Mortensen, W. B. and Sixsmith, M. (2015) 'The Power(s) of Observation: Theoretical Perspectives on Surveillance Technologies and Older People' *Ageing & Society* 35, 512.
Newcastle University (2017) *85+ Study.* Available at: http://research.ncl.ac.uk/85plus/
Nicholson, C., Gordon, A. and Tinker, A. (2016) 'Changing the Way "We" View and Talk about Frailty' *Age and Ageing* 46(3), 439.
Office for National Statistics (ONS) (2014) *Life Expectancy at Birth and at Age 65 by Local Areas in England and Wales: 2011 to 2013.* London: ONS.

ONS (2015) *Life Expectancy at Birth and at Age 65 by Local Areas in England and Wales: 2012 to 2014.* London: ONS.

ONS (2016) *Disability-free Life Expectancy (DFLE) and Life Expectancy (LE) at Age 65 by Upper Tier Local Authority.* London: ONS.

Sandel, M. (2012) *What Money Can't Buy: The Moral Limits of Markets.* London: Allen Lane.

Seshamani, M. and Gray, A. (2004) 'Ageing and Health-care Expenditure: The Red Herring Argument Revisited' *Health Economics* 13(4), 303.

Tronto, J. (1993) *Moral Boundaries: A Political Argument for an Ethic of Care.* New York: Routledge.

Twigg, J. (2006) *The Body in Health and Social Care.* Basingstoke: Macmillan.

Willetts, D. (2010) *The Pinch: How the Baby Boomers Took Their Children's Future – And Why They Should Give It Back.* London: Atlantic Books.

Chapter 4

Financial abuse of older persons

A criminal law perspective

Jennifer Collins

Introduction

Of growing concern is financial abuse of older persons, especially but not exclusively, by family members. This form of wrongdoing may merit a response in civil law (see Brammer, this volume). This chapter considers the role of the criminal law in England and Wales in regulating this form of wrongdoing. It argues that there are overlooked limitations in using the criminal law to address financial abuse of older persons. First, there is a lack of clarity as to what financial abuse of older persons amounts to within a wider category of elder abuse. As such, the wrong is remarkably difficult to reconcile with criminalisation principles. Second, an impulse to criminalise this form of wrongdoing must be weighed against the point that criminalisation is a blunt instrument. I therefore examine an alternative approach, appraising whether there is scope to interpret fraud by abuse of position in a vulnerable person-protective mode. This is an argument for levelling up protection for vulnerable persons generally rather than for older persons specifically.

In order to substantiate these arguments, the chapter is structured in the following way. The first section unpacks the complex and imprecise idea of financial abuse of older persons. Section 2 clarifies the distinctive nature of criminal law measures from those administered in the civil law. From this principled standpoint, the question to be addressed in section 3 is, what are the limitations in using the criminal law to address this form of wrongdoing? Arguments for criminalisation of financial abuse of older persons are less clear-cut and more complex than at first thought. With these limitations in mind, section 4 canvases an idea for reading fraud by abuse of position in a vulnerable person-protective mode.

1 What is financial abuse of older persons?

What does financial abuse of older persons amount to and include? My aim in this first section is to consider this question at a general level, before exposing the subject matter's complexities as it relates to English criminal law.

The first key point to note is that financial abuse of older persons can be regarded as a form of elder abuse. Reference to elder abuse loads the die at the outset with uncertainty and imprecision. Elder abuse is a complex phenomenon which encompasses a number of forms of wrongdoing. There is considerable variation between accounts which seek to define elder abuse. Anetzberger (2005, p. 7) defines elder abuse as 'the infliction of injury or suffering on a person age 60 years or older by her/himself or another person'. Action on Elder Abuse (2015) uses the definition of: 'a single or repeated act or lack of appropriate action occurring within any relationship where there is an expectation of trust, which causes harm or distress to an older person'. While the absence of a unitary account of elder abuse poses challenges when channelling arguments about law reform (Anetzberger 2005, pp. 3–4), it is not an analytical problem *per se*. Jonathan Herring (2009, p. 135) notes the similarity with domestic violence, which also 'lacks a precise definition'. Nevertheless, physical abuse and financial abuse can be identified at the core of a broad category of elder abuse (Anetzberger 2005).

Second, it is relevant to ask why any of these forms of abuse are significant in relation to older persons specifically. Older persons, particularly but not exclusively, may be victims of physical abuse or financial abuse, for example. What reasons justify this focus? An analysis of this point must first put in place a definition of who is recognised as an elder person. The World Health Organization's approach (WHO 2002) is to classify persons who are 60 or older as older persons. By contrast Jonathan Herring (2009, 138) argues that an individual becomes a candidate for elder abuse when they are 'subject to the social disadvantages and prejudicial attitudes that can attach to old age'. This in turn highlights one reason for focusing on a broad category of *elder* abuse rather than identifying different forms of abuse without such a tie to older persons. A focus on elder abuse recognises and challenges underlying structural and systemic issues of prejudice uniquely faced by older persons (Herring 2009).

Growing interest in elder abuse in the United States has been an important backdrop for focus on this issue in England and Wales. A strengthened public benefits system in the 1950s 'enabled more older people to live on their own in the community' (Anetzberger 2005, 2). These changes required a strong system of adult protective services for intervention in situations of impaired capacity, neglect, or exploitation. Legal provision in relation to elder abuse resulted – from the Older Americans Act at federal level, to elder abuse reporting laws at state level (Anetzberger 2005). Arguably there is now increasing public awareness and political will to tackle elder abuse as a broad category of wrongdoing on this side of the Atlantic, prompted by the House of Commons Select Committee Report on this topic in 2004.

Third, it is evident that financial abuse of older persons – a form of elder abuse – is similarly contestable in scope. Action on Elder Abuse (Crosby et al 2008, 12) defines financial abuse as 'stealing from, defrauding someone of, or coercing someone to part with, goods and/or property (Fitzgerald 2004)'. The Department of Health in *No Secrets* (2000) notes that financial abuse includes 'theft, fraud, exploitation, pressure in connection with wills, property or inheritance or financial transactions, or the misuse or misappropriation of property, possessions or benefits'. Both analyses identify a cluster of core concepts – such as 'exploitation' and 'pressure', among others – as important to a notion of financial abuse, though these concepts are not in themselves altogether stable and clear.

In any case there may be a danger in focusing on definitions of financial abuse of older persons in the abstract, while failing to explore what actually happens in these scenarios. This form of abuse involves an attack upon an older person's property interests. However, the gist of the wrong *is not limited* to an attack upon property interests and may involve an attack upon an older person's bodily interests. At this juncture we ought to reemphasise that older persons are not the only victims of financial abuse. However, a special interest in financial abuse of older persons may be justifiable in recognition of the impact that this form of abuse has. Smith (1999, 1–2) argues that older people who are victims of fraud 'have less time to recoup their losses and often are solely dependent upon their savings to finance their future'. It is also plausible that the 'personal, emotional and psychological consequences' for older persons are more significant, but it is important to further evidence this claim (Smith 1999,1–2).

A wide range of conduct may be used, which includes: coercion, force, threats, duress, undue influence, intimidation, harassment, deception, false pretence, false representation, and manipulation. Conduct may lie along a spectrum: at first conduct may be employed quite innocently but may become predatory as an abuser's goals develop. There will be variation in the seriousness of the conduct used and the level of fault held. What Wilson and Brown (2003 cited in Crosby et al 2008, 11) identify as 'inadvertent mismanagement' of an older person's funds will carry a lower degree of culpability than 'deliberated targeted abuse ... accompanied by threats and intimidation'. As noted in section 2 below, certain forms of conduct described as financial abuse of older persons may amount to criminal law offences in England and Wales.

A fourth preliminary point is to explain why the role of family members in this form of abuse is an interesting avenue to study. Some empirical evidence in the United States suggests a strong relationship between financial abuse and a pre-existing familial relationship. A study by Holfreter et al (2014 cited Jackson 2015, 63) identifies family members as the 'most frequent perpetrators of financial exploitation'. A close connection between elder financial abuse and family members was highlighted by the U.S. Senate Special Committee on Ageing in 2002 (Rabiner et al 2006, 54). Rabiner et al (2006, 54) point out that 'In the NEAIS report, over 60% of substantiated APS cases of financial abuse involved an adult child relative, compared to 47% for all forms of abuse'. Shelly Jackson (2015, 63) notes Acieno et al's research (2010) that, '5.2 per cent of adults aged 65 years and older living in the community had experienced financial exploitation by a family member'.

It is hardly feasible to suggest that we know how much familial elder abuse occurs, financial or otherwise. Some statistics suggest that around '57,000 people aged 66 and over' were victims of financial abuse in 2006–07 (O'Keeffe et al 2007 cited Crosby et al 2008, 4). Difficulties regarding the reliability of quantitative data in this context are well known. However, we can conjecture that older persons are particularly susceptible to financial abuse by family members. A starting point is to suggest that the nature of family relationships may mean that a predatory individual has ready access to an older person. Trust may already be built into a familial relationship, such as an adult child knowing their parent's bank details. Moreover, an aspect of entitlement may be a feature of familial relationships and a motivational factor for the abuse (Rabiner et al 2006, 54). The Centre for Policy on Ageing (2008) notes that '[f]inancial abuse, both at home and in residential care, is tied up with societal attitudes to inheritance'. The suggestion is that the family context provides ready-made opportunities for advantage-taking.

In procedural terms, a further significant feature of elder financial abuse perpetrated by family members is the difficulty it may create for 'detecting, stopping, and proving the abuse' (Rabiner et al 2006, 54). Predatory family members may be less likely to be held to account since older family members may be less likely to complain. It could be more difficult to establish a case based on the testimony and evidence of a family member. Legal redress may be difficult to establish if a fiduciary relationship is required. Given its perceived prevalence; unique features which provide opportunity for abuse; and difficulty for victims in accessing legal redress, the financial abuse of older persons by family members justifiably attracts special attention from theorists.

2 The role of the criminal law

We turn next to the role of criminalisation in responding to financial abuse of older persons. Civil and/or regulatory measures which address financial abuse of older persons do not preclude a criminal law response. Conduct may also merit law sanction, though strong justification for a criminal law offence will be required.

It is important at the outset to clarify the sense in which the criminal law is distinctive from civil law measures. The criminal law is a censuring institution which carries weighty implications for those who breach its prohibitions – in some cases supplying the justification for depriving a person of their liberty. Douglas Husak (2011, 102) states that 'The criminal sanction is the most powerful weapon in the state arsenal; the government is permitted to do nothing worse to its citizens than to punish them'. A state's decision to censure conduct publicly using the criminal law must explain 'the censure that punitive interventions communicate' (Kleinig 2016, 316). Not every example of state punishment 'is necessarily worse than any alternative mode of treatment' (Husak 2008b, 104). It is the *broad category* of criminal sanction, as a response to wrongdoing, which requires justification (Husak 2008b, 105). Because of the significant consequences of criminalisation there is strong support for minimalism in the state's use of the criminal law. Husak (2008a, 58) goes so far as to say that a citizen has a right not to be punished.

Given the coercive nature of criminalisation, any argument for criminalisation should be tested against clear, promulgated, and defensible principles. Two key general principles emerge as central. If we put to one side 'co-ordination offences', it is widely accepted that serious wrongdoing is a necessary prerequisite to criminalisation. This is because criminalisation is a condemnatory response to wrongdoing, communicating 'to the offender, the victims and the wider community that a public wrong was committed' (Duff and Green 2005, 9). It is manifestly unfair, even 'morally defamatory', 'to publicly convey that D acted reprehensibly having established nothing of the kind' (Edwards 2012, 75). Added to serious wrongfulness, is the need for conduct to cause harm, or the risk of harm, to others (Feinberg 1987). A harm threshold is crossed if the criminalisation of that conduct will proportionately prevent harm or prevent the risk of harm to others. Of course a harm threshold hinges on the meaning of 'harm' – a term notoriously difficult to elucidate. Feinberg's definition of harm to others as a 'setback to interests' (1987, 34) is one working definition, as is Andreas von Hirsch and Nils Jareborg's (1991, 1) argument that harm ought to be tied to the effects of criminal wrongdoing upon the 'living standard' of typical victims.

Even where thresholds to criminalisation have been met, further *constraints* grounded in the nature and purposes of the criminal law must be satisfied if a criminal offence is to be justified. Husak (2008a, 159) argues that the right not to be punished will only be outweighed by a need for criminal censure where a criminal offence requires: a substantial and legitimate 'governmental interest in enacting the law'; a clear trajectory toward achieving this purpose; and a proportionate criminal law response. These external justifications are required because of the costs involved to citizens in supporting a criminal justice system. These include the heavy financial implications of criminalisation – resources which could be deployed to good effect elsewhere in the economy – as well as the costs of wrongful convictions and abuse of power by officials (Husak 2008b, 109). The starting point, then, is that criminal censure by the state is 'extraordinarily difficult to justify from the perspective of citizens' (Husak 2008b, 109). It is also imperative that the criminal law complies with rule of law principles so that individuals are not ambushed by the criminal law. Ashworth and Zedner (2014, 114) argue that this requires 'maximum certainty of definition, fair warning and fair labelling' of criminal law offences. It should also be emphasised that any discussion about criminalisation must address the type and level of criminalisation in question.

Unlike many U.S. states which have enacted specific legislation to penalise financial abuse or exploitation, the current response of English criminal law has been to utilise existing offences for this purpose. These offences need not have been explicitly designed to penalise this form of wrongdoing, but may penalise certain aspects of financially abusive conduct and/or the result(s) of it. The Crown Prosecution Service (2009, Annex A) has noted the following as offences which may be directed at older persons: theft (s.1 Theft Act 1968), robbery (s.8 Theft Act 1968), blackmail (s.21 Theft Act 1968), fraud (s.1 Fraud Act 2006) and forgery (s.25 Identity Cards Act 2006; Forgery and Counterfeiting Act 1981). This discussion places us in a position to consider whether this approach is justifiable. I suggest below that the creation of new criminal law measures to penalise this form of wrongdoing is remarkably difficult to justify.

3 The limits of the criminal law

The previous section set out core principles for criminalisation. This section argues that reconciling financial abuse of older persons with these principles is especially problematic, highlighting in turn several limitations of the criminal law in dealing with this form of wrongdoing.

Imprecision at the heart of financial abuse of older persons

Arguments for criminalisation of financial abuse of older persons are undercut by the analytical complexities and uncertainty which characterise this broad category of wrongdoing. This contention has implications for adherence with rule of law principles. We consider arguments for new criminal law legislation to target financial abuse of older persons.

From the outset, financial abuse of older persons strikes us as a difficult case to justify the criminal law's involvement. Is there a *prima facie* case for criminalising this form of wrongdoing, leaving aside for now the type and level of criminalisation in question? Presumably initial thresholds to criminalisation can in principle be said to have been satisfied. We saw in section 2 above that a harm principle is a minimal threshold to criminalisation. While it would be preferable to have empirical evidence about actual harm to older persons through financial abuse, or the risk of such harm, an in principle argument is established. It is a further issue whether the state has a substantial interest in penalising such conduct. It is also relatively clear that a serious wrongfulness threshold to criminalisation is crossed in cases of financial abuse of older persons.

But even if, after superficial scrutiny, we can argue that these initial thresholds to criminalisation are satisfied, there are other factors which they must be weighed up against. A compelling criminalisation argument can only withstand scrutiny if it can be shown that it complies with rule of law principles. This is reinforced by Article 7 of the European Convention on Human Rights, which requires clearly promulgated criminal laws which are sufficiently certain. One reason why this form of wrongdoing is difficult to reconcile with criminalisation principles is that the notion of 'financial abuse of older persons' is opaque and imprecise.

One sense in which the term is imprecise lies in its inexact relationship with a notion of 'exploitation'. Financial abuse and financial exploitation of older persons are often referred to interchangeably (see Rabiner et al 2004, 65). At minimum, both ideas can be used as umbrella terms. But in order to avoid conceptual confusion it is important to establish the scope of financial abuse as opposed to financial exploitation. Both terms must be used precisely. It is well known that 'exploitation' of persons is a fiendishly difficult concept to define. The simple statement that 'A exploits B when A takes unfair advantage of B' is the general starting point for commentators who have written about interpersonal exploitation (Feinberg 1986, 179). I have argued elsewhere that 'exploitation' is not a clear-cut idea (Collins 2017). Firm explanation of the wrongfulness at the heart of exploitation is needed if it is to be illuminating. For example, in unpacking financial exploitation of older persons, is it significant if a person's characteristics are used (non-wrongful) as opposed to their personhood (wrongful)? What constitutes *serious* financial exploitation? It is necessary to engage with the real life complexity of financial exploitation of older persons, and this necessarily involves difficult boundary-drawing exercises.

This would suggest that there is currently a worrying trend toward the implementation of financial exploitation statutes in the United States, sometimes in relation to older persons specifically. Jackson (2015, 71) notes that 39 states in 2015 had 'enacted a criminal financial exploitation statute'. Notably the 'actions that constitute financial exploitation vary considerably from state to state and range from very specific to very vague actions' (Jackson 2015, 71). The element of circularity in appealing to a broad notion of financial abuse or financial exploitation of older persons must be acknowledged. This is hardly to penalise a clearly defined wrong. An argument for criminalisation must be balanced against this legal certainty counter-argument, together with a presumption against over-inclusive laws. A specific offence would be flawed if judges were unable to adjudicate on the true nature of the wrong of financial abuse of older persons because the offence was drafted too broadly (Edwards 2010).

In order to be workable as a principled criminalisation argument, there would need to be a precise definition as to what constitutes financial abuse of older persons. It is suggested here that there is nothing straightforward about identifying even the core features of serious financial abuse of older persons. What emerges from section 1 above is that relevant abusive conduct could range from strong coercive conduct to the use of subtler manipulative techniques. It could be argued that coercive conduct is necessarily more serious than manipulative techniques, therefore being at the core of this financial abuse of older persons. However, a subtler picture emerges given that coercion is a method which is morally wrong in its strong form, but which is more morally ambiguous as threats become less compelling (Berman 2002, 46). Arguably coercive conduct which relies upon a blend of threats, pressure, and intimidation might have the strongest connection with financial abuse of older persons. But there is reason to question whether the same holds true for weaker types of coercive conduct, which may involve the application of pressure without an accompanying threat, for example. In principle, strong manipulation could be just as serious as weaker coercive conduct. Even identifying the most serious conduct associated with elder financial abuse will be challenging.

In practical terms the most serious conduct, which is most strongly connected to a robust account of elder financial abuse, is likely to already come within the scope of existing criminal law offences. Existing property offences are the most likely possibilities. For example, dishonestly appropriating an older person's property interests, accompanied by an abuser's intention to permanently deprive them of that property, will be covered by the offence of theft. What are the ramifications of this? It could be argued that elder financial abuse simply involves property offences where older persons happen to be victims (cf Herring 2009, 134). This may present grounds for being rather more cautious about creating new criminal law offences so as to avoid overlapping criminal offences (Husak 2008a). If there is a case for distinguishing this form of wrongdoing on its own terms, there may be less obvious sense of what conduct a new specific offence exists to penalise. Presumably the targeting of an older person is significant, but this can be considered an aggravating factor at the sentencing stage. If the targeting itself is to be criminalised, there are important concerns about how are to do we do this while adhering to principles of legal certainty given that targeting conduct may be difficult to pinpoint.

Difficulties with implementing criminal law offences as having an older person-protective function

The argument advanced here is that there are difficulties in deploying the criminal law in an older person-protective mode. Criminalisation for this purpose is a blunt tool. The first difficulty is the coherence of singling out older persons for special treatment within the criminal law. The rationale *for implementing* criminal law legislation to penalise financial abuse of older persons is primarily concerned with protecting older persons as persons vulnerable to financial abuse. The Centre for Policy on Ageing's report (Crosby et al 2008, 28) notes that there is an assumption that 'older people require statutory protection because of the association of age with physical and/or cognitive impairments that increase vulnerability to abuse'. Criminal legislation would penalise defendants who perform conduct marked out in the statute with the required fault. Some statistics appear to support the view that old age exposes persons to the risk of financial abuse, especially by family members: a recent BBC report (2015) notes that one in three victims of fraud are aged 65 or over. AARP International (2006) identifies age as a risk factor for various forms of elder abuse because older persons are targeted for their 'financial security'.

Underlying vulnerability will be supported in some cases of financial abuse of older persons. But I cast doubt on the claim that we should use this as a rationale for justifying older persons-protective criminal law measures. It does not allow for the perfectly capable older person, instead imposing an analytical straightjacket as the justification for criminalisation. There is nothing in the nature of old age to say that older persons are more susceptible to financial abuse, especially by family members. Older victims of financial abuse may be active participants in financial abuse and may have sufficient knowledge and capacity to offer valid legal consent. Jackson and Hafemeister (2010, 288) have found that elderly victims of financial exploitation, when compared with the average elderly person, 'tended to have fewer communication problems, less cognitive confusion/dementia, less dependence on others, likely to be younger in age, and to not be experiencing poor social support'. Lack of capacity will not accompany every case of financial abuse. The concern expressed here is that we are too readily disposed to embrace vulnerability-based reasoning of older persons as the impetus and justification for new criminal law legislation. A link between older persons and vulnerability to financial abuse is inherently fragile.

In fact, enacting criminal law measures which penalise financial abuse of older persons may be damaging to older persons. Criminalisation could entrench actual or perceived vulnerability of older persons, for example by entrenching negative stereotypes about old age and cognitive impairment (see Palmore 1999, Kohn 2012). It could also lead to reductions in autonomy for older persons who wish to divest themselves of their property interests where certain 'indicators' of financial abuse exist. One example might be where an older person wishes to give a present of cash to be shared among carers in a nursing home. A robust argument for criminalisation cannot be based on the logic that older persons are necessarily more susceptible or vulnerable to financial abuse. It is a blunt normative choice to focus on the feature of age rather than on the reasons leading to vulnerable status. It is more plausible that 'the extent to which older persons are defrauded is directly proportional to the vulnerabilities that arise out of the circumstances in which they live' (Smith 1999, 1). We are in fact interested in identifying circumstances which make an older person vulnerable to financial abuse.

The focus ought surely to be upon justifying criminalisation on the basis that a body of persons who are vulnerable to financial abuse has been identified. Of course uncertainty abounds about how an idea of vulnerable persons is to be drawn (Herring 2016). We return to this point in section 4 below. But the targeting of vulnerable persons at least is the more compelling idea to drive forward an argument justifying criminalisation than one which classifies a whole category of persons as vulnerable with no clear reasoning backing this up. A focus on 'vulnerability' as a justification for criminalisation also has an important 'opening up' function. It requires criminal law theorists to explain the reasons *why* criminalisation is justified because certain individuals are considered vulnerable. Drawing on research by Thomas Hafemeister (2004, 391–393), AARP International (2006) underscores the need to identify reasons for 'specific cracks in victims' defences against exploitation', be they because of 'trust, financial naiveté, cognitive impairments, social isolation, dependency, fear, and embarrassment'. For example, a position of trust may leave one party vulnerable to another. This could be because of a power differential between persons, which means that one person is in a dominant position with the other more subservient. As we shall note below, a focus on vulnerability, if still within a conversation about justifying criminalisation, can only go so far. The criminal law cannot address reasons for this vulnerability. Moreover, it should be emphasised that this element of vulnerability may not need to be marked out in a proposed criminal law offence. It may be the rationale for penalising financially abusive conduct. Ostensibly, however, a criminal law measure may only penalise wrongful conduct undertaken by the defendant with fault. The offence itself need not require the deliberate targeting of vulnerable persons.

A possible counter-argument is that the criminal law ought to be dealing with structural prejudice toward older people. Herring (2009, 138) has carefully argued that elder abuse is conceptually distinct from targeting a person because they are vulnerable: it 'is a reflection of the attitudes of an individual, organization, or society towards older people in general, and older women in particular'. Moreover, 'non-vulnerable older people can suffer elder abuse on account of ageist attitudes and practices' (Herring 2009, 138).

Taking Herring's second point first, surely these types of cases ought simply to be dealt with using an existing property offence? There are a number of examples of 'non-pure' property offences in English law which penalise more than just an attack on property interests. These include the offences of robbery, burglary, and the general fraud offence. Such offences have links to the violation of property interests but also penalise attacks upon other rights (such as the right to bodily integrity). Moreover, while penalising the financial abuse of the vulnerable may justify the creation of a criminal law offence in the first place, there is no requirement that the element of targeting a vulnerable person in practice be marked out in the resulting offence. On the first point, there are also difficulties with this approach – for example, how do we determine that an individual has been targeted for ageist reasons? Herring argues (2009, 134) that we need to work out if the abuse is age-related. 'Strong' elder abuse will involve violent conduct and will reflect 'structural inequality relating to age', whereas 'weaker' elder abuse will 'involve any abuse of an older person in circumstances reflecting structural inequality' (Herring 2009, 134). But this could be very difficult to identify in practice, calling into question whether it is conceptually distinct in the way suggested.

There is a second strand to this section's argument about the bluntness of criminalisation. It concerns the implications of criminalisation for the protection of older persons specifically, and vulnerable persons more generally. Criminalisation, whether by a preventive measure or by a substantive offence is absolute in nature, expressing public censure and condemnation. Cathryn Costello (2015, 220) has argued powerfully in the context of forced labour that '[w]hile criminal law's expressive and punitive character singles out wrong-doers', criminalisation 'ignores how forced labour comes about'. Costello's argument (2015) is that the migration process and immigration law can create vulnerability conditions which are ripe for forced labour. But there is nothing in criminalisation that addresses the root cause of vulnerability (Costello 2015). The point is that it is important to identify and to address how vulnerability has been created, and criminalisation obscures this. It is a public policy concern to identify reasons for vulnerability and to address them. Can the civil law be used more nimbly to expose and address dynamics in families which make certain older persons susceptible to financial abuse, for example? Family lawyers may be able to bring a unique vantage point here.

4 The argument for fraud by abuse of position to be read in a vulnerable person-protective mode

There remain broad questions about whether the criminal law of England and Wales ought to tackle the issue of financial abuse of older persons by creating new specific offences. We have sketched a sceptical thesis in this chapter in response: first, by casting doubt on the possibility of sufficiently robustly resolving ambiguity within a concept of financial abuse of older persons for the criminal law; and, secondly, by highlighting that criminalisation is a blunt instrument in tackling this form of serious wrongdoing. By way of conclusion to this chapter, this section further develops one narrower issue: can an existing offence instead be used to address financial abuse of older persons? Specifically, can fraud by abuse of position provide a framework offence by which financial abuse of older persons can be penalised?

A focus on safeguarding older persons from opportunistic and predatory individuals was a theme in Parliamentary debates on the Fraud Bill. At the Committee stage (Stg Co Deb (20 June 2006) Co B, Fraud Bill col. 25–26), it was noted that legal protection for elderly persons from fraud by family members or workers would be undermined if fraud by abuse of position required a fiduciary relationship in order to establish a relevant position. The Solicitor-General (Stg Co Deb (20 June 2006) Co B, Fraud Bill col. 26) accepted that these were 'cases in which all of us would want the elderly to be safeguarded'. What has resulted in sections 1 and 4(1) of the Fraud Act 2006 does not require a fiduciary relationship (Law Commission 2002, para. 7.38). This form of the general fraud offence penalises a defendant who dishonestly abuses a position 'in which he is expected to safeguard, or not to act against, the financial interests of another person' (s. 4(1)(a)–(b)). A defendant must intend, by means of this abuse, to either make a gain for himself or another, or to cause loss or the risk of loss to another (s. 4(1)(c)). We noted in section 1 above the diversity of conduct which may be termed 'financial abuse of older persons'. In principle there appears to be scope to apply fraud by abuse of position to at least some core cases of financial abuse of older persons.

A more radical line of argument, tentatively advanced here, is that fraud by abuse of position can and ought to be interpreted purposively in a manner sensitive to protecting the financial interests of vulnerable persons. This is, protecting vulnerable persons should be more than a rationale for this form of the offence, but an interpretive driver. The focus is upon vulnerable persons rather than upon older persons specifically. The argument from section 3 above holds strength when we turn to fraud by abuse of position: we must be wary of the danger of entrenching actual or perceived vulnerability of older persons, in this context by interpreting the general fraud offence in an older person-protective mode. Instead, focusing on persons who are vulnerable for a variety of reasons identifies conditions of seriously unequal contest as our main concern. While it may be morally wrongful to intentionally hit a fit adult, there is something that is always morally wrongful about hitting a mentally disordered person or a young child. Some persons are less able to protect their own interests. A vulnerable party is simply not a match for the stronger party. One way of ensuring that this moral norm is respected is to acknowledge that some interactions between persons should not be pursued because the setting is one of unfair contest. Moreover, those who prey upon the vulnerable are likely to have a secondary reason for doing so, beyond the greater likelihood of succeeding in their goals. A vulnerable person may be less likely to report their ill-treatment and/or it may be difficult to build a case based upon their testimony and evidence.

Can the idea of a vulnerable person be made coherent? This task can only be touched upon here. Since we are all vulnerable to some degree – what Fineman (2008) identifies as 'ontological vulnerability' – we should want to single out reasons to say that a person is vulnerable if they are significantly or unusually vulnerable. This so-called 'institutional vulnerability' (Fineman 2008) can arise 'depending on an individual's economic and social relationships' (Rodgers 2016, p. 37). These are persons for whom Fineman argues the state has particular responsibility to provide care. For example, the mentally disordered and persons subjected to physical or mental abuse may be vulnerable in a context involving serious financial abuse. Alternatively an individual may be vulnerable because of their ambivalent legal status. Virginia Mantouvalou (2015, 50–51) highlights the 'legislative precariousness' of migrant workers, given the state's ability to opt-out of minimum labour law protections and because of immigration rules which tie workers to the employer with whom they entered the United Kingdom. A person may be vulnerable by their circumstances – even their legal position – or because of something linked to their personhood.

This suggestion that fraud by abuse of position should be read in this way is not altogether radical. There have been arguments that fraud by abuse of position can be linked with an anti-exploitation agenda (Simester et al 2016, Williams 2011). Moreover, recent developments in the criminal law, such as the Modern Slavery Act 2015, demonstrate a commitment to policing the most extreme instances of exploitative conduct, offering increased protection for vulnerable persons. The state has a substantial and legitimate interest in penalising the worst forms of interpersonal exploitation. A strong pressure point comes from a range of international obligations imposed upon the state (see Collins 2017). The argument here is complementary to this reasoning. While the role of the criminal law in policing exploitation is still very much open to debate, we here provide a cautious defence of levelling up protection for the vulnerable by developing vulnerable person-protective norms in the criminal law. This is an argument which should be taken seriously.

A link between abuse of a position of financial trust and vulnerable persons must be established. Notably, there is no explicit focus on the vulnerable within the fraud offence; the emphasis is on dishonest conduct which is undertaken with fault. There is scope for judicial development on this point. The Court of Appeal in *Valujevs* [2015], [41] has recently confirmed that the judge and jury must decide whether a reasonable person would hold an expectation that an individual will safeguard, or will not act against, the financial interests of another person. The dishonest targeting of a vulnerable person can therefore be taken into account when determining whether a relevant position of trust is held. It is well-known that the Explanatory Notes to sections 1(2)(c) and 4 of the Fraud Act 2006 draw few limits in making this determination: a fiduciary relationship is unnecessary and a relevant position may be held by a family member in relation to a vulnerable family member, for example (Explanatory Notes para. 7.38).

It bears highlighting that a defendant must occupy a position in which he is expected to protect, *or not to act against*, the financial interests of another person. It is not acceptable to include 'something as innocuous as failing to work for an employer as hard as one might' within this form of the fraud offence (Ormerod and Williams 2007, 133). But where there is scope for genuine debate as to whether a defendant occupies a relevant position, and an element of dishonesty is present, it may be convincing for a judge to leave fraud by abuse of position to the jury for interrogation. Moreover, if a judge takes a broad approach to what might in principle count as a 'position', it follows that the jury gets to make more of the decision based on dishonesty (Collins 2016). There is a strong argument for this approach where vulnerable persons are involved.

This discussion brings sharply to the fore the role of the courts in interpreting the offence in this way. What are the boundaries of fraud by abuse of position as judicially interpreted? In conclusion it cannot take for granted that this form of the general fraud offence will be deployed in a vulnerable person-protective mode. The Court of Appeal has demonstrated limited sensitivity to the plight of precarious migrant workers in *Valujevs* (see Collins 2016). In *Valujevs*, Fulford LJ narrowly based his reasoning that there was a case to answer in relation to fraud by abuse of position on the grounds that the defendants had assumed responsibility for, and control of, collecting the wages of their workers. The fact that the defendants charged excessive rent, withheld work, and lent money to ensure debt bondage, did not contribute to establishing a relevant position of financial trust. It was noted that individuals 'are entitled to and expected to look after their own interests' ([44]). This preoccupation with the interests of the free-market at the expense of vulnerable persons shows limited cognisance of recent trends in the criminal law to be responsive to extreme instances of exploitation. A commitment to vulnerable person-protective norms in interpreting fraud by abuse of position would require inclination from the courts, as *Valujevs* demonstrates.

References

American Association of Retired Persons (AARP) International (2006) *Keeping the Wolves From Grandma's Door: Financial Exploitation of the Elderly*. New York: International Network for the Prevention of Elder Abuse.

Action on Elder Abuse (2015) *What is Elder Abuse?* Available at: http://elderabuse.org.uk/what-is-elder-abuse/

Anetzberger, G. (2005) 'The Reality of Elder Abuse' *Clinical Gerontologist* 28, 1.

Ashworth, A. and Zedner, L. 2014. *Preventive Justice*. Oxford: Oxford University Press.
Berman, M. (2002) 'The Normative Functions of Coercion Claims' *Legal Theory* 8, 45.
British Broadcasting Corporation (BBC) (2015) *One in Three Fraud Victims 65 or Over, Charity Says*. Available at: www.bbc.co.uk/news/uk-34530586
Collins, J. (2016) 'Fraud by Abuse of Position and Unlicensed Gangmasters' *Modern Law Review* 79, 354.
Collins, J. (2017) 'Exploitation of Persons and the Limits of the Criminal Law' *Criminal Law Review* 3, 167.
Costello, C. (2015) 'Migrants and Forced Labour: A Labour Law Response' in A. Bogg et al (eds) *The Autonomy of Labour Law*. Oxford: Hart, 189.
Centre for Policy on Ageing (CPA) Briefing (2008) *The Financial Abuse of Older People* Available at: www.cpa.org.uk/policy/briefings/financial_abuse.pdf
Crown Prosecution Service (CPS) (2009) *Crimes Against Older People*. London: CPS.
Crosby, G. et al (2008) *The Financial Abuse of Older People: A Review From the Literature Carried Out by the Centre for Policy on Ageing on Behalf of Help the Aged*. London: Help the Aged.
Department of Health (DH) (2000) *No Secrets: Guidance on Developing and Implementing Multi-Agency Policies and Procedures to Protect Vulnerable Adults From Abuse*. London: DH.
Duff, R. A. and Green, S. P. (2005) 'Introduction' in R. A. Duff and S. P. Green (eds) *Defining Crimes: Essays on the Special Part of the Criminal Law*. Oxford: Oxford University Press, 1.
Edwards, J. (2010) 'Justice Denied: The Criminal Law and the Ouster of the Courts' *Oxford Journal of Legal Studies* 30, 725.
Edwards, J. (2012) 'Publication Review: Crimes, Harms, and Wrongs by A P Simester and Andreas von Hirsch' *Criminal Law Review*, 75.
Feinberg, J. (1987) *Harm to Others*. Oxford: Oxford University Press.
Feinberg, J. (1988) *The Moral Limits of the Criminal Law: Harmless Wrongdoing*. Oxford: Oxford University Press.
Fineman, M. (2008) 'The Vulnerable Subject: Anchoring Equality in the Human Condition' *Yale Journal of Law and Feminism* 20(1), 1.
Fitzgerald, G. (2004) *Hidden Voices: Older People's Experience of Abuse: An Analysis of Calls to the Action on Elder Abuse Helpline*. London: Action on Elder Abuse in association with Help the Aged.
Hafemeister, T. (2004) 'Financial Abuse of the Elderly in Domestic Settings' in National Research Council (ed.) *Elder Mistreatment: Abuse, Neglect and Exploitation in an Aging America*. Washington, D.C., MD: National Academies Press, 382.
Herring, J. (2009) *Older People in Law and Society*. Oxford: Oxford University Press.
Herring, J. (2016) *Vulnerable Adults and the Law*. Oxford: Oxford University Press.
House of Commons Health Committee (2004) *Elder Abuse*. London: The Stationery Office.
Husak, D. (2008a) *Overcriminalization*. Oxford: Oxford University Press.
Husak, D. (2008b) 'Why Criminal Law: A Question of Content?' *Criminal Law and Philosophy* 14, 99.
Husak, D. (2011) 'Reservations About Overcriminalization' *New Criminal Law Review* 14, 96.
Jackson, S. (2015) 'The Vexing Problem of Defining Financial Exploitation' *Journal of Financial Crime*, 22(1), 63.

Jackson, S. and Hafemeister, T. (2010) *Financial Abuse of Elderly People vs Other Forms of Elder Abuse: Assessing their Dynamics, Risk Factors and Society's Response.* Arlington, VA: Institute for Justice.

Kleinig, J. (2016). 'The Paternalistic Principle' *Criminal Law and Philosophy* 12, 315.

Kohn, N. (2012). 'Elder (In)justice: A Critique of the Criminalization of Elder Abuse' *American Criminal Law Review* 49, 1.

Law Commission (2002) *Fraud* (No 276). London: The Law Commission.

Mantouvalou, V. (2015) 'The Right to Non-Exploitative Work' in V. Mantouvalou (ed.) *The Right to Work: Legal and Philosophical Perspectives.* Oxford: Hart, 39.

O'Keeffe, M. et al (2007) *UK Study of Abuse and Neglect of Older People: Prevalence Survey Report.* National Centre for Social Research; King's College London. Available at: www.kcl.ac.uk/sspp/policy-institute/scwru/pubs/2007/okeefeetal2007ukstudyprevalence.pdf

Ormerod, D. and Williams, D. (2007) *Smith's Law of Theft*, 9th edn. Oxford: Oxford University Press.

Palmore, E. (1999) *Ageism: Negative and Positive*, 2nd edn. New York: Springer.

Rabiner, D., O'Keeffe, J. and Brown, D. (2004) 'Financial Exploitation of Older Persons: Policy Issues and Recommendations for Addressing Them' *Journal Of Elder Abuse and Neglect* 16(1), 65.

Rabiner, D., O'Keeffe, J. and Brown, D. (2006) 'Financial Exploitation of Older Persons' *Journal of Aging and Social Policy* 18(2), 47.

Rodgers, L. (2016). *Labour Law, Vulnerability and the Regulation of Precarious Work.* London: Edward Elgar Publishing.

Simester, J. R. et al (2016) *Simester and Sullivan's Criminal Law: Theory and Doctrine*, 6th edn. Oxford: Hart.

Smith, R. (1999) 'Fraud and Financial Abuse of Older Persons' *Australian Institute of Criminology* 132, 1.

Stg Co Deb (20 June 2006) Co B, Fraud Bill cols 25–26.

von Hirsch, A. and Jareborg, N. 1991. 'Gauging Criminal Harm: A Living Standard Analysis' *Oxford Journal of Legal Studies* 11, 1.

Williams, R. (2011) 'Cartels in the Criminal Law Landscape' in C. Beaton-Wells and A. Ezrachi (eds) *Criminalising Cartels: Critical Studies of an International Regulatory Movement.* Oxford: Hart, 289.

World Health Organization (WHO) (2002) *Views of Older Persons on Elder Abuse.* Geneva: WHO.

Cases

R v Valujevs [2015] 3 *WLR* 109

Chapter 5

Safeguarding in older age

Alison Brammer

Introduction

The abuse of older people as an issue of significant social concern emerged in the 1980s (Eastman 1984). Early professional focus was on elder abuse and has expanded to safeguarding of vulnerable adults, a term that may include older people, and most recently guidance has included domestic violence in the categories of abuse to which safeguarding applies. This is an area of practice, policy, and law that is growing in every sense. Practice in England developed in the absence of any specific legislation but inclusion of safeguarding provisions in the Care Act 2014, supported by Care and Support Guidance (DH 2016), marks a new era in this evolving field, placing safeguarding on a statutory footing for the first time in England. Older people statistically comprise the largest proportion of adults to whom safeguarding responsibilities apply, being amongst those adults with care and support needs. Older women are more likely to be victims of abuse than older men and are more likely to suffer from certain types of abuse. The latest guidance extends the categories of abuse adding self-neglect, organisational abuse, trafficking, and notably domestic violence. Campaigning groups have consistently articulated the view that much elder abuse is 'domestic violence grown old', however the main focus of domestic violence research has concerned younger women. This chapter will evaluate the new landscape for adult safeguarding from the perspectives of gender and ageing. Notions of autonomy and coercion are central to the conceptualisation of abuse and consequent safeguarding response and in particular the chapter will explore the inclusion of domestic violence of older women as a safeguarding issue.

A new era for safeguarding

The Care Act 2014 is legislation that is both consolidating and modernising. It was introduced following extensive work by the Law Commission (2008, 2010, 2011a, 2011b) and replaces a raft of outdated complex and contradictory adult social care legislation dating back to the National Assistance Act 1948. The Act restates some familiar principles but also signals a shift in policy and practice that centre the voice of the individual, who is the subject of concern. Specific provisions that place safeguarding adults on a statutory footing for the first time are included in the legislation. Previously a framework for practice in this area was provided by the *No Secrets* Guidance (DH 2000) together with reference to a range of intersecting legislation that might have some relevance to safeguarding, such as aspects of the criminal law and more recently the Mental Capacity Act 2005. The new legislation may be seen as a response to consistent calls for reform from various quarters. In 2009, CSCI described the existing legal framework for safeguarding adults as, 'neither systematic nor co-ordinated, reflecting the sporadic development of safeguarding over the last 25 years'. Another driver has been a concern that a hierarchy exists across safeguarding practice and a desire to address this at least in part to secure parity across adult and child safeguarding. Indeed, Baroness Hale, responding to the Law Commission consultation remarked, 'Statutory works tends to take priority over softer obligations. It is for this reason that adult safeguarding has been described as a "poor relation" to child protection' (Law Commission 2011b).

Detailed statutory guidance, *The Care and Support Statutory Guidance* (DH 2016) supports the Act with Chapter 14 as a replacement for *No Secrets.* The Guidance defines adult safeguarding as, 'protecting an adult's right to live in safety, free from abuse and neglect (14.7). It is important to note that the Care Act 2014 (and Guidance) applies to England only, with separate legislation applicable to adult safeguarding in Scotland, The Adult Support and Protection (Scotland) Act 2007, and in Wales, the Social Services and Well-being (Wales) Act 2014. The introduction of safeguarding legislation is still under consideration in Northern Ireland with support from the Commissioner for Older People for Northern Ireland. The challenge that such divergence in law relating to safeguarding across the UK as a consequence of devolution has been noted (Brammer 2014a), both conceptually and at a practical level in relation to individuals' subject to safeguarding and practitioners at the borders.

Provisions in the Act of specific application to safeguarding are few and must be viewed in the context of the wider care and support framework. As stated they are nevertheless a significant step in providing statutory recognition of safeguarding practice and lay down a framework setting some parameters for action and governance. Briefly, the following are relevant provisions.

Under s 42, the local authority has a duty to make (or cause to be made) enquiries to decide whether any action should be taken in a case where it has reasonable cause to suspect an adult who has care and support needs is experiencing or at risk of abuse or neglect which s/he is unable to protect him/herself from as a result of the care and support needs. Where such an adult is the subject of a safeguarding enquiry (or SAR), has 'substantial difficulty' in being involved in the process, and

there is no other suitable person to represent and support them, then under s 68 the local authority must arrange for an independent advocate to represent and support the adult. This provision exists alongside other avenues for advocacy support, including the IMCA, IMHA, and IDSVA. A formal structure for governance, coordination of multi-agency practice and 'learning lessons' is provided in s 43 which sets a statutory requirement for Safeguarding Boards to be established. One of the core functions of the Board is to arrange for a Safeguarding Adult Reviews under s 44 where an adult who has experienced, or died from, abuse or neglect. The Board also has discretion to review any other case involving an adult with care and support needs if there is cause for concern about how agencies worked together. Underpinning this governance structure, members of the SAB are required to contribute to reviews (s 44 (5)) and have broad duties to cooperate across the Act (ss 6–7). The Act exists as a gateway to a range of associated legislation and policy once the focus moves beyond investigation to certain responses, such as prosecution or employment-based disciplinary action.

For completeness, the specific safeguarding provisions must be understood in the context of the overall philosophy and intent of the Act, captured in the duty to promote well-being and associated principles. Limited caselaw to date portrays a somewhat cautious interpretation of well-being in these times of austerity, *Davey v Oxfordshire CC* [2017]. The Act lists a range of factors that contribute to well-being in s 2(2) including protection from abuse and neglect, alongside personal dignity, physical and mental health, and emotional well-being. One of the principles underpinning the Act, to which local authorities must have regard, is the need to protect people from abuse and neglect. Protection from abuse and neglect is therefore a consideration of much wider application than suggested by the limited specific safeguarding provisions. It is integral to all aspects of the Act. The first principle requires local authorities to have regard to 'the importance of beginning with the assumption that the individual is best placed to judge the individual's well-being (s. 1(3)(a)). This signals an important endorsement of changes to policy and practice prior to implementation of the Act, described initially as 'personalisation' in relation to assessment of need for community care services. It has developed into a commitment to person led and outcome focused work captured in the 'Making Safeguarding Personal' initiative (Manthorpe et al 2014).

Defining abuse

Formal definition of abuse of adults requiring a safeguarding response has been highly contested over the years (Brammer and Biggs 1998), particularly in relation to the description of the victim of abuse as a 'vulnerable adult' a term enshrined in *No Secrets* (Dunn 2014). *No Secrets* introduced a rights-based conceptualisation of abuse, 'Abuse is a violation of an individual's human and civil rights by any other person or persons' (DH 2000, 2.5), followed by a series of categories, about which a degree of consensus had emerged (physical, sexual, psychological, financial or material, neglect and acts of omission, and discriminatory abuse). Although the central definition refers to an individual, safeguarding activity is restricted to 'vulnerable adults'. A key theme of responses to a consultation on the *No Secrets* guidance (DH 2009) was critique of the term 'vulnerable adult', its link to community care services, and consequent 'welfarist approach to abuse' (Williams 2008) and exclusion from safeguarding of adults not eligible for community care services (Brammer 2014b). The term 'vulnerable adult' is not included in the new legislation but it is arguable that as the link to needs for care and support is a pre-requisite for a safeguarding enquiry, little has changed in substance.

In the Care Act 2014, abuse and neglect is further defined to include financial abuse in s 42(3). Other categories of abuse are listed in chapter 14 of the guidance. Familiar forms of abuse that featured in *No Secrets* are restated, with notable additions of four further categories of abuse gaining formal recognition for the first time, namely: modern slavery, organisational abuse, domestic violence, and self-neglect.

Such a neat categorisation of abuse is rarely presented in the complex reality of adult safeguarding and contrasts with Cambridge (2000)'s insight that, multiple abuse is a closer reflection of everyday practice. These 'new' categories represent a considerable extension to the boundaries of safeguarding practice and potentially incorporate scenarios that are unfamiliar, require expertise of bodies hitherto excluded form safeguarding, and require different responses. On closer examination the Guidance refers to domestic violence as incorporating psychological, physical, sexual, financial (each a category in their own right), with emotional abuse and so called 'honour'-based violence (14.17) It also notes that exploitation is a common theme across the various types of abuse and neglect. The move away from the much maligned term 'vulnerable adult' (although see Herring, this volume) and reluctance to offer an acceptable replacement, coupled with the breadth of types of abuse provided by the extension of categories suggests the demise of meaningful definition of adult abuse.

Safeguarding – what do we know about age and gender

The first detailed analysis of prevalence of abuse of older people on a national scale was published in 2007 (O'Keefe et al 2007). The survey involved interviews with 2,000 people over the age of 66, living in private households and representative of the UK population. Key findings were consistent with other international research (refs) and identified a prevalence rate of 4%. In the survey, interpersonal abuse (physical, psychological, or sexual) was more likely to be caused by men, comprising 80% of the perpetrators. Overall women were more likely to suffer mistreatment at 3.8% compared with 1.1% of men. Given that the survey excluded people living in residential settings it is perhaps not surprising that in the majority of cases the abuser was a member of the household, however it is notable that 51% were partners of the older person. When compared with safeguarding records held by local authorities the results suggest that only about 3% of abuse and neglect cases were coming to the attention of lead safeguarding agencies. For that reason and given the age of the survey it is worth also briefly considering the most recent statistic available on safeguarding (Adult Social Care Statistics 2016), based on the

Safeguarding Adults Return (SAR) data collected from local authorities covering the period 1 April 2015 to 31 March 2016 (the first collection since implementation of the Care Act 2014). The statistics cover concerns raised with local authorities about a risk of abuse and cases where an investigation is instigated under s. 42. Although elements of the return are mandatory there are also optional categories including the number of concerns as opposed to investigations. For this reason, together with the hidden nature of some abuse, and also as some safeguarding matters may be dealt with by other organisations the overall percentages are likely to represent a significant underestimate. In relation to age, 63% of all enquiries undertaken concerned a person aged over 65 and of that number 29% were over 85. As to gender, 60% of all cases concerned a woman. The place of abuse is most likely to be the individual's own home (43%) followed by a care home setting (30%). Where abuse takes place in the individual's own home, the source of risk in 63% of cases is a person known to the individual other than in a social care professional capacity, which would include family members and partners. The highest proportion of cases were recorded as neglect and acts of omission followed by 26% for physical abuse.

Although these statistics were collected following implementation of the Care Act 2014 and include investigations under s. 42, strangely the full range of types of abuse set out in the Care and Support Guidance are not covered. The omitted categories are self-neglect, domestic violence, and trafficking. Whilst some cases of domestic violence might be captured under the heading 'physical, sexual and/or psychological or emotional abuse', there is no evidence in the Report to indicate how many cases of domestic violence have in fact been recognised as a safeguarding matter, as the Guidance suggested, and proceeded to a s. 42 enquiry. As to further potential sources of data, disappointingly the British Crime Survey, which includes domestic violence, only covers age groups up to 59. Some further insight may be gained from smaller scale studies that have focused on particular types of abuse experience by those sharing particular characteristics, such as the study by Jeary (2004) of sexual crimes against older women.

Elder abuse or safeguarding

Safeguarding practice, or as it was more likely to be termed, adult protection services, initially focused on older adults. This was evident in the first policy publication, 'No Longer Afraid: the Safeguard of Older People in Domestic Settings' (Tomlinson 1993) and most local authority policies themselves focused on elder abuse. Gender considerations were largely missing with research into elder abuse described as 'gender neutral' (Penhale 2003). In 2000 *No Secrets* extended the application of adult protection, which gradually merged into safeguarding (ADASS 2005), to vulnerable adults. The safeguarding provisions introduced by the Care Act 2014 apply broadly in relation to adults with care and support needs. The only age related requirement is that it is applicable to those over the age of 18. Even this apparently straightforward demarcation by age can be more complex in practice, particularly in relation to the transition of individuals from childhood to adulthood, where seamless service provision between children's and adults' services may not be experienced by all; leaving care responsibilities under the Children Act 1989 continue up to the age of 25 and the Mental Capacity Act 2005 provisions apply from the age of 16 rather than 18.

Older age in itself is not a criterion under the Act. Unlike the HSPHA 1968 provision to promote the welfare of 'old people', the new duties to prevent needs for support and to promote well-being apply across the age range. A strong argument continues however, that there is a case for recognising abuse of an older person as different to, for example, the abuse of an adult with a learning disability in their mid-30s (Herring 2009).

As detailed above, there is a gender imbalance in consideration of elder abuse. In reality, most elder abuse victims are female. It has long been recognised that the majority of, though not all, perpetrators are male (Hightower et al 1999, Pritchard 2001). In part this may be an inevitable consequence of changing demographics. Women have a longer life expectancy then men and are also living longer than ever, frequently into their 90s and over. It appears however that being female is a risk factor for abuse.

Elder abuse or domestic violence

If an older woman suffers violence, is that domestic violence or elder abuse? Domestic violence of older women is largely missing from elder abuse literature and equally the position of older women is largely missing from domestic violence literature. It may be argued that domestic violence of older women has been marginalised and hidden within elder abuse, an invisible concern. Not surprisingly then, distinct discourse has developed around elder abuse and domestic violence and this is apparent in the relative lack of feminist analysis of elder abuse. An explanation may in part be offered by the origins of recognition. Whereas the emergence and recognition of domestic violence as a social problem is largely attributable to the voice of women and a grass roots movement, elder abuse largely lacks the voice of the victim and recognition can be traced to the actions of medical and social professionals.

Domestic violence suffered by older women may be distinguished from domestic violence suffered by younger women. It also presents in different forms for older women. Sometimes the abuse will have started earlier in life, may have been a longstanding presence in a relationship that has persisted into old age of the woman (and often of the perpetrator), sometimes referred to as 'graduated domestic violence' (Biggs et al 1995). Secondly the abuse may begin in old age within a longstanding relationship and thirdly the abuse may begin in older age within a later life partnership. The impact of the violence may differ in older age. For a woman who has become frail, physical violence may have a more severe effect. In other cases where the perpetrator may be unable to inflict a physical assault the behaviour may become more coercive and controlling, the dynamics of power and control remaining even though the physical violence may reduce. Domestic violence suffered by older women may exist in the context of a 'care-giving' relationship. Penhale and Goreham's analysis of interventions in intimate violence across seven police forces found that 11% of the victims were care providers and 20% were recipients of care from the perpetrator (2013). The same report highlighted that 'ownership' of the victim was a dominant feature of cases, characterised as including behaviours described as controlling, jealous, manipulative, oppressive, and dominant.

McGarry et al (2014) found that a lack of conceptual clarity between domestic abuse and elder abuse amongst agencies impacted on service delivery. Domestic violence of older women has an invisible quality. Lazenbatt et al (2013) suggest that 'service providers and policy makers often assume that DV stops at around 50' and Phillips (2000) is of the view that domestic violence of older women has been obscured by the gender neutral terms elder abuse and elder mistreatment. McCausland et al (2016) draw tentative conclusions from the limited research available suggesting that the incidence of domestic abuse increases where the victim is suffering from dementia, particularly where domestic abuse featured before the onset of dementia. One of the challenges in arriving at that conclusion was the tendency for all abuse of older people (male and female) to be captured within the term elder abuse and a lack of specific research on 'the subset of intimate partner abuse within the larger cohort of elder abuse' (ibid, 482).

A response to the act which is classified as domestic violence may be significantly different from the response if the act is classified as elder abuse. In domestic violence cases there is an expectation that some action will be taken by the victim, often an implicit or explicit assumption that the woman (most frequently the victim) will leave a violent partner. It may also include use of the private law to seek an injunction under the Family Law Act 1996. In fact this legislation provides an addition to the range of legal options that might provide a response to a wide range of cases including physical abuse since the extension to associated persons, including a wide range of relatives and same sex partnerships, but it remains primarily utilised in intimate partner abuse At governmental level the focus has been on strengthening criminal justice responses to domestic violence with the introduction of a discrete offence of coercive control in the Serious Crime Act 2015, s 76 (Bettinson and Bishop 2015). This offence also signals important recognition that domestic abuse does not always involve physical violence and is consistent with the Home Office cross-governmental definition of domestic violence and abuse as, 'any incident or pattern of incidents of controlling, coercive, threatening behaviour, violence or abuse between those aged 16 or over who are or have been intimate partners or family members regardless of gender or sexuality' (Home Office 2013). This emphasis on patterns of coercive behaviour is reflected in the new offence.

Effective intervention for domestic violence may include finding a safe space for the woman in the form of a refuge. Refuges focused on younger women with children may not have facilities for women with disabilities or for older woman.

The experience of an older woman in such a refuge may compound feelings of isolation. In this regard it is also important to acknowledge that it is incorrect to refer to 'older women' as a homogenous group. A woman of 65 will have very different needs and life experiences to an 85-year-old woman. A further consequence of differing approaches to domestic violence is that involvement of different agencies may be reflected in the label used to refer to the women e.g. Criminal Justice services refer to a victim whereas welfare agencies are more likely to use the term 'service user' (Robbins et al 2014).

The serious case review into the death of Mary Russell provides a poignant example of the invisibility of domestic violence suffered by an older woman (Southend SAB 2011). In 2010, aged 81, Mary Russell died from a bleed to the brain after being assaulted by her husband, Albert, aged 86. They had been married for 56 years. That was not the first assault. In the months leading to her death she had made 999 calls and had reported nine separate incidents of physical abuse by her husband, some to more than one agency, and for many there was corroborating evidence of injury. Despite this, police officers were unaware of the background when they responded to emergency calls and did not see a pattern of abuse. Neither the police nor social services had called a safeguarding strategy meeting and there was a lack of effective joint working. A conclusion of the review observed: 'Poor appreciation of the risks of domestic abuse in old age'. The Review also noted that, 'officers were aware of the undesirability of bringing a frail elderly man into custody', and subsequently the Crown Prosecution Service decided there was insufficient evidence to prosecute him. Lessons learned in the report include the statement that:

> This domestic violence review has highlighted issues about domestic violence in old age, especially in older old age and where older people have community care needs, which need to be incorporated in the training and development of staff. As the population ages the incidence of domestic abuse in older age will grow.
>
> (para. 4.1)

Domestic violence as a safeguarding issue

A joint report by the Local Government Association and ADASS (2014) stressed the need to make stronger connections between safeguarding and domestic abuse. Nevertheless, Robbins et al (2016) argue that there remains a lack of understanding amongst adult social workers in relation to domestic abuse as it is constructed as a children and families issue. Inclusion of domestic violence as an indicator of significant harm in the Children Act 1989 further focuses domestic violence as a child care issue. There are challenges to the social work education curriculum to ensure domestic violence is recognised by adult social workers as an adult social work issue rather than a matter only to be considered in child care cases.

Domestic violence can incorporate a range of harm – physical, sexual, psychological, and financial, all of which are recognised as categories of abuse in the Care and Support Guidance and it is pertinent to ask why the separate category has been included. Or, in other words what pushes a physical assault (for example) of an older woman into the category of domestic violence as opposed to the category of physical abuse. There are echoes of the debate between domestic violence and elder abuse. It is not simply a matter of nomenclature as the discussion earlier suggests that particular responses to domestic violence have become established practice. The distinction is also relevant in relation to investigation of concerns. For domestic violence the domestic abuse, stalking, and honour-based violence risk identification checklist (DASH-RIC) is routinely used as an assessment tool to identify and discuss risk with victims, and cases may then filter into consideration by the MARAC (Multi Agency Risk Assessment Conference) which considers individual high risk cases of domestic violence. The ADASS and LGA report notes however, that the tool is 'predisposed to assess risks for women with children and is known to have limitations for identification of the risk factors experienced by disabled and older people so professional judgement will be key'.

There are potential advantages of including domestic violence within safeguarding practice. These include helping the victim conceptualise their abuse and rendering the involvement of professionals of different agencies more acceptable. Older women may not conceptualise their experience as domestic violence. Lack of relevant information for older people may reinforce the stereotype that younger women are victims of domestic violence as awareness raising materials and those signposting related services typically depict younger women with children. Beyond recognition, there are many reasons why an older woman may not report domestic violence. Some may be similar to those cited by younger victims, such as fear of reprisal. In addition, the abuse may exist in a relationship where the women risks losing care provided by the abuser and may fear a move into residential care as an alternative. It may not be clear who to report the abuse to, with associated concerns about the stigma of involvement of the police. An older woman may have limited support networks and may fear the prospect of living alone.

It is possible that inclusion of domestic violence as a safeguarding issue could harness additional support for the woman beyond the responses of criminal justice agencies in a way that is more readily acceptable. For some older women targeted resources for care and support needs that are identified in a safeguarding enquiry might be accepted more readily than intervention, such as the offer of a refuge place. The fact that the local authority as a third party would lead the intervention rather than the expectation that the woman would take action might be well received and something of a relief for some women, although the paternalistic nature of this approach is apparent. There is also a greater emphasis on supporting the individual to recover from the abuse and develop resilience.

Multi-agency work is embedded in safeguarding and the involvement of social services in relation to care and support needs may result from a referral on a routine basis by a health professional and could also identify domestic violence that would otherwise remain concealed. Safeguarding may offer a way in given the hidden nature of domestic violence of older women. Again, in contrast to younger women, an older woman may not be working and lacks the visibility that responsibility for children carries, such as the school run. Injuries may also be disguised as and accepted as a consequence of falls.

Perhaps the most persuasive argument is presented in the form of 'making safeguarding personal'. This driver for a person-centred and outcomes-focused approach to safeguarding had its roots in personalisation. The merit of the approach here is the commitment to hearing the voice of the individual and establishing their preferred outcome. As the Guidance states:

> Making safeguarding personal means it should be person-led and outcome-focused. It engages the person in a conversation about how best to respond to their safeguarding situation in a way that enhances involvement, choice and control as well as improving quality of life, wellbeing and safety.
>
> (DH 2016)

Opposing argument would stress the welfarist approach of safeguarding. The case for separating domestic violence from safeguarding regardless of age and care and support needs includes the fact that the police are more likely to be the lead agency and criminalisation of the behaviour sends a stronger message that this is behaviour not to be tolerated in society. Reference back to the Mary Russell case highlights the weakness of this argument.

Conclusion

Considerations of age and gender are crucial in safeguarding practice. In effect they are risk factors. An older woman is significantly more likely to suffer abuse than a younger man and the abuse is more likely to be of an inter-personal than financial nature. The intersection of ageing and gendered domestic violence raises particular challenges. Reconceptualisation of domestic violence as a safeguarding concern partly addresses this challenge and may contribute to better outcomes for some victims.

The distinction between domestic violence as a safeguarding matter or a matter between individuals may be manifest in the legal response, on the one hand, 'welfarist' with an emphasis on support and prevention, on the other conviction of the perpetrator. This over-simplifies somewhat, but reflects differing agency involvement. A risk of including domestic violence in safeguarding is reinforcement of the message that behaviour against older women is described as abusive and a softer response is taken rather than recognition of the behaviour as criminal. On the other hand, its inclusion in safeguarding may reach older women suffering domestic violence who were previously invisible.

A further advantage of the safeguarding approach, with its emphasis on 'Making safeguarding Personal' is the focus on the outcome desired by victim. This has the potential to capture the largely silent voice and perspective of older women and may inform the development of responses, including joint or parallel rather than alternative activity by safeguarding teams and the police. The inclusion of domestic violence as a safeguarding issue should extend not restrict options for the individual. Safeguarding workers need to know about criminal options and injunctions whilst retaining an emphasis on support and prevention. For the police recognition of domestic violence of older women as different to the experience of younger women is important. Such changes in approach are likely to require considerable training to raise awareness of domestic violence of older women as a safeguarding matter.

It is too soon to tell what the impact of including domestic violence as a safeguarding category will be. The most positive outcome would be if this extension contributes to greater awareness of domestic violence as a concern irrespective of age or of care and support needs and that the voice of the woman dictates the outcome rather than the categorisation of the harm as a criminal justice or a safeguarding concern. A gap remains, however in that older women without care and support needs who are victims of domestic violence may not be well served by either model and are excluded from the support that safeguarding might offer, and the protection of the criminal law.

References

Adult Social Care Statistics (2016) *Safeguarding Adults: Annual Report, England 2015–16 Experimental Statistics*. London: NHS Digital.

Association of Directors of Adult Social Services (ADASS) (2005) *Safeguarding Adults: A National Framework of Standards for Good Practice and Outcomes in Adult Protection Work*. London: ADASS.

ADASS and Local Government Association (LGA) (2015) *Adult Safeguarding and Domestic Abuse: A Guide to Support Practitioners and Managers*, 2nd edn. London: ADASS and LGA.

Bettinson, V. and Bishop, C. (2015) 'Is the Creation of a Discrete Offence of Coercive Control Necessary to Combat Domestic Violence?' *Northern Ireland Law Quarterly* 66(2), 179.

Biggs, S., Phillipson, C. and Kingston, P. (1995) *Elder Abuse in Perspective*. London: Open University Press.

Brammer, A. (2014a) *Safeguarding Adults. Focus on Social Work Law Series*. Basingstoke: Palgrave Macmillan.

Brammer, A. (2014b) 'Safeguarding and the Elusive, Ever Inclusive Vulnerable Adult' in J. Wallbank and J. Herring (eds) *Vulnerabilities, Care and Family Law*. Abingdon: Routledge.

Brammer, A. and Biggs, S. (1998) 'Defining Elder Abuse' *Journal of Social Welfare and Family Law* 20(3), 285.

Cambridge, P. (2000) 'A Personal Touch: Managing the Risks of Abuse during Intimate and Personal Care' *Journal of Adult Protection* 2(4), 4.

Commission for Social Care Inspection (CSCI) (2008) *Raising Voices: Views on Safeguarding Adults*. London: CSCI.

Department of Health (DH) (2000) *No Secrets: Guidance on Developing and Implementing Multi-Agency Policies and Procedures to Protect Vulnerable Adults from Abuse.* London: DH.

DH (2009) *Safeguarding Adults: Report on the Consultation on the Review of No Secrets – Guidance on Developing and Implementing Multi-Agency Policies and Procedures to Protect Vulnerable Adults from Abuse.* London: DH.

DH (2016) *Care and Support Statutory Guidance.* London: DH.

Dunn, M. (2014) 'When are Adult Safeguarding Interventions Justified?' in J. Wallbank and J. Herring (eds) *Vulnerabilities, Care and Family Law*, Abingdon: Routledge.

Eastman, M. (1984) *Old Age Abuse.* London: Age Concern.

Herring, J. (2009) *Older People in Law and Society.* Oxford: Oxford University Press.

Hightower, J., Smith, M. J., Ward-Hall, C. A. and Hightower, H. C. (1999). 'Meeting the Needs of Abused Older Women? A British Columbia and Yukon Transition House Survey' *Journal of Elder Abuse & Neglect* 11(4), 39.

Home Office (HO) (2013) *Guidance: Domestic Violence and Abuse.* London: HO.

Jeary, K. (2004) 'The Victim's Voice: How is it Heard? Issues Arising from Adult Protection Case Conferences' *The Journal of Adult Protection* 6, 12.

Law Commission (2008) *Adult Social Care: Scoping Report.* London: Law Commission.

Law Commission (2010) *Adult Social Care: Consultation Paper No. 192.* London: Law Commission.

Law Commission (2011a) *Adult Social Care: Law Com No. 32*, London: Law Commission.

Law Commission (2011b) *Adult Social Care: Consultation Analysis.* London: Law Commission.

Lazenbatt, A., Devaney, J. and Gildea, A. (2013) 'Older Women Living and Coping with Domestic Violence' *Community Practitioner* 86(2), 28.

LGA and ADASS (2014) *Adult Safeguarding and Domestic Abuse: A Guide to Support Practitioners and Managers.* London: LGA.

Manthorpe, J., Klee, D., Williams, C. and Cooper, A. (2014) 'Making Safeguarding Personal: Developing Responses and Enhancing Skills' *The Journal of Adult Protection* 16(2), 96.

McCausland, B., Knight, L., Page, L. and Trevillion, K. (2016) 'A Systematic Review of the Prevalence and Odds of Domestic Abuse Victimisation among People with Dementia' *International Review of Psychiatry* 28(5), 475.

McGarry, J., Simpson, C. and Hinsliff-Smith, K. (2014) 'An Exploration of Service Responses to Domestic Abuse among Older People: Findings from One Region of the UK' *Journal of Adult Protection* 16(4), 201.

O'Keefe, M., Hills, A., Doyle, M., McCreadie, C., Scholes, S., Constantine, R., Tinker, A., Manthorpe, J., Biggs, S. and Erens, B. (2007) *UK Study of Abuse and Neglect of Older People: Prevalence Survey Report.* London: National Centre for Research.

Penhale, B. (2003) 'Older Women, Domestic Violence, and Elder Abuse: A Review of Commonalities, Differences and Shared Approaches' *Journal of Elder Abuse and Neglect* 15(3), 163.

Penhale, B. and Goreham, W. (2013) *Mind the Gap! Guidance of Social Support Practitioners.* Norwich: UEA.

Phillips, R. (2000) 'Domestic Violence and Aging Women' *Geriatric Nursing* 21(4), 188.

Pritchard, J. (2001) *Male Victims of Elder Abuse*, London: Jessica Kingsley.

Robbins, R., Banks, C., McLaughlin, H., Bellamy, C. and Thackray, D. (2016) 'Is Domestic Abuse an Adult Social Work Issue?' *Social Work Education* 35(2), 131.

Robbins, R., McLaughlin, H., Banks, C., Bellamy, C. and Thackray, D. (2014) 'Domestic Violence and Multi-agency Risk Assessment Conferences (MARACs): A Scoping Review' *Journal of Adult Protection* 16(6), 389.

Southend Safeguarding Adults Board (SAB) (2011) *Mr and Mrs A (Mary Russell) Serious Case Review*. Southend: Southend SAB.

Tomlinson, D. F. (2003) *No Longer Afraid: the Safeguard of Older People in Domestic Settings*. London: DH/Social Services Inspectorate.

Williams, J. (2008) 'State Responsibility and the Abuse of Vulnerable Older People: Is there a Case for a Public Law to Protect Vulnerable Older People from Abuse?' in J. Bridgeman, H. Keating and C. Lind (eds) *Responsibility, Law and the Family*. Aldershot: Ashgate.

Cases

Davey v Oxfordshire CC [2017] *EWHC* 354 (Admin)

Part 2

Rights and state institutions

Chapter 6

Accountability, social justice, and social care decision-making

Reflections on the responsive state

Beverley Clough

Adult social care has faced swingeing budgetary cuts, with funding reductions totalling £4.6 billion in the last five years, representing 31 per cent of real terms net budgets (ADASS 2015). Older adults have experienced the greatest reduction, facing cuts of 12 per cent in real terms (National Audit Office 2014). Whilst these trends precipitated the financial crash in 2008, the intensity of them has been increased by the coalition and subsequent Conservative government's austerity measures. This has had tangible consequences for the lived experiences of many older people who are reliant on services, as local authorities have sought to make savings across adult social care. As will be seen, reports are increasingly highlighting the increasing disadvantage, poverty, disempowerment, and loneliness facing many older people, primarily those who are also disabled.

Older people are the largest group of users of adult social care services and the NHS (The Kings Fund 2016) and as such it is important to consider the ways in which needs are assessed and met through the structures and institutions driving adult social care. In many situations, the choices available to individuals through the provision of social care can be the difference between remaining with family or kin in the community, or going into residential care. Meaningful participation and involvement in the community is impacted by the care packages offered. If such care packages are felt to leave particular needs unmet, perhaps because they are seen as ineligible or not sufficiently serious, then there is the potential to challenge this through legal mechanisms. The way in which the judges and the legal institutions of the state conceptualise and respond to these cases plays a crucial role in drawing the boundaries of responsibility for the subsequent experiences of those facing reduced provision of services. Judicial review is just one aspect of the overall institutional structures making up the state, but it is a key element in relation to the protection of human rights (Nedelsky 2008, 139). It is one of the most important forms of ensuring accountability for government or local authority decisions regarding access to resources. How this functions then, and the norms central to judicial review, warrants close analysis so as to enable a clear picture to develop regarding the role of the judicial institution and legal structures in facilitating enjoyment of rights. Insights from critical legal theory, and vulnerability theory in particular, help to illuminate the key role of the judiciary in endorsing or challenging entrenched power imbalances in this context, and importantly shift the emphasis and responsibility from the personal to the political and from the private to the public.

A key part of the conceptual apparatus in Martha Fineman's vulnerability theory is the idea of the responsive state, and considering the way in which the different institutions which constitute the state do and should work together to create or facilitate either resilience or disadvantage/disempowerment (2008, 2011, 2013, 2014, 2015). The way in which it responds, through the provision (and rationing) of health and social care services, has a direct impact on the choices and opportunities available to individuals. In considering the responsive state, it is important to engage with the socio-political context, and to think about the ways in which particular local authorities may respond to this in their adult social care duties under the Care Act 2014. This chapter, however, seeks to specifically consider the way in which accountability for adult social care decisions can be facilitated at present. In particular, judicial review of adult social care decisions and jurisprudence stemming from this will be highlighted as a context in which we see the stark institutional barriers to recognition and responsiveness.

This chapter will begin by outlining the disadvantage and disempowerment that is increasingly facing older people in society, and the role of the state in this. The case law and jurisprudence surrounding judicial review of decisions as to care packages will then be considered. It will be shown that the courts have, in the main, been hesitant to engage with close scrutiny of the substance of resource allocation decisions. The focus is primarily on the process by which decisions are made by local authorities, rather than a review of the substantive merits of the outcome of these. In response to concerns that we may have reached the limits of our jurisprudence, the concept of the responsive state is engaged with and fleshed out to suggest that the courts, as a core institution of the state, ought to be more responsive to the contextual realities of social care decision making and the structural barriers facing those reliant on services. Considering this through the lens of the responsive state is intended to provoke new lines of discussion as to the way that the structural machinery of our justice system has worked to exclude particular forms of disadvantage and enable them to persist. Whilst the focus in this chapter is on older people (a notoriously fluid and contested category) an important point to be emphasised here is that given our shared ontological vulnerability, these structural and institutional factors shape and impact on all of our lives, and as such should be a universal concern. Thinking about cases associated with older people through this lens enables us to challenge some of the foundational concepts of family law more broadly (such as the public/private divide, and where obligations and responsibilities are located) and to reframe some of the key questions.

Accessing adult social care services

As noted in the introduction, older people are the largest group of users of adult social care services. This is unremarkable, given that as we age our bodies change, alongside our needs for assistance to enable us to maintain our engagement with society. This may be compounded by disability or frailty, which intersects with age for many individuals. The way that services and those around us respond to our needs acutely impacts on our abilities and choices as we age.

The duties of local authorities to assess and meet the needs of adults are now enshrined in the Care Act 2014. The Care Act 2014 was enacted following a period of growing judicial and academic criticism of the complexity of adult social care law, and repeated calls for reform. The Act is governed by the overarching well-being principle which governs all acts of a local authority relating to an adult in need or a carer (s 1).

Despite the wide-ranging and positive elements covered by the well-being principle governing the Act, these depend heavily on sufficient government funding. As cuts to adult social care budgets have impacted on services, a number of reports have emerged highlighting the increasing disempowerment, poverty, and isolation faced by older people. Key links to the community, such as day centres and availability of support, are being reduced substantially as local authorities seek to make savings (Duffy 2013; Ginn 2013; QualityWatch 2014). The Equality and Human Rights Commission, in their 2011 report on Home Care, stated that most authorities were tightening eligibility criteria, so that they would only cover substantial or critical needs, leaving those assessed as having moderate or low needs having to fund and source their own care or manage without it (EHRC 2011, 18; also see QualityWatch 2014). They highlighted some appalling examples of 'care', including 'older people not being fed, or being left without access to food and water, or in soiled clothes and sheets. In numerous other instances older people were ignored, stripwashed by care workers who talked over them, confined to their home or bedroom, put to bed in the early afternoon and unable to participate in their community' (EHRC 2011, 27). The Kings Fund (2016, 3) have highlighted how the consecutive years of cuts to local authority budgets have seen 26 per cent fewer people get help and that given the stringent criteria, nobody has a clear picture of what has happened to those who are no longer entitled to publicly funded care or whose needs do not fit within the Care Act outcomes. A recent survey of directors of adult social services presented an increasingly bleak picture for older adults in particular, revealing that councils will struggle to meet their legal duties and that this will have serious consequences, particularly for those needing assistance with basic tasks such as getting out of bed, getting to the toilet, dressing, and eating (Butler 2016). The UKHCA have reported on the underfunding of home care across the UK and looks at the way that rates paid by local authorities to care providers is causing instability in service provision (UKHCA 2016), an issue which Ann Stewart addresses in Chapter 8 of this collection. The UN Committee on the Rights of Persons with Disabilities report, following their inquiry into the UK, highlighted a number of grave and systematic violations of the UNCRPD, with particular regard given to the Care Act 2014 and implications for Art 19 of the Convention (the right to live independently and be included in the community). Whilst they noted the laudable aims of the Care Act they suggested that the well-being principle 'fails to properly acknowledge the elements of autonomy and control and choice' (para. 88) and moreover that evidence pointed to increasing financial hardship due to tightening eligibility criteria at the local level, as well as a reduction in time and quality of social care services (para. 100). The Committee drew particular attention to evidence indicating that the level of care provision has diminished for older people with disabilities (para. 100). These reports are compounded by the overarching recognition of ageism in the provision of services, and a devaluing of the role of older people in society (Miller 2016; Moon 2006; Centre for Policy on Ageing 2009; Parliamentary and Health Service Ombudsman 2011) This has profound consequences for those who wish to remain in their homes, to engage in social and employment activities, to maintain personal relationships with family and friends, and participate in their communities. How an individual's needs and eligibility for services are assessed and responded to by local authorities is important, and their ability to challenge this if there is a refusal to fund certain care packages and thus hold the authority or state to account is crucial.

Accountability and the role of law

It is important to consider the way in which the state and its institutions can be held to account in relation to care decisions. In thinking about the way in which care packages can be challenged, it is important to hone in not just on what the law says on paper, but on the actual impact of this in practice and the opportunities that the legal system provides for particular individuals. As Palmer (2000, 68) suggests, there is a 'complex interplay of moral, clinical and economic judgements involved in individual cases of welfare rationing'. However, the administrative system pertaining to such decisions is equally complex, involving a multiplicity of actors, including the government, arms-length agencies, local authorities, NHS bodies, housing associations, and private contractors undertaking public functions. Collingbourne (2013, 476) argues that the way in which the administrative system works, and the way in which the law responds to this, will have a decisive impact on the enjoyment of rights, and in particular the right to independent living (476). She discusses the problematic web of 'discretionary powers' pervading the administrative system, which may be positive in terms of facilitating creative and individualised responses to need, but which may be detrimental to rights if left unchecked (477), due to the power imbalances that pervade this area.

Individuals can, in theory, hold local authorities to account for their decisions made under the Care Act 2014 and challenge these through the mechanism of judicial review. They may seek to utilise the Human Rights Act 1998 and argue that their human rights have been breached by the local authority. It is clear that care packages may engage and impact upon the enjoyment of human rights of older people, through limiting or facilitating their enjoyment and involvement in community life, impacting on their home, residence and personal relationships, and their liberty. Even the most basic care arrangements, such as getting out of bed, eating, and dressing can touch on the most fundamental rights of personal dignity, freedom from inhuman and degrading treatment, and health. However, as will be seen in the discussion in the following section, the ability to effectively hold authorities to account for these decisions is limited by practical barriers as well as institutional and systemic barriers.

One of the key challenges facing anybody seeking to challenge either health or social care provision is cost. One of the biggest challenges facing access to justice in recent years has been the enactment and coming into force of the *Legal Aid, Sentencing and Punishment of Offenders Act 2012* (LASPO). This has effected substantial cuts to the scope of civil legal aid available to challenge local authority decisions in community care law (MOJ 2016). Lord Neuberger, the President of the Supreme Court, has expressed concerns extra-judicially about legal aid cuts, which came into force in April 2013, and will result in a lack of financial provision being available in relation to claims affecting many older people in contexts such as benefits, welfare, and clinical negligence (BBC 2013). Whilst these changes impact on all in society, they may have a pronounced impact on older people who may also be experiencing poverty or disability. Moreover, knowledge of the law and routes of challenge, as well as having the mental and physical energy and determination to engage in an ongoing dispute present real systemic barriers for many older people. Judicial review is notoriously expensive, time consuming and, as will be seen below, unlikely to yield positive outcomes (Clements and Read 2005, 23; Donnelly 2010b, 275). The ability to challenge decisions may be further compounded by stress, exhaustion, poor health, lack of support, and a lack of choice or opportunity to do so (Clements and Read 2005, 24).

It thus appears that it is those who may have the greatest need to challenge care decisions are the ones left least able to do so. This feeds into the sense of instances of unmet need and poor care occurring 'off the radar'; as the Kings Fund report suggests, we do not have a clear picture of what happens to those older people who do not fit the criteria for care, nor what the human and financial costs are for them and those who care for them (Kings Fund 2016, 3). This is further reflected on by Carney and Beaupert (2015, 6) who argue that:

> isolated from the wider community and reliant on informal assistance of family or friends responsible for the problem, concerns are less likely to come to public attention, and much less to be remedied. Empirical evidence about these issues is scant.

This has the effect of privatising dependence and care and reinforcing the artificial boundary between the public and the private that has been the target of criticism from feminist legal theorists for a number of years (Boyd 1997; Munro 2007) and which emerges as a key theme across this collection.

Judicial review

Perhaps as a reflection of the difficulties in accessing the legal system in this context, there is a dearth of case law on older people and access to health or social care (Miller 2016; Clements and Read 2005). Aside from the practical barriers, the jurisprudence of the courts in itself can be viewed as a structural barrier to the rights of older people in this context. This section will consider some of the case law in this context, with a particular focus on the litigation culminating in *McDonald v UK* [2014], to demonstrate the limitations of the courts' jurisprudence, before going on to critique this from the perspective of the responsive state.

As the analysis below will demonstrate, the legal norms surrounding judicial review at present ensure that the focus remains on procedural issues, rather than more substantive equality. As Palmer suggests, 'at the core of judicial review lies the perennial struggle between the demands of deference towards the executive branches of government on one hand and the need for vigilance in controlling abuse of governmental power on the other' (2000, 69). There is a clear desire to avoid encroaching on the powers of the executive, particularly in the context of welfare and resource allocation. This is evident through analysis of case law, demonstrating the 'deeply embedded judicial conviction that matters of public finance are the preserve of the elected branches of government and not the courts' (Palmer 2000, 74). Such a desire manifests itself in the constraints in judgments touching on issues of social policy, within which the judiciary are careful not to engage with substantive human rights questions. Whilst procedure and process is undoubtedly of crucial importance in ensuring the protection of human rights of individuals affected by a particular decision, it is argued here that there is a need for both process rights *and* a close contextual engagement with the substantive impact of decisions on the enjoyment and realisation of core human rights.

One of the cases demonstrating this deferential stance is R *(on the application of McDonald) v Royal Borough of Kensington and Chelsea* [2011] UKSC 33. Here, the Supreme Court heard that Elaine McDonald was to have her home care package cut, and her night-time care withdrawn on the basis that she could use incontinence pads instead. Ms McDonald did not suffer from incontinence, but the combination of a small neurogenic bladder and difficulties with mobility meant that she needed assistance in going to the lavatory. The night-time care package enabled this assistance in getting to the toilet to happen. She was horrified at the thought of having to use incontinence pads as a substitute for this. Judicial review was sought on the basis of various grounds, including compliance with community care legislation, whether a review of her care package amounted to a reassessment of needs, and also for breach of her human rights. Ms McDonald argued that this cut to her night-time care package breached her Article 8 rights, amounting to an affront to her dignity. However, the Supreme Court (Lady Hale dissenting) refused to find this. Lord Brown noted that:

> There is no dispute that in principle [Article 8] can impose a positive obligation on a state to take measures to provide support and no dispute either that the provision of home-based community care falls within the scope of the article.
>
> (para. 15)

However, he went on to point to the wide margin of appreciation enjoyed by states in relation to the 'competing interests of the individual and of the community as a whole' (para. 16). Indeed, 'this margin of appreciation is even wider when … the issues involve an assessment of the priorities in the context of the allocation of limited state resources'. He described the effectiveness of an Article 8 claim here as 'hopeless' (para. 16). Ms McDonald appealed to the European Court of Human Rights in Strasbourg; however, it was difficult to see how the Article 8 claim can succeed against the backdrop of resource allocation arguments. The decision of the European Court of Human Rights confirmed this. Whilst a violation of Article 8 was indeed found, this was solely for a period of just under a year when *procedural* care planning procedures were not complied with. The remaining period where Ms McDonald was left without night-time care was held to engage Article 8, but to be proportionate and necessary in a democratic society because of the wide margin or appreciation afforded to State parties in this context. This is a matter of concern in the present climate in which cuts to services are being made due to budget constraints, alongside evidence that older people in society are among the hardest hit by austerity measures. In this, and other cases involving health or social welfare resources, the focus is essentially upon procedural matters – have certain processes been followed or assessments made? As O'Cinneide (2013) points out, 'little control is exercised over the substance of resource allocation decisions taken by public authorities' and so there is seemingly little scope or impetus to scrutinise the impact of decisions on the substantive rights or dignity of those affected by them. This litigation has been heavily criticised by many commentators (see Clements 2011; Pritchard-Jones 2015; Clough and Brazier 2014; Miller 2016).

The 'hollowness' of the norms of judicial review here create an accountability gap, where the substantive impact of these decisions is left unquestioned. Commenting on *McDonald*, Clements suggested that:

> had the court thought that the case engaged fundamental human rights it could have subjected the process to 'anxious scrutiny': see *R (Daly) v Secretary of State for the Home Department* [2001] UKHL 26, at paras [27]–[28]. Had the court wanted to, it could so easily have disposed of this case by reference to the irrationality of the council's reassessment process: *had the court wanted to.*
>
> (Clements 2011, emphasis added)

There is a palpable judicial reluctance to delve deeper into these cases and the stark human rights issues which they involve. There have, however, been some glimmers of hope within the existing legal framework. In *Price v UK* [2001] it was held that Article 3 had been breached when the prison authorities had failed to provide adequate care to meet the needs of a 4-limb deficient thalidomide victim in prison (also see *Napier v Scottish Minister* [2002]). But the threshold for Art 3 is high as it must be shown that the treatment or lack thereof, reaches the threshold of severity required of inhuman or degrading treatment. This threshold of severity was not met in a case in which a woman had to wait a year for a hip replacement (*R (on the application of Watts) v Bedford Primary Care Trust* [2006]), nor in a case in which a disabled woman was left confined to her living room, without access to a toilet for 20 months (*R (Bernard) v LB Enfield* [2002]). There is an apparent dividing line drawn here between the obligations in contexts where somebody is detained by the state in prison, and those owed to individuals in the community (Clements, 2011). Cases such as *Napier v Scottish Minister, Slyusarev v Russia* [2010], and *Dybeku v Albania* [2009] have firmly dismissed resources arguments as a relevant consideration in relation to Article 3 in the context of prisons or institutions detaining individuals. This can be contrasted with the approach taken in relation to health or social care in the community. There is instead a palpable resistance to recognising situations in the community as engaging Art 3 (see, for example, *North Yorkshire County Council & Another v MAG & Another* [2016] in which Cobb J described the raising of Art 3 as 'inflammatory and unhelpful' in a case involving a man having to crawl around his accommodation on his hands and knees due to the corridors being too narrow for his wheelchair). Clements (2011) further questions whether underpinning this dichotomy is an idea of a trade-off; that in return for community living other human rights must be waived or tempered. Here we can see a focus on the objective context of the individual – are they detained by the state? – with a concurrent lack of focus on the less overt but equally limiting factors which may prevent meaningful choice and inclusion in the community.

Interestingly, in *Bernard,* whilst the Art 3 argument failed, and Sullivan J was at pains to distinguish the community context from the prison context (para. 28), the Art 8 argument did succeed. Sullivan J placed emphasis on the family aspect of Art 8, and the fact that the living room that Mrs Bernard had to defecate and urinate in was shared by her husband and six children:

> the defendant was under an obligation not merely to refrain from unwarranted interference in the claimants' family life, but also to take positive steps, including the provision of suitably adapted accommodation, to enable the claimants and their children to lead as normal a family life as possible, bearing in mind the second claimant's severe disabilities. Suitably adapted accommodation would not merely have facilitated the normal incidents of family life, for example the second claimant would have been able to move around her home to some extent and would have been able to play some part, together with the first claimant, in looking after their children. It would also have secured her "physical and psychological integrity". She would no longer have been housebound, confined to a shower chair for most of the day, lacking privacy in the most undignified of circumstances, but would have been able to operate again as part of her family and as a person in her own right, rather than being a burden, wholly dependent upon the rest of her family. In short, it would have restored her dignity as a human being.
>
> (para. 33)

The extent to which the outcome in *Bernard* hinged upon motherhood and the importance of family needs to be further reflected on, particularly given the contrast to the way that Ms McDonald's Art 8 argument was dismissed. Such an approach may cause difficulties for older people – particularly those without dependents – seeking to assert their rights in this context, particularly if they are not considered by assessors or the judiciary as having dependents in this sense, or as not being central to a normative family unit.

Given the inconsistencies in these cases and the judicial dividing lines drawn between the prison and community contexts (and perhaps a discernible boundary around 'normal family life'?) the utility of judicial review in the context of community care decisions for older people is seemingly limited. O'Cinneide posits that the legal framework here embodies a liberal human rights discourse, built upon a particular view about individual rights and an individual's place in society and relationship with the state (2009, 164–166). There is a real struggle evident to enable this framework to fit these social care resource questions. With the accountability mechanisms focusing on ideas of notional equal subjects, rather than substantial, contextual, and embodied social justice issues, he sees little scope for engagement with socio-economic rights or social justice being furthered within this (O'Cinneide 2013, 39). As it may be legitimately argued that we have reached the limits of jurisprudence in relation to adult social care within this legal framework, questions can be raised about the fundamental conceptualisation of the legal subject and the relationship between the subject and the state. It is such fundamental questions that vulnerability theory seeks to address.

Vulnerability and older people

As has been discussed in other chapters in this collection, the notion of our shared ontological and universal vulnerability provides a powerful means to challenge aspects of our legal framework and the related structural and institutional elements of this. What is at the core of this is the recognition that all of us are shaped and impacted upon by our social, cultural, and political context. In her exposition of universal vulnerability, Martha Fineman has crucially focused attention on the state and its various institutions', structures', and resultant networks' function. In this way, Fineman has urged a focus attention not just on the concept of universal vulnerability, but also on the 'particular' in terms of the particularised, embodied experiences of individuals when structures work to expose their ontological vulnerability. The idea of the 'responsive state' is the normative strand of this understanding, which calls for the structures and institutions of the state to be (re)configured in order to respond to the pervasive (and often hidden) inequalities that result from particular understandings and perceptions of the role and scope of the state.

This focus on the contextualised experience resonates with the work of a number of feminist theorists and care ethicists who have similarly called for attentiveness and responsiveness from the state (Tronto 1993). What we see with this call to consider the context, rather than an abstracted liberal legal subject, is the way in which structures and institutions have a broad reach into our everyday experiences. Ideas as to freedom, autonomy, and choice are impacted by this context, challenging notions of clear lines dividing the public and the private. What is crucial, and sometimes overlooked, in discussions around vulnerability and the responsive state is the foregrounding of the recognition that the state is *already there* and always already shaping and constituting our experiences, beyond the narrow understandings of the confines of the state, or liberal ideas of the boundaries of the public/private divide. This echoes the idea that 'the personal is the political' (also see Benhabib 1992, 12–13).

What is also interesting and important to note here is that the notion of universal vulnerability allows us to move away from seeing categories or identity groups as somehow different and to expose the ways in which we are *all* shaped by these forces. This is not to say that we should ignore the very real marginalisation of particular groups in society – far from it. It is instead to suggest that institutional processes are working and interacting with certain groups and individuals in a way that exposes them to structural disadvantage. In recognising and bringing this to the fore, we can see the ways in which these can be reconfigured and responded to as well as thinking about how this structural scaffolding has become invisibilised when it works to produce accepted 'norms' and values. Similarly, whilst this chapter and collection is focused on older people, and the particular context and structures impacting upon them, of central importance is the need to foreground our shared ontological vulnerability, rather than rendering the structural norms that advantage certain groups in society invisible.

This echoes the work of MacIntyre who suggested that our recognition of dependence impacting upon all of us to unpredictable degrees and the consequent need to ensure attention to such needs 'is not a special interest, the interest of one particular group rather than of others, but rather the interest of the whole political society' (1999, 130). This is a vital counterpoint to the more individualistic conceptualisation of rights, such as those enshrined in Art 8, as necessitating a balance of '*competing* interests of the individual and of the community as a whole' (Lord Brown, *McDonald*, emphasis added).

Moreover, this recognition of our shared, universal vulnerability poses a stark challenge to the divide that we have seen between the way that cases involving access to services in prison are viewed as somehow qualitatively different to those in the community. As these dividing lines become blurred, and the reach of the state and its ability to expose vulnerability beyond the prison walls becomes clear, we can invite new perspectives on state obligations and the responsive state.

Moving towards substantive equality and social justice – the role of the judiciary?

The core idea here then is that the state, its structures, and institutions, can both entrench vulnerability and render people powerless, but also can facilitate resilience. In turning to think about law, legal institutions, and their role in society, the idea of the legal subject and the relationship between the legal subject and the state is thus of central importance. Using the vulnerable subject as the starting point, rather than the independent, rational individual underpinning some traditional liberal approaches, thus focuses attention of the state institutions and how they impact upon legal actors. This has profound implications for the traditional mainstream rights approaches we have seen above, and that O'Cinneide, among others, has criticised. Focusing on rights as a solution to the problems facing older people who are dependent on adult social care services can be seen as missing the contextual realities of their experience and situation. As Dodds put it:

> Attention to vulnerability ... changes citizens' ethical relations from those of independent actors carving out realms of rights against each other and the state, to those of mutually-dependent and vulnerably-exposed beings whose capacities to develop as subjects are directly and indirectly mediated by the conditions around them.
>
> (2007, 501)

There has been a longstanding dissatisfaction with rights in the care ethics literature and in the works of other feminist theorists. Much of this reflects what Dodds was touching on here – the idea that rights represent the concept of individualism and negative protection from interference in an otherwise unencumbered, atomistic subject position (see, for example, Holstein, Parks and Waymack 2011, xii; Munro 2007, 75). However, taking a more relational approach to rights (Nedelsky, 2006) allows us to think through more carefully the way that rights structure relationships and facilitate our capabilities in society (Nussbaum 1997). As Donnelly discusses, recognition of the way in which the state and the law have a role in facilitating autonomy and empowerment invites the development of a jurisprudence of positive rights (2010a, 271). In contrast to calls to abandon rights, what is needed here is a reconceptualisation of them aligned with the insights of relational approaches to law and society. Moreover, whilst some theorists (such as Smart) have expressed profound suspicion of using law as a site of change given its role in effecting oppression or disadvantage, it is argued that reconfiguring our approach to rights and legal structures and institutions will allow us to frame more progressive and transformative responses.

Importantly, the legal system, and the judiciary as part of this, need to be seen as a key part of these structures and institutions. It is important to note here, however, that this is not the *sole* site at which change needs to take place – this is just one context which can generate changes in other areas. Thinking about the institutional machinery of our justice system through the lens of vulnerability and the responsive state provokes challenging ideas about the way these configurations work together to produce and reproduce vulnerability. Judicial review can potentially enable useful institutional dialogue that brings this context to the fore and shines a spotlight on otherwise hidden substantive inequality.

The role of the judiciary

Arguments as to the role the courts can and should play in debates about substantive justice are not new and have been expertly engaged in by scholars such as O'Cinneide (2009, 2013), Fredman (2013), Palmer (2000), and King (2012). These have tended to decry the current reluctance to go beyond procedural analysis or 'apply heightened scrutiny to the substance of resource allocation decisions' (O'Cinneide 2013, 408) and have engaged with some of the core constitutional questions around Parliamentary Sovereignty, the Separation of Powers, and the reach and limits of democracy. As O'Cinneide points out, arguments as to democracy and the idea that resource decisions (or decisions to delegate these) ought to be made by elected officials are difficult to defend here. Whilst politicians may be accountable via the ballot box, the daily operation of the welfare state is complex and impenetrable and there is not much political capital to be gained by politicians probing deeply how the system treats marginalised individuals and groups (403). The lack of accountability in terms of social justice here is problematic, particularly in a context infused with inequalities in power, a lack of voice, and challenges in access to justice. As has been seen, this becomes all the more problematic when hidden sources of inequality are not seen as a 'rights' issue as part of the 'democratic process'. Further compounding this is the fact that decision making is, 'in practice skewed towards those with power in society, and even where majorities do make decisions, there is a risk they will override the rights of minorities' (Fredman, 2013, 107). This feeds into the idea that the boundaries drawn by a particular legal framework are a key dimension of the problem if they allow disadvantage and inequality to persist.

We need to see the judiciary as a vital part of the mechanisms for bringing about this transformative change. The lens of vulnerability theory and its focus on the interaction of the various institutions and structures of the state is also useful here for lending additional voice to ongoing attempts by feminist legal theorists to bring attention to the role that judges and judgments play in reproducing some of the 'fictions' underpinning our approaches to concepts like autonomy, responsibility, and equality (Hunter, McGlynn and Rackley 2010; also Fitz-Gibbon and Maher 2015). Indeed, the accountability gap that has developed as a result of the political norms shaping our society is enabled and reinforced by the judiciary. Seeing the totality of the interaction of the various structures and institutions constituting the state enables us to avoid seeing the courts and the judicial system as somehow outside of this, or as an 'objective' bystander (see Fitz-Gibbon and Maher 2015; Butler 1993; Tribe 1989). In addition, it ought also to be recognised that the way that state institutions interact here is not neutral, in the sense that it is a product of, and way of enabling, a particular view of the state and the legal subject.

In this context, whilst this is not to say that the judiciary should begin to re-write care packages, they can play a vital role in bringing otherwise obscured issues to light, such as powerlessness within processes of administrative justice, vacuums of accountability, and impacts of decisions on the lived experiences of individuals. In her dissenting judgment in relation to the application of the 'bedroom tax' to sanctuary schemes in *R (Carmichael and others) v Secretary of State for Work and Pensions* [2016], Lady Hale made the often overlooked point that:

> This is not a question of the allocation of scarce public resources: it is rightly acknowledged that public resources will have to meet this need one way or the other.
>
> (para. 77)

This is a crucial point that demonstrates the recognition that needs do not disappear just because they are not recognised through a particular assessment or judgment in a narrow context. Fredman has emphasised this point further in her exposition of multidimensional approaches to equality, looking at the interaction and synergies between disadvantage, stigma and stereotyping, participation, and difference (2016). In particular, she highlights that:

> From the perspective of substantive equality, the starting point must lie in the recognition that the question is not about how much to spend, but who should bear the cost. It is misleading to argue that it is too costly to accommodate difference or bring about structural change, since the cost is incurred in any event. The status quo, without legal intervention, requires the out-group to bear the full cost ... At the same time, little notice is taken of the fact that society does bear the cost of the specific characteristics of dominant groups, be they male, able-bodied, or in the ethnic majority. Working time, the built environment, or religious or cultural holidays and dress already cater for the dominant groups.
>
> (2016, 734)

There is an important role to be played here by the judiciary in shining a light on these issues and not allowing them to be kicked into an accountability vacuum.

Such an understanding resonates with a deliberative model of adjudication in which courts enable and ensure a robust form of accountability in their discourse with Parliament. Nedelsky, for example, has argued that judicial review is a necessary part of institutional dialogue (2008, 246). This can only be done effectively if the judges are robust in this and see themselves as part of the institutional and structural apparatus of the state. Such ideas echo Fredman's calls for an enhanced deliberative dimension of democracy (2013, 106) and a multidimensional concept of substantive equality (2016; 2014, 20). The way the judges enable this deliberation between facets of the state is thus crucial to bringing these issues to the fore and preventing them from being entrenched. Reflecting on the social care cases, it is clear that resources are an increasing problem for local authorities and their options are duly constrained. However, for the judiciary to hide behind due-process and fail to recognise the clear implications that these decisions have for the human rights of older people, and others, prevents the responsibility of the state in creating such conditions from being questioned.

Traditionally, such arguments are countered by suggestions that it is not the role of the court to make these 'polycentric' resource allocation decisions, or that to do so would circumvent democracy and usurp the role of Parliament (Waldron 2006; also see Gearty and Mantouvalou 2010). There is already a significant body of literature that engages with these issues in such terms. However, the argument here is not that the judiciary should be remaking these decisions. It is that the judiciary are part of the overall institutional machinery that enables inequality and disadvantage to persist, and their role in this ought to be recognised. Bringing such issues to the fore in turn enhances democratic decision-making as it enables a transparent discussion of what is at stake in these decisions. Accountability is lost when these decisions are allowed to be taken unchallenged and practices become entrenched. As Fredman cogently puts it:

> It could be argued that if the political system is defective in the extent to which ordinary people participate, the answer is to improve the political system rather than taking away more power from the people and giving it to the courts. However, this is a false juxtaposition. Parliament's ability to function as a robust forum of accountability might well be augmented by giving courts an appropriate role in insisting on such accountability. This can go hand in hand with political reform.
>
> (2013, 108)

Fredman illuminates here the way in which courts can strengthen, rather than detract from democracy by scrutinising decisions in terms of accountability, equality, and deliberative democracy. Indeed, participation and democratic accountability can be facilitated by giving voice to those whose interests are often marginalised by political processes (2016, 732). As she suggests, 'courts can reach decisions which, far from insulating an issue from further political debate, instead form a crucial part of that debate' (2008). This echoes arguments made by Benhabib in suggesting that in political decision-making, 'these decisions should not exclude the voice of those whose 'interests' may not be formulable in the accepted language of public discourse, but whose very presence in public life may force the boundaries between private needs and public claims, individual misfortunes and collectively representable grievances' (1992, 9). This is an important recognition of the way in which issues are framed in judgments and how these may mask the ways in which these frameworks work to privatise need and dependence, rather than bringing them to the fore in our political thinking and conceptualisation of the legal subject. Benhabib and Fredman in different ways support calls for expanded dialogue around questions such as needs and state responses in the context of adult social care, and for more discursive modes of justification in relation to judgments and the role of the courts.

Conclusion

It has been seen that against a background of cuts to services for older people, and a perceptible increase in reports of poverty, disadvantage, and isolation resulting from these, the judicial review process is failing to effect meaningful accountability. A focus on procedure over substance prevails, assisted by a focus on legal processes, margins of appreciation, and constitutional norms. The shift in approaches to justice offered by vulnerability theory and the responsive state offers an important substantive and multifactorial approach to equality and justice that can provide the tools to enable judges to press for accountability. This involves moving beyond the liberal legal subject and rights discourses that focus on procedure, rationality, and pitting individuals against each other. Moreover, such a shift requires more than superficial change, and requires such recognition to seep into and affect the institutions and structures that can give effect to this. It is important to think about this in terms of all of the institutions involved here, and the everyday spaces in which discretionary powers operate without meaningful accountability (see for example Collingbourne 2013; Revillard 2016). The judiciary are an important part of this machinery. If the 'rules' impacting on the responses of the judiciary are allowing or enabling disadvantage to persist and pushing it outside the margins of legal responses, then we ought to be asking questions of these rules and approaches. Recognition of this through the lens of vulnerability theory and the responsive state provokes new ways of engaging with and configuring the relationship between different state institutions.

Bibliography

Association of Directors of Adult Social Services (ADASS) (2015) *Budget Survey 2015 Report*. London: ADASS.

British Broadcasting Corporation (BBC) (2013) 'Lord Neuberger, UK's most senior judge, voices legal aid fears' *BBC News*, 5 March. Available at: www.bbc.co.uk/news/uk-21665319

Benhabib, S. (1992) *Situating the Self: Gender, Community and Postmodernism in Contemporary Ethics*. New York: Routledge.

Boyd, S. (1997) *Challenging the Public/Private Divide: Feminism, Law, and Public Policy*. Toronto: University of Toronto Press.

Butler, J. (1993) *Bodies that Matter: On the Discursive Limits of 'Sex'*. New York: Routledge.

Butler, P. (2016) 'Vulnerable adults at risk as councils face £1bn social care shortfall' *Guardian*, 13 July. Available at: www.theguardian.com/society/2016/jul/13/vulnerable-adult-social-care-risk-england-councils-face-1bn-shortfall Guardian Report.

Carney, T. and Beaupert, F. (2013) 'Public and Private Briocollage: Challenges Balancing Law, Services & Civil Society in Advancing CRPD Supported Decision Making' *University of New South Wales Law Journal* 36(1), 175.

Centre for Policy on Ageing (CPA) (2009) *Ageism and Age Discrimination in Social Care in the United Kingdom: A review From the Literature*. London: CPA.

Clements, L. (2016) *Care Act 2014 Overview (Revised 16th November 2016)*. Available at: www.lukeclements.co.uk/wp-content/uploads/2016/11/0-Care-Act-notes-updated-2016-11.pdf

Clements, L. (2011) 'Disability, Dignity and the Cri de Couer' *European Human Rights Law Review* 6, 657.

Clements, L. and Read, J. (2005) 'The Dog that Didn't Bark' in L. Lawson and C. Gooding (eds) *Disability Rights in Europe: From Theory to Practice.* Oxford: Hart Publishing.

Clough, B. and Brazier, M. (2014) 'Never Too Old for Health and Human Rights?' *Medical Law International* 14(3) 133.

Collingbourne, T. (2013) 'Administrative Justice? Realising the Right to Independent Living in England: Power, Systems, Identities' *Journal of Social Welfare and Family Law* 35(4), 475.

Dodds, S. (2007) 'Depending on Care: Recognition of Vulnerability and the Social Contribution of Care Provision' *Bioethics* 21(9), 500.

Donnelly, M. (2010a) *Healthcare Decision Making and the Law: Autonomy, Capacity and the Limits of Liberalism.* Cambridge: Cambridge University Press.

Donnelly, M. (2010b) 'Reviews of Treatment Decisions: Legalism, Process and the Protection of Rights' in B. McSherry and P. Weller (eds) *Rethinking Rights-Based Mental Health Laws.* Oxford: Hart.

Duffy, S. (2013) *A Fair Society? How the Cuts Target Disabled People.* London: Centre for Welfare Reform.

Equality and Human Rights Commission (EHRC) (2011) *Close to Home: An Inquiry into Older People and Human Rights in Home Care.* Manchester: EHRC. Available at: www.equalityhumanrights.com/sites/default/files/close_to_home.pdf

Fineman, M. A. (2008) 'The Vulnerable Subject: Anchoring Equality in the Human Condition' *Yale Journal of Law & Feminism* 20(1), 1.

Fineman, M. (2010) 'The Vulnerable Subject and the Responsive State' *Emory Law Journal* 60(2), 251.

Fineman, M. A. (2011) 'Elderly as Vulnerable: Rethinking the Nature of Individual and Societal Responsibility' *The Elder Law Journal* 20(2), 71.

Fineman, M. A. (2013) 'Equality, Autonomy and the Vulnerable Subject in Law and Politics' in M. A. Fineman and A. Grear (eds) *Vulnerability: Reflections on a New Ethical Foundaton for Law and Politics.* Aldershot: Ashgate.

Fineman, M. A. (2014) 'Vulnerability, Resilience, and LGBT Youth' *Temple Political and Civil Rights Law Review* 23(2), 307.

Fineman, M. A. (2015) 'Equality and Difference – The Restrained State' *Alabama Law Review* 66(3), 609.

Fitz-Gibbon, K. and Maher, J. (2015) 'Feminist Challenges to the Constraints of Law: Donning Uncomfortable Robes?' *Feminist Legal Studies* 23(3), 253.

Fredman, S. (2008) *Human Rights Transformed: Positive Rights and Positive Duties.* Oxford: Oxford University Press.

Fredman, S. (2013) 'Adjudication as Accountability: A Deliberative Approach' in N. Bamforth and P. Leyland (eds) *Accountability in the Contemporary Constitution.* Oxford: Hart.

Fredman, S. (2016) 'Substantive Equality Revisited' *International Journal of Constitutional Law* 14(3), 712.

Gearty, C. and Mantouvalou, V. (2010) *Debating Social Rights.* Oxford. Hart.

Ginn, J. (2013) 'Austerity and Inequality. Exploring the Impact of Cuts in the UK by Gender and Age' *Research on Ageing and Social Policy* 1(1), 28.

Holstein, M., Parks, J. and Waymack, M. 2011. *Ethics, Aging and Society: The Critical Turn.* New York: Springer Publishing.

Humphries, R. et al (2016) *Social Care for Older People: Home Truths*. London: The Kings Fund.

Hunter, R., McGlynn, C. and Rackley, E. (2010) *Feminist Judgments: From Theory to Practice*. Oxford: Hart.

Ismail, S., Thorlby, R. and Holder, H. (2014) *QualityWatch Report, Focus On: Social Care for Older People: Reductions in Adult Social Services for Older People in England*. London: The Health Foundation and Nuffield Trust.

Joint Committee on Human Rights (2007) *Human Rights of Older People in Healthcare. 18th Report of Session 2006–2007. Vol. 1, Report and Formal Minutes*. House of Lords and House of Commons. London: The Stationery Office.

King, J. (2012) *Judging Social Rights*. Oxford: Oxford University Press.

Law Commission (2008) *Adult Social Care: Scoping Report*. London: The Stationery Office.

Law Commission (2011) *Adult Social Care*. London: The Stationery Office.

MacIntyre, A. (1999) *Dependent Rational Animals: Why Human Beings Need the Virtues*. Chicago, IL: Open Court Publishing.

Miller, J. (2016) 'Dignity: A Relevant Normative Value in "Access to Health and Social Care" Litigation in the United Kingdom?' in A. Diver and J. Miller (eds) *Justiciability of Human Rights Law in Domestic Jurisdictions*. Amsterdam: Springer International.

Ministry of Justice (MoJ) and Legal Aid Agency (2016) *Legal Aid Statistics in England and Wales: October–December 2015*, 31 March. Available at: www.gov.uk/government/uploads/system/uploads/attachment_data/file/512577/bulletin.pdf

Munro, V. (2007) *Law and Politics at the Perimeter: Re-Evaluating Key Debates in Feminist Theory*. Oxford: Hart.

National Audit Office (NAO) (2014) '*Adult Social Care in England: Overview*' HC 1102 Session 2013–2014. London: NAO.

Nedelsky, J. (2006) 'Reconceiving Rights as Relationship' in C. Koggel (ed.) *Moral Issues in Global Perspective*, 2nd edn. Peterborough: Broadview.

Nedelsky, J. (2008) 'Reconceiving Rights and Constitutions' *Journal of Human Rights* 7, 139.

Nussbaum, M. (1997) 'Capabilities and Human Rights' *Fordham Law Review* 66(2), 273.

O'Cinneide, C. (2009) 'Extracting Protection For The Rights Of Persons With Disabilities From Human Rights Frameworks: Established Limits And New Possibilities' in O. M. Arnardóttir and G. Quinn (eds) *The UN Convention on the Rights of Persons with Disabilities: European and Scandinavian Perspectives*. Leiden: Brill Publishing.

O'Cinneide, C. (2013) 'Legal Accountabiltiy and Social Justice' in N. Bamforth and P. Leyland (eds) *Accountability in the Contemporary Constitution*. London: Hart.

Palmer, E. (2000) 'Resource Allocation, Welfare Rights – Mapping the Boundaries of Judicial Control in Public Administrative Law' *Oxford Journal of Legal Studies* 20(1), 63.

Parliamentary and Health Service Ombudsman (PHSO) (2011) *Care and Compassion? Report of the Health Service Ombudsman on Ten Investigations into NHS Care of Older People*. London: The Stationery Office.

Pritchard-Jones, L. (2015) 'Night-time Care, Article 8 and the European Court of Human Rights: A Missed Opportunity?' *Journal of Social Welfare and Family Law* 37(1), 108.

Revillard, A. (2017) 'Social Movements and the Politics of Bureaucratic Rights Enforcement: Insights from the Allocation of Disability Rights in France' *Law & Social Inquiry* 42(2), 450–478.

Tribe, L. H. (1989) 'The Curvature of Constitutional Space: What Lawyers can Learn from Modern Physics' *Harvard Law Review* 103(1), 1.

Tronto, J. (1993) *Moral Boundaries: A Political Argument for an Ethic of Care*. New York: Routledge

United Kingdom Homecare Association (UKHCA) (2016) *The Homecare Deficit 2016: A Report on the Funding of Older People's Homecare Across the United Kingdom* (Version 1). Surrey: UKHCA.

Waldron, J. (2006) 'The Core of the Case Against Judicial Review' *The Yale Law Journal* 115, 1346.

UN Committee on the Rights of Persons with Disabilities (2016) *Report of the Inquiry Concerning the United Kingdom of Great Britain and Northern Ireland carried out by the Committee under Article 6 of the Optional Protocol to the Convention*. Geneva: Office of the United Nations High Commissioner for Human Rights.

Cases

Dybeku v Albania [2009] 1*MHLR* 1

McDonald v UK [2014] *ECHR* 492

Napier v Scottish Minister [2002] *UKHRR* 308

North Yorkshire County Council & Another v MAG & Another [2016] *EWCOP* 5

Price v UK [2001] 34*EHRR* 1285

R (Bernard) v LB Enfield [2002] *EWHC* 2282

R (Carmichael and others) v Secretary of State for Work and Pensions [2016] *UKSC* 58

R (on the application of McDonald) v Royal Borough of Kensington and Chelsea [2011] *UKSC* 33

R (on the application of Watts) v Bedford Primary Care Trust [2006] *QB* 667

Slyusarev v Russia (Application No. 60333/00, 20 April 2010)

Chapter 7

Revisiting the feminist critique of rights

Lessons for a new older persons' convention?

Laura Pritchard-Jones

Introduction

In recent years, there has been growing concern about the violation of older peoples' human rights and their lack of protection in existing international human rights law.[1] Depictions of violations against older people such as abuse, discrimination, and enforced poverty, have resulted in the human rights of older people increasingly being discussed on the international stage. In 1982 the First World Assembly on Ageing in Vienna adopted the Vienna International Plan of Action on Ageing (VIPAA), followed ten years later by the United Nations Principles on Older Persons (UNPOP), and, subsequently, the Madrid Plan of Action on Ageing (MIPAA) in 2002. These documents, however, have no legal force,[2] and, as De Hert and Mantovani (2011, 402) have argued, such instruments have been largely unsuccessful in elevating the status of older people as full human rights' bearers. As Doron, Brown, and Somers claim:

> From a normative perspective ... the needs of older people have not been met by the Vienna Plan, the Madrid Plan or the UN Principles for Older Persons. In these plans, created over the course of nearly two decades, nations have set policies that have been ignored and action plans that have been abandoned.
>
> (2013, 169)

In light of such criticisms of existing laws and principles, in 2002, at the Second World Assembly on Ageing in Madrid, the Rwandan delegation to the Assembly proposed that the United Nations consider creating an international legal human rights convention directly concerned with the rights of older persons. As a result of this, and the later Chung Report (2009), the United Nations Department for Economic and Social Affairs established a Working Group, part of whose mandate was to consider the feasibility of such a convention.

The academic debate as to whether an older person's human rights convention is desirable is well rehearsed (Doron and Apter 2009; Williams 2011). Traditional criticisms of such a convention have questioned its possible utility; the difficulties of creating a single human rights treaty for the diversity of people we call 'old'; and, finally, the difficulty on agreeing a global consensus as to which rights should be protected for older persons. These criticisms are valid, but are not the focus here. Instead, this chapter seeks to advance this existing debate by considering human rights at a broader conceptual level, and, specifically, the very efficacy and utility of 'human rights' as a legitimate tool for older people. Its aim is to consider the extent to which existing feminist concerns – which form the theoretical framework for this collection – about the substance and structure of human rights laws can also be applied in relation to the application of human rights in old age. By viewing human rights through a feminist lens, it is suggested that a number of criticisms of the existing legal landscape emerge, and therefore the central aim of the chapter is to explore the question as to the extent to which drafters of a new convention for older people *could* and *should* listen to these existing feminist concerns over human rights law. As Binion (1995, 513) articulates, 'while the focus of [feminist] analysis is on women's experience, a feminist approach might have immediate implications for the rights of all disempowered peoples and raise questions about social organization generally'.

Feminist criticisms of human rights

Broadly speaking, there are two main strands into which feminist criticisms of human rights fall. The first is criticisms of the *utility* and *efficacy* of human rights laws specifically applicable to women, notably, treaties such as the Convention on the Elimination of All Forms of Discrimination against Women (CEDAW) and the Declaration on the Elimination of Violence Against Women (DEVAW). Given that this strand of existing literature is concerned with criticisms of these women-specific treaties *per se*, it is only of indirect relevance in a collection about old age and will not be discussed in any depth. The second strand of criticism is more applicable to the aims of this chapter, and postulates that 'human rights law' generally, as a substantive body of law, is of only limited utility in achieving equality and combatting abuses faced by women (and, arguably, other oppressed groups). Within this second strand are a number of ideas – however this chapter focuses on two in particular – the overly individualistic paradigm of the legal subject who is the traditional bearer of human rights, and the implications this first criticism has for the public–private debate. It is necessary to briefly explain these ideas in more detail, and how they have been articulated by feminists, in order to explore how such criticisms might be interpreted in the context of old age and a specific human rights convention for older persons.

Feminist critiques of human rights, as Charlesworth, Chinkin, and Wright (1991, 635–638) elaborate, are multi-faceted and have a number of manifestations, all of which arguably result in a limitation on the level of protection that human rights can offer women as *individuals*, but also impact how much protection they can afford women collectively as an oppressed *group*. As noted above, one of the main criticisms of human rights law is the idea that traditional human rights formulations are premised on a legal subject who embodies a particular set of characteristics. This is the legal subject who represents the masculine public persona; someone who is detached and individualistic, or as Brown (2000, 239) notes, '...a discourse that presumes an ontologically autonomous, self-sufficient, unencumbered subject'. In effect, it is argued by feminists that the international human rights law system in both substance and structure is inherently gendered, and favours masculine interests that gives priority to – and even deifies – the 'public individual' over the 'private relational' being.

How, then, does such an argument come about and how is it arguable that human rights law does this? First, human rights operate in such a way that human rights discourse effectively reduces complex power relations down to a very simplistic model whereby such problems are seen as 'solved' once a particular right is acquired. Once the right to, for example, be free from discrimination is acquired,[3] it is assumed that such discrimination is unlawful and that it will be effectively eradicated by virtue of such international laws. Yet such an approach does not pay sufficient scrutiny to types of discrimination, its pervasiveness particularly in the private sphere, and whether simply 'eradicating' discrimination is the best solution. Moreover, priority in international human rights law has historically been given to securing civil and political rights for individuals – rights such as freedom from discrimination, suffrage rights, and freedom of religion. Indeed, some substantive civil and political rights themselves – such as the right to privacy, explored in greater depth later – may even operate to the detriment of oppressed individuals, or be rendered down by treaties and by the courts interpreting these treaties, to a simple binary between the public and the private domains. Securing these 'types' of rights, as Bunch (1990, 488) argues, may in fact be seen as less of an issue among some groups – such as women – than securing socio-economic rights, especially given that women may find their socio-economic rights violated more frequently than their civil and political ones. Interestingly, and again this is a point that this chapter will return to later, there is also some limited evidence to demonstrate that this may also be a significant factor in older peoples' perceptions of human rights as legal tools – such as the Human Rights Act 1998 in England and Wales – and that they therefore do not resonate greatly with older people. A poll conducted with older people in 2005 found that many of the participants felt disengaged from the types of rights – predominantly civil and political rights – protected by such laws (Lewis and Morris, 2005).

Furthermore, it is argued that current human rights laws do not adequately reflect women's experiences, and that they are impervious to the structural reality of abuses that women face because of precisely how they operate. Rights, as they currently operate in law, rely on *individuals* raising possible violations in order to seek redress – which, as a result of negative socio-economic conditions – many women may not be in a position to do. Human rights operate in such a way as to construct a zone of defence, pitting the individual in conflict with the state, against whom they are seeking to enforce their right. This approach is epitomised in Dworkin's (1977) famous 'rights as trumps' model – which also has the effect of reducing human rights to a simple conflict between an individual and the state. Failing to provide effective mechanisms by which women can raise possible violations not only serves to entrench even further the types of structural and private conditions that render women voiceless in the 'human rights' arena, but may, in turn, mask more complex relationships surrounding the rights-bearer that may enhance or frustrate human rights – particularly in the private domain – indeed rights are not simply affected by an individual's engagement with the state, but also with other organisations, and other individuals.

Moreover, given that human rights are cast in such individualistic terms, mechanistically providing a particular *individual* with a certain right does little to enhance the position of that *group* more generally. As Mégret (2011) argues, providing all members of that group with identical rights may be seen to indicate that there is a singular identity to that group which can be remedied by a one-size-fits-all approach to their human rights. Such an approach may in fact gloss over or misrepresent the heterogeneity of such 'groups'; these may include groups such as women, disabled people, children, and older people whose global identities may be – and frequently are – very diverse. In effect, the way human rights as a legal framework have traditionally been structured and substantiated has meant that they are predominantly concerned with a legal subject that is both free from relationships other than with the state, and an individual who has the resources – personal, societal, and economic – to be able assert its power against the state. From a feminist perspective, such an image is seen by many to be unrealistic and 'dangerously one-sided' (Nedelsky 1993, 13).

Ultimately – and as Carol Smart (1989, 138–159) argues – given the number of limitations inherent within human rights one could question whether they can ever be of any real use in remedying the injustices faced by women, or indeed of any oppressed group. One of the reasons for this line of criticism is that the language of rights in particular may be antithetical to women (Binion 1995). As Gilligan (1982) famously asserted, women may be less likely to think in terms of rights and more in terms of relationships, and consequently their responsibilities that flow from these relationships. The reality, however – as many have pointed out notably throughout this edition – is that while humans are individuals, they are also 'relational beings' (Gergen 2009). They are situated within a network of crucial relationships with other individuals, organisations, and the state. Feminist critiques of human rights law are therefore twofold. First, they criticise the substance of human rights by arguing that the individualistic conceptualisations of the self that they promulgate fail to account for the ways in which people are essentially and substantively relational beings – in other words they 'ignore the relational nature of social life' (Tushnet 1989, 410). Second, feminists go beyond a simple critique, and offer modes of thinking about human rights that begin from a different normative perspective – one that sees relationships as ontologically prior to the individual, and which prioritises women's own experiences as the starting point, or, to quote Charlesworth and Chinkin, challenges the 'narrow referential universe of the international legal order' (Charlesworth and Chinkin 2000, 211) within which rights discourse exists. As Binion (1995, 511) further notes of feminist jurisprudence more widely, '[it] has certain defining characteristics that are shared with feminist studies generally. These include a focus on women's experience, especially the disempowerment that has been ubiquitous'.

Linked to this masculine paradigm flows a second criticism, and one which features heavily throughout this book. This second strand of criticism argues that because of the individualistic paradigm of the public persona at the centre of human rights law, and because this body of law is only concerned with activity explicitly regulated or undertaken by the state[4] i.e. the public domain, it not only masks violations that happen beyond that – that is, those that occur in the private domain[5] – but also fail to pay adequate attention to structural conditions that also enable the perpetuation of such 'private' violations. As a result, it is argued that because some of the worst abuses that women suffer – violations such as sexual violence, domestic abuse, and forced marriage – take place within the private realm, human rights laws perpetuate women's inequality because, quite simply, they do not concern themselves with these areas (see also Brammer, this volume). As Wright argues:

> It is … the basis on which the State is obliged to refrain from interfering in certain 'natural' human rights, such as expression, religion, assembly, association or privacy itself … The State is obliged to refrain from interfering in 'private' matters … the innermost 'private' arena of home and family remains inviolate …
> (1989, 248)

As many feminists have suggested (Bunch 1990; Chinkin 1999; Brown 2000), one example of human rights law creating this division between the public and the private spheres is the through the right to privacy, which appears in many major human rights treaties.[6] The right to privacy, depending on its interpretation, 'can be seen to both advance or deter emancipation – to cloak inequality or procure inequality' (Brown 2000, 236). If, for example, the right to privacy is used as a mechanism of avoiding state intrusion into private spheres, thereby allowing the perpetuation of violations such as domestic violence – an argument treated less favourably by recent judgments, especially in the European Court of Human Rights[7] – then this represents one obvious example of a frustration of women's human rights in the name of the right to privacy.

As well as through substantive masculine-framed rights, such as the right to privacy, the abstention of human rights law from the private domain also operates on a more structural level. Because statistically women still find themselves predominantly engaged in activities that essentially remain consigned to the private domain – such as care or domestic work – they naturally do not fall within the purview of traditionally formulated human rights law. In the 2011 Census, for example, in England and Wales 57.7% of informal or unpaid caregivers were women, compared to 42.3% of men (Office for National Statistics 2013). This is a figure that is replicated with an even greater statistical margin between men and women on a global scale, and has led to the Special Rapporteur on Extreme Poverty and Human Rights to report that '[s]tates' neglecting or failing to address women's disproportionate unpaid care workload can be seen as a major failure to comply with the obligations regarding equality and non-discrimination which are the pillars of international human rights law' (United Nations 2013, para. 19).

Given increasing life expectancies in both developed and developing states, increasing prevalence of chronic health conditions in old age, and a move towards home care in old age in many countries, a similar trend may be beginning to emerge in relation to older people. Again, during the last census, the provision of unpaid care increased with age in England and Wales. Statistically, the highest amount of unpaid care was provided by those aged between 50 and 64, and those aged 65+ a close second. Furthermore, more individuals within the over-65 age group were providing more than 50 hours of care per week, compared to any of the other age groups (Office for National Statistics 2013). Yet, Otto criticises this failure of human rights law to engage with the disproportionate burden of care work resting on women – and as shown from the statistics above, arguably older people – by suggesting that this is due to the masculine paradigm outlined in the previous section:

> The paradigm of formal equality … does not challenge gendered domestic arrangements because its masculine standard limits its scope to equality in the public sphere … for the equality principle to achieve women's full inclusion in humanity, it needs to destabilise the masculine universal …
>
> (2005, 109–110)

In light of this, most feminist critics of human rights law do not argue for a version of formal equality that simply requires 'adding women and mixing' (Charlesworth and Chinkin 2000, 50), which would simply require extending the same rights to women, and has arguably been the dominant ideology in human rights law thus far, even in women-specific human rights treaties. Article 3 of CEDAW, for example, states that women are guaranteed 'the exercise and enjoyment of human rights and fundamental freedoms on a basis of equality with men'. Instead, it is convincingly suggested by many – notably once again by Otto (2005) – that human rights laws *must* recognise and acknowledge differences between women and men in order to effectively tackle such abuses, and the structural denial of rights that also facilitate such abuses. Only when this is done is it possible to rebuild 'basic concepts of international law in a way that they do not support or reinforce the domination of women by men' (Charlesworth and Chinkin 2000, 61). As O'Hare summarises:

> The exclusion of women's voices from defining the content of human rights discourse has in turn meant that human rights law has evolved along a gendered 'fault-line' that distinguishes between the public and private spheres for the purpose of legal regulation.
>
> (1999, 367)

The brief précis thus far has touched upon the many criticisms by feminist writers on the public–private divide in international human rights law as it has served to perpetually mask private violations of rights experienced by women. As Eisler (1987) points out, this gendered division between men and women has particularly deep historical roots that perhaps do not exist in relation to other oppressed groups, such as older people. Yet if we look beyond the 'women-specific' elements, it is possible to discern certain core concepts that emerge from these criticisms that may be transferrable to the debate around an older person's human rights convention. Ultimately, what the criticisms outlined above demonstrate is that first, human rights convey a particularly individualistic ideology that not only fails to reflect the reality of lived experiences for many, but that this ideology also works in such a way as to have the effect of reinforcing and continuing the subordination of an oppressed group who, by virtue of particular circumstances, fail to meet this notion of the individualistic ideal. The second fundamental assumption that emerges from the critiques offered above is that human rights laws create an artificial divide between two realms – the public and the private – viewing only the former within its remit. Moreover, human rights laws fail to provide any justification for maintaining – or question the validity of – this ideology, and the distinction it creates between the public and the private domains. As Thornton indicates:

> the fiction of separate spheres remains normatively and ideologically significant and it may be that a simplistic division offers an appealing, albeit treacherously false sense of security in the face of complex and elusive phenomena that operate at a number of levels of meaning.
>
> (1995, 4)

Yet a large number of the issues that face older people in particular – many of which are elaborated on within this book (e.g. Clough, Herring, Stewart this volume) – call in to sharp relief the validity of the individualistic paradigm at the centre of human rights law, as well as calling into question the conceptual basis for the division between the public and private realms.

Feminist criticisms and old age

There are two interwoven questions that need raising in relation to the feminist criticisms of human rights laws identified above and how they might be applied to the situation of older people. The first is whether – factually – such criticisms are still valid. *Does* human rights law operate in such a way when it comes to its engagement with older people? Does human rights law apply an individualistic conceptualisation of the self, which thinks in terms of discrete categories, and therefore maintains a distinction between the public and the private spheres? The second issue is a normative one. What can feminist criticisms teach us about what human rights law specifically for older people – as is suggested under a new convention – *should* look like?

There is a dearth of research on older peoples' perceptions of human rights law, yet an analysis of the broader sociological and legal sources indicates that certainly in the application of human rights – and in relation to the principles than underpin them such as autonomy and dignity – the criticisms articulated above may well hold true in relation to old age. It is well documented in many of the chapters contained within this edition – and indeed elsewhere (Mikołajczyk 2013) – that existing human rights law as it applies to older people fails to recognise the complexity of an older person's relationships, and therefore has, at its heart, an individualistic outlook. As Clough explains in her chapter, in *McDonald v UK* [2014] Elaine McDonald argued that the continued provision of carers to assist her in using the toilet was crucial to her psychological well-being, and therefore both her Article 3 and Article 8 rights under the European Convention on Human Rights. In light of this, she argued that her local authority's decision to replace her night-time carers with incontinence pads was a violation of both Article 3 and 8. As Clough further notes, both the Supreme Court (*R (MacDonald) v Royal Borough of Kensington & Chelsea* [2011]) and the European Court of Human Rights (*MacDonald v UK* [2014]) were less than amenable to this argument[8] – Lord Brown going as far as describing the argument under Article 8 as 'hopeless' (*R (MacDonald) v Royal Borough of Kensington & Chelsea* [2011], [16]). Such an approach to the human rights arguments laid before the court – particularly the Supreme Court – betray what Clements (2011, 680) calls, an 'able-bodied view of the world'. This may be a view of the world that is not shared by many older people, who face increasing levels of disability and impairment; both physical and cognitive (Giordano 2012), and renders the older person 'other' (Higgs and Gilleard 2014) to the dominant able-bodied perspective. Moreover, such a view of the world is individualistic in that it fails to recognise the importance attached to relationships of care in securing fundamental human rights for older people (Herring 2009; Herring 2014) – a point I shall return to in due course – or a desire to engage itself in private or intimate issues (Carr 2012).

A similar approach can also be discerned in the European Court of Human Rights Case of *HM v Switzerland* [2002]. This case concerned the alleged unlawful deprivation of liberty in a residential home under Article 5 of the European Convention of HM, of an 84-year-old woman living in 'intolerable conditions of hygiene' (*HM v Switzerland* [2002], [18]) in her own home, which she shared with her son. In finding that there had been no deprivation of liberty under Article 5, the Court noted that 'the applicant had the possibility of staying at home and being cared for by the Lyss Association for Home Visits to the Sick and Housebound, but she and her son had refused to cooperate with the association' (*HM v Switzerland* [2002], [44]). In effect, because HM failed to comply with the demands of the caregivers – the Lyss Association – she was removed, ostensibly against her will, to a care home, and moreover under the Court's legal interpretation of Article 5, she was not 'deprived of her liberty' whilst living at the care home. In effect, her failure to comply with what was expected of her in the (able-bodied) eyes of the Court – acceptance of the home care – meant that she was also deprived of any positive protection of her rights under Article 5 of the European Convention when she *was* taken in to a care home. Ultimately, whether an older person has legally been deprived of her liberty is in fact an entirely separate issue from the fact of their refusal of social care at home. Yet in *HM v Switzerland* this latter point – the refusal of home care – is conflated with the legal issue of whether there has been a deprivation of liberty under Article 5, and is used by the Court as justification for finding none, and therefore denying HM any protection under Article 5.

The points raised above highlight how the central feminist criticisms of rights considered earlier – the individualistic and idealistic paradigm – may also play out in relation to older people who bring human rights claims to court. Yet, interestingly, when interpreted in an alternative light, the cases also highlight the second part of the feminist critique of rights; that human rights, as they currently operated through the courts, remain resistant to disturbing the artificial distinction between the public and the private realms, and therefore fail to pay sufficient regard to the *need* for relationships – and particularly relationships in the private domain – in old age. Relationships of *care*, for example, may be central to an older person's own conceptualisation of autonomy and dignity – values that underpin human rights – and therefore to the relevance of human rights to the older person. Elaine McDonald's central argument, for example – that the replacement of carers to assist her to use the toilet in favour of incontinence pads was a violation of her rights – demonstrates that central to her conceptualisation of her rights under Article 3 and Article 8, and consequently her interpretation of what autonomy and dignity meant to her, were ultimately relationships of care. In Ms McDonald's view, it was these relationships with the night-time carers that secured her dignity, autonomy, and personal integrity – and therefore respect for her rights – not incontinence pads. Furthermore, as some have argued (Pritchard-Jones 2015), the failure of both the domestic courts and the European Court of Human Rights to engage with the human rights arguments advanced by Elaine McDonald represents a failure to take the rights of older people seriously, and moreover, represents a marked reluctance to seriously engage with, or recognise, the relational meaning of autonomy and dignity to older people.

Indeed, one of the most fundamental and obvious ways in which old age may challenge the clarity of the distinction that human rights law has drawn between the public and the private is in fact through issues that arise in relation to care. While human rights law prefers to cast the public and the private into two discrete categories, issues around care in old age call into question the clarity between the public and the private. Such issues fundamentally demonstrate the artificiality of this distinction and the fluidity with which the two domains mix when an older person faces, for example, a move from their own home into a care home. As Twigg argues (1999, 388) '[d]isability and its consequences disrupt this traditional ordering, in some cases imposing a radical reordering'. If their own home is the ultimate signifier of this 'private realm' then a care or residential home – where life, and traditionally private activities such as 'bodywork',[9] or sexual intimacy (Twigg 1999, 391; Twigg 2000), for example, become heavily regulated and controlled – signifies the public paradigm. Moving from a private home to a care home or residential home therefore represents a 'symbolic reversal' (Twigg 1999,

394) of the private and the public domains. When such a move occurs then a tension arises between the public and the private as activities traditionally confined to the private domain must now fit within, and be carried out, in a very 'public' arena (Willcocks, Peace, and Kellaher 1987; Twigg 1999).

Indeed, literature suggests that for older adults, maintaining any element of privacy in care homes is not only important, but also frequently publicly undermined (Willcocks, Peace, and Kellaher 1987; Bauer et al 2013; Simpson et al 2017). These are not insignificant issues given the current statistics on care homes. In the UK alone, approximately 426,000 adults live in care or nursing homes, and the overwhelming majority – around 405,000 – are over the age of 65 (Age UK 2016). Yet as well as highlighting the fluidity of and possibly disrupting the division between the two domains – the public and the private – care issues also highlight a tension that many feminist scholars fail to address; notably, that there is a deep meaning to older people of their 'private' sphere, and desire to retain control, when faced with ever increasing threats to it. This is evidenced in part by a reluctance to leave their own home and a desire to move back there where they have had to move in to a care home (Wilkin and Hughes 1987; Lee 1997; Thein, D'Souza, and Sheehan 2011).

This argument – that relationships are at the core of rights for older people – also finds support in any analysis of broader sociological and legal literature. Human rights – and especially the values of autonomy and dignity that underpin them – are 'relational' in that they are upheld, enhanced, and sometimes desecrated through relationships held by the older person. These may be relationships on both a *macro* level, for example with the state through the provision of state-funded care, or organisations such as the Church. Or, they may be relationships on a *micro* scale – with other individuals such as family, friends, and caregivers – or even with themselves, that is, 'self-relations'. This point resonates with the particular feminist critique – outlined earlier – that traditionally formulated human rights focus too heavily on an individual's relationship with the state. While an older person's relationship with the state will be of importance, particularly in jurisdictions where care in old age may be funded by the state, it is only one among many important relationships that may affect that older person's rights. As Charlesworth and Chinkin (2000, 209) argue in a feminist context, '[t]o assert a legal right … is to mischaracterise our social experience and to assume the inevitability of social antagonism by affirming that social power resists in the state and not in the people who compose it'. In effect, human rights have historically assumed that the state bears the only responsibility for violations of a person's human rights. Yet this disguises one crucial link between the individual whose rights have been violated and the state – other individuals and organisations who perpetrate these violations whether or not imputable to the state.

A wholesale analysis of empirical data in relation to older people and their perception of human rights and the values that underpin them is, of course, outside the remit of this chapter, yet a brief analysis serves to demonstrate the point made above. First, as mentioned earlier, while there is a paucity of literature on older peoples' perceptions of human rights as formal legal mechanisms, empirical research across a multitude of disciplines strongly supports the assertion that the *language* of rights, and the values that underpin them – including autonomy and dignity – are important for older adults, particularly when faced with either personal or structural conditions that might threaten them. These may be physical or cognitive conditions which threaten their ability to live independently, for example, or may require their move into a care home or hospital facility thereby sacrificing some fundamental rights they may have enjoyed at home (Joint Committee on Human Rights 2007; Kontos et al 2016), such as increasing frailty, or the onset of dementia. Or, they may be structural conditions which pervade institutions, such as elder abuse neglect, or ageism[10] and are perceived – rightly – as threats to the older person's autonomy and dignity (Phelan 2008; Herring 2012; Naughton, Drennan, and Lafferty 2014). In the words of one 76-year-old participant in a study conducted by Black and Dobbs (2014, 1304), '[a]s one is able to accomplish less and less, one's sense of worth is worn away and with it, the dignity with which one is treated and which one feels'. This approach is also evidenced by a range of other studies involving older people (Becker 1994; Heathcote 2000; Woolhead et al 2004; Hollcoat-Nallétamby 2014; Lloyd et al 2014).

Yet crucially, such studies also evidence the way in which these values are upheld – and therefore the way that rights are upheld – for older people, is through the maintenance of relationships. It is not only empirical data that recognises this 'relational' element to human rights; it is also how they have been increasingly recognised in certain areas of domestic law. *Re GC* [2008] for example, involved a decision from the England and Wales Court of Protection concerning the residence of GC, an older adult with dementia, who lacked capacity under the Mental Capacity Act 2005. In deciding that it would be in GC's best interests to return to live at home, rather than in a care home, Hedley J notes that 'in residence decisions for the elderly, there is … an importance in place which is not generally recognised by others; not only physical place but also the relational structure that is associated with place' (*Re GC* [2008], [21]). In effect, the maintenance of valuable relationships – individual, spatial, and temporal – becomes increasingly important in upholding the human rights of older people, when such relationships may come under increasing threat from both personal and societal factors. This is a dimension that existing formal human rights laws do not adequately take into consideration, and arguably requires a conceptual shift from viewing rights as 'trumps' (Dworkin 1977), to viewing rights as 'relationships', a contention advocated by Nedelsky (1993).

The literature considered above on older persons' experiences of autonomy, dignity, and human rights in old age suggests that many of the early criticisms of human rights that were raised by feminists may still be relevant in relation to the construction of human rights and their underlying principles in old age. These arguments suggest that while human rights *could* be useful as a mechanism for framing the violations experienced by older people – and it has been shown how human rights do retain a certain importance for older people – in their present form they rely on a particular legal paradigm that is overly individualistic, failing to situate the older person within their network of relationships. It is also arguable that more recent developments in human rights law – such as that evidenced by the United Nations Convention on the Rights of Persons with Disabilities (UNCRPD)[11] – represent a shift towards an understanding of human rights that places a higher priority on relationships that could be developed in a new convention for older persons. The emphasis placed on the need for support to exercise legal capacity in the UNCRPD under Article 12(3), or on the need for gender and age specific assistance and support for persons with disabilities and their family and caregivers to avoid exploitation, abuse, and violence under Article 16(2), for example, highlight the importance of the need for relationships of support in order to fully realise rights for traditionally oppressed groups.

Moreover, as both Brennan (1999) and Tomasi (1991) note, a relational approach is not in itself antithetical to the notion of human rights. Both authors highlight how relationships are, in fact, at the heart of human rights. As the latter argues, '… individual rights are fundamentally relational concepts' (Tomasi 1991, 527). This is because human rights laws – at their core – are used to regulate the power relationships between different actors. As such, those responsible for drafting a new convention for the protection of older people may be wise to heed feminist concerns about the legal subject that historically lies at the heart of traditional human rights formulations.

Conclusion

While 'rights function to articulate a need, a condition of lack or injury' (Brown 2000, 239) it is also arguable that neither can such injuries 'be fully redressed or transformed by rights' (Brown 2000, 239). In effect – and much as Smart (1989) argued that the language and structure of human rights might be useful in delineating the issues faced by women – human rights do have the potential to help us understand the issues and violations that older people face. Yet, at present, we must not be quixotic about the potential of human rights laws; they are not, after all, a panacea. They cannot, in their current forms, provide all the answers to the issues faced by older people. This is because, first, they are currently structured in such a way as to venerate a legal paradigm that is endowed with particular characteristics – a criticism made by feminist scholars of rights more generally, and picked up in relation to older people in this chapter. Moreover, human rights create a distinction between the public and the private domain, but fail to scrutinise the justification for this line with any degree of seriousness or rigour. Yet, as this chapter has also sought to demonstrate, old age brings with it certain issues, and complexities, that requires proper scrutiny of the validity of this distinction between the public and private, and may call into question its very existence.

Charlesworth, Chinkin, and Wright (1991, 614) note that, 'at bottom, feminism is a mode of analysis, a method of approaching life and politics, a way of asking questions and searching for answers, rather than a set of political conclusions about the oppression of women'. Expanding on this, Chinkin (1997, 13) argues that the 'paramount objective' of feminist interventions into international human rights law and discourse has been to develop 'a more inclusive international legal system that takes seriously the interests of all women'. If this is indeed the case, then there is no reason why drafters of a new convention for the protection of the rights of older people could not learn from the methods of these feminist critics in order to also develop an international legal system that also takes seriously the interests of all older persons. In realising this goal, it is therefore important that any drafters of a new convention listen to feminist concerns about human rights. It is time to displace the independent ideal and the reification of the public–private divide historically situated at the centre of human rights law, in favour of a model of human rights that better reflects the lived experiences of old age. This chapter has suggested that, in this regard, human rights law in relation to older people may have much to learn from feminism.

Notes

1 The right to non-discrimination and equality of treatment in Article 26 of the International Covenant on Civil and Political Rights, and Article 2 of the International Covenant on Economic, Social, and Cultural Rights, for example, include protection on the grounds of 'race, colour, sex, language, religion, political or other opinion, national or social origin, property, birth or other status', but do not explicitly refer to age.
2 In Wales, however, the Older Person's Commissioner's mandate specifically includes reference to UNPOP (Commissioner for Older People (Wales) Act 2006, s 25), as does the recent Social Service and Well-being (Wales) Act 2014 (s 7(1)).
3 See, for example, CEDAW Article 1.
4 See, for example, s 6 of the Human Rights Act 1998, which makes the Act only applicable to public authorities, or those exercising functions of a public nature (s 6(3)).
5 A full discussion on the public-private divide from a feminist perspective is beyond the remit of this chapter, and earlier chapters have sought to uncover the falsity of this divide as it applies to older people. This chapter therefore only concerns itself with how this divide has been played out in human rights and their accompanying feminist critiques.
6 See, for example, Article 8 of the European Convention on Human Rights, and Article 17 of the International Covenant on Civil and Political Rights: 'No one shall be subjected to arbitrary or unlawful interference with his privacy, family, home or correspondence, nor to unlawful attacks on his honour and reputation'.
7 Recent developments in the European Court of Human Rights suggest that that Court at least may be placing much greater emphasis on the need for states to take their positive obligations seriously towards victims of domestic violence, at least where Article 3 (right to be free from inhuman or degrading treatment and torture) and Article 14 (the right to be free from discrimination) rights under the European Convention are concerned. *TM and CM v Moldova* [2014] involved an application to the European Court of Human Rights that a failure to take the claimants' complaints about domestic violence seriously amounted to a breach of their Article 3 and Article 14 rights. The Court found that the failure by the domestic authorities to intervene when they had knowledge of the risk of further violence represented a violation of Article 3, and violation of Article 14 in conjunction with Article 3 in that it represented condoning violence and a discriminatory attitude towards women.

8 Although the European Court did recognise a procedural violation of McDonald's Article 8 rights in relation to the period of time where the local authority had not acted in accordance with a procedure prescribed by law in changing her care plan.
9 'The term "bodywork" has commonly been applied to the work that individuals undertake on their own bodies, often as part of regimens of health and wellbeing' (Twigg, 2000, 411).
10 Ageism may be considered to be attitudes towards an individual, or group, solely based on their age – in relation to older people, this attitude that underlies ageism may be that they are less able and of a lower status. As Butler (1975, 35) enunciates, 'senile, rigid in thought and manner, old-fashioned in morality and skills…'.
11 The United Kingdom has both signed and ratified the UNCRPD.

Bibliography

Age UK, 2016. *Later Life in the UK*. Available at: www.ageuk.org.uk/Documents/EN-GB/Factsheets/Later_Life_UK_factsheet.pdf?dtrk=true

Bauer, M., Fetherstonhaugh, D., Tarzia, L., Nay, R., Wellman, D. and Beattie, E. (2013) '"I Always Look Under the Bed for a Man". Needs and Barriers to the Expression of Sexuality in Residential Aged Care: The Views of Residents With and Without Dementia' *Psychology & Sexuality* 4(3), 296.

Becker, G. (1994) 'Autonomy in the Face of Frailty' *Journal of Aging Studies* 8(1), 59.

Binion, G. (1995) 'Human Rights: A Feminist Perspective' *Human Rights Quarterly* 17(3), 509.

Black, K. and Dobbs, D. (2014) 'Community-Dwelling Older Adults' Perceptions of Dignity: Core Meanings, Challenges, Supports and Opportunities' *Ageing and Society* 34(8), 1292.

Brennan, S. (1999) 'Reconciling Feminist Politics and Feminist Ethics on the Issue of Rights' *Journal of Social Philosophy*, 30(2), 260.

Brown, W. (2000) 'Suffering the Paradoxes of Rights' *Constellations* 7(2), 230.

Bunch, C. (1990) 'Women's Rights as Human Rights: Towards a Re-Vision of Human Rights' *Human Rights Quarterly* 12, 486.

Butler, R. (1975) *Why Survive? Being Old in America*. New York, Harper & Row.

Carr, H. (2012) 'Rational Men and Difficult Women – R (On the Application of McDonald) v. Royal Borough of Kensington and Chelsea [2011] UKSC 33' *Journal of Social Welfare and Family Law* 34(2), 219.

Charlesworth, H. and Chinkin, C. (2000) *The Boundaries of International Law*. Manchester: Manchester University Press.

Charlesworth, H., Chinkin, C. and Wright, S. (1991) 'Feminist Approaches to International Law' *The American Journal of International Law* 85(4), 613.

Chinkin, C. (1997) 'Feminist Interventions into International Law' *Adelaide Law Review* 19(1), 13.

Chinkin, C. (1999) 'A Critique of the Public/Private Dimension' *European Journal of International Law* 10(2), 387.

Chung, C. (2009). *Working Paper prepared by Chinsung Chung, Member of the Human Rights Council Advisory Committee*, 4 December. A/HRC/AC/4/CRP.1.

Clements, L. (2011) 'Disability, Dignity, and the Cri de Coeur' *European Human Rights Law Review* 6, 675.

De Hert, P. and Mantovani, E. (2011) 'Specific Human Rights for Older Persons' *European Human Rights Law Review* 4, 398.

Doron, I. and Apter, K. (2010) 'The Debate around the Need for an International Convention on the Rights of Older Persons' *The Gerontologist*, 50(5), 586.

Doron, I., Brown, B. and Somers, S. (2013) 'International Protection for the Human Rights of Older People: History and Future Prospects' in P. Brownell and J. J. Kelly (eds) *Ageism and Mistreatment of Older Workers: Current Reality, Future Solutions*. London: Springer.

Dworkin, R. (1977) *Taking Rights Seriously*. London: Bloomsbury.

Eisler, R. (1987) 'Human Rights: Towards an Integrated Theory for Action' *Human Rights Quarterly* 9(3), 287.

Gergen, K. (2009) *Relational Being: Beyond Self and Community*. Oxford: Oxford University Press.

Gilligan, C. (1982) *In a Different Voice*. London: Harvard University Press.

Giordano, S. (2012) 'Is a Gray World Desirable?' in H. Lesser (ed.) *Justice for Older People*. Amsterdam: Rodopi.

Heathcote, G. (2000) 'Autonomy, Health and Ageing: Transnational Perspectives' *Health Education Research* 15(1), 13.

Herring, J., 2009. 'Losing It? Losing What? The Law and Dementia' *Child and Family Law Quarterly* 21(1), 3.

Herring, J. (2012) 'Elder Abuse: A Human Rights Agenda for the Future' in I. Doron and A. M. Soden (eds) *Beyond Elder Law: New Directions in Law and Ageing*. London: Springer.

Herring, J. (2014) 'The Disability Critique of Care' *Elder Law Review* 8, 1.

Higgs, P. and Gilleard, C. (2014) 'Frailty, Abjection and the "Othering" of the Fourth Age' *Health Sociology Review* 23(1), 10.

Hollcoat-Nallétamby, S. (2014) 'The Meaning of "Independence" for Older People in Different Residential Settings' *Journal of Gerontology* 69(3), 419.

Joint Committee on Human Rights (2007) *The Human Rights of Older People in Health-care: Eighteenth Report of Session 2006–07, Vol. 1 – Report and Formal Minutes*. London: The Stationery Office.

Kontos, P., Grigorovich, A., Kontos, A. and Miller, K. (2016) 'Citizenship, Human Rights, and Dementia: Towards a New Embodied Relational Ethic of Sexuality' *Dementia* 15(3), 315.

Lee, D. (1997) 'Residential Care Placement: Perceptions Among Elderly Chinese People in Hong Kong' *Journal of Advanced Nursing* 26(3), 602.

Lewis, M. and Morris, J. (2005) 'Rights for Real: Research on Attitudes of Older People Towards Human Rights' in F. Butler (ed.) *Rights for Real: Older People, Human Rights, and the CEHR*. London: Age Concern.

Lloyd, L., Calnan, M., Cameron, A., Seymour, J. and Smith, R. (2014) 'Identity in the Fourth Age: Perseverance, Adaptation and Maintaining Dignity' *Ageing and Society* 34(1), 1.

Mégret, F. (2011) 'The Human Rights of Older Persons: A Growing Challenge' *Human Rights Law Review*, 11(1), 37.

Mikołajczyk, B. (2013) 'Is the ECHR Ready for Global Ageing?' *The International Journal of Human Rights Law* 17(4), 511.

Naughton, C., Drennan, J. and Lafferty, A. (2014) 'Older People's Perceptions of the Term Elder Abuse and Characteristics Associated with a Lower Level of Awareness' *Journal of Elder Abuse & Neglect* 26(3), 300.

Nedelsky, J. (1993) 'Reconceiving Rights as Relationships' *Review of Constitutional Studies*, 1(1), 1.

O'Hare, U. (1999) 'Realizing Human Rights for Women' *Human Rights Quarterly* 21(2), 364.
Office for National Statistics (ONS) (2013) *Full Story: The Gender Gap in Unpaid Care Provision: Is there an Impact on Health and Economic Position?* Available at: www.ons.gov.uk/peoplepopulationandcommunity/healthandsocialcare/healthandwellbeing/articles/fullstorythegendergapinunpaidcareprovisionisthereanimpactonhealthandeconomicposition/2013-05-16
Otto, D. (2005) 'Disconcerting "Masculinities": Reinventing the Gendered Subject(s) of International Human Rights Law' in D. Buss and A. Manji (eds) *International Law: Modern Feminist Approaches.* Oxford: Hart.
Phelan, A. (2008) 'Elder Abuse, Ageism, Human Rights, and Citizenship: Implications for Nursing Discourse' *Nursing Inquiry* 15(4), 320.
Pritchard-Jones, L. (2015) 'Night-Time Care, Article 8 and the European Court of Human Rights: A Missed Opportunity?' *Journal of Social Welfare and Family Law* 37(1), 108.
Simpson, P., Horne, M., Brown, L., Brown, C., Dickinson, T. and Torkington, K. (2017) 'Old(er) Care Home Residents and Sexual/Intimate Citizenship' *Ageing & Society* 37(2), 243.
Smart, C. (1989) *Feminism and the Power of Law.* London: Routledge.
Thein, N., D'Souza, G. and Sheehan, B. (2011) 'Expectations and Experience of Moving to a Care Home: Perceptions of Older People with Dementia' *Dementia* 10(1), 7.
Thornton, M. (1995) 'The Cartography of Public and Private' in M. Thornton (ed.) *Public and Private: Feminist Legal Debates.* Oxford: Oxford University Press.
Tomasi, J. (1991) 'Individual Rights and Community Virtue' *Ethics* 101(3), 521.
Tushnet, M. (1989) 'Rights: An Essay in Informal Political Theory' *Politics and Society* 17, 403.
Twigg, J. (1999) 'The Spatial Ordering of Care: Public and Private in Bathing Support at Home' *Sociology of Health & Illness* 21(4), 381.
Twigg, J. (2000) 'Carework as a Form of Bodywork' *Ageing and Society* 20(4), 389.
United Nations (2013) *Extreme Poverty and Human Rights.* A/68/293.
Wilkin, D. and Hughes, B. (1987) 'Residential Care of Elderly People: The Consumers' Views' *Ageing & Society* 7(2), 175.
Willcocks, D., Peace, S. and Kellaher, L. (1987) *Private Lives in Public Places.* London: Tavistock Publications Ltd.
Williams, J. (2011) 'An International Convention on the Rights of Older People' in M. Odello and S. Cavandoli (eds) *Emerging Human Rights in the 21st Century: The Role of the Universal Declaration on Human Rights.* Abingdon: Routledge.
Woolhead, G., Calnan, M., Dieppe, P. and Tadd, W. (2004) 'Dignity in Older Age: What do Older People in the United Kingdom Think?' *Age and Ageing* 33(2), 165.
Wright, S. (1989) 'Economic Rights and Social Justice: A Feminist Analysis of Some International Human Rights Conventions' *Australian Yearbook of International Law* 12, 241.

Cases

HM v Switzerland [2002] *ECHR* 157
McDonald v UK [2014] *ECHR* 492
R (MacDonald) v Royal Borough of Kensington & Chelsea [2011] *UKSC* 33
Re GC [2008] *EWHC* 3402 (Fam)
TM and CM v Moldova [2014] *ECHR* 81

Chapter 8

Impoverishing care

Ann Stewart

> The dystopian prospect is of an oligopolised sector dominated by financialised chains whose operating subsidiaries are financially fragile as they provide institutional care in a high cost format which is socially unaffordable and of inconsistent quality because their workforce is under resourced, ill paid and ill trained.
>
> (Burns et al 2016)

Introduction

The Health Act 2009, section 2 requires health bodies, including the Care Quality Commission (CQC) as the key regulator of the health and social care sectors to have regard to the NHS Constitution. Its first key principle is as follows:

> The NHS provides a comprehensive service, available to all irrespective of gender, race, disability, age, sexual orientation or belief. It has a duty to each and every individual that it serves and must respect their human rights. At the same time, it has a wider social duty to promote equality through the services it provides and to pay particular attention to groups or sections of society where improvements in health and life expectancy are not keeping pace with the rest of the population.
>
> (DH 2015)

'It is difficult to think of a more explicit statement of a human rights- and social solidarity-based approach' to guide regulation (Prosser 2010, 134). No such ringing statement of social purpose informs the work of the CQC in relation to its social care responsibilities. Its primary objective is 'to help protect and promote the health, safety and welfare of people who use health and social care services' (Health and Social Care Act 2008, s 3(1)).

As many of the contributions to this collection stress it is important not to reinforce ageist constructs which align growing older with vulnerability and frailty or alternatively with independence and an impossibly vigorous self-reliance (Bedford) which requires older people to fight rather than celebrate their changing bodies (Herring). While it is the case that overall the 'baby boomer' cohort (those born between 1945 and 1965) is much better placed than their parents' generation to shape what ageing means and to age well, this chapter focuses on those who have substantial care needs and on the highly contentious issue of the way in which social care is presently provided. It addresses the darker side to being old in contemporary Britain. The way in which social care is provided has profound effects on the lives of those in receipt of the care and on those who love and care for them. Other contributors to this collection address issues relating to accountability in the allocation of public resources (Clough and Bedford)

This chapter assesses the extent to which state provision has been able to ameliorate the effects of inequalities generated over life courses in older age. Ageing tends to deplete the social, economic, and political capital of those who need and provide significant amounts of care. However, those that have been less able to accumulate assets over their life course, often women, are most affected by the vagaries of the social care market (see Easton for a discussion of the way in which state provision for older prisoners also exacerbates such inequalities). This chapter shows how the present market which depends, to a large extent, on public funding is failing to provide decent services for all. It is reproducing and exacerbating existing socio-economic inequalities. The way in which we care for our elderly often impoverishes not only those in need of care but also those who provide it either as informal carers or as paid care workers, again the majority of whom, but by no means all, are women. The social care system does not provide its key resource, the workforce with decent conditions and wages.

The chapter explores the way in which the social care market has developed to demonstrate the complex melding of the public and private in social care provision as increasing numbers of individuals (and their families) are obliged to fund their own care costs in a market still dominated by local authority (LA) tendering processes. In particular it looks at the evolving relationship between the state which funds social care for those who are eligible, those who provide institutional forms of care and those who are responsible for regulating the market which now include LAs.

It is clear that many individual providers offer good care but the sector as a whole is unable to provide consistently high quality services. It is argued by influential stakeholders that those who provide care services are also being impoverished by the lack of funding. While the majority of services are provided by debt burdened and under-capitalised small providers who often struggle to make a reasonable level of profit, the social care market is becoming more dependent upon and influenced by large private equity financed providers whose investors expect to make a return of 11–12%. It is argued in this chapter that the market is developing in ways that suggest that inequalities will deepen as consolidation increases. Individuals able to pay well for services are likely to have choices and to receive better care although such care is not necessarily guaranteed given the business model presently adopted by market leaders. Those reliant on state funding or who have limited resources will find their options even more constrained.

The chapter then moves on to consider the role of regulation. To what extent can the parlous state of affairs relating to increasing inequalities and precarious provision in the social care market be tackled through interventions in the market? The public interest in and funding of the provision of care for vulnerable adults ensures that this has become a heavily regulated sector which raises questions about the nature of regulation and the extent to which decent care services can be provided to all within a regulated market? If so what form of regulatory intervention is most likely to support this objective? This chapter explores the role of the CQC and LAs with new responsibilities under the Care Act 2014 to shape, oversee and regulate the market.

Despite the absence of the political will to treat entitlement to care in the same way as health, it is argued that substantial levels of public intervention are essential if elderly vulnerable adults and those who care for them are to be treated with the respect and dignity to which all citizens are entitled. The chapter ends with suggestions as to how this might be achieved.

Inequality in older age

There are 11.6 million people aged 65 or over (18.5% of the total UK population). This group is projected to rise by over 40% in the next 17 years to over 16 million. By 2040, nearly one in four people in the UK will be aged 65 or over. 1.5 million people are aged 85 or over. There are more people in the UK aged 60 and above than there are under 18 years of age (Office for National Statistics 2016). These statistics are often associated with words like 'burden' or concepts such as 'dependency ratio' in policy circles. Yet older people are healthier and wealthier than ever before. They contribute to society in a wide range of ways including caring for their contemporaries and future generations.

Not all elderly people are vulnerable and in need of social care and not all elderly people are poor. Indeed, increased rates in state pensions, more people contributing to private/company pensions and working for longer, and importantly more women working and contributing to their future security has ensured that poverty in 'young pensioners' has decreased significantly (Corlett 2017). There is a growing view that the 'baby boomers' (born approximately between 1946 and 1964) are entering older age having benefited disproportionately or at the expense of the younger generation (Leach et al 2008; Willetts 2011).

While these broader developments have ameliorated pensioner poverty, they do not compensate for differences in life courses. Intra-generational and inter-generational inequalities have been growing since the 1980s (Corlett 2017). Those who are poor during their working lives, whose work is precarious and/or interrupted by caring responsibilities or by health or other problems, have far fewer resources to enable them to be resilient in older age. They also tend to be less healthy and to live in environments which are less supportive. '1.6 million (14% of) pensioners in the UK live below the poverty line and less than 26% of pensioner couples have more than £1500 in savings' (James and Spruce 2015,

468). The very elderly, the majority being women, are the poorest cohort of pensioners and still among the poorest in society. They tend also to be in need of considerable support. For others a sudden life changing event such as a stroke or a longer-term condition such as dementia can have a devastating social and economic effect.

Caring for adults is still highly gendered although significant numbers of men particularly in older age care. Women:

> care for longer hours and for a longer duration than men and are more likely to give up work as a result … are more likely to be dual-carers … who care for their children and elderly dependants … more likely to care during the 'peak age' for caring (Corlett 2017, 45–64), when caring is likely to have the most significant impact on their careers and earning power.
>
> (James and Spruce 2015, 466–7)

Withdrawal from the labour market creates potential long-term vulnerability:

> In a UK study of 4000 carers, almost half cutback on essentials such as food (43%) and heating (44%) and ended up in debt in order to make ends meet; two in five carers who have given up paid work or reduced their working hours reported that they were between £10,000 and £20,000 a year worse off.
>
> (James and Spruce 2015, 468)

Addressing poverty: the evolution of social care policy

The means tested social care system has been a key source of support for poor adults and in recent times their carers. Social care was not part of the original post-war welfare state settlement. 'Personal social services' only emerged as a legal concept and into an important area of activity for Local Authorities (LA) with the implementation of the Local Authority Social Services Act in 1970. The nature of the support and the way in which it has been provided has changed radically since 1945.

The first stage (1945 to 1980s) involved the LA as direct provider of 'old people-s'homes' and 'home helps' and other targeted services. The work force were public sector employees who through collective bargaining were able to negotiate reasonable terms and conditions of employment. Stage two which began in the 1980s, involved a move to privatisation and choice for individuals. The 1990 National Health Service and Community Care Act re-cast local councils as 'enabling authorities' which were required to spend 85% of funding on commissioned services (Hudson 2016). Care workers became predominately non-unionised private sector workers.

The resulting change in ownership was rapid: 'in 1979 64% of residential and nursing home beds were still provided by local authorities or the National Health Service; … by 2012 it was just 11%'. The 'bulk of the adult social care workforce – around 72% – is now employed in the private and voluntary sectors, along with another 14% employed by individual service users making use of "personal budgets", leaving just 14% employed by local authorities' (Hudson 2016, 7, 8).

The third stage in the development of the relationship between the state and the market, reflected in the Care Act 2014 has been to place individual well-being at the heart of policy-making. This is achieved through direct payments to eligible individuals to purchase the services they need although LAs still procure significant numbers of services. State support is still means tested (excluding anyone with assets over £23,250 not including their home in the case of domiciliary care and potentially including in the case of residential care). LAs have expanded responsibilities to 'broker' services for all who have identified care needs (Sloan 2016) and to ensure that an appropriate/functioning market exists to enable them to purchase care services.

In summary, despite the huge changes that have occurred in the way in which social care has been delivered, the original fault lines between a national service funded through taxation and free at the point of delivery (the NHS) and a means tested local service available only those on very limited means and subject to changing policy prescriptions and resourcing persists.

Deepening inequalities through austerity

While needs are rising, the ability of LAs to meet these is increasingly constrained by reductions in the funds available to them. Since 2010 austerity measures, imposed by central government, have resulted in a real 5% decrease (Jarrett 2017). These funds are not ring fenced within LA budgets and must compete with statutory obligations and other services. One million fewer people now receive services (Humphries et al 2016). Given that state social care provision is means tested these cut backs hit the least able to absorb them – those in need of care and their carers.

The growing crisis in social care has come to public attention resulting in a number of policy responses including permission for LAs to raise a 'social care precept' on council taxes amounting to no more than 6% over 3 years until 2019. The £380m generated in 2016 amounted to less than two-thirds of the £600m that was needed to maintain services due in large part to the introduction of the National Living Wage (NLW) (ADASS 2016). The promised increase in 2020 will add a total £2.3bn to wage costs (D'Arcy and Kelly 2015). In poor areas the amount raised will be substantially less than in more affluent areas while the need for services in these areas is higher. The result is greater social and economic impoverishment in already less affluent areas.

The perceived unfairness of this means tested system of public support for care was addressed in the Dilnot Inquiry (2011, discussed in Hopkins and Laurie 2015). The costs of a life-changing event such as a severe stroke or the long-term effects of dementia can impoverish an individual with modest to reasonable assets. One in ten will need to spend £100,000 on care although it is impossible to predict who this will be. Care must be privately funded until such time as such funds are reduced to the level which attracts public funding. The revised proposals incorporated into the Care Act 2014 have been shelved for the time being (officially until 2020 but many suspect kicked into the long grass) ensuring that for some although not all, care costs still have a devastating effect (Sloan 2016).

Entrenching poverty: impoverishing providers and workers?

Until the mid-1990s, care home operators were mostly a combination of small, family firms operating one or a couple of homes, using the medical or nursing experience of the owners, some non-profit making/charitable associations, and LA run homes. In 2016 there were about 18,000 care homes in Britain (roughly 487,000 beds) and 7,000 domiciliary care agencies reflecting the change in policy to provide services at home. The bulk of these are still small privately owned and run businesses. The proportion of nursing homes has increased to cater for the growing number of people who are living longer with multiple health conditions and in particular with dementia.

New providers have entered the market: financialised operators who have built up chains of homes because the activity has been seen to generate reliable state-backed cash flows. Contrary to the earlier providers who use their properties as a means to provide care – their business is caring, the business model of these operators is property based with rents provided through their care services. The ten largest providers account for around 20% of the care home market whilst the top 20 providers account for around 28% of the market. In some parts, such as nursing home beds in London, the big chains already provide a majority of the beds available (Hudson 2016).

LAs are seeking wherever possible to reduce the price they pay for commissioned services. Providers argue that LAs are driving down the price below the cost of the level of provision that is required to meet CQC quality standards. There is a huge need for investment (in excess of £15bn) to upgrade facilities to meet such standards and rising consumer expectation. It is estimated that 85% of the sector is using buildings over 50 years old which are now close to obsolescence. There is however a chronic shortage of finance available to smaller providers. 'High street' banks are unwilling to lend partly because the businesses are already heavily indebted. Owners must resort to riskier, higher interest loans adding to their indebtedness. Industry analysts confirm that profitability in the sector is low. Research undertaken for the BBC found that 5,871 individual owners make, on average, about £60,000 profit as operators and that on average, each care home makes £17,647 in profit before tax (BBC Radio 4 2016). They have also had to absorb the increased cost of staffing, constituting 60% or more to total costs, which result from the introduction of the NLW and its proposed increase, raising serious questions as to the ability of providers to continue to absorb these costs through price rises or profit reduction. About 5,000 homes are at risk of closure because they carry too much debt and do not make enough profit to cover loan repayments.

41% of residents pay privately, 37% are fully funded by the state, 12% are paying fees topped up by LAs, and 10% funded by the NHS (Hudson 2016, 12). Overall private funding accounts for £10 billion while public funding accounts for £14 billion per year (Hudson 2016, 12). Where possible, providers rely on self-funded clients who are estimated by sector analysts LaingBuisson to be paying 43% more for exactly the same level of provision, thus cross-subsidising their publicly funded counterparts.

This is not fair on self-funders, particularly given the present low cap for public funds, and has the effect of potentially creating a two-tier market.

While the evidence relating to the vulnerable position of the smaller providers is compelling, the position of the new large entrants is much less clear. They have undoubtedly contributed to investment to the sector, around £30 billion, and created over 350,000 beds in care homes (Hudson 2016, 9). However, there is considerable evidence to suggest that their financing model involving debt-based financial engineering is creating unnecessary risk and high profit taking. The model evolved in the early 2000s when interest rates were low and bond holders required lower rates of return than shareholders. Debt was relatively cheap.

> The purchase of care home businesses could be funded by selling debt; this caps returns on that portion of capital to the benefit of the private equity fund which has unlimited equity rights to the upside from operating or selling on. Their shareholders expect to make a return of 11–12% which is the 'going rate' for high risk, high return finance sectors.
>
> (Burns et al 2016, 4)

The aim is to bring earnings forward and pass liabilities on. Complex multi-level company structures use tax havens making tax difficult to trace. The business can easily change form. It is possible to make use of an op co/prop co structure:

> where the care home operator pays rent to a property company for homes which it previously owned. The cash released by selling property can be taken out of the business or used to fund rapid expansion through buying smaller care home businesses.
>
> (Burns et al 2016, 5)

Recent building of new residential and nursing homes in a standard format, designed to minimise labour costs, with 60 or more en-suite bedrooms has been dominated by the chain operators. There are huge pressures on working practices to reduce costs. One recent study identified a range of changes including restricting annual leave, reducing the numbers of qualified nursing staff, increasing resident–staff ratios, removing sick pay, moving to unpaid on-line training to be completed at home, removing paid breaks, and no longer paying for handover meetings at the start and end of shifts (Hudson 2016, 9). Such employment practices are not restricted to the residential sector. The recent case involving SevaCare, a major home care provider, revealed the extent of bad practice (Bradley 2016). Workers were required to provide 24-hour care to care users with severe dementia but only paid for their waking hours. The migrant workers involved said they felt like slaves.

Crisis?

Last year the CQC found a third of care homes required improvement and 7% were 'inadequate'. A recent survey of almost half of all LAs in England responsible for social care commissioning found that 77% had experienced provider failure in the year 2015/16, and 74% thought another failure likely in the coming year. Up to 37,000 beds could be lost by 2020/21 with a possible 50% of care homes thought to be 'non-viable'. Domiciliary service providers are also vulnerable:

> Two of the top five providers (Care UK and Saga) recently decided to pull out of the market … the largest not-for-profit care provider – Housing and Care 21 – [is] pulling out of the home care business it has been providing in over 150 local authority areas.
>
> (Hudson 2016, 14)

Mears has withdrawn from contracts in the North West, claiming that the fees being paid by LAs amounted to 'encouragement to providers to breach the National Living Wage'.

Significant regional differences are emerging. In areas like the North East where there is much greater reliance on LA funded residents the large companies are not providing services and choices are much more limited. In the South West and East where average incomes are much higher and with more privately paying clients, LAs are less able to place and a two-tier system is developing. In London, the majority of residential places are publicly funded while the large players dominate the market. Here it may be the case that the large players are able to inflate their prices.

The market as presently structured is at risk of structural failure while some are 'minting' it (Laing 2017). It is struggling to provide decent standards of care for its elderly clientele, decent wages and conditions for its work force, and a sustainable business model for its providers. It is also producing not addressing inequalities. The poor are increasingly vulnerable to poor conditions while those with more resources are not necessarily immune from the pressures on decent levels of service.

Addressing inequalities and impoverishment though regulation

Black (2002, 20) defines regulation as the 'sustained and focused attempt to alter the behaviour of others according to defined standards or purposes with the intention of producing a broadly identified outcome or outcomes, which may involve mechanisms of standard-setting, information-gathering and behaviour-modification'.

> Social and economic regulation has been designed to promote economic efficiency, to redistribute resources in a public-spirited fashion, to reduce or eliminate social subordination, to reflect collective aspirations, to protect future generations from irreversible losses, and to alter preferences that are produced by various motivational or cognitive defects …
>
> (Sunstein, quoted in Prosser 2010, 11)

Thus regulatory laws may not be limited to correcting a market: they may 'serve to constitute market relations' as 'prior to, not secondary, to the market' (Baldwin et al 2012, 22) and can be used to achieve distributional justice. Prosser (2010, 12) points to two regulatory visions: 'regulation as an infringement of private autonomy, emphasizing rules, predictability and regulatory independence' and regulation 'as an enterprise, emphasizing collaboration with government, discretion, and responsiveness'. He favours the latter which is the way in which the 'pluralistic regulatory landscape' operates in relation to social care. He identifies four rationales that 'can be used to classify regulatory activities' and to provide 'the basis of normative arguments about how regulators should act': to maximise efficiency and consumer regulation; to promote human rights; to promote social solidarity; and as a means for deliberation and resolution of contending arguments.

Applying these rationales, a combination of which can be adopted by any regulator, facilitates an assessment of the role of regulation in tackling the tendency to impoverish and to entrench social and economic inequality. The fourth rationale which identifies the contribution of regulation to resolve problems and build consensus through procedural means will not be addressed specifically although this deliberative role forms an important part of the work of both the CQC and the LAs. It will emerge in discussion of the other three.

Both the CQC and LAs 'shape', 'oversee', and 'regulate' the market, all of which activities can fit within each rationale. 'The idea of shaping the market goes beyond the notion that the role of the state is to "fix" or somehow forestall market failure; rather the role of the state is to act as a catalyst for innovation' (Hudson 2016, 15). We have seen the way in which the state has been involved in creating the market. Privatisation and 'personalisation' create customers. They encourage a change in normative understanding of older people: no longer vulnerable passive recipients of state services but active individuals who take responsibility for and plan for their later years (Herring; Bedford). As customers they seek choice of services to meet their needs (recast perhaps as desires) (Stewart 2012). Both commissioning and brokerage shape the market. The austerity budgets shape the market by creating significant fee differentials between state supported and self-funded customers contributing to the creation of a two-tier market.

The Care Act 2014 and its guidance provides a specific meaning of market shaping and supports Prosser's first economically focused rationale. It repositions the state's role from one of control to one of co-production and collaboration with other parties. LAs are required to promote the efficient and effective operation of a market in services for meeting care and support needs with a view to ensuring that any person in its area, however funded, wishing to access services in the market has a variety of providers and high quality services from which to choose and sufficient information to make an informed decision about how to meet the needs in question (s 5(1)). The Statutory Guidance stresses the positive facilitative role that each LA has in shaping its local market (para. 4.2). It is to 'signal to the market the types of services needed now and in the future … encourage innovation, investment and continuous improvement …' (para. 4.7).

The duty requires LAs to be aware of the needs of carers and 'the importance of fostering a workforce whose members are able to ensure the delivery of high quality services (because, for example, they have relevant skills and appropriate working conditions)' (para. 5.2). Thus the workforce, both informal and formal, is recognised as a key 'factor of production'. The LA duty is best met through the production of a Market Position Statement which is created in close collaboration with providers, service users, carers, and other relevant bodies (para. 4.6). It requires a move beyond market engagement to market intelligence and market influence (Institute of Public Care 2016).

In principle, this duty supports considerable intervention to promote human rights and social solidarity as well as market efficiency. If used to full effect, it might be able to influence the market in ways that would ensure that all can access decent services. It could ensure that care workers have decent work and that unpaid carers' needs are catered for. However, there are severe limitations on use in this extended way not least of which are the budgetary constraints on LAs and the reliance on the present private providers to deliver services. Whether a 'shaping' duty could support restructuring of the market is a point developed later.

While LAs in collaboration with others shape the market, the CQC 'regulates' it in a number of ways including through its market oversight obligations in relation to the large providers. As Prosser identifies, there are debates over regulatory visions but risk management is thought currently to achieve 'better regulation' (Black and Baldwin 2010). This form starts with identifying the risks to be managed not the rules to be complied with and focuses attention on the quality of the firm's internal controls. It is often described as 'meta regulation' and responsive approaches to regulation (Baldwin et al 2012). Understanding risk in the present context is important. The model adopted by chain providers is high risk, offering the possibility of a good rate of return for equity holders. In this sense it is a 'good' financial risk at the level of the organisation but can threaten the structural integrity of the market. The 'social' risk is not good: it can result in the collapse of a large care provider which cannot be replaced easily. Business failure among small providers is not as socially or structurally risky as long as all do not fail at once.

The Care Act supported by Regulations establishes the CQC's duties and functions.[1]

> The criteria are designed to be met by those care providers that, because of their size or concentration, Local Authorities would find difficult to replace were they to fail. The criteria relate only to how difficult a provider would be to replace and bear no relation to any judgement of actual or potential risk of failure.
>
> (Care Quality Commission 2015)

They cover both residential and domiciliary providers. The CQC assesses the financial sustainability of the providers within the scheme and informs LAs where business failure is likely to mean a provider may become unable to carry on the regulated activity for which it is registered.[2] Notification triggers the temporary duties placed on LAs to meet the care and support needs of adults or of carers (Care Act 2014, s 48).

The CQC (2015, 14) recognises that this new function: 'financial oversight of private, "for profit" providers of adult social care has not routinely been carried out by a public body …'. It aims to minimise the burdens on those affected and to ensure that the process itself does not contribute to the potential for failure. Evaluation is staged, enabling the organisation involved to resolve the problems internally through, for instance, rescheduling debt or restructuring within a wider corporate group. Only at the last sixth stage is there external notification to the LA. Individual service users are not notified at any stage.

There is a separate requirement in the Health and Social Care Act 2008 (Regulated Activities) Regulations 2014 that all directors of registered providers are responsible for the overall quality and safety of that care under the 'fit and proper person' requirement. Registered providers or their partners must be of good character, possess the right competencies and skills, and be physically and mentally fit to carry out the management function (reg 4). Directors of companies join nominated individuals (responsible for supervising the management of the regulated activity and liaising with the CQC) (reg 6) and registered managers (reg 7) as regulated persons.

While this form of market regulation is an acknowledgement of the precarious nature of the care services market, the regulator has no powers to intervene to prevent a company collapsing. It is an early warning system for LAs. Oversight does not change the business model or behaviour of these providers or influence the level of risk they take. While market oversight allows the business to fail, the responsibility for dealing with the 'social fall out' does shift to the public sector. The 'moral hazard' associated with a guaranteed public 'bail out' remains.

The fit and proper person test is likely to have little impact on the potential for market failure in the care home sector. To deliver consistently high levels of care requires highly skilled personnel with specialist management knowledge. It is not as easy as providing the routinised 'excellence' practised in the hospitality/hotel industry. The CQC cannot prosecute for breach of the regulations, although ultimately it can deregister a provider. Much responsibility is in reality devolved to the 'registered manager' for the particular care service. However the average annual salary for managers is £27,700 (Sodha 2016). One in four leave each year. This form of regulation cannot address issues and does not ensure decent work, including career progression for care workers and managers. It does not address the overall cost to fee paying clients (whether publicly or personally funded) of a high risk/high return model. This form of meta regulation seems to offer very little in relation to human rights and social solidarity objectives.

The oversight duty sits uneasily with the rights-based normative rationale of the CQC (2014) which 'put[s] human rights principles and standards at the heart of policy and planning'. To ensure compliance with legislative requirements under the Human Rights Act (HRA) 1998, the Equality Act 2010, and UN Conventions, this involves the promotion of equality, diversity, and human rights to ensure that all health and care services provide people with 'safe, effective, compassionate and high-quality care, and to encourage them to make improvements' (CQC 2014, 4). The CQC is not inspecting for compliance with the HRA or with the Equality Act but to see how providers perform in relation to five key service questions: are they safe, effective, caring, responsive to people's needs, and well led; and to check that providers do not fall below the fundamental standards required by regulations.[3] The CQC is mindful of its role in relation to 'self-funders' given that the HRA only protects those who receive care when the care is commissioned or at least partially funded by a LA (CQC 2014, 8). It uses the principles that 'are considered to underpin all international human rights treaties': Fairness, Respect, Equality, Dignity, and Autonomy (choice and control) and 'weaves' these into the key lines of enquiry which are used to guide inspections (CQC 2014, 7, 16). The approach uses 'Intelligent Monitoring to identify where the risks are for people using services – based on data and evidence and information from people' (CQC 2014, 18).

As we have seen the individual in need of care services is now at the heart of the policy agenda and the normative base for the Care Act. The CQC's rights approach to regulation supports this policy agenda although it achieves this through routinised and bureaucratised registration and inspection of care providers. It grades providers against the five service questions (outstanding, good, requires improvement, or inadequate). These ratings must be published by the provider and by the CQC, and in this respect, adds to the economic objective of consumer choice. The CQC has powers to intervene to require cessation of services if there is a risk to safety or through deregistration of the provider if improvements do not occur. The CQC does not have powers to pursue individual complaints. This role is fulfilled by the Local Government Ombudsman if there is a public role in the individual's care provision.

Much has been written on the ability of regulation to provide either a reliable indicator of quality or a means to improve it (e.g. Black and Baldwin 2010). Risk-based methods and meta regulation in part are responses to earlier critiques of rule-based methods (Gray and Hamilton 2006). It means that there is a reliance on monitoring of provider processes to prompt organisational responses. It results in infrequent inspection of many providers not thought to be at risk. There is deep scepticism as to whether the present method is able to ensure decent (human rights compliant) and consistent quality of care (Burton 2017). Critics point to the inability of a centrally organised CQC to spot abuse and neglect in local homes with cases coming to light through other means and to the very high level of poor quality provision. Generally, market informed mechanisms do not work well in a sector where 'distress purchasing' tends to be the norm. There is little scope for shopping around even if the care is privately funded.

The cost of regulation has a differential impact on small and large providers. While the large organisations are able to use specialists within their ranks to produce the necessary information and responses, the smaller providers must rely on their own skills or buy them in. To reduce its reliance on public funding, the CQC now charges for inspection: in effect 'each resident in the small home will pay £627 and each resident in the large home will pay £530 for one inspection visit and report' (Burton 2017, 14). At a wider level, it is argued that the large providers use their power and influence within the sector to shape, in their own image, an understanding of what constitutes good social care – hotel style, thus stifling innovation including the provision of what could be considered more socially risky but positively and if wished 'homely' care.

It is very difficult to see how this form of individualised human rights-based regulation could be used to tackle wider structural inequalities. The workforce is marginalised in this rights framework. While providers are required by the CQC to recruit 'fit and proper' staff and to have enough suitably qualified, competent, and experienced staff who must be given the support, training, and supervision they need, its fundamental standards have nothing to say in relation to labour rights and protection.

Yet this workforce is central to maintaining a functioning market because:

> care possesses the distinct characteristics of service work, that is, simultaneous production and consumption, intangibility in demands and the customer's presence in the labour process. Much of the customer's sense of satisfaction is gained from this direct interaction with workers.
>
> (Cunningham 2016, 652)

There is often an inverse ratio between improving productivity through rationalisation and care quality. Technological innovation can be inconsistent with caring. '"Hard" HRM [human resource management] sees labour as a factor of production and a resource to be exploited and manipulated. "Soft" HRM sees labour as a resource to be nurtured in order to encourage commitment' (Cunningham 2016, 653). The large providers tend to adopt the 'hard' approach, bureaucratising care relationships to achieve standardised excellence. As we have seen the most significant regulatory intervention in relation to the workforce has been the introduction of the NLW, providing an average pay rise of 9.2% for 57% of frontline workers although it has 'bunched' them with little potential to progress up the pay ladder (Gardiner 2015). With the planned increase in 2020, a low wage, high return model of social care will become even more unsustainable.

In Prosser's third rationale, regulation is directed to achieving social solidarity. This approach, which seeks to avoid the fragmenting effects of markets and to promote universal access to public services of consistent quality, informs the work of the CQC in relation to health provision given its different roots within the welfare state. There is little scope in social care where it is so sorely needed. CQC is not Offcare. It has no powers to set uniform 'tariffs'/prices or limit geographical disparities. An unimplemented section in the Equality Act 2010 offers a glimmer of possibility. Public authorities would have a duty 'in taking strategic decisions to have regard to the desirability of exercising them in a way designed to reduce inequalities of outcome resulting from socio-economic disadvantage' (s 1).

Intervention to support social solidarity and distributive justice

The manifest problems in the social care market provoke a critical assessment of regulation to address social solidarity and distributive justice objectives. While there is public support for regulation to protect adults in need of social care, there is much less consensus on the way in which such care should be provided. The move from state provider to state broker/market shaper is further muddying public understanding of social care. Social care was a targeted public service provided primarily to the poor. It is still associated with and dependent on public assessment of need via the Care Act 2014 and public funding, and to a great and probably growing extent reliant on non-market familial provision. However, it is increasingly transforming into a market-based, price-differentiated consumer service.

Market-based governance:

> causes bureaucrats to reform or 'translate' aspects of social welfare that previously may have been expressed in the language of need, vulnerability or harm into the language of market failures or market distortion. Not only does this translation tend to silence certain critical modes of demanding justice, particularly those that rely on moral or distributive values, but the institutional solutions which bureaucrats advance to secure the 'translated' social welfare values render them politically vulnerable.
>
> (Morgan 2003, 490).

Social care regulation provides a good example of this translation. The present forms of market shaping and oversight will not redress the way in which this fragile market is developing with growing reliance on forms of financing that provide 11 or 12% return on capital. Oversight is addressed through the social consequences of failure, not because it is an unacceptable way of providing an essential social service. There is a pressing need to finds ways of providing care which values those who are poor and coming to the end of their lives while also caring for those who care for them. More generally the provision of care must be rooted in social welfare values of social solidarity and distributive justice. In theory, the market shaping duties of LAs could support such innovation but politically and financially they are not in a position to support alternative visions.

What could be done given that there is no appetite for social care to be provided free at the point of delivery, supported through general taxation, as part of an extended and reshaped NHS? There is equally no likelihood of the social care market being replaced by state provision. However, below are a number of proposals made recently which would contribute significantly to restructuring provision (Burns et al 2016). They make full use of Prosser's fourth model of 'deliberative' regulation assuming that far more transparency and accountability could shape debate and encourage a new consensus of what constitutes a functioning and caring market.

- LA as a public body, to make the contents of contracts with private providers fully transparent;
- ownership details of companies providing public services under contract to the public sector to be available for public scrutiny;

- private companies in receipt of public services contracts to be domiciled in the UK and subject to UK taxation law;
- all providers required to comply with minimum labour standards and accept collective bargaining rights.

A further more radical suggestion is to give local electorates powers to call to account any provider judged to be providing an inadequate service thereby offering a much more direct and political form of intervention than the bureaucratised form used by the CQC.

LA shaping could extend into restructuring. Organisations with a social purpose could be designated as preferred providers of care and support services. The state could challenge the high risk/high return model by seeking to replace it with a low risk/low return model that is not reliant on debt-based financial engineering but on social funding with low cost capital. A start on this would be made through setting an upper limit on what constitutes a reasonable return (say 5%) on investment in contracts with private companies. This would reduce 'private equity investors' interest' and help 'to re-balance the market between state, voluntary and private provision' (Hudson 2016, 4).

A more positive approach would be to use the ability of the public sector to access low cost finance. LAs can borrow at 4–5% from the Public Works Loan Board although present Treasury policy seeks to limit investment in social infrastructure. Burns et al suggest using LA pension funds:

> Currently many local authority pension fund investments earn no more than 5% net return (interest and capital gain) annually. Why not a national scheme in which local authority pension funds invest in the building of care homes which could provide 5% returns at very low risk?
>
> (2016, 10–11)

This would enable the state, using 'mission oriented public investments' (Mazzucato 2012) to underwrite 'imaginative new experiments in social care rather than simply police the standardised provision by the chains' (Burns et al 2016, 9). With a 5% return (rather than 11 or 12%) it would also be possible to add a levy specifically dedicated for staff development and training.

Conclusion

As presently constituted and funded the adult social care system can impoverish those who have modest funds ensuring their increased vulnerability while not protecting all those who should be eligible for support. The tension, accentuated by the present lack of funding within the public system, between providing decent quality care which is also profitable passes the risk on to others including carers and care workers. Present regulatory measures which involve light touch market oversight by the CQC and limited capacity to market shape by LAs are inadequate. What is needed to tackle structural inequalities and the impoverishment of care is a rebalanced relationship between the market and the state with more aggressive measures to encourage socially responsible providers and innovation in the ways in which care is provided. Although LAs are 'shaping' local social care markets and the CQC nationally is regulating the business practices of providers, tackling the impoverishment associated with care for the elderly requires far more radical interventions in the market.

Notes

1 Care Act 2014 sections 53 to 57; Care and Support (Market Oversight Criteria) Regulations 2015; Care and Support (Market Oversight Information) Regulations 2014.
2 The Care and Support (Business Failure) Regulations 2015 define the meaning of business failure.
3 Health and Social Care Act 2008 Regulations 2014.

Bibliography

Association of Directions of Adult Social Services (ADASS) (2016) *Annual Budget Survey Association of Directors of Adult Social Services.* London: ADASS. Available at: www.adass.org.uk/adass-budget-survey-2016-full-report

BBC Radio 4 (2016) *You and Yours,* 4 May.

Baldwin, J., Cave, M. and Lodge, M. (2012) *Understanding Regulation: Theory, Strategy and Practice.* Oxford: Oxford University Press.

Black, J. (2002) 'Critical Reflections on Regulation' (LSE Centre for the Analysis of Risk and Regulation Discussion Paper 4, 2002). Available at: http://eprints.lse.ac.uk/35985/

Black, J. and Baldwin, J. (2010) 'Really Responsive Risk-Based Regulation' *Law and Policy* 132(2), 81.

Bradley, P. (2016) 'Minimum wage and working time for care providers' 26 September. Available at: www.wrighthassall.co.uk/knowledge/legal-articles/2016/09/26/minimum-wage-and-working-time-care-providers/

Burns, D., Cowie, L., Earle, J., Folkman, P., Froud, J., Hyde, P., Johal, S., Rees Jones, I., Killett, A. and Williams, K. (2016) *Where does the Money Go? Financialised Chains and the Crisis in Residential Care.* London: Centre for Research on Socio-Cultural Change (CRESC).

Burton, J. (2017) *What's Wrong with CQC? A proposal to reform the regulation of social care.* London: The Centre for Welfare Reform.

Care Quality Commission (CQC) (2014) *Human Rights Approach for our Regulation of Health and Social Care Services.* London: CQC.

CQC (2015) *Market Oversight of 'Difficult to Replace' Providers of Adult Social Care. Guidance for Providers.* London: CQC.

Corlett, C. (2017) *As Time Goes By: Shifting Incomes and Inequality Between and Within Generations.* London: Resolution Foundation.

Cunningham, I. (2016) 'Non-profits and the "Hollowed Out" State: The Transformation of Working Conditions through Personalizing Social Care Services During an Era of Austerity' *Work, Employment & Society* 30(4), 649.

D'Arcy, C. and Kelly, G. (2015) *Analysing the National Living Wage Impact and Implications for Britain's Low Pay Challenge.* London: The Resolution Foundation.

Department of Health (DH) (2015) *The NHS Constitution: The NHS Belongs to Us All.* London: DH.

Dilnot Inquiry (2011) *Fairer Care Funding The Report of the Commission on Funding of Care and Support.* Available at: http://webarchive.nationalarchives.gov.uk/20130221130239/; www.wp.dh.gov.uk/carecommission/files/2011/07/Fairer-Care-Funding-Report.pdf

Gardiner, L. (2015) *Care to Pay? Meeting the Challenge of Paying the National Living Wage in Social Care.* London: Resolution Foundation.

Gray, J. and Hamilton, J. (2006) *Implementing Financial Regulation: Theory and Practice.* London: Wiley and Sons.

Hopkins, N. and Laurie, E. (2015) 'Social Citizenship, Housing Wealth and the Cost of Social Care: Is the Care Act 2014 "Fair"?' *Modern Law Review* 78(1), 112.

Hudson, B. (2016) *The Failure of Privatised Adult Social Care in England: What is to be Done?* London: The Centre for Health and the Public Interest.

Humphries, R., Hall, P., Charles, A., Thorlby, R. and Holder, H. (2016) *Social Care for Older People: Home Truths.* London: King's Fund/Nuffield Trust.

Institute of Public Care (2016) *Market Shaping Review: What is Market Shaping?* Oxford: Oxford Brookes.

James, G. and Spruce, E. (2015) 'Workers with Elderly Dependants: Employment Law's Response to the Latest Care-giving Conundrum' *Legal Studies* 35(3), 463.

Jarrett, T. (2017) *Social Care: The State of the Care Home Market (England)* Briefing Paper Number 07463. London: House of Commons Library.

Laing, P. (2017) *The Bottom Line.* BBC Radio 4, 4 February.

Leach, R., Phillipson, C., Biggs, S. and Money, A. (2008) 'Sociological Perspectives on the Baby Boomers Quality' *Ageing* 9(4), 19.

Mazzucato, M. (2012) *The Entrepreneurial State: Debunking Private v Public Sector Myths.* London: Anthem.

Morgan, B. (2003) 'The Economization of Politics: Metaregulation as a Form of NonJudicial Legality' *Social and Legal Studies* 12(4), 489.

Office for National Statistics (ONS) (2016) *Overview of the UK Population: February 2016.* London: ONS.

Prosser, T. (2010) *The Regulatory Enterprise: Government, Regulation, and Legitimacy.* Oxford: Oxford University Press.

Sloan, B. (2016) 'Adult Social Care and Property Rights' *Oxford Journal of Legal Studies* 36(2), 428.

Sodha, S. (2016) 'Underfunded and overstretched – the crisis in care for the elderly' *The Observer*, 10 December.

Stewart, A. (2012) 'From Family to Personal Responsibility: The Challenges for Care of the Elderly in England' *Journal of Social Welfare and the Family Law* 34(2), 179.

Willetts, W. (2011) *The Pinch: How the Baby Boomers Took Their Children's Future – And Why They Should Give it Back.* London: Atlantic Press.

Chapter 9

Older prisoners, gender, and family life

Susan Easton

Introduction

Older prisoners take into prison with them the same challenges faced by older people outside prison. However, the problems of loneliness, depression and isolation in old age may be exacerbated inside prison as maintaining family bonds may be particularly difficult for older prisoners and imprisonment *per se* is an isolating experience and form of social exclusion. Prison visits are crucial as part of this family contact, but it may be difficult for older relatives to visit elderly prisoners beause of health and mobility problems or financial reasons.

In some cases, families may break contact, for example, the adult children of elderly sex offenders may avoid contact because of concerns over stigmatisation. Prisoners themselves may avoid contact where there is a history of violence from another family member, or they may not want their children or grandchildren to visit them inside.

However, some older prisoners feel less isolated inside prison because there is more social contact than in the community. Some prisoners interviewed by the Prison Reform Trust said they would actually prefer to stay in prison as there was no one else to go back to outside:

> I committed my last offence to get back inside – I didn't really do any crime – just couldn't be bothered to turn up to see my probation officer, which I knew would get me recalled. Truth is I have no relations or friends on the outside and no interests – they're all here. I have spent most of my life inside that by the time I was given my parole I had great difficulty surviving by myself. I was also getting so ill trying to cope … there wasn't anybody there to help or support me. So now I'm in my 70s and back 'home' and this is where I'm going to die – not that I want to spend the end of my life in prison but what else is there for me?
>
> (PRT 2008, 12)

Some elderly prisoners, when released, find it difficult to deal with isolation in the community. One prisoner in the PRT study said he was so lonely living in sheltered accommodation that he wished he was back inside (ibid, 13). In cases where prisoners have lost contact with their families, prisoners may seek to create families inside and other inmates may become their families.

Older people may be vulnerable outside prison, but this vulnerability also may be increased inside men's prisons. Studies of older prisoners have found that some older prisoners have experienced bullying because of their frailty and are apprehensive when surrounded by younger prisoners. Prisons, in recent years have become more dangerous places with an increase in the frequency and seriousness of acts of violence in male prisons (HMCIP 2016, 22).

The declining health status of older people may also be exacerbated inside prison. The definition of an older prisoner is usually over 50 which is lower than might be expected but reflects the fact that prisoners generally age faster than the wider population because of their poorer health and because of the impact of imprisonment. Offenders may have an unhealthy lifestyle before entering prison, but being in prison may speed up the ageing process. However, for those leading chaotic lives before prison, health may actually improve in custody.

The over-50s now constitute 15 per cent of the prison population, with 12,577 prisoners aged 50 and over, and 4,373 aged over 60 (HMCIP 2016, 8). The over-60s are the fastest growing group within the prison population with the numbers tripling since 2001 (PRT 2016, 8). The number of sentenced prisoners aged 60 and over increased by 164 per cent between 2002 and 2015 (PRT 2015, 5). Although in 2015–16 the prison population declined slightly, the number of older prisoners remains relatively high and is also expected to increase. The projections for 2016–2021 for England and Wales predict the prison population will be 84,300 by the end of March 2021 (Ministry of Justice 2016a). The over-50 prison population is projected to grow from 12,700 on 30 June 2016 to 13,900 by end of June 2020, with the over-60 population projected to grow from 4,500 to 5,400 and the over-70 population from 1,400 to 1,900 in the period 2016–21 (ibid).

The number of older prisoners in the prison population in England and Wales has increased since the 1990s, for a number of reasons. Older prisoners are more likely than younger prisoners to be serving longer sentences because of the type of offences committed, with a large number of older prisoners serving sentences for sex offences, including non-recent sex offences. By 2015, 42 per cent of prisoners aged over 50 were serving sentences for sex offences. The ageing of the prison population has mirrored the demographic changes in the wider society, but the increase in numbers also has to be seen in the wider context of penal expansion, with an increase in longer determinate sentences, as well as increased use of indeterminate sentences compared to the early 1990s. Although the Imprisonment for Public Protection (IPP) sentence has now been abolished, there are still IPP prisoners being held in prison beyond their tariff date. Those serving mandatory life sentences are also spending longer in custody than 20 years ago as sentence length has increased. Some older prisoners have grown old in prison serving long sentences. The expansion also reflects increased punitiveness, which has been extended to older offenders, so sentencers and society are now more willing to prosecute and punish older offenders.

In the UK the recent expansion of the older prison population since 2000 has been attributed principally to the rise in the number of prisoners sentenced for non-recent sex offences, which inevitably mean the offender is quite old by the time the sentence is served. For example, Max Clifford was aged 71 when he was sentenced in 2014 for 8 years for a series of indecent assaults committed in the 1970s and 80s. Also in 2014, 84-year-old Rolf Harris was sentenced to 5 years and 9 months for indecent assaults committed between 1969 and 1986. From 2002 to 2015, there was an increase of 164 per cent in number of prisoners sentenced for historical sex offences. In addition, there are older prisoners growing old in prison because they are serving long sentences for serious crimes committed at a younger age, those serving short sentences for a first offence and persistent offenders returning to prison repeatedly during their criminal careers.

This rise in the number of older prisoners has occurred at a time of shrinking prison budgets and increased violence and instability in prison. In England and Wales, budget cuts have been achieved through cuts in staffing which have affected the experience of imprisonment of all prisoners, but which have had a disparate impact on the experience of imprisonment of older prisoners including women prisoners. While the 2016 White Paper *Prison Safety and Reform* does announce the government's intention to increase staffing to deal with the current crises of violence, assaults, and use of psychoactive drugs, the concerns are primarily over younger male prisoners rather than the elderly or women prisoners and the problem of staff retention is not addressed (Ministry of Justice 2016b).

Despite the expansion of the older prison population, there has been relatively little research on this group until recently, possibly reflecting the marginalisation of older people found in the wider society as well as the relatively small size of the group. Within criminology the focus has been on the elderly as victims of crime and on their fear of crime rather than as perpetrators.

However, there has been more interest in recent years with a Thematic Review of older prisoners from the Prison Inspectorate in 2004, *No Problems – Old and Quiet,* which recommended changes to their treatment (HMCIP 2004) and the follow-up review in 2008 (HMCIP 2008). The Prison Reform Trust has also considered the problems faced by older prisoners in *Growing Old in Prison* (2003) and *Doing Time: The Experiences and Needs of Older People in Prison* (2008). The House of Commons Justice Committee also conducted an inquiry into older prisoners in 2013. There have also been studies by Wahidin (2004), Crawley and Sparks (2005) and Mann (2012), considered below. which have enhanced our knowledge and understanding of older prisoners. The experience of imprisonment may be affected by the intersectionality of age, gender, ethnicity and disability. These differences may affect access to services inside prison. However, the primary focus of research on ethnicity and imprisonment has been on the experiences of young male BAME prisoners (see, for example, Young 2014).

The expansion of older prisoners raises problems for prison regimes in dealing with their needs, but also for the prisoners themselves. It is generally agreed by those working with older prisoners and researchers studying this group that older prisoners experience the pains of imprisonment more intensely. Crawley and Sparks (2005) also conducted research on elderly male prisoners in four prisons, observing their experience and conducting in-depth interviews. They highlight the 'institutional thoughtlessness' of prison regimes in dealing with elderly prisoners and note the low status of this group many of whom as sex offenders are already low in the prison hierarchy. More recently Mann (2012) conducted research on older male prisoners, interviewing 40 prisoners and 10 officers in three prisons, and found that older prisoners' experienced the pains of imprisonment more severely than younger prisoners. The 2008 HMCIP study also noted inconsistency between prisons in their levels of support. However, older prisoners were generally more positive than younger prisoners regarding prison life, although they were also more likely to report victimisation because of their age, disability or the nature of their offence.

Furthermore, because older prisoners are seen as 'old and quiet' their needs are more likely to be overlooked. Prison regimes are primarily geared to young male prisoners. For example, older prisoners may also be subject to higher levels of security than may be necessary. Because of the nature of the offence committed, they may be held in a high security estate, even though they may be frail and with limited mobility. However, there have been some escapes by older prisoners so the prison authorities will tend towards caution. Rules on security aimed at younger prisoners may be applied generally, but make life more difficult for older prisoners. Prisoners will be expected to respond promptly to requests to move around the prison but older prisoners may take much longer and find it hard to fit into prison routines. Education and resettlement programmes are primarily geared to younger prisoners and designed to prepare them for the job market while older prisoners need preparation for coping with isolation and retirement. Family contact, health, and social care issues also need to be considered. Payment by results programmes are primarily focused on younger prisoners and success is measured in terms of the reduction of reoffending, but older prisoners are already less likely to reoffend. However, it was made clear in the response to the Justice Committee's report that resettlement services should be available to older prisoners regardless of potential employment or reoffending benefits (Ministry of Justice 2013, para. 23). Resettlement for those who have served long sentences is very challenging and they will need advice on how to avoid isolation outside, as well as practical information on access to healthcare and state pensions.

Maintaining family links

Being old in prison may make it harder to maintain family ties, particularly if prisoners are allocated to a prison far from the family home. Contact with family members is seen as an important element in prisoners' rehabilitation as it maintains contact with the outside world and can contribute to reintegration of the offender on release. Regular contact with families may also reduce tensions within prison. A key principle in the European Prison Rules (EPR 5) is normalisation, that is, conditions inside prison should be as close as possible to the positive aspects of life outside in the community and maintaining family contact is an important element of this. The right to family life is also recognised and protected by Article 8 of the European Convention on Human Rights and Article 12, the right to marry and found a family. But these rights may be limited, if there are security issues or a risk of crime (Arts 8(2) and 12(2)). So visits are refused for security reasons and the limits will be assessed on the principle of proportionality. There may be restrictions on particular visitors because of security concerns or where there are child protection issues (Easton 2011).

While visitors can receive some financial assistance under the Assisted Visitors scheme, visiting may be difficult for elderly visitors if visiting facilities are not accessible or long journeys are involved, especially for those with limited mobility or in wheelchairs. Elderly visitors may find travelling difficult or impossible. On visiting day, it may take some time to process visitors, which will be more difficult for elderly or infirm visitors. For foreign national prisoners, the problems of maintaining bonds through visits or phone contact may be even harder. They can have a free five-minute phone call per month if they have not had a social visit, but obviously this is not enough to deal with family issues. Arranging visits can be difficult for all prisoners and the Prison Inspectorate has highlighted delays and problems with the visits booking system in prisons, as well as delays entering prison. In one prison, visitors were observed entering the prison 45 minutes after the scheduled time for the visit, despite arriving early (HMIP 2016, 50). These problems will be even harder for elderly or inform visitors. Older prisoners may also find using phones difficult, for example, if they have hearing problems or are arthritic. The treatment of visitors may also raise Article 8 issues if they are subjected to body searches as in the case of *Wainwright v UK* App. No. 12350/04 (26 September 2006). Families may also suffer stigmatisation and social exclusion through imprisonment of family members.

The right to family life should be taken account of in allocating or transferring prisoners, but this may be seen as most relevant to younger women prisoners with dependent children. The offender has no right to be allocated to a prison nearer his or her home. For Article 8 to be breached, distance from home would not count unless the distance were extreme or the family members were disabled. A decision to allocate an offender to a particular prison may be deemed proportionate despite the adverse effect on family visits, for example if there are security issues or certain programmes are only available in a particular prison.

The prisoner's categorisation will also be a key factor in determining the allocated prison. Security issues will affect their classification, but for elderly infirm prisoners clearly the likelihood of escape or absconding is less likely. This was considered in *R(P) v Secretary of State for the Home Department* EWHC 1018

Admin 2002, where an elderly and unwell prisoner had been placed in category A, despite being unlikely to be able to escape because of his age and infirmity. The court held that the Prison Service should consider prisoners' cases on an individual basis and if the escape risk could be managed at a lower level of security then it would be unlawful to rule out that out of consideration of this. However, sometimes prisoners may be subject to higher security than necessary because a decision has been made to allocate them nearer home.

Those prisoners who have grown old inside serving long sentences may be especially isolated, and may have lost contact with younger family members, especially if held far from home. One prisoner interviewed by the PRT had been inside for nearly 30 years and had lost contact with friends and did not know if any of his family was still alive (PRT 2008, 1). Another prisoner said:

> I started my sentence before my grandchildren were born and because I've been moved around so much and now am at the other end of the country; I have not seen them or my daughter for six years ... We write occasionally but as time has gone on it has become less ...
>
> (PRT 2008, 10)

Similar findings were noted in the Report of the House of Commons Justice Committee: 'Prison staff reported to us that in their experience of holding older prisoners frequently all contact had been lost with their family and friends' (House of Commons 2013, 43).

Older prisoners may lose their parents while in prison and this can pose problems in organising funerals and disposing of family possessions and acting as executors of the will. Prison visitors may offer assistance in such cases. For example, a volunteer with a local advocacy project helped arrange storage of items from the parental home to await his release and passed on his wishes for the funeral arrangements (NACRO 2009b, 38). There may also be inheritance issues to deal with while incarcerated. As Monk (this volume, p. 190) has noted inheritance issues impact more people than ever with the expansion of property ownership and changing values of property. So prisoners may find themselves dealing with these issues at a distance.

For those serving long sentences the prison becomes their home. In the absence of family ties, some prisoners will form close bonds with other prisoners to create close ties. In some cases, women officers will become proxy figures for families and prisoners' attitudes to the treatment of staff may reflect what they see as appropriate treatment for family members. This was also found in Crewe's study of a Category C prison, where women officers concurred that they were treated as maternal surrogates for younger prisoners (Crewe 2006, 409). Crewe also found friendship networks became important as a means of countering isolation in prison and surviving the sentence, with bonds formed through regional affiliations or other links (Crewe 2009). Mann (2012) found that older male prisoners sometimes assumed a father figure role with younger women officers. Establishing surrogate family relationships may offer an alternative notion of masculinity to the dominant notion of masculinity in prison which is physical toughness, bullying, and predatory behaviour, which means that older male prisoners will be positioned low in the prison hierarchy.

However, the responses of older prisoners to loss of family contact may vary. Crawley and Sparks (2005) found that some lifers in their study coped better if they had no contact with families outside or no families, while those worried about spouses and families found the separation more unbearable.

Could the problems of maintaining family contact be ameliorated? Extended visits for partners and family members would enable relatives to make longer less frequent visits. Special days can be designated for grandparents. These have been offered, for example, at HMP Downview for women to re-establish links with their grandchildren. Facilities for older and disabled visitors also could be improved. Visitors and pen pal schemes for older prisoners may also be beneficial. Release on temporary licence may be given to prisoners to deal with urgent family matters or to attend family funerals or other purposes, but it may be refused for security. But the number of ROTLs has declined in recent years because of security concerns following some high profile failures.

The loss of family bonds may also impact on housing and resettlement, as older prisoners are less likely to have accommodation on release. Sex offenders may have had to leave their home area and will be prohibited from returning there as part of their licence conditions. Older prisoners with health or social care needs may be particularly difficult to resettle. They may have lost their homes while in prison and will find it difficult to access local authority accommodation on release. Some may enter hostel accommodation but may be apprehensive about bullying by younger residents. Sex offenders relocated in sheltered housing may be isolated and avoid contact with their neighbours because of fears they will find out about the nature of their offence.

Gender issues

The most striking feature of the prison population is the large number of male prisoners, who constitute 95 per cent of the prison population in England and Wales. Although the number of women prisoners has increased since the early 1990s, their numbers are still relatively low. The number of women prisoners over 50 increased from 92 in 1996 to 316 in 2008, of whom nearly half were foreign national prisoners, many of whom were serving sentences for drug importation (PRT 2008, 1). On 2 December 2016 there were 3,936 female prisoners in England and Wales. For older women prisoners, the most common offences are violence against the person and drugs offences. The reasons for the gender disparity have been well documented elsewhere (see, for example, Berberet 2014). But it is only relatively recently that the differences between the needs of male and female prisoners have been acknowledged and gender specific policies have been formulated. Women prisoners are more likely to have experience of domestic violence before entering prison and more likely to be socially excluded. Many women lose their homes on imprisonment while male prisoners' partners and children may stay in the family home. But while women have gradually become more visible, older women's voices have rarely been heard. Older women have received less attention than men and the reason often given is that this is because their numbers are much smaller (Crawley and Sparks 2005).

The concerns of prison reformers and researchers investigating female imprisonment have focused primarily on younger prisoners and on women as prime carers of young children and have highlighted the vulnerability of women prisoners, The Corston Report, the major report on women prisoners, did not consider older prisoners. Women's prisons are now assessed against the *Expectations for Women Prisoners* formulated by the Prison Inspectorate and published in 2014 (HMIP 2014). These were influenced by the Bangkok Rules, the UN 2010 Rules for the treatment of women prisoners. The *Expectations* recognise that women prisoners' needs may be distinct from men's needs and that prison regimes have been primarily geared towards the needs of male prisoners. They focus on a range of issues, including healthcare, security, and respect. Judging prisons against these Expectations, the Prison Inspectorate has found that generally women's prisons perform better than men's prisons (HMCIP 2016, 9). While successive governments have recognised the need for gender specific policies and gender specific standards, the All Party Parliamentary Group on Women in the Penal System (2011) has noted that progress has been relatively slow in meeting many of the suggestions of the Corston Report. The House of Commons Justice Committee on Women Offenders (2015) welcomed the improvements and the decline in the numbers of women in prison, but was critical of the lack of funding for women's centres and cuts in release on temporary licence for women prisoners.

Prison regimes are primarily geared to male prisoners and it is only relatively recently that gender specific policies have been developed. This meant women prisoners were marginalised and older women even more so. For example, women have been subjected to higher levels of security and cuts in home leave because of the actions of male prisoners. Prisons are also geared to younger prisoners in good health, so older women with health problems may find the experience of prison particularly difficult. The Corston Report found that women prisoners had higher rates of mental health problems than women outside prison or male prisoners (Corston Report 2007, 19). Women prisoners with disabilities are disadvantaged compared to male prisoners with disabilities, as there are fewer prisons offering programmes, so it is harder to make reasonable adjustments for them. If gender discrimination intersects with age discrimination, older women prisoners are even more marginalised. Older women who have run homes and families will find the infantilising experience of imprisonment and the loss of privacy in prison especially difficult to accept.

The Prison Service Order on Women Prisoners (PSO 4800) gives guidance on gender specific standards for the treatment of women prisoners (Annex K). It does include an annex on older women, but is just one page long and refers to their healthcare needs and the need for grandparent days to facilitate contact with families, the fact that their learning needs may be different, and the pace may need to be slower. It also refers to older women's supportive role in relation to younger prisoners.

Women may held further from their families than male prisoners because there are fewer prisons for women, although it is recommended that they be situated as close to their homes as possible. Women prisoners were transferred to Downview and Bronzefield in Surrey following the closure of Holloway in 2016, which meant it was further for family members to travel on visiting days. Distance from home may also have implications for healthcare, for example, in attending hospital appointments made before imprisonment. While some prisons do allow extended family visits and have facilities for children to visit and stay overnight, this is designed for prime carers of young children rather than for older women prisoners. For foreign national women prisoners maintaining family contact will be more challenging (HMCIP 2004).

While the majority of women prisoners serve short sentences, there is also a small group of female lifers, including one prisoner, Rosemary West, serving a whole life sentence for ten murders – including one of her children, as well as sexual assault, and child cruelty.[1] Older women may also find themselves acting in a surrogate mother role to younger women prisoners. Establishing surrogate families in women's prisons has been seen as a way of helping women negotiate the pains of imprisonment, although their functionality has been debated, as women may bring to these new families similar behaviours to those they exhibited in their own families prior to imprisonment outside (see van Wormer 2011). Some of the issues litigated in relation to family life have primarily affected younger women with dependent children. However, women reaching the end of their reproductive lives may face the loss of a future family.[2]

There will also be specific health issues for older women for example, problems of access to cervical screening and mammography services. Some women prisoners undergoing HRT treatment for the menopause before entering prison, may find it difficult to continue with treatment and suffer if they have to stop treatment suddenly. Experiencing night sweats also will be difficult if sheets are changed only once a week.

In Wahidin's (2004) study, older women dreaded being ill, because of the problems of access to treatment and fact that medical facilities were under resourced, and if held in the hospital wing would be isolated from the activities of the prison. They also dreaded hospital visits where they would be handcuffed or visibly accompanied by prison officers. Older women also suffered derogatory comments about their appearance from male officers. She visited 16 prisons and conducted 35 independent semi structured interviews in four women's establishments. At the time of her research women made up 4.6 per cent of the female prison population and while these prisoners were more likely to suffer from health problems, they found it difficult to access healthcare.

Older women may have quite different interests from younger female prisoners. At Styal, for example, there is an over-50s forum for older women, with arts and crafts such as knitting, in partnership with Age Concern (NACRO resource pack, 36). This is useful as generally regimes are geared to younger prisoners, for example, yoga and mindfulness courses aimed at detoxification.

However, in some respects conditions in women's prisons are better than in men's prisons, including visiting facilities. Recent reports from the Prison Inspectorate suggested that women's prisons were found to be good or reasonably good in the prisons inspected and women's prisons generally perform better than men's prisons (HMCIP 2016, 9). For example, there is less violence and bullying than in men's prisons and better relationships with staff

In some women's prisons, additional provision is made for older prisoners. At HMP Downview a special over-50s unit for older women opened in 2008, because older women felt intimidated by younger prisoners (NACRO 2009b, 31). It also provided more milk and fruit to women and thicker mattresses and exchanged visiting orders for PIN credit for phone calls for women whose elderly parents who could not easily travel and offered separate yoga and gym sessions for older women.

Health and social care issues

Most of the discussion of older prisoners' problems relates to health and disability. For both male and female older prisoners, healthcare will be a particular problem in prison. Mental health services focus on younger prisoners. The prison system is designed for healthy younger men, rather than older men whose health problems and health needs may be quite different and the cost of healthcare services to older prisoners will be substantial. The availability of healthcare will be affected by the availability of prison officers, so if staff are not available appointments may be missed. The 2016 Report of the Prison Inspectorate which examined healthcare found that '(T)he care of older prisoners required improvement at several prisons, including Humber and Leicester ...' (HM Chief Inspector of Prisons 2016, 35).

The health status of older prisoners is generally worse than young prisoners (Department of Health 2009, House of Commons Justice Committee 2013). The challenges of ageing, physical, and other disabilities, may be exacerbated inside prison. Social care and healthcare requirements increase with age and may impose considerable financial costs on the prison. Chronic diseases, such as diabetes and lifestyle-related ill-health, are more likely in older prisoners. For prisoners imprisoned for the first time in late life the shock of being in prison may lead to anxiety and depression (Crawley and Sparks 2005).

Fazel et al's study of the healthcare needs of a group of older prisoners in Oxford and the surrounding area found high levels of chronic illness with similar findings by other studies (Fazel et al 2001). The health of elderly male prisoners was worse than that of the general population and worse than that of younger prisoners. Fazel et al estimated 30 per cent of older prisoners had a personality disorder and 30 per suffered from depression. In that study there was a high incidence of mental health disorders, including drug and alcohol misuse, and anxiety in the 50–59 group but it was lower over the age of 60. However, depression was higher in older prisoners than in the same age group outside prison. A study using data from the Surveying Prisoner Crime Reduction Survey found that the 115 older prisoners examined had higher levels of ill health and physical disabilities than younger prisoners, but were less likely to have a history of drug problems (Omolade 2014).

The Prison Reform Trust study of older prisoners in 2008 found differences between healthcare services received in prison and the care they would have received outside, although the principle of equivalence demands parity (PRT 2008). As well as higher morbidity rates for physical illnesses, there were also high levels of depression and problems of accessing medication. Older prisoners have a higher risk of cancer and may have a history of poor nutrition and a lifestyle predisposed to health problems. Since 2008, there have been changes in the responsibility for healthcare which has passed to NHS trusts. Commissioning is now undertaken by NHS England at a national level.

Older prisoners have reported problems in accessing healthcare, delays in seeing nurses or GPs, difficulties in obtaining medications, keeping hospital appointments, being handcuffed during appointments, or being transferred mid-sentence disrupting treatment. While prisoners should not normally be transferred during a period of treatment and although medical staff can request this, these requests do not always succeed.

There are also cases of dementia within the older prison population. However, it is likely that number of prisoners with dementia is greater than recorded. In the early stages, the organisation of the prison and rigid routines may actually make it easier for dementia to pass unnoticed. Moll argues that the structured regime of prisons may help people cope with the onset of dementia so they are less likely to be diagnosed (Moll 2013, 12). Moreover, as in the wider population, forgetfulness may be seen as an inevitable aspect of old age rather than as something more serious. In the early stages dementia may display itself in depression and withdrawal, so is less likely to attract attention than florid symptoms of mental illness. What is needed is routine screening for older prisoners, better staff training, the engagement of external bodies, including charities, in making suggestions on ways their experience may be improved and appropriate modifications to prison environments where possible, for example, clear signposting for facilities. Local authorities are now responsible for the social care needs of prisoner under the Care Act 2014. Given the ageing population within prison, the issue of dementia in prison is likely to become more important and most costly and will need to be addressed.

Some prisoners may die in prison, in their cells or in the prison healthcare centre, while receiving palliative care. While it is possible to release terminally ill prisoners on compassionate grounds if they are expected to die within three months, there may be a reluctance to do so, especially after the Lockerbie Bomber case, where the prisoner remained alive for much longer. The view of many prison staff is that this option is underused (Department of Health 2007, 10). It has been argued that a one-year deadline would be more appropriate (PRT 2008, 4). There have also been cases of elderly prisoners being subject to restraint during end of life care because of security concerns.

Accommodating older prisoners with disabilities

Older prisoners, like prisoners as a whole, are a diverse group and may include those who are physically and mentally active, as well as those requiring considerable support. However, there is a higher incidence of disability among older prisoners. Cognitive decline associated with ageing will affect older prisoners. The problems facing prisoners with learning disabilities have been well documented by Loucks (2007) and the Bradley Report (Department of Health 2009).

Physical disabilities will also make life for older prisoners challenging, especially in older prisons which are less suited to accommodating infirm or disabled prisoners. Prisons have a duty not to discriminate against those with disabilities formerly under the Disability Discrimination Act 1995 and now under the Equality Act 2010. There is a statutory duty to make reasonable adjustments to services, so that they are accessible to all who use them. As the House of Commons Justice Committee observes: 'while an environment which is appropriate to older prisoners has been facilitated in modern prisons, it simply does not exist in older prisons' (House of Commons Justice Committee, 2013, para. 29).

A Prison Estate Transformation Programme is being undertaken to modernise the estate by closing older prisons and replacing them with more efficient modern ones, which are better able to house such prisoners. Modern prisons are better designed for access for those with physical disabilities than older prisons which are harder to adapt. There may be problems of moving around the prison and using stairs and bunk beds in shared cells as well as a lack of social care. Older inmates may rely on younger prisoners to help with social care through a buddy system. Although these helpers cannot undertake personal care because of the risk of abuse, they can perform a range of other tasks.

Accessibility is important for these prisoners as it may be necessary to complete Offending Behaviour Programmes and Sex Offender Treatment Programmes as a move towards their release. It may also be harder for older prisoners to take educational classes if there are physical barriers or materials are not available in large print. The Prison Inspectorate has highlighted the lack of age specific activities including education. Mann's (2012) study also found activities primarily geared to younger prisoners. There may also be problems in participating in work, if there is no light work available for older prisoners, increasing their isolation.

The Department of Health published a toolkit for good practice in caring for older prisoners in 2007. The Prison Service Orders on Disabilities and Women also include guidance on older prisoners on making prison more accessible (PSO 2855, PSO 4800). However, the Prison Service Instruction 32/2011 on disabilities does not make any specific recommendations on older prisoners.

Impact mitigation for older offenders

If, as we have suggested, older prisoners suffer the pains of imprisonment more sharply, it raises the question of whether there should be impact mitigation for age or disability, at the point of sentencing. If older prisoners find punishment more difficult, they are effectively punished twice, for their offence and for being older. The question of whether incarcerating a very elderly and infirm prisoner amounts to inhuman and degrading treatment or punishment, was considered by the Strasbourg Court in *Papon v France* App. No. 64666/01 (7 June 2001). Papon was 88 when he was given a 10-year sentence for aiding and abetting crimes against humanity, in the 1940s as an official in Vichy France, where he was involved in the arrest and imprisonment of French Jews deported to their deaths in Germany. He was 90 when his case came before the Chamber and argued that an extended sentence, given his age combined with poor health, constituted a breach of Article 3. The court rejected this claim although it stressed the need for appropriate conditions in prison. Moreover, the President could exercise a prerogative of mercy under French law, or he could be given parole for medical treatment, if his condition worsened in future. In fact the French Appeal Court did release him when his health deteriorated in 2002 and he died in 2007 following heart surgery.

Mann (2012) argues that incarceration is not the most economic or effective way of punishing elderly offenders. This obviously raises difficult issues of impact mitigation, which have been discussed elsewhere (Piper 2007, Easton 2008, Easton and Piper 2016, 225–38). Chiu, for example notes that early release for older inmates may offer cost savings but 'the practice can be at odds with other criminal justice goals, such as retribution or incapacitation' (Chiu 2010,10). There may also be political barriers to releasing older prisoners if this measure is unpopular with the public.

But even if impact mitigation at the sentencing stage is unlikely, age must be taken account of in prison. Age is now a protected characteristic under equality law so prisons are obliged to take older prisoners' needs into account and have a duty not to discriminate on grounds of age or disability, gender, sexual orientation, or any other protected characteristic. While prisons have a duty to promote equality under the Equality Act, and to ensure support for prisoners from all groups with protected characteristics, the focus has in the past been principally on race and gender rather than age. However, the current approach is a generic approach to equality and diversity and to reducing unequal outcomes.

Conclusion

As we have seen, there are particular challenges facing prisoners growing older in prison. While there are examples of good practice in engaging and integrating older prisoners, including, older prison forums which can reduce isolation and give older prisoners a voice, and cases where education and work is available and a buddy system for younger prisoners to help older prisoners and centres for older prisoners, provision is variable through the prison estate.

An example of good practice may be found at HMP Leyhill, where with the help of Age Concern, a Day Centre was set up to offer activities to older prisoners

(NACRO 2009a, 43). Leyhill also created a special wing for older prisoners which offers a calmer space, but prisoners still have access to main services. It also has a dedicated older offender liaison officer role and offers adapted exercise classes for older prisoners. The staff who run the day centre for older prisoners at Leyhill were also allowed to take an NVQ in Health and Social Care. There is also a separate wing for older prisoners at HMP Wynott (Fry 2005). But the problem is the variability of provision as not all prisons have effective policies. Mann (2012) found only 18 prisons had age-related initiatives or programmes. The Isle of Wight prison offered a referral process for staff concerned about a prisoner's memory and dementia awareness training is available at Exeter and Dartmoor (Moll 2013).

In addition NACRO, Age Concern, and the Department of Health have published recommendations and guidance toolkits to improve the treatment of older prisoners (NACRO 2009a, 2009b). The organisation RECOOP (Resettlement and Care for Older Ex-Offenders and Prisoners) was asked by NOMS (National Offender Management Service) to assist prisons in promoting the well-being of older prisoners and to encourage their engagement in activities and has also devised programmes for older prisoners.

Because prisoners have been seen as 'old and quiet' and less troublesome than younger prisoners, and are less likely to be disruptive or to self-harm, or cause disciplinary problems, their needs are more likely to be overlooked. This is reflected in the failure to develop a national strategy for this group. The absence of such a strategy means prisoners in prisons without an effective policy will suffer. All prisons should have an older prisoners' policy and protocols for assessment. So far the response from the Ministry of Justice has been that this is not appropriate because of the diversity of the older prison population (Ministry of Justice 2013). The Government has instead stressed the need for an individual approach: 'A requirement for every prison to have an older prisoner policy detailing age specific regimes would reduce the ability of prison governors to provide regimes which reflect the actual and specific needs of prisoners' (ibid, para. 6). But while acknowledging the diversity of the older population, there are, as we have seen, common needs which should be addressed.

Age-related policies and provision, proper assessment and assistance for resettlement and an accredited prisoner helper scheme would advance the treatment of older prisoners. Proper training for staff involving specialists in health and social care and the designation of staff with specific responsibility for older prisoners would enable staff to recognise mental health problems. Some of the measures needed could be achieved quite cheaply, such as extra bedding, locating prisoners on the ground floor, and in lower bunks. Greater use could be made of ROTL and compassionate release, but while those who have committed very serious offences need to be retained in prison, they still need to be given appropriate care.

It has been mooted that older prisoners should be held in separate units although some are already segregated from other prisoners because of their offences. This separation would make it easier to provide specialist care. It may also be more cost effective to held them separately to concentrate resources. Others favour the integration of older prisoners with the wider community and it is thought that older prisoners, who are less volatile, have a calming effect on younger prisoners. Separation may cut older prisoners off from prison routines which may be detrimental and stigmatising. But older prisoners may be reluctant to mix with other prisoners on the wing because of fears of bullying and the Prison Inspectorate has noted that support for victims of bullying is generally poor (HMCIP 2016, 22). Providing day centres or a separate space within the main prison offers an alternative to segregation or integration. Whichever route is selected, it is important that the needs of older prisoners are not overlooked in the current climate of prison instability.

Notes

1 West is held at HMP Low Newton which runs the Primrose Programme for women with dangerous and severe personality disorders. Given the nature of her offence, preservation of family contact may seem less relevant, but West has received family visits and was transferred temporarily to HMP Woodhill in 2005 to facilitate such visits.

2 The implications of Article 8 for prisoners' access to artificial insemination were considered in *Dickson v UK* App. No. 44362/04 (4 December 2007) where the Grand Chamber of the European Court of Human Rights decided that a refusal to support such a request did breach Article 8. In Dickson's case there were no child welfare, security, or cost issues and a right should not be lost simply because giving effect to it might offend public opinion.

References

All Party Parliamentary Group on Women in the Penal System (2011) Women *in the Penal System: Second Report on Women with Particular Vulnerabilities in the Criminal Justice System*. London: Howard League.

Berberet, R. (2014) *Women, Crime and Criminal Justice*. Abingdon: Routledge.

Chiu, T. (2010) *It's About Time: Ageing Prisoners, Increasing Costs and Geriatric Release*. New York: VERA Institute of Justice.

Corston Report (2007) *The Corston Report: A Review of Women with Particular Vulnerabilities in the Criminal Justice System*. London: Home Office.

Crawley, E. and Sparks, R. (2005) 'Surviving the Prison Experience? Imprisonment and Elderly Men' *Prison Service Journal* 160.

Crewe, B. (2006) 'Male Prisoners' Orientation towards Female Officers in an English Prison' *Punishment and Society* 8, 394.

Crewe, B. (2009) *The Prisoner Society*. Oxford: Oxford University Press.

Department of Health (DH) (2007) *A Pathway to Care for Older Offenders: A Toolkit for Good Practice*. London: DH.

DH (2009) *The Bradley Report: Lord Bradley's Review of People with Mental Health Problems or Learning Disabilities in the Criminal Justice System*. London: DH.

Easton, S. (2008) 'Dangerous Waters: Taking Account of Impact in Sentencing' *Criminal Law Review* 2, 105.

Easton, S. (2011) *Prisoners' Rights, Principles and Practice*. Abingdon: Routledge.

Easton, S. and Piper, C. (2016) *Sentencing and Punishment: The Quest for Justice*, 4th edn. Oxford: Oxford University Press.

Fazel, S., Hope, T., Donnell, I., Piper, M. and Jacoby, R. (2001) 'Health of Elderly Male Prisoners: Worse than the General Population, Worse than Younger Prisoners' *Age and Ageing* 30(5), 403.

Fry, D. (2005) 'Managing Older Prisoners at HMP Wymott' *Prison Service Journal*, 160.

House of Commons Justice Committee (2013) *Older Prisoners: Fifth Report of Session 2013–14.* HC 89. London: The Stationery Office.

House of Commons Justice Committee (2015) *Women Offenders: Follow-up*, HC 314. London: The Stationery Office.

HM Chief Inspector of Prisons (HMCIP) (2004) *No Problems – Old and Quiet: Older Prisoners in England and Wales.* London: HM Inspectorate of Prisons (HMIP).

HMCIP (2008) *Older Prisoners in England and Wales: A Follow-up to the 2004 Thematic Review by HM Chief Inspector of Prisons.* London: HMIP.

HMCIP (2016) *Annual Report 2015–16.* London: HMIP.

HM Inspectorate of Prisons (HMIP) (2014) *Expectations: Criteria for Assessing the Treatment of and Conditions for Women in Prison.* London: Ministry of Justice (MoJ).

Loucks, N. (2007) *No One Knows: The Prevalence and Associated Needs of Offenders with Learning Difficulties and Learning Disabilities.* London: Prison Reform Trust.

Mann, N. (2012) *Doing Harder Time? The Experiences of an Ageing Male Prison Population in England and Wales.* Aldershot: Ashgate.

Ministry of Justice (MOJ) (2013) *Government Response to the Justice Committee's Fifth Report of Session 2013–2014: Older Prisoners*, Cm 8739. London: The Stationery Office.

MoJ (2016a) *Prison Population Projections 2016–2021 England and Wales, Ministry of Justice Statistics Bulletin.* London: MoJ.

MoJ (2016b) *Prison Safety and Reform*, Cm 9350. London: MoJ.

Moll, A. (2013) *Losing Track of Time: Dementia and the Ageing Prison Population: Treatment Challenges and Examples of Good Practice.* London: Mental Health Foundation.

National Association for the Care and Resettlement of Offenders (NACRO) (2009a) *Working with Older Prisoners Workshop.* London: NACRO.

NACRO (2009b) *A Resource Pack for Working with Older Prisoners.* London: NACRO.

Omolade, S. (2014) *The Needs and Characteristics of Older Prisoners: Results from the Surveying Prisoner Crime Reduction (SPCR) Survey.* London: MoJ.

Piper, C. (2007) 'Should impact constitute mitigation? Structured discretion versus mercy' *Criminal Law Review* 141.

Prison Reform Trust (2003) *Growing Old in Prison.* London: Prison Reform Trust.

Prison Reform Trust (2008) *Doing Time: The Experiences and Needs of Older People in Prison.* London: Prison Reform Trust.

Prison Reform Trust (2015) *Bromley Briefings: Prison Factfile.* London: Prison Reform Trust.

Prison Reform Trust (2016) *Bromley Briefings: Prison Factfile.* London: Prison Reform Trust.

van Wormer, K. (2011) 'Female Prison Families: How are they Dysfunctional?' *International Journal of Comparative and Applied Criminal Justice* 11(1–2), 263.

Wahidin, A. (2004) *Older Women in the Criminal Justice System: Running Out of Time.* London: Jessica Kingsley.

Young, Baroness (2014) *The Young Review: Improving Outcomes for Young Black and/or Muslim Men in the Criminal Justice System.* London: Black Training and Enterprise Group (BTEG).

Cases

Dickson v UK App. No. 44362/04 (4 December 2007)
Papon v France App. No. 64666/01 (7 June 2001)
R(P) v Secretary of State for the Home Department [2002] *EWHC* 1018 (Admin)
Wainwright v UK App. No. 12350/04 (26 September 2006)

Part 3

Relationships in old age

Chapter 10

Ageing, love and family law

Jonathan Herring

Introduction

This chapter looks at how older people understand their family and intimate lives. It seeks to explore what kind of issues are important to them and what role, if any, family law might play. I will start by looking at the nature of identity in old age and what the experience of old age tells us about personal identity and hence the values that should underpin family law. Second, I will explore the role of relationships in old age, which reveals aspects of relationships which tend to get overlooked in family law writing. Third, I will explore issues around sex and sexiness in old age. I believe that looking at family life in old age in these ways opens up a new vista for the nature of family law for generally.

Old age and identity

I confess to sometimes finding it difficult to remember exactly how old I am.[1] Nor am I quite sure what age category I fit into. I would say I am middle aged, but that is a blurry concept and according to some definitions I'm not.[2] Certainly, if I was asked to describe myself I doubt I would make any reference to my age. But, at the ends of the age spectrum these matters are more fixed. Children know how old they are and the lines between toddler, child, tweenager, teenager, and young person are relatively well defined. Children attach significance, even pride, to these changes. For them, age is an aspect of identity (Weiss and Lang 2012a). So too, although in complex ways, is age part of self-definition for older people. In complex ways because, as we shall see, old age is commonly portrayed as something that should be fought against and rejected. Successful old age is about not being old. Hence, the common comment, 'I don't feel as old as I am' (Uotinen et al 2006). This view of old age, being a battle against being old, is one which will be rejected in this chapter. But, first, I will explain that popular conception.

Ageism and aged identity

Simon Biggs (2004, 46) has convincingly claimed that we live in a 'climate of considerable cultural confusion' on old age. Extended life expectancy and improved healthcare means that people no longer expect to survive only a few years of retirement before death. Yet, the portrayal of old age as a time of ill-health, dependency, and frailty prevails. David Weiss and Frieder Lang (2012) claim 'older adults are often perceived as being senile, incompetent, and unattractive. Consequently, older adults may feel that they are socially devalued'. Angie Williams and Jon Nussbaum (2001) refer to a large number of studies finding that younger adults talk to older people in a way which assumes failing physical and cognitive capabilities. Of course, it would be wrong to think that the stereotypes of old age are entirely negative. Warmth, friendliness, and being willing to help might be associated with old age (Diehl, Owen and Youngblade, 2004). Nevertheless, even these are often associated with vulnerability and weakness, and so slightly presented as 'double edged' positives: friendly, but gullible, for example.

These negative beliefs about old age are the cornerstone of ageism. Ageism is commonly presented as a set of negative assumptions about people, based on their age. Robert Butler (1995) claims that ageism is manifested though:

> stereotypes and myths, outright disdain and dislike, or simply subtle avoidance of contact; discriminatory practices in housing, employment and services of all kinds; epithets, cartoons and jokes. At times ageism becomes an expedient method by which society promotes viewpoints about the aged in order to relieve itself from the responsibility towards them, and at other times ageism serves a highly personal objective, protecting younger (usually middle-aged) individuals – often at high emotional cost – from thinking about things they fear (aging, illness and death).

It must be added that when considering ageism, it is important to appreciate its intersection (Ward and Bytheway 2008) with sex, race (Walker and Northmore 2006) sexual orientation (Kimmel, Rose and David 2006; Heaphy, Yip and Thompson 2004), disability (Sargenat 2005) and other forms of oppressive power within society (Squire 2008). For example, it is often reported that a woman's attractiveness is judged against an extremely youthful ideal (Sontag 1978). While men are commonly said to be capable of being attractive even while showing signs of ageing, a woman's attractiveness requires removal of visible signs of ageing (Binstock, Fishman and Johnson 2006). Older women report being invisible and irrelevant (Hofmeier et al 2016). Indeed, it is notable that people throughout their adult lives report anxiety about the ageing of their bodies (Sargent-Cox, Rippon and Burns 2014, 201). Ageism, therefore, impacts not just older people, but younger people fearing the ageing process.

One notable manifestation of ageism is the widespread marketing of and use of cosmetic surgery or beauty treatments, aimed at older people (Fernand 2008). Jill Chonody and Barbra Teater (2016) report that from 2003 to 2013 there has been a five-fold increase in the 'anti-aging treatment' industry, with 90% of these performed on women. Newspapers repeatedly run articles on how a particular celebrity looks young or old for their age. The *Daily Mail* recently had a headline: 'Would YOU dare ask a computer how old you look? Eight brave women try out the terrifyingly simple new internet craze' (Ley 2016). The bravery, presumably, is because you are told you look (to the computer!) older than you really are. Notably 'looking one's age' is rarely seen as a complement.

Clash of outer and inner: masks and masquerades

Many gerontologists explain that the ageist attitudes just described lead to an uneasy tension for older people. They do not recognise the description of old age being a time of loss of capacity and physical frailty and do not want to adopt the role that is expected for older people. They therefore seek to deny that they belong to the group older people, or at least disguise the fact the do. Interestingly, the description of old age is accepted, as it is 'natural, and thus beyond dispute' (Calasanti and Slevin 2006, 18). It is just that the older person does not accept it for themselves (Hummert et al 1994). They do not 'feel old'. Mike Hepworth positions this contradiction in terms of inner youthfulness and bodily age:

> At the heart of the difficulty of explaining what it's like to be old lies the awareness of an experiential difference between the physical processes of ageing, as reflected in outward appearance, and the inner or subjective 'real self'.
>
> (1991, 93)

In the literature it is suggested that the standard response to the tension between the 'youthful self' in the 'ageing body' is the use of masks or masquerades, whereby the older person seeks to take on the appearance of a younger person and so escape the negative stereotypes associated with age (Featherstone and Hepworth 1989). These masks can range from cosmetic surgery to styles of dress, speech, or behaviour. It can also include socialising with younger people in order to seek identification with them. Indeed, a substantial market in services is now available offering a range of products, procedures and life style options which enable a 'youthful' old age. Simon Biggs (1997) separates the use of masks and the concept of masquerade, where you act out the role of the younger person. The image of the mask presents the 'real old person' hiding behind a youthful presentation; while in the masquerade the older person is seeking to be accepted as younger. Biggs (1997) writes that the way 'we "story" or "perform" our way through structure and experience helps us to understand relations between generations and between genders'.

This idea of seeking to disguise age is particularly relevant for older women. Martha Holstein (2006) argues:

> If we older women fail to care for our bodies so that we can meet normative expectations to age 'successfully,' we may be viewed askance – at the simplest level for 'letting ourselves go' when 'control' is putatively within our grasp – and, more problematically, as moral failures for being complicit in our own

> aging. We lose our cultural relevance. The belief in the possibility for, and moral obligation to, control and also contribute to delegitimating old age as the foundation for policy responses. If old age can be just like middle age – if only we had behaved differently – why should public policy single out the old for political attention.

The impact of ageing on masculinities raises interesting issues too:

> The men pictured in the anti-aging advertisements drive themselves into expensive and strenuous fun, translating the achievement orientation of the labor market into those of recreational consumption. Banned from the competition for salaries and promotions, they struggle for status by spending the wealth and strength they have to play as young men do in their attempts to appear as vigorous as possible.
>
> (Calasanti and Slevin 2006, 4)

These understandings conceive of 'the social world as a source of attack either through pressure to conform or as the site of actively hostile attitudes toward mature identity' (Biggs 1997).

While this presentation of old age as a youthful self, trapped inside an ageing mask, is widespread in the academic literature and the popular press, it is one I wish to challenge in two ways. First, it devalues the bodily and relational nature of the self. Second, it implies the 'ageist assumptions' are false, where I will, perhaps shockingly, argue they are true.

The relational and bodily self

I reject the argument that we should understand older people as using a mask or masquerade behind which the real youthful self hides because it downplays the relational and bodily nature of the self. As Julia Twigg (2009) suggests it reinforces a Cartesian split of body and mind. It appears to reflect an assumption that there is a 'real self', a youthful self, which is independent from the actual body. The body becomes the enemy as it is danger of forcing the mask to slip or the masquerade to become a farce. This Cartesian split is widely rejected in modern thought. Nowadays it is generally acknowledged that the self and the body are closely entwined and it makes no sense to think of a self independently from the body. To argue that there is a 'youthful self trapped beneath an ageing mask' (Biggs 1997, 566) is a manifestation of the attitude Simone de Beauvoir (1970) identified: 'that will never happen to us – when that happens it will no longer be ourselves that it happens to'. The real us will remain young. It is our bodies that will age and we can use masks to disguise us. Yet, the truth is that our identity and our bodies are intertwined.

The image of the youthful self hiding behind a mask also promotes a highly individualised concept of the self: one where the true inner self exists and then one presents a different self to the outside worlds and one's relationship with others. I would argue that, in fact, one's identity comes from one's relationships and interactions with others (Foster and Herring 2017). That is that the self is inevitably relational and social. As Settersten (2015) puts it:

> We organize our lives around other people and ask them to organize their lives around us. Individual lives are often at odds, and friction must be resolved if relationships are to be maintained. Big life course decisions are generally made jointly, not singly. Relationships enter into decisions and affect opportunities related to where to go to school, where to live, with whom to partner and parent, what kind of work to take, hours and years worked, when to have children, how many to have, how they are spaced, and the like. These are often carefully negotiated – and compromised – within the context of relationships.

With this understanding it is clear that seeing ageism as a challenge to identity which needs to be resisted underplays the impact of ageism. Ageism is a more powerful force than that because it infects relationships and interactions with others and thereby challenges the very self.

Even our understanding of age is relational. As Martha Holstein (2006) puts it:

> We understand our experiences relative to others: We compare ourselves to other people our age. To where our parents were when they were our age. To how old we will be when we experience something we expect in the future. To how long we will have been together, or how much time we will have left.

We cannot, therefore separate out the real us from the us as we are treated as and related to. There is no self that can exist outside the relational and social context we live in. Clearly much more needs to be said and such a claim needs far more substantial justification than I can give it here (see Foster and Herring 2017).

An interesting manifestation of this point found noted by Weiss and Lang (2012b) who found that the negative stereotypes appear associated with chronological age, rather than generational identity. When people were asked about their generation (a war-time baby; a child of the sixties etc.) people spoke in far more positive terms than when they were asked about people in relation to age (e.g. people in their 80s). This demonstrates particularly powerfully that it is the assumptions tied to a particular age, rather than the mere fact of age which is significant. One important reason for this is that the identification with a generation is communal. You are defined in relation to a group, rather than the stereotypes of old age which focuses on individualised characteristics.

Combatting ageism

As was said earlier, much has been written of the negative images of old age. The glorification of youth means than old age is seen as a loss of all that is good, particularly in terms of bodily functioning (Cruikshank 2009). Butler (1995) regarded ageism as a by-product of a fear of ageing and creating a barrier between the desirable young and the less desirable old. Old age was seen as carrying stigma. Hence, we have a substantial literature on the concept of a successful ageing, which is centred around the themes of activity, autonomy, and lifestyle. The aim being to live the kind of life we might, but for the burdens of work, have live in middle age. As Toni Calasanti and Neal King have succinctly put it:

> Successful aging means not aging and not being old because our constructions of old age contain no positive content.
>
> (2005, 7)

Simone de Beauvoir (1970) writes:

> When we look at the image of our own future provided by the old we do not believe it: an absurd inner voice whispers that that will never happen to us – when that happens it will no longer be ourselves that it happens to.

A standard response to ageism is, therefore, to deny that old age means a loss of youth; to claim that older people are capable of being as autonomous, capacitous, and independent as younger people; and to promote a 'youthful' old age. That response is, I suggest, misconceived.

The stereotypes of old age: mental and physical frailty; dependence on others; gullibility; and terror of loneliness are the reality we all face and cope with throughout our lives. I suggest we are all, regardless of age presenting an image of good physical and mental health; emotional security; sound judgement; controlled bodies. It is, ironically, only in old age that the stereotypes match the reality. Yet by then we have been hiding and denying that reality for too long. I suggest therefore, not that we need to change the stereotypes of old age, so much as change our stereotypes of middle age and youth.

We need, then, to recognise the vulnerability and dependence that is the essence of human nature. It is not that in old age we enter a time of incapacity and need for care; but rather that has always been then there, just better disguised by the provision of social service and a wide range of social structures.

As Betty Friedan puts it:

> … Seeing age only as decline from youth, we make age itself the problem – and never face the real problems that keep us from evolving and leading continually useful, vital, and productive lives. Accepting that dire mystique of age for others, even as we deny it for ourselves, we ultimately create or reinforce the conditions of our own dependence, powerlessness, isolation, even senility.
>
> (1993, 25–6)

Indeed, it may be that this explains why despite the popular perception, in fact sociologists have found that old age tends to bring with it increases in well-being (Ryff, Singer and Love 2004). Interestingly the popular perception of middle age as being the prime of life is not reflected by many studies finding those aged around 40 as being at the bottom of a U shaped curve of assessments of well-being (Blanchflower and Oswald 2004). Many psychologists have sought to explain the increase in old age well-being in terms of older people having better coping mechanisms than younger people, rather than seeing any positives in old age (Diener and Suh 1997' Laslett 1989). That explanation is itself revealing because it assumes that old age brings with it negatives, with which people need to cope. Perhaps the comfort of old age is that the need to pretend is less.

Relationships in old age

I move on to explore the role relationships have in old age. When looking at the significance of marriage or long-term relationships, it is interesting to note what is often cited as at the heart of marriage: the potential to create children; the creation of a stable environment for raising of children; and the formalisation of commitment are commonly cited (Herring 2017). These matters may be important for younger married couples but a study of long-term relationships in old age reveal other benefits, that tend to get overlooked when considering what marriage is for.

As Settersten (2015) suggests 'When relationships have long duration, we experience each other at new ages and in new life periods. There are no clear scripts for how relationships are supposed to look or feel'. Hollywood romances typically end with the couple driving off into the sunset after the wedding. They have arrived, we are told, but there are few films on couples who have been married a long time and those tend to paint stale relationships, certainly not fulfilling ones (for a rare exception see Haneke 2012). What, exactly, once you have found the love of your life, are you meant to do with them?!

As described earlier, old age can be a disturbing experience. People reject the assumptions others make about them and feel the real self is being betrayed by the older body. Older people can be excluded from social spaces and provision. The glorification of youth can lead to alienation and loneliness. This can be exacerbated by a loss of contemporaries. Bernice Neugarten (1995) talks of the 'costs of survivorship' and a 'thinned social landscape'. A particular loss can be that:

> We lose people with whom we shared many experiences, who are central to our identities, and who are no longer there to validate – or to question – our memories or accounts. This kind of identity loss also occurs with the death of older generations, as we are pushed up the family ladder and, once at the top, become orphans in time.

For those whose long-term relationships survive into old age these can provide a central role to identity. As Settersten (2015) puts it:

> All of life's ups and downs, and its major milestones, involve or are shared alongside other people – whether with individuals, in small groups, or in

whole communities. The experiences of others become ours, and ours theirs. Relationships are subject to social expectations and judgments, rituals and memory, reinforcements and punishments; they can ensure life's vitality or destroy it.

Jan Baars sees an important part of ageing being the telling of stories. She explains its significance:

> We can live and tell others about our experiences and actions. And to record a narrative or to write it down is also a possible enrichment: the narrative becomes accessible outside the small circle of those who are directly present and opens, invites and facilitates opportunities to interpret the meanings of the text. Narrative brings experience to language, into the world of others.
>
> (2012, 155)

In particular, through our stories with others we can appreciate who we are in terms of a continuity. We are a story. We have changed and changed over time. Who we are not just who will be. Atchley explains the essence of continuity theory:

> Continuity theory is evolutionary. It assumes that the patterns of ideas and skills, which people use to adapt and act, develop and persist over time; that a course of developmental direction can usually be identified; and that the individual's orientation is not to remain personally unchanged but rather consistent with the individual's past …
>
> (1993, 5–6)

This understanding of the self emphasises that the self is a process and that we develop in terms of who we are and what our values are. As Featherstone and Hepworth (1989, 143) put it 'the previous life of the old people … acts as a background and context for their expectations and experience of old age'. This emphasises an important role for relationships: they enable the narrative of the continuity of the self to be told. To share the stories and make sense of them with one who has journeyed with you is something precious and good. This important role is often overlooked in discussions of family life. Perhaps in part because in youth the story is seen as primarily lying in the future. Time is spent planning for the future and investing for activities to come, in old age the focus can in longer term relationships involve both a looking back and looking forward.

Hagestad and Settersten (2017) capture these points well:

> We see personal meaning as interpersonal. A sense of self is created and maintained through social mirrors, in webs of interdependent lives that span family generations and historical time. As societies change, so do socially constructed meanings. Consequently, the older individuals get, the more likely it is that they have core meanings that are not shared by many people around them, and they

> have few witnesses who know where they have been. To some extent, then, they become strangers to other people and even to themselves.

It is here that partners, friends, and families can play a crucial role. They help maintain the self in its historical place. They use a language which can be used to self-define in the past, but in a way which may be little understood by those of a different generation. De Beauvoir (1970: 283) writes that 'old age is particularly difficult to assume because we have always regarded it as something alien, a foreign species'. Having relationships which know us as we were as well as we are is an important part of overcoming that alienation.

This means that relationships in old age can have a very particular value. But it is not limited to giving context (Hagestad and Settersten 2017). Knowledge that life will end in the foreseeable future can give life a sense of urgency and piquancy. That can give old age relationships a particular flavour:

> That is, the temporary and fleeting state of our lives and relationships is what bringsmeaning. Time is precious because it is limited. In anticipating our own ends, we may get more strategic about the relationships in which we invest. Knowing that a relationship is time bound might affect what or how much we put into it – whether we give it our all while we have it, or whether we hold back from it knowing it will leave us. Encounters with life threatening illnesses may leave us acutely aware that a relationship is running out of time, or death may take it away before we were ready.
>
> (Hagestad and Settersten 2017)

The possibility of death terminating the relationship, while always true, is particularly pertinent: As Torbjörn Bildtgård and Peter Öberg (2017) put it:

> The certainty of death is a challenge to the individual to live life deliberately. One way of putting this might be that time wasted on inauthentic existence (not acknowledging the meaning of one's existence) cannot be regained.

They note that older people can have an acute awareness that although in one sense they have more time (the children have left home; employment responsibilities are over, or greatly reduced) but in another they have less time. It can be seen as a luxury of having time with a loved one. They report one married women saying:

> Love is amazing, but I don't think that you can experience it before you reach our age. I really don't think so. Not this intensively and close. Because there is really nothing that gets in the way. You don't need to work, you don't need to get up in the morning. You have no kids, no parent–teacher conferences to attend. There are so many things that you have to do in life, and now that you have done them and can enjoy retirement, it's just wonderful!
>
> (Bildtgård and Öberg 2017)

That quote should stop and make us think and not just to think how lucky she is. What is it about contemporary life that is preventing this kind of love?

Sex and old age

There has been a considerable amount of work in recent years on sexual relationships in old age. There is increased awareness of sexual satisfaction in old age. As John Williams (2015) writes, in the past sexuality was:

> believed to decline and eventually disappear as part of ageing. Alternatively, any sexual activity by an older person is considered unnatural and distasteful conjuring up images of the 'dirty old man'. Older people are either 'asexual or hypersexual'.

No one writing in the field would suggest that now. I suggest two observations on our increased understanding on sex in old age.

First, it is notable how many older people talk in positive terms about sexual relationships in old age. However, this is not in terms of the kind of values which are all too commonly used to assess the success of sex: prevalence; range of activities; passion; energy. Rather the attributes of tenderness, intimacy, and comfort are emphasised. Much is made of the importance of cuddles and touch; of simply being physically intimate (Potts et al 2006). The fact there is less penetrative sex does not mean it is of lower quality. Potts et al (2006) claim that:

> The experience of ageing (and of erectile changes) may give some men opportunities to experiment with alternative sexual lifestyles. Men who take advantage of these opportunities often report that sex in mid-to-later life does not change in quality for the worse, and in fact they are 'doing more of the kind of sex they want. They are more considerate to women; they are more competent at giving pleasure'

Second, and in distinction to this, there is the weight of attention placed on medical interventions designed to improved 'sexual performance': particularly Viagra. The marketing and public discussions of Viagra commonly present erectile difficulties in terms of a decline or loss, which can be overcome with medical intervention (Potts et al 2006). It suggests that 'proper' youthful sexual behaviour can be restored. Viagra is said to ensure that there is adequate 'sexual performance' and sex lives are 'strengthened'. All of this is predicated on an assumption that sexual penetration with a firm and enduring erection is required for a successful sex life. There is much that can be written about the heterosexist and patriarchal assumptions here. These are similar to assumptions that underpin the law on consummation, which I have critiqued elsewhere (Herring 2017). Yet, as already indicated although erectile dysfunction is portrayed as a major problem and source of anxiety for men and their partners is not clear how much that is simply a pressure created by marketing (Tiefer 2004; McHugh and Chrisler 2015). Katz and Marshall (2003, 8) argue that 'the commercial successes of pharmaceutical and mechanical remedies for sexual dysfunction rest on a recent cultural-scientific conviction that lifelong sexual function is a primary component of achieving successful aging in general'. Linn Sandberg (2013) writes:

> Although men in my study narrated how erectile changes and sometimes loss of erectile function altogether were experienced as distressful and as a hardship, few of them expressed straightforward wishes to regain their former sexual function or the sexual practices they had engaged in earlier life. Instead, many seemed to hold highly negotiated positions vis-à-vis their changing bodies, not only when it came to erectile function but to bodily changes overall. Particularly, one narrative was highly salient, and participants repeatedly used it to make sense of their later-life sexual subjectivities: that of the significance of intimacy and touch. When the men's bodies changed due to ageing, and not only in terms of erectile function, several men in my study narrated a (re)discovery of other body parts, practices and pleasures.

Third, I suspect one reason why researchers assumed that older people did not have sex was that older bodies were seen as unsexy: greying; wrinkling and saggy; the body in decay (Chonody and Teater 2016). One older woman said:

> I am ashamed of my aging body and ashamed that I am ashamed. I believe women pay an enormous price for cultural biases related to gender and age.
>
> (quoted Hofmeier 2016)

This assumption of the unsexiness of the ageing body reflects an utterly false image of the body as being constrained, controlled, and owned. The body that droops and spills challenges this, but the image of the leaky body is a far more accurate representation of all bodies. Linn Sandberg (2013) writes:

> At the very heart of this discourse on old age as negation is the ageing body as unbounded, leaky, fragmented and lacking control. The ageing body has consequently been discussed as a threatening disruption to identity and self.

In fact, the contrast between the firm youthful body and the wrinkled older body is a false contrast. There is an irony that those characteristics are in fact reflected in what is commonly portrayed as the heart of man's power: the wrinkly, saggy penis and scrotum. Maybe, here in the male imagination the older body ridicules phallocentricism and so generates hatred.

It is not surprising that among older people their bodies are sites of negotiation of multiple and contrasting meanings, including loss, pleasure and desire (Thorpe et al 2015). Most believed that long-term partners regarded them with love and affection regardless of appearance and they attached importance to their partners' perceptions (Montemurro and Gillen 2013). Sandberg (2013) writes of Gustav who developed male breasts following medical treatment, but this opened up for him new ways of appreciating this body and interactions:

> What is initially experienced as a loss of manhood subsequently becomes an opening a new way of experiencing a pair of soft and spongy male breasts. Gustav's story is interesting in how it presents the agency and capacities of ageing bodies to shape new subjectivities and experiences of pleasure. But it is also interesting in how it opens up for ways of rethinking masculinity. Gustav does not start to experience himself as a woman; rather, the categories of man/woman, femininity/masculinity become obsolete – what matters concerning the ageing body is its capacity to produce pleasure.

Conclusion

This chapter has explored the nature of identity in old age and the role of family life in that in order to open up new understanding about the nature of families and the proper scope of family law. I have highlighted three points. First, the popular image of the 'older self' disguising its identity behind a 'youthful mask' provides too individualised an understanding of the self and fails to appreciate the way that relationships with other constitute the self. This makes the ageist assumptions about people all the more serious because not only do they become forces against which the self must battle, they impact on the very nature itself. They create the older person. This has broader messages for family law because it highlights the very serious harm of abusive relationships: they are not just challenges which the self must be shielded from they are attack on the very self.

Second, I have argued that the ageist assumptions that older people lack capacity, are frail and vulnerable, are in fact perfectly true. The lie is the assumption that younger people do not equally share these characteristics. Societal responses to old age make more visible characteristics of the human nature which have always been there: that we are vulnerable, interdependent selves. The problems with ageism are not that they make false assumptions about old age, but they make false claims about youth. Family law, needs then to be based on a model which prioritises not the values of autonomy, individualised rights, and independence but rather relationships, care, and mutuality.

Third this chapter has explored the role of relationships in old age. It has sought to highlight the role that relationships can play in providing a narrative shape for lives and a common language which can play a key role in identity.

Finally, the chapter has looked at sex and sexiness in old age. It has explored how academic and medical discourses have reflected some of the heterosexist and masculinist assumptions about the nature and role of sex that can be found in other areas of family law, such as the requirement for consummation of marriage.

Notes

1 At the time of writing I am 48.
2 The Oxford English Dictionary cites 45–60 being middle aged. But a survey of the British general public suggests that they believe middle age starts at 55 (BBC 2012).

Bibliography

Atchley, R. (1993) 'Continuity Theory and the Evolution of Activity in Later Adulthood' in J. Kelly (ed.) *Activity and Aging: Staying Involved in Later Life*. London: Sage.

Baars, J. (2012) 'Critical Turns in Age, Narrative and Time' *International Journal of Ageing and Later Life* 7, 143.

British Broadcasting Corporation (BBC) (2012) 'Middle age begins at 55 years, survey suggests'. Available at: www.bbc.co.uk/news/education-19622330

Biggs, S. (1997) 'Choosing Not To Be Old? Masks, Bodies and Identity Management in Later Life' *Ageing and Society* 17, 553.

Biggs, S. (2004) 'Age, Gender, Narratives, and Masquerades' *Journal of Ageing Studies* 18, 45.

Bildtgård, T. and Öberg, P. (2017) 'New Intimate Relationships in Later Life: Consequences for the Social and Filial Network?' *Journal of Family Issues* 38, 381.

Binstock, R., Fishman, J. and Johnson, T. (2006) 'Anti-Aging, Medicine and Science' in R. Binstock and L. George (eds) *Handbook of Aging and the Social Sciences*. Cambridge, MA: Academic Press.

Blanchflower, D. and Oswald, A. (2004) 'Well-Being Over Time in Britain and the USA' *Journal of Public Economics* 88, 1356.

Butler, R. (1995) 'Ageism' in G. Maddox (ed.) *The Encyclopaedia of Aging*. Dordrecht: Springer.

Calasanti, T. and King, N. (2005) 'Firming the Floppy Penis: Class and Gender Relations in the Lives of Old Men' *Men and Masculinities* 8(1), 3.

Calasanti, T. and Slevin, K. (eds) (2006) *Age Matters*. Abingdon: Routledge.

Chonody, J. and Teater, B. (2016) 'Why do I Dread Looking Old?: A Test of Social Identity Theory, Terror Management Theory, and the Double Standard of Aging' *Journal of Women & Aging* 28, 112.

Cruikshank, M. (2009) *Learning to be Old: Gender, Culture, and Aging*, 2nd edn. Lanham, MD: Rowman & Littlefield.

de Beauvoir, S. (1970) *Old Age*. London: Penguin.

Diehl, M., Owen, S. and Youngblade, L. (2004) 'Agency and Communion Attributes in Adults' Spontaneous Self-Representations' *International Journal of Behavioral Development* 28, 1.

Diener, E. and Suh, E. (1997) 'Subjective Well-Being and Age. An International Perspective' *Annual Review of Gerontology and Geriatrics* 17, 304.

Featherstone, M. and Hepworth, M. (1989) 'Ageing and Old Age: Reflections on the Postmodern Life Course' in B. Bytheway, T. Keil, P. Allatt and A. Bryman (eds) *Becoming and Being Old: Sociological Approaches to Later Life*. London: Sage.

Fernand, D. (2008) 'Women Who Date Younger Men'. *Sunday Times*, 18 May.

Foster, C. and Herring, J. (2017) *Identity, Personhood and the Law*. Dordrecht: Springer.

Friedan, B. (1993) *The Fountain of Age*. London: Jonathan Cape.

Hagestad, G. and Settersten, R. (2017) 'Aging: It's Interpersonal! Reflections From Two Life Course Migrants' *Gerontologist* 57, 136.

Haneke, M. (2012) *Amour.*

Heaphy, B., Yip, A. and Thompson, D. (2004) 'Ageing in a Non-Heterosexual Context' *Ageing and Society* 24, 881.

Hepworth, M. (1991) 'Positive Ageing and the Mask of Age' *Journal of Educational Gerontology* 6, 93.

Herring, J. (2017) 'Why Marriage Needs to be Less Sexy' in J. Miles, P. Mody and R. Probert (eds) *Marriage Rites and Rights.* Oxford: Hart.

Hofmeier, S., Runfola, C., Sala, M., Gagne, D., Bronley, K. and Bulik, C. (2016) 'Body Image, Aging, and Identity in Women over 50' *Journal of Women and Aging* 29, 3.

Holstein, M. (2006) 'On Being an Aging Woman' in T. Calasanti and K. Slevin (eds) *Age Matters.* Abingdon: Routledge.

Hummert, M., Garstka, T., Shaner, J. and Strahm, S. (1994) 'Stereotypes of the Elderly Held by Young, Middle-aged, and Elderly Adults' *Journal of Gerontology* 49, 240.

Katz, S. and Marshall, B. (2003) 'New Sex for Old: Lifestyle, Consumerism, and the Ethics of Aging Well' *Journal of Ageing Studies* 17, 3.

Kimmel, D., Rose, T. and David, S. (2006) *Lesbian, Gay, Bisexual, and Transgender Aging.* New York: Columbia University Press.

Laslett, P. (1989) *A Fresh Map of Life.* London: Macmillan.

Ley, R. (2016) 'Would YOU dare ask a computer how old you look? Eight brave women try out the terrifyingly simple new internet craze'. *Daily Mail,* 24 October. Available at: www.dailymail.co.uk/femail/article-3868712/Would-dare-ask-computer-old-look-Eight-brave-women-try-terrifyingly-simple-new-internet-craze.html

McHugh, M. and Chrisler, J. (2015) *The Wrong Prescription for Women.* Westport, CT: Praeger.

Montemurro, B. and Gillen, M. M. (2013) 'Wrinkles and Sagging Flesh: Exploring Transformations in Women's Sexual Body Image' *Journal of Women and Aging* 25, 3.

Neugarten, B. L. (1995) 'The Costs of Survivorship' *Center on Aging Newsletter* 11, 1.

Potts, A., Grace, B., Vares, T. and Gavey, N. (2006) '"Sex for Life"? Men's Counter-Stories on "Erectile Dysfunction", Male Sexuality and Ageing' *Sociology of Health & Illness* 28, 306.

Ryff, C., Singer, B. and Love, G. (2004) 'Positive Health: Connecting Well-being with Biology' *Philosophical Transactions, Royal Society* 259, 1383.

Sandberg, L. (2013) 'Affirmative Old Age: the Ageing Body and Feminist Theories on Difference' *International Journal of Ageing and Later Life* 8, 11.

Sargenat, M. (2005) 'Disability and Age – Multiple Potential for Discrimination' *International Journal of the Sociology of Law* 33, 17.

Sargent-Cox, K., Rippon, M. and Burns, R. (2014) 'Measuring Anxiety About Aging across the Adult Lifespan' *International Psychogeriatrics* 26, 135.

Settersten, R. (2015) 'Relationships in Time and the Life Course: The Significance of Linked Lives' *Research in Human Development* 12, 217.

Sontag, S. (1978) 'The Double Standard of Ageing' in V. Carver and P. Liddiard (eds) *An Ageing Population.* Sevenoaks: Open University Press.

Squire, J. (2008) 'Intersecting Inequalities: Reflecting on the Subjects and Objects of Equality' *Political Quarterly* 79, 53.

Thorpe, R., Fileborn, B., Hawkes, G., Pitts, M. and Minichiello, V. (2015) 'Old and Desirable: Older Women's Accounts of Ageing Bodies in Intimate Relationships' *Sexual and Relationship Therapy* 30(1), 156.

Tiefer, L. (2004) *Sex is not a Natural Act.* Boulder, CO: Westview Press.

Twigg, J. (2009) 'Clothing, Identity and the Embodiment of Age' in J. Powell and T. Gilbert (eds) *Aging and Identity: A Postmodern Dialogue*. New York: Nova Science Publishers.

Uotinen, V., Rantanen, T., Suutama, T., and Ruoppila, I. (2006) 'Change in Subjective Age among Older People over an Eight-year Follow-up: "Getting Older and Feeling Younger"?' *Experimental Ageing Research* 32, 381.

Walker, A. and Northmore, S. (eds) (2006) *Growing Older in a Black and Minority Ethnic Group*. London: Age Concern.

Ward, R. and Bytheway, B. (2008) *Researching Age and Multiple Discrimination*. London: Central Books.

Weiss, D. and Lang, F. (2012a) '"They" Are Old But "I" Feel Younger: Age-Group Dissociation as a Self-Protective Strategy in Old Age' *Psychology and Ageing* 27, 153.

Weiss, D. and Lang, F. (2012b) 'The Two Faces of Age Identity' *Journal of Gerontopsychology and Geriatric Psychiatry* 25, 5.

Williams, A. and Nussbaum, J. (2001) *Intergenerational Communication Across the Life Span*. Mahwah, NJ: Lawrence Erlbaum.

Williams, J. (2015) 'Intimate Relationships between Older People in Institutional Settings: Ageism, Protection or Fear?' *Ethics, Medicine and Public Health* 1, 194.

Chapter 11

Which ageing 'families' count?

Older lesbian, gay, bisexual, trans* and/or queer (LGBT*Q) – relational legal in/exclusions in (older age) family law

Sue Westwood

Introduction

There has been extensive recent discourse and debate about the socio-legal construction of lesbian, gay, bisexual, trans*,[1] and/or queer (LGBT*Q) families in relation to parenting and partnership recognition (Harding 2011; Barker and Monk 2015a). Indeed, it has been argued that term 'family' itself tends to reinforce heteronormative notions of biological kinship (Barker 2006; Barker 2012), thereby excluding more diverse non-normative kinship constellations, including 'families of choice' 'chosen family' and/or 'families of friends' (Roseneil and Budgeon 2004). However there has been far less attention given to *ageing* lesbian, gay, bisexual, trans*, and/or queer (LGBT*Q) family forms. Many older LGBT*Q 'families' include a wide range of relationships, involving constellations of biological family, friends, lovers, ex-lovers, partners, ex-partners, and various connections with children via those relationships (Cook-Daniels 2006; Almack et al 2010; Croghan, Moone and Olson 2014; Traies 2015; Westwood 2016). Yet family law has so far paid little attention to these diverse relationships.

This inattention is located within the wider exclusion of friendship (Leib 2007; Rosenbury 2007; Gelzinis 2011) and non-familial caring relationships (Sloan 2012) in law:

> Despite calls for increased legal recognition of diverse families, few scholars have considered whether family law should recognize care provided outside of the home, and no scholar has considered whether family law should recognize the care provided and received by friends.
>
> (Rosenbury 2007, 189)

This chapter interrogate law's normativity with regard to ageing 'families' (see also Herring, this collection). I argue that law has failed to keep up with changing 'family' forms, specifically close friendships. I locate my arguments in relation to law and older people in the United Kingdom (UK) and propose increased recognition of non-normative families in general and close friendships in particular in order to redress legal exclusions and inequalities in later life.

Law and the family in older age

Traditionally, critiques of family law have tended to focus on parenting issues and intimate partnership recognition, primarily orientated towards younger adults couple formation (Diduck and O'Donovan 2006). Only more recently has family law begun to be recognised as also interacting with the domain of older age (Herring 2016). Indeed. it could be argued that in later life family law is more salient than at any other part of the lifecourse. In later life, incapacity, morbidity, and mortality trigger important issues which invoke issues of family recognition. Incapacity necessitates the need for others to represent the views and wishes of the person with failing capacity. Morbidity prompts the need to make preparations for passing on one's estate. Mortality invokes a wide range of inheritance issues (see Monk, this collection).

As I have argued elsewhere (Westwood 2014; 2016), family law, particularly in relation to law and the older person, privileges the conjugal couple and biological/adopted family, and lacks legal mechanisms which enable recognition of other relationship forms. There is now a four-tier structure of relationship recognition in law relating to the older person (see Figure 11.1).

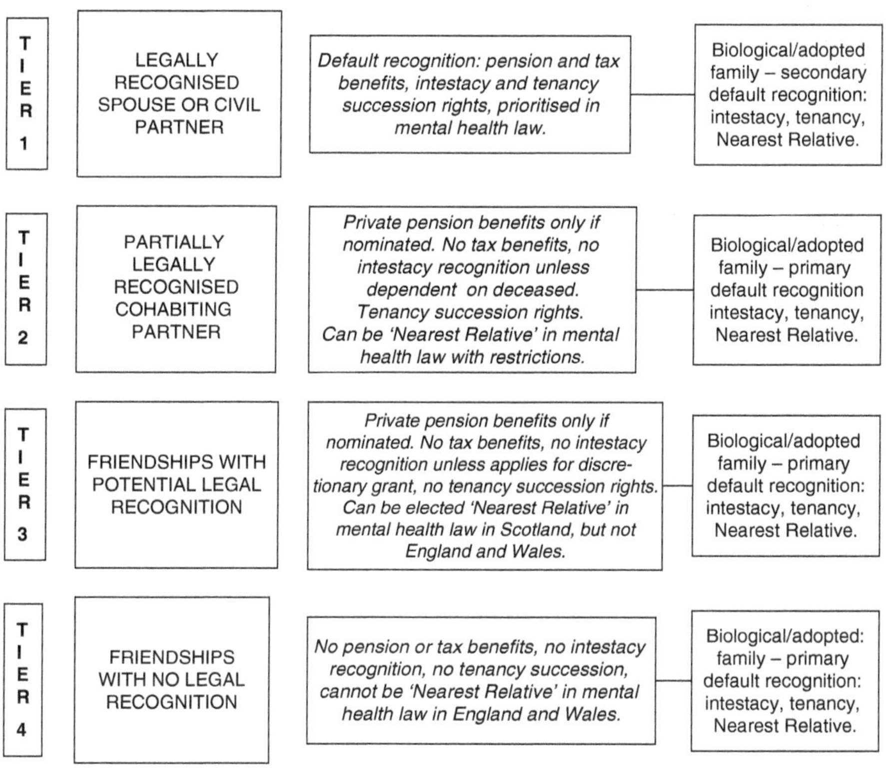

Figure 11.1 Four-tier relationship recognition in law and the older person in the United Kingdom (Westwood 2013 and 2016)

At the top, most privileged, tier is the formally legally recognised couple, which benefits from default recognition in relation to pension benefits,[2] tax benefits (in life[3] and in death[4]), intestacy[5] and succession tenancy rights.[6] At the next tier down is the partially legally recognised couple, i.e. cohabiting partners who have not had their relationship formally recognised in law (via civil partnership and marriage). Such relationships enjoy far fewer legal recognitions[7] particularly in relation to intestacy rules. At the same time, running in parallel to the privileging of the formal legal conjugal couple are enduring biological/filial family defaults in many areas of law, including intestacy law and tenancy rules (Westwood 2014). Moving further down the tier of relationship recognition is friendship. There is no formal default legal recognition for friends in terms of pensions, tax, inheritance etc. and only partial legal recognition for some friends in those circumstances where an older person can opt friends in, for example nominating them as beneficiaries in wills (Monk, this collection; Westwood 2015 and 2016).

When a person dies, their surviving friends have few rights as 'inheritance family' (Douglas et al 2011, 254) unless they have been made beneficiaries in a will (Monk 2016). Unlike partners, they enjoy: no pension rights (unless the deceased person has named them as beneficiaries in private pension schemes), no tax benefits while the deceased person was alive and no Inheritance Tax privileges once the person has died. They also have no tenancy claims. In England and Wales, when someone dies, tenancy succession rights to council and housing association tenancies is limited to spouses, civil partners, and 'family members' which comprise cohabiting partners, children, parents, siblings, and most other 'close relatives'. Friends are not included.

Friends also have few rights in terms of making claims upon the deceased person's estate. They are not recognised in intestacy rules.[8] They have also very limited options to make a claim under the Inheritance (Provision for Family and Dependants) Act 1975, which apply if they can show that the deceased person had assumed responsibility for their maintenance prior to death. Very often, when an older person is nearing the end of their lives, friends are providing that person with support, rather than the other way round (Coore, this collection). However, a relationship of support given to the now-deceased person, rather than support received from that person, is not automatically recognised in inheritance provisions (Anderson 2011), although a discretionary grant could be awarded by the Crown under application (The Treasury Solicitor 2008).

Incapacity is particularly relevant for older people, relating to a range of age-related conditions, not least of which is dementia, which is of particular concern to older LGBT*Q people (Westwood and Price 2016). In terms of incapacity law, an individual can delegate Powers of Attorney to anyone of their choosing,[9] as well as nominating others in Advance Directives and Advance Decision-Making,[10] and this includes friends. However, friends often experience a lesser status and influence with these powers, and/or as next of kin compared with biological/adopted family members, particularly in terms of end-of-life decision-making (Almack et al 2015; Marie Curie, 2016). Furthermore, while in Scotland, friends can be nominated as Nearest Relative under mental health legislation,[11] in England and Wales, they cannot.

In these various ways, then, friendship is marginalised/excluded in relation to law and the older person. Resources, recognition, and representation (Westwood 2016) in later life and upon death are directed towards the conjugal couple and biological/filial family members, privileging and reinforcing the normative recognition of these relationship forms (Auchmuty 2009). They are directed away from friendships and from informal care providers (Sloan 2012) including friendship carer. This reproduces and reinforces the cultural devaluation of care in society (Barnes 2012) and law (Herring 2013) and exacerbates the marginalisation and material/societal disadvantages experienced by friends and friendship carers (see also Pritchard-Jones, this collection).

Law and LGBT*Q 'families'

The past few decades have seen dramatic improvements in the UK in anti-discrimination rights for people with minority sexualities[12] and on the basis of gender identity[13] and in gender identity recognition rights[14] (Sharpe 2007). There has also been a seismic shift in the recognition of same-gender[15] relationships in terms of parenting (Harding 2011) and partnership recognition (Barker and Monk 2015b). In the UK, same-gender partners can now have their partnerships recognised via both civil partnership[16] and marriage.[17] Same-gender couples can also now adopt[18] and co-parent via IVF.[19] In the build up to these major landmarks, alongside those campaigning for these legal recognitions, were those who offered the counter-argument that they risked further marginalisation of other relationship forms (Barker 2006; Harding 2011; Barker 2012). The relationship networks of LGBT*Q people in particular comprise a complex, and variable mixed membership, including:

> Non-normative intimacies – between friends, non-monogamous lovers, ex-lovers, partners who do not live together, partners who do not have sex together, those which do not easily fit the 'friend'/'lover' binary classification system.
>
> (Roseneil and Budgeon 2004, 138)

Crucially, and often unrecognised, these significant relationships are a vital source of care and support (Hash and Mankowski 2017), particularly in later life. There is not as yet a word to describe such non-normative relationships (Almack, Seymour and Bellamy 2010). In my recent research on ageing, gender and sexuality, I coined the term SLIFs in an attempt to encompass them:

> I have chosen to deploy the acronym 'SLIFs' (Supportive and Loving Intimate Friendships) to describe them, not out of a wish to categorise in a reductionist sense, but for conceptual convenience and to aid comparison.
>
> (Westwood 2016, 16)

For those older LGBT*Q people who have experienced lifelong social exclusion, prejudice and discrimination, including from their biological families, SLIFs take on added significance, offering a crucial web of relationships which have acted as a buffer and source of resistance to stigmatisation and marginalisation and their consequences (Cook-Daniels 2006; DeVries and Megathlin 2009; Traies 2015). Older trans* people who have transitioned in later life often experience additional familial exclusion when they do so (Bailey 2012), making friends even more significant.

In later life SLIFs not only provide community and friendship but are also vital sources of practical, material, and emotional care and support provided by and for older LGBT*Q people (Witten 2009; Cronin et al 2011; Knauer 2016; Orel 2017). Yet such caring relationships often go unrecognised in law and society (Shiu, Muraco and Fredriksen-Goldsen 2016):

> Chosen family also lacks legal recognition. The default rules governing substituted decision making, guardianship, and inheritance still privilege the interests of relatives defined by blood, marriage, or adoption. Marriage equality has made it possible for LGBT older adults to marry their partners, but it does not in any way alter their legal relationship with other members of a chosen family … in the absence of advance planning documents, it remains likely that chosen family will be considered mere legal strangers without legal standing to consent to or refuse medical treatment or make other decisions on behalf of their chosen family member.
>
> (Knauer 2016, 159)

Thus SLIFs, so important to older LGBT*Q people, are the very relationships which are at the bottom of the relationship recognition tier in terms of law and the older person.

Legal in/exclusions in later life

To return to the title of this chapter – 'Which ageing "families" count?' – it would seem that the conjugal couple and biological/adopted relationships are those which are recognised, and privileged, in law relating to the older person. SLIFs – friends, informal carers, and other non-conjugal, non-biological close relationships – are not recognised in many areas of relevant law. They are thereby excluded from the associated material, financial, and decision-making benefits of such recognition. Given that SLIFs are of particular importance to older lesbian, gay, bisexual, trans*, and/or queer (LGBT*Q) people, this suggests profound inequalities associated with relational legal exclusions in (older age) family law.

This is not to suggest that being included in law is always a good thing: with recognition comes regulation (Harding 2011) and staying out of law's way has allowed friendships to flourish on their own (voluntary) terms:

> Friendship thrives on lack of state recognition, but that lack also makes friendship suspect. The placement of friendship outside the law gives individuals the freedom to experience multiple forms of friendship and to create new forms of friendship, but that freedom also means that individuals can view friendship as more open to fraud than those intimate adult relationships recognized by the state. The state, by omission, defines friendship as a relationship with no legally enforceable obligations, and that definition necessarily shapes the benefits, risks, and experience of friendship for all.
>
> (Rosenbury 2007, 206)

So friendship, in its legal exclusions, is nonetheless shaped by law, through what cannot flow to it in terms of legal rights. Friendship and law are already in a relationship, albeit a rather silent one:

> The law makes possible and structures friendships, whether it does so consciously or not. Accordingly, pretending that the law has nothing to do with our friendships is not a plausible posture. As cultural environments and their enabling conditions within the law change, so do friendship patterns and processes. And the forms of intimacy friendships display in any cultural context are no doubt affected by the law and legal categories.
>
> (Leib 2007, 265)

Moreover, we are not talking here about 'just' friendship, but about a particularl kind of friendship, involving friends as family, friends who possibly co-habit, friends as reciprocal care providers, and friendships based on support, love, intimacy, and commitment. While these are not exclusively the domain of older LGBT*Q people, they do have a unique particularity among older LGBT*Q people, forged as they have been against a backcloth of prejudice, discrimination, social exclusion, and marginalisation. These are 'friends' who may be as close as, or even closer than, spouses, civil partners, and biological family (Westwood 2015) and who yet have very few comparative rights in law. This is an inequitable state of affairs.

The marginalisation of SLIFs in law intersects with the socio-legal cultural devaluation of care, particularly informal care (Herring 2013). As highlighted in relation to private law in particular by the work of Brian Sloan (2012), informal non-biological carers have very few legal rights and recognitions, particularly in relation to inheritance. This exclusion is exacerbated when those informal carers do not conform to traditional notions of family:

> Rights for carers require an intelligible model of the family that has no space for non-standard intimacies: polyamory, non-standard parental relationships, independent financial arrangements between partners, and close ties between friends.
>
> (Conaghan and Grabham 2007, 20)

With increasingly reliance by the retreating state (Daly and Westwood 2017) upon a dwindling supply of informal carers (Pickard 2015) this is a significant concern. As Brian Sloan has argued:

> The strain under which societal resources will be placed and the need for justice for informal carers render it vital to at least consider the specific recognition of such carers in private law, even in the absence of unconscionable dealing, and even for entirely altruistic carers.
>
> (Sloan 2012, 245)

The current lack of justice for informal carers with specific regard to intestacy involves the following: 1) it means that the conjugal couple and the biological family benefit financially with no conditions based upon quantity and quality of care provided to the deceased person before their death; 2) it means that someone who is dependent on the older person, i.e. has been supported by them before death, can claim for that continued support after the person has died, irrespective of whether there has been any reciprocal care provided; 3) it means that a person who is not a spouse/civil partner or a biological/adopted family member, but who is a SLIF, and has provided the person with care, perhaps a very high level of care, before they died (without any promise of reward) has no automatic claim on the person's estate, including the home in which they may have both been living. This, as Brian Sloan has argued is '*unconscionability of outcome*' (Sloan 2012, 241) which privileges marriage and civil partnership and biological/adopted relationships and dependency upon the deceased over all other relationships of care and support and dependency on the part of the deceased. It makes the conjugal couple, the biological/adopted family line, and material dependency upon the deceased *what matters*, with the provision of care and support to the deceased not counting at all. This can be located within feminist critiques of law (Hunter, McGlynn and Rackley 2010) specifically, here, that law fails to take into account the relational, the private, the lived experience of women and the (gendered) provision of care.

The case for expanding legal recognition

There is, then, I propose, an urgent need to expand the legal recognition of relationships to incorporate friendship, SLIFs or 'close friends' (Knauer 2016) in particular, and the provision of informal care and support. While this is of particular relevance to older LGBT*Q people, given the increasingly complex later-life 'families' including blended families among all older people (Pezzin, Pollak and Schone 2013), it is increasingly relevant to all society. This is further reinforced by the growing significance of friendship for non-LGBT*Q as well as LGBT*Q people (Gray 2009), particularly the growing numbers who are ageing without children (Deindl and Brandt 2016):

> While the law does much for family members, extending certain legal measures to friends would be a realistic acknowledgement that, in times of difficulty, we often depend on the selfless acts of friends as well as family.
>
> (Gelzinis 2011, 548)

The Law Commission of Canada proposed radical revisions to the legal recognition of relationships going 'beyond conjugality' (Law Commission of Canada 2001) noting in particular relationships which involved economic and emotional support among 'families of friends' and their importance to LGBT*Q people and to older people, especially older women. The Commission argued that 'the state must provide adequate legal structures that support the relationships that citizens develop' (Law Commission of Canada, 2001 xiv–xv). Ultimately the Commission did not pursue this approach, although there are various forms of non-conjugal, non-biological/adopted relationship constellation recognitions across the world (see Barker 2012, for a detailed exploration). At the time, Nicola Barker observed:

> The Law Commission is missing an opportunity to ask important questions about the nature and purpose of relationship recognition. It is in the answers to these questions that a just and equitable model of relationship recognition must be found.
>
> (Barker 2006, 256).

Such considerations are also needed to engage with issues of care and, more specifically:

> Whether remedies should be granted not on the basis that the care recipient indicated that the care provider would receive anything, but because the carer's work is perceived to merit a remedy in any event.
>
> (Sloan 2012 241)

The following six actions would go a long way towards remedying the inequities which have been identified in this chapter:

1 Remove tax privileges, in life and in death, for couples. This immediately levels the playing field and ceases to reinforce compulsory coupledom and its associated privileges (Auchmuty 2009).
2 Include close friends – SLIFSs – as potential claimants under intestacy rules.
3 Include close friends – SLIFSs – as potential claimants under tenancy succession rules.
4 Include those who provided the deceased person with informal care and support – emotional, instrumental, practical material, financial – as having an equal right to claim as dependents under the Inheritance (Provision for Family and Dependants) Act 1975.

5 Formalise the legal recognition of next-of-kin and make it clear this should be based on the person's own choice, or, if they lack capacity, the closest tie, rather than privileging the conjugal couple or biological/adoptive ties. This may be complex to implement, but there are ways and means of doing so (Royal College of Nursing 2003).
6 Amend mental health legislation in England and Wales, to come in line with mental health legislation in Scotland, enabling friends to be nominated as Nearest Relative, as had been previously considered but discounted by the government prior to the Mental Health Act 2007 (Hewitt 2007).

There can be many objections raised to the increased inclusion of friendship care and friendship carers in law, not least of which that, with recognition, comes regulation of a relationship which is often based on voluntarism, altruism, and trust. The counter-argument to this is that voluntarism does not preclude reward. It is also possible that a frail older person could acquire suddenly enthusiastic new friends and new informal carers, if there is a financial incentive. But, to be brutal, if the friendship and care is good, then it is better than no care at all, and perhaps it should be financially rewarded, whatever its origins. If it is not good, then of course it should not be rewarded, there should be no 'undue profit' (Horton 2008, 67), and so the quality of a friendship and of care should always be rebuttable in law.

There is also the concern that informal/friendship carers can have the opportunity to exert undue influence on the person they are supporting, particularly if they are in a position of power and the older person may be vulnerable to such undue influence due to dependency (Horton 2008). I would propose that every older person who is physically and cognitively disabled should have an advocate (who could not make a claim on their estate) to give voice to the older person which would include guarding against this. Pollyanna-ism in times of austerity, perhaps, but adult protection issues cannot be ignored any more than child protection issues, even when resources are tight (Brammer, this collection).

Ultimately, friendship and friendship care need to be brought to the table in relation to law both generally and more specifically, in the context of this chapter, law, and older people. This does not have to involve the wholesale formalisation of friendship. As Leib has observed:

> Even if we choose to retain friendship's core as a private relationship rather than one with public recognition that carries duties and privileges, there remains good reason to give the legal system competence to recognize friendship-even if only to keep a hands-off policy to it.
>
> (Leib 2007, 265)

Recognition could include both a hands-off policy and a hands-on one according to context. This would make possible the inclusion of friendship and that of friendship carers, under those circumstances when to not do so would produce inequitable outcomes, such as those I have outlined in this chapter.

Conclusion

This chapter has considered which relationships count in UK family law relating to older people. I have argued that the conjugal couple and biological/adopted relationships are privileged over friendship and friendship carers. This privileging occurs within the wider exclusion of friendship and non-familial caring relationships in law. This adherence to traditional familial relationship forms is failing to keep up with increasingly diverse relationship constellations, including in later life. In particular, it under-recognises the significance of friends, especially 'close friends' or SLIFs, to LGBT*Q older people specifically, and many non-LGBT*Q older people as well. It also reproduces and reinforces the undervaluing of informal care in law and society.

Traditionally, critiques of family law have tended to focus on parenting and partnership issues. As this chapter, and this entire edited collection demonstrate, family law is extremely pertinent in relation to older people and later life issues and concerns. It might be over-simplistic to suggest that the under-attention to ageing issues in family law might be a symptom of institutional ageism, but this is probably a relevant factor. So too is the fact that the later life relationship constellations which are most relevant to older LGBT*Q people – families of friends – are those which are most excluded in law relation to older people. Undoubtedly, heteronormativity (the assumption that heterosexual identities and relationship formations are the norm), heterosexism (the systematic privileging of heterosexual identities), cisnormativity (the assumption that binary cisgender[20] identities and relationship formations are the norm) and cisgenderism (the systematic privileging of cisgender identities) have also played a part. However, rather than bemoan this normativity and its consequent exclusions, it is far better to find ways forward.

I have proposed six strategies which would promote increase inclusion of friends/SLIFs in law relating to the older person: 1) Remove couple tax privileges; 2) Include close friends – SLIFSs – as potential claimants under intestacy rules; 3) Include close friends – SLIFSs – as potential claimants under tenancy succession rules; 4) Allow those who provided the deceased person with informal care and support to claim under the Inheritance (Provision for Family and Dependants) Act 1975; 5) Formalise the legal recognition of next-of-kin and strengthen the place of close friends; and 6) amend mental health legislation in England and Wales, so that friends can be nominated as Nearest Relative.

Increasing the recognition (and thus regulation) of friendship in this way risks undermining its voluntarism and 'freedom' from law. But as this chapter has argued, friendship has never been 'free' from law, just pushed out on the margins by it. It is time for friendship and friendship carers, to be brought in from the cold, and be afforded the recognition, resources, and rights they deserve.

Notes

1 Trans* is an umbrella term which covers the gender identity spectrum: including (but not limited to) transgender, transsexual, transvestite, genderqueer, genderfluid, non-binary, genderless, agender, non-gendered, third gender, two-spirit and bigender (Tompkins 2014).
2 Married couples and civil partners are entitled to State Pension on the basis of a spouse's/civil partner's National Insurance contributions. Surviving spouses/civil partners are entitled to the deceased spouses'/civil partners' occupational pension.
3 Spouses and civil partners born before 5 April 1935 can claim the Married Couple's Allowance and tax benefits, enabling the transfer of savings to a spouse/civil partner who pays no tax or tax at a lower rate.
4 Under the Inheritance Tax Act 1984, which applies across the UK, a surviving spouse is exempt from Inheritance Tax. Following the Civil Partnership Act 2004 (CPA) this benefit was also extended to civil partners (Tax and Civil Partnership Regulations 2005).
5 Under the Inheritance Tax Act 1984, which applies across the UK, a surviving spouse is exempt from Inheritance Tax. Following the Civil Partnership Act 2004 (CPA) this benefit was also extended to civil partners (Tax and Civil Partnership Regulations 2005). In cases of intestacy, the spouse/civil partner is allowed to apply to become an executor of the deceased partner's estate and to inherit under intestacy rules: Administration of Estates Act 1925, England and Wales; English Inheritance and Trustees' Powers Act 2014; Succession (Scotland) Act 1964, as amended by the Law Reform (Miscellaneous Provisions) (Scotland) Act 1968 and the Succession (Scotland) Act 1973. Spouses and civil partners are also entitled to make a claim under the Inheritance (Provision for Family and Dependants Act) 1975 (England, Wales and Northern Ireland) (as amended by the Law Reform (Succession) Act 1995) and Family Law (Scotland) Act 2006.
6 In terms of tenancy rules (Housing Act 1988 – England and Wales; Housing (Scotland) Act 2001; Housing (NI) Order 1983), spouses and civil partners are entitled to take over a deceased spouse's/civil partner's council tenancy and housing association tenancy, but not private assured shorthold tenancies (unless their name is also in the tenancy agreement). They may be entitled to succeed under assured and regulated private tenancies.
7 Cohabiting partners who are not married or in a civil partnership do not receive the same pension rights (although they can be named as beneficiaries in private pension schemes under which anyone can be nominated as a beneficiary), tax benefits or Inheritance Tax privileges. Cohabiting partners are also not recognised under intestacy rules which, whilst recognising spouses and civil partners, then default to a hierarchy of potential beneficiaries which privilege biological and adopted family members. Cohabiting surviving partners can take over a deceased partner's council tenancy and housing association tenancy, but not private assured shorthold tenancies (unless their name is also in the contract).
8 English Inheritance and Trustees' Powers Act 2014.
9 The Mental Capacity Act 2005 (England and Wales) and the Adults with Incapacity (Scotland) Act 2000 enable, through Lasting Powers of Attorney (LPAs) (Property and Financial Affairs/ Personal Welfare) in England and Wales, and a Power of Attorney in Scotland, a person to nominate those who can make decisions about their property and finances and about their care should they lose the capacity to do so for themselves.
10 Advance Decisions in England and Wales (Mental Capacity Act 2005, ss 24–26) and Advance Directives in Scotland (Adults with Incapacity (Scotland) Act 2000 s 47(2)) enable a person to make decisions on another's behalf with regard to medical treatment at end of life. In England and Wales, an advance decision is legally binding and must be

respected by medical teams (although it can be overridden under the Mental Health Act 1983). In Scotland, advance directives are not legally binding, but must be taken into account by medical teams and others making decisions on a person's behalf.

11 Under the Mental Health (Care and Treatment) (Scotland) Act 2003, a person over 16 can nominate a 'named person' to support him/her and to protect his/her interests in any proceedings under the Act. This can be a friend if they wish.

12 Under the Equality Act 2010, which provides protection from direct and indirect discrimination, sexual orientation is a protected characteristic.

13 Under the Equality Act 2010, which provides protection from direct and indirect discrimination, gender identity is a protected characteristic.

14 Under the Gender Recognition Act 2004, transgender people who meet certain criteria can change their legal gender, and have their birth certificates altered to reflect this.

15 'Sex' and 'gender' are often conflated and/or confused in law, and it is often more common to refer to 'same-sex' couples. However, I am intentionally using 'gender' in this paper, to avoid essentialist, biologically driven binary understandings of 'female' and 'male', and to locate sex/gender in performative contexts (Butler 2011).

16 Civil Partnership Act 2004.

17 Marriage (Same Sex Couples) Act 2013; Marriage and Civil Partnership (Scotland) Act 2014.

18 Following the Adoption and Children Act 2002 for the first time same-sex couples and lesbian, gay and bisexual individuals were permitted to adopt children.

19 The Human Fertilisation and Embryology Act (2008) sets out who a child's legal parents will be when they are conceived through artificial insemination and allows co-parenting for same-sex couples.

20 Cisgender (or cis) is a term for people whose gender identity matches the sex/gender they were assigned at birth.

References

Almack, K., Seymour, J. and Bellamy, G. (2010) 'Exploring the Impact of Sexual Orientation on Experiences and Concerns about End of Life Care and on Bereavement for Lesbian, Gay and Bisexual Older People' *Sociology* 44(5), 908.

Almack, K., Yip, A., Seymour, J., Sargeant, A., Patterson, A. and Makita, M. (2015) *The Last Outing: Exploring End of Life Experiences and Care Needs in the Lives of Older LGBT People: A Final Report.* Nottingham: University of Nottingham.

Anderson, K. L. (2011) 'Intestacy in Scotland: The Laughing Heir' *Aberdeen Student Law Review* 2(1), 52.

Auchmuty, R. (2009) 'Beyond Couples' *Feminist Legal Studies* 17(2), 205.

Bailey, L. (2012) 'Trans Ageing' in R. Ward, I. Rivers and M. Sutherland (eds) *Lesbian, Gay, Bisexual and Transgender Ageing: Biographical Approaches for Inclusive Care and Support.* London and Philadelphia, PA: Jessica Kingsley Publishers.

Barker, N. (2006) 'Sex and the Civil Partnership Act: the future of (non) conjugality?' *Feminist Legal Studies* 14(2), 241.

Barker, N. (2012) *Not The Marrying Kind: A Feminist Critique of Same-sex Marriage.* Basingstoke: Palgrave Macmillan.

Barker, N. and Monk, D. (eds) (2015a) *From Civil Partnership to Same Sex Marriage: Interdisciplinary Reflections.* Abingdon, Routledge.

Barker, N. and Monk, D. (2015b) 'From Civil Partnership to Same-sex Marriage: A Decade in British Legal History' in N. Barker and D. Monk (eds) *From Civil Partnership to Same Sex Marriage: Interdisciplinary Reflections.* Abingdon: Routledge.

Barnes, M. (2012) *Care in Everyday Life: An Ethic of Care in Practice*. Bristol: The Policy Press.

Butler, J. (2011) *Gender Trouble: Feminism and the Subversion of Identity*. New York: Routledge.

Conaghan, J. and Grabham, E. (2007) 'Sexuality and the Citizen Carer' *Northern Ireland Legal Quarterly* 58, 325.

Cook-Daniels, L. (2006) 'Trans Ageing' in D. Kimmel, T. Rose and S. David (eds) *Lesbian, Gay, Bisexual and Transgender Ageing*. New York: Columbia University Press.

Croghan, C. F., Moone, R. P. and Olson, A. M. (2014) 'Friends, Family, and Caregiving among Midlife and Older Lesbian, Gay, Bisexual, and Transgender Adults' *Journal of Homosexuality* 61(1), 79.

Cronin, A., Ward, R., Pugh, S., King, A. and Price, E. (2011) 'Categories and Their Consequences: Understanding and Supporting the Caring Relationships of Older Lesbian, Gay and Bisexual People' *International Social Work* 54(3), 421.

Daly, M. and Westwood, S. (2017) 'Asset-based Approaches, Older People and Social Care: An Analysis and Critique' *Ageing and Society* 1–13.

Deindl, C. and Brandt, M. (2016) 'Support Networks of Childless Older People: Informal and Formal Support in Europe' *Ageing and Society* 36, 1.

DeVries, B. and Megathlin, D. (2009) 'The Meaning of Friendship for Gay Men and Lesbians in the Second Half of Life' *Journal of GLBT Family Studies* 5(1–2), 82.

Diduck, A. and O'Donovan, K. (eds) (2006) *Feminist Perspectives on Family Law*. Abingdon: Routledge-Cavendish.

Douglas, G., Woodward, H., Humphrey, A., Mills, L. and Morrell, G. (2011) 'Enduring Love? Attitudes to Family and Inheritance Law in England and Wales' *Journal of Law and Society* 38(2), 245.

Gelzinis, P.P. (2011) 'Do Friends Need the Law? Examining Why Friendship Matters and What Governments Can Do for this Important, through Overlooked Relationship' *Suffolk University Law Review* 45, 523.

Gray, A. (2009) 'The social capital of older people' *Ageing and Society* 29(1), 5.

Harding, R. (2011) *Regulating Sexuality: Legal Consciousness in Lesbian and Gay Lives*. Abingdon: Routledge.

Hash, K. M. and Mankowski, M. (2017) 'Caregiving in the LGBT Community' *Annual Review of Gerontology and Geriatrics* 37(1), 77.

Herring, J. (2013) *Caring and the Law*. Oxford: Hart.

Herring, J. (2016) 'Family Law and Older People in a European Perspective' in J. Scherpe (ed.) *European Family Law*. Cheltenham: Edward Elgar.

Hewitt, D. (2007) 'Relative Progress?' *The New Law Journal*, 157(7257), 1.

Horton, D. (2008) 'The Uneasy Case for California's Care Custodian Statute' *Chapman Law Review* 11.

Hunter, R., McGlynn, C. and Rackley, E. (eds) (2010) *Feminist Judgments: From Theory to Practice*. London: Bloomsbury Publishing.

Knauer, N. J. (2016) 'LGBT Older Adults, Chosen Family, and Caregiving' *Journal of Law and Religion* 1.

Law Commission of Canada (2001) *Beyond Conjugality: Recognizing and Supporting Close Personal Adult Relationships*. Available at: www.samesexmarriage.ca/docs/beyond_conjugality.pdf

Leib, E. J. (2007) 'Friendship and Law' *UCLA Law Review* 54, 631.

Leib, E. J. (2010) 'Contracts and Friendships' *Emory Law Journal* 59, 649.

Marie Curie UK (2016) *Hiding Who I Am – The Reality of End of Life Care for LGBT People.* Available at: www.mariecurie.org.uk/globalassets/media/documents/policy/policy-publications/june-2016/reality-end-of-life-care-lgbt-people.pdf

Monk, D. (2013) 'E M Forster's Will: An Overlooked Posthumous Publication' *Legal Studies* 33(4), 572.

Monk, D. (2016) '"Inheritance Families of Choice"? Lawyers' Reflections on Gay and Lesbian Wills' *Journal of Law and Society* 43(2), 167.

Orel, N. A. (2017) 'Families and Support Systems of LGBT Elders' *Annual Review of Gerontology and Geriatrics* 37(1), 89.

Pezzin, L. E., Pollak, R. A. and Schone, B. S. (2013) 'Complex Families and Late-life Outcomes among Elderly Persons: Disability, Institutionalization, and Longevity' *Journal of Marriage and Family* 75(5), 1084.

Pickard, L. (2015) 'A growing care gap? The supply of unpaid care for older people by their adult children in England to 2032' *Ageing and Society 35*(1), 96.

Rosenbury, L. A. (2007) 'Friends with Benefits?' *Michigan Law Review*, 106, 189.

Roseneil, S. and Budgeon, S. (2004) 'Cultures of Intimacy and Care Beyond "The Family": Personal Life and Social Change in the Early 21st Century' *Current Sociology* 52(2), 135.

Royal College of Nursing (2003) *Lesbian, Gay, Bisexual and Transgender Patients or Clients: Guidance for Nursing Staff on Next-of-kin Issues.* Available at: www2.rcn.org.uk/__data/assets/pdf_file/0014/623201/6pp-leaflet_final-signe-pages-72dpi.pdf

Sharpe, A. N. (2007) 'Endless Sex: The Gender Recognition Act 2004 and the Persistence of a Legal Category' *Feminist Legal Studies* 15(1), 57.

Shiu, C., Muraco, A. and Fredriksen-Goldsen, K. (2016) 'Invisible Care: Friend and Partner Care Among Older Lesbian, Gay, Bisexual, and Transgender (LGBT) Adults' *Journal of the Society for Social Work and Research* 7(3), 527.

Sloan, B. (2012) *Informal Carers and Private Law.* Oxford: Bloomsbury Publishing.

The Treasury Solicitor (2008) *Discretionary Grants in Estates Cases.* London: The Treasury Solicitor.

Tompkins, A. (2014) 'Asterisk' *TSQ: Transgender Studies Quarterly* 1(1–2), 26.

Traies, J. (2015) 'Old Lesbians in the UK: Community and Friendship' *Journal of Lesbian Studies* 19(1), 35.

Westwood, S. (2014) '"My Friends are my Family": An Argument about the Limitations of Contemporary Law's Recognition of Relationships in Later Life' *Journal of Social Welfare and Family Law* 35(3), 347.

Westwood, S. (2015) 'Complicating Kinship and Inheritance: Older Lesbians' and Gay Men's Will-writing in England' *Feminist Legal Studies* 23(2), 181.

Westwood, S. (2016) *Ageing, Gender and Sexuality: Equality in Later Life.* Abingdon: Routledge.

Westwood, S. and Price, L. (eds) (2016) *Lesbian, Gay, Bisexual and Trans* Individuals Living with Dementia: Concepts, Practice, Rights.* Abingdon: Routledge.

Witten, T. M. (2009) 'Graceful Exits: III. Intersections of Ageing, Transgender Identities and the Family/Community' *Journal of GLBT Family Studies* 5, 36.

Chapter 12

'Inheritance law matters'

Daniel Monk

Inheritance law is a bit of a poor relation in the family law curricula, often addressed in a cursory way, if at all. This is a pity. For the question 'who will inherit?' has always been at the heart of the ideological underpinnings of 'the family' and, indeed, of society as a whole. In post-revolutionary France and America succession law was the most hotly debated issue of the day; as defining and distinguishing of national values and political identities as issues such as Brexit or gay marriage are today (Blumenthal 2006; Counter 2010). Many of these debates were expressed in literary form and in 1897 the British literary critic L. S. Lewis wondered, 'Goodness only knows what novelists and dramatists would do without wills' (1897: 441). A classic example of this genre is George Eliot's *Middlemarch*, where wills provided the key to her critique of marriage and the status of women.

In the modern age the last two novels that utilise inheritance to speak of the wider human condition – and especially that of women – are Daphne du Maurier's *My Cousin Rachel* (1951) and Muriel Spark's *Momento Mori* (1959). The dates here are significant. 'Will-plots' appear to have gone out of fashion at the same time as 'French window' dramas were being swept off the British stage by angry young men (Rebellato 1999); both perceived as 'class ridden' and 'melodramatic'. As a vehicle to throw a light on character and as a defining component of status, inheritance had all the wrong connotations for a new wave of thinking that sought to celebrate independence and individuality; and there was perhaps an implicit assumption that a society that enables equal opportunities for all, simply has no place for it. The relative silence about inheritance also resonates with the compelling thesis, albeit contested, that it is death and not sex which is the dominant taboo of modern society (Walter 1991).

The most recent legal reform, the Inheritance and Trustees' Powers Act 2014, was informed by a Law Commission consultation (2011), which initiated a renewed interest in inheritance amongst socio-legal scholars (Williams et al 2008; Douglas et al 2011). The reform enhanced the status of surviving spouses in the intestacy rules, but attracted relatively little attention. Yet inheritance law impacts on more people now than ever before, primarily as a result of increased property ownership; as a result more *elderly* people have more wealth to transfer on death than ever before. Yet rather than extending owner-occupation, inheritance practices are one factor in the stalling and indeed the actual reversal of the trend (Hood and Joyce 2017).

At the same time, the generation that led the way in shifting traditional marital, familial, and sexual practices are now ageing. Consequently, there are more step-parents, half-siblings and step-siblings, cohabitees, and single person households than ever before; and in these new 'blended families' the convention of vertical transmission of wealth from a married couple to their children is not straightforward. Alongside these generational dimensions are the wider implications of an ageing population. Individual disputes about the capacity of testators and familial and social debates about responsibilities for elder care all impact on inheritance – and, in particular, on understandings of 'the family home'; all the more so in the context of increasing inequality and a shrinking state.

This chapter provides an overview of some of the key contemporary debates about inheritance and in doing so highlights the ways in which they represent a key site for the negotiating and troubling of ideas about family, kinship, and care and in different ways grapple with the legacies of both social and economic liberalism.

Inheritance practices

In 2007 the National Consumer Council published a report, which recommended that urgent action was needed to encourage people to write wills (Brooker 2007). While it found that a large number of people had no will, the research revealed significant demographic differences that reflected 'a stark social divide' (2007, 18). Age and social class, not surprisingly, were both key factors, with 70% of people over 65 and 70% of those in socio-economic categories AB making wills, compared to only 3% amongst 16–24 year olds and 27% in socioeconomic categories DE. Widows and married couples and divorced couples were more likely to have made a will than separated, cohabitant, and single people. An underlying premise of the report's recommendations was that will-making is a good thing – a responsible act – primarily because 'intestacy can have a devastating human cost' (2007, 11). But while there is undoubtedly wide ignorance of the intestacy rules, the assumptions about the benefits of will-writing overlook the extent to which the functions of inheritance law are varied and disputed.

'Estate-planning'

One of the reasons why richer people write wills is to reduce the burden of inheritance tax. It is a major part of what is referred to as 'estate planning'. Like 'family planning', this is a polite euphemism: they discretely veil the genteel taboos of money and sex. But acknowledging the motive of tax avoidance would suggest that *less* will-writing might lead to an increase in tax revenues, and, as a result, a greater redistribution of wealth. While inheritance tax is paid on only a small number of estates, the aspiration to leave the family home to children (for most people their main and only major asset), combined with the significantly increased property prices, was critical to the Conservative government's introduction in 2015 of a transferable main residence allowance enabling married couples to, in effect, bequeath £1m free of tax.

The main function of effective 'estate planning' is to place assets outside of wills and as a result outside of the taxable probate estate. The result has been a 'non-probate revolution', whereby the primary vehicle for wealth transmission is 'will-substitutes'. The subject of much analysis in the US (Leslie 2014) they have, received little academic attention in England and Wales, despite the fact that their use, notwithstanding their varied functions, risks undermining the whole purpose of having rules regulating succession (Braun and Röthel 2016). In the context of avoiding legal obligations to others, Herring has recommended extending anti-avoidance measures available in divorce law to inheritance provisions (2016). While tax avoidance is without any doubt a key motive for their use, one way, paradoxically, of restoring wills to the centre of inheritance practices would be to simply abolish inheritance tax and replace it with more effective mechanisms of wealth taxation (Lee 2007). The point here is to highlight that the 'devastating human cost' of intestacy assumes a private and 'familial' rather than a public and social cost.

'Doing-the-right-thing'

The hope that will-making will reduce familial conflict and provide appropriate protection for individuals, wrongly assumes that giving effect to testators' desires will necessarily be more likely to achieve these ends than the default application of the intestacy rules. Indeed, it is precisely because of this that the Inheritance (Provision for Family and Dependants) Act 1975, albeit on a highly restricted basis, permits challenges to wills *and* the effects of intestacy: both might result in 'unreasonable' outcomes. Moreover, assumptions that testators will 'do the right thing', assumes there is a consensus about what that might be. But motivations that might be considered reasonable – alleviating need, the equal treatment of children, and the recognition of both love and care – will often point to contradictory dispositions.

Tate has argued that a contemporary justification for unrestricted testamentary freedom is that it enables elderly people to reward family members who are care-givers. On the basis of demographic changes that have increased the need for and expense of elder care, and as a critique of the 'windfall' nature of inheritance, he argues that discrimination between a testator's children or relatives is justified. Distinguishing this discrimination from past practices he notes that:

> Once a punishment inflicted primarily on wayward progeny, disinheritance of adult, non-disabled descendants has become an unfortunate but necessary consequence of the need to reward those who care for their ageing parents or grandparents.
>
> (Tate 2008, 134).

This attempt to connect testamentary freedom and elder care can be challenged on a number of fronts. A continental law perspective would emphasise how upholding the rights of children to inherit equally has a positive impact on familial relations (Lamarca I. Marquès 2014). Significantly this approach reflects contemporary public opinion in England and Wales. Finch and Mason found that 'the principle of equal treatment of children reigns supreme when it comes to the division of major assets (2000, 77). Douglas et al's research confirmed this and noted that exceptions were only found to be acceptable 'in order to preserve the "ancestral" home or particular heirlooms' (2011, 269).

Conversely, others supportive of enhancing the legal recognition of care have called for limiting testamentary freedom to be restricted by extending the grounds of post-mortem challenges to include the provision of care (Herring 2016; Westwood 2013). This moral and pragmatic proposal may have unintended consequences. Incentivising care for wealthy elders may exacerbate inequalities, as the friends and relatives of the rich may already be more privileged; enhancing the legal privatising of care offers little to those most in need. It might simply shift rather than relieve tensions within families and could expose vulnerable elders to the attentions of 'professional' care-chasing. The point here, however, is that while Tate's argument supports and, indeed, like the National Consumer Council report, encourages will making, these conflicting approaches reveal the ethical contingencies of the practice.

A more fundamental problem with the assumed benefits of will making is that the principle of testamentary freedom legitimises *unworthy* motivations. In the much-cited judgment in *Frere v Peacocke* (1846), Sir Herbert Fust held that:

> Because a man does *not duly appreciate the acts of feelings which generally influence mankind*, that, therefore he is to be considered mad, and unfit to make a disposition of his property, is not the law of the country.
>
> (at 456, emphasis added)

Subsequent statutory reform tempered this absolutist position, but while this case makes a clear distinction between mental as opposed to moral incapacity, in practice the line between the two is often blurred and this has important implications for an increasing number of elder people. The issue of 'unworthy' or 'unnatural' wills highlights a debate about the extent to which the law should uphold testamentary wishes contrary to dominant moral values or understandings of 'responsible' behaviour. And gender has often been central to this debate.

Gender and discrimination

In 2014 the Law Society published guidance for its members about how to write sharia-compliant wills, which require that sons and daughters be treated differently. In response to the ensuing media storm, the President of the Law Society publically apologised and the guidance was removed from the Society's website

(Cross 2014). The basis of the objections was unclear; there is nothing, *per se*, unlawful about parents treating children unequally – on the basis of gender or otherwise – and the intention was simply to help legal practitioners better understand the requirements of some of their Muslim clients. Broader concerns about the possible influence of sharia law on family justice were clearly present, alongside questions about the appropriateness of the Law Society, as a quasi-public body, being perceived as condoning gender inequality. But while the guidance was publically criticised by government ministers (Bowcott 2014), what was missing from the media coverage was any mention of the fact that the possibility of extending human rights provisions to testamentary provisions had been considered and explicitly rejected by policy makers at the early stages of the drafting of the Equality Act 2010.[1]

The law addresses the issue of explicit discrimination in the context of conditional gifts. In England and Wales, the grounds on which a condition will be held to be contrary to public policy, and as a result void, are narrowly construed (Kerridge 2009). Particularly relevant to women, but not exclusively, are conditions which represent an attempt to control potential beneficiaries' personal relationships (Monk 2011). But located firmly in the 'private sphere', human rights provisions have had no impact on such conditions (Chalmers 2007).

Grattan and Conway argue that courts should have the power to strike out conditions which impact on rights to privacy, marriage, and freedoms of religion and association (2005). But testamentary conditions can be understood to be little more than 'bribes': beneficiaries have the choice not to be bound by them. Consequently legal intervention would, in effect, not be upholding fundamental rights, rather, simply a right to inherit. A right explicitly rejected in *Marckx v Belgium* [1979]. Moreover, if one accepts Tate's argument noted above, the threat of disinheritance is a legitimate tool for elders in securing and rewarding much needed care. But context is all. In supporting extending anti-discrimination measures to inheritance law, Grattan and Conway point to the ways in which conditions have legitimised apartheid and helped sustain sectarian inequalities (2005), whereas Cooper and Herman (1999) identify how conditions have enabled minority groups to sustain their distinctive identity.

The moral outcry about the sharia guidance says much about the very particular position of one minority group, the Muslim community in contemporary Britain. This particularity is reinforced by contrasting media coverage, at precisely the same time, of the death of the Duke of Westminster. Much attention was paid to the fact that his vast fortune would be inherited by his only son and youngest child. An example of highly effective 'estate planning', it also highlighted the continued practice and legality of male primogeniture. This was remarked on in the media. For example, the headline in the *Evening Standard* was: 'Duke of Westminster's eldest daughter misses out on £9 billion fortune – because she's female' (Simpson 2016). In contrast to sharia wills, this practice did not result in any ministerial statements.

Aristocratic inheritance practices may seem outdated, but they have a significant impact on land ownership. Moreover, taking a long view is critical to understanding contemporary debates. The celebrated principle of testamentary freedom in wills only makes sense if located alongside the practices of strict settlement of land, marriage settlements, and dower rights (Fellows 1991, 148).

Women and will-writing

While married women were once prevented from writing wills (Fellows 1991), research indicates that will-writing is 'no longer a male dominated practice' (Hacker 2010, 333) and that women are now not only more likely to write them than men (Brooker 2007), but that the process itself is now largely dominated and driven by women, perceived as constituting 'domestic, and therefore arguably women's work' (Hasson 2013, 14). Men, it would appear, treat wills rather like visiting a doctor, something to be put off, whereas women, 'less in thrall to the illusion of immortality' (Hasson 2013, 8) view will making as part of taking responsibility for the well-being of the family and protecting children is the main motivation. Hasson argues that will-making 'can provide space and opportunities for women to experience power and exercise authority over men' (2013, 14).

An alternative feminist perspective is provided by Fellows (1991). In a powerful critique of the liberal progressive account, she argues that women's central role in protecting and ensuring that their children inherit, and taking responsibility for this, supports the view that married women, in practice and despite the legal changes, remain active participants in ensuring that they, paradoxically, remain vehicles, conduits and vessels for inheritance:

> In practice wives are not considered worthy of being property owners or of exercising their rights to make wills. Fathers want a Kingdom where they retain the prerogative to be the property-givers to their children and grandchildren.
>
> (159)

The reference to 'grandchildren' here is significant. Women's wealth is far more likely than men's to be inherited; consequently in cases where the wife is richer than the husband, the protection of her inherited wealth enables grandfathers to sideline potentially problematic sons-in-laws and ensure that 'family money' remains so. A classic case in this respect is the pre-nuptials dispute in *Radmacher v Granatino* [2010] for the judgment in favour of the much richer wife, while much vaunted as respecting the autonomy of the parties to a marriage, arguably simply masks the effective upholding of the quasi-testamentary power of the grandfather (see Taylor and Kaganas and Piper in this collection).

Inheritance disputes

There are two ways to challenge a will. A person who believes the testator ought to have included them in the will can only argue that *explicitly* by way of an application under the Inheritance (Provision for Family and Dependents) Act 1975. Challenges on this basis are limited by restrictions on who is eligible to apply and awards are based on discretionary assessments of 'reasonable provision'. An alternative route is provided by the doctrinal rules relating to 'capacity', 'revocation', 'certainty', or 'undue influence'. Challenges on the basis of these rules, in principle, protect rather then restrict testamentary freedom. Yet while very distinct, the motives underlying these two types of challenges may be the same. For example, in practice allegations of 'undue influence' are almost exclusively made by those with a vested interest in such a finding, and often by those ineligible to make a complaint under the 1975 Act. Moreover, judicial values determine the outcome of both kinds of challenge.

'Sitting in the armchair of the testator'

In applying the doctrinal rules about the validity of a will, the role of the judge is to 'sit in the armchair of the testator'. Critiques of this liberal subjectivist position have suggested that it masks the moral judgment of the judges; and consequently the outcomes in the cases can both reflect and produce gendered, raced, and 'familial' societal norms (Leslie 1996).

In re Strittmater's Estate [1947] is poignant example. The testator, a single woman with no children, bequeathed her estate to an early feminist organisation, of which she had been an active member for many years. Her will was successfully challenged on the grounds of her alleged incapacity, by her distant relatives who benefited as a result. This was established by notes she had made in the margins of books which the court deemed evidence of 'her morbid aversion to men' and 'feminism to a neurotic extreme' (at 95, 53 A 2d at 205). As Fellows comments, 'what the court left to be considered for another day was whether any level of feminism could avoid the label of extremism and mental instability' (1991, 143).

The underlying judicial values are often more subtle. In some cases the relationship with the testator and the disappointed heirs may be a factor. In *Kostic v Chaplin* [2007] a testator bequeathed his considerable fortune to the Conservative Party. While those of a different political persuasion might question the wisdom underlying such a gift, the finding of mental incapacity was based on evidence of the testator's delusions about his relatives, which it was held 'poisoned or distorted' his 'natural affections'. As a result the testator's son inherited and, arguably, it was the perceived reasonableness and normality of a parent bequeathing an estate to a child that informed the 'subjective' assessment of the testator.

Judicial values can of course be progressive. In *Rowe v Clarke* [2005] the same-sex partner of the deceased testator was unable to locate the will in which he was named sole beneficiary, and requested the court to grant probate on the basis of a copy. The brother of the deceased, who would have been the sole beneficiary under the intestacy rules, contested the application and relied on the revocation presumption that an original will not forthcoming at death is presumed to have been intentionally destroyed by the testator (Kerridge 2009, para. 7–23). The key factor supporting the rebuttal of the presumption was the view reached by the judge about the nature of the relationship between the deceased and his brother, in particular the latter's homophobia which, in the judge's view suggested that the deceased would not have been 'prepared to allow his estate to pass to his brother' (para. [60]).

In ascertaining the testator's intention the judge effectively acknowledges that for lesbians and gays, particularly those from non-supportive backgrounds, wills are an effective device for privileging the 'logical' over the 'biological' family (Monk 2016). The Civil Partnership Act 2004, an explicit legislative rejection of the values of the brother, came into force within two months after the hearing of *Rowe*. Consequently it is hard not to read the judgment, at least in part, as a sympathetic conferring of posthumous legal recognition of the same-sex relationship.

Questions of undue influence are particularly pertinent for vulnerable and elderly testators. Here too the cases arguably reveal underlying judicial values premised on the privileging of particular relations.

In *Carapeto v Good* [2002], the judgment records that Good was a 'prolific will maker' (2). Unmarried, childless, and with a physical disability since childhood resulting from polio, at the age of 67 she employed Carapeto, a Portugese woman, as her housekeeper and this enabled Good to remain in her home until her death 20 years later. Good bequeathed the bulk of her £1.4M estate to Carapeto. Alleging 'undue influence' the will was challenged by Good's half-brother and her six nieces and nephews, the people who would have inherited under the intestacy rules. In finding against them Rimer J observed that, 'I can well understand how the family's suspicions have been aroused [but] It must not be overlooked that the Carapeto family had by 1999 played a central and close role in Miss Good's life for some 20 years' (para. 126–7).

The outcome of this case coheres with research into public attitudes, as non-nuclear family members are viewed as appropriate beneficiaries only 'in the absence of a created family' – couples or children (Douglas et al 2011, 256). On the other hand, Good's wealth was largely inherited, and public attitudes attach a degree of significance to 'family money', and this may have informed the relatives' sense of disappointment; in other words her nieces and nephews may have seen the estate as their grandfather's money as much as their aunt's. What is debatable is whether the judge would have reached the same decision had the defendants been her children, rather than more distant relatives. Moreover, had Good bequeathed a smaller legacy to Carapeto, as opposed to the bulk of the estate, this would have been in keeping with an earlier established practice whereby bequests to carers, or domestic servants in an earlier terminology, were not unusual (Monk 2013). With an increase in live-in care, often as in the Carapeto case provided by foreign workers, the practices of these gifts, questions of 'appropriate' size, and allegations of undue influence, justified or otherwise, are likely to increase.

In *Edwards v Edwards and others* [2007] the allegation of undue influence was made by one brother against another in relation to their mother's will, under which only one of them benefited. Emphasising the orthodox position, the judge made clear that 'the question is not whether the court considers that the testator's testamentary disposition is fair', but 'whether in making his dispositions, the testator has acted as a free agent' (para. 47). He went on to find that there had been undue influence, that the respondent brother had, 'poisoned his mother's mind by making deliberately untruthful accusations against [the applicants] and that the effect of his doing so was to cause her own discretion and judgment to be overborne' (para. 55).

A sad tale and the point here is not that the decision is in any way wrong. But, as with *Carapato*, what is notable is that the outcome, in this case the equal treatment of the testator's children, coheres with public attitudes and the prevailing social norms. In both cases in the objective reasonableness of the will is a factor determining an explicitly subjective test.

In cases where someone has prepared a will for a person under which he or she has benefited, there is no clear presumption of fraud or undue influence. Kerridge has suggested that in these circumstances the onus should be on the propounder of the will and even if a challenge is unsuccessful in such cases he should pay the costs, 'unless the allegations are wholly unmeritorious' (88, 5–38). Other countries, such as Israel, have gone further by rendering void any gift made to a beneficiary who is any way involved. The Law Commission is currently undertaking a review of the law relating to wills, but it remains to be seen whether these proposals will be introduced.[2]

Reasonable provision

Judicial values are explicit in cases determined under the jurisdiction of the Inheritance (Provision for Family and Dependants) Act 1975; it intentionally establishes a discretionary regime. In the extensive case law, particularly contentious and complex are claims by independent adult child.

In *Re Coventry (dec'd)* [1980] the judge set a high threshold for such claimants in holding that 'the mere fact that the son found himself in necessitous circumstances was not by itself sufficient to establish his claim'. Here the estate passed to the deceased's wife, despite the fact they had separated many years before and the son had lived with his father, and as a result of the decision moved into a caravan. The combination of the necessity of elder care to enable people to remain in their home and the difficulties facing younger people seeking a home means that intergenerational households are likely to increase, which may be detrimental as well as benefical to elders. This might impact on the 'valued judgment' in similar cases in the future. Moreover gendered assumptions about the virtues of 'male' independence and 'feminine' care may also be underlying factors, as, arguably, they are in other areas of family law· Applications by daughters are particularly revealing in this respect.

In *Garland v Morris* [2007] a daughter was unsuccessful in challenging the will of her father who had left his whole estate to her elder sister. The claimant had benefited under the will of her mother, who had separated from her father, but by the time of her father's death was dependent on social security. The judge's decision was informed by his finding that she 'could not be bothered' to meet her father, who disapproved of her lifestyle as an unmarried mother and there was little contact between them in the 15 years before his death. Douglas comments that 'the poor relationship' between the two 'was held to justify her exclusion' (2014: 239).

Similarly, in *Wright v Waters* [2014], the mother's letter in which she had stated that her daughter had been 'a constant source of trouble to me' and had 'shown no interest in my welfare whatsoever', was critical in finding against the daughter: the judge holding that 'my value judgment is that [her] conduct outweighs all of the factors in her favour'.

However, in the most recent case of *Ilott v The Blue Cross and others* [2017], a non-dependent daughter *was* successful in her claim against her mother's estate. This was despite the fact that she had been estranged from her mother for almost 26 years and had no expectation of benefiting as her mother had explicitly forewarned her of her exclusion from her will. The High Court awarded her the sum of £50,000, approximately one-fifth of the estate, and the Court of Appeal raised the award to £143,000. The daughter's claim attracted much sympathy. Aden LJ described the mother as having acted in 'an unreasonable, capricious and harsh way towards her only child' (para. [51]). In support of the Court of Appeal's judgment, under the headline 'Thicker than Water', the leader in *The Times* stated that 'the imminence of death should of itself confer no special right to be cruelly or unfairly whimsical' (2015); a reference in part to the fact that the mother had left her entire estate to animal charities to which she had shown no particular interest in her lifetime.

However, in a unanimous decision, the Supreme Court restored the initial award by the High Court. For those who perceived the Court of Appeal's judgment as an unjustifiable incursion on testamentary freedom, the decision will be welcome. And will be relived by Lord Hughes finding that:

> Some judges might *legitimately* have concluded that the very long and deep estrangement had meant that the deceased had *no* remaining obligation to make any provision for her independent adult daughter.
>
> (para. 35, emphasis added)

Moreover, the judgment makes clear that judges should not determine these cases by weighing the respective needs and expectations of claimants against those of a testator's beneficiaries: an important finding for charities reliant on bequests. A critical issue in this case was the fact that the daughter was in receipt of means-tested state benefits. The Supreme Court held that it was legitimate to take into account the impact of a legacy on such benefits, but that in this case the High Court had done so. However, Lady Hale noted that a factor that could *not* be taken into account was 'the public interest in family members discharging their responsibilities towards one another so that these do not fall upon the state', and in doing so highlighted a distinction between inheritance and divorce law (para. 63).

Lady Hale held that in this case 'a respectable case could be made for at least three very different solutions', including awarding nothing, as noted above by Lord Hughes. Critical of the law's failure to provide 'guidance as to the factors to be taken into account in deciding whether an adult child is deserving or undeserving of reasonable maintenance', her judgment concludes with an expression of regret that the Law Commission 'did not reconsider the fundamental principles underlying such claims when last they dealt with this topic in 2011' (para. 65).

In the absence of legal reform in determining these cases judges are 'thrown back on "common sense" and his or her own understanding of appropriate family behaviour and norms' (Douglas 2014, 240). What is effectively being adjudicated on are performances of parental and filial responsibility. Rather than demarcating clear legal obligations, law here legitimises an invasive examination of emotions. A similar shift is evident in adjudications of statutory wills, where the imposition of a best interests test has the ability to severely challenge individual autonomy (Harding 2015).

Conclusion

For good or for ill inheritance touches on more people's lives than ever before. This chapter has provided an overview of some of the current debates in the field and without attempting to resolve them has endeavoured to demonstrate that they reflect wider concerns. This is a field of law and practice in which the intensely personal and the political interlock, it brings materiality into conversation with emotions and the economies of care into conversation with the function of the family and the role of the state. These connections and the very awkwardness of the subject, the discomfort it frequently provokes is why policy and decision making in this field is so fraught. But it is also why it matters and cannot be ignored. Much of this is not new. But in the current socio-economic context of increased privatisation of care and collapse of social mobility (Dorling 2014) the long-standing tensions are particularly acute. In this context inheritance matters more and the cases implicitly acknowledge the extent to which, in contemporary western societies, the nineteenth century's literary obsession with inheritance as a vehicle to throw a light on character and as a defining component of status looks eerily familiar.

Notes

1 Personal conversations with legal practitioners at the Equality Human Rights Commission.
2 'Wills to be reviewed by the Law Commission'. Available at: www.thegazette.co.uk/wills-and-probate/content/219

References

Blumenthal, S. (2006) 'The Deviance of the Will: Policing the Boundaries of Testamentary Freedom in Nineteenth Century America' *Harvard Law Review* 119, 959.

Braun, A. and Röthel, A. (2016) *Passing Wealth on Death: Will-substitutes in Comparative Perspective*. Oxford: Hart.

Bowcott, O. (2014) 'Law Society Withdraws Guidance on Sharia Wills' *Guardian*, 24 November.

Brooker, S. (2007) *Finding a Will: A Report on Will-making Behaviour in England and Wales*. London: National Consumer Council.

Chalmers, J. (2007) 'Testamentary Conditions and Public Policy' in K. Reid, M. de Waal and R. Zimmerman (eds) *Exploring the Law of Succession*. Edinburgh: Edinburgh University Press.

Cooper, D. and Herman, D. (1999) 'Jews and other Uncertainties: Race, Faith and English Law' *Legal Studies* 19, 339.

Cownie, F. and Bradney, A. (2003) 'Divided Justice, Different Voices: Inheritance and Family Provision' *Legal Studies* 23, 566.

Cross, M. (2014) 'Society Withdraws Sharia Wills Note' *Law Society Gazette*, 25 November.

Counter, A. (2010) *Inheritance in Nineteenth-century French Culture*. London: Maney/ Legenda.

Douglas, G. (2014) 'Family Provision and Family Practices' *Oñati Socio-Legal Series* 4(2), 224.

Douglas, G. et al (2011) 'Enduring Love? Attitudes to Family and Inheritance Law in England and Wales' *Journal of Law and Society* 38, 245.

Dorling, D. (2014) *Inequality and the 1%*. London: Verso.

Fellows, M. L. (1991) 'Wills and Trusts: "The Kingdom of the Fathers"' *Law and Inequality* 10, 137.

Finch, J. and Mason, J. (2000) *Passing on: Kinship and Inheritance in England*. London: Routledge.

Grattan, S. and Conway. H. (2005) 'Testamentary Constraints in Restrain of Religion in the Twenty-first Century: An Anglo-Canadian Perspective' *McGill Law Journal* 50, 511.

Hacker, D. (2010) 'The Gendered Dimensions of Inheritance: Empirical Food for Legal Thought' *Journal of Empirical Legal Studies* 7(2), 322.

Harding, R. (2015) 'The Rise of Statutory Wills and the Limits of Best Interests Decision-Making in Inheritance' *Modern Law Review* 78(6), 945.

Hasson, E. (2013) '"Where There's a Will There's a Woman": Exploring the Gendered Nature of Will-making' *Feminist Legal Studies* 21(1), 21.

Herring, J. (2016) 'Will-Substitutes and the Claims of Family Members and Carers' in A. Braun and A. Röthel (eds) *Passing Wealth on Death: Will-substitutes in Comparative Perspective*. Oxford: Hart.

Hood, A. and Joyce, R. (2017) *Inheritances and Inequality Across and Within Generations*. London: Institute for Fiscal Studies.

Kerridge, R. (2009) *The Law of Succession*. London: Sweet and Maxwell.

Lamarca, I. and Marquès, A. (2014) 'We are not Born Alone and We Do Not Die Alone: Protecting Intergenerational Solidarity and Refraining Cain-ism through Forced Heirship' *Oñati Socio-Legal Series* 4(2), 264.

Law Commission (2011) *Intestacy and Family Provision Claims on Death*. London: Law Commission.

Lee, N. (2007) 'Inheritance Tax – An Equitable Tax No Longer: Time for Abolition?' *Legal Studies* 27(4), 678.

Leslie, M. (2014) 'Frustration of Intent in the Wealth Transmission Process' *Oñati Socio-Legal Series* 4(2), 283.

Leslie, M. (1996) 'The Myth of Testamentary Freedom' *Arizona Law Review* 38, 235.

Lewis, L. (1897) 'Some Peculiar Wills' *Strand Magazine* 14, 441.

Monk, D. (2011) 'Sexuality and Succession Law: Beyond Formal Equality' *Feminist Legal Studies* 19(3), 231.

Monk, D. (2013) 'E M Forster's Will: An Overlooked Posthumous Publication' *Legal Studies* 33(4), 572.

Monk, D. (2016) 'Inheritance Families of Choice? Lawyers' Reflections on Gay and Lesbian Wills' *Journal of Law and Society* 43(2), 167.

Rebellato, D. (1999) *1956 and All That: The Making of Modern British Drama*. London: Routledge.

Simpson, F. (2016) 'Duke of Westminster's eldest daughter misses out on £9 billion fortune – because she's female' *Evening Standard*, 10 August.

Tate, Joshua C. (2008) 'Caregiving and the Case for Testamentary Freedom' *University of California, Davis Law Review* 42, 129.

Walter, T. (1991) 'Modern Death: Taboo or not Taboo?' *Sociology* 25, 293.

Westwood, S. (2013) '"My Friends are my Family": An Argument about the Limitations of Contemporary Law's Recognition of Relationships in Later Life' *Journal of Social Welfare and Family Law* 35(3), 347.

Williams, C. et al (2008) 'Cohabitation and Intestacy: Public Opinion and Law Reform' *Child and Family Law Quarterly* 20(4), 499.

Cases

Carapeto v Good [2002] *EWCA* Civ 994
Edwards v Edwards and others [2007] *EWHC* 1119 (Ch)
Frere v Peacocke (1846)
Garland v Morris [2007] *EWHC* 2 (Ch)
Ilott v The Blue Cross and others [2017] *UKSC* 17
In re Strittmater's Estate (1947) 140 *N.J. Eq.* 94
Kostic v Chaplin [2007] *EWHC* 2298
Marckx v Belgium (1979) *2 EHRR* 330
Radmacher v Granatino [2010] *UKSC* 42
Re Coventry (dec'd) [1980] Ch 61
Rowe v Clarke [2005] *EWHC* 3038 (Ch)
Wright v Waters [2014] *EWHC* 3614 (Ch)

Chapter 13

Looking after grandchildren

Unfair and differential impacts?

Felicity Kaganas and Christine Piper

Many grandparents are busy people and, for some, that it is because of their 'grandparent duties'. These 'duties' may be undertaken full time, as a regular weekly commitment or on particular days such as school holidays, or when a grandchild or her parent is ill. And while caring for grandchildren is for many a source of pleasure, they may also speak of a sense of moral obligation and, in some cases, feelings of being 'put upon' and being 'too old for all this'.

You may hear it remarked that it is because there are more families with both parents working full time or more parents divorcing and living apart that grandparents now have more of these 'grandparent duties'. Such anecdotal evidence raises important questions. Has there been an increase in the use of grandparent care, whether full-time or part-time? If so, what are the reasons? Are there similar trends in other countries? Do grandparents feel they have a choice? And, importantly, are there any problematic issues relating to gender and to the age of the grandparents?

This chapter will first consider the research evidence for any significant trends in care-giving by grandparents – placing this in the context of what is known about grand-parenting in the recent and more distant past – and evaluating the reasons. It will then focus on any differential effects in terms of gender and age before analysing the development – within the context of law and policy – of what emerges as the most important issue, that of grandparent care for those children who would otherwise be in the care of the state.

A growing trend?

One might assume that the trend would be towards less involvement by informal carers such as grandparents because of the increase in formal care:

> Since the late 1990s formal childcare has become both more available and more affordable across the UK as a consequence of initiatives such as free entitlement to part-time early education for all three and four year olds, the

> development of children's centres and subsidies for childcare costs through Working Tax Credits.
>
> (Rutter and Evans 2012, 8)

However, in 2013 the Grandparents Plus charity reported that 'the amount of childcare provided by grandparents is increasing' (Grandparents Plus 2013). Mooney and Statham noted that surveys of mothers' use of childcare showed that, by the end of the twentieth century, care by relatives, and particularly by grandparents, was the most common (2002, 2). Research 'investigating grandparents who provide regular informal child care is still within its infancy' (Kirby and Sanders 2012) but, in the UK, it has identified a range of levels of involvement 'from occasional babysitting through regular help with child care to being the sole or main provider of childcare while parents work' as well as full-time care 'for grandchildren whose parents are unable or unwilling' to provide care (Statham 2011, 4).

Informal/part-time care

In the UK, a survey of 7,100 parents receiving child benefit in 2008 concluded that, although 2008 saw an increase in the take-up of out-of-school services (such as breakfast and after-school clubs), '[t]he take-up of informal childcare (such as grandparents) has remained stable over the period 2004–2008'. The average time spent by grandparents on childcare was found to be 6.5 hours per week (Speight et al 2009, 1–2). The percentage of working lone parents who used informal care provided by grandparents was 29%, exceeding the use of ex-partners (23%); similarly, 27% of couples with both parents working used grandparent care (Speight et al 2009, 165, table C2.2). This study therefore concluded that 'informal carers such as grandparents continue to play a prominent role in providing childcare' and that 'Pre-school age children were particularly likely to receive care from grandparents, which was for relatively large amounts of time and often for economic reasons (i.e. so that parents could work or study)' (ibid, 137). Further, a review of research data on grandparents in the UK providing childcare (excluding sole carers) found that 'Grandparents were the main child care arrangement for 35 per cent of families where the mother was working or studying when the child was nine months old, ahead of all other types of care' (Statham 2011, 2). And it seems that it is grandmothers, in particular, who are the main carers:

> Younger grandmothers (eg aged 50 to 64) who are fit, healthy and with younger grandchildren are the most likely to be providing care for their grandchildren, often to enable parents, and especially mothers, to work.
>
> (Grandparents Plus 2013, 1)

Research indicating that grandparent part-time care is increasing can be found in other jurisdictions too. For example, in Australia:

> A significant change in recent years is the increasing numbers of grandparents who are providing child care for their grandchildren. Australian grandparents are the biggest providers of informal child care for children between birth and 12 years, but particularly for babies and toddlers while their parents are in the workforce or studying.
>
> (ABS 2006)

Similarly, in the USA, 'One-fifth of children aged below five with employed mothers benefit from grandparent provided child care as their main source of daycare' (Ho 2015, 359) and Mauk (2016), summarising recent research in relation to grandparents engaging in part-time or full-time care of grandchildren, concludes, 'These statistics represent a growing trend in American culture'. Dutch research also found an increase in care by grandparents aged 58–68 (Guerts et al 2015).

Full-time care

In the UK, it is in relation to full-time care that research has revealed the most significant change. An analysis of the 2001 census data showed that 173,200 children were being raised by relatives (Nandy et al 2011), a significant increase from 1991 (Aziz et al 2012, 4), and research indicates that it is primarily grandparents who are kinship carers (Aziz et al 2012, para. 4.8; Ashley et al 2015, 6, 7; Hunt and Waterhouse 2012, 7). Aziz et al found that 70% of their research sample of 493 family and friends carers were grandparents and that most were caring for one or two children, while some were raising three or more (2012, 3). In the Bristol University sample of 80 children and their carers 61.25% of kinship carers were grandparents (Selwyn et al 2013, 5, 6). Forty-five per cent of all the kinship carers had other caring responsibilities too – 40% had responsibilities outside the home for another adult and 5% were caring for their spouse or partner at home (ibid, 7). A research sample of 32 grandparents aged 65 and over who were raising their grandchildren had the following characteristics: 74% were women and 26% were men, 58% were living with a partner, while 22% were single carers (separated or divorced), 19% were widowed, and four were still working (Wellard 2011, 10). Again, the evidence is that it is grandmothers who are most involved.

The trend towards more 'skipped generation' families (see Herlofson and Hagestad 2012) or 'Grand Families' (AARP 2010) can also be found in the USA. In 1999 Bryson and Casper wrote that, 'In 1970 a little over 3% of all children aged under 18 were living in a home maintained by their grandparents. By 1992 this percentage had increased to nearly 5% … In 1997 [to] … 5.5 percent' (Bryson and Casper 1999, 23). In 2010, AARP reported, 'The number of children living in a grandparent's home has increased significantly over the past decade, according to … the U.S. Census Bureau'. The Department of Health and Human Services in the USA also reported that, out of the 44.7 million people who were over 65 in 2013, 'a total of about 2.2 million … lived in a household with a grandchild present. About 536,000 of these grandparents over 65 years old were the persons with primary responsibility for their grandchildren who lived with them' (AOA 2014, 2, 5). Livingston and Parker (2010) cite research showing that, 'One child in 10 in the United States lives with a grandparent', and that 41% of those children were being cared for primarily by the grandparent.

Ethnic group variations

There are clearly variations among ethnic groups in the amount and type of grandparent care. For example, researchers at the University of Bristol found that, 'Children from Asian, black, mixed, Chinese and other ethnicities were all over-represented in the kinship population' and the prevalence rates were particularly high for black African and Pakistani children (Nandy and Selwyn 2013, 1657). The researchers speculate that varying 'expectations of a "duty" to care for members of the extended family are likely to be a factor' (ibid). Similarly, in the USA, 'The phenomenon of grandparents serving as primary caregivers is more common among blacks and Hispanics than among whites' (Livingston and Parker 2010). Reasons of space preclude a focus in this chapter on these ethnic variations but there is some suggestion that the sharpest recent rise in grandparent care has been among the white population: 'The number of white grandparents primarily responsible for their grandchildren rose by 9% from 2007 to 2008, compared with an increase of just 2% among black grandparents and no change among Hispanic grandparents' (Livingstone and Parker 2010).

Explanations

Research suggests that parents tend to use informal childcare in six different ways. It may be used as the main type of care for babies and toddlers; as an affordable supplement to nursery; as regular after-school and holiday childcare; and as emergency cover or when a child is ill. It may also be used as short-term childcare for parents who are studying or looking for work. Finally, parents who work outside normal office hours may use informal childcare as their main form of childcare (Rutter and Evans 2012, 9).

Research also suggests that the increase in the use of part-time care can be attributed to a combination of parental separation and more mothers working or studying.[1] Grandparents offer support to children and grandchildren after marriage or relationship breakdown (FMI/University of Hertfordshire 2009, 3; Timonen et al 2009, 31). They also step in when mothers are working or to give parents 'parental time', enabling parents to do domestic activities, go shopping or to socialise (Speight et al 2009, 3, Table C4.1, 171). In addition, there are many grandparents providing care simply because the adult child – the parent – is not able/no longer able to find affordable housing or maintain mortgage payments and so moves back 'home'.[2]

For many years one reason for full-time grandparent care in countries across the globe has been that grandparents have taken over when parents have migrated to find work but have not been able or willing to take their children with them. Herlofson and Hagestad reference research on rural Asian and African areas (2012, 28); Baker and Silverstein (2012) discuss similar migration of the middle generation in skipped generation families in China and the USA; Ingersoll-Dayton et al (2015) examine this phenomenon in Thailand. In South Africa grandparents have long played such a role, but one on which HIV/AIDs has impacted: grandmothers now have a crucial role in looking after grandchildren when their adult child is ill or dies of AIDs (Chazan 2008; see also Raniga and Simpson 2010).[3] However migration does not feature among the most common reasons identified in the UK for grandparent care when the parent is 'absent'. Rather, the reasons often attest to complex and troubled family circumstances.

Aziz et al, in their survey of full-time kinship carers (70% of whom were grandparents) found four main reasons: parental drug abuse (41%); neglect (51%); parental mental illness (21%); and domestic violence (21%) (2012, 21).[4] The researchers comment that these figures corroborate findings in other studies:

> children living with family and friends carers had usually suffered multiple adversities before being placed with their carers, … the level of adversities suffered was equal to if not greater than the level of adversities suffered by children entering the care system.
>
> (ibid, referencing Hunt et al 2008 and Farmer and Moyers 2008)

Also, often overlooked in the general statistics, is the fact that children are in grandparent care because their mother is in prison. This is not an insignificant subgroup. Research exploring the experiences of children in Scotland who had a family member in prison noted that, 'Each year in Scotland, more children will experience a parent's imprisonment than a parent's divorce' (Loureiro 2010, 5).

'Research from the UK and US suggests that around half of imprisoned mothers and fathers lived with their children before imprisonment' (Williams et al 2012, 19) but, in a Ministry of Justice survey, 77% of mothers in prison reported that their children were living with a family member who was not the other parent, compared with 10% of fathers in prison (Ministry of Justice 2004; see also Dodd and Hunter 1992). Studies in 2007 similarly reported that over three-quarters of male prisoners' children lived with their (the child's) mother but that during maternal imprisonment, the alternative primary caregivers were often the grandparents or other female relatives (see Williams et al 2012, 19).

In 2011 it was estimated that 6,000 of the 17,000 children separated from their mothers by imprisonment were in kinship care (Prison Advice and Care Trust 2011). Galloway et al (2014) point out that this is in line with earlier findings that a majority of children affected by maternal imprisonment were in kinship care, 'looked after either by grandparents (25%) or other family members or family friends (29%) … compared with 2% of children of male prisoners' (2014, 19, referencing HMIP 1997). Often grandmothers had also been responsible for grandchildren before their adult child was imprisoned because of issues such as drug abuse (Galloway et al 2014, 19). It is maternal grandparents, particularly grandmothers, who bear the burden, leading academics in the USA to refer to grandmothers with daughters in prison 20 years ago as 'some of the nation's neediest older persons' (Dressell and Barnhill 1994, 685).

How different from the past?

The accepted truth appears to be that, 'The 20th century modern period of social change largely destroyed the extended family in Britain replacing it with the nuclear family living in geographical and social isolation' (FMI/University of Hertfordshire 2009, 28). Certainly, the growth of university education in the second half of the twentieth century led to relationships being established between partners from different parts of the country whilst the growth of larger and often global businesses has entailed employment moves to other parts of the country or abroad. Social mobility has, then, meant that extended households are less common.

However, another prevalent 'truth' is that the industrial revolution of the late eighteenth and early nineteenth centuries was responsible for the break-up of extended families:

> Family and kinship relations were perceived as the primary structuring features of small scale, pre-industrial society, producing basic goods and services and ordering roles and obligations … Industrialisation was identified by many as having sounded the death knell for this way of life, destroying extended families and undermining communities.
>
> (Gillies 2003, 3)

From the mid-eighteenth century many adult workers moved to the growing towns either because the agricultural revolution led to a shortage of employment in rural areas or because of the increasing need for labour in the new mills.[5] Normally the migration was to a town nearby: the 1851 census showed that most of the emigrants to Liverpool, Manchester, and Bolton came from Lancashire, Cheshire, or Ireland (Deane 1965, 145–146). Nevertheless, that could well be a sufficient distance to make close links with extended families difficult. And many moved further afield to find work. The entrepreneurs in the first cotton mills advertised for labour over a wide geographic area. For instance, in 1771 Richard Arkwright advertised in Derby, Nottingham, and Manchester for his new mill in Cromford, Derbyshire (Fitton 1989, 30). But while mill owners employed whole families– men, women, and children (Fitton and Wadsworth 1968)[6] – three-generational groups were not the norm. Research on the industrial revolution based on 600 working class autobiographies shows 34 families – a minority – where there were representatives of three generations for part of the autobiographer's childhood (Humphries 2010, 157).

Further, it is now clear that the early textile mills relied very heavily on child labour (Humphries 2010, 2015) and that many of those children were orphans, often sent to the Midlands and further north, and apprenticed to mill owners who provided board and lodging (Honeyman 2007; Humphries 2015). Even after the Poor Law Amendment Act 1834 and the establishment of workhouses, this practice continued. Not all these pauper apprentices were orphans but, even if there was a parent or grandparent still living they clearly could not care for the children because they were working, or could not financially support them because they themselves were in the workhouse. The sheer numbers of apprentices involved – over 300 at Cressbrook Mill for example (Chapman 1992) – attests to an acute lack of available grandparent care.

The view that extended families were prevalent until they were destroyed as a result of industrialisation is contentious. Research based in several disciplines has undermined the idea of an earlier golden age of extended family living and provided evidence that the extended family as a household disappeared – if it ever existed – long before industrialisation. Laslett showed that family households of four or five persons (average of 4.75) were the norm in England by the 1540s when parish records began (Laslett 1965; Wrigley and Schofield 1989) and that it was 'not true that industrialization brought the simple nuclear family with it' (Laslett 2015, 91). In any case, as he pointed out, 'You could not with any confidence expect to see your grandchildren' (Laslett 1971, 103; see also Ward 1990); average life expectancy at birth was 35–40 in the eighteenth century (Mercer 2014, referencing Wrigley and Schofield 1989). Rosenthal's research (1996),[7] using Inquisitions Post Mortem in the late medieval period, found that only one-third of the families in his sample extended into three generations.

More recent research suggests that there were diverse – but remarkably stable – regional variations in family patterns (Todd 1990 referenced in Duranton et al 2008, 6 *et seq*) and that, in the UK, the nuclear family was dominant in southern and eastern England and eastern Scotland, with the multi-generational family type prevalent in the west of the British Isles (Duranton et al 2008, 13).[8] The suggestion, then, is that the nuclear family form long preceded industrialisation in much of the UK. Things started to change, Laslett argues, in the 1850s and 1860s when registers show that the poor had more kin living with them (Laslett 2015, 96). Indeed, Ruggles asserts that 'the frequency of extended families roughly doubled between about 1750 and 1900' (1987, xvii). In this later stage of industrialisation, the next generation had kin nearby or even sharing their rooms but, given continuing high early death rates, other (younger) extended family members might more often provide substitute care than did grandparents (Anderson 1995; Humphries 2010, 156–158). In any event, until the various nineteenth-century factory and mines Acts reduced the hours of work for children, or made such work illegal, only the very youngest children in industrial areas would have needed informal child care, a situation which continued with the introduction of universal free primary education in the last decade of the nineteenth century.[9]

By the early twentieth century, however, because of improvements in living standards and public health, the median age at death had risen: in 1910 it was

63.[10] So more grandparents were alive – and well enough – to care for grandchildren. Working class mothers often still needed to work and evidence in biographies suggests grandmothers provided part- or full-time care.[11] Indeed, one historian asserts that the period between the late nineteenth century and the mid-twentieth century was 'a kind of "golden age" of working class kinship' (Lynch 2010, 189) but there is a dearth of research with regard to care by grandparents. The focus of much of the analysis of trends in the twentieth century is on care for, not care by, the older generation (see, for example, Wall 2010).

The situation was different for the middle classes where the professional or industry owning grandparents might have had considerable social and economic power and little time for grandparenting; care would have been provided by servants. Later, middle class women fought for the right to work and increasingly did work although immediately after the Second World War mothers in the middle and working classes were encouraged to be full-time mothers and housewives (Donnelly 1999, 43). As the twentieth century progressed more mothers chose employment outside the home (Social Issues Research Centre 2011, 5–6) but, at the same time, there was increasing provision of child care by the state, as well as Third Sector and for-profit companies. Researchers have noted that, whilst research has been published in the last decade or so in relation to grandparent care, 'we are a little more in the dark about … the trends that have occurred over previous decades' (ibid, 7). One development was that grandparents were increasingly discussed as an emotional rather than practical or financial resource for grandchildren with a corresponding focus on opportunities for contact with them (Kaganas and Piper 1990, especially 32–33).

It is not, therefore, possible to see an overall progression in the twentieth century either towards or from part-time grandparent care. It has been important to a lesser or greater extent in various decades. In relation to full-time care, however, there is no evidence of a trend towards greater use of such care until relatively recently. In the last decade or so, however, the greater use of grandparents for full-time care has been a significant development.

The effects on grandparent carers of the recent trend

This generation of grandparents has been referred to as the 'pivot generation' because not only might they be juggling care of grandchildren with employment but – because of increased longevity – they might also have care-giving responsibilities towards their own parents (Mooney and Statham 2002). The difficulties for full-time carers – especially those who are caring for grandchildren who would otherwise be in local authority care – are particularly acute.

The children

Aziz et al (2012, 3) found that the children in their study had, in most cases, experienced traumatic events or neglect in the past:

> 51% of the children came to live with the carers as the result of experiencing neglect, 30% because of emotional abuse and 21% physical abuse. Some children had suffered multiple abuse. Most cases featured parental drug and/or alcohol abuse, parental mental ill health or parental death.

The children tended to be particularly needy or vulnerable with nearly half having a 'disability or special need such as emotional and behavioural problems' (Aziz et al 2012, 3; Ashley et al 2015, 6; Hunt and Waterhouse 2012, 12, 15). Ashley et al report that half the children in their study had a long-term illness or special needs. Forty-three per cent were judged by carers to have emotional and behavioural problems (2015, para. 3.1). Similarly, Aziz et al found that 38% of the carers asked said the child in question had behavioural and emotional problems. Twenty-one per cent referred to special educational needs. Carers also reported that children had learning disabilities, physical disabilities, and chronic illness (2012, para. 4.7) Mercer et al's review found that children cared for by family and friends had suffered similar 'adverse experiences' to those experienced by children cared for by local authority foster parents in the care system. They also observe that there is research showing that those with the most challenging children to raise receive little help (2015, para. 1.3)[12]

Age and vulnerability

In the study by Aziz et al, 29% of the children were living with at least one carer over the age of 60. Twenty-six per cent of all the carers had a long-term illness or disability and 24% had a partner with a long-term illness or disability (Aziz et al 2012 para. 4.8).

In Wellard's sample of 32 grandparents aged 65 or over, 24 of the carers had a long term health condition or disability, of which arthritis was the most common, followed by heart disease and high blood pressure:

> 57% of those with a health condition, or 13 individuals, describe the impact of the health condition as 'moderate or severe', 13 (50% of those who answered the question) describe themselves as 'stressed', with 10 rating their personal wellbeing as 'good'. Just one respondent receives help with their condition from adult social services. Eight respondents say their partners have a long term health condition, for whom four are providing care and support. Four are providing care and support for an elderly relative or neighbour.
>
> (Wellard 2011, 10)[13]

Wellard also found that older grandparents had less support: 'It was striking that the [older] grandparents who felt they were coping least well were less likely to have strong support networks and that having someone who understands their situation and can offer emotional support is vital for their wellbeing' (ibid, 33).

Poverty and employment

There are also serious financial consequences. In 2005 Gray pointed out that, 'Raising employment rates amongst the over 50s is an established objective of government policy, yet it may conflict with the role of younger grandparents in childcare' (2005, 557) and that has proved to be so. In one survey it was found that, 'Almost half (49%) of kinship carers have had to give up work permanently to care for the kin child, and a further 18% had to give up work temporarily' (Ashley et al 2015, 2).[14] Others reduced their hours or took a lower grade job. Some reported that their partners had increased their hours or delayed retirement (Aziz et al 2012, para. 6.2). The authors observe:

> The income data partly explains why so many family and friends carers who completed the survey feel that life is a continual financial struggle. This is made harder for many who cannot increase their income by working extra hours or taking on a job because of the responsibilities of caring for the kin child/ren, and yet many are also having to pay out significant sums to cover the extra costs of the children.
>
> (para. 6.7)[15]

The impact was only slightly less in the sample interviewed by Mooney and Statham:

> Three in five of those who had not already retired when they took on the role of caregiver had not had to make any changes to their work. That still left two out of five employees who had needed to make specific changes.
>
> (2002, 17)

So it is at least partly because of their caring responsibilities that 'Family and friends carers emerge ahead of the general population in many of the indicators of poverty or low income (Aziz and Roth 2012, 3).

Contact

There are also implications for grandparent carers arising from the fact that not all siblings live with the same relatives when their parents are unable or unwilling to care for them. Aziz et al found that 56% of family and friends carers were raising children who had at least one sibling living elsewhere (2012, 16; see also Hunt et al 2008). Often siblings in these families were placed with other members of the extended family (Farmer and Moyers 2008; Hunt et al 2008) and this allowed for a 'high level of contact' (see Aziz et al 2012, 16). However, Aziz et al found that 'only one in nine of the siblings living elsewhere are living with other relatives. Almost three times as many children had siblings who had either been adopted or were living in unrelated foster care' (2012, 16). This may make contact more difficult to negotiate. Research also provides a less than rosy picture of contact between children and their parents:

> Two of the grandparents had to return to court repeatedly because parents of the children they are looking after were seeking greater contact. One grandmother felt that her grandson's father, who is unemployed and able to get legal aid, uses court proceedings as a weapon against her.
>
> (Wellard 2011, 32).

These kinds of difficulties emerged also in a small qualitative Australian study:

> Grandparents reported that arguments, tension, and communication difficulties were common problems that would arise between themselves and the parents. This result highlighted that although parenting may prepare you for caring for your grandchildren it does not prepare you for working in a co-parenting team with adult children (the parents).
>
> (Kirby and Sanders 2012, Discussion section).

Gender

The American research of Wang and Marcotte (2007), using a nationally representative sample of 3,240 grandparents who were heads of households, found that grandparents in 'skipped-generation families' – looking after grandchildren without the children's parents in the household – were 'older and frailer, limiting opportunities in the labor market'. They relied 'less on the earnings of the grandchildren's parents to pay for expenses' but needed to work to finance caring (2007, 21). The authors comment, in relation to such grandparents, 'The families with the least power and fewest resources are most often put in this position. And within these families, women appear to make the most substantial accommodation and sacrifice' (ibid, 22). Similarly, Livingston and Parker, writing in the USA, found that, 'Some 62% of grandparent caregivers are female, and 38% are men' (Livingston and Parker 2010).

In the UK, 90% of those responding to the survey of friends and family carers undertaken by Aziz et al were women. More than a third of them were raising the child(ren) alone, compared to 4% of men (2012, para. 4.8). In Gautier and Willard's study, nine out of 10 kinship carers responding to the researchers' questions were grandparents and 92% of these were women (2014, 6). Selwyn et al found that the majority of kinship carers were grandparents and most of them were single women (2013, 3). Selwyn and Nandy report that '[a]mong grandparent kinship carers, 86% of grandfathers lived in a couple, compared to only 24% of grandmothers' (2014, 44). Broad's research revealed that 42% of kinship carers were grandparents and 68% of kinship carers were female (2004, 216). The picture painted by these findings confirms prevailing assumptions that it is women who are responsible for caring and, more particularly, caring for children.

What emerges from the evidence above is that, not only is there a relatively recent clear trend to more full-time grandparent care in the UK, but that this is also not a return to the 'normal' situation of earlier times. As we will explain, there are also very specific legal reasons for this development which themselves create further problems for grandparent carers.

Kinship care, local authorities and the law

Legislation has now been enacted requiring local authorities to prioritise kinship/family and friends care over fostering by unrelated carers and institutional care. Section 22C, introduced into the Children Act 1989 in 2008, creates a hierarchy of placements for children who are looked after by local authorities, whether under a care order or a consensual arrangement. Near the top of this hierarchy are family members and friends.

First preference is given to arrangements whereby the child lives with parents, someone with parental responsibility or, where a child arrangements order specifying with whom a child should live subsisted in respect of a child subsequently made the subject of a care order, the person in whose favour that s 8 order was made.[16] The duty to comply with these provisions is removed where to do so would not be consistent with the child's best interests or would not be reasonably practicable.[17] In such cases the local authority must place the child in a placement they consider to be the most appropriate.[18] In making this judgement, the local authority should give preference to a 'placement with an individual who is a relative, friend or other person connected with [the child] and who is also a local authority foster parent'.[19] It is also possible to place a child with a grandparent who is not a foster parent.[20]

Government policy that led to the enactment of s 22C was clearly informed by the view that kinship care is best for most children who cannot remain with their parents: it is 'much better for most children than entering care, and children have told us they believe the same' (HM Govt 2006, para. 2.29). Kinship placements enable children to stay with people they know and trust and provide a 'stable, safe and nurturing' environment (DfES 2007, para. 2.34). During the parliamentary debate concerning what would become s 22C, MP Tim Loughton observed that, 'Most people acknowledge that there are clear advantages to kinship caring and placements with family members'.[21]

However, there may be other reasons for the increased reliance on kinship care, including a move to reduce cost and to shrink the role of the state (Broad 2004, 212; Hunt 2003). O'Brien suggests that one explanation lies in necessity; it is:

> the demise of institutional care; a preference for fostering and simultaneously a shortage of such carers; and – perhaps most importantly – a better understanding of what extended families can provide to children in need of care. However, the increase in the kinship care placement rate reflects a development evolving more out of a scarcity of alternative care options than a coherent, childcentred policy that prioritised or aimed at developing this care option.
>
> (2012, 128)

The increased emphasis on kinship care means that more grandparents are approached by local authorities to take on the care of their grandchildren. They play a pivotal role in the privatisation of child care represented by s 22C. This has implications for the autonomy of those grandparents; their autonomy is curtailed by their new childcare responsibilities, particularly if they have no financial or practical help.[22] Grandparents may give up work and pension prospects, leaving themselves financially vulnerable in old age. Finances generally, social lives, and relationships with partners can be affected. Holidays may no longer be an option and space can be a problem (Roth et al undated, para. 2.8).

As Aziz et al observe, typically relatives and friends who take on the care of children need to be able to make decisions about how the child is raised and they need financial and other support (Aziz et al 2012, para. 3.1). However, these needs are often not met. Grandparents who take on care of their grandchildren as a result of a private arrangement without any involvement of the local authority, or where the local authority simply facilitates a private arrangement, are particularly ill served; the local authority has financial and other obligations only to 'looked after' children. These are children who are in care under a care order or accommodated by the local authority under s 20 of the Children Act 1989 with the consent of those with parental responsibility.[23]

Research studies mentioned by Hunt and Waterhouse observed that local authority support appeared to be determined by the child's legal status rather than need. Also, it is the local authority that assesses whether the child has been placed with the carer under s 20 or not and the designation of arrangements as private, or as giving rise to looked after status, and so necessitating local authority support, seemed arbitrary. Finally, kinship carers were often not aware of the alternatives available to them or were in a weak position to challenge local authority decisions (2012, 5).

'Looked after' grandchildren

Since local authorities have a duty to maintain only 'looked after' children, whether or not grandparents become entitled to any assistance from the state and also what kind of assistance they get depends on the circumstances in which they undertake the care of their grandchildren and on the nature of their legal relationship with them.

Local Authorities have a duty in terms of s 17 of the Children Act 1989 to provide services for children in need within their areas. There is also a duty on local authorities under s 20 to provide accommodation for children in need in their area who require it because there is no-one who has parental responsibility for the child; the child has been lost or abandoned; or the person caring for the child has been prevented, whether temporarily or permanently, and for whatever reason, from providing suitable accommodation or care. Section 22(3) provides that local authorities have a duty to 'safeguard and promote' the welfare of any child being looked after by that local authority. Section 22A re-enacts the duty of local authorities to provide accommodation for children in their care. Section 22B places a duty on local authorities 'to maintain a child they are looking after in other respects apart from the provision of accommodation'. Section 22(1) of the

Children Act 1989 defines a looked after child to include a child who is in care or one who has been accommodated under s 20, but the definition expressly excludes a child receiving services under s 17. The effect of these provisions is that if a child is in care or if a child in need is accommodated in terms of s 20, the local authority has a duty to maintain that child. That duty may persist in some instances: 'a child who is looked after and is placed with a relative, friend or other person connected with the child in accordance with section 22C(5) continues to be looked after' (DfE 2011, para. 3.15).

In the case of looked after children, the local authority is required to support the arrangement and the placement is treated like any other foster placement. This includes payment of a non-means tested foster allowance which meets the national minimum. If a child is accommodated under s 20, the child qualifies as a looked after child and is visited by a social worker who oversees his or her welfare. A weekly fostering allowance is paid but there is no entitlement to Child Benefit or Child Tax Credit. The foster carers must be offered training and support. The local authority must provide support to meet the child's needs including an education plan, a health plan and training as well as support for the foster carers (Hunt and Waterhouse 2012, 4). Support, including financial support for carers may continue until the young person is 21 and the young person may receive support for educational and training purposes until the age of 25 (ibid).

In all other cases local authority support is discretionary.

Grandchildren who are not 'looked after' – discretionary payments

In the case of private arrangements where the local authority is not involved,[24] or merely facilitates the private arrangement, financial support is restricted to state benefits, including child benefit and, where appropriate, means tested benefits and tax credits. If the child is a child in need, there may also be support from the local authority under s 17(6) of the Children Act 1989.[25] If a child in need is supported under s 17, the child is not classified as a looked after child and there is no entitlement to financial assistance; the local authority has a discretion. Family income may be taken into account since the local authority must have regard to the means of the child and parents under s 17(8) CA 1989 (DfE 2011, table 1). Support under s 17 may take the form of advice, guidance and counselling and s 17(6) provides that assistance may be given in kind or in the form of financial help.[26] Discretionary support may take the form of regular payments but these cease when the child reaches the age of 18 (ibid).

According to the statutory guidance for local authorities dealing with family and friends care, the majority of family and friends arrangements are informally agreed between those with parental responsibility and the carers:[27]

> Most such arrangements remain entirely private without the need for the involvement of children's social care services, although where a child is

> assessed as being in need support may be provided under section 17 of the 1989 Act.
>
> (DfE 2011, para. 3.1)

In cases where the local authority is involved, whether or not the child falls into the category of looked after children depends on whether the local authority placed the child or simply assisted with a private arrangement. In *Southwark LBC v D*, [28] the court said that, while there may be cases where the local authority facilitates a private arrangement, in cases where a local authority plays a major role, it is likely to be seen as fulfilling its statutory duty under s 20 and the child is a looked-after child:

> **[49]...** If the local authority is facilitating a private arrangement, it must make it plain to the proposed foster parent that she or he must look to the parents or person with parental responsibility for financial support. The local authority must explain that any financial assistance from public funds would be entirely a matter for the discretion of the local authority for the area in which the foster parent is living. Only on receipt of such information could the foster parent give informed consent to acceptance of the child under a private fostering agreement. If such matters are left unclear, there is a danger that the foster parent (and subsequently the court) will conclude that the local authority was acting under its statutory powers and duties and that the arrangement was not a private one at all.

The Guidance states that:

> It may not always be easy to determine whether a child who is cared for by family or friends requires accommodation for the purposes of section 20(1) or whether that child's needs should be met by providing support under section 17 of the 1989 Act. In any event, where the local authority has instigated the arrangement for a child to live with a friend or relative, the local authority should provide an appropriate range and level of support for those arrangements.
>
> (DfE 2011 para. 3.16)

If a child is a looked after child, it is unlawful to discriminate against family or friends foster carers; they are entitled to be paid in the same way as and those who are unrelated.[29] However this is not so if the arrangement is a private one and government has expressed concerns that support should be adequate:

> No child or young person should have to become a looked after child ... for the sole purpose of enabling financial, practical or other support to be provided to the child's carer. Authorities must seek to provide any necessary support services without the child becoming looked after unless the child

> meets the criteria at section 20(1) of the 1989 Act and requires accommodation. Neither should the fear of losing support be allowed to become an obstacle to family and friends carers taking over responsibility for the long term care of a looked after child through applying for a residence order[30] or special guardianship order. Decisions by a local authority that a child should become looked after, or cease to be looked after, must be based on an assessment of the child's needs and circumstances.
>
> (DfE 2011, para. 2.19)

Some relatives choose to apply for special guardianship or a child arrangements order.[31] These orders offer the only means by which carers gain the status to operate as autonomous decision-makers. Either of these orders will confer parental responsibility on the carer and a special guardian may exercise parental responsibility to the exclusion of all others.[32] However while some grandparents appreciate the freedom from local authority supervision[33] that these orders provide, others are encouraged or pressured[34] into applying for them in order to relieve the local authority from paying foster allowances. Hunt and Waterhouse quote one grandparent:

> Foster allowances are paid only for a short term period; authorities are not prepared to pay grandparents a foster allowance until the children reach the age of 16 years old. Once the short term period has expired grandparents are expected to sign a binding contract to either accept residency/special guardianship. This is so unjust … You love and adore the children and want to keep them part of the family unit. The authorities involved, knowing these bonds, ties and attachments have been cemented, make available one get out option 'give the children up to be fostered out to strangers' … I consider this to be emotional blackmail.
>
> (2012, 75)

The government has extended the Adoption Support Fund to special guardians in cases where children were previously looked after (DfE 2016b, 41; DfE 2016c). In addition, in the case of a child who was being looked after immediately prior to the making of a special guardianship order, the child, special guardian, or parent has the right to be assessed for support services such as counselling or financial assistance.[35] Financial support is payable to a special guardian or prospective special guardian to facilitate arrangements for special guardianship where the local authority considers such arrangements to be in the child's best interests and to support the continuation of such arrangements.[36] However the requirement to provide support is qualified in Regulation 6(2). Support is payable only where the local authority consider it 'necessary to ensure that the special guardian or prospective special guardian can look after the child'; where the local authority 'consider that the child needs special care … because of his illness, disability, emotional or behavioural difficulties or the consequences of his past abuse or neglect'; where the local authority consider that it is appropriate to contribute to legal costs; and where the local authority consider it 'appropriate to contribute to the expenditure necessary for the purposes of accommodating and maintaining the child' which might include paying for 'furniture and domestic equipment, alterations to and adaptations of the home', transport, clothing, toys, and other necessary items.

The Guidance states that:

> 49. It is important that children who are not (or were not) looked after are not unfairly disadvantaged by this approach. In many cases the only reason that the child is not looked after is that relatives stepped in quickly to take on the responsibility for the child when a parent could no longer do so.
>
> (DfE 2016a)

However, although Regulation 11 confers a discretion on local authorities to offer assessments to the child, special guardian or prospective special guardian or parent, among others, even where the child has not been a looked after child, there is no right to be assessed in these cases.[37]

Assessments for support follow the Assessment Framework and so take into account the child's developmental needs as well as the parenting capacity of the special guardian (DfE 2016, para. 56). When assessing financial support, the means of the special guardian will normally be taken into consideration. Regulation 13 requires the local authority to take account of:

a the person's financial resources, including any tax credit or benefit, which would be available to him if the child lived with him;
b the amount required by the person in respect of his reasonable outgoings and commitments (excluding outgoings in respect of the child);
c the financial needs and resources of the child.

There is also no right to assessment where a relative is caring for a child in terms of a child arrangements order. The local authority has a discretion to make contributions to the child's accommodation and maintenance.[38]

Hunt and Waterhouse sum up the position:

> Looked after status, the only one which provides entitlement to support, is an increasingly reliable passport to a comprehensive package of services for both carers and children. The statutory framework for special guardianship means that it is usually a better option than a residence[39] order, but since support is discretionary, very much inferior to kinship foster care. Informal arrangements are the least well supported. Carers who act on their own initiative to protect children are often discriminated against in terms of accessing support.
>
> (2013, 3)

In short, most grandparent carers are left out in the cold. The position of grandparents caring full-time for children who are not looked after is exacerbated by the

Welfare Reform and Work Act 2016; this introduces a benefit cap and limits child tax credit to two children.[40]

Choice and autonomy

While there is little historical evidence that grandparents have traditionally acted as substitute full-time carers in this country, it is clear that, despite the hardships that ensue, this is a role they, and more particularly grandmothers, are now expected, and see themselves as duty-bound, to play. As one grandparent quoted by Wellard said:

> People say to me, 'I don't know how you do it' and I say 'but if you're in the situation you've got to, what choice have you got. If the situation comes to you and it's your own, what choice have you got?' You don't have any choice, do you, you do it.
>
> (Wellard 2011, 36)

This perception of inevitability and lack of choice can be contrasted with the contemporary emphasis on choice and control in the decision to become a parent; with the availability of contraception and abortion, parenthood is a status that is now, more than ever, one that is assumed voluntarily. Boyd et al (2015, 8) have written about the increased reproductive choices that have become available to women since the 1970s, and they go on to focus on perhaps one of the most deliberate and carefully planned types of parenthood. They coin the phrase 'autonomous motherhood' to describe the situation of women who choose to raise a child alone (14). The researchers deploy a relational conception of autonomy rather than one rooted in liberal individualism (15). While acknowledging the agency of the individual, they highlight the importance of relationships with others in enhancing and facilitating autonomy; supportive relationships and networks are what enable these mothers to parent alone (15, 28, 173, 175).

These networks are particularly important because of the expectation that single mothers should be economically self-sufficient and should eschew dependency; neo-liberal ideology demands that responsibility for raising children be privatised (11, 21 and 178). Prior to embarking on autonomous motherhood, women set about establishing networks, saving money, and also gauging the extent of potential help from family (186). For these women, then, becoming a parent is a choice. While their autonomy is constrained by childcare responsibilities and while economic factors may shape decisions, they are able to make preparations for taking on the responsibility and exercise it autonomously (19).

For grandparents who take on the full-time care of their grandchildren, things are very different: 'Whatever the circumstances that brought grandchildren into the home of their grandparents to be raised, it can come as a shock to the older adults who find themselves in this situation' (Mauk 2016). The transition to kinship care is 'often sudden and crisis-driven' (Selwyn et al 2013, 10). Hunt and

Waterhouse (2012, 8) report that, in their study, fewer than a third of the carers said that responsibility for children was assumed as part of a planned move; most said it had 'all happened suddenly, in a crisis'. Most said that, had they not stepped in, the child would have gone into local authority care. Others said they did not know what would have happened (8, 28). Selwyn et al report that some carers felt they had little choice. Most said they did not want the child to go into care and that they felt a sense of obligation (2013, 13).

The decision is typically one taken in haste and without good advice or sufficient preparation. In one study, over 75% of carers said that, at the time of taking on the responsibility of full-time childcare, they did not have enough understanding of the legal position to make an informed decision (Aziz et al 2012, para. 5.6).[41] Carers wanted to 'do the right thing' by taking in the child but were 'largely unaware of the legal options and consequences of what they were doing' (ibid). It seems that social workers did not give them information. Moreover, the potentially helpful role of family justice professionals in redressing the imbalance of power between the local authority and the carers is reduced. This is because carers cannot afford legal advice or representation, because of the variability of expertise among solicitors and because there are no guardians in private law proceedings (Hunt and Waterhouse 2013, 7). Restrictions on Legal Aid imposed by the Legal Aid, Sentencing and Punishment of Offenders Act 2012 exacerbate the problem.

In addition, once the decision is made, carers often are left to their own devices without help. Carers participating in research studies reported an unmet need for emotional support (Aziz et al 2012, 3; Ashley et al 2015, 16). They also needed, but did not get, respite care, counselling and help with managing children's behavioural and emotional difficulties (Roth et al undated, para. 2.7; Selwyn et al 2013, 61) Carers felt they would have benefited from meeting other kinship carers and this, say Ashley et al, highlights 'the isolation and struggle many face alone' (2015 16).[42] Carers may have to contend with interference from troubled parents and even applications for specific issue or prohibited steps orders. They may also be faced with having to manage, alone, contact, and even risky contact, between the child and his or her parents (Selwyn et al 2013, 38).[43]

So, while the adult children of these grandparents may differ from Boyd's autonomous mothers in that their parenthood may not be planned or supported,[44] grandparents who step in to take on care of their grandchildren are also far removed from that situation. They do so with little choice, with no chance to build networks and they are expected to be financially and emotionally self-sufficient.

Conclusion

A significant number of grandparents, and more specifically grandmothers, are engaged in the care of their grandchildren, whether full-time or part-time. This they do at considerable cost to themselves in many instances, although many report very positive experiences of watching their grandchildren grow and thrive. Grandparents who become full-time carers perhaps gain the most satisfaction and also sacrifice the most.

Yet grandparents are not autonomous agents when deciding to take on the responsibility of parenting their grandchildren; they are left with little choice if they do not want their grandchildren to go into care. Many care for their grandchildren, not only because they love them, but because they feel they have a duty to do so. Indeed, that they should feel this way is now an expectation held by social workers and endorsed by the law. In particular, it is grandmothers who consider themselves responsible for caring for grandchildren. Local Authority social workers implementing the preference in policy and legislation for kinship care also appear to see grandmothers as the prime candidates. And since social workers do not appear to inform grandparents of their options and entitlements, grandparents are not in a position to choose the terms on which they assume responsibility; many do not have access to reliable legal advice. They do not have the time and space to prepare for parenthood and they do not have access to support, whether practical, financial, or emotional. In taking on childcare full-time, they sacrifice their autonomy in terms of financial self-sufficiency, lifestyle, social relationships, activities, and even in terms of their intimate relationships. They are expected to cope alone with troubled children as well as the troubled parents of those children. Many are not in good health and many are forced to face poverty.

Calasanti has observed the extent to which poverty is exacerbated by 'structural adjustment policies that assume that "families" can absorb the costs' (2010, 146). While this observation was made in the context of the global south, it is relevant to grandparent care in Britain. That financial and other support for most grandparent and other family and friends carers is discretionary and often not forthcoming might be attributable to an assumption that these carers should be acting out of altruistic motives, out of a sense of duty, or a combination of both. It is perhaps an assumption that grandparents ought to be responsible for their grandchildren that sets them apart, even in the eyes of some grandparents themselves, from stranger foster parents. As Beverly Hughes, the then Minister of State for Children, Young People and Families, said in the debate on the 2008 amendments to the Children Act:

> We want to see more relative carers receiving financial and other support from local authorities when it is needed. The serious problem with the amendment is that it would, in effect, remove the discretionary aspect of section 17 for this category of children and family carers and effectively give family carers an entitlement in law that birth parents, who may have similar difficulties, currently do not have.
>
> We have to be very clear that it is not the role of local authorities to provide general income maintenance for families, and nor are they resourced to do so.[45]

Friends and family, then, are regarded as being in a similar category to parents. Yet they, and more specifically, grandparents, have not been seen in this light in the past. There is no historically established expectation – in the UK or, indeed in many other western countries – that grandparents care full time for grandchildren. Moreover, there is a difference between the children whose grandparents cared for them in the past and the children put in friends and family care today; the children that modern grandparents are raising are often challenging and with special needs. We are not returning to an age of close extended families. This is new and the burden borne by contemporary grandparents is heavier.

Grandparents, particularly grandmothers, are a significant resource in the neoliberal climate of privatisation of childcare responsibility. And this resource is exploited by local authorities as cheaply as possible.

Notes

1 See, for statistics, Speight et al (2009, 198, Table C9.1).
2 See, for example, www.caba.org.uk/help-and-guides/information/keeping-peace-live-adult-children. Livingstone and Parker (2010) refer to a sharp rise in the number of children living with grandparents during the 'Great Recession'.
3 It is also worth noting that in South Africa, 'coloured workers often paid their parents to care for their children' (Burman 1996, 585).
4 In the USA the increase in full-time care by grandparents has been attributed to 'the growth in drug use among parents, teen pregnancy, divorce, the rapid rise of single parent households, mental and physical illness, AIDS, crime, child abuse and neglect, and incarceration of parents' (Bryson and Casper 1999, 23).
5 Although 'The true exodus from the land did not develop until the second half of the nineteenth century' (Deane 1965, 139).
6 Indeed, women and children dominated the labour force: at Arkwright's Cromford mills in 1789: 150 men were employed out of a total labour force of 1150 (Humphries 2015, 49).
7 See the review of this book by J. Bennett, in *The Medieval Review*. Available at: https://scholarworks.iu.edu/journals/index.php/tmr/article/view/14467/20585
8 See, also, Nash (1982, 135) for research on Denbighshire in Wales where grandchildren were boarded out to help grandparents.
9 The Elementary Education Act 1880 made attendance at school compulsory only for 5–10 year olds, raised to 11 in 1893, 12 in 1899 and 14 in 1918 but education was not free until the 1890s.
10 www.ons.gov.uk/peoplepopulationandcommunity/birthsdeathsandmarriages/deaths/articles/mortalityinenglandandwales/2012-12-17
11 See, for example, the biography of Catherine Cookson by Kathleen Jones (1999).
12 See also Selwyn et al (2013, 17).
13 In the USA: 'Overall grandparent primary caregivers are relatively young – more than two-thirds (67%) are younger than age 60, with 13% younger than age 45' (Livingston and Parker 2010).
14 See also Aziz et al (2012, para. 6.2).
15 The position of carers is likely to be exacerbated by the provisions of the Welfare Reform and Work Act 2016 (Ashley et al 2015, 14).
16 S 22C(2) and (3).

17 S 22C(4).
18 S 22C(5).
19 S 22C(7).
20 S 22C(6)(d).
21 Hansard 2008 col 769; Public Bill Committee Debates, Children and Young Persons Bill [Lords] Col 49. Available at: www.publications.parliament.uk/pa/cm200708/cmpublic/children/080624/pm/80624s02.htm
22 See also Selwyn et al (2013, 52–4, 67).
23 But see *London Borough of Hackney* v *John Williams and Adenike Williams* [2017].
24 See *R (on the application of Cunningham)* v *Hertfordshire County Council & Anor* [2016].
25 See Aziz et al (2012) para. 3.2.
26 See DfE (2011) para. 3.6.
27 Provided they are relatives in terms of s 105 CA 1989, there is no need to notify the local authority.
28 [2007] 1 FLR 2181.
29 *R (on the Application of L and Others) v Manchester City Council; R (on the Application of R and Another) v Manchester City Council* [2001]; *R (on the application of X) v London Borough of Tower Hamlets* [2013].
30 Now a child arrangements order.
31 See Aziz et al (2012) para. 3.3.
32 See DfE 2011 para. 3.23.
33 Without these orders and where children are not subject to care orders, carers need to get permission from those with parental authority, usually the parents, in making any decisions other than those relatively minor ones covered by s 3(5) of the Children Act 1989.
34 See Bowyer et al (2015, 26); Selwyn et al (2013, 9, 13, 58).
35 Regulations 3 and 11 Special Guardianship Regulations 2005; s 14F Children Act 1989. See also DfE (2016a) para. 22.
36 Regulation 6(1).
37 See also s 14F Children Act 1989.
38 Children Act 1989, sched 1 para. 15.
39 Now Child Arrangements Order.
40 See Ashley et al (2015, 14ff).
41 See also Ashley et al (2015, 2, 20); Hunt and Waterhouse (2012, 41).
42 See also Selwyn et al (2013, 51, 67).
43 See Bowyer et al (2015, 35–36).
44 We are indebted to Daniel Monk for this observation.
45 Hansard Public Bill Committee Debates 2008 Children and Young Persons Bill [Lords] Col 77. Available at: www.publications.parliament.uk/pa/cm200708/cmpublic/children/080624/pm/80624s07.htm

Bibliography

AARP (formerly the American Association of Retired Persons) (2010) 'More grandparents raising grandchildren'. Available at: www.aarp.org/relationships/grandparenting/info-12-2010/more_grandparents_raising_grandchildren.html

Australian Bureau of Statistics (ABS) (2006) *Child Care, Australia, June 2005* (Catalogue No. 4402). Canberra: Australian Bureau of Statistics.

Anderson, M. (1995, republished 2007) *Approaches to the History of the Western Family 1500–1914*. Cambridge: Cambridge University Press.

Administration on Aging (AOA), U.S. Department of Health and Human Services (2014) *A Profile of Older Americans 2014.* Available at: www.aoa.acl.gov/aging_statistics/profile/2014/docs/2014-Profile.pdf

Arber, S. and Timonen, V. (eds) (2012) *Contemporary Grandparenting: Changing Family Relationships in Global Context.* Bristol: Policy Press.

Ashley, C., Aziz, R. and Braun, D. (2015) *Doing the Right Thing; A Report on the Experience of Kinship Carers.* Available at: www.frg.org.uk/images/Kinship_Care_Alliance/151013%20Report%20on%20kinship%20carers%20survey.pdf

Aziz, R., Roth, D. and Lindley, B., edited by Ashley, C. (2012) *Understanding Family and Friends Care: The Largest UK Survey.* Available at: www.frg.org.uk/images/e-publications/ffc-report-3.pdf

Baker, L. and Silverstein, M. (2012) 'The Well-being of Grandparents Caring for Grandchildren in Rural China and the United States' in S. Arber and V. Timonen (eds) *Contemporary Grandparenting: Changing Family Relationships in Global Contexts.* Bristol: Policy Press.

Bowyer, S., Wilkinson, J., Tapsfield, R., Gadsby Waters, J. and Corrick Ranger, H. (2015) *Special Guardianship. Qualitative Case File Analysis.* London: Department for Education (DfE).

Boyd, S., Chunn, D., Kelly, F. and Wiegers, W. (2015) *Autonomous Motherhood?: A Socio-Legal Study of Choice and Constraint.* Toronto: University of Toronto Press.

Broad, B. (2004) 'Kinship Care for Children in the UK: Messages from Research, Lessons for Policy and Practice' *European Journal of Social Work* 7, 211.

Bryson, K. and Casper, L. (1999) *Coresident Grandparents and Grandchildren.* Washington, D.C., MD: U.S. Census Bureau, Current Population Reports, 23–198.

Burman, S. (1996) 'Intergenerational Family Care: Legacy of the Past, Implications for the Future' *Journal of Southern African Studies* 22(4), 585.

Calasanti, T. (2010) 'Gender and Aging in the Context of Globalization' in D. Dannefer and C. Phillipson (eds) *The Sage Handbook of Social Gerontology.* London: Sage.

Chapman, S. (1992) *The Early Factory Masters: The Transition to the Factory System in the Midlands Textile Industry.* Aldershot: Gregg Revivals.

Chazan, M. (2008) 'Seven "Deadly" Assumptions: Unravelling the Implications of HIV/AIDS among Grandmothers in South Africa and Beyond' *Aging and Society 28*, 935.

Deane, P. (1965) *The First Industrial Revolution.* Cambridge: Cambridge University Press.

Department for Education (DfE) (2011) *Family and Friends Care: Statutory Guidance for Local Authorities.* London: DfE.

DfE (2016a) *Special Guardianship Guidance. Statutory Guidance for Local Authorities on the Special Guardianship Regulations 2005* (as amended by the Special Guardianship (Amendment) Regulations 2016). London: DfE.

DfE (2016b) *Adoption. A Vision for Change.* London: DfE.

DfE (2016c) *Adoption Support Fund.* Available at: www.adoptionsupportfund.co.uk/FAQs

Department for Education and Skills (DfES) (2007) *Care Matters. Time for Change.* Cm 7137 Executive Summary. London: DfES.

Dodd, T. and Hunter, P. (1992) *The National Prison Survey, 1991: a report to the Home Office of a study of prisoners in England and Wales carried out by the Social Survey Division of OPCS.* London: Office of Population Censuses and Surveys (OPCS).

Donnelly, M. (1999) *Britain in the Second World War.* London: Routledge.

Douglas, G. and Ferguson, N. (2003) 'The Role of Grandparents in Divorced Families' *International Journal of Law, Policy and the Family* 17, 41.

Dressel, P. and Barnhill, S. (1994) 'Reframing Gerontological Thought and Practice: The Case of Grandmothers with Daughters in Prison' *The Gerontologist* 34(5), 685.

Duranton, G., Rodríguez-Pose, A. and Sandall, R. (2008) *Family Types and the Persistence of Regional Disparities in Europe*, SERC Discussion Paper 9. London: Spatial Economics Research Centre (SERC), London School of Economics.

Farmer, E. and Moyers, S. (2008) *Kinship Care: Fostering Effective Family and Friends Placement*. London: Jessica Kingsley.

Fitton, R. S. (1989) *The Arkwrights, Spinners of Fortune*. Manchester: Manchester University Press.

Fitton, R. S. and Wadsworth, A. (1968) *The Strutts and the Arkwrights 1758–1830: A Study of the Early Factory System*. Manchester: Manchester University Press.

FMI (Family Matters Institute) and the University of Hertfordshire (2009) *Do Grandparents Matter? The Impact of Grandparenting on the Well-being of Children*. St Albans: FMI/University of Hertfordshire.

Galloway, S., Haynes, A. and Cuthbert, C. (2014) *An Unfair Sentence, All Babies Count: Spotlight on the Criminal Justice System*. London: NSPCC.

Gautier, A. and Willard, S. (2014) *Disadvantage, Discrimination, Resilience: The Lives of Kinship Families*. London: Grandparents Plus.

Gillies, V. (2003) *Family and Intimate Relationships: A Review of the Sociological Research*. London: South Bank University.

Grandparents Plus (2013) *Grandparents and Childcare*. May Policy Briefing 04. Available at: www.grandparentsplus.org.uk/wp-content/uploads/2013/05/Briefing-paper-on-grandparental-childcare.pdf

Gray, A. (2005) 'The Changing Availability of Grandparents as Carers and its Implications for Childcare Policy in the UK' *Journal of Social Policy* 34(4), 557.

Geurts, T., van Tilburg, T., Poortmand, A.-R. and Dystra, P. (2015) 'Child Care by Grandparents: Changes Between 1992 and 2006' *Aging and Society* 35(6), 1318.

Hansard (2008) House of Commons, Children and Young Persons Bill, 16 June.

Herlofson, K. and Hagestad, G. (2012) 'Transformation in the Role of Grandparents across Welfare States' in S. Arber and V. Timonen (eds) *Contemporary Grandparenting: Changing Family Relationships in Global Contexts*. Bristol: Policy Press.

HM Government (2006) *Care Matters. Transforming the Lives of Children and Young People in Care* Cm 6932. London: DfE.

HMIP (Her Majesty's Inspectorate of Prisons) (1997) *Women in Prison: A Thematic Review*. Available at: www.revolving-doors.co.uk

Ho, C. (2015) 'Grandchild Care, Intergenerational Transfers, and Grandparents' Labor Supply' *Review of Economics of the Household* 13(2), 359.

Honeyman, K. (2007) *Child Workers in England 1780–1820: Parish Apprentices and the Making of the Early Industrial Labour Force*. Aldershot: Ashgate.

Humphries, J. (2010) *Childhood and Child Labour in the British Industrial Revolution*. Cambridge: Cambridge University Press.

Humphries, J. (2015) 'The Industrial Revolution: Factories, Families, Foundlings' in C. Wrigley (ed.) *The Industrial Revolution, Cromford, The Derwent Valley and The Wider World*. Cromford: The Arkwright Society.

Hunt, J. (2003) *Family and Friends Carers: Scoping Paper Prepared for the Department of Health*. London: Department of Health (DH).

Hunt, J. and Waterhouse, S. (2012) *Understanding Family and Friends Care: The Relationship between Need, Support and Legal Status. Carers' Experiences.* London: Family Rights Group (FRG).

Hunt, J. and Waterhouse, S. (2013) *It's Just Not Fair! Support, Need and Legal Status in Family and Friends Care. Summary.* London: FRG.

Hunt, J., Waterhouse, S. and Lutman, E. (2008) *Keeping Them in the Family: Outcomes for Children Placed in Kinship Care through Care Proceedings.* London: British Association for Adoption and Fostering (BAAF).

Ingersoll-Dayton, B., Punpuing, S. and Tangchonlatip, K. (2015) 'Skipped Generation Households in Thailand: Pathways to Grandparents' Provision of Care' *The Gerontologist* 55 (Suppl 2), 607.

Kaganas, F. and Piper. C. (1990) 'Grandparents and the Limits of Law' *International Journal of Law and the Family* 4, 27.

Kirby, J. and Sanders, M. (2012) 'Using Consumer Input to Tailor Evidence-Based Parenting Interventions to the Needs of Grandparents' *Journal of Child and Family Studies* 21(4), 626.

Laslett, P. (1965) *The World we have Lost.* London: Routledge.

Laslett, P. (1971) *The World we have Lost.* London: Routledge.

Laslett, P. (2015) *The World we have Lost, Further Explored.* Abingdon: Routledge

Legacy Project. Available at: www.legacyproject.org/guides/gptoday.html

Livingston, G. and Parker, K. (2010) 'Since the Start of the Great Recession, More Children Raised by Grandparents', 9 September. Available at: www.pewsocialtrends.org/2010/09/09/since-the-start-of-the-great-recession-more-children-raised-by-grandparents/

Loureiro, T. on behalf of Scotland's Commissioner for Children and Young People (SCCYP) and Families Outside (2010) *Perspectives of Children and Young People With a Parent in Prison.* Edinburgh: SCCYP.

Lynch, K. (2010) 'Kinship in Britain and Beyond for the Early Modern to the Present: A Postscript' *Continuity and Change* 25(1) 185.

Mauk, K. (2016) 'Grandparents Raising Grandchildren: A Growing Trend' *Senior Care Central,* 6 February. Available at: https://senior-care-central.com/grandparents-raising-grandchildren-trend/

McCloskey, D. (2001) 'Paid Work' in I. Zweiniger-Bargielowska (ed.) *Women in Twentieth-Century Britain: Economic, Social and Cultural Change.* London: Longman/Pearson Education.

Mercer, A. (2014) *Infections, Chronic Disease, and the Epidemiological Transition.* Martlesham: Boydell and Brewer.

Mercer, A., Lindley, B. and Hopkins, A. (2015) *Could do Better… Must do Better… A Study of Family and Friends Care Local Authority Policies.* London: FRG.

Ministry of Justice (MoJ) (2004) *Prisoners' Childhood and Family Backgrounds: Results from the Surveying Prisoner Crime Reduction (SPCR) Longitudinal Cohort Study of Prisoners.* London: Home Office.

Mooney, A. and Statham, J. with Simon, A. (2002) *The Pivot Generation, Informal Care and Work after Fifty.* Bristol: Policy Press.

Nandy, S. and Selwyn, J. (2013) 'Kinship Care and Poverty: Using Census Data to Examine the Extent and Nature of Kinship Care in the UK' *British Journal of Social Work* 43, 1649.

Nandy, S., Selwyn, J., Farmer, E. and Vaisey, P. (2011) *Spotlight on Kinship Care: Using Census microdata to examine the extent and nature of kinship care in the UK at the turn of the twentieth century.* Bristol: University of Bristol.

Nash, R. (1982) 'Family and Economic Structure in Nineteenth-Century Wales: Llangernyw and Gwytherin in 1871' *Welsh History Review* 11(2), 135.

O'Brien, V. (2012) 'The Benefits and Challenges of Kinship Care' *Child Care in Practice* 18, 127.

Prison Advice and Care Trust (2011) *Protecting the Welfare of Children When a Parent is Imprisoned*. London: PACT.

Raniga, T. and Simpson, B. (2010) 'Grandmothers Bearing the Brunt of HIV/AIDS in Bhambayi, Kwazulu-Natal, South Africa' *The Social Work Practitioner-Researcher* 22, 1.

Rosenthal, J. (1996) *Old Age in Late Medieval England*. Philadelphia, PA: University of Pennsylvania Press.

Roth, D., Aziz, R. and Lindley, B. (undated) *Relative Poverty: Family and Friends Care in London*. London: FRG.

Ruggles, S. (1987) *Prolonged Connections The Rise of the Extended Family in Nineteenth-Century England and America*. London: The University of Wisconsin Press.

Rutter, J. and Evans, B. (2012) *Improving Our Understanding of Informal Childcare in the UK*. London: Daycare Trust.

Selwyn, J. and Nandy, S. (2014) 'Kinship Care in the UK: Using Census Data to Estimate the Extent of Formal and Informal Care by Relatives' *Child and Family Social Work* 19, 44.

Selwyn, J., Farmer, E., Meakings, S. and Vaisey, P. (2013) *The Poor Relations? Children & Informal Kinship Carers Speak Out*. Bristol: University of Bristol.

Social Issues Research Centre (2011) *The Changing Face of Motherhood*. Oxford: SRIC.

Speight, S., Smith, R., La Valle, I., Schneider, V. and Perry, J. with Coshall, C. and Tipping, S. (2009) *Childcare and Early Years Survey of Parents 2008*, Research Report DCSF-RR136. London: National Centre for Social Research, Department for Children, Schools and Families (DCSF). Available at: www.natcen.ac.uk/media/173883/childcare-and-early-years-survey-of-parents-2008.pdf

Statham, J. (2011) *Grandparents Providing Child Care, Briefing Paper*. London: Childhood Well-Being Research Centre. Available at: www.gov.uk/government/uploads/system/uploads/attachment_data/file/181364/CWRC-00083-2011.pdf

Timonen, V., Doyle, M. and O'Dwyer, C. (2009) *The Role of Grandparents in Divorced and Separated Families*. Dublin: School of Social Work and Social Policy, Trinity College Dublin.

Todd, E. (1990) *L'invention de l'Europe*. Paris: Éditions du Seuil.

Wall, R. (2010) 'Economic Collaboration of Family Members Within and Beyond Households in English Society, 1600–2000' *Continuity and Change* 25(1), 83.

Wang, Y. and Marcotte, D. (2007) 'Golden Years? The Labor Market Effects of Caring for Grandchildren' *IZA Discussion Papers* 2629. Bonn: IZA.

Ward, J. (1990) 'Wealth and Family in Early 16th-century Colchester' *Essex Archaeology and History* 21, 110.

Wellard, S. (2011) *Too Old to Care? The experiences of older grandparents raising their grandchildren*. Available at: www.grandparentsplus.org.uk/wp-content/uploads/2011/03/GP_OlderGrandparentsOnline.pdf

Williams, K., Papadopoulou, V. and Booth, N. (2012) *Prisoners' Childhood and Family Backgrounds, Results from the Surveying Prisoner Crime Reduction (SPCR) Longitudinal Cohort Study of Prisoners*, Ministry of Justice Research Series 4/12. London: MoJ.

Wrigley, E. and Schofield, R. (1989) *The Population History of England 1541–1871*. Cambridge: Cambridge University Press.

Cases

London Borough of Hackney v John Williams and Adenike Williams [2017] *EWCA* Civ 26.

R (on the application of Cunningham) v Hertfordshire County Council & Anor [2016] *EWCA* Civ 1108

R (on the Application of L and Others) v Manchester City Council; R (on the Application of R and Another) v Manchester City Council [2001] *EWHC* Admin 707

R (on the application of X) v London Borough of Tower Hamlets [2013] *EWHC* 480 (Admin)

Southwark LBC v D [2007] 1*FLR* 2181

Chapter 14

Grandparents and grandchildren

Relatedness, relationships and responsibility

Rachel Taylor

Introduction

Whilst many grandparents play a vitally important part in their grandchildren's lives, the law takes an ambivalent approach to their role. Grandparents have no legal rights to a relationship with their grandchildren, yet are often the lynchpin for children unable to live with their parents. Given the extent to which grandparents are relied on as a resource, there are often claims that grandparents ought to have access to greater legal rights to safeguard those relationships. These claims will be considered in two key areas in which grandparents' relationship are particularly vulnerable: seeking to maintain relationships with grandchildren against the opposition of the parents; and seeking to oppose adoption to maintain legal and social ties with grandchildren.

Despite the strong claims of some grandparents, it will be argued that giving greater legal rights to grandparents would be undesirable. The current law is sufficiently flexible to recognise and support grandparents where intervention will be of benefit to the child. Additional procedural rights would risk unnecessary and harmful litigation. Greater substantive rights risk detracting from the essential question of the welfare of the child. This risk is particularly evident in the repeated attempts to introduce presumptions in favour of biological relatedness in determining who should care for a child. Such presumptions risk distorting children's welfare by prioritising biology over practical care. The notion that there is a presumption in favour of biological relatives has caused distortion in the practical application of the law, despite the fact that such presumptions have repeatedly been rejected by the higher courts. The background of financial cuts to children's services has exacerbated these problems. Kinship care by relatives, such as grandparents, often provides a cheaper and quicker alternative to public care for those children who cannot be safely accommodated with their parents. Although in many cases this may be the best outcome for children and grandparents, the ideological emphasis on biology has often been used to prioritise kinship even in cases where it is not the best or even safe option for children. In this way the focus on biology has transferred the burden of public care onto grandparents, sometimes to the detriment of both children and grandparents. It will be argued here that the law is best understood as prioritising relationships of primary responsibility rather than biological relatedness itself. Further, that the priority for children and grandparents is not greater legal rights for grandparents but greater practical and financial support for those who do take that primary responsibility.

Preserving relationships: conflict with parents

The campaign for recognition

As grandparents play an increasing role in caring for grandchildren, their relative absence in legislation may seem outdated. Certainly there has been significant political pressure for greater legal recognition and financial support for grandparental relationships. As Kaganas and Piper detail in this volume, grandparents who act as primary carers under a private arrangement are particularly neglected in the current law and often find themselves suffering significant financial detriment with little state support for their role. Campaigns for greater employment rights and financial support for caring grandparents seek to give support, which can alleviate the hardship that many such grandparents face.

Campaigns for greater legal rights in preserving relationships with grandchildren have proved more controversial (Kaganas 2007). Grandparents as a distinct category are largely absent from the legislation that governs children's contact and residence arrangements. Unlike parents, grandparents must first obtain the leave of the court before applying for a child arrangements order. If leave is obtained then there is no statutory presumption, as there is for parents, that a child's welfare will be enhanced by the involvement of grandparents in her life. Grandparents are particularly vulnerable to loss of relationship with their grandchildren if the relationship between the child's parents breaks down. The Grandparents' Association has estimated that one million children have lost contact with their grandparents in this way (Grandparents Plus 2011). Grandparents' groups have long campaigned for removal of the leave requirement and a presumption in favour of contact to aid these grandparents.

For a time these campaigns looked likely to succeed. In 2010 the outgoing Labour government announced plans to remove the leave requirement and to aid grandparents seeking contact (Department for Children, Schools and Families 2010). A few months later, the new Deputy Prime Minister, Nick Clegg, considered that it was 'crazy' that many grandparents did not feel 'empowered' to step in after parental break up as (Clegg 2010). Despite the apparent political consensus in favour of rights for grandparents, the status quo has remained. The turning point was the Family Justice Review (Ministry of Justice 2011), which recommended retaining leave to prevent 'hopeless or vexatious applications' and rejected talk of grandparents' rights that may detract from the rights of the child. The Government accepted this recommendation, against a wider background of encouraging the resolution of disputes outside of court (Ministry of Justice 2012). The campaign for legal rights for grandparents seems unlikely to succeed in the current climate. Given the overall policy of increasing barriers to access to the court in private family cases it would surprising to find barriers being lowered for grandparents. More fundamentally the retention of leave is consistent with priority being given to non-interference with those responsible for primary parenting.

The leave requirement

A 'fundamental principle' for the Law Commission in drafting what would become the Children Act 1989 was that 'primary responsibility for the upbringing of children rests with their parents'. The leave requirement reinforced this by acting 'as a filter to protect the child and his family from unwarranted interference in their comfort and security, whilst ensuring that the child's interests are properly respected' (Law Commission 1988). These fundamental principles can be seen in the detailed legislation, which privileges not just parents but those who have, or might be expected to have, taken primary responsibility for the practical care of the child. Those who can apply without leave include: guardians; special guardians, step-parents with parental responsibility; any person with whom the child has lived for at least three of the five previous years; and a foster parent or relative with whom the child has been living for at least a year. Under these provisions, a grandparent who has acted as a primary carer will usually be able to apply without leave, whether that care was established through a formal court order or through *de facto* caring for the child for the required period of time. Any person who does not fall into these categories of primary carers, including grandparents and other relatives, must obtain the leave of the court.

In this way the requirement of leave recognises the prima facie responsibility of those with primary responsibility for the child. This is particularly important given that the leave requirement applies not just to cases where the applicant seeks contact with the child but also in those cases where primary care is sought. The latter form of child arrangements order represents a draconian interference with the parents' responsibility and the enjoyment of family life. Such applications also have considerable potential to disrupt public proceedings, including adoption, and delay alternative permanent placement for the child. By requiring that the applicant has either acted as a primary carer or obtained leave, the current law offers some protection from such threats of interference.

For those who have not acted as primary carers, the leave requirement is unlikely to pose too great a hurdle for those grandparents who have a strong relationship with the child and who seek a relationship that does not cause significant disruption to the child's life. The courts have been particularly keen to ensure that leave does not impose too high a burden on grandparents if they have a relationship amounting to 'family life' for the purpose of Article 8 ECHR (*Re J* [2002]). Together these requirements offer a flexible discretion to the court to deal with the diversity of potential applications. The primary caring relationships are protected from vexatious and harmful applications, whilst the grandparent with a relationship with the child and a prospect of success is likely to succeed. This approach reflects that elsewhere in the law of granting prima facie protection to primary caring relationships but granting a broad discretion to the court to protect other relationships that are in the child's welfare.

Making child arrangements orders

Campaigns concerning leave have tended to focus on grandparents estranged from their grandchildren following the breakdown of a parental relationship. In reality many of the cases that reach court concern far more complex situations in which there are welfare concerns akin to public law proceedings and significant questions over the children's future living arrangements. For this reason it is not possible to treat grandparents' child arrangements cases as a monolithic group. In these cases the tensions between the triangle of primary parenting responsibility, relatedness, and relationships interact very differently depending on the facts. A perennial difficulty has been the question of whether parents have any additional status to grandparents and whether there is a presumption that children are best brought up by their natural parents. The cases show that, rather than protecting parents as such, the courts will usually protect functioning relationships of primary responsibility and their importance to the child's welfare.

The leading case in this area is *Re B* [2009], in which the Supreme Court upheld the maternal grandmother's role as primary carer for her 3-year-old grandson whom she had cared for since birth, rejecting the father's attempt to take over that responsibility. Lord Kerr's judgment for the court stressed the pivotal importance of welfare as 'the dominant and overriding factor that ultimately determines disputes', and rejected attempts to distort that test by considering the supposed right of the child to be brought up by his natural parents. Whilst it might ordinarily be best for a child to be brought up by biological parents, this assumption had no role to play in litigated cases, which rarely involved such ordinary situations. In this way a unanimous Supreme Court delivered what appeared to be a terminal blow to any attempt to assert a presumption in favour of natural parents in residence disputes or any automatic preference for parental care.

The limited weight given to biology can be seen in the Court of Appeal decision in *Re T* [2010] in which there was no biological relationship between the 'grandparents' and one of the children. The children, aged 10 and 7, had been living with the paternal grandparents of the elder child for 6 years. The grandparents had taken over their care with the consent of the mother, who was suffering from alcohol addiction and unable to care for them. Six years later, having recovered from her addiction and established a new family, the mother sought return of the children. In finding for the grandparents, the Court of Appeal rejected the view that the biological link was a 'stand-alone feature' instead it was only relevant in so far as it impacted on the welfare of the children. As there was no evidence that the grandparents treated the younger child differently, the absence of a biological connection played virtually no role in the decision. The case is a good illustration of the importance given to maintaining the primary caring relationship, despite the absence of a biological link between the grandparents and one of the children and despite the fact that the biological mother had maintained substantial contact with the children.

At first sight, the observation of the Court of Appeal in *Re B* [2012](b), that 'manifestly grandparents are not on equal footing with parents' seems to be tension with these cases. In that case the nearly 5-year-old child had been brought up by her mother throughout her life. The relationship with the father was 'turbulent' and the paternal family were regarded by the mother as 'abusive and dangerous'. The mother, who had borderline capacity to litigate, had refused to comply with contact orders in favour of the grandmother that had initially been made when she was neither present nor represented. The trial judge had ordered transfer of residence from the mother to the grandmother in order to ensure that contact took place. The Court of Appeal overturned this decision, stressing the difference between grandparents and parents without care. Whilst transfer of residence might be appropriate as a 'weapon of last resort' in contact disputes between parents, the court knew of 'no case in which such a dire sanction has been exercised against an obdurate parent to transfer the primary care to a grandmother'. The difference between parents and grandparents was underlined by the requirement of leave, to which we might now add the absence of a statutory presumption that the child will benefit from grandparental involvement. The apparent conflict between the statements of the Supreme Court and Court of Appeal on the relative position of parents and grandparents is best seen as reflecting the protection of relationships of responsibility. Whilst grandparents will not be at a disadvantage in retaining their primary caring position, grandparents without primary responsibility will find it difficult to use private law to disrupt the child's primary care.

Both *Re B* [2009] and *Re T* [2010] are examples of grandparents stepping in to a situation that might otherwise have required local authority intervention. Research by Maebh Harding and Annika Newnham suggests that such cases are typical of child arrangements cases involving grandparents (Harding and Newnham 2015). Their analysis of county court applications for private children's orders showed that non-parents, primarily grandparents, were the applicants in 12% of cases. These cases were overwhelmingly concerned with residence and the child was almost always already living with the non-parent. These non-parents seeking residence orders were almost always successful in obtaining sole residence, with the two cases in which they were not resulting in shared residence. Strikingly, the cases contained features that might be more traditionally associated with public, rather than private, proceedings. In almost all of the cases there were serious welfare concerns and doubts as to the mother's ability to provide secure full-time parenting. Further, in more than half of the cases, the local authority was actively involved with the family before the residence application was made, often having encouraged, or even insisted on, that application. In those cases where child did return to the mother's care, the local authority was heavily involved in supporting and monitoring that transfer. Whilst the research does not purport to be a representative sample, the findings fit with Bainham's observation that the binary division between public and private proceedings is becoming blurred in practice (Bainham 2013).

As Kaganas and Piper observe in this volume, there are significant incentives for local authorities to encourage arrangements in private law rather than using care proceedings. Harding and Newnham's research also seems to confirm that applications for residence by grandparents and other non-relatives often function as an alternative to public law applications. Kaganas and Piper demonstrate the disadvantages that this can have for grandparents caring for children without the obligations that would attach to looked after children. There are also potential disadvantages to the child in that grandparents obtaining private orders will not be subject to the same assessments as foster carers in public proceedings (Department of Education 2010). Further, the severe restriction on legal aid in private family disputes means that both parents and non-parents are likely to find themselves without legal representation. For grandparents this can mean that the financial consequences of proceeding through private law orders are not fully understood, whilst parents find themselves at risk of losing care of their children without legal representation. Similarly, the child is unlikely to be separately represented in private proceedings. The consequences for parents in losing the primary care of their child in these cases can be materially identical to those under a care order. The Children Act 1989 was premised on the clear demarcation between public and private law, with the threshold criteria standing as the barrier to removal of a child against the parent's will. It is with good reason that local authorities are prohibited from using private law orders to avoid public law proceedings. The current approach risks removing children from parental care without the substantive and procedural protections that are available in public law proceedings. If local authorities are encouraging such private applications as a means of avoiding public proceedings, there is clearly a risk that the Article 8 rights of parents and children will not be sufficiently protected, particularly in the absence of legal advice. In such cases, the flexible leave requirement, together with the application of welfare that gives no 'stand-alone' consideration to the parental relationship may be insufficient to justify intervention with those Article 8 rights (Bainham 2013). The privatisation of what are effectively public law cases has significant risks for all participants.

Preserving relationships: adoption

It is the prospect of adoption that perhaps raises the greatest threat to the relationship between grandparents and grandchildren. An adoption order not only risks social and psychological relationships that may already exist but breaks the legal ties and kinship networks that form the heart of the law's construction of the family. The role of adoption in providing care for children has been a point of considerable political and legal contention in recent years. The Government has consistently promoted adoption as a means of providing a stable home for children who would otherwise remain in the care system (Department for Education

2016). At the same time, the UK has come under sustained international scrutiny over the questionable suggestion that it is out of line with prevailing European practice on non-consensual adoption (Fenton-Glynn 2016) and assertions that the law in this jurisdiction is too ready to break existing legal and biological ties.

The European Court of Human Rights has confirmed that English adoption law is not incompatible with the European Convention on Human Rights (*YC v UK* 2012). Nonetheless, the tension in the Court's judgment between the principle 'that family ties may only be severed in very exceptional circumstances' and the fact that 'it is in the child's best interests to ensure his development in a safe and secure environment' is often difficult to apply in practice. The domestic courts' attempts to clarify the law have exacerbated much of the complexity in this area, most notably the Supreme Court judgment in *Re B* [2013] including Baroness Hale's observation that:

> ... it is quite clear that the test for severing the relationship between parent and child is very strict: only in exceptional circumstances and where motivated by *overriding requirements* pertaining to the child's welfare, in short, where nothing else will do.

Together with the subsequent decision Court of Appeal in *Re B-S (2013)*, this case appears to have generated an understanding that the Supreme Court intended to change the law and elevate the importance of biological ties. If this were the case it would have considerable implications for grandparents seeking to offer alternatives to adoption outside the family. Whilst the senior judiciary have repeatedly stated, both judicially (*Re R* [2014]) and extra-judicially (McFarlane 2016), that the cases were not intended to change the law, nonetheless the 'nothing else will do' mantra appears to have had a significant impact on many areas of practice.

Adoption: grandparents and the statutory framework

In adoption, as in private cases, the statutory framework does not give grandparents any specific rights or recognition. The gateway to adoption is governed by the consent of those with primary legal responsibility for the child's upbringing. Before an adoption can take place, the consent of the parents with parental responsibility or the guardian or special guardian, must be obtained or dispensed with. It follows that it is only the people within these categories who can formally oppose the making of an order by seeking to withdraw that consent. In this way the statutory scheme is based on the protection of the primary relationship of responsibility, although it is tightly focused on primary legal responsibility and does not extend to the de facto responsible carers who are able to apply for child arrangements orders without leave. Collectively these provisions mean that grandparents have no direct means of challenging the adoption or placement order unless they are also guardians. Nonetheless, the absence of specific legislative rights does not erase grandparents from the adoption process: indeed relationships with grandparents can be determinative in practice. Relationships with grandparents can be relevant: in offering alternatives for care; as part of the welfare assessment; and through contact. The possibility of grandparents as alternative carers is of particular importance in adoption cases. The sections below consider first grandparental care under special guardianship as an alternative to a plan for placement for adoption outside the family and second the possibility of grandparental care as a means of resisting an adoption order. Whilst both of these scenarios raise similar issues around the importance to be attributed to care within the birth family, in the latter situation the child will already have been placed with potential adopters. In these cases the primary responsibility of the original parents has been relinquished or forfeited, so the tension between the importance of relationships and relatedness becomes particularly difficult to resolve.

Special guardianship and adoption

As Kaganas and Piper detail in this volume, local authorities have both legislative obligation and financial incentive to place children with kinship carers. The role of special guardianship is particularly important in considering kinship care as an alternative to adoption. Special guardianship was introduced in 2005 as a means of offering permanent placements for children without terminating their existing legal ties to their parents. The special guardian obtains parental responsibility and is able to exclude the exercise of the parental responsibility of others, but, unlike adoption, the existing parents retain their legal status and parental responsibility for the child. Although, special guardianship is not limited to kinship carers, it seems that the majority of special guardians are related to the child, with the largest single group being grandparents. For example, in Wade et al's 2014 review of 230 cases, 90% of special guardians were related to the child, with just over half being grandparents. Special guardianship was originally intended to be used to provide permanence for children for whom adoption was not appropriate, for example for older children who did not want to break their existing link to their parents. There is, however, concern that it is now being used in preference to adoption, even in cases where that is not likely to secure a stable outcome for the child. Anecdotal evidence suggests that some local authorities have reacted to the 'nothing else will do' judgments of *Re B* and *Re B-S* by viewing special guardianship as the 'default option' (Department for Education, 2015). This is supported by the recent rapid increase in the number of special guardianship orders being made, particularly for children leaving care. In 2015/16, 3,830 children left care through a special guardianship order, an increase of 78% since 2012 (Office for National Statistics 2016); at the same time there has been a significant drop in placement orders for adoption (Department for Education 2016). Further, increasing proportions of children under one are being accommodated through special guardianship, rather than being placed for adoption (Harwin et al 2015). Together these findings suggest that special guardianship is increasingly being used as an alternative to adoption in finding permanent placements for children, even if those children are very young.

There is insufficient research at present to confirm the reasons for this shift and whether they are likely to be long term. In particular, it is not yet clear whether this change is linked to an increased emphasis on the importance of birth families following the *Re B/Re B-S* line of cases, although there is some evidence that this is the perception within children's services (Bowyer et al 2015). Whether special guardianship provides a preferable alternative to adoption will, of course, depend on the individual circumstances of the child concerned. There are, however, good reasons for concern that special guardianship may be being used in circumstances in which it may not provide a safe permanent home for the child. Certainly there has been a notable increase in the use of supervision orders in conjunction with special guardianship, suggesting that these may be placements in which there is on-going concern as to the guardian's ability to provide a safe home. Around a third of special guardianship orders were accompanied by a supervision order in Harwin et al's 2015 study of special guardianship in public law proceedings. Further, Bowyer et al's 2015 research on local authority use of special guardianship noted that interviewees considered that the orders were being made in more 'fragile' placements than was originally the case. Wade et al's in depth review of special guardianship also found that in a significant minority of cases the assessment of special guardianships was rushed and inadequate (Wade et al 2014). The Government has taken these concerns seriously and issued the Special Guardianship (Amendment) Regulations 2016 to improve assessment, but it remains to be seen whether this will have a significant impact, particularly given the time pressure placed on decision-making by the public law outline.

Although special guardianship is not unique to grandparents, the high representation of grandparents means that these trends are of particular importance to them. Special guardianship can provide a secure and stable means of providing children with a permanent home. Nonetheless, recent experience suggests that they are being used in situations where they might be inappropriate. There is certainly a perception that this is related to the pressure to find kinship placements that 'will do' before finding placement outside of the family. There is a risk that the emphasis on the importance of relatedness will undermine the chances of some of those children finding secure, permanent homes.

Grandparents challenging adoption orders: Re W

The tension between recognising the importance of relatedness and finding its limits has been particularly acute in cases where the child has already been placed for adoption and developed relationships with her potential adoptive parents. The tangled question of how the law values parenting relationships as against the preservation of links with the biological family was raised particularly sharply in the case of *Re W*. Whilst the outcome of any single case will depend closely on the specific facts, it is worthy of careful consideration for the guidance of the Court of Appeal on the misunderstandings that had flowed from the 'nothing else will do' case law and in the contrasting decisions of the judges who heard the case before and after that Court of Appeal decision.

The case concerned a little girl, A, born on 1 May 2014 and placed with foster parents the following day. Her natural parents, both of whom had significant learning disabilities, had never cared for A and had no wish to do so. At the age of 7 months she moved to live with the prospective adopters, Mr and Mrs X, under a placement order. At every stage in the case that placement was described as a great success and a close and loving attachment had clearly been built between A and Mr and Mrs X, whom A regarded as her parents. The paternal grandparents, Mr and Mrs G, only discovered A's existence when they took on the care of the birth parents' subsequent child, E, shortly after his birth. Mr and Mrs G quickly sought the care of A and also offered the prospect of a close and loving home, albeit one not yet tested, and additionally could provide an upbringing with A's biological sibling and wider family. In the meantime the X family had lodged their adoption application. By the time the case came before Mr Justice Bodey (Re W [2016] (a)) A was 2 years old and had lived with Mr and Mrs X for 17 months. He was then faced with the 'judgment of Solomon' to decide between two prospective secure homes: one offering an upbringing within the biological family and the other providing the only parenting relationship that A had ever known. In this way, as Judith Masson (2016) observes, the case raised a sharp conflict between caring relationships and biological relatedness. In deciding for the grandparents, Bodey J was clearly influenced by the reports of the children's guardian and the independent social worker, both of whom worked from the assumption that if the grandparents were willing and able to provide a secure home for A, she ought to be placed with them, indeed that she had a *right* to be placed with them.

The Court of Appeal (*Re W* [2016](b)) set aside the decision and was deeply critical of the determinative weight that the reports gave to placing A within her biological family. Lord Justice McFarlane, giving the leading judgment, was determined to dispel any notion of right or presumption to be brought up within the 'natural' family, tracing this back to a misunderstanding of the *Re B/Re B-S* 'nothing else will do' approach:

> The phrase is meaningless, and potentially dangerous, if it is applied as some freestanding, shortcut test divorced from, or even in place of, an overall evaluation of the child's welfare. Used properly, as Baroness Hale explained, the phrase 'nothing else will do' is no more, nor no less, than a useful distillation of the proportionality and necessity test as embodied in the ECHR and reflected in the need to afford paramount consideration to the welfare of the child throughout her lifetime … The phrase 'nothing else will do' is not some sort of hyperlink providing a direct route to the outcome of a case so as to bypass the need to undertake a full, comprehensive welfare evaluation of all of the relevant pros and cons.

When considering the welfare evaluation at the placement stage, that assessment would naturally tilt to good quality care within the family, as no relationship with the potential adopters would yet have been established. Where this relationship had been established and the child had formed secure attachment to the potential adopters that balance would naturally change and the child's welfare could not be determined simply by looking at the existence of the viable family placement. Instead, the status quo and the child's existing attachment to their primary carers would play a significant part in the welfare assessment.

Rehearing the case with the benefit of new and extensive expert reports, Mr Justice Cobb (*Re W* [2016](c)), considered that it was not finely balanced. Short-term damage would be inevitable if A moved to her grandparents. There was also a 'serious possibility of medium-term and long-term emotional and psychological damage to A by the traumatic severing of the secure attachments which she has formed with the Xs' and no recommended route to transferring her care in a way that could realistically mitigate against those harms. Given the significant risks of severing those secure attachments, it was clear that her welfare was best served through adoption with the X family. In reaching this decision, Cobb J did not consider the convention rights of the parties in detail but noted that it was unlikely that the paternal grandparents had Article 8 rights through their blood relationship with A alone. It was recognised by all parties to the case, including Mr and Mrs X, that contact with the paternal grandparents and the creation of a relationship would be of benefit to A in the future. In this way there was a continuing recognition of the importance of biological relatedness, nonetheless the value given to this link was far outweighed by preserving the primary parenting of the X family. Cobb J considered that it would not be better for A if a contact order were made, instead the Xs should be in control of that contact without the need for court intervention. In this way the case again reflects the importance given to the primary parenting relationship.

The case of *Re W* is important for its firm re-statement of the importance of a full welfare analysis, unimpeded by presumptions as to the value to be placed on biological relationships alone. Protection for the rights of the birth family is not found in this final welfare assessment but in the statutory structures and guidance around parental consent and the priority given to kinship care. The tragedy for Mr and Mrs G was not found in an absence of legal rights but in the delay in informing them of A's birth.

Conclusions

From the perspective of grandparents, the law on protecting the grandparental relationship may appear to be inconsistent and place unfair burdens upon them. Whilst grandparents play a significant role in practical care for their grandchildren, there is no automatic right to apply to the court to protect that relationship. From the position of grandparents this may put them in a vulnerable position: often asked to make considerable sacrifices for their grandchildren's care but with little legal protection for that relationship if things go wrong. Whilst grandparents without care have little standing in private cases, in public law the position seems very different. If the child is to be removed from parental care, it is often the grandparents who play a pivotal part in providing an alternative home. In contrast to the position in private law, the law's approach in public cases is to prioritise kinship care to avoid placement outside of the family. Again there is often inadequate practical and financial support for grandparents who have undertaken the considerable burden of caring for a grandchild in these circumstances.

Nonetheless, the law makes far more sense when seen as a means of prioritising the relationship of primary care and responsibility for the child. By giving prima facie priority to this relationship and protecting the primary carer from interference, the law protects the relationship that is likely to be of primary importance to the child herself. Where the grandparent has undertaken primary responsibility they will be in a strong position, both in applying for private orders and resisting interference from others seeking to disrupt that caring relationship, even the child's biological parents. The grandparent without care is placed under additional burdens to show that it is in the child's best interests for that primary care to be disrupted. The difference between the position of grandparents without care in private and public cases is best explained by this importance given to the responsible carer. In private cases there will usually be a parent, or other primary carer who has prima facie protection from interference; in public cases that primary carer is either unwilling or unable to continue to provide safe primary care and so the question becomes replacing rather than protecting that primary relationship.

The fallout from the misunderstanding of *Re B/Re B-S* demonstrates the risks inherent in using presumptions in finding the best care for children. The reassertion of the welfare principle, unimpeded by such shortcuts, brings advantages and disadvantages to grandparents depending on whether the case concerns the child's parents or care outside of the family. The real problem in these cases is not in the absence of enforceable relationship rights for grandparents but in the resourcing of family justice. In particular, Grandparents are placed under considerable burdens by the privatising of what would be public family cases. The use of private orders can release local authorities from the need to provide financial and practical support. The cuts to legal aid and resources within the private family courts leave complex cases without access to sufficient legal advice, assessment support and representation for the child. Cases involving grandparental care often involve children in circumstances of conflict and risk of harm, the solution to these cases is more likely to be found in greater resources than legal rights.

Bibliography

Bainham, A. (2013) 'Private and Public Children Law: An Underexplored Relationship' *Child and Family Law Quarterly* 25(2), 138.

Bowyer, S., Wilkinson, J. and Gadsby Waters, J. (2015) *Impact of the family justice reforms on front-line practice phase two: special guardianship orders* (Research Report DFE-RR478B).

Clegg, N. (2010) 'Why it's time for families to come first' *Daily Mail*, 17 June.

Department for Children, Schools and Families (DCSF) (2010) *Support for All: The Families and Relationships Green Paper*. London: DCSF.

Department for Education (DfE) (2010) *Family and Friends Care: Statutory Guidance for Local Authorities'*. London: DfE.

DfE (2015) *Special Guardianship Review: Report on Findings*. London: DfE.

DfE (2016) *Adoption a Vision for Change*. London: DfE.

Fenton-Glynn, C. (2016) *Adoption Without Consent, Update 2016*, EU PE 556.940. The Hague: European Parliament.

Grandparents Plus (2011) *Policy Briefing Paper 01*. Available at: www.grandparentsplus.org.uk/wp-content/uploads/2011/03/Policy-Briefing-01-paper-statistics-Feb-2011.pdf

Harding, M. and Newnham, A. (2015) *How do County Courts Share the Care of Children Between Parents? Full Report*. London: Nuffield Foundation.

Harwin, J. et al (2015) *A National Study of the Use of Supervision Orders and Special Guardianship over Time (2007–2016), Briefing Paper Number 1: Special Guardianship Orders*. London: Nuffield Foundation.

Kaganas, F. (2007) 'Grandparents' Rights and Grandparents' Campaigns' *Child and Family Law Quarterly* 19, 17.

Law Commission (1988) *Family Law Review of Child Law Guardianship and Custody*. London: Law Commission, 594.

Masson, J. (2016) 'Relationships and Relatedness in Family Law' *Journal of Social Welfare and Family Law* 38(4), 456

McFarlane, A. (2016) *Nothing Else Will Do, Keynote Address to the Family Law Bar Association National Conference*. Available at: www.judiciary.gov.uk/wp-content/uploads/2016/10/lj-mcfarlane-flba-keynote-221016.pdf

Ministry of Justice (MoJ) (2011) *Family Justice Review: Final Report*. London: MoJ.

MoJ (2012) *The Government Response to the Family Justice Review*. London: The Stationery Office.

Office for National Statistics (ONS) (2016) *Children Looked After in England Year Ending 31 March 2016*. London: ONS.

Wade, J., Sinclair, I., Stuttard, L. and Simmonds, J. (2014) *Investigating Special Guardianship: Experiences, Challenges and Outcomes*. London: DfE.

Cases

Re B [2009] *UKSC* 5

Re B (A Child) [2012](a) *EWCA* Civ 737

Re B (A Child) [2012](b) *EWCA* Civ 858

Re B (Care Proceedings: Appeal) [2013] *UKSC* 33

Re B-S (Adoption: Application of s 47(5)) [2013] *EWCA* Civ 1146

Re J (Leave to Issue Application for a Residence Order) [2002] *EWCA* Civ 1364

Re R (Adoption) [2014] *EWCA* Civ 1625

Re T [2010] *EWCA* Civ 1644

Re W [2016](a) *EWHC* 2437 (Fam)

Re W (A Child) [2016](b) EWCA Civ 793

Re W (Adoption: Contact) [2016](c) *EWHC* 3118 (Fam)

YC v UK (2012) 55*EHRR* 967

Index

ADOLESCENT STORM AND STRESS

An Evaluation of the Mead–Freeman Controversy

James E. Côté
University of Western Ontario

Routledge
Taylor & Francis Group
LONDON AND NEW YORK

First published 1994 by Lawrence Erlbaum Associates, Inc.

Published 2018 by Routledge
2 Park Square, Milton Park, Abingdon, Oxon OX14 4RN
52 Vanderbilt Avenue, New York, NY 10017

First issued in paperback 2018

Routledge is an imprint of the Taylor & Francis Group, an informa business

Cover design by Kate Dusza

Library of Congress Cataloging-in-Publication Data

Côté, James E.
Adolescent storm and stress : an evaluation of the Mead-Freeman controversy / James E. Côté.
p. cm. --(Research monographs in adolescence)
Includes bibliographical references and indexes.
ISBN 0-8058-1506-6 (cloth)
1. Adolescence. 2. Adolescent psychology. 3. Nature and nurture.
4. Mead, Margaret, 1901-1978. 5. Freeman, Derek. I. Title.
II. Series.
GN483.C68 1994
305.23'5--dc20 **93-45835**
CIP

ISBN 13: 978-1-138-87331-5 (pbk)
ISBN 13: 978-0-8058-1506-1 (hbk)

This book is dedicated
to the young people
currently struggling to
"come of age in Samoa."

A firm knowledge of their history is particularly critical for young people who must make their life choices in the context of the present clash between tradition and a form of modernity that . . . negates and undermines the authentic values of their past. . . . [A] firm knowledge of the past choices made by their forbears . . . [is] enormously important if young people are to maintain a sure sense of identity as they face the difficult constraints and choices of the present.

—Leacock (1987, p. 180)

Contents

Series Foreword

Research Monographs in Adolescence is a series of theoretically grounded empirical works in the form of authored monographs. Drawing from the knowledge and expertise of scholars in multiple disciplines, such as psychology, sociology, and anthropology, the books in this series are written by leaders in the field for their peers in the academic community. These original and state-of-the-art works will be useful as archival material and will serve as valuable resources for upper level undergraduate and graduate courses. The monographs will not only advance our understanding of adolescence through the finest research possible, but will provide information necessary to design useful intervention strategies and to direct social policy.

The premier book in this series, *Adolescent Storm and Stress: An Evaluation of the Mead–Freeman Controversy*, by sociologist James Côté, is an excellent example of the scholarship to which this series aspires. By providing a compelling and careful examination of critical arguments in the Mead–Freeman controversy, this volume makes a significant contribution to our understanding of adolescent development and the transition to adulthood, while shedding light on the politics of the debate.

Nancy L. Galambos
Nancy A. Busch-Rossnagel

Preface

In 1928, Margaret Mead published her first book, entitled *Coming of Age in Samoa*, in which she described to the Western world an exotic culture where people passed through adolescence with a minimum of difficulties. *Coming of Age* brought her instant acclaim and stands as the "most widely read anthropology book ever published," having sold millions of copies in 16 languages (Muuss, 1988, p. 139). This book also launched her career as the best-known and most outspoken anthropologist of the century.

For more than 50 years, images from Mead's pioneering book permeated Western public consciousness of life in so-called simpler societies. Among the public, an image apparently prevailed that Samoa was a veritable paradise, where casual attitudes marked most social relationships, including sexual ones. In addition, Mead's conclusion that Samoan adolescents experienced little "storm and stress" was widely accepted in academic circles.

In 1983, Derek Freeman, an Australian anthropologist, published a book in which he systematically attacked Mead's conclusions about that culture and the way people came of age. Aside from attacking the most famous anthropologist of the century, Freeman took on the cultural anthropology "establishment" by questioning the integrity of its role in the "great debate" of the 20th century—the perennial "nature–nurture" debate. Since then, Freeman's book, entitled *Margaret Mead and Samoa: The Making and Unmaking of an Anthropological Myth*, has received so much attention that one observer remarked that Freeman had sparked "the biggest debate in the social sciences for years" (Crocombe, 1989, p. 38).

On the one hand, one could dismiss the whole matter as that of one person's word against another's. On the other hand, there are important implications to this controversy. Most generally at stake is the nature–nurture debate itself, and the presumption that Freeman has scored a victory for the "nature" side. More specifically at stake are assumptions about the period we call "adolescence and youth," and the belief that adolescence is inevitably a period of "storm and stress"—of biological/hormonal disequilibrium. But, perhaps most important are the implications of this controversy for young people in all societies, including contemporary Samoa. I refer here to the social expectations and economic policies that affect their well-being and life chances. If these expectations and policies are to be fair, they must be based on sound knowledge about the intrinsic nature of adolescence, and not on hastily drawn conclusions clouded by territorial academic disputes. For these reasons, I set out to carefully analyze the questions raised by Freeman and evaluate the charges he has leveled against Mead.

When I first began investigating the Mead–Freeman controversy, I had no intention of writing such a detailed manuscript on the matter. However, I did not anticipate the complexities involved in sorting out the many claims made in the affair. As I was sorting things out, however, for the reasons just stated, I became convinced that a book had to be written to help other interested parties evaluate these claims. To keep my investigation from being sidetracked by the complexities of the Mead–Freeman controversy, I remained focused on Mead's original research question. This question was whether coming of age was easier in Samoa than in the United States during the 1920s. I refer to it as Mead's "coming-of-age thesis." In assessing this thesis, two issues must be settled: To what extent are her various *conclusions* plausible? To what extent were her *observations* accurate?

The evidence I accumulated to tackle these issues is presented throughout the eight chapters of this book, each of which assesses Freeman's criticisms from a different perspective.

Chapters 1 through 3 present a comprehensive evaluation of the charges made by Freeman regarding Mead's coming-of-age conclusions. Over the span of these three chapters, the scientific quality of Freeman's charges is assessed against the plausibility of Mead's coming-of-age thesis. As we see, when the pertinent evidence is examined, very few of Freeman's charges persuade us to reject Mead's thesis.

In chapters 4 through 6, the accuracy of Mead's coming-of-age observations is evaluated with a sociohistorical analysis of Samoan culture. Freeman's case against Mead hinged on his assertion that she was largely wrong in her contentions about adolescence because she had a limited and biased perspective regarding Samoan culture. He claimed that he has a more thorough and accurate knowledge of the culture. In order to evaluate this crucial aspect of Freeman's critique, we undertake a sociohistorical analysis that traces the trajectory of social change initiated by missionaries in the 1800s (chapters 4 and 5). Based on written documents, this analysis allows us to determine if we can pinpoint the "Samoa" that Mead recorded in the 1920s (chapter 6). Again, we find little written evidence that leads us to seriously question the validity of Mead's observations.

Chapter 7 rounds out the sociohistorical evaluation of Mead's coming-of-age thesis by providing a glimpse at the "coming of age" experienced by contemporary Samoan youth. When we compare what prevailed in "precontact" Samoan culture with the circumstances confronting Samoan youth today, we find an insidious and inexorable disenfranchisement of young people there. What was once a place where most young people apparently came of age with relative ease, has become a place where many young people experience great difficulty finding a place in their society. This problem is now so serious that Western Samoa has one of the highest youth suicide rates in the world. But, Freeman denied the relevance of social change for the way Samoans come of age, claiming that adolescence has been stressful since before contact with the West. By doing so, he overlooked the possibility that much of what he witnessed during the 1960s (when he did most of his research) was a product of social change that had taken place since the 1920s. Thus, the missing component in this aspect of the controversy is the social change that was set in motion by the missionaries during the 1800s. And, herein lies the crux of the controversy—it is only within its context that we can understand the controversy itself, and the context is the social change and cultural disenfranchisement that has altered the way Samoans come of age. In light of what has happened as a result of contact with the West, this chapter ends with a set of policy recommendations regarding what might be done to rectify the cultural disenfranchisement of Samoan youth.

The concluding chapter (chapter 8) completes the interdisciplinary evaluation of Mead's coming-of-age thesis by examining from a sociological perspective the "Samoa" Mead described, and evaluating her claim that it would have provided an ease of passage from childhood to adulthood. We see here how her pioneering study introduced questions that are still pertinent to the study of adolescence. Although crucial elements of the Mead–Freeman controversy as they pertain to Mead's central thesis are resolved in this chapter, several questions are raised as to what is happening to young people in contemporary Samoa and what will happen there in the future (e.g., on the issue of "choosing" one's identity). The chapter ends with a set of recommendations for future research that will help us to continue to address these questions, both in terms of understanding the "adolescent process" and in terms of comprehending the social disorganization that young people in places like Samoa now face as a result of Western influence.

All told, my investigation of the Mead–Freeman controversy led me to the conclusion that Mead's coming-of-age thesis is quite plausible when viewed from a variety of perspectives, and when viewed in the context of the "Samoa" she studied. Yes, there are problems with some of what she wrote in *Coming of Age*. But there is little reason to believe that she was wrong in most of what she reported—contrary to what Freeman claimed and despite the mythology surrounding her book. With respect to my ability to arrive at a reasonable conclusion in this matter, I believe the fact that I am an "outsider" to both the anthropological community and Samoan culture has helped me to see the controversy in a way that provides a unique and useful contribution to the literature on Samoa: As a sociologist, I am not bound by an allegiance to the anthropological community; and as a non-Samoan I am not bound by a code that prevents me from discussing what some see as the less flattering aspects of Samoan culture. Instead, I am free to apply my expertise unrestrained by the partisanships that have marked some attempts to make sense out of Mead's work in Samoa and Freeman's criticism of her work.

ACKNOWLEDGMENTS

I would like to thank my close colleagues, Anton Allahar, Charles Levine, and Benjamin Singer, for their helpful comments on a previous draft of this manuscript as well as for their continuing personal support. I am also indebted to Dean Emoke Szathmary for her encouragement from the beginning of this project, and to Gerald Adams for his ongoing sound advice. In addition, it was a delight to work with the editors of the Research Monographs in Adolescence series, Nancy L. Galambos and Nancy A. Busch-Rossnagel. I appreciate their sharp insights and competent guidance. Finally, the assistance of the J. B. Smallman Publication Fund, Faculty of Social Science, The University of Western Ontario, is acknowledged.

James E. Côté

CHAPTER ONE

The Mead–Freeman Controversy: Mead on Trial

THE CONTEXT OF MEAD'S RESEARCH

Mead undertook her study during a period when it was widely believed that "adolescence" was associated with a period of turmoil caused by biological instabilities stimulated at puberty. As Freeman (1983) has noted, this belief was a cornerstone of the "nature" side of the nature–nurture debate. An implication of this position is that adolescence is an "affliction" that inevitably occurs regardless of social or cultural circumstances. Accordingly, it was argued that it does not matter what experiences and opportunities are available to the young, all pass through a period of what was dubbed *storm and stress* (from the German *Sturm und Drang*). In the introductory chapter to *Coming of Age in Samoa* Mead (1928) described the climate that prevailed in the 1920s:

> a great mass of theorizing about adolescence is flooding the book shops; so the psychologist in America tried to account for the restlessness of youth. The result was works like that of Stanley Hall of "Adolescence," which ascribed to the period through which the children were passing, the cause of their own conflict and distress. Adolescence was characterized as the period in which idealism flowered and rebellion against authority waxed strong, a period during which difficulties and conflicts were absolutely inevitable. (p. 2)

Mead was skeptical of this position because of obvious empirical variations in adolescent "turmoil," even within Western societies (e.g., German youth in the post-World War I era, and young immigrants to the

United States; Mead, 1928, p. 2). Moreover, there was no *scientific* evidence to support the universal storm-and-stress position. In particular, this position was not based on rigorous experimentation, where potential causes are systematically controlled, and eliminated if nonsignificant (p. 3).

Based on her anthropological training, Mead believed this experimentation could be simulated by systematically comparing cultures in terms of how adolescence was structured and experienced. If dissimilar structures produced different experiences—differing amounts of turmoil, or none at all—then the biological position would be called into question on scientific grounds. Thus, the anthropologist could ask the question: "Are the disturbances which vex adolescents due to the nature of adolescence itself or to the civilization?" (p. 11).

The remainder of Mead's position and experimental strategy is discussed in chapter 2, so need not be stated here. Based on the study she conducted, however, she concluded that because few of her Samoan informants showed signs of behavioral problems brought on by puberty, "adolescence is not necessarily a time of stress and strain, but . . . cultural conditions [can] make it so" (p. 234). In addition, she found that the experience of puberty made no significant characterological difference. In her words:

> The adolescent girl in Samoa differed from her sister who had not reached puberty in one chief respect, that in the older girl certain bodily changes were present which were absent in the younger girl. There were no other great differences to set off the group passing through adolescence from the group which would become adolescent in two years or the group which had become adolescent two years before. (p. 196)

Mead argued that the difficulties affecting the adolescent of the 1920s United States were caused by "conflicting standards and the belief that every individual should make his or her own choices, coupled with a feeling that choice is an important matter" (pp. 234–235). In contrast, she asserted that in 1920s Samoa:

> The growing child is faced by a smaller dilemma than that which confronts the American-born child of European parentage. The gap between parents and children is narrow and painless, showing few of the unfortunate aspects usually present in a period of transition . . . essentially the children are still growing up in a homogeneous community with a uniform set of ideals and aspirations. (p. 273)

With this evidence of dramatic cultural differences in the prevalence of adolescent difficulties, Mead concluded that storm and stress cannot be considered a biological inevitability. She was the first to provide evidence for this conclusion, and as we see here, this conclusion has held even as it has been put to the test with contemporary theory and methodology.

THE CONTROVERY SPARKED BY FREEMAN'S BOOK: MEAD ON TRIAL

Not one to mince words, Freeman (1983) asserted that "Mead's account of Samoan culture and character is fundamentally in error" (p. xii). In diametric opposition to Mead's account, Freeman argued that Samoan culture was/is anything but casual: There was/is a high level of aggression and violence among Samoans; that Samoans idealize(d) premarital chastity, but also commonly engage(d) in rape; and that they were/are highly competitive and easily insulted. In a move that escalated the controversy and kept it alive for the past decade, Freeman placed Mead's study squarely in the middle of the nature–nurture debate. He did this by arguing that Mead was at some level trying to please her mentor, Franz Boas, by giving him conclusive evidence that culture, not biology, determined adolescent behavioral disturbances.

Freeman declared that his book provides "detailed empirical evidence to demonstrate that Mead's account of Samoan culture and character is fundamentally in error" (p. xii). He also said that this evidence "has the specific purpose of scientifically refuting the proposition that Samoa is a negative instance" of adolescent storm and stress because it shows "that the depictions on which Mead based this assertion are, in varying degree, mistaken" (p. xiii). The literature reacting to these and other claims in Freeman's book now comprises hundreds of commentaries, including dozens of journal articles, reviews, rejoinders and letters, a few books (see Caton, 1990), a documentary film (Heimans, 1988), and even the "Phil Donahue Show" (Holmes, 1983a).

The fact that Freeman's arguments often stand in stark contrast to Mead's account is just one indication that an evaluation of the controversy is not a simple task. Furthermore, he has managed to attract a number of followers who have taken up his cause (see especially Appell & Madan, 1988; Caton, 1990). To deal with the polarization of opinion on this matter, it is necessary to consider various claims in light of possible ulterior motives.

Complicating matters further is the fact that life on the remote island Mead studied has changed dramatically. Life there is now rather "Americanized," replete with a high school, television reception, popular Western music, ghetto blasters, pickup trucks, and air service twice a day (cf. Holmes & Holmes, 1992). Because we obviously cannot go back in time to 1925, we have no choice but to rely on inferences derived mainly from written documents and to arrive at judgments of the plausibility of certain evidence and arguments.

In getting to the heart of the matter, therefore, we must stand back and look at the controversy itself, and the characters involved in it. Unfortunately, Mead died in 1978 and did not leave a very extensive defense of her position. In attempting to conceive of what she might say now in her own defense, we run the risk of adopting an overly sympathetic stance toward her work. On the other hand, many reviewers of Freeman's book argue that it is difficult to sympathize with him. This is so in terms of how he originally presented his criticisms and how he has responded to commentary about his criticisms. As Brady (1991) argued, "Freeman has made it difficult to discuss his work without discussing him. . . . There is in many of Freeman's responses a verve, a relish to fight, a sense of retribution far beyond the ordinary. . . . He conveys the distinct impression . . . that to disagree with him is to be morally wrong . . ." (p. 449).

Based on my review of his critique of Mead's work (e.g., Côté, 1992), I am of the opinion that Freeman's intransigence would be more fathomable if he had "hard" evidence supporting tight arguments. As we see in the chapters to follow, however, his evidence often has obvious limitations and his arguments often have alternative conclusions. He did not acknowledge either possibility. Thus, it is hard to sympathize with an unrelenting campaign against Mead's work, which is supposedly simply trying to set the record straight. Incidentally, it is interesting to note that a book critiquing her work was released in the same year, but its author apparently did not believe it necessary to launch a crusade against her to make his point (Goodman, 1983).

The unrelenting nature of Freeman's campaign leaves one with the impression that he is settling a score—but then again perhaps he is. For instance, he openly admitted that he wrote his book partly at the urging of some of his chiefly Samoan friends who were displeased with the image of Samoans that Mead supposedly created (Freeman, 1983, p. xv). As argued here, his disclosures in this regard suggest that he may be playing the role of the Samoan chief who is trying to preserve the honor of Samoans against Mead's perceived negative portrayals. If this is the case, Freeman might have been too close to the culture to have given us the dispassionate analysis he claims to have given.

THE CENTRAL FIGURES IN THE CONTROVERSY

Both of the central figures in this controversy are dynamic and colorful individuals. The debate stimulated by their works undoubtedly reflects their respective characters. It is therefore useful to consider the role played by both figures in this affair. It is also helpful to frame this dispute in terms of a legal metaphor, because it involves charges laid by one person against another. Moreover, the alleged "crime" took place some time ago, and there is little direct or material evidence upon which to assess "guilt" or "innocence." Accordingly, readers are asked to play the role of jury members for this section, and for the remainder of the book. This role requires readers to: (a) assess the plausibility of arguments, (b) determine the admissibility and validity of certain forms of evidence, (c) judge critically the statements of "witnesses," and (d) decide the extent of culpability of the parties involved.

The Prosecutor: Derek Freeman

Many observers of this controversy have pondered over Freeman's behavior in the matter, particularly his persistence and intransigence (e.g., Brady, 1991). Previously, a connection was drawn between the nature–nurture debate and the appeal of Freeman's book for some of his followers. In this section, we look deeper into Freeman's behavior and speculate as to why he undertook his crusade against Mead in the first place; why he has been unwilling to revise any of his criticisms despite obvious evidence to the contrary; and why he persists in trying to prove himself absolutely right and Mead (and others) absolutely wrong.

Freeman, now Professor Emeritus at Australian National University, began his research in Western Samoa in the 1940s when he was in his 20s. During a 2-year stay, he became fluent in the language; was "adopted" by a Samoan *matai* (a titled family head, or chief); and was even granted a symbolic chiefly Samoan title, thereby giving him access to the *fono* (village assemblies of *matai*). This placed him, he claimed, "in an exceptionally favorable position to pursue [his] researches into the realities of Samoan life" (p. xiv).

If we assume that Freeman has identified strongly with the *matai* role and has appropriated that perspective, then we can surmise that he has also internalized the concern with maintaining the ideals of the culture by ensuring that transgressions of the social order are properly dealt with. Primarily, *matai* are invested with the authority and responsibility to direct daily economic and social activities. This includes the assignment of work projects, the distribution of food and available resources, and the meting out of fines and punishments. Secondarily, *matai* are expected to assume an ahedonic, circumspect posture in engaging in the day-to-day life of the community (Holmes, 1987), and to maintain a certain "detachment" from their families, especially from children and young people (cf. Schoeffel & Meleisea, 1983).

In understanding Freeman's motivations in this controversy, then, it is useful to know that his reference group in Samoa is that of the *matai*; much of his knowledge of Samoa is derived from the perspective of its male culture; and he is likely to have been socially and emotionally removed from Samoan young people. Thus, we can understand in part why his portrayal of Samoan society dwells on violence and crime as well as on its authoritarian features. Readers will also recall that Freeman divulged that he had been asked to correct Mead's portrayal of Samoa. In his words, some "educated Samoans . . . entreated [him] . . . to correct [Mead's] mistaken depiction of the Samoan ethos" (p. xv). But, one final piece of information helps to complete the picture. He also disclosed that he knew for several decades that he was going to attack Mead's work. In his words: "By the time I left Samoa in November 1943 I knew I would one day face the responsibility of writing a refutation of Mead's Samoan findings" (p. xiv). Note that he spoke of a *refutation*, not a critical evaluation. In other words, his conclusion had already been formed in 1943. With these statements, Freeman seems to have admitted that long before he wrote his book, he had accepted an assignment as a *matai* to neutralize what was perceived as a blight on Samoan honor perpetrated by Mead.

Samoan author Wendt saw Freeman's motivation in terms of carrying out a "mission." In A. Wendt's (1983) view, Freeman is "a *matai* who takes his mataiship seriously. Most importantly, he has deep love and respect for us. This I think helps explain his almost *obsessive quest to correct what he deems was the wrong Margaret Mead did to us*." Wendt also argued that Freeman's book is "apt justification for his life, his *mission*, his search to belong. To us " (pp. 12, 69, italics added).

This "mission" would help to explain why Freeman has been determined to disgrace Mead and her associates. At the very least, as mentioned earlier, the degree of his involvement in the *matai* role raises questions about his capacity for detachment and objectivity in the controversy. Indeed, in a documentary film discussed in chapter 2, Freeman is shown weeping during a *fono* meeting (in Western Samoa) in response to the numerous expressions of praise and honor bestowed upon him by his *matai* friends.

Freeman's identification with the *matai* role and his acceptance of this mission also help to account for his intransigence in the controversy. This is especially the case with regard to the issues of sexuality and virginity, and his insistence that social changes between the 1920s and 1960s are irrelevant to the controversy. Modern Samoa is devoutly Christian, and the *matai* and pastors share village power. As part of contemporary Christianized Samoa, the *matai* therefore have a responsibility to ensure that Christian ideals are protected. However, as is seen in chapters 4 and 5, the missionaries encountered a culture they considered "heathen" and "immoral," so they set out to "Christianize" it and to remove all vestiges of this "heathen immorality." Therefore, for Freeman to admit that pre-Christian Samoans practiced any thing other than Christian sexual behavior would be to undermine the current *matai*-pastor power sharing and to violate the mandate of the *matai* role, because it would validate this "heathen" past.

To continue this line of reasoning, it would appear that Freeman "the scientist" cannot admit that Samoan sexual practices were significantly different before Christianity, because Freeman "the *matai*" cannot admit that Christianity has had any significant impact on elements of Samoan society related to sexual and social mores. Thus, it appears that Freeman has had to draw a line of defense on these points, because any other position would compromise his stature as a titled Samoan, even though it is a symbolic title. Incidentally, it is of interest to note that O'Meara (1990) observed, in the village he recently studied, that most people "describe their own, pre-Christian past as the time before they 'saw the light.' They rarely speak of that time, and then only with some embarrassment" (p. 47).

Brady (1991) drew a similar conclusion, linking Freeman's motivation regarding this mission on behalf of Samoans with his position on the nature–nurture debate. He noted as well that some of Freeman's supporters recognize this: "that Freeman has been on a heroic and highly personalized mission—a 'double-edged' quest—to discredit Mead, first on behalf of what he declares is superior science and second on behalf of some very conservative Samoans who have found Mead's characterizations of their attitudes about sex embarrassing and offensive" (p. 499).

To put Freeman's strategy in a context more familiar to Westerners, his tactics resemble those of an aggressive prosecuting attorney who does what is necessary to win a "case." For example, in his book, he based some of his critique on the premise that Mead was young (age 23), inexperienced, and apparently anxious to please her mentor, "Papa Franz" (Boas). This, he said, led her to draw some hasty conclusions in order to provide Boas with much needed evidence for his position in the nature–nurture debate. Such *ad hominem* aspersions are irrelevant and unprofessional, and have contributed to a degeneration of this "scientific debate." This *ad hominem* reasoning could just as easily be turned back on Freeman with similar irrelevant charges. For example, although I would not do so, someone could just as easily cite him as an eccentric old man trying to live up to Karl Popper's reputation, the person to whom he dedicates the book. But, such name calling accomplishes nothing for science.

More recently, Freeman (1991) chronicled what he claimed to be the history of Mead's involvement before, during, and after her research in

Samoa. In a serious departure from academic protocol, Freeman's "historical analysis of the Samoan researches of Margaret Mead" can be described as little more than "soap opera science." Although this judgment may seem harsh, readers will find in that article rumor and innuendo, hearsay and gossip, and unsubstantiated insinuations about Mead's character. Is it really germane to a scientific dispute whether or not Mead had a one night stand at a conference, whether she and Ruth Benedict had "an intimate Sapphic relationship" (p. 105), or whether she danced barebreasted when in Samoa? I think not. In fact, there is no solid scientific evidence in that article that can be said to resolve anything, other than prurient and voyeuristic desires.

Others have objected to Freeman's patronizing attitude toward Mead. Turnbull (1983), for example, argued that "[w]ith a revealing show of male chauvinism, Freeman even mentions how this 'young female student' included as part of her field equipment some 'cotton dresses.' This irrelevant piece of information he gleaned from his avid reading of Mead's writings, scholarly, popular, and private, randomly mixed to cast her not only as a mindless Boasian, but as a rather empty-headed, silly girl" (p. 33).

As we see, Freeman's evidence against Mead is circumstantial. Although he postulated a motive (he argued that she was attempting to please her mentor, Franz Boas) and opportunity (her selection of a research site that she thought in advance would likely validate her hypothesis), he did not have any material or direct evidence from Ta'u in the 1920s pertaining to most of the matters involved (except for the flawed testimony of one person, described in the next chapter). Therefore, he did the two things that any ambitious prosecutor would do: (a) he provided as much circumstantial evidence as can be mustered; and (b) he raised questions about the character, morality, and competence of the accused. With a skillful presentation, he attempted to sway the jury of public opinion to convict Mead of his charges. As is seen in this volume, however, when a reasonable defense is provided for Mead, his evidence is far from convincing or conclusive.

The Defendant: Margaret Mead

The second principal figure in the controversy is Mead herself. In this section we see how her own behavior appears to have contributed to both the current bad press about her book and the loss of reputation she has suffered personally. As we see, the extent to which she wrote *Coming of Age* as a popular book has contributed to this controversy, as has the way she handled criticisms of that book since it was published. We also see, however, that these failings do not justify the serious indictments raised by Freeman.

As an academic, Mead could have handled matters much better, beginning with the initial publication of her book in 1928. This is the wisdom of hindsight, however, and for the young academic the prospect of publishing can make other concerns seem unimportant. At the time, she was new to the scene and this book was to lead to immediate recognition and acclaim. To make the book marketable, her publisher apparently urged her to write additional chapters in a popular style, and it is primarily the content of these chapters that has been the object of criticism. Certainly, these chapters contain some generalizations that are difficult to defend academically (see chapters 3 and 6, this volume).

To put the issue of marketability into perspective, Mead's (1930/1969) scholarly report of her Samoan research, *Social Organization of Manu'a* would never have been published in place of *Coming of Age* by a popular press. If she had wished to stay academically "pure," however, she should have only published something like *Social Organization*. In any event, academics who are dissatisfied with the offending chapters from *Coming of Age* should read, for example, the following segments from *Social Organization*: "Daily Life in Manu'a" as a substitute for "A Day in Samoa", and "Dominant Cultural Attitudes" as a substitute for "Our Educational Problems in the Light of Samoan Contrasts."

It also appears that Mead did not understand Samoan culture as well as she thought (Holmes, 1987; Schoeffel & Meleisea, 1983). Although she did spend 9 months intensively and directly studying the culture, even after years of study, elements of any culture may not be fully appreciated by an outsider. In particular, she may not have fully understood the "casualness" of Samoans, but she would not be the only one to have had this problem (Swaney, 1990). Clearly, Westerners accustomed to a time-managed, hurried, compartmentalized existence have a difficult time understanding the "laid-back" nature of some non-Western cultures. It is common that apparently "relaxed" behaviors and attitudes are mistaken by Westerners for laziness or dullness, or in Mead's case, an emotional shallowness. From the accounts of Samoans commenting on the controversy, however, Freeman may not be any closer to understanding the "true" Samoan character, if any such thing exists (cf. Ala'ailima, 1984; Schoeffel & Meleisea, 1983; A. Wendt, 1983; F. Wendt, 1984).

Eventually, Mead did entertain the notion that her informants provided her with a skewed view of Samoan culture. Unfortunately, she should have considered this problem much sooner, and she should have at least warned readers in the preface of later printings. After all, much of her information came from young women who were "coming of age" and by Mead's own account were experiencing the best years of their lives. Her informants were temporarily free from many responsibilities and obligations, and most were able to experiment socially in a playful fashion.

One's culture can look very benign from this point of view. Such a "moratorium period" is by definition one where individuals are largely free from responsibilities and irreversible commitments (Mageo, 1988; cf. E. Erikson, 1968). During a moratorium the "stakes" are often not "high" for those involved, because they are relatively free to casually move from one interest to the next.

The possibility that Mead's perspective was somewhat askew does not mean, however, that Freeman's was any more accurate. As we saw in the last section, Freeman's appropriation of the *matai* role and his mission to counteract Mead's supposed influence may have produced a narrow lens through which he viewed both Samoan culture and scholarly criticisms of his work.

Finally, although it is possible to give Mead the benefit of the doubt in most instances, she was undoubtedly in error in stating that "because one girl's life was so much like another's, in an uncomplex uniform culture like Samoa, *I feel justified in generalizing* although I studied only fifty girls in three small neighboring villages" (Mead, 1928, p. 11, italics added).

Not only is it unclear to whom she is generalizing, it is also unclear as to where and when. She wrote that she went to Ta'u "as a corrective for the degree of culture contact" elsewhere in American Samoa (Mead, 1930/1969, p. xv). Thus, there is an obvious flaw in her logic if she selected the island of Ta'u because of its remoteness, but still felt justified in generalizing to the rest of Samoa. Why bother going to Ta'u when by the logic of the quotation just cited she could have found the same thing anywhere in Samoa? Logically, she cannot have it both ways. Moreover, she was also aware that what she observed on Ta'u was no longer completely "traditional" either, and that the culture there was undergoing changes when she conducted her study. Given the uniqueness of Ta'u, then, there are grounds to question some of Mead's generalizations to the rest of Samoa. But, by the same token, Freeman's contention that Ta'u in 1925 would have been no different from Western Samoa in the 1960s is questionable (we explore this further in chapter 3). In Appendix III of *Coming of Age*, Mead discusses the historical uniqueness of the "Samoa" she studied on Ta'u.

As for the "real" Samoa, I do not think that anyone, even Samoans themselves, can lay claim to a complete understanding of Samoan culture in all of its forms in all places and times. If anything, Freeman may have simplified it as much as Mead is thought to have (Ala'ailima, 1984; Bock, 1983; Feinberg, 1988; Hooper, 1984; Levy, 1984; A. Wendt, 1983; F. Wendt, 1984). Moreover, the resolution to the controversy is not likely to be found "somewhere in between" the two versions, as some have suggested (e.g., Swaney, 1990). Rather, it appears to lie in part with a complex and flexible culture that survives and maintains its integrity by appropriating the forces that seek to change it, and by defying easy definition and understanding (cf. Laing, 1987). The protective strategy of incorporating an influence as much as possible before the influence incorporates the culture was noted by Mead, and has since been noted by others (e.g., Baldauf & Ayabe, 1977). This is believed to be the case with Christianity, for example. A number of observers have remarked that it is difficult to say whether Samoa was Christianized, or whether Christianity there was "Samoanized" (e.g., Hanson, 1973; Holmes, 1980a, 1980b; Meleisea, 1987a; Stanner, 1953).

In any event, it is important to note that Samoan culture is complex and is based on a long history of intricate and subtle customs and oral traditions. It currently has a reputation as the most conservative of the Polynesian cultures (Hanson, 1973; Holmes, 1980a), and Samoans proudly refer to their way of life as *fa'a Samoa* (the Samoan way).

In light of these considerations, had Mead initially titled the book something like *Coming of Age on Ta'u*, and not engaged in wholesale generalizations to other Samoan islands and to other historical periods, there would not likely be a controversy today about her work. Indeed, in a later scholarly publication, she exercised more caution in stating that her generalizations regarding Samoan should be "understood to refer to Manu'a specifically" (Mead, 1931, p. 545). Nevertheless, there is a controversy. In the next chapter we begin the task of judging the merits of the charges made by Freeman that stimulated one of the greatest disputes in the history of anthropology.

METHODOLOGIES APPROPRIATE TO THE EVALUATION OF MEAD'S COMING-OF-AGE THESIS

Given the extreme and disparate positions in this case, how do we go about evaluating Freeman's charges, as well as Mead's original work? Before proceeding, it is appropriate to apprise readers of the methodologies I employed to evaluate the controversy.

As mentioned earlier, because life has changed dramatically at Mead's research site, there is little point in attempting to replicate her study there. Instead, we are confronted with the task of piecing together available evidence until enough of an understanding is developed to allow for a conclusion to be drawn. What I have done, therefore, is to undertake an interdisciplinary analysis, utilizing a number of different qualitative and quantitative methodologies.

In chapter 2, where Freeman's case against Mead is laid out, I "deconstruct" the politics of the controversy, to discover that it is in many ways yet another battle in what is for many people a sort of "nature–nurture war." Indeed, when we systematically examine the components of the arguments and evidence that have been assembled in the case against Mead's coming-of-age thesis, we find that a number of interesting maneuvers have been undertaken. One such maneuver is a documentary film that claims to resolve the controversy. When this film is deconstructed, however, and the *scientific* merit of the evidence presented in this film is examined, a different conclusion can be drawn about what this film means for the Mead–Freeman controversy.

In chapter 2, I "unpack" the statistics Freeman produced to attempt to refute Mead's coming-of age thesis. Freeman presented a number of statistical arguments concerning crime and delinquency that he believes exposes Mead's coming-of-age thesis as erroneous. To evaluate his critique, these statistical arguments are critically examined with state-of-the-art empirical knowledge regarding adolescence and human development. This critical evaluation is carried out on the data that were collected by Freeman in Samoa, as well as on comparative data he used from other countries. Similarly, the crude crime rates Freeman used to argue that Mead's thesis was wrong, are algebraically converted into estimates of what life would be like on a daily basis in a given Samoan village. Thus, Freeman's statistical case against Mead is examined in terms of statistical realism and errors of statistical conclusion.

In chapter 3, several forms of evidence are examined, including expert opinion and material evidence I gathered during a fact-finding visit to Western Samoa and Mead's research site in American Samoa. This material evidence, which includes geographic, topographic, and photographic material, provides us with reference points with which to evaluate Freeman's claims.

Chapters 4 and 5 undertake a sociohistorical analysis of adolescence in Samoa since contact with the West. Based on textual analyses of the detailed diaries kept by Christian missionaries and the ethnographies of early anthropologists, a trajectory of social change is mapped out, giving us a working knowledge of adolescence in Samoan culture over the past 150 years. Chapter 6 presents a summary and analysis of "Mead's Samoa" of the 1920s. With the working knowledge gained in chapters 4 and 5, we are then in a position to judge whether "Mead's Samoa" reasonably fits with this historical trajectory. In this chapter, I also analyze data collected by Mead that were never formally crosstabulated, apparently because Franz Boas told her not to bother. When these data are carefully examined, conclusions can be drawn regarding the normative structure of the villages she studied.

The remaining two chapters of this book deal with the situation that currently obtains in Samoa. Statistics and textual accounts are presented in these chapters that reveal what has happened to how young Samoans come of age since Mead conducted her study in the 1920s. This empirically derived understanding of contemporary Samoa provides a basis for policy recommendations, as well as recommendations for future research, with respect to the problems confronting those currently struggling to come of age in a rapidly changing Samoa.

CHAPTER TWO

Freeman's Case Against Mead

THE PREMISE OF FREEMAN'S CASE: ADOLESCENT BIOLOGY

Freeman (1983) believes he has proven that Mead "was at error in her depiction of the nature of adolescence in Samoa." Based on this belief he declares that "her much bruited 'negative instance' [regarding adolescent "storm and stress"] is . . . no negative instance at all" (p. 268). In other words, Freeman argued that Mead did not find a culture where adolescence was free of storm and stress, so he believes she did not have evidence that refuted the biological argument of adolescent turmoil. He did not waver from this position, and more recently referred to Mead's coming-of-age thesis as "preposterous" (1985, p. 910) and "egregious" (1987a, p. 930) with its conclusion that adolescent storm and stress is not primarily biological in origin.

When the basis of this strong condemnation is examined, however, it appears that Freeman misconstrued Mead's conclusion. From his reconstructions of Mead's writings, Freeman appears to be attempting to portray her as professing that "biology" has no relevance for adolescent behavior or disturbances in behavior during adolescence. In one place he "quoted" her as saying that " 'we cannot' . . . 'make any explanations' in terms of the biological process of adolescence itself" (1985, p. 910); in another he contended she said that " 'we cannot make any explanation' of the 'disturbances' of adolescence other than 'in terms of' the 'social environment' " (Freeman, 1987a, p. 930).

The reader will note that these are not direct quotes; rather, they are collages of passages that, as we see later, do not accurately represent Mead's conclusion. Freeman has these "creative" collages throughout his book. To make this matter more problematic, he provided all of the references from each paragraph in single endnotes, so that it appears in his text that the quoted passages are from one source. This technique produced more than 50 pages of endnotes. Moreover, in many of these collages, Freeman is not quoting from Mead's *Coming of Age*, but from other sources, published for vastly different audiences over her 50-year career. This unusual referencing style makes it difficult for the reader to judge the validity of Freeman's reconstructions of Mead's thoughts. As Rappaport (1987a) noted, "Professor Freeman seems to have combed Mead's corpus for phrases and sentences that can be construed in ways convicting her of his charges" (p. 304). See McDowell (1984) for a thorough critique of Freeman's writing and referencing style.

As we saw in chapter 1, Mead's conclusion is actually quite different. She simply said that because the biological processes associated with adolescence are the same for Samoans and Americans, many difficulties experienced by U.S. adolescents may be attributed to characteristics of U.S. culture that are absent in Samoan culture. This reasonable conclusion was stated as follows by Mead (1928):

> If it is proved that adolescence is not necessarily a specially difficult period in a girl's life—and proved it is if I can find any society in which that is so—then what accounts for the presence of stress and storm in American adolescents? First, I may say quite simply that there must be something in the two civilizations to account for the difference. *If the same process takes a different form in the two different environments, I cannot make any explanations in terms of the process, for it is the same in both cases.* But the social environment is very different and it is to it that I must look for an explanation. What is there in Samoa which is absent in America, what is there in America which is absent in Samoa, which will account for the difference? (pp. 197–198, italics added)

A fair reading of this full quotation suggests that Mead is simply saying that the biological processes associated with adolescence are the same in both cultures, not irrelevant. In other words, she identified the biology of puberty as a *constant* and social environment of adolescence as a *variable*. Mead (1928) provided the following justification for taking this position:

> For the biologist who doubts an old hypothesis or wishes to test out a new one, there is the biological laboratory. . . . Keeping all the conditions but one constant, [the biologist] can make accurate measurement of the effect of one. This is the ideal method of science, the method of controlled experi-

> ment, through which all hypotheses may be submitted to a strict objective test. (p. 5)

Thus, Mead was aware of the requirements of the experimental method and of biological research in this area. Her design was sound unless one is willing to argue that pubertal biology is linked with "racial" differences. That is, a potential flaw in the logic of her design is that the variable of "race" is not held constant in her comparison between U.S. and Samoan cultures. Although some of Freeman's supporters have suggested that this may be a problem (Appell, 1984; Buchholz, 1984), they should heed Sprinthall and Collins (1984) who concluded that "racial and ethnic differences in puberty are minor" (p. 74). In any event, Freeman has not taken her to task on this matter.

Interestingly, in his original critique, Freeman did not paraphrase Mead's conclusion; instead, he provided it verbatim. After doing so, he stated the following:

> In other words, any explanation in biological terms of the presence of storm and stress in American adolescence was totally excluded. . . . Instead of arriving at an estimate of the relative strength of biological puberty and cultural pattern . . . Mead dismissed biology, or nature, as being of no significance whatsoever in accounting for the presence of storm and stress in American adolescents, and claimed the determinism of culture, or nurture, to be absolute. (Freeman, 1983, p. 78)

Freeman's interpretation of Mead's conclusion raises questions about his understanding of both research design and biological research on adolescents. As just argued, Mead had, in principle, a sound research design. More specifically, U.S. society constituted the control group and Samoan society the experimental group; the independent variable was cultural institutions governing adolescence (known to differ) and the dependent variable was the ease/difficulty of coming of age. If a difference were found on the dependent variable, it would be attributable to cultural institutions, because the biological processes of puberty were essentially held constant.

In spite of this reasonable research strategy, Freeman (1983) contended that Mead was not "scientifically equipped to investigate the subtle and complex interaction, in Samoan behavior, of biological and cultural variables" (p. 75). These criticisms are unconstructive because of their vagueness, however. For example, he never specified just what she should have done to assess biological variables. In 1925, the state of knowledge regarding the biology of adolescence was totally theoretical and there was virtually no technology available to measure relevant physiological variables.[1] In fact, little scientific attention has been paid to the relationship between puberty and adolescent behavior until quite recently. As noted by Brooks-Gunn and Reiter (1990):

> until the 1980s almost no developmental work on the meaning or effects of puberty had been conducted. . . . Then in the 1980s, starting with a 1981 conference on girls at puberty, this topic came into its own. During that decade at least six conferences were held on early adolescence, with the topic of puberty having a prominent place in each. (p. 19)

Freeman also claimed that Mead did not carry "out any systematic comparison of hereditary and environmental conditions" (p. 76). To the contrary, with puberty defined as the onset of menstruation (Mead, 1928, pp. 283–284), Mead assembled a sample to represent prepuberty (n = 11), imminent puberty (n = 14), and postpuberty (n = 25) and she noted that there were no major characterological or psychopathological differences among these three groups. If puberty is the "hereditarian condition" responsible for adolescent storm and stress, such differences should have been observed among such a grouping of informants. This research strategy is apparently inadequate for Freeman, however. Again, just what he expected her to do is unclear, as is what he would expect of someone conducting such research today with current knowledge and technology.

In view of these considerations, Freeman's critique of Mead's treatment of the biological factors affecting adolescence is questionable. If we assume that he is not being obtuse in his reading of Mead, we might conclude that he is naive regarding the difficulties of understanding and documenting the interplay between biological and cultural factors. Moreover, at no time in her career did Mead dismiss the relevance of biological factors (cf. Rappaport, 1987a, 1987b). If she were able to participate in this debate today, she probably would clarify her position by arguing that cultural factors can stimulate certain biological reactions in adolescents that are part of a chain of causation in some of the storm and stress associated with this period. She was simply implying that in the absence of certain cultural factors, these biological reactions are not stimulated and that therefore the storm and stress can be considered neither natural nor inevitable.[2] She would therefore probably not have

---

[1]In fact, Mead did look for some sort of technology to help her, but all that was available at the time was the newly developed instrument to measure galvanic skin response. She concluded that it would not have been suitable for the task, however, partly because it would only measure gross emotional responses (Mead, 1972).

[2]See Paikoff and Brooks-Gunn (1991) for a discussion of research models that need to be tested to sort out such issues.

argued that biological factors are "of no significance in accounting for the presence of storm and stress in American adolescents" (Freeman, 1983, p. 78), but that they constitute intervening rather than independent variables. As Rappaport (1987a) noted:

> Mead clearly recognized the biological character of puberty, never claimed that biological factors had nothing to do with behavior, and simply stated that differences in the emotional and cognitive correlates of "the same [biological] process" in "different environments" are to be accounted for by environmental differences. *Hardly preposterous*. (p. 160, italics added)

Ironically, recent research undertaken with state-of-the-art theory and technology supports Mead's conclusion that biological factors do not directly affect most adolescent behavior or disturbances (e.g, Adams, Montemayor, & Gullota, 1990; Montemayor, Adams, & Gullota, 1990). Referring to the notion that hormones are primarily responsible for emotional turmoil among adolescents, Brooks-Gunn and Warren (1989) noted that in the empirical literature "hormone-affect associations, when found, . . . are small. . . . No direct effects of pubertal status were found" (p. 47). In their own study of the negative affect of 100 females, age 10–14, Brooks-Gunn and Warren (1989) found that "endocrine system factors . . . accounted for no more than 4% of variance in negative emotional expression . . . [while] social factors accounted for more variance (8% and 18% for depressive and aggressive affect, respectively) than biological factors" (p. 47). They concluded from these findings that "hormonal activation effects in humans may not be large . . . and may be overshadowed by environmental events."

Other experts in this area agree. For example, after reviewing the relevant literature, Montemayor and Flannery (1990) concluded that the evidence indicates "that pubertal effects, by themselves, account for a relatively small proportion of the variance in early adolescent behavior" (p. 294). Sprinthall and Collins (1984) provide this elaboration of the implications of state-of-the-art research:

> biological changes [associated with puberty] seem to influence psychological development through the subjective meanings that the changes have for adolescents themselves and for adults and peers around them. . . . [Thus] the effects of the primary physical changes of adolescence are *socially mediated* by the reactions of self and others. In this view one's self-image and self-esteem reflect one's own and others' subjective reactions to biological maturation. And these reactions are determined by sociocultural standards, norms, and expectations about physical characteristics that are widely held in a society or culture. (p. 79)

Finally, in specific reference to the Mead–Freeman controversy, Muuss (1988) maintained that:

> [Freeman's] argument for a synthesis between biological and cultural determinism seems to come too late to have a major impact. The synthesis has already taken place. Although proponents of culture or biology may emphasize one more than the other, most contemporary theorists view development as an interaction between nature and nurture. ***Adolescent turmoil, storm and stress, and crises are no longer considered inevitable, not even for adolescents growing up in the United States.*** And regardless of whether or not Mead was correct about Samoa, other anthropologists have observed societies in which adolescence is not turbulent. Thus, the physiological changes of puberty and sexual maturation alone are not categorically responsible for adolescent difficulties. Anxieties, insecurities, social pressures, social expectations, and cultural, educational, and family factors may all contribute to adolescent stress. (p. 142, italics added)

In summary, when critically examined, Freeman's critique of Mead's treatment of biological factors amount to straw arguments. As Rappaport (1987a) noted: "The conclusion that Freeman asserts was Mead's [conclusion] is indeed, preposterous, ***but it verges on the preposterous to attribute [that conclusion] to her***" (p. 304, italics added).

Why did Freeman go to such great lengths to construct this argument? The answer appears to lie with his position on the nature–nurture debate and the perception that Mead's study constitutes a cornerstone of the nurture side of that debate. If we assume that he had already set out on the mission to redeem the "honor" of Samoans (as argued in chapter 1), the inclusion of this argument gave him the opportunity to attempt to score a victory against those whom he thinks have given insufficient attention to the biology of human development. In doing so, he was apt to gain allies from those who favor nature explanations of human behavior. We see in the next section how Freeman gained allies by attacking Mead's coming-of-age thesis, thereby creating the perception that he has delivered a blow to the nurture side of the nature–nurture debate.

THE POLITICS OF THE CONTROVERSY

The politicking behind the controversy is an interesting sociological phenomenon on its own. As such, it deserves detailed consideration here, because it helps us understand why a small study done more than 60 years ago commands so much attention today. In this controversy, the world has witnessed anthropologist pitted against anthropologist, publicly insulting and discrediting each other. Throughout the brouhaha that ensued from the highly publicized release of Freeman's book in 1983, the central focus of Mead's study has often been ignored; instead, her book became symbolic of much larger fractures within the anthropological community—in fact, within the social scientific community. As we see, when viewed in terms of possible ulterior motives, the "real reason" for much of the attention given to the Mead–Freeman controversy appears to be that it is yet another battle in the nature–nurture war, if you will, that began over a century ago.

Freeman prefaced his attack on Mead's research with a four-chapter treatment of what he believes to be somewhat of a cultural determinist conspiracy that has fabricated evidence for the nurture side of the debate. To counteract this conspiracy, he seemed to think it is important to refute Mead's study because it provides a "negative incidence" that discredited the nature position of absolute biological causation regarding adolescent storm and stress. Readers of his book must wade through this material before they get to the substance of his critique of Mead's actual research. Yet curiously, Freeman eventually acknowledged after some 255 pages that "research on ordinary adolescents has generally failed to substantiate claims of the inevitability and universality of adolescent stress" (Freeman citing Katchadourian, 1977). In other words, Freeman admitted the validity of Mead's basic coming-of-age conclusion!

Why, then, did he write his book? To answer this question we could fall back on the explanation that he is really trying to settle a score for his chiefly Samoan friends, as mentioned earlier. Although this does appear to account for some of his motivation, had his book simply focused on the dissatisfaction of some Samoans with Mead's portrayal of Samoan culture, I doubt that it would have been published in the first place, or that it would have drawn so much criticism and support. In short, there seems to be something more potent to this controversy—something that has drawn otherwise circumspect social scientists into a rather unpleasant row. Thus, one is left with a strong suspicion that it is the nature–nurture debate that provides much of the potency for the controversy.

Given his attack on the nurture side of the debate, one would predict that Freeman's followers in the controversy would be nature advocates. In fact, Freeman's "exposé" of Mead can be seen as a counterstrike to the bad press the nature side of the debate has received over the years. This bad press includes recent revelations that the British psychologist Sir Cyril Burt published fraudulent results during his lifelong quest to prove that intelligence is for the most part genetically inherited (see Broad & Wade, 1982; Gould, 1981). What Freeman's work promised was that finally a "victory" could be scored against the nurture side, and for once it would not be the nature side being accused of deceit.

This possible ulterior motive in Freeman's "refutation" of Mead would account for why he painted such a dark portrait of Samoan culture and character in spite of the risk that it would displease Samoans who object to such harsh portrayals of them and their culture. That is, to appease nature advocates he may have been trying to prove that traits such as aggressiveness are universal human "biological imperatives" that cannot be mitigated by culture, contrary to what Mead's study implied.

The appeal of Freeman's attack on Mead can be seen in some of the commentary provided by his followers. For example, shortly after the controversy began, Caton (1984) claimed that in working through the "Mead Problem" (p. 29), anthropology will likely "undergo a complete reorientation" (p. 29). By exposing Mead and returning "Samoa to reality," Caton submitted that anthropology will be reformed. His logic is stated as follows:

> Those who accept Freeman's refutation affirm a set of observations that exhibit cross-cultural constants operating throughout Samoan culture. The refutation consequently entails rejection of cultural determinism, which denies those constants. One is obliged to accept a model that predicts and explains the constants. That model, Freeman amply documents, is the interactionist model of nature and nurture, based upon behavioral biology.
>
> The other option is to defend Mead's fantasy. That defence must take the way of disingenuous evasions, and pay the price of bad conscience; or else it must become intransigent obscurantism fighting with epithets and dirty tricks. In America especially obscurantism has been highly visible. (pp. 30–31)

These are strong words, but Caton continued railing against the U.S. anthropological "establishment" for its reaction to Freeman's book:

> We see here operating the obscurantist mind that equates behavioral biology with conservatism on the ground that acknowledging significant biological control of behavior is incompatible with social improvement. *This is the gut issue. The Americans are paranoid about biology*, and indeed about any facts inconsistent with the wish to improve the species out of sight. *What's the matter with them? Why are they so discontent with the species as it is?* (p. 31, italics added)

There certainly is much that can be unpacked from this tirade. But, aside from the fact that he did not specify exactly what it is from "behavioral biology" or Freeman's interactionist model that we should wholeheartedly embrace, one has to wonder how he can be so smug about a species that is potentially so destructive, particularly when that species clearly exhibits cross-cultural variation in its tendency toward destructiveness. One does not have to be a social scientist to be aware of the ameliorating effect of particular cultural arrangements on the darker side of "human nature" or on the *potentials* of human behavior. Undoubtedly, few in the U.S. anthropological "establishment" would disagree that the darker side of human nature emerges when stimulated by particular circumstances, and that "human potential" can be stimulated by other circumstances.

Caton (1990) more recently published *The Samoa Reader: Anthropologists Take Stock*, an anthology of articles and news clippings related to the Mead–Freeman controversy. He claimed this book presents a "range of opinion" (p. 1) on the subject. As one reads *The Samoan Reader*, however, it appears that selective evidence is provided in favor of Freeman's critique. This is not surprising because some of the material was provided by Freeman from his personal library (Caton, 1990, p. v). Moreover, Caton, the editor, wrote a section clearly intended to discredit Mead and her supporters (entitled "Did Margaret Mead Speak Samoan?", pp. 158–164. See Brady, 1991, for a review of this book).

Other statements and actions in defense of Freeman have been similarly problematic. For example, Appell and Madan (1988) provided what appears to constitute a position statement for some of Freeman's followers:

> Many of us who view anthropology as a scientific and scholarly discipline have been shaken to our intellectual foundations by the response Freeman's book has received in American anthropology. The attempts to silence him, to deprive him of the right of adequate reply to published criticism, the failure to weigh the issues critically and put them to Popperian test, the conscious and unconscious misreading of his argument including denial of the facts on which it is based, and the attempts to divert attention from his refutation by *ad hominem* attacks have astonished many of us. We find these reactions counterproductive in a discipline that is supposedly seeking the truth. For all those skilled in social analysis and willing to turn this analysis upon their own social lives, *such reactions are the reactions of a belief system that is out of touch with the real world and unresponsive to change*. (p. 23, italics added)

In other words, Appell and Madan seem to believe not only that criticisms of Freeman are unfair, but that criticisms are the result of anthropologists being afflicted with some sort of pathological dogmatism (cf. Rokeach, 1960). Freeman himself is apparently preparing his own sociological analysis of the controversy based on Leon Festinger's sociopsychological classic *When Prophecy Fails* (Freeman, 1987b). He contended that Mead's supporters are exhibiting what he called "the Festinger reaction" because they still support her work "despite the presence of unequivocal and undeniable evidence" to the contrary (pp. 392–393). More recently, Freeman (1991) claimed that Mead was "cognitively deluded" during her study and *Coming of Age* spread her delusion, producing one of "the more spectacular and instructive instances of collective cognitive delusion in the history of the human sciences" (pp. 118–119).

In example after example, the actions of Freeman and some of his followers come across more as a take-no-prisoners attack on Mead and cultural anthropology, than as a dispassionate analysis of the general merits and limits of her work. For instance, among Freeman's followers there have been attempts to support Freeman's blanket claim that Mead was simply "wrong" and that there is little merit in her book. In an early commentary, Appel (1984) said that he "found Freeman's argument to be completely convincing" (p. 189) and several pages later proclaims that "anyone who can read with a discerning mind would have seen that Mead's *Coming of Age* was just plain rubbish" (p. 205).

Appell, an ex-student of Freeman, has since co-edited a book entitled *Choice and Morality in Anthropological Perspective: Essays in Honour of Derek Freeman* (Appell & Madan, 1988). In the first chapter of that book the editors attempt to explain some of Freeman's bullying behavior while at the same time admonishing Freeman's critics for being unfair to him. In their defense of Freeman they noted that although he is sometimes perceived to be "dogmatic and self-assertive," these traits should really be seen "as dedication, enthusiasm, and an unrelenting pursuit of the truth" (p. viii). They also argued that part of Freeman's character is a "deep sense of moral responsibility to espouse the cause of those, whether individual or groups, whom he believes to be the victims of caprice, prejudice, or persecution" (p. ix). As for Freeman's response to criticisms of his attack on Mead, they claimed that he has responded in a dignified manner to "attacks on his work and personal integrity" by answering "each point of criticism in the serious manner befitting a scholar" and that he has "never returned abuse for abuse" (p. ix).

Yet another reviewer announced that Freeman's book constitutes "our most up-to-date and reliable account of Samoan culture" (Badock, 1983, p. 606). This is a most curious statement because Freeman's book is not an ethnography, as he clearly pointed out (Freeman, 1983, p. xii). Such commentaries are unproductive because it is obvious that many of their authors have little or no direct knowledge of Samoan culture or history, or of adolescent development, upon which to assess the plausibility of Freeman's claims. Instead, as suggested earlier, their support for Freeman appears to originate with his attack on the nurture side of the debate and their common complaint that the nature side has not been sufficiently acknowledged by the U.S. anthropological establishment.

It appears that support for Freeman gained enough momentum to spawn a documentary film to support his case against Mead (Heimans,

1988). The film, entitled *Margaret Mead and Samoa*, begins with the narrator claiming that the controversy "will be resolved by startling new evidence presented in this program" (see Freeman, 1989a, 1991, 1992, for his discussions of this "startling new evidence"). To the uninformed, uncritical viewer, the film would appear to present an objective account of the controversy. For example, interview segments are presented with those who seem to represent both sides of the debate. However, an informed, critical examination reveals something quite different. A critical examination uncovers a rather slick production that carefully orchestrates what information is presented, and the pace of its presentation. Moreover, disclosures about the controversy are selective and far more interview segments are presented in support of Freeman's position in the controversy. The few interview segments with those who support Mead's position tend to present only ambiguous or potentially discrediting information about her.

The first portion of the film provides a protracted *ad hominem* portrayal of Mead, referring to her presumed personality characteristics, weaknesses, and frailties as a woman. She is said, for example, to have overcompensated because of her plain looks, to have searched for a mentor, and to have had a terrific need to be accepted by others. Essentially, a negative impression of Mead the person—the woman—is created. This is done presumably to create suspicions about her academic integrity and abilities. Nowhere in the film is there an analysis of Freeman's personality, or an implication that his gender somehow compromises his intellectual integrity and ability. In addition, Ruth Benedict, Mead's close friend and colleague, is described as an unhappily married woman who had done a number of things but had never found fulfillment. The tendency to disparage women who step out of traditional roles may be widespread, but it certainly cannot be excused because of its prevalence, especially in what is supposedly a scientific debate.

With Mead's credibility undermined, the film pretends to represent her Samoan research. However, it focuses almost entirely on the issue of female Samoan premarital sexual behavior, rather than Mead's central thesis—the issue of whether adolescence was problematic for her informants. In presenting this slanted view, a number of points are made that seriously misrepresent both Samoan culture and her research there. Two examples of this are cited here.

In one interview, we witness a curious leap of logic based on the reasoning that because Mead did not report any pregnancies in her book, there must not have been any sexual activity taking place. Not only is such a statement naive, it is ill-informed because it ignores the ample evidence of premarital and extramarital sexual behavior in precontact and contemporary Samoan culture, as well as the continuing practice of the casual adoption of children from unwed mothers (Schoeffel & Meleisea, 1983). The fact is that Mead (1928) cited several examples of "illegitimacy" in her book (pp. 54–55, 56, 153, 168, 181), as well as the technique used for inducing a miscarriage (p. 153).

In another excerpt in the film, someone identifies the double standard in contemporary Samoan society by which males attempt to have sex with as many women as possible, while at the same time protecting their sisters from the sexual advances of other males. The conclusion is drawn for us, however, that females are not having sex before marriage. Although this double standard undoubtedly now exists, as it does in many societies, logic dictates that if some males are having sex, some females must also be having it (the issue is heterosexual activity). In his haste to support Freeman, this "expert" is ignoring Freeman's (1983) own data that reveal that 27% of a sample he drew of unmarried Samoan female adolescents were nonvirgins. Those unfamiliar with the details of this controversy are truly misled by such arguments.

By dwelling on the issue of sexual behavior, and presenting witness after witness who declares that Samoans do not engage in premarital sex, the film builds to a "climax" where the controversy is supposedly resolved by what Freeman (1989a) called "crucially important new evidence." When this evidence is critically analyzed, however, it is obvious that scientifically it is neither reliable nor valid.

With respect to its reliability, it is based on the testimony of a witness of doubtful credibility. The informant, Fa'apua'a Fa'amu, declares that although she and her agemates treated Mead like a *sister*, they also lied to her about their sexual behavior (Freeman, 1989a, cited her as Mead's "very closest Samoan friend," p. 1018). Therefore, despite her contention during the interview of having lied in the past to Mead, we are supposed to believe that the resolution of this scientific controversy rests with her present "truthful" testimony. The film also claims that this was Mead's "chief informant," but according to Freeman (1989a), she was too old to have been one of Mead's actual informants (the informants Mead studied to evaluate her coming-of-age thesis were all between the ages of 8 and 20). She was apparently the same age as Mead at the time, so they simply developed a friendship (both she and Mead were born in 1901; Freeman, 1989a, p. 1018).

But, it is also unclear just how deep this friendship was. Mead wrote that Fa'apua'a principally resided in a village that was several miles from her research site. Mead (1928) acknowledges her as "the Taupo of Fitiuta" (p. viii; i.e., the ceremonial virgin of the village of Fitiuta on the opposite side of Ta'u from where Mead stayed) and seems to have spent time with her only during formal intervillage visits (*malaga*; Mead, 1977). Further, Fa'apua'a recently told a newspaper reporter that in 1925–1926 she did not know Mead was an anthropologist, although she also said that Mead "was always going around with a notebook and writing things on it" (Caton, 1990, p. 163; Freeman, 1989a). Mead's occupation is a rather important detail of which Mead's "very closest Samoan friend" would be unaware. Whether she really did not know at the time, or she had forgotten Mead's principal reason for being there, such disclosures further call into question this informant's credibility as a witness in the matter. In any event, the reliability of any testimony given some 60 years after the fact must be viewed with caution, especially if it supposedly settles a controversy in a scientific manner.

Aside from these problems, the fact is that Mead's book describes the sexual behavior of many of her informants and others in the villages she studied, not just Fa'apua'a Fa'amu's, so even if information about her is false, her current recanting does nothing to address the other material in Mead's book. Moreover, Mead's descriptions of sexual behavior are often based on information that most young villagers would have known at the time if they kept up with local affairs, so she would not have had to rely solely on personal accounts. Readers can evaluate this on their own, simply by perusing Mead's book.

If we focus on the scientific validity of this "crucial evidence," we find that no safeguards were used during this data collection to eliminate the possibility that the information obtained was contaminated by the method of collection.

Freeman (1991) constructed the events leading up to the interview to suggest that Heimans, the filmmaker, just stumbled upon her testimony. He wrote at the beginning of his article that "[w]hen he reached Fitiuta . . . Heimans was approached by a dignified Samoan lady, dressed as though she were going to church. She told him, through an interpreter, that she had a confession to make and would like to have it recorded on film so that all might know of it" (p. 104). Later in the article he claimed that "when she heard that an Australian filmmaker was coming to Manu'a, she decided, being a devout Christian, to make a formal confession" (p. 116).

This "serendipity" (Freeman, 1991, p. 104) stretches credulity, especially when it appears that Freeman was with the camera crew that recorded the "confession."[3] Thus, he was present, or at least nearby, before and during the interview, so it is possible that his presence, just 4 years

[3]This is deducible from references provided by Freeman. He gave the following reference for the interview discussed in his 1989a article: "Fa'apua'a Fa'amu 1987 Interviews with Galea'i Poumele and D. Freeman, on November 13. Fitiuta, Manu'a, American Samoa" (Freeman, 1989a, p. 1022). However, in a separate article, he provided a reference for the interview in the film: "Fa'apua'a Fa'amu 1987 Transcript of interview of 13 November with Frank Heimans of Cinetel, Sydney, Australia. Galea'i Poumele, Secretary of Samoan

after the publication of his controversial book, had some effect in terms of what she sensed was expected of her. In fact, according to Freeman (1991, p. 122), she had lived "in Hawai'i from 1962 to 1986," so it is also likely that she had heard about the controversy while living there, especially because it had been well-publicized by the U.S. media, including "the 'Phil Donahue Show' and the CBS morning news show" (Holmes, 1983a, p. 541). At the very least, a camera crew investigating the controversy must have heightened her expectations in some way.

But, more importantly, the consensus in the Ta'u area had been for some time that Mead was duped by mischievous informants, so local residents were well aware of a controversy over Mead's work, even without Freeman stirring things up. Being the last person alive from that era would mean that she would have been "fingered" by local residents as partly responsible for the embarrassing things Mead wrote about residents of the island. Thus, when the Heimans' film crew arrived, it is possible that she was pressured to make her "confession." Under these circumstances, not to deny that she had been "promiscuous" when young would have contradicted this consensus and perpetuated the embarrassment. Cranberg (1983a) described the consensus about Mead on the island where she conducted her study—note that this disdain for Mead predates the release of Freeman's book:

> Based on my one-year experience as a medical doctor on the island [during 1979–1980], it was surprising to learn that much of the wondering [about Mead] is petulant, irritated, and contentious. Many Ta'u natives today wonder why she should have earned generous royalties while reporting from freely given sources of information. . . . Some wonder why she did not wait to write her book until after all its characters had died. Far from being a hero on the island, she appears to be a source of embarrassment to its people. Mention of her name is a touchy subject, and her book is treated as if it were best forgotten quickly. (p. 182)

Although we could excuse such vagaries of data collection on the presumption that some circumstances are beyond anyone's control, when we examine the conditions under which the interview portrayed in the film was conducted, it is hard to overlook the strong possibility of other "interviewer effects." For example, the interviewer in the film was a High Chief and the Secretary of Samoa Affairs, Government of American Samoa. The fact that a High Chief who was also a high-ranking government official was interviewing her on a sensitive sexual subject in front of a camera

---

Affairs, Government of American Samoa, interviewer" (Freeman, 1989b, p. 761). Note that both interviews took place on the same day on the island of Ta'u. This is not evident in his 1991 article.

raises additional questions regarding how frank Fa'apua'a Fa'amu could be under those circumstances. Furthermore, it appears that the interviewer is the son of someone else who was also a young woman on Ta'u when Mead was there, and was friends with Fa'apua'a during that time. This is deducible from the transcript of the interview provided by Freeman (1989a, p. 1020), when Fa'apua'a Fa'amu said to Galea'i Poumele, "Then, your *mother* Fofoa and I would pinch one another and say: "We spend the nights with boys, yes, with boys!" (italics added). Thus, by implication she would have been charging that the mother of the interviewer had been (what is now defined as) "promiscuous" as well. And, finally, later in the film the interviewer expresses his strong negative opinions regarding Mead's book. Several scenes later in the film, the interviewer says: "I think [Mead] made up her mind that she's going to write that theory according to what she believed, but not according to what the people are living here."

Under these circumstances, why should this person admit on camera and in the presence of authority figures that she engaged in *what is now* considered immoral behavior? Quite likely, as word about Mead's book got back to her informants, who found themselves in an increasingly Christianized culture (cf. Gerber, 1975), they became upset and denied the "whole thing." Evidently, Fa'apua'a Fa'amu had been a devout Christian most of her adult life and her father had been a lay preacher (Freeman, 1989a, p. 1018). To admit to premarital sexual activity would constitute an admission of hypocrisy and immorality, as well as invite public disgrace in front of her community, children, and grandchildren (cf. Schoeffel & Meleisea, 1983). In fact, Fa'apua'a Fa'amu is on record as saying that "she was very displeased with Mead after she heard the things she said in her book" (Caton, 1990, p. 13).

Understandably, then, the young women described by Mead have likely never forgiven her for telling the world that they engaged in premarital sex, therefore shaming them as well as their families and villages. After all, there is no question regarding which villages she studied and there were only 25 postpubertal adolescent females in the villages at the time. Accordingly, in spite of her use of pseudonyms, many of the sexually active informants could have been identified by those familiar with the villages. With information from Mead's vivid case history presentations (e.g., family background, social reputation, and dominant personality characteristics), in conjunction with information in Appendix V of *Coming of Age* (which provides information such as age, family structure, and whether time had been spent in the "pastor's household"), the identity of many of her informants could surely have been recognized. In fact, with information from Freeman's (1989a) article, it was obvious to me who Fa'apua'a Fa'amu is in Mead's book. If I could identify her in this way, surely anyone from her community could have identified her and the others described by Mead. Incidentally, Mead's account of Fa'apua'a Fa'amu occupies less than one page of her book.

Thus, it is entirely plausible that it was far easier for Fa'apua'a Fa'amu to lie on camera and to say that what she said 60 years ago was a lie. It is also plausible that she now believes that what she told Mead was a lie. Sixty years of reflection can lead to all sorts of "mental acrobatics," ranging from repression to cognitive dissonance reduction (cf. Festinger, 1957). This would account for the fact that she has sworn on a bible to attest she is now telling the truth (Freeman, 1991, p. 116).

In view of these plausible alternative explanations for this testimony, there is ample reason to dismiss Freeman's (1989a) conclusion that "there is now an adequate, empirically based explanation of why it is that Margaret Mead's account of sexual mores and behavior in Samoa is radically at odds with the accounts of all other ethnographers" (p. 1021). On the contrary, his "evidence" can be seen in the context of a general desire of some Samoans to "deny" Mead's account of this period in their past (cf. Gerber, 1975; Schoeffel, 1986). There have been enough Samoans who have gone on record as being upset with Mead's "exposé" for this to be a plausible explanation for the discrepancy mentioned by Freeman, and for this "crucially important new evidence" to be called into question (cf. F. Wendt, 1984).

Finally, it is highly doubtful that Popper (1968), himself, would be impressed with the claim that this interview is key evidence in a refutation. In fact, from the following passage it is likely that Popper would dismiss it as a "non-reproducible single occurrence" and "a few stray basic statements:"

> We say that a theory is falsified only if we have accepted statements which contradict it. This condition is necessary, but not sufficient; for we have seen that non-reproducible single occurrences are of no significance to science. Thus, a few stray basic statements contradicting a theory hardly induce us to reject it as falsified. (p. 86)

In spite of all of these problems with this evidence, Freeman (1989b) declared that he has "claimed closure of the controversy" (p. 760) and that his refutation of Mead is "now fully vindicated" (Freeman, 1992, p. 2). But, this supposed "resolution" of the controversy represented by this interview with Fa'apua'a Fa'amu must be dismissed for lack of scientific rigor, and the film that claims to resolve the Mead–Freeman controversy appears to be little more than propaganda produced to support Freeman's "mission" to discredit Mead. It is ironic, therefore, that in the film Freeman states: "The scientific truth is something that cannot be settled politically. It's something that depends on the evidence" (Heimans, 1988).[4]

With this understanding of the political context of the controversy, we now turn to an examination of the specific evidence presented by Freeman in his claim that Mead's conclusion concerning her coming-of-age thesis was "preposterous."

FREEMAN'S EVIDENCE: ADOLESCENT STORM AND STRESS

The thrust of Freeman's statistical critique of Mead's coming-of-age thesis is based on three arguments. One is that she contradicted herself in her own work; a second is based on assertions that crime and delinquency are, and were, rampant in all parts of Samoa; and a third is based on his conversations with a handful of "highly educated Samoans."

Argument 1: Apparent Contradictions in Mead's Work

Freeman argued that Mead contradicted herself in her own work and that she really described a situation where adolescent storm and stress was more common than in Western countries. In pointing out this supposed contradiction, he noted that Mead identified several informants who were exhibiting delinquent behavior, and he posed the question "what can be concluded about delinquency among Samoan female adolescents from the information Mead herself has provided?" (1983, p. 255). Indeed, in a chapter entitled "The Girl in Conflict," Mead discussed in detail seven individuals who exhibited various forms and degrees of social deviance. Let us begin with an examination of Mead's definitions of deviance and delinquency, and how she applied these definitions to these seven informants.

Mead defined the *deviant* as someone who departs from the pattern of behavior prescribed by his or her group (p. 169). From this reference point, Mead noted two types of deviance in her sample: *downward* deviance and *upward* deviance.

---

[4]Those interested in reading the various commentaries about the Mead–Freeman controversy can consult a number of sources from both "sides" that: (a) support Freeman (e.g., Appell, 1984; Appell & Madan, 1988; Caton, 1984, 1990; Leach, 1983; Tribe, 1984); (b) criticize him (e.g., T. Baker, 1984; Brady, 1983, 1991; Ember, 1985; Goodale, 1984; Handler, 1984; Kuklick, 1984; Laing, 1987; Leacock, 1988; Murray, 1990, 1991; Nardi, 1984; Patience & Smith, 1986; Paxman, 1988; Rappaport, 1986; Reyman, 1985; Scheper-Hughes, 1984; Schoeffel & Meleisea, 1983; Shore, 1983; Turnbull, 1983); and (c) both support and criticize him (e.g., Badock, 1983; Buchholz, 1984; Hooper, 1984; Muensterberger, 1985).

The downward deviants in Mead's (1928) view were *delinquents*. She used this term "to describe the individual who is maladjusted to the demands of her civilization, and who comes definitely into conflict with her group, not because she adheres to a different standard, but because she violates the group standards which are also her own" (pp. 171–172).

The upward deviants, on the other hand, were stimulated to move "beyond" their culture resulting in the "wish to exercise more choice than is traditionally permissible" (p. 171). This desire to make nontraditional choices was "encouraged by the educational system inaugurated by the missionaries" (p. 171), so it would therefore have been less common in traditional Samoan culture. Of the seven deviants in Mead's sample, three were classed by her as upward deviants (p. 171; their pseudonyms are Ana, Lita, and Sona). It is important to note that Mead concluded that these three individuals were managing adequately within their community by utilizing the options available to them.

The other four deviants were not so easily classifiable, as the following passage reveals: "were there really delinquent girls . . . girls who were incapable of developing new standards and incapable of adjusting themselves to the old ones? My group included two girls who might be so described . . ." (Mead, 1928, pp. 172–173). Thus, only two informants clearly fit Mead's definition of delinquency. Of these two, one (Mala) had just reached puberty, whereas the other (Lola) was 2 years past puberty. But Mala had exhibited behavioral difficulties since early childhood, while Lola had done so for at least 4 years (pp. 177–179).

The other two deviants were marginally delinquent: One (Sala) had not yet encountered "serious conflict with her community" except that she had been expelled from the pastor's house for "sex offenses" (p. 181); and the other (Siva) was a "delinquent in the making" who was only 11 years old and had not yet reached puberty.

The main problem with the inferences Freeman drew from these qualitative descriptions is that he made inappropriate and inexact statistical comparisons with other cultures. These comparisons are based primarily on statistics from Great Britain, which Freeman argued indicate that the "delinquency rate" in Ta'u would have actually been "about ten times higher than that which existed among female adolescents in England and Wales in 1965" (p. 258). This startling assertion is based on the claim that if "among the twenty-five adolescents [Mead] studied there was *one* delinquent act per annum, this is equivalent to a rate of forty such acts per thousand" (Freeman, 1983, p. 257). Note that all that he did here was to use the algebraic equation "1/25 = x/1,000," where "x" equals 40 upon solution (1,000/25), and to cite the statistic that the delinquency rate in England and Wales in 1965 was 4.00 per 1,000.

Freeman claimed that this statistical sleight of hand is a "conservative" assumption, but it is actually a specious one because not only is he inappropriately extrapolating from a small sample to a large one, but he is setting up a "zero-tolerance" standard of deviance that no culture can meet. In other words, by his reckoning, only 1 of Mead's 25 informants had to commit a delinquent act to conclude that Samoan culture is rife with delinquency, because the resulting statistical rate would indicate ten times the delinquency rate of the Western countries compared.

But, add to this specious argument the fact that Freeman's statistics are for *indictable offenses* in England and Wales, and there is little left to his claim that Mead contradicted herself. This use of these indictment statistics ignores the well-established finding that far more crime takes place in Western societies than is reflected in such statistics. For example, in the criminology literature it is known that:

> not all offenses result in a charge being laid; and not all charges result in a conviction. Indeed, only about one known victimization in 100 comes to a conviction, if attention is confined to crimes against persons such as assault or rape, only one victimization in ten is reported to the police and only one such report in ten results in a conviction. (Tepperman, 1977, pp. 7–8)

Thus, Freeman's statistical argument suggests something close to the *minimum* estimate for one culture (Western), whereas Mead's account would represent something close to the *maximum* estimate for another (Samoan). Moreover, her cases involve mainly the violation of social mores that often do not lead to indictments in Western countries (cf. Young & Juan, 1985). The fact that a minority of her sample engaged in some delinquency stands in stark contrast to Gold and Petronio's (1980) observation that more than "80% of American adolescents admit to committing one or more delinquent acts . . . in the course of a few years of adolescence" (p. 523).

Using Gold and Petronio's figure of 80% to establish a more appropriate estimate for Western countries (their figure summarizes research from the 1960s and 1970s, whereas Freeman's estimate is taken from the 1960s), we can evaluate various estimates from Mead's sample. For example, we could count the two informants who had minor delinquency problems (Sala and Siva) along with the two Mead more clearly classed as delinquent (Mala and Lola). Even so, including all of Mead's 50 informants would mean that only 8% of her sample engaged in some form of delinquency. Note as well that this estimate includes all causes, none of which appear to have had their genesis after puberty. We can arrive at another, more liberal, estimate if we count only the 25 informants between 15 and 19 years of age. (This is the age range Freeman uses for delinquency statistics from Great Britain.) This produces a rate of 12% (3/25), because only three of Mead's informants were "delinquent" or "potential delinquent" in this age range (recall that Siva was only 11). Clearly, these figures are much lower than the 80% estimate that applies to U.S. society.

Freeman (1983) introduced another, equally problematic argument, when he implied that Mead's "four delinquents and three 'upwards deviants,' . . . together, make up 28 percent of her sample of twenty-five female adolescents" (p. 258) and should be considered to have experienced adolescent storm and stress. He did not specify any means of confirming these as cases of storm and stress. Instead, he simply claimed that Mead engaged in a "decidedly unscientific maneuver" by not pursuing this issue. Freeman did not pursue the issue of how and why these cases should be thus classified; instead, this argument is tagged onto the argument regarding crude delinquency statistics.

Had he wanted to ensure that he was being "decidedly scientific," he should have sought ways to operationalize storm and stress, and he could have done this by examining the contemporary literature that directly assesses the difficulties that Western adolescents can encounter in coming of age. He would have found that this literature reveals rather high levels of such difficulties. For instance, in their longitudinal study of a sample of U.S. male adolescents, Offer and Offer (1975) classified only 23% as experiencing a conflict-free, "continuous" growth, that would be comparable to that described by Mead. Although only 21% of their sample were classified as experiencing what they termed *tumultuous* growth—severe turmoil—another 35% were classified as experiencing *surgent* growth—moderate difficulties in emotional adjustments. Thus, some 56% of their sample experienced a variety of conflicts and emotional difficulties, ranging from moderate to severe. Similarly, other researchers have found that a majority of U.S. young people at some time have problems in terms of developing and sustaining a sense of commitment and belief (e.g., Marcia, 1980). In addition, up to two thirds of those in samples of Canadian young people have experienced problems with parental conflict, a lack of a sense of direction in life, and an uncertainty of belief (Côté, 1986; Pfeiffer & Côté, 1991).

If we return to Mead's account of her cases of "girls in conflict," we can gain a better sense of what these cases mean for her coming-of-age thesis. First, the two cases that Mead actually classified as delinquent were not exhibiting symptoms of an adolescent storm and stress somehow associated with puberty, because one informant had exhibited behavioral difficulties since early childhood, and the other had done so for at least 4 years but was only 2 years past puberty. Thus, they exhibited what were likely problems of childhood that persisted into adolescence (Freeman appeared to consider adolescence the postpubertal period). In fact, Mead (1928) did not report any serious behavioral problems that began after puberty, with puberty defined as the onset of menstruation (pp. 283–284).

It is also important to note that, despite Freeman's charge that Mead was a cultural determinist, Mead actually implied that an important cause of the problems faced by her two delinquents was biological, or in her words "temperamental." As we see from the following passage, Mead argued that their problems stemmed from an incompatibility between their temperaments and the constraints of Samoan culture:

> Lola and Mala both seemed to be the victims of lack of affection. They both had unusual capacity for devotion and were abnormally liable to become jealous. Both responded with pathetic swiftness to any manifestation of affection. At one end of the scale in their need for affection, they were unfortunately placed at the other end in their chance of receiving it. Lola had a double handicap in her unfortunate *temperament*. . . . Her *temperamental defects* were further aggravated by the absence of any strong authority in her immediate household. . . . So it would appear that their delinquency was produced by the combination of two sets of causal factors, unusual emotional needs and unusual home conditions. Less affectionate children in the same environments, or the same children in more favourable surroundings probably would never have become as definitely outcast as these. (p. 180, italics added)

Ironically, this is the type of "interactionist" thinking that Freeman claimed is lacking in Mead's analysis. In reality, Mead made note of the limitations of the range of temperaments Samoan culture could accommodate (see especially Mead, 1930/1969, pp. 80–86; see also Mead, 1928, pp. 127-130, 247). Although Mead did not provide a definition for her usage of the term *temperament* in *Coming of Age*, she did so in a later publication (Mead, 1937), stating that she used

> the word temperament in the accepted technical sense for those aspects of the personality which are physiologically "given," as opposed to *character*, the latter being that part of the individual personality which is the result of the interaction between native equipment—or temperament—and cultural conditioning. (p. 558)

In other words, Mead was operating under the assumption that individuals have certain, sometimes idiosyncratic, genetic dispositions which they take with them into social situations. This is the meaning that is implied in *Coming of Age*, yet Freeman still felt justified in calling her a cultural determinist.

Contrary to the mythology that Mead painted a simple, idyllic picture of life in Samoa, the fact is that throughout *Coming of Age* Mead described various social and personal unpleasantries she witnessed while there. Included in these descriptions were instances of adjustment problems experienced by 7 of her 50 informants. Rather than constituting examples of adolescent storm and stress, as Freeman claimed, they more closely resemble conflict-produced adjustment problems that might be found in any culture. The fact that Mead documented these cases so carefully attests to the credibility and thoroughness of her research. Had she really been intent on presenting a distorted image of Samoan adolescence, she surely would not have devoted a full chapter to these problems. Instead, she showed us how individuals with certain temperaments and experiences found it difficult to come to terms with the constraints imposed by Samoan culture.

In evaluating this aspect of Freeman's "refutation" of Mead's work, therefore, it is clear that his evidence is itself easily refuted and his argument is poorly conceived: He did not provide definitions for the basic but controversial concepts of adolescence or storm and stress; he did not offer a theory that links social deviance or delinquency with adolescent storm and stress; and he did not evaluate Mead's research against the vast repertoire of theory and research on youth and adolescence that has accumulated since she carried out her pioneering work.

Argument 2: Delinquency Rates

Freeman presented another statistics-based argument in his attempt to refute Mead's claims that the adolescence she witnessed was one of relative ease. He first cited data that he said he collected in Western Samoa, documenting 746 convictions for crimes of violence committed by persons age 12 to 22 between 1963 and 1965 (he did not explain the methodology he used in collecting these data). In discussing these data, he stressed that the peak age for the convictions was 16, but he did little more than to imply that there is some sort of biological cause for the association between age and conviction rate. This implication is delivered with a citation of Katchadourian's (1977) *The Biology of Adolescence* as evidence that "the attainment of puberty is marked by steady and rapid improvement in physical strength, skill and endurance, and this development is also marked by involvement of adolescents in aggressive encounters of various kinds" (Freeman, 1983, p. 260).

Freeman continued with a presentation of more statistics that he said he compiled from Western Samoan police records. The offenses include: "assault and other crimes of violence; the 'provoking of a breach of peace'; theft and other offenses against property; trespass; rape and indecent assault; abduction; obstructing the police; uttering threatening insulting or indecent words; drunkenness; and perjury" (pp. 264–266).

He then compared these figures with those published by Sir Cyril Burt in 1925 for crimes in England. Burt's figures exhibit similar characteristics, especially a peak rate at age 16 with the highest rates occurring during the ages 15 to 19 years. From these comparisons he concluded that "it is clearly evident that the adolescent period in Samoa, [is] far from being 'untroubled' and 'unstressed' " (Freeman, 1983, p. 268).

When carefully scrutinized, however, this impressive statistical evidence argument loses its force rather dramatically, in terms of (a) a misrepresentation of Samoan culture and history (especially as it applies to the island of Ta'u), (b) methodological vagueness, and (c) vague application of human developmental theory.

Samoan Culture and History. From the point of view of Samoan culture and history, most of the crimes Freeman listed are irrelevant to communities based on communal sharing where there was virtually no private property or consumer items, no local police or courts, and no alcohol, as was the case before contact with the West. When applied specifically to the island of Ta'u in the 1920s, Freeman's case is weak. In fact, much of his overall critique rests on the tenuous assumption that Ta'u in 1925 would not have been significantly different in terms of day-to-day life from Western Samoa in the 1960s. He contended that all of the islands in the Samoan archipelago have been plagued with high rates of crime and delinquency for some time.

This contention is problematic given the historical, geographical, and political differences among the Samoan islands (discussed in more detail in the next chapter). For example, Western Samoa comprises two large islands, which in 1965 had a population of about 131,000 living in over 300 villages and one small city, compared with Ta'u in 1925–1926 comprising four villages with a population of about 1,200. In effect, then, Freeman claimed that the small island of Ta'u, with its modest population living in closely knit villages, was as crime-ridden as Western Samoa in 1965 and England in 1925. Holmes (1983b), who is discussed more in the next chapter, took Freeman to task on this issue early in the controversy:

> Freeman should have compared Ta'u with Ta'u. When I visited there in 1954, I found little of the deviant behavior he describes, and I can only assume that it was even rarer in 1925. William Green, the principal of the government school in American Samoa, in 1924, observed, "There has been no murder case in American Samoa since our flag was raised in 1900. Natives will suffer indignities for a long time before resorting to a fight." (p. 17)

Figures 2.1 and 2.2 give readers an idea of the relative size of islands in the Samoan archipelago.

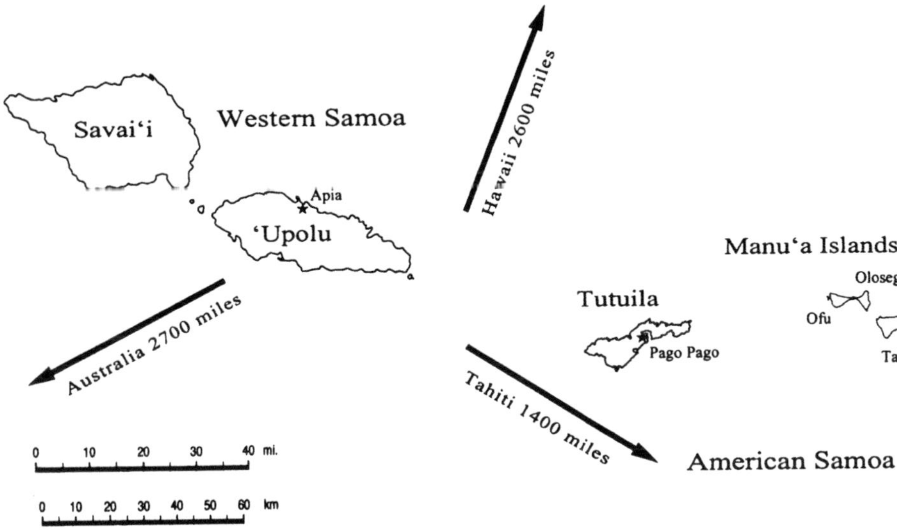

FIG. 2.1. The Samoan Archipelago.

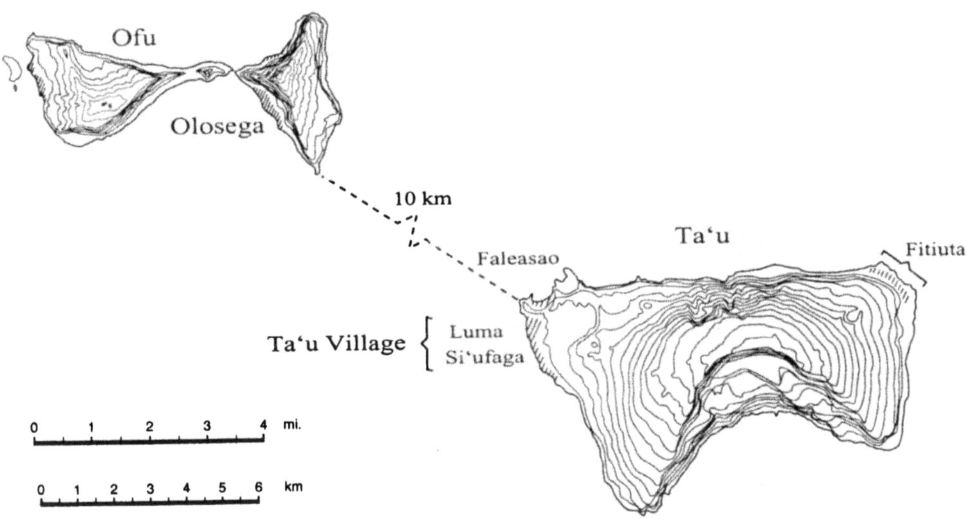

FIG. 2.2. Manu'a Islands

It is difficult to fathom how Freeman could ignore the element of cultural change with this argument, even in Western Samoa. For instance, O'Meara (1990) wrote that a major change over just one generation in the Western Samoan village he studied was the incidence of theft. In contrast to Freeman's claims, he noted that a

> generation ago or more theft was uncommon or even rare. . . . Today nothing is left in the plantations unless it is well hidden, and the crops themselves are frequently pilfered. When the family goes to church or to some other village affair, one member must always stay behind to . . . "guard the house" (pp. 69–70)

Interestingly, Freeman endorsed O'Meara's book as being "empirically exact" (cited by Spindler & Spindler, 1990).

Holmes is especially critical of Freeman on this point, noting that "nearly 70 per cent of the reported crime is said to be committed among the 18 per cent of the population which lives" in Apia—the only city in Western Samoa (Holmes, 1983c, p. 4). In another article Holmes (1983b) expanded on this:

> While Freeman is correct that Samoans share a common culture throughout the archipelago . . . [t]here is a great deal more criminal and deviant behavior in urban centers, such as Apia or Pago Pago, than in the smaller, more isolated communities in remote parts of Savai'i or the Manu'a Islands. In metropolitan areas, family heads and village councils of chiefs no longer hold control, and young men who migrate from outer villages to these areas, seeking work and excitement, often become intoxicated with their newfound freedom and behave in very non-traditional ways. (p. 17)

Methodological Vagueness. Freeman (1983) provided no discussion of his methodology other than to say that a "method was open to [him] . . . to compile from police records, a *random* sample of convicted offenders . . . The sample [he] compiled in this way totaled 2,717 convicted offenders" (p. 264), The vagueness of Freeman's account regarding his methodologies makes it difficult for other social scientists to evaluate his claims, especially given his contention to be "scientifically" refuting Mead. For example, he said these figures were for offenses committed in "the early 1960s, predominantly by inhabitants of the island of Upolu" (p. 266; elsewhere he said "c. 1963–1965," p. 263). The population of Western Samoa 15 years of age and over was about 63,937 in 1966 (Department of Statistics, Western Samoa, 1989, p. 3). This suggests that at least 4.25% of the adult population had been convicted of a criminal charge during the early 1960s (i.e., 2,717 divided by 63,937). Moreover, because he spoke of a random sample, we may assume that the actual population of convicted offenders from which he drew his sample must have been many times larger than 4% of the population, otherwise why bother to draw a sample, let alone a "random" one? How much larger is this population of convicted offenders? Are we talking about a society of ex-cons? I think not.

This vagueness is a problem throughout the book. For example, at one point he stated that "in the course of [his] fieldwork [he] observed fifty-six individuals aged 19 and under being physically punished by a parent, older sibling, or other senior member of a family . . . seventeen [of whom] were between the ages of 11 and 19" (p. 260). In presenting this as social scientific evidence, he should have supported it with, for example, accounts of (a) the period of time comprising his observations, (b) the contexts in which the incidents occurred, (c) the number of similar incidents that did not evoke punishments, and (d) comparisons with other cultures.

Human Developmental Theory. Finally, from the perspective of theories of human development, to say that physical development is "marked by" aggressive encounters is both vague and problematic, as is the suggestion that the "attainment of puberty" is related to these aggressive encounters. Had Freeman consulted the available literature on the topic before publishing his book, he would have encountered a literature review which concludes that "[a]n explanation of . . . delinquent behavior in terms of the onset of puberty seems weak . . ." (Gold & Petronio, 1980, p. 523).

In all likelihood, the conviction statistics he cited are related to the social structure of adolescence in 1960s Western Samoa. As we see later in this book, he should be aware that in precontact Samoan society, males would have undergone their rites of passage (tattooing and entry into the *'aumaga*—the group of untitled men) at age 16 and would be subsequently engaged in a meaningful participation in Samoan society (e.g., Turner, 1861/1986). By the 1960s, however, as economic, religious, and educational forces continued to transform Samoan society, many males no longer had the opportunity to experience these rites of passage. With no substitute for them, the traditional basis for developing a sense of identity was undermined and the transition to adulthood was becoming increasingly ambiguous and prolonged.

Sociologically speaking, these changes have resulted in a "cultural disenfranchisement" of Samoan youth. Having dislocated the young in the continuity of generational inheritance, it has become increasingly necessary for Samoan society to impose Western-style social control mechanisms to suppress and contain the disaffection among the young. The hostility and resentment among the young in response to the imposition of arbitrary adult authority is captured by Freeman in an anecdote he presented to support his case against Mead:

> From early adolescence onward Samoan youths may be observed grimacing and making threatening gestures at their elders, including chiefs, behind their backs, especially after having been punished or reprimanded; *with the attainment of puberty*, youths will occasionally lose control and openly attack those in authority over them. For example, in April 1965 a 31-year-old chief, patrolling a village of Savai'i to enforce the ten P.M. curfew, came upon a group of five male adolescents *who were breaking this curfew by playing a guitar and singing*, and he at once set about chastising them with a board. Instead of scattering, as would children, at this show of chiefly authority, one of these youths hurled a stone at the chief with such a force as to expose the bone of his forehead and put him in hospital for a fortnight with a concussion. (Freeman, 1983, pp. 261–262, italics added)

Note how Freeman associated "the attainment of puberty" with this incident of aggression. But numerous questions are left unanswered by this anecdotal evidence: We do not know how reliable Freeman's account is; we do not know how common such incidents are; and we do not know the actual age of the individual who allegedly threw the stone. Furthermore, is the behavior of the stone-thrower really attributable to the "attainment of puberty?" If so, how? What are the physiological mechanisms involved? Do they constitute proximal or distal causes? As part of his chapter on adolescence, Freeman cited crime statistics for persons ranging in age from 12 to 22. Are we to believe that all such individuals are "afflicted" with an inability to control their aggressive impulses against authority? If all are not afflicted, what saves those who are not? Freeman did not address any of these concerns.

If we take Freeman's word that his statistics and anecdotes are reliable, then at least part of their explanation must include factors associated with the social disorganization affecting the time and place of their origin. When we do so, we can consider the possibility that social factors constitute "proximate" causes of deviant behavior, and biological factors constitute potential "distal" causes of deviance (cf. Harris, 1983). Accordingly, without an immediate provocation, various biologically based potentials such as anger or aggression are not triggered, even if a particular individual is more prone to such reactions than is another individual. Such biologically based potentials do not operate at random or in a void, except in the cases of serious medical or organic psychiatric disorders, and adolescence is not a disorder.

To provide an example, the imposition of curfews is a postcontact social development—a social control mechanism that became necessary in certain areas to keep the now culturally disenfranchised and frustrated young person under supervision. In this light, we can understand Freeman's reports of the resentment and aggression on the part of some young people to be triggered by the imposition of arbitrary adult authority. Moreover, Western influence introduced the notion that childhood and adolescence can be periods of idleness and leisure. This notion of youth as a time of leisure stands in contrast to the well-documented fact that young people in precontact Samoa (and most agrarian societies) played an integral role in the division of labor. Therefore, it is not surprising that in the modern era some Samoan youth would now experience their life as one of "servitude" (Freeman, 1983, p. 259). In chapter 4, I examine the precontact circumstances that would have made adolescence a more rewarding period of life than it now is.

Given Freeman's own call for an "interactionist anthropology" that considers the interaction between culture and biology (e.g., Freeman, 1987c), he must be willing to entertain the question of how the social environment can produce biological reactions such as aggression. The deleterious effects of this social disorganization on Samoan youth have been analyzed by several social scientists (P. Baker, Hanna, & T. Baker, 1986; Leacock, 1987; MacPherson & MacPherson, 1985; O'Meara, 1990; Pitt & MacPherson, 1974; Yusuf & Peters, 1985). They have also been characterized in A. Wendt's (1973, 1977, 1979) fictional accounts of Western impact on Samoan society and Samoan youth.

Argument 3: Expert Samoan Opinion

Freeman's third piece of evidence regarding adolescence is clearly the weakest. This evidence comes from his account of casual conversations he had with several Samoans. Normally, this type of evidence is inadmissible as scientific evidence. Undoubtedly, even a court of law would dismiss it as "hearsay." Nevertheless, it must be examined here because some observers have apparently been swayed by it (e.g., Muuss, 1988, p. 142, wrote that this piece of evidence "devastates Mead's conclusions").

Freeman (1983) stated that he had never met "a Samoan who agrees with Mead's assertion that adolescence in Samoan society is smooth, untroubled, and unstressed" (p. 259). To substantiate his claims, he cited conversations with four "highly educated Samoans" and an unspecified number of Samoan adolescents whom he and his wife "came to know particularly well" (p. 259). From these informal sources he felt justified in concluding that "it is clearly evident that not a few Samoans, during adolescence, are subjected to psychological stress'' (p. 260).

Although it is impossible to verify Freeman's ''data'' from most of his ''informants,'' one ''informant'' wrote a review of his book, and certainly did not endorse it. In the context of Freeman's claim, her comments are quite illuminating:

> I have seen days (and nights) like Margaret Mead's and moments of mayhem like Freeman's. No one who has lived in Samoa long could doubt the existence of both. My only problem is with people who, like the blind men and the elephant, feel for one aspect or another and draw conclusions about what Samoans really ''are.'' (Ala'ailima, 1984, p. 91)

Freeman also cited this source as having recorded ''that Samoan adolescence is . . . 'a period of 'Sturm und Drang' '' (Freeman, 1983, p. 259). However, in her lighthearted book describing some adventures she had adjusting to Samoan life, she mused that Mead must have been wrong because of several experiences she had with young people in her charge (Ala'ailima, née Calkins, 1962—she was an American who married a Samoan in the 1950s). It is ironic for Freeman's argument, however, that most of the incidents she described involve the attempts of these young people to engage in premarital sexual activity without their adult custodians finding out.

More to the point, however, even if a number of Samoans are of the opinion claimed by Freeman, so what? No one in Samoa is an expert on adolescence in 1920s Ta'u as far as I know and Freeman named none. To put this in another context, would it carry any weight if I went to a particular area and asked four people what they thought about something, and then reported their opinions to the social science community? I think not.

Although I am reticent to engage in hearsay, to make my point regarding the reliability of opinion, I informally asked similar questions in Samoa, but got different answers than did Freeman. The consensus of these answers was that young people in contemporary Samoa are no different from young people elsewhere. There is a sense of ongoing change, however, but this should come as no surprise given the extent of Western influence, especially in American Samoa, which has strong ties with Hawaii and California. In American Samoa, there seems to be a growing concern about the importation of gang mentalities from these U.S. centers, and an increase in violence as a result. In Western Samoa, the concern seems to growing about the lack of jobs available to the young when they graduate from high school and the inability of some young people to find a place in Samoan society because of recent economic and social change. These problems are explored in chapter 7.

LIES, DAMNED LIES, AND STATISTICS[5]

As we saw previously, Freeman's case against Mead's portrayal of Samoan culture is partly based on comparisons of Samoan crime statistics with those from other countries. In presenting his case against Mead, he also presented statistics pertaining to all ages, not just adolescents. It is with these statistics that he made his most forceful arguments about the "darker side" of Samoan culture. In doing so, however, he has left the impression with some readers that Samoans are "a race of sex-starved rapists" (Levy, 1984), or that they are a "violent . . . delinquent, rape and suicide prone . . . people" (F. Wendt, 1984, p. 95). Marshalling this statistical evidence, Freeman seems to have swayed a number of people to his side, creating the impression that Mead was a fool for not having noticed these "obvious" traits and behaviors among Samoans. But, let us step back for a moment and consider his statistics in a different context.

Most of the statistics used by Freeman are crude rates, in which crimes are counted per year against a population denominator of 100,000. For instance, from his own research he stated that

> In 1966, when the total population of Western Samoa was about 131,000, the number of forcible and attempted rapes reported to the police in Western Samoa was thirty-eight. This is equal to a rate of about sixty rapes per 100,000 *females* per annum, a rate twice that of the United States and twenty times that of England. (pp. 248–249, italics added—note the rate is per female)

Setting aside the potential problems with the accuracy of Freeman's statistics for a moment, we must ask what these statistics say about what life was/is like for the average Samoan female, particularly one coming of age? Samoan villages range in size from 200 to 500 (Meleisea, 1987b, pp. 5–6), so we will assume that the average village has a population of about 350.[6] Using basic algebra, when we convert the overall probability of 60/100,000 to a specific probability of x/175 (assuming that roughly one half the population of a village was/is female), we find that there was a probability of .105 rapes or attempted rapes being reported in a given village in Western Samoa during 1966. In other words, there may have been one reported incident of rape or attempted rape for every 10 villages, over an entire year! The intention of stating these figures in this

---

[5]This phrase is taken from Mark Twain (1924, p. 246) in reference to his being perplexed by the use of statistics.

[6]A feature of Samoan social organization is that a village will not grow beyond a certain size without out-migration taking place. Presumably villages do not grow much larger than the 500 figure cited by Meleisea, although O'Meara (1990) cited 600 as the upper limit.

way is not to diminish the severity of rape as an offence, but one is left with a much different impression of daily life in Samoan culture.

Freeman nevertheless felt justified in alleging that "rape is unusually common in Samoa" (p. 249). Although he did say that he is aware of the problem of engaging in the cross-cultural comparisons of such statistics (p. 164), I am not convinced that he has taken these problems seriously. Clearly, he placed no *scientific* restraints on his comparisons. For example, it is very difficult to compare cultures in terms of the rate at which a crime like rape is reported to police. In Canada, for instance, it has been estimated that only 1 in 10 incidents of rape is reported to the police (Tepperman, 1977). Freeman contended that "in Western Samoa a very considerable proportion of forcible and surreptitious rapes are, in fact, not reported to police." He does not, however, give us any evidence for this assertion or how this rate of reporting compares with other countries.

Returning to Mead's study, based on Freeman's rates, using the population figure of 600 for the three villages she studied (Mead, 1928, p. 260) and dividing it by 2 to estimate the number of females, there would have been a probability of .18 rapes or attempted rapes being reported in the three villages she studied on Ta'u during 1925–1926. In other words, using Freeman's figures, one would expect a report perhaps once every 5 years. Because Mead was there for only about 6 months, the probability of her encountering an incidence of rape or attempted rape would be one half the figure just cited. Accordingly, using Freeman's statistics, there was a statistical probability of only .09—a 1 in 10 chance—of a rape or attempted rape being reported while she was there.

But, add to these considerations differences in time and place, and the probability of an occurrence diminishes even further. For example, Freeman vaguely referred to missionary accounts of rape, and accounts of rapes during the first three decades of the 20th century (p. 249). However, Rowe (1930) provided the following account of a rape in Apia, Western Samoa, during the 1920s:

> A circumstance which created a considerable sensation about the end of 1922, and ruffled a period of calm, was that one of the white sisters from the hospital was raped by a Samoan on the lonely stretch of up-hill road. . . . *It was an occurrence, I think, entirely unprecedented in Samoa.* (p. 133, italics added)

Rowe's (1928) account is totally consistent with Mead's own statement that "[e]ver since the first contact with white civilization, rape, in the form of violent assault has occurred occasionally in Samoa" (p. 93). Freeman (1983) cited Mead as writing that "the idea of forceful rape . . . is completely foreign to the Samoan mind'' (p. 244), but this is taken from Mead's (1931) article ''The Role of the Individual in Samoan Culture'' in which she explicitly restricts her generalizations about Samoan practices ''to refer to Manu'a specifically'' (p. 545).

Holmes (1983c) said the following about Freeman's rape statistics:

> The statistics which Freeman maintains could not be obtained until 1981 [after Mead's death] reveal the fact that in American Samoa some fourteen rapes per year occurred from 1975 to 1980. Freeman also states that court records from American Samoa show 'numerous cases' of rape recorded for the first three decades of this century. . . . I know for a fact that there are no records of rapes occurring in Manu'a at the time of Mead's research and none for 1954 when I was doing my restudy of Mead. (p. 4)

Instead, Holmes attributed occurrences of rape largely to the Naval personnel stationed at Pago Pago and to other Western/urban influences—to ''social disorganization brought on by cultural change and not a biological disposition toward aggression inherent in the Samoan make-up'' (p. 4).

Finally, although Freeman (1983) cited Rowe elsewhere, he conveniently omitted Rowe's reference to how unusual rape was. In view of these arguments, although rape undoubtedly occurred and occurs in Samoa, as in most other countries in world, Freeman appears to have blown its significance out of proportion in his quest to discredit Mead. Unfortunately, he also simultaneously discredited Samoan culture.

This technique of evaluating Freeman's statistical arguments can be applied to the other statistics he presented regarding murder, assault, and assault causing bodily harm.

For murder, his estimate of 6.6 per 100,000 in Western Samoa in 1977 translates to a probability of .0231 murders in a given village of 350 in a given year. Therefore, there might have been one murder for every 50 villages that year. My own check of Western Samoan records reveals two murders reported in 1964 and one in 1965 (Police and Prisons Department, Western Samoa, 1965). Although Freeman used data from the mid-1960s for his other comparisons, he curiously did not do this for this crime, despite the fact that the report just mentioned is available at the Nelson Library in Apia, Western Samoa. The fact is that this crime shows great fluctuations there. For instance, Freeman reported 10 murders for 1977, but more recent statistics reveal only 6 murder charges in 1985, 7 in 1986, 2 in 1987, and 7 in 1988 (Department of Statistics, Western Samoa, 1989, p. 81).

For ''affrays,'' or feuds that erupt into violence between families, Freeman cited a statistic of 40 per 100,000, which translates to a probability

.14 affrays per village of 350 in a given year. Therefore, there might have been one affray reported for every seven villages that year.

Finally, Freeman's figures from the mid-1960s in Western Samoa for "assault causing bodily harm" translate from 105.1 per 100,000 to .37 per village of 350 per year. Those of common assault translate from 773 per 100,000 to 2.71 per village per annum. Thus, there might have one serious assault reported for every three villages that year, and about three minor assaults per village.

Consistently, when we analyze Freeman's statistics by applying their probabilities, we get a much different picture of daily life than the bleak one painted by him. Clearly, using his own statistics, the average Samoan neither engaged in violence nor would have been in daily fear of it. Yet, Freeman has succeeded in swaying large numbers of people to his dark view of Samoan culture. His eloquent prose together with his use of anecdotes of incidents that took place over great amounts of time makes for dynamic reading, but not for good science.

Undoubtedly, tempers flare and violence occurs in Samoa, but to hold Samoa up as an extreme example is highly misleading to the world, and highly insulting to Samoans. In his attempt to discredit Mead for not emphasizing these things in her research, Freeman also disparaged Samoan culture by making it sound like Samoans beat on each other as a daily practice.

Finally, in reference to Mead's coming-of-age thesis, when we review Freeman's statistics in the above light, there is nothing in them that places Mead's conclusion in question.

CONCLUSION

To conclude this investigation of Freeman's case against Mead, in the final analysis, Freeman's "refutation" is itself easily refuted. His criticism that Mead ignored biological factors is not only erroneous, it is empty, because he himself did not suggest ways in which she might have examined such factors any more than she actually did. His evidence concerning storm and stress among Samoan adolescents is weak and can easily be interpreted in ways other than the one he has chosen as part of his quest to discredit Mead. Most problematic is his contention that Ta'u of the 1920s can be understood with observations and statistics collected elsewhere during the 1960s. Further, Freeman did not examine the issues involved from the appropriate social scientific perspectives. Had he done so, and examined human development and sociological literature, he would have developed a more sophisticated position on the matter of adolescent storm and stress. Therefore, he could have considered the plausibility of Mead's formulations in light of the dramatic social and economic forces that have affected Samoan culture during the 20th century. Finally, Freeman's use of crime statistics seriously distorts Samoan culture, and has few implications for Mead's coming-of-age thesis.

CHAPTER THREE

Mead's Culpability

Now that we have reviewed the heated controversy stimulated by Freeman's book and evaluated Freeman's case against Mead, we can move toward a "verdict" on Mead's coming-of-age thesis. In this chapter, we look beyond the arguments presented by Freeman and examine Mead's coming-of-age thesis based on several independent sources of evidence. This "cross-examination" begins with the "testimony" of expert witnesses, none of whom have any apparent political axe to grind. Following their testimony, we inspect the only available "material evidence" in the case. Finally, we review what Mead said in her own defense, in response to early criticisms of her book.

EXPERT WITNESSES

Lowell Holmes

The first witness is Lowell Holmes. Holmes is an American anthropologist whose doctoral thesis was a restudy of Ta'u during the 1950s. For almost 40 years, his career has been devoted largely to the study of Samoan culture, particularly in the Manu'an group of islands (see especially Holmes, 1957a, 1957b, 1974, 1980a, 1987; Holmes & Holmes, 1992). No other anthropologist has studied Manu'a as extensively. Thus, Holmes is the most qualified anthropologist to consult in this case.

Based on his research, Holmes has no hesitation endorsing most of Mead's findings. When the controversy first erupted, Holmes (1983b) spoke in her defense, saying that despite

> the great possibilities for error in a seminal scientific study, [he] found Mead's Samoan research remarkably reliable. The differences between [their] findings that could not be attributable to change were relatively minor and, in most cases, involved *not discrepancies in data but differences in interpretation* . . . (p. 16, italics added)

In *Quest for the Real Samoa*, Holmes (1987) confirmed that he found "the validity of her Samoan research remarkably high." Moreover, he can "confirm Mead's conclusion that it was undoubtedly easier to come of age in Samoa than in the United States in 1925" (p. 103; see also Holmes & Holmes, 1992, pp. 143–144).

In evaluating Holmes' credibility here, it is most interesting that during the 1960s he advanced several criticisms of Mead's work, and was consequently embroiled in a public controversy with her (e.g., Mead, 1961, 1930/1969). As he explained, he therefore has no reason to rush to her defense, but he also saw no reason to deny the validity of the bulk of her work, or to personally discredit her. In fact, Holmes (1983b) remarked that the

> truth is that I would have loved to play the 'giant killer', as Freeman is now trying to do. (What graduate student wouldn't?) But I couldn't. I had found the village and behavior of its inhabitants to be much as Mead had described. *Coming of Age in Samoa* was like a map that represented the territory so well that I met few surprises when I arrived. (p. 15)

With respect to his points of disagreement with Mead, Holmes (1987) stated the following: "What I did find in an exhaustive review of Mead's writings on Samoa was that the culture was not quite as simple as she would have had us believe. In other words, she often overgeneralized, a common failing among novice fieldworkers" (p. 103).

At the same time, Holmes was quite critical of Freeman's claims about Samoan culture, and he devoted a chapter of his book to a critique of Freeman's refutation. Holmes (1987) said, for example, he "never saw the society as inflexible nor the Samoans as aggressive as Freeman characterizes them. Actually, [he] saw the society as one in which people went to extremes to avoid conflict and to arrive at compromises" (p. 104).

Although Holmes believes that Mead was correct with respect to her coming-of-age thesis, he does not feel that he can support her contentions regarding several other features of Samoan culture and character. These features include her claims regarding the absence of *intense* sexual/romantic relationships and the extreme casualness of Samoans (i.e., that there are no "high stakes," no "fights to the death," or little competition). However, he does not think that these bear upon the issue of coming of age. Holmes believes, as do I, that it was unnecessary for Mead to have made such arguments about Samoan culture and Samoan character to support her coming-of-age thesis. In other words, even if she were wrong on these cultural and characterological matters, she could have been right on the coming-of-age issue.

Finally, it is worth mentioning that Holmes reviewed the extensive personality testing that has been conducted on Samoans. Holmes (1987) concluded that there emerges "a profile of Samoans very much at odds with that put forth by Derek Freeman. [It is] strongly supportive, however, of Margaret Mead's conceptualizations" (p. 136). This profile depicts a low level of creativity, high conformity and benevolence with low independence, and strong tendencies for deference, order, self-abasement, and endurance (pp. 127–136).

Schoeffel and Meleisea

The research team of Penelope Schoeffel and Malama Meleisea conducted several joint and independent studies of Samoan culture (Meleisea, 1987a, 1987b; Meleisea & Meleisea, 1980; Schoeffel, 1979, 1986; Schoeffel & Meleisea, 1983). Based on their academic and personal knowledge of Samoan culture, they produced one of the clearest evaluations of Mead's work in response to Freeman's critique. Although their evaluation does not always bear directly on her coming-of-age thesis, it is worth considering their joint testimony, because it helps us put into context Mead's observations and conclusions concerning Samoan culture and character.[1]

Schoeffel and Meleisea (1983) prefaced their commentary on Mead's work with the assertion that there is a "dualism inherent in Samoan culture" (p. 58). This dualism involves the distinction between "actual individual behavior," as acted out by Samoans in their day-to-day lives, and "ideal social behavior as it would be described by Samoans, particularly adult Samoans of high rank" (p. 59). They argued that although Mead glimpsed this dualism, she did not fully understand it and she tended to confuse the two. They also noted, however, that Freeman has done the same thing. For instance, Freeman's position regarding sexual behavior

[1]The following self-description explains why Schoeffel and Meleisea (1983) can be considered experts on the matter:

> Our contribution will be respectively that of an anthropologist who carried out four years of research on the status of women in Samoan social structure and culture, and that of an historian who has devoted the past four years to the formal study of twentieth-century changes in Samoan lands and titles and also "came of age" in Samoa between 1948 and 1972 in a village where his ancestors had lived for the preceding seven generations. (p. 58)

is argued at the level of *ideal* behavior, whereas Mead's is at the level of *actual* behavior. Schoeffel and Meleisea (1983) explained this as follows:

> Freeman disputes the testimony of Mead's informants on the grounds that sexual topics are not freely discussed by Samoans and that her informants deliberately duped her with their accounts. Schoeffel's field notes suggest [1979], to the contrary, that Mead was not duped and that clandestine love affairs, not dissimilar to those related by Mead, are not in the least uncommon. But the crucial point is that they are clandestine and, as Freeman points out, severely punished if they become publicly known. The general Samoan attitude is that, without careful surveillance, adolescent girls and boys will engage in illicit sexual relations. Female virginity is an aristocratic value and, in so far as all Samoans like to consider themselves of aristocratic descent (regardless of their actual rank), family prestige can be enhanced or damaged by public evaluation of the chastity of its unmarried family members. (pp. 59–60)

They continued by saying that "Mead's contention that there was 'passive acceptance' by Church authorities of premarital sex accords well with [their] own observations" (p. 62). Thus, Schoeffel and Meleisea found Mead's observations regarding the *incidence* of sexual behavior to be quite plausible and they have witnessed similar behaviors themselves. It appears that Mead simply did not understand sufficiently the dualism of the culture. This issue is discussed again in chapter 6.

In addition to corroborating Mead's observations regarding the incidence of premarital sexual behavior, Schoeffel and Meleisea stated that "[t]here are many other instances of Mead giving a fairly accurate description of common practice which does not accord to formal ideology" (p. 62). For instance, Freeman argued against Mead by declaring that a voluntary change of residence was *not* possible for Samoan children or young people (Freeman, 1983, pp. 204–205; cf. Mead, 1928, p. 40 ff.). On this matter, Schoeffel and Meleisea (1983) stated the following:

> We have several case studies of this: Malama Meleisea once left home and went to another family (to whom he was related by structural definition rather than by close blood ties). He did this when he had shamed and angered his parents in consequence of defying the village pastor. He went to another family until his father's anger had cooled and his father fetched him home a few weeks later. Malama's foster brother attached himself to the Meleisea family, of his own choice, when he was in his early teens. The arrangement gradually became permanent over the years and eventually Malama's father formally adopted the young man so that he could use the family name as his own. Malama's personal experience accorded well with the many biographical accounts collected by Penelope Schoeffel from Samoan informants. (p. 63)

Although the practice has been commonplace until quite recently,[2] Schoeffel and Meleisea noted that it "is also perfectly true that in terms of formal ideology Samoan children are not supposed to disobey their parents and that the transfer of children between households should be a formal transaction between or among the adult members of the family" (p. 63).

This testimony provided by Schoeffel and Meleisea assures us that Mead's book is not "all rubbish" as some would have it. Moreover, it supports the observations presented earlier in this book that Mead and Freeman viewed Samoan culture from different perspectives. Although Schoeffel and Meleisea are particularly critical of Freeman for not acknowledging the dualism of Samoan culture, and despite their general support for Mead's observations, they do criticize her work in a way that helps to identify areas where she might have erred. In reference to the "dualism" they believe that Mead overlooked, they wrote:

> The essential weakness of Mead's analysis is her confusion or failure to distinguish between actual and ideal categories of behavior. The actual sexual conduct of adolescent girls was confused with ideal rules about how adolescent girls ought to behave. But when it came to their emotions, she reversed the error. In her contention that there was an absence of poignant choices, deep emotions and conflict in the lives of Samoan adolescents, she was echoing the prescriptive, formal, public demand that they should not *display* strong emotion or conflict. Mead's own abundant data confirms the existence of gloomy or passionate emotion and violent conflicts in adolescent girls. Her classification of the cases as 'deviant' conforms neatly to the *Samoan* ideal that people, particularly young people, ought not to display evidence of emotion; that such feelings ought to be contained, repressed or denied. (p. 67)

All told, the expert testimony does two things: It corroborates Mead's coming-of-age thesis (Holmes), and it helps to clarify the criticisms raised by Freeman concerning Mead's account of Samoan behavior and ethos (Schoeffel and Meleisea). Another source of evidence is available that helps us to arrive at a verdict in this case. This evidence is obtained with a return to the scene of the alleged crime and with an examination of the geographical and historical factors relevant to the controversy.

---

[2]It is now less economically viable for families to take in young people. This trend will increase because of the introduction of education (and associated school fees and expenses) and the changing nature of childhood in a wage economy. Thus, as in other countries affected by the West, Samoan children and young people are changing from being economic assets for families to being economic liabilities. This is the case because their decreased contribution of domestic labor is not proportionately replaced by wage labor, and there are outside expenses associated with raising them.

MATERIAL EVIDENCE

Geography and History

Freeman has steadfastly maintained his position that Mead's observations on the island of Ta'u in the 1920s can be evaluated with evidence from other Samoan islands collected several decades later. The following passage appears to represent his position:

> I do *not* believe . . . that the communities studied by Mead and myself have ever been exactly "the same." . . . What I do consider, however, is that as historically related communities with a common language and a common culture, they are, for a wide range of behavioral and cultural phenomena, sufficiently similar to make comparisons between them *in respect of these phenomena*, rationally justified and empirically significant. (Freeman, 1985, pp. 912–913)

Many commentators on the controversy find it difficult to accept such a claim, however. For example, Schoeffel and Meleisea (1983) remarked that they "have the greatest difficulty in believing that there have not been major changes in Samoan society and behavior from one decade to another, let alone over the past fifty-five years since Mead commenced her study" (p. 63). Certainly, my training as a sociologist leads me to have great difficulty in believing that there would be no differences in behavior, particularly deviant behavior, on an island like Ta'u (Mead's reference point) in comparison with an island like Upolu (Freeman's reference point), in spite of a shared culture (cf. Turnbull, 1983).

Let us begin, then, with a look at the geographical differences between the two reference points that might account at least in part for the contradictory conclusions drawn by Mead and Freeman. In chapter 2, two maps of the Samoa archipelago were provided. These are meant to help readers understand how the geography of the Samoan islands might have affected the *possibilities* and *limitations* of Samoan culture and behavior over the centuries.

Referring to Fig. 2.1, it is immediately obvious that Ta'u is much smaller than Upolu. In fact, Ta'u is only 28.5 square kilometers (Hunt & Kirch, 1988, p. 156),[3] whereas Upolu is 1,115 square kilometers. Thus, Upolu is over 30 times larger than Ta'u. Moreover, Ta'u has proportionately more mountain slope in relation to arable and habitable land. With its highest point at 965 meters and only 41% of its area having less than a 30% slope, a mere 12 square kilometers is usable. With respect to

[3] Other sources estimate its size to be 39 square kilometers (e.g., Swaney, 1990).

population, in the 1960s Upolu had a population of 90,000 living in over 200 villages, compared with Ta'u in the 1920s comprising 4 villages with a population of about 1,200.[4] Thus, the population of Freeman's reference point is some 75 times greater than that of Mead's reference point.

The ruggedness of the islands in which Mead carried out her research is described by Hunt and Kirch (1988) in the following manner:

> The Manu'a Islands of Ofu, Olesega, and Ta'u form a separate cluster at the eastern end of the Samoan archipelago. Mutually intervisible, they are separated from Tutuila to the west by 100 km of often turbulent ocean which reduced the frequency of voyaging contacts with the larger islands. . . . Ofu, Olesega, and Ta'u are remarkable in their *dramatic topography; steep-sided, majestic volcanic cones thrust out of the turbulent waters, with summits often shrouded in clouds* . . . The smallest of the principal Samoan islands, *their steep topography offers little area suitable for settlements and gardens . . . Coastlines are rock-bound, with narrow fringing reefs only in places*, restricting the possibilities of marine subsistence. (p. 155, italics added)

In contrast, Upolu, the island upon which most of Freeman's research was carried out, "extends about 72 km from east to west and up to 24 km from north to south . . . [and it] . . . has a chain of volcanic peaks running from one end of the island to the other, with hills and *coastal plains on either side*" (Douglas & Douglas, 1986, pp. 510–511, italics added). Thus, although rugged in areas, Upolu has far more area suitable for habitation. The ruggedness of Ta'u can be seen with the contour lines in Fig. 2.2, as can that of Ofu and Olesega (the three islands constitute all of Manu'a).[5]

---

[4]Ta'u's population was about the same in 1980—Hunt and Kirch (1988) put it at 1,146. An estimate from 1854 placed the entire population of Manu'a at 1,275 versus 15,587 for Upolu (Ward, 1967, p. 365). Another source (Park, 1980) traced the population pattern of Manu'a over this century, specifying a range of 1,756 in 1900 to a peak of 2,800 in 1950. For 1926, Park estimated it at 2,060.

It should be noted that population estimates for Samoa are generally considered rather unreliable, and that many estimates are likely inflated through the inclusion of people who have moved but who are still considered family members (e.g., they may actually be residing on Tutuila or have emigrated to Hawaii or San Diego). Hunt and Kirch (1988, pp. 155–156) argued that for all of Manu'a "the resources of the land and sea are sufficient to support a modern population of 1,700 persons and it is certain that the late prehistoric population was several times greater than this figure." Thus, the most liberal estimate of the population that all of Manu'a could ever sustain would be about 5,000 people. Assuming that Ta'u would sustain 60% of Manu'a's potential population of 5,000, Ta'u could still sustain only one thirtieth the population of 1960s Upolu.

[5]According to Hunt and Kirch (1988), Ofu and Olesega are 3.4 and 4.5 square kilometers, respectively; their highest points are 638 and 494 meters, respectively; their areas with less than a 30% slope are 9% and 10%, respectively; and in 1980 their respective populations were 254 and 340.

Two photographs taken during my visit in February 1991, bring these maps to life. Figures 3.1 and 3.2 show much of Mead's research site. Although the buildings have changed many times since as a result of hurricane damage, the size of the villages has not. Figure 3.1 captures about one half of the village of Luma, the village in which Mead lived while she did her research. Note how small this village is, being squeezed between the ocean and a marsh (the unused area in the left of the photograph is marshland). Note, as well, the proximity of the houses, which affords little privacy. Figure 3.2 provides a view of about half of the village of Faleasao, situated over a hill from Luma. Observe, as well, its small size and the proximity of all of the dwellings. Note, also, that there is no room for this village to grow—it is situated on a beach immediately below the cliffs of an old volcano cone. Together these two figures depict about one half the area of the villages in which Mead's informants lived. Such a tightly knit setting hardly looks like the "hotbed" of delinquency and psychological malaise claimed by Freeman; on the contrary, this is the type of setting in which one would expect a high level of community control over behavior. It is hard to imagine how such small communities would have survived over the centuries if disruptive deviance were not somehow minimized.

Obviously, this topographical and photographic evidence does not constitute "proof" of anything, but it does give the reader a frame of reference

FIG. 3.1. Luma Village.

FIG. 3.2. Faleosao Village.

with which to evaluate other claims. Accordingly, with this knowledge of Ta'u, we can now more easily consider other information about Ta'u that highlights its uniqueness in comparison with the rest of Samoa, particularly during Mead's visit. These unique circumstances, all of which cast doubt on the reasonableness of Freeman's critique, include the following historical and political factors.

American Samoa had not experienced any wars for several decades, and it had been annexed by the United States at the turn of the century. Manu'a, of which Ta'u is a part, had recently seen its long-reigning line of royalty end, so an authority void would have existed. In addition, Mead noted repeatedly how Christianization, still in progress at the time, had tempered many harsh practices found in the traditional culture as well as ameliorating intervillage and interisland hostility. Thus, the period before, and during, her visit seems to have been one of political harmony.

After presenting a similar analysis, and concluding that "things were pretty quiet while Mead was there," Schoeffel and Meleisea (1983) acknowledged that they "have some sympathy with the problems of those who carry out brief research in quiet times" (p. 64). They state this because Schoeffel studied a village between 1976 and 1982 that had been investigated by B. Lockwood (1971) 10 years earlier, and

> [s]he was amazed at the difference between her own observations and those of Lockwood; apparently in the space of ten years a progressive, prosperous, well-governed and peaceful community had become a strife-torn, faction-ridden, economically stagnant village in which leadership was virtually absent. (p. 64)

The differences observed by two investigators in the same village only 10 years apart should make us wary of claims such as Freeman's that radical differences in behavior are not to be expected in different parts of Samoa, especially at different points in time. Schoeffel and Meleisea accounted for the differences in the following manner:

> While Schoeffel's first impression was that Lockwood must have mixed up his villages or his field notes, Meleisea's longer experience with the events of the past and those of Schoeffel's particular ethnographic present, led [them] both to realize that the two highest ranking chiefs of the village had been in the prime of their political careers, both nationally and locally, when Lockwood conducted his inquiries. In 1978 they were aged and ill, and the village was in the grip of a series of successive rivalries among a collection of aspiring chiefs and would-be chiefs which had disrupted the economic prosperity and social tranquillity of the village. (pp. 64–65)

The geographical and historical analysis given here, along with earlier analyses of Samoan culture, make it clear that, as in other cultures, Samoan behavior can take many forms. Like other cultures, therefore, Samoan culture can manifest itself in a myriad of ways, depending on the forces influencing it at a particular time and place. But this should come as no surprise for those who are not operating at the level of stereotypes. In the context of Schoeffel and Meleisea's just mentioned experiences, an observer might find "Freeman's Samoa" in one village, whereas another observer might find "Mead's Samoa" in the next; neither observer would be wrong, and both would have seen different facets of the "same Samoa." Indeed, as Meleisea (1987a, p. 31) noted, Samoan culture is a "living culture" in which "nothing is ever fixed; small changes and adjustments are constantly taking place so that the actual situation often differs from the ideal model which people may have of society and its rules."

Another way to evaluate Freeman's claim is for readers to consider how conditions have changed in their own culture since the 1830s—when the missionaries first arrived in Samoa; or since the 1920s—when Mead did her research. For example, consider how much life has changed since 1920 for those "coming of age" in California or Colorado, in Ontario or Quebec, in New South Wales or Victoria, or in England or

Scotland. Consider, as well, how sexual mores and childrearing practices have changed. Sexual mores and childrearing practices are aspects of the same culture but it is unreasonable to assume there have not been significant differences over such spans of time and place.

Three very important conclusions can be drawn from the evidence just presented with respect to the Mead–Freeman controversy. First, given the actual and potential uniqueness of Ta'u, there is sufficient reason to doubt Mead's blanket generalizations from Ta'u to the rest of Samoa, as well as Freeman's contention that coming of age on Ta'u in 1925 would have not been significantly different from doing so in Western Samoa in the 1960s. The second conclusion pertains to Freeman's claim that Samoan culture is essentially homogeneous and can be understood from one research site at one point in time. His position on this matter is contradicted by the research of other scholars of Samoan culture. The third conclusion is that if Mead had initially titled the book something like *Coming of Age on Ta'u*, and not generalized to other Samoan islands, there would have been little basis for a critique. In her scholarly work, Mead did restrict her generalizations to Manu'a (e.g., 1931, p. 545) and the companion book to *Coming of Age* specifically restricts itself to Manu'a—indeed, it is called *The Social Organization of Manu'a*. However, these do not nullify the inappropriate generalizations made in *Coming of Age*.

Mead's Own Defense

Minor criticisms of Mead's work had been circulating throughout the anthropological community for some time before Freeman's book was published (e.g., Shore, 1982; Stanner, 1953). But criticism is supposed to be "healthy" in science—evidence that scientists are doing their job of scrutinizing each other's work. Although Mead responded to these criticisms on several occasions, she apparently did not feel that any major revisions of her book were necessary, and she never provided a full defense of her position. She did, however, provide two partial responses to criticisms of her work. The first is in the introduction and conclusion to the 1969 edition of *Social Organization*, and the second is in the Preface of the 1973 printing of *Coming of Age*.

In the latter source, Mead commented on encounters she had with Samoan university students who were embarrassed by her frank and sometimes uncomplimentary portrayal of their grandparents (cf. F. Wendt's, 1984, criticisms of the book). She lamented that they and other readers tended to disregard the fact that the study was carried out in the 1920s and describes life then. In her own defense, she stated: "It seems more than ever necessary to stress, as loud as I can, this is about the Samoa . . .

of 1926–1928. When you read it remember this. Do not confuse yourselves and the Samoan people by expecting to find life in the Manu'an islands of American Samoa as I found it."

She continued in that Preface to note that she did not want to alter the contents of the book (despite its many reprintings) because it was a historical document and she did not want to change its style of writing. In her words:

> I can emphasize that this was the first piece of anthropological fieldwork that was written without the paraphernalia of scholarship designed to mystify the lay reader and confound one's colleagues. . . . *I did not write it as a popular book*, but only with the hope that it would be intelligible to those who might make the best use of its theme . . . (italics added)

Despite her protestations, however, Mead was not being entirely forthright. The book has been widely read by the general public; in fact, it is "the most widely read anthropological book ever published [with] sixteen translations and millions of copies sold" (Muuss, 1988, p. 139). Moreover, it would appear that she wrote in a way to make it marketable, particularly with the inclusion of the academically controversial chapter entitled "A Day in Samoa." This is the second chapter of the book and was likely placed near the beginning so as to grab readers' interest before they encountered the more mundane details of her account. In this chapter, she employed the now familiar popularizing technique of providing a composite sketch of daily life. Unfortunately, to imply that all of those events could happen in one day is misleading (cf. Holmes, 1983b) and not ethnographically acceptable. On the other hand, Mead instructed that "[f]or the scholarly reader, there is a new edition of *The Social Organization of Manu'a* . . . revised in the light of contemporary ethnographic theory" (Preface, 1973 printing of *Coming of Age*).

Yet, contrary to these declarations, it seems that Mead was occasionally embarrassed about *Coming of Age* because of its nonacademic style. For example, in the introduction to *Social Organization* (1969) she noted that "I incorporated in [*Coming of Age*] a section originally intended for this monograph, called 'A Day in Samoa,' which I had decided was too literary in character for the style of a Bishop Museum monograph!" (p. xvii). And, when it was subjected to academic scrutiny by Lowell Holmes, Mead equivocated in terms of how authoritative she saw the book to be:

> Holmes' quotations are from reprints of paperbacks which make the whole dating system into pulp. I wrote *Social Organization of Manu'a* (1930) after I wrote *Coming of Age in Samoa* (1928), and the former should therefore be regarded as the more complete and definitive. (p. 224)

In *Social Organization*, Mead went on to comment on what was then mounting criticism of her characterization of Samoan "character" as one of "mildness and low affect" (p. 226). She raised two possibilities regarding the discrepancy between her own analyses and those of others. The first possibility was that the Ta'u that she witnessed in the 1920s was a historical anomaly in which there was a "temporary felicitous relaxation of the quarrels and rivalries, the sensitivity to slights and insults, and the use of girls as pawns in male rivalries" (p. 228). The second was that she saw the culture through the eyes of her informants—young females. In Mead's (1930/1969) words:

> The other possibility is that to the young girl, herself either a virgin but not a *taupou*, or experimenting quietly with lovers of her own choosing, uninvolved in the rivalries that were related to rank and prestige, moving gently, unhurriedly into adulthood, the preoccupations of the whole society may have seemed more remote than they would have appeared from any other vantage point. *And this is the vantage point from which I saw it*. I was alone, very slight and smaller than the Samoan adolescent girls. My subject of research called for my spending the largest proportion of my time with them. . . . My primary task was to get to know and understand adolescent girls; the ethnography of this monograph was a by-product, an extra dividend. (p. 228, italics added)

Those who now stand in judgment of Mead's work have a responsibility to acknowledge her admission regarding the possible discrepancies noted here regarding Samoan character and to appraise her explanation for them. Her admission also requires, however, that the generalizability of some of her findings beyond Ta'u of the 1920s and beyond the experiences of those "coming of age" be viewed with caution. In chapters 4 and 5, I act on this caution and carefully examine the social history of adolescence in Samoa since early missionary contact.

Finally, Freeman and some of his supporters make much of the fact that Mead did not live in a Samoan household. In reality, she lived in a medical dispensary in the village of Luma (see Fig. 3.1). In one of her letters written shortly after her arrival, Mead (1977) said that the "people in these villages are right at my very doorstep" (p. 36). This lodging gave her an excellent *neutral* site from which to study all of the inhabitants of the villages, not just those who happened to be members of a household in which she might have stayed. Had she stayed in a Samoan household, she would have likely been constrained in her movements to other households for fear of offending her hosts (cf. Swaney, 1990), and, as she said, she might have been caught up in the various intra- and inter-*aiga* (family) rivalries that characterized village living. As she wrote in the acknowledgment section of *Coming of Age*, the dispensary furnished her "with an absolutely essential neutral base from which [she] could study all the individuals in the village and yet remain aloof from native feuds and lines of demarcation." Thus, she managed to find what she described as "an excellent arrangement."[6] Here is how Mead (1977) described her quarters—note how it allowed her to interact with her young informants on their terms:

> My room is half of the back porch of the dispensary quarters building. There is a loosely woven bamboo screen which divides my room from the porch outside the dispensary and here the Samoan children gather to peek through the holes and display a few English words or chatter endlessly in Samoa about Makelita's various belongings. . . . At night I push back the curtain which divides my room off at the other end, put away the chairs, push back the tables and there is plenty of room for a small *sivasiva*—dance. The young people bring their guitars and ukuleles and dance for me. A few new ones come every night and it gives me an excellent opportunity to gradually learn their names . . . (p. 37)

A number of observers condone Mead's decision to carry out her research in this way. Turnbull (1983), for example, argued that

> on such a small island, to have settled in with one family in one village would have placed her in special and perhaps restricted relationships with other families and other villages. Further, given the open architecture of the traditional Samoan house (a roof with neither outside walls nor inner partitions), no privacy would have been possible; and for her inquiries into the delicate topic of the adolescence of girls, Margaret Mead judged correctly that both she and the girls would require privacy. She knew perfectly well what limitations this imposed. Even today a comparable choice would by no means be uncommon, and better by far than any pretence of "going native." (p. 33)

In the final analysis, the issue of Mead's choice of residence is really a red herring with respect to her coming-of-age thesis. The fact is that her primary concern was not an ethnography of village life. Rather, her primary concern was with the experiences of the young females in three villages. From her base of operations, she was able to interact with and interview these informants, without being distracted by the "domestic politics" of any one Samoan household.

[6]Dr. Lee Cranberg, who worked as a physician in the village of Luma during 1979–1980, found village life there to be "transparent" and easy to integrate into. He had little doubt that Mead could have developed a clear picture of village life (personal communication, November 27, 1991). In his words, "[t]hat she shared accommodations in the midst of the village with an expatriate American couple would not have prevented her from sharing her day-to-day life with Samoan neighbours" (Cranberg, 1983b, p. 19).

A VERDICT ON MEAD'S COMING-OF-AGE THESIS

Before readers deliver a verdict based on the evidence presented here, it is appropriate to deliver several charges to them as the "jury."

First, we cannot go back in time to the Ta'u of 1925–1926, a time during which Mead was the only record keeper there. Indeed, it is fruitless to try to assess her thesis today with ethnographic or quantitative social/psychological measurements because life on Ta'u has changed significantly (cf. Holmes & Holmes, 1992). Therefore, in evaluating Mead's claims about that time and place we must rely on inference and plausibility, as well as on corroboration from other observers, particularly those who were closest in time and place to her research site.

Second, it is unrealistic to expect her study to be flawless, especially given the pioneering nature of her research. The recognition that some of her observations cannot be verified, or that some of her conclusions are tenuous, certainly does not justify dismissing the entire book (cf. Appell, 1984, p. 205). It is this type of unreasonableness that has generated more "heat than light" (Feinberg, 1988, p. 656) in this controversy. Thus, with very little prior research to go on, it is understandable that she might have overlooked some matters and overemphasized others. What many of her critics seem to have forgotten is that this was one of the earliest studies of adolescence and she therefore had very little prior biological or social research on which to base her work. In short, it is easy to sit in harsh judgment a half century later and ignore the fact that she blazed a trail that has led to a body of knowledge that can now be used to judge her work.

Third, we must keep in mind that even if Mead was wrong in some of her characterizations of Samoan culture, character, and ethos, she still may have been right in her conclusions about coming of age. After all, the study was subtitled *A Psychological Study of Primitive Youth for Western Civilization*, so it was primarily a psychological study of adolescence, not an ethnography of Samoan culture. Moreover, she may have been right about the ease of adolescence but she may have been wrong in her reasons for arriving at this conclusion.

Finally, it must be remembered that what is at issue here is ethnographic-type research, a research technique that can be high in internal validity (accuracy), but low in external validity (generalizability). As Bernard (1988) noted, two of the principal weaknesses of ethnographic research are that "(a) it is difficult for other researchers to replicate an ethnographer's findings . . . ; [and] (b) whatever an ethnographer learns about one village or island may have little to do with other villages or islands in the same general cultural region" (p. 146). Mead's research is vulnerable to both weaknesses, but it is hardly appropriate to hold her personally responsible for the shortcomings of a research method.

With these qualifications in mind, and after weighing all of the evidence presented thus far, I believe a reasonable verdict lies in favor of Mead's coming-of-age thesis. In these inquiries, little reason could be found to doubt that Mead reported accurately what she saw and was told during her study; to suspect "fudging" on her part; or to assume "duping" by her informants. Moreover, Freeman's claims regarding a storm and stress ostensibly characterizing Samoan adolescent behavior on Ta'u in the 1920s are weak and the evidence he presents can be interpreted in ways that do not contradict Mead's conclusion. Finally, not only are Freeman's arguments regarding adolescence easily refuted themselves, there is also sufficient corroboration of Mead's conclusion from other sources. More corroborative evidence is examined throughout the remainder of this book.

Although there is little in Freeman's critique that constitutes an actual scientific refutation, it nevertheless appears that Mead compromised several canons of social science by sensationalizing parts of her account to make her book more marketable. In addition, she appears to have capitalized on romantic notions about the South Seas and sexual stereotypes about Polynesians, although not nearly to the extent claimed by some of her critics. We have also seen evidence that she engaged in some unsubstantiated speculation regarding why "coming of age" there was one of ease, and she had insufficient grounds for assuming that her observations and conclusions could be generalized to the rest of Samoa. Thus, although her main thesis appears to be supported by the evidence, it seems that she did not exercise what is now considered the appropriate scholarly restraint expected of an academic in presenting and interpreting findings. On the other hand, she said that she wrote the book for "teachers, parents, and soon-to-be parents" (p. 1973 edition), and she was ostensibly trying to convey a message to that audience.

It is unfortunate that the controversy has focused on a few notions about Mead's book, thereby overlooking what is otherwise a "rich and sensitive" account (Feinberg, 1988, p. 656). Even with its faults and limitations, if it is read as a semi-popular, pioneering study with cross-cultural implications, it can be appreciated as a valuable historical document and a landmark study. As such, it advanced the understanding of adolescence in its time, and anticipated later developments in the field (such as the concept of the moratorium period and the socioeconomic forces prolonging youth and adolescence). Chapter 6 reconstructs her portrait of how Samoans would have come of age at the time. From this reconstruction we get a much better idea of how rich and sensitive her work is.

In view of a verdict in favor of Mead's thesis, what do we have to say to Freeman about his years of work on these issues? First, his critique has alerted us to the limitations of Mead's research, and potential problems with its generalizability. For this we are grateful. And, second, he has inadvertently sounded the alarm of an unfolding tragedy in modern Samoa; namely, the difficulties facing many young Samoans because of the cultural disenfranchisement brought on by Western influences. For this we are also grateful.

Were it not for this latter implication of the controversy, we could reasonably end this book here. But, in chapter 7, I take up the issue of the cultural disenfranchisement of Samoan youth, after constructing a social history of adolescence in Samoa. This allows us to better understand what has happened as a result of contact with the West. At the same time, it gives us the opportunity to assess the historical veracity of Mead's work. Completing this task allows us to draw a conclusion as to whether Mead "fabricated" a Samoan culture, out of touch with the rest of the culture, as some have charged. As we see, these two issues actually dovetail because, in assessing the historical accuracy of Mead's research, we come to understand how drastically "coming of age in Samoa" has changed. Thus, it is within the context of Samoan history that we come to fully understand the Mead–Freeman controversy.

CHAPTER FOUR

A Social History of Adolescence in Samoa: Precontact Culture

Freeman contended that Samoan culture is, and has been, essentially homogeneous throughout the archipelago and that very little change relevant to the controversy took place between the time of Mead's study and his own research. In a similar vein, he insisted that adolescence has been stressful in Samoa since before Mead's study and before contact with the West. The evaluation presented here casts Freeman's case into serious doubt. But, that appraisal was based largely on evidence of a more *inferential* nature, so it could be argued that the review of Freeman's case is not complete. In order to more decisively judge this aspect of the controversy, it is appropriate to examine evidence of a more *descriptive*, historical nature that allows us to draw conclusions regarding social change and stability in Samoa (chapters 4 and 5) and the plausibility of "Mead's Samoa" (chapter 6). The purpose in carrying out this comparison is to determine whether Mead's Samoa fits with the "trajectory" of social change set in motion by contact with the West and the social engineering undertaken by the missionaries.

In compiling this historical evidence it became clear to me that not only does Mead's Samoa fit the pattern of change, but that the direction of this change has continued to the present. It also becomes clear that Freeman's assumption of an absence of significant social change simply begs the very important sociological question of the *nature* of the changes affecting this region. Indeed, as we see, the following sociological investigation of the history of adolescence in Samoa reveals a fascinating yet depressing saga of the demise of a well-structured and meaningful adolescence before contact with the West, and the creation of a conflictual and alienating adolescence after a century and a half of contact with the West. By denying the relevance of social change in Samoa for the Mead–Freeman controversy, Freeman overlooked the possibility that the turmoil he witnessed among Samoan youth in the 1960s was a product of this change. As is seen later, the culmination of this change has been disastrous for many of those now coming of age there.

Many written sources have been consulted in reconstructing this social history of Samoan adolescence: the accounts of missionaries, written mainly in the 1800s; the results of studies conducted by anthropologists during the 1900s; fictionalized writings and poetry representing the Samoan "spirit"; and, contemporary documents including government reports, newspaper articles, and documentary films. Much of this evidence is presented verbatim from these sources. Consequently, some readers may find the long quotations tedious to read. Given the controversial nature of this topic, however, it is appropriate to reduce my synthesis of this material, and to let readers judge it for themselves.

COMING OF AGE IN PRECONTACT SAMOA

The available written documentation reveals a number of features of precontact Samoa that should have provided for a relatively continuous and stress-free passage from childhood to adulthood.[1] Perhaps most crucial to the issue of continuity was the fact that Samoan children were not protected from the hardships and "evils" of the world. In contrast to the child-centered conventions of contemporary Western societies, Samoan children were not indulged in a protected fantasy world that left them wholly dependent on adult supervision and care; they were not an economic liability to the household, rather they were an economic *asset* and investment; and they lived in the real world of adults, witnessing most of what adults witnessed. In short, by their teen years Samoan young people were already "worldly" individuals in their own right, with a working knowledge of that world, and they possessed socially recognized capacities and skills upon which to build an adult sense of identity (cf. Holmes, 1987). In short, there was a well-established *quid pro quo* between the young and adults that dictated that all individuals contributed

[1]I am purposely excluding Mead's writings from most of the present chapter, because one of the objectives of this chapter is to assess the plausibility of Mead's account of Samoan adolescence by estimating what conditions were like for those coming of age in precontact society. As we see, Mead's research provides the first *thorough* record of Samoan childhood and youth before the Samoan life cycle was drastically altered by Western influences. As we also see, Mead's *Coming of Age* is important because she made reference to many of the things that had been, or were being, altered by the missionaries.

to the collective to the extent that they were capable, and all received their share as they needed. There is little of a *quid pro quo* between adults and children in Western societies, and it is being lost in contemporary Samoa, as we see later in this book.

Those familiar with the topic will know that most "primary" cultures expose their young to the "real-world" conditions of the adult culture. But Samoan culture had the added advantage of a relatively fruitful natural environment. Thus, although young Samoans contributed labor to their family and community, the amount of labor was minimized for all Samoans by the benign climate and lush environment. This allowed Samoan culture to give those coming of age the time to slowly learn the tasks of the culture, and to gradually increase their labor contribution as they entered adulthood. Such a "moratorium," as it is now called, can play a crucial role in alleviating the stresses of life that might otherwise accompany major life transitions (cf. Erikson, 1968; and chapter 8, this volume) .

On the matter of this natural "affluence," Holmes (1987) estimated that on Ta'u an average family could "provide itself with ample food by working its plantations only about three days a week" (p. 34). He also noted that "[w]ithin the memory of the Manu'an people there is only one occasion, a hurricane, when there was a shortage of food. . . . In Samoa no one goes hungry. The extended family provides for all its members" (p. 34). The labor of children, however minor the tasks involved, made it possible for all members of the community to enjoy the benefits of this benign environment. This is corroborated by Greksa, Pelletier, and Gage (1986) who, after reviewing the relevant literature, concluded that "productive males in precontact Samoa probably needed to expend no more than 6–12 hours of work per week in agricultural labor. Even if one assumes a highly conservative estimate of 15–20 hours of agricultural labor per productive male per week, this is not a great deal of work" (p. 303).

Meleisea (1987a) presented a similar portrait of life in precontact Samoa. In his words:

> Everything we know about Samoa in the early 19th century indicates that the Samoan people had achieved a very abundant comfortable way of life in which everyone was well fed and well housed. Things looked so good to European seamen in the 19th century that many of them ran away from their ships to live with the Samoans. T.H. Hood . . . remarked: "on the whole, a happier race of people could not be found than the Samoans. A scowling and discontented face is seldom seen; want or poverty is unknown, and nature has showered upon their country her choice gifts." (p. 26)

The inclusion of such descriptions is not intended to romanticize or idealize precontact Samoan culture, but to give readers some idea of the type of *environment* in which young Samoans would have come of age. The point of including these descriptions is to outline the felicitous environment that made it possible for certain social institutions to arise that were not oriented directly to group subsistence. Let us now examine these institutions.

We know much more about the way males came of age in precontact Samoan society than we do about the coming of age of females. For males, the principal rite of passage on the path to full adulthood occurred at age 16. The initiation entailed experiencing the long and painful process of body tattooing, from the waist to below the knees. The missionary George Turner (1861/1986) wrote of the importance of the tattoo for the adult male social identity:

> the man who was not tattooed . . . was not respected. . . . Until a young man was tattooed, he was considered in his minority. He could not think of marriage, and he was constantly exposed to taunts and ridicule, as being poor and of low birth, and having no right to speak in the society of men. But as soon as he was tattooed, he passed into his majority, and considered himself entitled to the respect and privileges of mature years. When a youth, therefore, reached the age of sixteen, he and his friends were all anxiety that they should be tattooed. . . . On these occasions, six or a dozen young men would be tattooed at one time. . . . In two or three months the whole is completed. The friends of the young men are all the while in attendance with food. (pp. 87–89)

Marquardt (1899/1984) reported at the turn of the century that males who were not tattooed were considered cowards and were highly stigmatized:

> Especially the women despised them and the chiefs refused to accept food from their hands which they called stinking. The contempt for men who lack the national adornment has been weakened little by the influence of the missionaries but nevertheless continues until this day. An untattooed man is still not popular and many a father refuses him his daughter's hand. It is no rarity that young people who are being prepared for the mission service turn their backs on the mission schools for the only reason that the "students" are forbidden to get tattooed. (p. 8)[2]

When this tattooing was complete, the male became a member of the *'aumaga*, the group of "untitled men" in the village. The *'aumaga* was

---

[2]Grattan's (1948) record supports Turner's and Marquardt's observations: "In earlier custom an untattooed young man was not regarded very seriously either by his fellows or the girls of the village" (p. 112).

responsible for accomplishing work projects and daily maintenance of the village. Through hard and skillful work and service (*tautua*), the untitled man could earn respect and reputation in the community, and perhaps eventually gain greater status by being elected a *matai* (chief) by his *'aiga*. Each *'aiga* had at least one *matai* who headed their branch of the family and represented them at the *fono* (village council of chiefs).

Young women had a corresponding institution that structured their adolescence—the *aualuma*. Meleisea (1987b) described the importance of the economic and social role played by the young women of the *aualuma*:

> The *aualuma* represented the honour of the *nu'u* [village], for example when a *nu'u* or a district went to war, a high ranking maiden would march at the head of the party. Also, when *malaga* (visiting parties) came to the *nu'u*, the *aualuma* would decorate the guest houses of the *nu'u* and see to the reception and entertainment of the guests. Whereas household goods such as tapa, sleeping mats and thatch pieces were made by groups of wives (who were regarded as being comparable, although somewhat lower status to the *'aumaga*), objects of great value such as *'ie toga* (fine mat) and *'ie sina* (a cloth with a shaggy surface woven from bleached fibers) were made by the *aualuma*. The titular leader of the *aualuma* was the *sa'o tama'ita'i*, a girl or woman from the family of the highest ranking *ali'i* who held a title derived from the name of an important ancestress. (p. 7)

Meleisea also described the correspondence of the positions of young males and females in precontact Samoan culture:

> Work outside the immediate sphere of the *'aiga* was carried out by corporate groups: the *'aumaga*, to which the untitled men belonged; and the *aualuma*, to which all the girls and women of the *nu'u* (as distinct from in-marrying wives) belonged. Each group had its own dwelling houses in the *nu'u* and both were internally stratified according to the rank and status of the *matai* titles of one's *'aiga*. These groups reflected the division of labor and status between brothers and sisters in *aiga*. The *'aumaga* were the *malosi o le nu'u* ("the strength of the village"), its army, fishermen, horticulturalists, cooks and sportsmen. (p. 7)

Of great interest in itself, but also in the context of the Mead–Freeman controversy, is the fact that females also underwent a tattooing ritual. Moreover, knowledge of this practice has been all but lost, due no doubt to the influence of the missionaries and a desire to suppress knowledge of the "heathen" past. Fortunately, a monograph written in 1899 has preserved knowledge of the practice. According to Marquardt (1899/1984), the tattooing of women was still widespread at the time in German-administered Western Samoa. He estimated that about 60–70%

of women sported these tattoos. Marquardt speculated that it was done because whereas "[m]en had themselves tattooed to please women . . . women [did it] to increase their attractiveness to men" (p. 16).[3] The fact that it was "usually carried out at the time of beginning puberty" could be explained, according to Marquardt, because it was "at this time sexual feelings start to develop. A girl wants to please a man and therefore she asks for the means to achieve this purpose and she obtains them" (p. 17). He also recorded that it was done at the same time as the chief's sons were tattooed and that it was "always carried out by male tattooing masters, usually between the girls' fourteenth and sixteenth year. The complete tattooing of the thighs usually takes five to six days" (p. 22). Figure 4.1 shows the types of frontal designs recorded by Marquardt that would typically be sported by males and females (from Ngan-Woo, 1985, p. 67; see Marquardt, 1899/1984, for detailed drawings and photographs of the various components and designs).

During their teenaged years, young Samoans would learn or hone most of the skills, and perform most of the tasks, considered part of the "common-sense" knowledge of the adult world. In addition, many would adopt a specialization that would constitute a foundation of their adult identity. According to Meleisea (1987a):

> Although every adult Samoan knew how to perform the basic economic tasks appropriate to their sex in order to survive, there were dozens of specializations recorded by early observers. The basic economic tasks for men were agriculture, carpentry, hunting and fishing; and for women, weaving, tapa making and oil making. The specializations were based upon elaborate artistic refinements of these basic activities; for example fishing and pigeon hunting were technically very complex and diverse and associated with a lot of ceremony which turned them into gentlemanly sports instead of mere food-getting activities. The master fisherman or master hunter took charge of these activities and used their specialized knowledge to organize large groups of less skilled people. The same was true of house-building, boat-building, wood-carving, tattooing and many other activities. Among women there were specialists in manufacturing the most valuable kinds of mats, tapa cloth, medicines and oils. (p. 33)

Thus, several specializations were open to both males and females within the village division of labor. Status could be gained equivalent to that of a "master" of these specializations through apprenticeships with an established expert. Turner (1861/1986) provided an account of how the Samoan technique of *fale* building was transmitted from one generation to the next:

---

[3]O'Meara (1990, pp. 75–76) also reported that he was told that it was done to increase sexual attractiveness, but he knew of no recent instances of it being carried out.

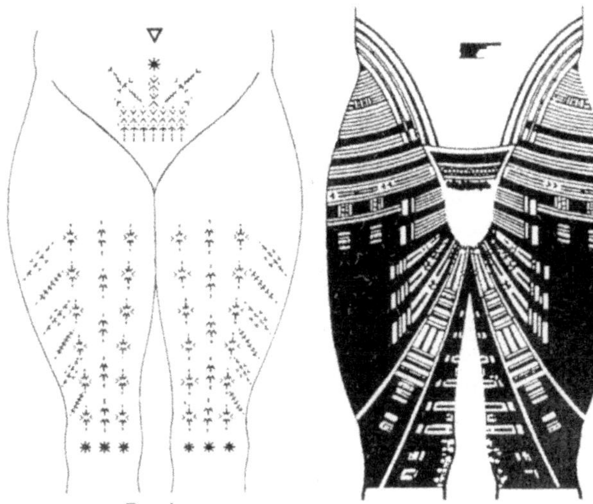

FIG. 4.1. Traditional frontal tatoo designs (from Ngan-Woo, 1985).

> house building . . . is a distinct trade in Samoa; and perhaps, on average, you may find one among every three hundred men who is a master carpenter. Whenever this person goes to work, he has in his train some ten or twelve, who follow him as journeymen, who expect payment from him, and others as apprentices, who are principally interested in learning the trade. When a young man takes a fancy to the trade, he has only to go and attach himself to the staff of some master carpenter, follow him for a few years, until he thinks he can take the lead in building a house himself. (p. 167)

Ceremonies apparently marked the entrance of the young person into the *'aumaga* or *aualuma*, but the records regarding precontact Samoa are not clear. For males, tattooing was definitely a necessary requirement, but it is unclear whether a village feast was held for each male for the actual recognition of membership. Holmes (1987, p. 118) noted, however, that in 1950s Ta'u, the "*matai* accompanies the boy to the village council [*fono*] and presents [a] kava root so that his son will have village recognition when he joins" the *'aumaga*. With respect to entrance into the *aualuma*, the record is also unclear, but Turner (1861/1986) seems to be describing this ceremony in the following passage:[4]

> About the time of entering into womanhood, their parents and other relatives collect a quantity of fine mats and cloth, prepare a feast, and invite

[4]The meaning of this ceremony is verified by Mead's (1928) account when she wrote that formerly "[t]he girl's entrance into the *Aualuma* was always, not just occasionally, marked by a feast" (p. 275).

> all unmarried women of the settlement. After the feast the property is distributed among them, and they disperse. None but females are present. It is considered mean and a mark of poverty, if a family does not thus observe the occasion. (p. 90)

In precontact Samoa, a man would leave the *'aumaga* only upon being conferred with a *matai* title. Otherwise, he would remain in it for life. Although most males probably aspired to acquire such a title, especially as they approached middle age, some apparently did not experience this ambition (cf. Mageo, 1988). However, Grattan (1948) noted that "progress from untitled to titled rank is the normal aspiration sooner or later of most adult males" (p. 14), and implied that this was the case in precontact culture. Women would leave the *aualuma* upon marriage. We see in the next chapter how this has changed.

ANALYSIS

In sociological terms, it is critical to the continuity and stability of a culture that the young be recruited into adulthood as welcomed and willing participants. The less they are welcomed, the less accepting the young will tend to be of the conventions of the culture awaiting them as adults. Consequently, the less responsible they will feel about willingly passing on the culture as they found it. This was apparently not a problem in precontact Samoa, although it now is in many Western societies, particularly for women. In fact, notwithstanding the changes discussed in chapter 5, in some respects Samoan culture is still considered the most stable and conservative of the Polynesian cultures (e.g., Hanson, 1973; Holmes, 1980b; Stanner, 1953). As we see later, however, the missionaries did introduce significant changes into Samoan culture by altering the way the young are socialized and recruited into adulthood. They learned very early that the way to change a culture is to alter the way the young "come of age."

The previous description of precontact Samoa presents a picture of well-structured socialization processes governing the coming-of-age process. In particular, the *'aumaga* and *aualuma* should have ensured that behavior was quite well regulated among the young. And these processes seem to have worked well, because the culture has survived for centuries more or less in the form encountered by the missionaries. Although undoubtedly some young people found these processes stressful and some probably engaged in what we call delinquency, if life had been as stressful and delinquency-prone as Freeman argued, there would be far more evidence of such problems. For example, the early missionary accounts make no mention of either excessive stress or delinquency. Had there been problems in these respects, the missionaries surely would have given them as much attention as they did other "evils." If anything, the earliest records emphasized the opposite in terms of the quality of life available (cf. Meleisea, 1987a, p. 34).

In addition to these structures, precontact Samoan culture had other characteristics and mechanisms that would have minimized behaviors that might have threatened community integrity and cultural stability. An examination of these confirms the view of a well-regulated society—one that would remain intact over dozens of generations.

As we see, precontact Samoan communities employed a number of mechanisms that were apparently effective in minimizing the incidence of social deviance, and remedying much of the damage that might have been caused by this deviance. Again, this is not to say that precontact Samoa was a paradise. Most notably in contrast to this image were the wars that apparently occurred with some frequency (Freeman, 1983). But, again, our concern is with the institutions that would have consistently affected how the young would come of age, and to these we look *within* communities, not between them. There is no indication that these institutions were affected by any constant war-readiness.

First, villages averaged about 350 inhabitants. Thus, precontact Samoan culture did not have to deal with the types of deviance associated with anonymity or excessive population density. Moreover, as Gilson (1970) described, any threat to village integrity was dealt with immediately:

> when a village was irreconcilably divided on any important issue, local or otherwise, the weaker party might be driven out in order to restore village unity. Individuals who committed serious offenses were treated no less harshly. When travellers or visitors stirred up trouble or acted disrespectfully toward the village, even unintentionally, they were liable to immediate attack and expulsion by the *'aumaga*. The Samoans were so sensitive about village honour and the enforcement of local customs and regulations that their reaction against transgressors was inclined to be hasty and violent. (p. 48)

Second, a well-defined authority structure (the *fono*) existed that was replicated in all villages. Part of its mandate was to coordinate relationships among villages. The *matai* was the undisputed head of the *'aiga*, which could include more than 60 persons. Membership in the *'aumaga* required the observance of the principle of the *tautua*; namely, service to the *matai*. Through this service, young men gained respect and status in the eyes of the adult community, and could perhaps eventually earn a *matai* title. Associated with this service was the requirement that the authority of the *matai* not be challenged. If dissatisfaction over some thing was felt, it was a "privilege" to raise it with the *matai*, not a "right" (MacPherson & MacPherson, 1985).[5] The decision of the *matai* on the matter was final, however, and any questioning of the decision was considered childish (*fia pepe*) or immature (*ma fau*) (MacPherson & MacPherson, 1985). Physical punishment of young people occurred when other avenues of control failed, but was apparently required on an infrequent basis (Holmes, 1987).

Third, if a young person found his or her *matai's* decisions unacceptable, or day-to-day living a problem, he or she could sometimes change households within the village or go to another village. "Adoptions" were common for younger individuals, but anyone appearing in an *'aiga's fale* (house) who was in need of shelter was taken in (cf. Schoeffel & Meleisea, 1983).

Finally, to remedy damage caused by more serious forms of deviance committed between *'aiga* (and villages), an apparently effective mechanism referred to as the *ifoga* was employed. The *ifoga* seems to have provided a means of shaming the offender as well as producing a reparation that was not too disruptive of community life. According to this custom, the offender and his or her *matai* would go to the doorstep of the offended *aiga* and ask for forgiveness. They would do so early in the morning, cover themselves in "fine mats" and stay there all day, or for several days if necessary. This would be done until either forgiveness was forthcoming and they were invited into the household, or physical revenge was taken on them (Filoiali'i & Knowles, 1982). This custom survives today, although a Western-style legal system now officially attends to matters of justice.

Given these cultural characteristics and mechanisms, it is unlikely that serious delinquency, or other forms of seriously disruptive deviance, existed to any great extent. Readers are reminded of the examination of Freeman's statistical and anecdotal evidence in chapter 2. There it was concluded that even if "high" cross-culturally, the various forms of social deviance were likely sporadic occurrences in a given village. Of course, there are no written records from precontact culture to quantify these behaviors. In light of this discussion, however, it is *implausible* that village life was highly problematic or stressful, particularly on the small, isolated island of Ta'u.

SEXUAL PRACTICES IN PRECONTACT SAMOA

The issue of Samoan sexual habits has been associated with Mead's book since it was first published. Soon after it was released, some critics called it scurrilous for the attention given to the sexual behavior of young women

---

[5]This is a recent source describing a surviving convention, but the convention appears to be so fundamental to *fa'a Samoa* that it undoubtedly predated Western contact.

(Cassidy, 1982). A. Wendt (1983) believes that the "instant worldwide popularity of Mead's Samoa was due largely to her delectable portrayal of free love without guilt under the huge swaying palms" (p. 10).

As we saw in chapter 1, this is the issue upon which many Samoans have focused. Consequently, many view Mead's work with contempt because of its incongruence with contemporary Christian Samoa. Unfortunately, this issue has overshadowed the many other important matters raised by Mead's work. Thus, the current mythology encourages the belief that the focus of her book was about adolescent sexual habits rather than about coming of age.

Despite what some contributors of the Mead–Freeman controversy have claimed, the issue of sexual behavior is not crucial to Mead's coming-of-age thesis. Furthermore, she never asserted in *Coming of Age* that casual sexual relations were a necessary component to an ease of coming of age. In fact, it is plainly there for anyone to read that of "the twenty-five girls past puberty, [only] eleven had heterosexual experience" (Mead, 1928, p. 151). Because she argued that the other 14 also had an ease of passage, she obviously did not see sexual experimentation as a necessary component of this ease of passage. As we see in chapter 6, she found sexual experimentation to be an *option* for some, not an expectation or a requirement. On the other hand, as we see later, it is likely that young Samoan females had more sexual freedom before Mead's time—before they lost rights in the *aualuma*, and before many were sequestered into the pastor's house where their chastity was required.

Therefore, although it is actually tangential to Mead's coming-of-age thesis, I am taking the time to deal with the issue of sexuality in this book because of the emotionally charged mythology surrounding it. Freeman brought worldwide attention to this issue, probably to the horror of some conservative Samoans, by arguing that Mead was wrong in her accounts of premarital sex among her informants because she took seriously a teasing (or "duping") by her informants on sexual matters (Freeman, 1983, pp. 289–290, 1989a). By examining the available writings about the matter, the issue can perhaps be put to rest. At the very least, the concern over Mead's credibility can be addressed, given that her book was made possible by her rapport with these young women. Accordingly, it is worthwhile to consider whether her reports of such behaviors are plausible.

We begin this analysis with evidence provided by the first missionary to make written records of precontact Samoa—John Williams (cited in Moyle, 1984).

Williams found a Samoa in which polygamy was widespread. In his 1830 and 1832 journals he pondered over what to do about polygamy because it was "inconsistent with Christianity" (p. 142). However, he did not want to immediately impose the Christian practice of monogamy because it was mainly the chiefs who practiced polygamy—"some have two others have as many as six" wives (p. 142)—and if he threatened the chief's interests they might turn against him and Christianity. His dilemma was expressed in the following way:

> it is . . . a subject fraught with perplexity. In many instances a man has two wives with whom he has lived for many years & has a family by each feels an attachment to both, & of course is at a loss which to put away. If he is allowed to keep his two others will make it a pretext for keeping half a dozen so that prudence & consideration must be exercised in the management of this affair. I have thought that in some instances perhaps it might be well to allow them to retain their wives & yet admit them into Christian communion, *but the wild young Chiefs who have so many wild young girls to none of which he is lawfully married according to the customs of the country* of course the putting of them away would be attended with no difficulty for that is frequently done. For when a young Chief wishes to marry a *maitai* or lady she will not hear of his proposition until he puts away all his other wives. This he does without hesitation. (pp. 142–143, italics added)

Actually, according to Meleisea (1987a), the missionaries' social engineering was more complicated than Williams thought because the

> changing of one custom often led to a series of changes. For example, . . . [c]hiefs wishing to become Christians were asked to choose one wife for the rest of their lives . . . Since the main reason for chiefs contracting so many marriages was the Samoan political system. . . . changing that custom also greatly changed the political system of Samoa. It was another eight years after 1830, before Samoans really accepted the new teachings on marriage, and when they finally did, the conferring of *taupou* titles became less important. This is because the institution of the *taupou* was closely associated with chiefly marriage, which linked families and villages all over Samoa through the multiple marriages of chiefs to high ranking ladies. (p. 68)

With respect to general sexual behavior, Williams recorded the following impression of the Samoans he encountered in the early 1830s: "I should certainly on the whole consider them a people of lascivious habits far more like the Tahitians than the Tagnatabuans to whose female population the palm of modesty must be conceded by all the ladies of the Eastern groups even to the Sandwich Islands" (p. 233).

On the matter of premarital sex, Williams recorded a practice that institutionalized a free sexuality for unmarried females. He described this practice as follows:

> It is also a common thing for [unmarried] young women to be publicly deprived of their virginity by a young respectable Chief in the same way

> as at the marriage ceremony [a public, manual rupturing of the hymen]. This is considered an honour & no person objects to marry a young woman who has been thus treated. The Chief who ruptures the Hymen will frequently give the young woman a great name which will gain her respectability but *I suspect the reason why this singular system prevails is the young females are tired of submitting to the restraints their virginity imposed on them & by being thus honourably deprived of their virginity they have full liberty to gratify their wishes & also escape the disgrace of being looked upon as common prostitutes.*
>
> The Teachers inform me that six young females had been thus treated within a short space previously to my arrival by the son of Malietoa. These occasions are always attended with dancing & merriments of every description. (pp. 256–257, italics added)

This passage suggests a *tolerance of premarital sexuality even greater than that reported by Mead*. This would make sense given that Mead's observations were made after some 80 years of Christian influence. But, perhaps the greatest corroborating evidence for Mead's account comes from Williams' statement that "[t]he young females I have heard have a great objection to marriage[,] a roving commission being more congenial to their feelings" (p. 233). As we see later, Mead (1928, p. 195) also indicated that some of her informants reported wanting to delay marriage as long as possible, and instead engage in casual sexual encounters.

Williams continued by noting that although he was told that adultery was rare and was punishable with death, he was skeptical. The reader will note here that the ideal of chastity apparently existed then, but was also likely violated regularly.[6] Williams stated the reason for his skepticism that the cultural ideal actually translated into behavior:

> I am not a convert to this opinion for I know too much of the natives of the South Seas generally to allow me to suppose that chastity could be maintained under the circumstances in which the Samoa females live. It is a very common thing for one Chief to have from two to six or more wives. The rule established is that each female is to lie with husband three successive nights. Now allowing that the husband has six wives it will be fifteen nights again before she is admitted to his bed. During these fifteen nights she sleeps where she likes or generally speaking sleeps in an adjacent house where all the persons of the establishment men & women sleep promiscuously together under one cloth so that at least there are fifteen chances against the alleged chastity of some. (pp. 233–234)

---

[6]He suspected that when punishment was meted out it was likely only for those who had violated some other norm or who threatened the interests of certain chiefs. Western culture had a similar practice with the burning of witches in England and the United States (Karlsen, 1987).

A number of other entries made by Williams gives us some idea of the social atmosphere that might have prevailed in 1830s Samoa with respect to sexual mores. For example, in the following account, we glimpse something of the precontact idea of decorum in formal dining among chiefs and their honored guests:

> This afternoon I had the honour of being surrounded at tea time by his Majesty's five wives three of which are about five & forty or fifty years of age the other two are girls about seventeen or eighteen. On being invited to partake they drew nearer & formed a circle dropping their little round abouts off their loins on to the ground. They curled the small end of it into the lap just barely concealing the only part that they even make a pretension to conceal. Having asked a blessing they eat heartily and cheerfully of what was placed before them. This is the first time I have had the honour of eating with *five naked* queens. The natives appear to take the greatest pride in exposing their persons. (pp. 143–144)

Obviously, Samoan conceptions of modesty were quite different from the conception Williams took with him from his native land. We see this in more detail in the following passage:

> The females however are by no means as careful about concealing their persons as the men. At the Samoa Islands the care is on the part of the men. I have seen a man demand from a female a lavalava or round about to cover his person while she is obliged to go naked. Clothing of every kind appears a burden to them. If a person should jeer a young woman as she might be passing by remarking freely on her person saying she was diseased or ill formed she would instantly throw off her cloth & expose herself in every possible direction & pass on. A respectable young man who had been residing among them some time informed me that when he first went on shore among them the females in great numbers gathered round him & some took off their mats before him exposing their persons as much as possible to his view. Perceiving him bashful the whole of the women old & young did the same & began dancing in that state before him desiring him not too bashful or angry it was Faa Samoa or Samoa fashion. (p. 232)

Thus, from Williams' journals it appears that the standards of modesty, decorum, and sexual conduct obtained in contemporary Christian Samoa would not be found in precontact Samoa. In fact, as we see in chapter 5, the missionaries worked for decades to "Victorianize" Samoans and it took generations to totally eradicate some practices. Accordingly, one of their earliest objectives was to convince Samoans to wear clothing: "Some few Samoans who have embraced Christianity have taken to wear cloth entirely. On Sabbath days also the Teachers have succeeded in inducing the whole congregation men & women to attend properly clothed & decently covered" (p. 231).

Turner (1861/1986) also provided us with records of Samoa before Christianity was more fully adopted (the 1840s and 1850s). With respect to premarital sex, he wrote the following:

> Chastity is ostensibly cultivated by both sexes; but it is more a name than a reality. From their childhood their ears are familiar with the most obscene conversation; and as a family, to some extent, herd together, immorality is the natural and prevalent consequence. There are exceptions, especially among the daughters of persons of rank; but they are the exceptions, not the rule. Many native teachers and other consistent characters, seeing the evil, have now separate sleeping apartments in their dwellings; and their better regulated families are becoming models to their countrymen of an improved and improving community. (pp. 90–91)

Note in the latter portion of this account that the missionaries by this time were beginning to have an impact and that some Samoans were ostensibly altering their behavior, at least for the sake of the missionaries. With respect to extramarital sex, Turner wrote the following:

> Adultery, too, is sadly prevalent, although often severely punished by private revenge. If the injured husband seeks revenge in the blood of the seducers, no one thinks he has done wrong. But the worst feature of the law of private revenge is, that the brother, or any near relation of the culprit, is as liable to be killed as he himself is. Fines are now being substituted; but occasionally, revolting murders are committed on account of the crime. (p. 91)

Turner recorded the emotion of jealously and the custom of revenge for adultery, matters that Freeman raised. Undoubtedly, these were components of precontact Samoan culture, but it does not appear that they were simple matters. Indeed, the nature of jealousy and the definition of adultery both appear to be situational in nature and are dependent on the nature of the agreement between the couple. Thus, in explicitly monogamous relationships, these prescriptions probably prevailed for most couples, and the missionaries undoubtedly cultivated the emotion of jealousy to increase the chances that couples would stay in "Christian unions." For polygamous unions, however, other standards likely applied. For instance, if we return to Williams' records, we find an account of the following practices:

> The husband appears passionately fond of his wife for a short time. Sometimes it will continue for a year or two sometimes until she becomes preg-

nant. Generally at the end of a year or eighteen months the wife will not only give her consent but expect her husband to take another female as wife as well as herself, & it frequently occurs that the wife herself will go to her own tribe & seek from her friends & relations the female who is to share with her affections of her husbands. *This perhaps may be one reason why generally speaking copartnership in husbands by Samoan females is attended with so little jealousy & quarrelling*. The universal rule established among them of giving to each wife in rotation her three days & three nights supremacy may also tend to promote union & good feeling among the wives toward each other. (p. 258, italics added)

Another account from this period of Samoan sexual behavior comes from Stair (1897/1983), who lived in Samoa from 1838 to 1845. Stair's account verifies Williams' record:

Polygamy at one time was largely prevalent, many chiefs having seven or eight or even more wives at a time. There were generally one or more principal wives, who kept the others in subjection, often exerting their authority with a very high hand. Formerly, a discarded wife of a chief, or one who had voluntarily left her husband, was prohibited from marrying another man, unless the latter were powerful enough to set this prohibition in defiance. As illustrating a custom common at one time in Samoan society, I may mention that many women have assured me that when it is seen that the husband was resolved upon adding another wife to his harem, the principal wife often selected her own sister or sisters, and endeavoured to get them added to the family roll of wives, so that she might have some control over them. This plan was frequently adopted to avoid strangers being brought into the family. (p. 175)

Finally, Williamson (1939/1975) carried out an extensive review of all of the early accounts of Polynesian cultures, including Samoan culture. Based on these varied sources he found it reasonable to draw the following conclusions: With respect to virginity, he stated that like other Polynesian cultures "virginity is a social asset rather than a moral virtue, and is rigorously preserved only in the case of the taupou [ceremonial village virgin]" (p. 324). With respect to premarital sex in general, he said that in Samoa:

According to Turner and Brown, chastity in either sex, prior to marriage, though ostensibly cultivated, was more of a name than a reality, and the lack of it was not regarded as a very serious offence; but, according to Turner, exceptions to this general rule were found, especially among the daughters of persons of rank. D'Urville says that girls were entirely free to dispose of their persons till married, and La Perouse tells us that girls were, before marriage, mistresses of their own favors, and their complaisance did not dishonour them. (p. 156)

Williamson also found evidence of the complexity of the Samoan mores discussed by Schoeffel and Meleisea (see chapter 3):

> A ceremony on marriage for testing the virginity of the bride was . . . performed not only in the case of daughters of chiefs, but in that of the commoner people also; and even among the latter, a girl who did not emerge successfully from the test was regarded as disgraced, and might be beaten; though the disgrace to her seems to havė been nothing compared with that of a chief's daughter, who might be killed. This suggests that immorality, even among the humbler classes was not as general as some writers make it out to have been; ***but it cannot be doubted that girls of these classes were much more lax than were the daughters of chiefs***. (pp. 156–157, italics added)

Although it is possible that some women were punished or killed after they failed the test of manual defloration, it appears that provisions could be made so that even nonvirgins could pass the test. As Holmes (1957b) said, "informants state that many a girl has been saved embarrassment by the substitution of a chicken bladder full of blood for that normally produced by the broken hymen" (p. 413). Indeed, much of the anger at someone failing the test would be over the foolishness of submitting to the test unprepared when one was not a virgin, because this would cause shame to the *aiga* and invalidate any economic arrangements surrounding the marriage. On this matter, Mead (1928) wrote that

> [a]lthough the virginity-testing ceremony was theoretically observed at weddings of people of all ranks, it was simply ignored if the boy knew that it was an idle form, and "a wise girl who is not a virgin will tell the talking chief of her husband, so that she be not shamed before all the people." (p. 98)

In reference to polygyny, Williamson noted that the practice, common among chiefs, was reported by most observers:

> There were generally . . . one or more principal wives, who kept the others in subjection, often exerting their authority with a very high hand; and when the husband proposed to add another wife to his establishment, his principal wife often secured the selection of her own sister, thus structuring her control and avoiding the introduction of strangers into the family. When a woman married (presumably only one of the upper or wealthier classes), it was usual for her to take with her to her husband one, two, or three concubines. . . . The concubines, though only regarded as secondary wives, were not usually despised, and any of them might eventually be taken as a wife without further ceremony. Kramer explains it by saying that it was not usual for a woman to return to her husband for six months after the

> birth of her child; so she brought with her at marriage some of her women relations, to prevent her husband from going to other women during the interval of separation. (pp. 178–179)

From these many accounts, there can be little doubt that sexual behavior in Samoa before it was Christianized was more casual for virtually *everyone, including young females* (see also Howard & Kirkpatrick, 1989, pp. 78–84). The denial of this by Freeman and some contemporary Samoans can be understood in terms of the concerted efforts of missionaries and the local pastors to first create, and then maintain, a hegemony of Victorian sexual values and practices. These efforts have been so successful that the very thought of precontact "promiscuity" appears to be anxiety provoking for many Samoans, so various defenses are employed to deny it.

Freeman's "mission" can be understood as part of this collective denial. In fact, his own reconstruction of precontact behavior is highly selective (see Freeman, 1983, chapter 16). For example, he cited a portion of a sentence from Williamson's account (that "virginity is a social asset rather than a moral virtue"; 1983, p. 230), but he conveniently omitted the remainder of the sentence; namely, that virginity "is rigorously preserved only in the case of *taupou*." Freeman made no mention of the additional documentation provided above from Williamson, nor did he mention the passages from Williams, Turner, or Stair. Furthermore, Freeman's own conduct in this matter stands as starkly hypocritical when we find that he has admonished Boas for not verifying Mead's account by checking these sources. In his words:

> What can be said with certainty is that if Boas, as the instigator and supervisor of Mead's Samoan researches, had taken the elementary precaution of consulting the readily available ethnographic literature on Samoa, as, for example, the writings of *Williams, Turner*, Pritchard, Stuebel, and Kramer, he would have very quickly found accounts of the sexual and other behavior of the Samoans that are markedly at variance with Mead's picture of life in Manu'a. . . . (Freeman, 1983, p. 291, italics added)

CHAPTER FIVE

A Social History of Adolescence in Samoa: Changes in Samoan Culture

MISSIONARIES AND THEIR IMPACT

Missionaries like George Turner and John Williams played a key role in initiating the changes wrought by the West on Samoan culture. Conveniently, they kept records of their perceptions regarding what they found, and of their intentions regarding what they set out to change, so we can now trace their influences on contemporary Samoa.

When reviewing Turner's (1861/1986) record, one is struck by his disdain for the culture he found in Samoa. For example, he (and many other missionaries) viewed many Samoan customs as "evil," so he set out to eradicate that evil and to teach the "heathen natives" (p. 4) to live by what he believed to be the morally superior principles of Euro-Christian culture. Moreover, in what some would today consider delusional, Turner believed that "Satan . . . [held] . . . dominion in Samoa [and he was not going to give it up] without a struggle" (p. 7). Turner described several "schemes" (p. 9) that he believed Satan had devised to prevent Samoans from embracing Christianity. Here, we examine Turner's struggles with Satan and the negative impact of the outcome of these struggles on young Samoans. First, it is enlightening to place the whole of the missionary effort in a sociological context.

Gilson (1970) provided a thorough review of the changes that took place in Samoa during the 19th century. Included in this review is the following summary of the agenda of the London Missionary Society

(LMS),[1] the strongest Christian influence in Samoa and the sect that prevailed on Ta'u when Mead was there. According to Gilson, the ultimate goal the LMS set for itself in Samoa was "to ban the activities and relationships, social and personal, that by mission standards were immoral or tainted with 'heathenish' associations, and to prescribe the ethics and conventions of puritanism" (p. 96). In reaching this goal, many Samoan customs had to be eradicated. Given priority in their agenda was the "Christianization" of "sex and family relations," including the following:

> the abolition of polygamy and, in most cases, divorce, the celebration of monogamous marriages in church; the prohibition of certain customary marriage rights, including the exchange of goods and the public test of virginity; the prevention of political marriages and of marriages between Christian and non-Christian; the prohibition of adultery, fornication and prostitution; the prohibition of obscenity in word and action; the imposition of new standards of dress, including "full coverage" for women and, when at worship, shirts or coats for men, but not shoes for either; the adoption of hair styles "appropriate" to the individual's sex, meaning long for women and short for men, the reverse of traditional styles; [and] the internal partitioning of houses and more liberal use of the external blinds. (p. 96)

Also given priority was the inculcation of "Christian" values and habits. The most extensive of these included the insistence that "the Sabbath should be strictly kept and that *habits of industry* should be encouraged. In the latter aim was enshrined the *dignity of work*, and with it the assurance that the people would be able to clothe and house themselves properly and contribute to the *support of their mission and church*" (p. 97, italics added). We see this agenda in the following passage taken from Turner (1861/1986). Here he described his experiences in attempting to instill the values of individualism among Samoans:

> The system of a common interest in each other's property . . . is clung to by the Samoans with great tenacity. . . . This common property system is a sad hinderance to the industrious, and eats like a canker-worm at the roots of individual or national progress. No matter how hard a young man may

[1]The London Missionary Society (LMS) was a nondenominational Protestant sect whose sole reason for existence was "to spread the knowledge of Christ among heathen and other unenlightened nations" (Moyle, 1984, p. 2). Initially, most of the financial support for the LMS "came from the Congregational Church with whom, in later years, the [LMS] became exclusively associated. The Congregational Church was different from other non-conformist churches because it preferred decisions concerning church government to be made by the congregation rather [than] by bishops or ministers" (Meleisea, 1987a, p. 55). The LMS "created the first independent church in the South Pacific with a fully indigenous ministry and administration. Today it is called the Christian Congregational Church of Samoa" (Meleisea, 1987a, p. 60).

be disposed to work, he cannot keep his earnings: all soon passes out of his hands into the common circulating currency. (p. 170)

It is not clear what the "national progress" was that Turner was thinking of for these island-bound people who had done quite well for centuries before his arrival. Surprisingly, however, Turner did display an inkling of comprehension of how Samoans recognized the benefits of their communal system:

> The sick the aged, the blind, the lame, and even the vagrant, has always a house and home, and food and raiment, as far as he considers he needs it. A stranger may, at first sight, think a Samoan one of the poorest of the poor, and yet he may live ten years with that Samoan and not be able to make him understand what *poverty* really is, in the European sense of the word. "How is it?" he will always say. "*No food!* Has he no friends? *No house to live in!* Where *did* he grow? Are there no houses belonging to his friends? Have the people there no love for each other?" (pp. 170–171)

Thus, included in the missionary agenda was the goal of diminishing the Samoan concern for collective welfare, and replacing it with Western individualism. As someone who was raised to take the teachings of Christ seriously, I find this part of the agenda to be a curious hypocrisy for those claiming to be emissaries of Christ. But, then, the (largely Protestant) missionaries functioned as the "shocktroops" for the onslaught of Western economic practices based on the profit motive, such as wage labor, "middle class individualism" (Meleisea, 1987b, p. 18), and careerism. Samoans were told that initiative and individual striving were what pleased God, not looking after each other's welfare; they were also told that their primary concern for the collective was misguided, although it was acceptable as a subsidiary social concern. Meleisea (1987a) framed the missionary mind-set in the following manner:

> The first missionaries to Samoa were of the lower middle classes of England, the backbone of the Evangelical movement there. They believed that hard work was the duty of a Christian. They thought Pacific Islanders lazy because the hours that people worked were so different to those of the English. For example, Samoans worked very hard at times of planting and harvesting, but there were also times when there was plenty of leisure. The missionaries wanted to make Samoans more industrious. One way of doing this was by introducing new goods to the people which necessitated their working for wages, or selling products, in order to obtain them. The idea which the missionaries had of the way Samoans should live, was based upon the ideals of the middle classes of England; where households consisted of the married couple and their children. The man was the breadwinner, and produced the food, working regular hours outside the home.

> The woman was the home-maker, and cooked and sewed clothes in the house for the family. (p. 67)

On point after point, the missionaries told Samoans that their customs were sinful and that they should feel guilty when they behaved in ways that offended God. These were not easy things to impress upon people from a culture that did not recognize one God, let alone one that was so punishing and vengeful when offended (cf., Holmes, 1987, pp. 59–60). Observers agree that most Samoans remained ambivalent to the Protestant work ethic and material accumulation, something that continually frustrated Western entrepreneurs (Oliver, 1961). But, guilt-driven motives were not easy notions to instill in a shame-based culture (cf. Gerber, 1975).[2] In fact, this latter point may help explain why many of the changes instituted by missionaries seem to be more a matter of word than deed. The strong evidence of "dualism" discussed in chapter 3 supports this notion; namely, that in certain matters some Samoans may go through the motions of conformity to avoid being shamed, but not feel guilty for "discrete" violations of Christian conventions, such as breaking the convention of sexual abstinence.[3]

Completing the agenda for the Christianization of Samoa was to be no small task, largely because of the resistance of Samoans, so the missionaries gave themselves generations to accomplish it. The missionary agenda ultimately succeeded in converting Samoans to a *form* of

---

[2]The concepts of *sin* and *guilt* appear not to have had wide currency in the traditional culture. Indeed, it appears that the missionaries promoted these concepts, with some difficulty, as described later. Instead of guilt, the primary emotion motivating approach-avoidance behavior seems to have been shame. Thus, if one violated a norm, one brought shame onto one's self, but also onto one's *aiga* and one's *matai*. Given the fact that privacy was not valued and that little norm violation went unnoticed, this would constitute a stronger social control mechanism than guilt, as employed by Western culture, because guilt is much more private and can be controlled psychologically (although with "neurotic consequences"). Moreover, the *fono* would levy fines against the offender's *aiga* and *matai*, not just the offender. Therefore, would-be offenders would know that they would have to account for their behavior to their extended family as well as the village.

[3]As a point of interest, Somerset Maugham (1985) provided a caricature of this attitude in his famous short story, "Rain," set in Samoa:

> "When we went there they had no sense of sin at all," [Reverend Davidson] said. "They broke the commandments one after the other and never knew they were doing wrong. And I think that was the most difficult part of my work, to instill into the natives the sense of sin." (p. 256) "You see, they were so naturally depraved that they couldn't be bought out of their wickedness. We had to make sins out of what they thought were natural actions. We had to make it a sin, not only to commit adultery and to lie and thieve, but to expose their bodies, and to dance and not to come to church. I made it a sin for a girl to show her bosom and a sin for a man not to wear trousers." (p. 258)

Christianity—the hundreds of churches that are the center of communities throughout the islands are a testimony to this success. Yet, in spite of 150 years of concerted effort, many Samoan traditions have survived in some form and many Samoans are still proud of this "*fa'a Samoa*" (the Samoan way of life). See Holmes (1980a, 1987) and Meleisea (1987a, 1987b) for analyses of how and why Samoans embraced Christianity.

The complexity of Christian-Samoan culture can be attributed in part to the fact that the conversion of Samoa was the culmination of numerous *rational* choices. These choices were made in the *fono* of virtually every village in Samoa. Therefore, the view that Samoans were passive throughout the conversion process is a simplistic one. The decisions to embrace Christianity was often based on the promise, however implicit, that material advantages would follow. As Holmes (1987) argued, in "exchange for all [the] prohibitions the Samoans . . . probably expected . . . that ultimately they would also acquire some of the white man's magic for getting material wealth" (p. 61). Consequently, contemporary Samoan life is more complex than it may appear based on a superficial analysis, and some practices continue to exist along side of Western *religious* conventions (as with tattooing) and Western *legal* conventions (as with the *ifoga*) (cf. Hanson, 1973; Holmes, 1980b; Meleisea, 1987a; Oliver, 1961; Stanner, 1953).

Without this complexity in Samoan culture, I doubt the Mead–Freeman controversy would have emerged at all. Although this complexity is confusing to outsiders, it also seems to have become a source of confusion for many Samoans, particularly those now attempting to come of age. For those interested in pursuing this matter, I highly recommend A. Wendt's (1973, 1977, 1979) novels and short stories, in which he portrays the complexities of 20th century Samoan culture and the resulting confusions experienced by some Samoans.

MISSIONARY IMPACT ON COMING OF AGE

The missionaries' desire to recreate Samoan culture in the image of Victorian-European culture represents a distinct lack of sensitivity to the validity, and an appreciation of the beauty, of that culture. Holmes (1987) noted in this regard that "the early English missionaries seemed to be unable to separate their religious beliefs from their culture and values" (p. 60). As a part of their "mission" to Christianize Samoa (and the world) and as a consequence of their insensitivity to the institutional balances in the culture they were transforming, many of the changes instituted by the missionaries have proven to have been harmful to Samoans, particularly young Samoans. From the point of view of the interests of the young people who are inheriting the transformed culture, the influences of the missionaries are harmful to the extent that they destroyed some of the best traditions of Samoan culture and allowed them to be replaced with some of the worst practices of European culture.

These criticisms of missionary activities are not intended as a claim that missionaries are solely responsible for all that has happened to Samoan culture since the 1830s. Nor am I denying that the missionaries had what many would see as a positive impact, such as health care and literacy. Nevertheless, to complete their "mission," they felt they had to eradicate "heathenism," and to do so it was necessary to transform the culture. It appears that their strategy of culture transformation was to target how Samoans would come of age. Had they preserved the existing institutions governing coming of age, the society would have remained largely intact. As indicated earlier, the surest way to change a culture is to change what the young are taught and how they are socialized—thereby changing what they *value*. Accordingly, as we see in this section, the missionaries set out to destroy most of the social institutions that guided young Samoans through childhood to adulthood. In doing so, they also diminished the status of young people in Samoan society—culturally disenfranchised them—because the institutions they destroyed had guaranteed them basic rights as persons. With diminished status and rights, many of those coming of age have had a lower sense of purpose, more difficulty developing a sense of identity, and less affinity with their culture. I explore the ramifications of these problems in chapter 7. For now I focus on the specific changes initiated by the missionaries.

One of the missionaries' first objectives was to eradicate the practice of tattooing. Turner (1861/1986) provided the following justification for doing so—note the disregard of the fact that tattooing had marked a rite of passage for Samoan youth for several centuries:

> The waste of time, revelling, and immorality connected with the custom have led us to discountenance it; and it is, to a considerable extent, given up. But the . . . youth still thinks it is manly and respectable to be tattooed; parental pride says the same thing; and so the custom still obtains. It is not likely, however, to stand long before advancing civilization. European clothing, and a sense of propriety they are acquiring daily, lead them to cover the tattooed part of the body entirely; and, when its display is considered a shame rather than a boast, it will probably be given up, as painful, expensive, and useless; and then, too, instead of tattooing, age, experience, common-sense, and *education* will determine whether or not the young man is entitled to the respect and privileges of mature years. (pp. 89–91, italics added)

Given his disdain for the practice among men, Turner must have been horrified with the tattooing of women. Undoubtedly, the tattooing of women would have been considered even more "evil" by the early missionaries because of its immodesty (see Fig. 4.1), and their efforts were likely more concerted in the case of women. Although the practice seems to have been consequently eradicated among women, it was to be impossible to eliminate among men. As late as the 1920s, many missionaries were apparently still consumed with the notion of abolishing it. This was recorded by the New Zealand administrator Rowe (1930), who noted that "the missionaries—with the exception of the Catholics—hated it, and still hate it as a relic of 'heathenism.' It matters nothing apparently to them that, while the custom stands, it militates against immature mating; and that *it is the one test in these islands, where life is so easy, that the youth has to go through*" (p. 85, italics added).

Note from the emphasized portion of Rowe's passage his intuition that the attack on this practice was negatively affecting youth. Rowe continued by noting that the best tattooers were on Savai'i, where missionary influence was weaker, and that "the population of Manu'a was likely to be reduced by this cause [getting tattooed], as those who indulged in the fashion were forbidden by law to return" (p. 73). It is of interest to note that this coincides with a minor detail from Mead's (1928) study, which was conducted during the same decade. She reported that "[t]attooing has been taboo on Manu'a for two generations, so only part of the population have made the necessary journey to another island in search of a tattooer" (p. 267).

The situation in contemporary Samoa is proving Turner wrong regarding the entitlement of respect and privilege that accompanies "advancing civilization." For example, for many young people in Western Samoa, education does not now "determine whether or not the young man is entitled to the respect and privileges of mature years" in their culture (Turner, 1986/1861, pp. 89–91). Rather, education seems to drive a wedge between many young people and their ancestral culture. As for tattooing, this practice is enjoying a resurgence in popularity, probably as a direct response to the deteriorating circumstances confronting young males. Indeed, recently, "more and more [young men] are deciding to undergo this painful procedure to display their Samoan identity" (McGovern, 1988, p. 28; see also Holmes, 1987, p. 76).

O'Meara (1990) suggested that tattooing is popular today partly because:

> the tattoo is quintessentially Samoan, and wearing one is a matter of cultural pride. . . . The tattoo ceremony also marks the beginning of adulthood. In addition, *it brings a great deal of attention and praise to young*

unmarried women be encouraged to live in the pastor's house under his and his wife's supervision (of course, they were only accepted if they were still virgins, or had been forgiven for their "immorality").

Third, with the demise of the *taupou* tradition, there was also less legitimation for the *aualuma* in terms of an appeal to traditional authority, so through time less social value would have been attached to it by adult male Samoans. In this context, we can place Keesing's (1934) remarks about the resistance to empowerment of the new Women's Committee in the 1920s: "At the same time resistance has been generated among many of the male titleholders against enhancement of women's authority. This forms another of the currently critical areas of conflict in modern Samoan society" (p. 56).

And, finally, because their function was more "expressive" than that of the "instrumental" *'aumaga*, it would have been less disruptive economically to disband the *aualuma*. All these factors would have operated in the opposite direction in terms of maintaining the basic structure of the *'aumaga*. The *'aumaga* did not threaten patriarchal or puritanical sentiments, it was not tied to the *taupou* tradition, and it was necessary for the day-to-day operation of the agrarian economy.

Eventually, however, the *'aumaga* would diminish in importance as well. But its collapse was to take much longer, and has only taken place recently, largely because of the imposition of the wage economy and mass education. It is important to recognize therefore that while the demise of the *aualuma* seems to have been a direct result of missionary efforts, the demise of the *'aumaga* was more likely an *indirect* result of their efforts, to the extent that they laid the basis for and encouraged the wage economy.

Holmes (1957b) provided an account of the *'aumaga* of the 1950s. We can note from his description that, as late as the 1950s, young males were still formally welcomed to both adulthood and to the local polity. Moreover, their activities in the *'aumaga* were still basically the same as they had been for centuries:

> When a boy has completed his schooling he is eligible to enter . . . the *'aumaga*. His family head (matai) may suggest *'aumaga* affiliation or in some cases a boy goes to his family head and expresses his desire to join. If the family head agrees that he should, he goes with the boy, bringing a kava root in his name to the village council. This presentation represents the official recognition by the village council that a young man may enter the untitled men's society.
>
> After being thus recognized by the village council, he prepares for his actual entrance into his society. At their next meeting the boy goes by himself with his gift of food (*momoli*), which usually consists of a six pound tin of corned beef and other food such as taro, breadfruit and . . . *palusami*.

> After placing his gift in the center of the floor the boy takes a seat in the back of the house and waits patiently while the business of the group is discussed. Finally he is recognized in a welcoming speech by one of the "Talking Chief's sons" (*tamato'oto'o*). He replies with a speech, after which one of the Talking Chief's sons distributes his food, and he is officially accepted as a member of the group. Thereafter he takes a seat at a post corresponding to the rank of his family head . . . (pp. 408–409)

Just three decades later, however, we find that throughout most of Samoa, the *'aumaga* appears to exist mainly in name only. According to Shore (1982), during the 1970s, the *'aumaga* in the village he studied in Savai'i still functioned to do the bidding of the *fono* and it provided a route to *matai* titles through *tautua*. Its function seems to have been more "socioemotive" than "instrumental," however. For example, although Shore noted that it functioned to encourage "in its members the development of skills and attitudes appropriate for young men" (p. 102), its members did things such as checking taro quotas once a month and cleaning village and school grounds one day a month.

For the most part, then, villages no longer engage in cooperative labor, except in the service of the village pastor (O'Meara, 1990). Instead, individual wage labor has replaced cooperative village labor. Now, most teenaged males (and females) attend secondary school and many move out of the village upon graduation, in search of the wage labor they have been taught to want. Most move either to larger urban areas of Samoa or to other countries (as is seen in chapter 7). Consequently, even many remote villages have been depopulated, particularly of young males (O'Meara, 1990; Yusuf & Peters, 1985). Accordingly, work projects are rarely communal enterprises any longer:

> A few young men occasionally form temporary clubs, working each other's plots in turn or hiring out to work on their families' plots. Sometimes the few families who are short on labor but have money to spare also hire a few neighbour youths for a single day of labor. Otherwise, each nuclear family or each unmarried man usually works his own taro plots independently. (O'Meara, 1990, p. 60)

The point to be taken here is that the *'aumaga* has declined in importance as secondary education has transformed both social relations in each Samoan village and the values held by the young attempting to come of age. The nontraditional values send many of the young off on a search for wage labor in pursuit of the material benefits believed to accrue from this labor. There is little sign that this transformation will slow in pace, or undergo a reversal.

Hence, as was the intention of the missionaries (Turner, 1861/1986,

p. 91), one of the most enduring influences on adolescence and the transition to adulthood has been mass education. Originally, the missionaries were concerned only with teaching adults to read well enough so that they could read the bible themselves (during the many prayer times established as part of the daily routine). At the same time, they needed to solidify their own base of operations and ensure their perpetuity. Meleisea (1987a) described how their plan unfolded:

> Education was a major programme of the mission. The policy was to educate men as pastors to take care of the parishes in the villages, so that when every village had a Samoan pastor, the English missionaries could devote themselves to teaching in the church schools and colleges, and take care of the administration of the church.
>
> The pastors and their wives ran schools for both children and adults in villages throughout the nineteenth century and, up until the 1950s, most Samoans were educated by village pastors. . . . The pastor taught the boys whatever practical skills he had learnt, while his wife taught the girls *papalagi* domestic arts. (pp. 59–60)

When the state assumed support for education in this century, primary schooling became almost universal. The majority of those in their teen years now attend secondary schools in both Western Samoa and American Samoa. Although it is true that mass education has many social and personal benefits, in the case of Western Samoa, it has some very discernibly negative side-effects, given the limitations placed on this society by its geographical and economic circumstances. As Schoeffel and Meleisea (1983) noted, Mead (1928, e.g., pp. 28–29) recorded the first stages of the social disorganization caused by mass education in the 1920s.

Most devastating to Samoan culture is the fact that mass education has led to a decline in respect for ancestral wisdom, and for those who possess it. The respect for the elder that was once a mark of this culture is diminishing as children learn competing sources of wisdom and knowledge. The world views explicitly and implicitly inculcated through education sometimes come into direct conflict with the world view of the *aiga* or *matai*. This can be a source of great difficulty for everyone concerned, especially if the young person must then live under the authority of the *matai* (cf. O'Meara, 1990).

As a consequence of the decline of the importance of the *'aumaga*, the expansion of the secondary school system, and a loss of respect for ancestral customs, many young Samoans have sought out nontraditional sources of meaning. Unfortunately, not many other forms of meaningful activity have become available. As is seen in chapter 7, wage unemployment in Western Samoa is widespread, but it is particularly high among the young. For a time, emigration to New Zealand from Western Samoa was easily accomplished and constituted somewhat of a rite of passage (MacPherson & MacPherson, 1985). However, this avenue has now been largely cut off by the financially beleaguered New Zealand government (Immigration Division, New Zealand, 1982; Yusuf & Peters, 1985). Educated to think beyond the *'aumaga* and *aiga*, but with few viable options, many young Samoan men have felt extreme desperation (cf. Leacock, 1987; MacPherson & MacPherson, 1985; Norton, 1984).

To summarize this chapter thus far, succeeding generations of young Samoans, having been denied traditional rites of passage by the missionaries, were told that they could "prove themselves" as individuals by being successful economically in an occupation or career. They were also told that Western-style, disciplinary, mass education made the person "better," and better able to understand the world to come. Young people were taught to "strive" in this system. But this Western obsession with accomplishment has reduced the value of striving defined in terms of traditional *fa'a Samoa*. Traditionally, men displayed their ambition through hard work within the *'aumaga*, by earning respect through the *tautua*, developing oratory skills, and perhaps earning the title of *matai*. Instead, successive generations have learned to sell their labor outside the *'aumaga*, and to keep the fruits of that labor for themselves and perhaps their *'aiga*. In doing so, many feel they have lost their Samoan identity.

MISSIONARY IMPACT ON SEXUAL PRACTICES

As we have seen, much has changed since the missionaries set out to reform the "heathen immorality" of Samoans. In particular, the rights and privileges of young females have suffered. Collectively, they seem to have gone from having membership rights associated with a group that had solidarity and semiautonomy in the *aualuma*, through to being sequestered by the local pastor to "protect" their chastity, to being peripheral to a nominal "committee." In other words, they have been culturally disenfranchised by changes initiated by missionaries, and their status has decreased significantly in Samoan society as a result. Some of the stages of this transformation can be culled from the writings of missionaries, diplomats, and scholars.

The only relevant missionary account from the present century comes from Brewer (1930/1975), who was posted to Tutuila from 1920 to 1923. We can detect from his record both the missionary influence in altering Samoan public behavior and traces of traditional customs that might have been practised when the missionaries were *not* a part of group activities. For example, he wrote of an experience where he encountered a *malaga* (visiting party) on its way to Pago Pago:

> In the forefront was the taupou . . . She was really prancing along, and *she didn't have a single solitary stitch on her*! She stopped, and *when she saw we were missionaries*, she immediately grabbed her lava lava . . . and threw it around herself, pulling over her shoulders a little shawl that she had been carrying on her hand. (p. 27, italics added)

Also writing at this time was a New Zealand administrator, N. A. Rowe (1930). He related a similar experience from Western Samoa during his stay there during the 1920s:

> Sometimes, going along a road through the dripping forest in Samoa, one comes upon a party of girls, bare-breasted, wearing the sufficient lavalava, and carrying their frocks upon their arms. At the sight of a white man they will stop and struggle into the redundant garments, or hurriedly, as they pass, will hide their breasts in simulated shame. *This is one of the major triumphs in Samoa, of religion*. (p. 47, italics added)

Those familiar with contemporary Samoa will recognize that "sociosexual" conditions have changed considerably. Rowe (1930) appears to have sensed these changes and their deleterious effects, as the following quotation from the Colonial Office Report (1924–1926) suggests. Note in this passage the perception that Christian morals were producing forms of sexual deviance and a moral "decadence" that had not existed in precontact Samoa:

> The spirit of the old severe system is gone; it has been replaced by the mere letter of the new, to which the native accords lip-service without understanding. He is a man deprived of moral landmarks. *Clothes, covering bodies which once went naked and unconscious, have contributed to his moral decadence by stimulating nasty curiosities, which never before existed.* (pp. 48–49, italics added)

We can gain from these selections a sense of the practices that likely prevailed in precontact Samoa and the changes in these practices initiated by missionaries. Yet, during the first 100 years of contact with missionaries, change was apparently not uniform throughout the Samoan islands. Rather, it is quite likely that various combinations and permutations of precontact and imported-Christian practices would have been found in different locations throughout the islands. In the 50 years since, however, a greater homogeneity of practices seems to have been brought about through the concerted efforts of religious authorities, and has been aided by modern mass communication and transportation.

Thus far, little has been reviewed that places Mead's account of the incidence of premarital sexual behavior during the 1920s in doubt.

Moreover, we can even move past the period when Mead made her observations, and gain a glimpse of how some precontact practices survived as far as the mid-1900s. Holmes (1957b) provided the following account of what he found in the village of Ta'u during the 1950s:

> Sex activity in Manu'a centres around the boy's intermediary (*fa'asoa*) who approaches the girl and arranges a rendezvous with the boy. . . . Such meetings take place after the families of the principals have retired, when they slip out of their houses to a specified rendezvous. . . . *Samoan girls enjoy a considerable amount of sexual freedom without the conflict as that confronting the American teen-aged girl.* Promiscuity is condemned by the church but winked at by the family. An unmarried girl who finds herself pregnant will face a certain amount of verbal abuse from her family, but the matter is soon forgotten, and the newborn child is welcomed with open arms, without any stigma attached to it. (pp. 409–411, italics added)

It is unclear to what extent these attitudes and practices have survived intact in the 1990s, but Schoeffel and Meleisea's account suggests they have (see chapter 3).

One area where the missionaries seem to have succeeded fully is with instilling the puritanical obsession with covering the human body—an uncomfortable thing to do in a tropical climate. By the 1960s, many Samoans seemed to have fully embraced Christian attitudes toward the body. For example, based on his experiences as a school teacher in Western Samoa, Irwin (1965) wrote:

> Samoan girls are much more conservative in their dress than European girls. They dress colourfully and attractively but never daringly. Clothes are meant to hide the figure, particularly between the hips and knees. No Samoan girl wears shorts or a bathing costume. If she did, everybody would know she was a bad girl like those who come ashore half naked from passing ships. (p. 54)

This is indeed quite a different Samoa than the one recorded by the early missionaries. Now, the free-spirited, half-naked women are *palagi* ("European") tourists, and the people being offended by the lack of modesty are Samoans. In this respect, it appears that Europeans have traded places with Samoans, in the sense that Samoans have imitated elements of European culture of the Victoria era (e.g., modesty) and Europeans have imitated elements of precontact Samoan culture (e.g., immodesty). It is interesting to note that in the original edition of her book, Mead provides a photograph of a young woman wearing only "the bark costume of long ago" (caption of photo, between pages 160 and 161). This young woman did not appear shy in baring her breasts for the photographer.

Although the photographer is not identified, it was likely Mead herself, and the subject was likely one of her informants.

The Victorian prudishness acquired from Europeans apparently even extends to the clothes worn to school, at least for Samoans now living in New Zealand. The following passage from a monograph prepared for the New Zealand Office of Race Relations (to help New Zealanders understand Samoans) explains this:

> In co-educational schools, embarrassment may be felt if the school insists on certain uniform requirements for girls. Samoan girls do not always feel comfortable in short physical education skirts or in rompers. In particular they are sensitive about wearing swimming costumes in the presence of boys, and if they do, the boys too can feel embarrassed. (Ngan-Woo, 1985, p. 21)

Undoubtedly, we are seeing the "ideal" of the Christian-Samoan culture in that passage. We also see the ideal in the following passage regarding what is claimed to be the "real" sexuality of Samoan women:

> Samoan female adolescents are aware of the taboo placed on their womanhood. The *aiga* take pride in its daughters. Virginity is to be yielded only at marriage. Brothers or male cousins exercise an active surveillance over their women's whereabouts, but will avoid their women's physical presence. They take an active interest in activities entered into by women, especially those at night. . . . The Samoan ideal of chastity for females before marriage is rigidly upheld and it becomes a source of pride for an *aiga*. Thus a son's ***triumph in marrying a virgin is seen as especially significant***. (Ngan-Woo, 1985, p. 24, italics added)

That it would be a "triumph" to marry a virgin, if virginity were a universal custom in the culture, is of course a logical contradiction. However, we see something of the *reality* in a passage following shortly after the statement just cited: "In fact however, some Samoans do produce 'illegitimate' children, but the woman is still able to marry. In other words, faaSamoa recognises human frailty, and is willing to forgive" (p. 24).

Based on the material just examined, together with material from chapters 3 and 4, there is little reason to doubt the basic details of Mead's account: We may take exception with how she expressed certain things and how she explained other things, but there is little reason to doubt the likelihood that some of her informants engaged in a certain amount of casual sexual behavior that was passively accepted by their communities. We have seen strong evidence that such behaviors would have been found in precontact Samoa and we have examined the influence that was changing them when Mead conducted her study (the Christianization undertaken by missionaries). But even with the greater impact of Christian influence in contemporary Samoa, such behaviors apparently still occur (Schoeffel & Meleisea, 1983), and have even been documented by Freeman (1983) himself. Accordingly, in the concluding section of the next chapter I attempt to understand the logic by which Freeman could muster a case against Mead on this issue.

CHAPTER SIX

Mead's Samoa

IS IT PLAUSIBLE IN TERMS OF THE HISTORICAL EVIDENCE?

With the historical perspective developed in chapters 4 and 5, we are now in a position to judge whether "Mead's Samoa" of the 1920s can be pinpointed along the trajectory of social change initiated by the missionaries in the 1830s. Using this technique, we have another means by which to assess the plausibility of Mead's coming-of-age thesis. As discussed previously, the controversy over Mead's work has tended to ignore the substance of her book; namely, the coming-of-age thesis regarding the psychological processes and social structures associated with adolescence in 1920s Ta'u. Chapter 4 presented a reconstruction of the institution of adolescence as it might have existed in precontact Samoa, and chapter 5 traced the changes in that institution initiated by missionaries. This chapter provides a review and analysis of what Mead actually wrote about the Samoa she observed.

Qualifications Placed by Mead Upon Her Findings

Before examining Mead's Samoa it is important to gain an appreciation of the limitations that she herself put on the validity and generalizability of her findings.

To be specific, Mead's (1928) *Coming of Age in Samoa* is about 50 young women between the ages of 8 and 20 who were growing up in three small villages on the island of Ta'u in 1925–1926. The subtitle, *A Psycho-*

logical Study of Primitive Youth for Western Civilization, conveys Mead's intention to focus on the psychological world of these young women and to compare it with the world confronting young American women.

Moreover, the book can actually be read as two overlapping books. The first comprises 14 chapters written for the general public. It is partly because of the literary license used by Mead in these chapters that various interpretations and misunderstandings of the book have emerged. Clearly, one has to read these chapters keeping in mind the fact that Mead was trying to "sell" the book and reach a popular audience with a particular message. The "second book" can be found in the appendices, which present much of the technical, social-scientific, as opposed to the popular, record of her research. Quite possibly, her publisher had her squeeze this information into these appendices to make room for more stimulating material. These appendices provide more exacting details of her research as well as a series of qualifiers regarding her analysis and conclusions.

In Appendix II, Mead presented most of the restrictions that she thought should be taken into account in reading her study. But, of course, as Freeman's critique reveals, she did not always make these restrictions explicit when she described her informant's experiences. Had she done so, the controversy over her work either might not have arisen at all in the first place or it might not have been as complex.

Mead dealt first in Appendix II with the problem of the transitional nature of the culture she was studying and how this made it "impossible to present a single and unified picture of the adolescent girl in Samoa." Thus, she grappled with the problem of including

> descriptions of customs which had fallen in partial decay under the impact of western propaganda and foreign example . . . [and the] double necessity of describing not only the present environment and the girl's reaction to it, but also of interpolating occasionally some description of the more rigid cultural milieu of her mother's girlhood, [all of which] mars to some extent the unity of the study. (p. 259)

We can see here the dilemma Mead faced in providing an accurate account of the experiences of her informants while not letting her research shift to a study of social change.[1] This was to be the decision that in-

[1] In Appendix III, Mead provided an analysis of the social change that places her study in historical context. Although much of this is helpful and apparently accurate, in reading it we must bear in mind Schoeffel and Meleisea's criticism that Mead sometimes confused the ideal culture with actual behavior. Thus, for example, her citation of traditional harsh punishments for sexual impropriety (p. 273) must be interpreted in light of what we reviewed in chapters 4 and 5. Yes, such punishments were possible because of stipulations originating in the ideal culture, but it is more likely that they were employed infrequently, and that sexual license was more widely enjoyed.

vited the current controversy and it is something that must be kept in mind when reading her passages about the "typical" experiences of her informants.

A second qualifier specified the limitations of her perspective. She acknowledged that given the qualitative nature of her study with its case history method, "[t]he conclusions are also all subject to the limitation of the personal equation. They are the judgements of one individual upon a mass of data, many of the most significant aspects of which can, by their very nature, be known only to herself" (p. 261). In chapter XIII, she also admitted the possibility for error, but attempted to minimize it in her work by focusing on the ways that "aspects of Samoan life[,] which irremediably affect the life of the adolescent girl[,] differ from the forces which influence [American] girls" (p. 198).

A third qualifier was that, because of her focus on young women and the necessity of keeping her analysis simple, she provided details of Samoan culture *only as they were relevant to her young informants*. In her words: "Although knowledge of the entire culture was essential for the accurate evaluation of any particular individual's behaviour, a detailed description will be given only of those aspects of the culture which are immediately relevant to the problem of the adolescent girl" (pp. 262–263).[2]

Thus, Mead's description of Samoan culture in *Coming of Age* was *tailored* to the experiences of her informants, although she certainly did not make this clear throughout her book. It also appears that she may have forgotten this stipulation herself when she wrote about Samoan culture in some of her later works.[3] Decades later, in the 1969 edition of *Social Organization of Manu'a*, she was to repeat this specification when she acknowledged that she likely saw the culture largely through the eyes of her young informants (see chapter 1, this volume).

A final stipulation involved the fact that the transitional culture placed further restrictions on her sample size of "average girls." Important to the Mead–Freeman controversy is the fact that about one third (9 out of 25) of her postpuberty sample were directly under "European" influence

[2]In fact, she stated this in a similar fashion in the introduction to her book (pp. 11–12), but the implications of that passage are easy to miss.

[3]Barnouw (1983) noted that "Mead had an unfortunate tendency, of which Freeman takes advantage, to make stronger and broader assertions in later publications than she did in her original study" (p. 428). On the other hand, Barnouw also noted that after he had "finished Freeman's book, [he reread *Coming of Age*]. In this reading it did not seem to [him] that Mead's generalizations were phrased as strongly as [he] had come to expect. The explanation for this discrepancy appears when one examines Freeman's citations. Although the focus of [Freeman's] book is on *Coming of Age in Samoa*, many of the Mead quotations come from later works of hers" (p. 428).

with their residence in boarding schools run by the village pastors.[4] This limited the pool of "traditional" respondents on which many of her generalizations are based, but it also gave her a "rough control group," as she described:

> The existence of the pastor's boarding-school for girls past puberty provided me with a rough control group. These girls were so severely watched that heterosexual activities were impossible; . . . they lived a more ordered and regular life than the girls who remained in households. The ways in which they differed from other girls of the same age and more resembled European girls of the same age follow with surprising accuracy the lines suggested by the specific differences in environment. (pp. 264–265)

In this passage we see that Mead's generalizations about the "passive acceptance" of premarital sexual behavior obviously did not apply to the one third of her sample living in the pastors' houses. However, although virginity and chastity were required of these young women, these restrictions were apparently not the source of "adolescent turmoil," as is seen later.

With these qualifications in mind, we can now examine and interpret what Mead wrote about how her informants experienced their coming of age. Thus, we should bear in mind that: (a) she was describing a culture in transition; (b) she had a limited view of the culture; (c) she tailored her discussion of the culture to those aspects most relevant to the lives of her informants; and (d) within her sample of her postpuberty informants there were actually "two adolescences"—one closer in nature to precontact Samoa, and one corresponding to the pastors' attempt to recreate Victorian-European culture.

Female Adolescence

According to Mead, the process of coming of age was a gradual one, begun very early in life. After weaning, infants of both genders were usually put under the care of a girl aged 6 or 7 (p. 22) who, with the aid of others, essentially mentored the young one. The girl's duties included keeping the younger child out of mischief and "housebreaking" the child, by using both verbal and physical punishments. For girls, this tutelage

[4]The pastors of each village boarded teenagers whose "parents wished them to have three to four years of superior educational advantage and stricter supervision" (p. 68). On Tutuila there was a large boarding school for girls and boys, referred to as the Missionary Boarding School. These "trained many boys as native pastors and as missionaries for other islands, and many girls to be pastors' wives" (Mead, 1928, p. 270). Mead also noted that the missionary schools "were regarded as a social rather than a religious adventure" (p. 161).

lasted until they were sufficiently trained and socialized themselves to become nursemaids.

After this time, the young girl learned various skills such as the rudiments of weaving, collecting and breaking coconuts, spreading copra to dry, playing games and singing, house cleaning, preparing pandanus leaves for weaving, and running errands. Partly because of her young charges, and partly because of discouragements from young boys, the younger girl did not learn how to deal with the reef or "the more adventurous forms of work and play" (p.27). For these reasons, the girl also tended not to engage in cooperative activities and therefore did not learn the principles of group organization as well as did boys. On the issue of play for Samoan children, Mead wrote that despite the assignment of work tasks to them ("which have a meaning in the structure of the whole society"), this did not mean "that they have less time for play than American children who are shut up in schools nine to three o'clock every day" (pp. 226–227).

When the young girl became strong enough, she was relieved of her nursemaid duties, and could work on the plantations and carry produce back to the village. This usually occurred just before puberty. According to Mead:

> It may be said with some justice that the worst period of their lives is over. Never again will they be so incessantly at the beck and call of their elders, never again tyrannised over by two-year-old tyrants. All the irritating, detailed routine of housekeeping . . . is . . . performed by children under fourteen years of age. (p. 28)

Released from baby-tending, young women now learned more complicated skills related to the carrying and preparation of food. Then, if they proved themselves capable of completing tasks competently, they could go on fishing expeditions and engage in all of the preparations for these. They could also learn the techniques of harvesting forest products for weaving, clothing and ornaments. The most important skill acquired was weaving the "fine mat," considered "the high point in Samoan weaving virtuosity" (p. 32). (In general, woven mats are very important in daily Samoan life, being used for sitting, sleeping, eating, and privacy, whereas fine mats have a complex exchange value in Samoa culture; see Linnekin, 1991.) These fine mats should only have taken 1 to 2 years to weave, but for the adolescent who was not yet an accomplished weaver, a longer period was allowed. Begun at puberty, these mats were often not finished until age 19 or 20, after which they became part of the girl's dowry. The quality of the mat became "a testimony to the girl's industry and manual skill" (p. 32).

The period during which the fine mat was being woven can be considered a moratorium—a socially permitted delay of adulthood (Erikson, 1968, discussed in chapter 8, this volume; cf. Mageo, 1988). The social permission existed in the sense that the young woman could not marry until the fine mat was completed, because it was part of her dowry. On the one hand, this seems to have been a period of psychological preparation and of proving qualifications of marriageability. On the other hand, this period was the freest of the young woman's life, particularly in being relieved of child-tending responsibilities. In reference to the first characteristic of this period Mead wrote that:

> Throughout this more or less systematic period of education, the girls maintain a very nice balance between the reputation for the necessary minimum knowledge and a virtuosity which would make too heavy demands. A girl's chances of marriage are badly damaged if it gets about the village that she is lazy and inept in domestic tasks. But after these first stages have been completed the girl marks time technically for three to four years. (p. 33)

This "marking of time" involved completing basic required tasks and demonstrating a "pass proficiency" (p. 37) in terms of competence and industry—and therefore marriageability. To excel would end the moratorium period, by inviting marriage and children, and she would be denying herself the opportunity for freedom and experimentation. Mead described this as follows:

> She does the routine weaving, especially of the Venetian blinds and carrying baskets. She helps with the plantation work and the cooking, she weaves a very little on her fine mat. But she thrusts virtuosity away from her as she thrusts away every other sort of responsibility with the invariable comment, *'Laititi a'u'* ("I am but young"). All of her interest is expended on clandestine sex adventures, and she is content to do routine tasks. . . . (p. 33)

Obviously, not all of Mead's informants were expending all of their interest on "clandestine sex adventures," because one third were under the supervision of the pastor, specifically to prevent such behavior. Again, it is important to read Mead with the qualifications just discussed in mind.

In terms of preparation for adulthood, most instrumental task learning had already taken place by this point. However, although marriageable,

> the seventeen-year-old girl does not wish to marry—not yet. It is better to live as a girl with no responsibility, and a rich variety of emotional experience. This is the best period of her life. . . . The long expeditions after fish and food and weaving materials give ample opportunities for rendezvous.

> Proficiency would mean more work, more confining work, and earlier marriage, and marriage is the inevitable to be deferred as long as possible. (p. 38)

Readers are reminded that in chapter 4, missionary John Williams (cited in Moyle, 1984) was quoted as writing that "young females I have heard has a great objection to marriage[,] a roving commission being more congenial to their feelings" (p. 233).

Although the account thus far describes a more "traditional" coming of age, the question arises as to what was taking place for those boarding at the pastor's house. One would think that the imposition of European standards of conduct would introduce stress and conflict into the lives of these young women as they struggled with the conflicting requirements of two cultures. Mead dealt extensively with this issue, and concluded that although some conflicts had been experienced by several young women (her "upward deviants" who wanted to move beyond traditional Samoan culture), these conflicts were not a source of sustained personal distress for them. On the other hand, she predicted that this would not be the case in the future, as institutions such as mass education drew young Samoans away from traditional culture. In her words:

> while religion itself offered little field for conflict, the institutions promoted by religion might act as stimuli to new choices and when sufficiently reinforced by other conditions might produce a type of girl who deviated markedly from her companions. That the majority of Samoan girls are still unaffected by these influences and pursue uncritically the traditional mode of life is simply a testimony to the resistance of the native culture, which in its present slightly Europeanized state, is replete with easy solutions for all conflicts; and to the apparent fact that adolescent girls in Samoa do not generate their own conflicts, but require a vigorous stimulus to produce them. (pp. 170–171)

The primary fact of life introduced for those who wished to reside in the pastor's house was the requirement of chastity, something that appears to not have been required of most young women in precontact Samoan culture (chapter 4). But, as Mead wrote, "[t]he lives of the girls who lived in the pastor's household differed from those of their less restricted sisters and cousins only in the fact that they had no love affairs and lived a more regular and ordered existence" (pp. 156–157). If the requirement of chastity was unacceptable to the young women, or if the living arrangement was unpleasant, she simply had to break an important rule of the pastor's household and she would be expelled (p. 163). In fact, Mead reported that almost all of her older informants had spent some time in a pastor's house (p. 161). However, a number of her informants apparently found the experiences in the pastor's house to be pleasant, and life to be more leisurely there than with their families, so they obeyed the rules. In Mead's words, their fascination with the experiences in the pastor's house "was usually a sufficient bribe to good behaviour, at least to discretion" (p. 163). In a sense, then, a balance was struck to maintain the moratorium period of precontact culture by which restrictions on sexual behavior were exchanged for other freedoms and rewards.

As for the missionary attitude toward chastity, Mead contended that a blind eye was turned toward the premarital sexual behavior of those not residing in the pastor's house, as long as it was discrete (as noted earlier, forms of discretion also appear to have been necessary in precontact Samoa). The "passive acceptance . . . of pre-marital irregularities went a long way towards minimizing the girls' sense of guilt" (p. 161) and it went a long way in preventing stress in the lives of the young. As Mead noted, the introduction of Christian values regarding sexuality could "have provided a real setting for conflict" (pp. 163–164). However, as late as the 1920s, the pastors were not enforcing those values, except through residence in the pastor's house. As Mead explained, pastors did not then require church membership or attendance among the young. Had they imposed religious observance on the young, "crises in the lives of the young people would very likely have occurred" (p. 164). Instead,

> the whole religious setting is one of formalism, of compromise, of acceptance of half measure. The great number of native pastors with their peculiar interpretations of Christian teachings have made it impossible to establish the rigour of western Protestantism with its inseparable association of sex offenses and an individual consciousness of sin. And the girls upon whom the religious setting makes no demands, makes no demands upon it. They are content to follow the advice of their elders to defer church membership until they are older. *Laititi a'u. Fia siva* ("For I am young and like to dance"). The church member is forbidden to dance or to witness a large night dance. (p. 164)

Thus, we can see the unique mixture of Samoan traditions and Victorian Protestantism in 1920s American Samoa. Samoan-born pastors were faced with the dilemma of *imposing* "imported" values on their own people. Undoubtedly, the imposition of such values on an unwilling population would have been at great cost or it might have had a "boomerang effect" leading to forms of resistance. As we saw in chapter 5, however, the missionaries had an ambitious, long-term agenda of transforming the entire culture. Accomplishing a goal of this significance takes generations, and must be done at a pace that does not estrange the people being changed. From Mead's record, we see that they chose to transform the culture through the formal education of the young, where they could isolate the young from their families and indoctrinate them with Christian values and European knowledge.

The residential arrangements in the pastor's house appear to have replaced the *aualuma* of precontact culture as a significant force in the socialization of young women. The *aualuma* provided the young woman with a peer group and a meaningful, structured, daily existence, both of which were now rendered by the pastor. Those who did not live in the pastor's house, therefore, were more on their own, and were left more to their devices, as Mead documented. Indeed, Mead attributed some "individual peculiarities" of personality among some of her informants to the absence of a homogenizing effect of a socializing institution like the *aualuma* (p. 140).

In reference to the *aualuma* of 1920s Ta'u, Mead documented its state of decay as an institution. She noted that formerly "[t]he girl's entrance into the *Aualuma* was *always, not just occasionally*, marked by a feast" (p. 275, italics added). By the time of her study "the formal entry into the *Aualuma* is often neglected and is more a formal fee to the community than a recognition of the girl herself" (p. 80). When formal entry was observed, it was often not until 2 to 3 years past the girl's puberty. Even then it might simply involve her *matai* sending "an offering of food to the house of the chief *taupo* of the village, thus announcing that he wishes the daughter of his house to be henceforth counted as one of the group of young girls who form her court" (pp. 76–77). Of course, with the *taupou* tradition obsolete, there was little concrete justification for maintaining the *aualuma*. In fact, when Mead was there, in "many parts of Samoa[,] the *Aualuma* has fallen entirely to pieces and is only remembered in the greeting words that fall from the lips of a stranger" (p. 77).

This account constitutes the outline of the institution of adolescence available to Mead's informants. With respect to entry into adulthood, the process was straightforward—find a suitable mate, or have one arranged, and get married. This generally happened at age 20 or 21. If it did not happen voluntarily at this age, social pressures were brought to bear upon the woman, and her attitude changed:

> The girl of twenty-two or twenty-three who is still unmarried loses her laissez faire attitude. Family pressure is an effective cause in bringing about this change. She is an adult, as able as her married sisters and her brother's younger wives; she is expected to contribute as heavily as they to household undertakings. (p. 185)

Therefore, it was the need for the young woman's domestic labor that in part forced an end to her moratorium period and pushed her to marry. Therefore, she turned her attention to marriage and "settled down to increase her value as a wife'' (p. 185). Once married, life was highly structured, but it was apparently generally satisfying, and Mead believed ''[t]he young married women of twenty to thirty [to be] a busy, cheerful group'' (p. 190). Mead noted an exception to this with Manita, who was 27 and still unmarried. Manita was mentioned as an example of an ''upward deviant,'' although she was not in Mead's sample of 50 informants. Manita was considered the most beautiful woman in the village and had many ''suitors and lovers,'' but ''she was of a haughty and aggressive nature and men whom she deemed worthy of her hand were wary of her sophisticated domineering manner'' (p. 166).

Based on the observations just outlined, Mead concluded that most of her informants experienced their adolescence to be relatively unstressful. Mead attributed this to the ''general casualness of the whole society'' (p. 198) and to the ''primitive'' or uncomplicated nature of the society. In interpreting her conclusion, however, we must bear in mind the qualifications placed on her study. For example, she was studying a culture in transition, so her conclusions apply more to the traditional structures and customs, than to the Western customs being introduced by the missionaries.

With this in mind, we can more readily accept her conclusion that the remnants of precontact Samoan society provided a relatively straightforward socialization process for the young as they came of age. Contributing to this would have been an absence of competing belief systems as well as a lack of ambiguity regarding the roles that constituted the adult identity (both of which the missionaries were chipping away at, however, as Mead recorded). With little to produce stress and confusion in making choices, the young would come of age in a community where the practices and beliefs in one family or village were very much like the practices in other families or villages. All of this, along with the Samoan extended family (large numbers of siblings and relatives to diffuse emotions and tensions), appears to constitute a formula for an adolescence uncomplicated by psychological distress or an acting out of conflicts. There was simply very little that would produce much ''emotional turmoil'' to get in the way of individuals enjoying their moratorium and then accepting their adult roles.

Mead mentioned sexual freedoms, of which the young could take advantage, in the context of the ease of passage through adolescence. Although it does appear that a number did exercise this franchise, a significant proportion did not, yet according to Mead they too experienced an ease of passage. Logically, then, sexual freedom or the potential for experimentation would not have been crucial to an ease of passage. In fact, Mead did not include sexual freedom as a requirement for an ease of passage. Still, precontact Samoan culture appears to have had a more consistent sexuality morality for both men and women than the morality being introduced by the missionaries. Traditionally, sex was viewed to be a "natural, pleasurable thing" (p. 201), and women were not stigmatized for playing their natural role in it. However, it was also the case that they and their partners had to be discrete about it. In addition, their activities could not be seen as a threat to community interests. Accordingly, these young women should not have been confused or traumatized over conflicting standards for sexual behavior. Because of the controversial nature of these assertions, this issue is examined in more detail here.

Male Adolescence

Mead described female adolescence as constituting a predictable set of steps delivering the individual relatively painlessly from childhood into adulthood. Although her study was specifically about females, she also provided considerable detail about the coming of age of males. But, because her informants were female, she did not have access to the psychological world of the young male. Rather, she had to rely more on her observations of the social structures to which they were conforming, and she had to draw inferences about their experiences from these observations. In contrast to the changes affecting female adolescence, male adolescence had been less drastically transformed by the missionaries. This appears to have been the case because (a) it stood in contravention of fewer Victorian morals, and (b) it was more instrumental to the material well-being of the community. However, we see from Mead's account that the passage into adulthood was often more dramatic and more structured for young men, presumably as a precursor for their more dominant roles in that society.

Early childhood was very similar for boys and girls. By mid-childhood, however, differential opportunities emerged, as Mead described:

> Very small boys also have some care of the younger children, but at eight or nine years of age they are usually relieved of it. Whatever rough edges have not been smoothed off by this responsibility for younger children are worn off by their contact with older boys. For little boys are admitted to interesting and important activities only so long as their behaviour is circumspect and helpful. Where small girls are brusquely pushed aside, small boys will be patiently tolerated and they become adept at making themselves useful. (p. 28)

These young boys would form themselves into groups of four or five and place themselves under the supervision of a group of older males in order to learn various skills, such as reef fishing. These experiences would have also taught them how to quickly organize themselves into cooperative work groups. The learning of cooperative work habits was an important socialization influence in preparing the young male for the requirements for "success" in this culture. These cooperative work habits were important qualities that would eventually carry young males into adulthood. In contrast, as mentioned earlier, with the demise of the *aualuma*, young girls were no longer exposed to these types of group-bonding experiences. This deficit undoubtedly made it more difficult for women to achieve a role of high status in the culture (women could earn titles, but it was rare). During their middle childhood, the boys also learned how to prepare food and cook it in the *umu* (an outdoor oven made by covering food with hot rocks and banana leaves). Males were expected to perform this task for the duration of their lives, so long as they remained "untitled" (i.e., not a *matai*).

Tattooing, the principal rite of passage of precontact culture, was prohibited of young males by the missionaries while Mead was on Ta'u. Thus, Mead (1928) noted that "tattooing has been taboo on Manu'a for two generations, so only part of the population have made the necessary journey to another island in search of a tattooer" (p. 267). She also observed that "today, scarcely half of the young men are tattooed" (p. 275). As we saw in chapter 4, in precontact Samoa, tattooing took several months; it was done in mutually supporting groups; and it was a prerequisite for entry into the *'aumaga*.

With tattooing banned at the time of her study, Mead did not specify whether there were any formal prerequisites for entry into the *'aumaga*. (Holmes, 1987, noted that in the 1950s, finishing school was the entry requirement.) She did note, however, that:

> When the boy is old enough to enter the *'aumaga*, the head of his household either sends a present of food to the group, announcing the addition of the boy to their group, or takes him to a house where they are meeting and lays down a great kava root as a present. Henceforth the boy is a member of a group which is almost constantly together. (p. 76)

Although tattooing was not part of their rite of passage, young men were apparently prepared in terms of skill acquisition for early adulthood. According to Mead:

> the seventeen-year-old boy is not left passively to his own device. He has learned the rudiments of fishing, he can take a dug-out canoe over the reef safely, or manage the stern paddle in a bonito boat. He can plant taro or transplant cocoanut, husk cocoanuts on a stake and cut the meat out with a deft turn of the knife. Now at seventeen or eighteen he is thrust into the *'aumaga*, the society of the young men and the older men

> without titles, the group that is called . . . "the strength of the village." (pp. 33–34)

Thus, the experiences in the *'aumaga* were important for socializing the young man to develop the skills and responsibilities associated with adulthood. In addition to a sense of competency and accomplishment, he also derived a sense of belonging in his community and a realization that his family and village needed him. Mead described these socializing experiences, and how they differed from the experiences of young women:

> Here he is badgered into efficiency by rivalry, precept and example. The older chiefs who supervise the activities of the *'aumaga* gaze equally sternly upon any backslidings and upon any undue precocity. The prestige of his group is ever being called into account by the *'aumaga* of the neighbouring villages. His fellows ridicule and persecute the boy who fails to appear when any group activity is on foot, whether work for the village on the plantation, or fishing, or cooking for the chiefs, or play in the form of a ceremonial call upon some visiting maiden. Furthermore, the [male] youth is given much more stimulus to learn [than are females] and also a greater variety of occupations are open to him. (p. 34)

From these accounts, it is clear that males underwent experiences that were more group structured than did females and that they had more choice about what they would learn and do as an "occupation." Occupational choices included house building, fishing, carving, and oratory. Important to the coming-of-age issue is Mead's inference that the period following entry into the *'aumaga* could constitute a moratorium, if the individual so chose. As was the case for females, a young man could make this time a moratorium by not excelling too much, for to do so would make him eligible for higher status, marriage, and perhaps a chiefly title. Accordingly, the young man could "bide his time," carrying out his responsibility but not outdoing his peers.

Thus, membership in the *'aumaga* marked the young man as "grown up and ready to assume adult responsibilities" (p. 55). Although doing his share of the work was important, he should not excel in his duties unless he was ready to accept a title. Once a title was offered, if it was refused, it would never be offered again (p. 36). Consequently, the young man would squander his ultimate chances for advancement. When a title was accepted, however, the freedoms of the moratorium were relinquished and the titled person was expected to become very serious and circumspect, and not engage in open hedonistic activities. Mead did not identify any cases where these pressures caused serious problems of the storm and stress variety for young men. However, she did identify a 27-year-old *matai* who described the burden it had been for him being a *matai* for the past 4 years. Moreover, she noted that "the boy is faced by a far more difficult dilemma than the girl" (p. 37) in trying, on the one hand, to keep the freedom of youth while, on the other hand, meeting his obligations. For he needed to maintain a reputation that would later allow him to find a good marriage partner and to earn a title.

The *'aumaga* also appears to have provided a very effective socialization setting within which to learn the requirements of the formal leadership roles in the community, particularly those of the *fono* (village council), with its esoteric rituals and language. Mead described this in detail: "The *'aumaga* mirrors the organization of the older men. Here the young men learn to make speeches, to conduct themselves with gravity and decorum, to serve and drink the kava, to plan and execute group enterprises" (p. 76).

According to Mead, the practice of entering all young men into the *'aumaga* had the effect of creating a population that was homogeneous in behavior and outlook. As Mead noted, "the many years' apprenticeship in the *'aumaga* formed an excellent school for disciplining individual peculiarities" (p. 140). In terms of the sanctioning of behavior, normative pressures were directed against "the inept, the impudent, and the disobedient among the young" and they encouraged the young to "work industriously and skilfully, not [to] be presuming, [to] marry discreetly, [to] be loyal to their relatives, not [to] carry tales, not [to] be trouble makers" (p. 130).

This discussion provides the essentials of Mead's description of the coming of age for young males. Readers can draw their own conclusions as to whether it was experienced as pleasant for the typical Samoan male. However, this well-structured adolescence and young adulthood is basically the "coming of age" that would have been experienced for numerous generations prior to Mead's study (except the schooling requirements and the prohibition on tattooing). The young men did appear to face a certain amount of competition, rivalry, and bravado, but whether these were experienced by them as psychologically unpleasant or stressful is not clear. Mead did not record any incidents of serious delinquency or personality disorders among the young men, but she did not intensively interview any young men either. What is clear, however, is the crucial point that their coming of age was structured and orderly, and they therefore should have been prepared cognitively and emotionally as children for their adolescence; as adolescents they should have been prepared cognitively and emotionally for their youth; and as youth they should have been prepared cognitively and emotionally for their adulthood.

Comparing Mead's Account of Sexual Practices With Freeman's Criticisms

Freeman (1983) claimed that "Miss Mead" (p. 226)[5] depicted Samoans "as a people for whom free lovemaking is 'expected' among adolescent girls" (p. 240). On the contrary, Mead actually wrote that "sex activity is never urged upon the young people" (p. 232). Disregarding Mead's actual account, then, Freeman argued that

> this conclusion is indeed so preposterously at variance with the realities of Samoan life that a special explanation is called for; as I shall discuss further . . . all the indications are that the young Margaret Mead was, as a kind of joke, deliberately misled by her adolescent informants. (p. 240)

Freeman rightly noted that Mead identified about one half her sample of postpuberty females to be virgins (Freeman, 1983, p. 238). He also argued that "the furtive sexual liaisons in which a minor proportion of adolescent females became . . . involved were recognized by all concerned as shameful departures from the well-defined ideal of chastity" (p. 240). He applied this latter statement to his own research in the 1960s in which he identified 27% of a sample of teenaged Samoan females as nonvirgin, but implied that the statement applies to Mead's sample from the 1920s.

Given what we have already examined in chapters 3, 4, and 5, one may ask whether it is worth considering Freeman's critique any further on the matter of premarital sexual behavior. I believe it is, because it is on this issue that much of the mythology about Mead's book is centered, and it is on this issue that "Samoans are perturbed by Mead's depiction of them" (Freeman, 1983, p. 240). So let us backtrack a bit before examining *exactly* what Mead wrote in *Coming of Age* about this issue.

As discussed in chapter 3, Schoeffel and Meleisea found Mead's descriptions of the sexual behavior of her informants to be quite plausible, even in terms of their own recent experiences in Western Samoa. The prevalence of such behavior in precontact Samoa was verified in chapter 4 from the records of missionaries, and in chapter 5 we saw how the missionaries set out to systematically eradicate this semi-autonomous sexuality. Mead's account therefore accords well historically, and she appears to have described a transitional culture at the point where the pastors had not yet fully enforced Victorian standards on all of the young women.

How, then, do we account for Freeman's vehemence regarding this issue? The reader will recall that Freeman has held an honorary chiefly

[5]Mead was actually married at the time. As noted earlier, Freeman patronized Mead in this manner throughout his book.

title since the 1940s (Freeman, 1983, p. xiv). Schoeffel and Meleisea attributed Freeman's disagreement with Mead partly to the fact that his "chiefly rank imposed an insurmountably difficult impediment to his direct knowledge of the private experiences and informal behaviour of young adolescent females." This is because interaction "between persons of different ranks and statuses, particularly those structurally 'opposed' in Samoan culture, is very restricted and formal" (p. 67).

Testimony from another Samoan supports Schoeffel and Meleisea's view. A. Wendt (1983) argued that "[i]n our culture it has always been taboo to discuss sexual matters publicly or freely or in mixed company. The Church's strict Victorianism merely reinforced this" (p. 13). In addition, Wendt clearly believes that Freeman erred in his argument regarding sexual mores, as is evident in the following passage:

> he is correct in stating that we place a great priority on female virginity, we institutionalize it in the taupou, we forbid pre-marital and extra-marital sex and promiscuity. *But it does not mean that a lot of all these various types of sex do not go on.* As in other societies, what we preach publicly to be our standard or morality does not necessarily reflect how we actually behave. There are a great deal of double standards in all societies. In this instance, *Freeman accepts too readily the evidence of our elders, the guardians of our public morality, who, if they are really human, often break, clandestinely, the very standards they set up.* . . . Even in the 1920s Samoa wasn't anywhere near "all virginity," as it were. (p. 14, italics added)

Wendt explained Freeman's error in the following way: "The easily discernible flaws in Freeman's book stem from its polemical form. To prove Mead wrong some of his claims tend towards exaggeration and idealisation. (This idealisation is also perhaps the result of his profound trust in us)" (p. 14).

It is most curious that Freeman's (1983) own evidence clearly shows that virginity was not strictly enforced even in the 1960s. Only 73% of his sample of 43 teenagers were virgins, a figure that is consistent with the historical trajectory of the social change we have traced in the last three chapters. Moreover, among 19-year-olds, only 40% of his sample were still virgins—hardly representative of a well-enforced norm. Freeman (1991) inadvertently acknowledged that his research supports Mead's findings on the issue of premarital sex, when he wrote that "Mead's own data . . . 'reveal' that 52% of her sample of 25 [postpubertal] girls were virgins, *a conclusion not significantly differently from my own*" (p. 120, italics added). He appears to have missed the implications of such a statement (i.e., that 48% were not virgins) because he simply went on to claim that Mead's data were "*quite at odds* with her misinformed statements about the prevalence in Samoa of premarital promiscuity" (p. 120).

The most obvious conclusion one can draw on the matter is that Freeman must be blind to the evidence on this issue, and its implications, because of the "mission" he has undertaken to rescue Samoan honor, as defined for him by his Samoan associates who entreated him to "correct [Mead's] mistaken depiction" of their culture and ethos (Freeman, 1983, p. xv). If Freeman's representation of Mead's account is erroneous, what then did she write? First, let us see how she gauged the impact of missionaries at the time.

Mead said that "there is a definite inverse correlation between residence at home and chastity" (p. 147), although she did not conduct any statistical tests on her data. When we turn to Appendix V of her book (p. 285) we find a table of figures that allows us to evaluate this statement. From the information provided in this table it is possible to conduct these statistical tests and to use residence in the pastor's household as an operationalization of Christian influence on traditional premarital behavior. I conducted these tests and have provided the results in Tables 6.1 and 6.2. In these procedures, residence in a pastor's household is the independent variable and heterosexual experience is the dependent variable.

In Table 6.1 we can see the statistically significant association (Phi = .37) between these variables in terms of the pattern of cell frequencies. Most obvious is the finding that 10 (62.5%) of those not living with the pastor had heterosexual experience, whereas 7 (77.8%) of those living

TABLE 6.1
An Examination of the Influence of Christianity on Premarital Sexual Behavior: Mead's 25 Postpuberty Informants

Count *Column Percentage* *Total Percentage* *Adjusted Residual*		*Residence in Pastor's Household*	
		Yes	*No*
Heterosexual experience	Yes	2 22.2% 8% − 1.9	10 62.5% 40% + 1.9
	No	7 77.8% 28% + 1.9	6 37.5% 24% − 1.9

Chi-Square:
Pearson = 3.74, $p < .05$.
Fisher's Exact Test, $p = .06$.
Phi = .37, $p < .05$.

TABLE 6.2
An Examination of the Influence of Christianity on Premarital Sexual Behavior: Mead's Informants 1 Year or More Past Puberty

Count *Column Percentage* *Total Percentage* *Adjusted Residual*		*Residence in Pastor's Household*	
		Yes	*No*
Heterosexual experience	Yes	1 16.7% 5.6% − 2.7	10 83.3% 55.6% + 2.7
	No	5 83.3% 27.8% + 2.7	2 16.7% 11.1% − 2.7

Chi-Square:
Pearson = 7.48, $p < .01$.
Fisher's Exact Test, $p = .01$.
Phi = .64, $p < .01$.

with the pastor had no heterosexual experience. On the one hand, one might be inclined to dismiss these figures because chastity was a *requirement* for boarding with the pastor. On the other hand, if we look for a norm of sexual abstinence from the community, we do not find a strong one, because only 6 (37.5%) of those not boarding with the pastor had no heterosexual experience. Sociologically speaking, then, the fact that most of those not boarding with pastor had sexual experience suggests that the pastors, not the community, set the norm of sexual abstinence.

It is possible to examine the community norm regarding premarital sex more directly if we restrict the analysis to informants who were 1 year or more beyond puberty (defined by Mead as time since first menstruation). This is justified with Mead's statement that puberty was not the "immediate forerunner of sex experience. Perhaps a year, two or even three years would pass before a girl's shyness would relax, or her figure appeal to the roving eye of some older boy" (p. 146). Accordingly, in this analysis the variable "heterosexual experience" is less affected by biological factors.

When we conduct this analysis, the statistical relationship becomes much stronger, with the measure of association (Phi) jumping from .37 to .64 (Table 6.2). In this more biologically mature sample, 83.3% of those *not* living with the pastor had heterosexual experience, whereas 83.3% of those living with the pastor had no heterosexual experience. If we look for a norm of sexual abstinence from the community for this sample, we do not find one because only 16.7% of those living in the community (i.e., not boarding with the pastor) had no heterosexual experience. Indeed, in this case the *behavioral norm* is clearly with heterosexual experience, as Mead's generalizations suggest.

We can interpret these statistics to reflect the attempt by religious authorities to institute the norm of premarital chastity. They also suggest that chastity was *not the community norm*, especially for those 1 year or more past puberty. In other words, virginity was enforced mainly by the pastor, not by the community.

But what exactly did Mead write in deciphering these behaviors? Well, *nowhere* did Mead contend that the Samoans are "a people for whom free lovemaking is 'expected' among adolescent girls," as Freeman claimed (p. 240). Instead, she said that "free experimentation [was] *permitted*" (p. 150, italics added). In addition, she noted that this "permission" applied to the "average" or "plebian young people" she studied, but that the *taupou* was "excepted" (i.e., excluded from) from this "free and easy experimentation." In fact, she wrote that virginity "was a legal requirement for" the *taupou* (p. 98).[6] Quite clearly, the statistical analyses just cited support her contention that the typical "plebian" did engage in premarital sexual behavior.

On the other hand, there are several passages from *Coming of Age* that are questionable. As we review these, it becomes clear that Mead must shoulder some of the blame with respect to the mythology now surrounding the sexual content of her book (cf. Feinberg, 1988). Among her references to her informants' sex lives, we see Mead's tendency to embellish her account with flowery prose, presumably to maintain the interest of her nonacademic audience. From an academic point of view, her descriptions sometimes amount to overstatements and it is clear from her other references to sexual practices that not all of her informants did all of the things she described. Indeed, her use of anecdotes often create the impression that certain practices were more common than was likely the case. Among her more embellished passages are the following:

> As the dawn begins . . . lovers slip home from trysts beneath the palm trees. (p. 14)
>
> . . . then at last there is only the mellow thunder of the reef and the whisper of lovers, as the village rests until dawn. (p. 19)[7]

---

[6]Mead's sense about the complexity of Samoan sexual mores is evident with her remark that the Samoan "attitude towards virginity is a curious one" (p. 98).

[7]Undoubtedly, these first two incidents happened, but it is unlikely that they occurred on a nightly basis.

> To live as a girl with many lovers as long as possible and then marry in one's village, near one's own relatives and to have many children, these were uniform and satisfying ambitions. (p. 157)[8]

> Familiarity with sex, and the recognition of a need of a technique to deal with sex as an art, have produced a scheme of personal relations in which there are no neurotic pictures, no frigidity, no impotence, except as a result of severe illness, and the capacity for intercourse only once in a night is counted as senility. (p. 151)[9]

> Samoans rate romantic love and fidelity in terms of days or weeks at most, and are inclined to scoff at tales of life-long devotion. (p. 155)[10]

But in her book we can also find credible descriptions and analyses of the Samoan sexual ethos. For example, she submitted that for Samoans

> sex is a natural and pleasurable thing; the freedom with which it may be indulged in is *limited by* just one consideration, *social status*. Chiefs' daughters and chiefs' wives should indulge in no extra-marital experiments. Responsible adults, heads of households and mothers of families should have too many important matters on hand to leave them much time for casual amorous adventures. *Everyone in the community agrees about the matter*, the only dissenters are the missionaries who dissent so vainly that their protests are unimportant. *But as soon as sufficient sentiment gathers about the missionary attitude with its European standard of sex behaviour, the need for choice, the forerunner of conflict, will enter in Samoa society.* (pp. 201–202, italics added)

We can see in this passage Mead's record of the resistance of Samoans in relinquishing a more pleasurable aspect of their traditional culture, as well as her prediction that the missionaries would eventually prevail. From the testimony of Samoan scholars presented earlier, it appears that the missionaries have still been only partially successful in altering *actual* behavior. Nevertheless, they seem to have been more effective in producing a consensus about the *ideals* of continence.

---

[8]These are many ambitions to place together in one generalization. Clearly, they did not all apply to those in the pastor's house.

[9]Obviously Mead was not qualified to make such clinical judgments, especially epidemiological conclusions regarding all of the inhabitants of the villages she studied. She probably picked up the notions of technique and stamina from boasting (male?) informants and took liberties in drawing the clinical conclusions.

[10]This statement was prefaced with the observation that she found "only one example of prolonged and intense passion . . . in the three villages" she studied (p. 155).

Mead also appears to have understood the way in which sexual relations were socially organized, and she classified these relations as follows:

> Besides formal marriage there are only two types of sex relations which receive any formal recognition from the community—[a] love affairs between unmarried young people . . . whether leading to marriage or merely a passing diversion; and [b] adultery.
>
> Between the unmarried there are three forms of relationship: [a] the clandestine encounter, "under the palm trees," [b] the published elopement, *Avaga*, and [c] the ceremonious courtship in which the boy "sits before the girl" . . . (p. 89)

This description of the first two forms of sex relations between the unmarried reveals that those who engaged in them faced several obstacles that did not facilitate the "free love" atmosphere she ostensibly promoted. Instead, it appears that she was describing the freedom more from the perspective of some of her informants, than from a community consensus that simply called for people to "look the other way" (cf. Schoeffel & Meleisea, 1983). It appears that the clandestine encounters had to be just that—done in secret—and they were restricted to "those of humbler birth" (pp. 99–100). In describing how the young woman dealt with these circumstances, Mead remarked that all of "the adult and near-adult world is hostile, spying upon her love affairs in its more circumspect sophistication, supremely not to be trusted. No one is to be trusted who is not immediately engaged in *similarly hazardous* adventures" (p. 68, italics added). Moreover, children apparently took sport in trying to catch young lovers in the act "under the palms" (pp. 135–136). The hazards presumably were associated with gossip and gaining a reputation as "promiscuous" (e.g., p. 181). Nevertheless, an apparently elaborate system existed by which a *soa* (a friend—a confidant and "ambassador"; pp. 89–90) arranged for two would-be lovers to meet surreptitiously.

The second form of sex relation was apparently less common, as Mead described:

> Elopements are much less frequent than the clandestine love affairs because the girl takes far more risk. She publicly renounces her often nominal claims to virginity; she embroils herself with her family, who in former times, and occasionally even today, would beat her soundly and shave off her hair. Nine times out of ten, her lover's only motive is vanity and display . . . (pp. 103–104)

Again, in both of these forms of sex relations, it does not appear that anything approaching a free love ethos prevailed. Those who advocate the mythology that Mead's book describes such an ethos would do well to give *Coming of Age* a careful reading.

We now have a much better picture of what Mead actually wrote in *Coming of Age* about the sexual behavior of her informants. Freeman seems to be inaccurate in much of his representation of what she wrote. Moreover, the mythology that this is simply a book about adolescent sexuality is just that—fiction. Although Mead discussed intimate details of her informants' lives, there is far more to the book than this, as we have seen in her description of the coming of age of young Samoans.

To return to the main concern in this book, Mead's coming-of-age thesis emerges from the examination given here as entirely plausible. It has not been seriously contradicted by any evidence, notwithstanding Freeman's often selective use of evidence and recurrent misrepresentation of her position. Indeed, "Mead's Samoa" fits with a trajectory of social change that one would expect for the island of Ta'u, as it came under increasing missionary influence. Moreover, on the basis of the evidence examined in this book, Mead's record of the experiences of her young female informants stands as valid in its basic details.

CHAPTER SEVEN

Coming of Age in Contemporary Samoa

WESTERN INFLUENCE AND THE CULTURAL DISENFRANCHISEMENT OF SAMOAN YOUTH

What has been forgotten in the furor surrounding Freeman's critique of Mead's study is the plight of young Samoans currently struggling to come of age. As we have seen, the young people of Samoa have lost most of the institutions that once guided them on a sure path from childhood to adulthood. The degeneration of these institutions began when the missionaries took it upon themselves to drive "Satan" from the islands. Inadvertently acting as the "shocktroops of capitalism," many missionaries set out to instill values and attitudes conducive with wage labor and capital accumulation.

The changes they set in motion have been accelerating in latter part of the 20th century with the entrenchment of mass consumption, mass production, mass education, and mass communications. Moreover, mass transportation has removed protective barriers from Samoan culture, both physical and psychological, so the basic conception of the realm of possibility has been drastically altered for the young Samoan. Most certainly, missionary influences are not responsible for all that has happened in the past 150 years to young Samoans, but the part they played in setting the stage is significant nonetheless.[1]

[1]See Oliver (1961) for a broader, political-economy discussion of historical influences in Western Samoa. Gailey (1987) provided a similar discussion of Tonga, bringing out gender issues, as did Lockwood (1993) in reference to Tahiti.

In a sense, the crux of the current "youth problem" in Samoa is that although the *conception* of the realm of possibility has changed for many young people in Samoa, the *reality* of what is possible has not changed significantly. What emerged from the sociohistorical analysis presented earlier is that at the heart of these changes is a "cultural disenfranchisement" of young people by which they have been robbed of their rich cultural heritage, and given poor "Western" economic prospects in return.

For example, the propitious institution that once saw to the coming of age of young women (the *aualuma*) was stripped of its mandate soon after the missionaries were securely established, probably because it offended missionaries' puritanical and patriarchal values regarding the autonomy of women—sexual and otherwise. Young women of contemporary Samoa are not only denied this aspect of their heritage, they also face a denial that there was anything different for Samoan women before contact with the West. Thus, they have lost part of their cultural heritage and been misled about their loss. As is seen in this chapter, there is now a "crisis" in gender roles in contemporary Samoa associated with a loss in the status of women introduced by Western religious and economic influences. Interestingly, it is this turn of events in which Mead's work has been caught, because Freeman took up the cause of a denial of Samoa's non-Christian past.

In addition, changes initiated by the missionaries that set the stage for the introduction of the wage economy eventually led to the disintegration of the auspicious institution that saw to the coming of age of young men (the *'aumaga*). In 1928, Mead predicted that should the *'aumaga* ever be disbanded "Samoan village life would have to be entirely reorganized," because the entire village depends on their work and support of ceremonies (p. 76). Moreover, Mead (1928) predicted that Western influences would be devastating for Samoan culture:

> economic instability, poverty, the wage system, the separation of the worker from his land and his tools, modern warfare, industrial disease, the abolition of leisure, the irksomeness of bureaucratic government—these have not yet invaded an island without resources worth exploiting. (pp. 276–277)

It is difficult to say what the ultimate outcome of these changes will be, but it is hard to be optimistic about how well things will turn out in the short run. What is clear, as is seen later, is that many young people in contemporary Samoa no longer have the benefit of the benign transition from childhood to adulthood described by Mead. The structures that have replaced the traditional coming-of-age institutions leave much to be desired in terms of guiding the young from childhood to adulthood.

Unfortunately, along with other Western practices, Samoan society has increasingly adopted the practice of making childhood and adolescence into a period of emotional and economic dependency. In doing so, many of the basic rights and privileges of its youngest people have been taken away. Meanwhile, many adults themselves have become dependent on Western economic, social, political, and religious institutions. Consequently, the *quid pro quo* (reciprocal exchange) that existed between young people and adults in precontact culture has been upset. Indeed, as we see, young people have lost much in the span of a few generations, particularly much of the cultural heritage that once saw to their basic emotional and material needs. What they have lost has been replaced for many with unfulfillable dreams imported through Western institutions.

Analysis is restricted in this chapter to the situation currently facing young people in Western Samoa. It is necessary to consider Western Samoa separate from American Samoa because the two countries are distinct political entities. As such, they have experienced different economic and political forces over the century. The islands of Samoa were divided between the colonial powers of Germany and the United States in 1900. Upolu and Savai'i (now Western Samoa) went under German rule, whereas Tutuila and the Manu'a Group went under American rule. The latter constitute American Samoa, still a U.S. territory, while the former passed under New Zealand rule during World War I, and became an independent state in 1962.

In terms of the extent of Western influence, although no region is untouched, in Western Samoa, the island of Savai'i has been less affected by the modern wage economy than has the island of Upolu. The greatest Western influence on Upolu is in Apia area, the capital city (and only city) with a population of 45,000. American Samoa has been highly "Americanized," especially around Pago Pago harbor, the capital area—there are no cities per se in American Samoa, rather parts of the island of Tutuila are becoming "suburban." More remote villages and islands in the Manu'a Islands (comprising Ofu, Olesega, and Ta'u) retain some of their traditional lifestyle, but less so than in more remote areas of Western Samoa.

The common thread of their joint Samoan heritage remains, but at present they are on two distinct trajectories into the future. In many respects, those coming of age in American Samoa are far better off materially than their "poorer cousins" in Western Samoa. There are more educational opportunities, including free primary and secondary education as well as opportunities to attend U.S. universities. Because all American Samoans are also American nationals, there is the option of emigrating to the United States, especially Hawaii or California. In addition, many males join the U.S. armed forces (cf. North, 1991). In contrast, Western

Samoa ranks close to Bangladesh in terms of gross national product (GNP), although its largely intact subsistence economy makes the comparison invidious (Meleisea & Meleisea, 1980).

In terms of social problems, there does not appear to be an unusually high suicide rate (King, 1981) or crime rate in American Samoa. Among those who emigrate, some develop problems associated with living in U.S. inner cities, and those who have returned recently have brought back the gang mentality found among some minority youths in the United States. Consequently, there is some current concern on Tutuila about an increase in violence associated with this gang mentality. Incidentally, some of the gang mentality is now finding its way to Western Samoa via American Samoa.

In view of these differences, I am not dealing in detail with the problems of coming of age in contemporary American Samoa because these problems now very much resemble those found among the young in many parts of the United States. Coming of age in American Samoa certainly has changed dramatically since the time of Mead's study, and consequently any research conducted there now would not shed much light on the controversy over her work. But, in choosing between which "coming of age" to discuss in this book, I have selected the situation in Western Samoa because the problems facing the young there appear more pressing than those facing the young in American Samoa. For a treatment of the situation in contemporary American Samoa, see Holmes and Holmes (1992).

COMING OF AGE IN WESTERN SAMOA, 1990

One hundred and sixty years of contact with the West has dramatically altered daily life in Western Samoa, even in remote villages. As was seen earlier, the missionaries set out beginning in the 1830s to change the values and attitudes associated with fundamental notions like individualism versus collectivism, and profit versus sharing. Then, with some difficulty, entrepreneurs introduced practices such as wage labor, making way for capital accumulation (see Oliver, 1961, for Samoan resistance to these influences). As we also saw, generational replacement has facilitated the process of social change, for it was by gradually affecting each subsequent generation that the "heathen" traditions of old Samoa were gradually transformed or eradicated. This gradual change meant that Mead still witnessed many precontact practices in the 1920s. Now, many struggle with the contradictions of trying to honor the remnants of old values from *fa'a Samoa* while simultaneously living with the realities of the new practices.

O'Meara (1990, pp. 69–70) provided a detailed account of how life has changed over the span of just one generation in a village he recently studied on the island of Savai'i. Included in these changes are: an increase in population,[2] less isolation, more travel (to Apia, American Samoa, and New Zealand), "new needs and desires," a "perception of scarcity" of material goods, more theft, and more family dispersion.[3] Many of these changes have led to a decreased sense of morale and an increased sense of frustration, particularly among the young who find certain aspects of village life less than satisfactory. As Meleisea and Meleisea (1980) argued, each "year thousands of young people graduate from secondary school but few find jobs and most feel that village farming is a poor return for their years in school" (p. 37).

In reference to how the "new" religion has transformed life in the village he studied on the island of Savai'i, O'Meara provided the following description of life in one of the more "fundamentalist" villages:

> Some church rules have a significant effect on village life. The Methodists are rather puritanical compared to most other denominations in Samoa. They allow precious little in the way of entertainment. The Church does not permit dancing at night (and discourages it during the day). It bans card playing of any kind, day or night, and strictly forbids the drinking of alcohol. . . . During the Christmas and New Year's holidays . . . several entrepreneurial families ran bingo games . . . by the light of gas lanterns in their homes or on the cricket pitch. The pastor banned the popular games after only two nights. (p. 44)

Admittedly, this village represents an extreme to which religious influence has transformed life in some villages, and the extent to which

---

[2]Meleisea and Meleisea (1980) noted that "the population of [Western Samoa] has grown from early 19th century estimates of 40,000 to approximately 160,00 in 1977, with something like a 3% annual increase. The consequence is a growing strain on land and inner reef marine resources" (pp. 36–37). From more recent records it is evident that the rate of population growth is declining. Between 1966 and 1971, the population increased by about 12%; between 1971 and 1976, the increase was only 4%; between 1976 and 1981, the increase was 3%; and between 1981 and 1986 it was only 1% (cf. Department of Statistics, Western Samoa, 1989). Although this "plateauing" should relieve some strain, it means that there is a population "bulge" now coming of age. In 1966, only 24% of the population were between the ages of 15 and 29 (31,510 people). As of 1986, 31% of the population were in this age range (48,495 people).

[3]O'Meara noted that a "generation ago families were still united, in good times and in bad. . . . Today migration is often expected and in many cases desired—yet it is also feared. Parents become separated from their children, friends are lost, and brothers and sisters scatter as they disappear into awaiting airplanes" (p. 70). He also noted that some of this family separation is caused by the necessity of family members going off to engage in wage labor to support their families. It is not uncommon for fathers, and especially sons, to work in Apia or American Samoa, but to only visit their families every few weeks.

Samoans no longer enjoy various forms of carefree activity and physical releases—such as dancing. Still, there are almost 24,000 practicing Methodists in Western Samoa (Meleisea, 1987a, p. 67). It is interesting to note in this context that Mead devoted a chapter to the importance of the *siva* (dance) "in the development of individuality and the compensation for repression of personality in other spheres of life" (p. 121).

Despite the prohibitions on hedonistic activities, some young people still engage in these emotional and physical outlets as part of a village "underground." O'Meara described some of this:

> All of these prohibitions apply to villagers wherever they are, but slackness sometimes creeps in when people travel to Salelologa, Apia, or overseas. Young men sometimes even hold clandestine poker games or drinking parties behind the village, though *matai* almost never attend these affairs. Villagers are generally willing to overlook breaches of proper conduct *as long as violators remain discreet*. If misconduct leads to a public outburst or to fighting, however, the village council imposes heavy fines on offenders. (pp. 44–45, italics added)

Many young people experience these restrictions as oppressive, particularly those who compare their own lives with the lives of young people in Western culture as portrayed in movies and magazines. For example, apparently many find the nightly curfew that has been instituted in most villages to be unreasonable (cf. Freeman, 1983, pp. 261–262). To violate the curfew brings a sometimes heavy fine for all except the *matai*, who are exempt because it is their duty to patrol the village (it begins at 9 or 10 p.m., depending on the village). O'Meara recorded that the curfew is in place "to assure that schoolchildren get to bed early; to prevent theft, *clandestine meetings of unmarried people*, and other elicit behaviors that might go undetected in the darkness . . ." (p. 56, italics added).

In relation to "Mead's Samoa," then, life in contemporary Samoa is obviously quite different—more repressive—as Freeman inadvertently brought to our attention. He also inadvertently brought to our attention the *deteriorating* situation facing young people there. As was seen in chapter 5, the *'aumaga* and *aualuma* now exist in name only, with few exceptions. Consequently, the primary village supports that once gave a sense of meaning and future purpose to the lives of the young have weakened. And, increasingly, the generations that once lived together in cooperation and mutual benefit now find family relationships increasingly strained. As Leacock (1987) argued, "the immediate source of stress for many young people is a perceived lack of empathy and concern on the part of stern and demanding parents, while parents who become angry over the perceived lack of proper respect on the part of the young may be excessively abusive'' (p. 182).

Hence, many of the young are in no-win situations. They are formally educated, and informally socialized, to expect certain material and emotional gratifications, but their prospects for realizing these expectations are often not good. There is now less opportunity for those who try to take the nontraditional, wage-labor route. For those who do take the traditional route, a less than satisfactory situation is increasingly encountered. In 1980, Meleisea and Meleisea characterized these problems in the following manner:

> The greatly increased educational facilities which have been available for Samoan children since the 1950s have created rising expectations among the younger generation, a dissatisfaction with village life and a longing for wage employment in Apia or a chance to emigrate . . . Returning migrants are another source of dissatisfaction with village life and the predominantly subsistence economy, as well as a source of new values and aspirations. (p. 37)

More recently, O'Meara (1990) summarized these problems by saying that ''the cycle of *tautua* is broken'' (p. 162). With this expression he meant that the traditional *quid pro quo* that existed in precontact society between the ''young'' and the ''adult'' has disintegrated, as he explained:

> The system of authority and service is organized largely on seniority—those who are younger serve and obey those who are older. Ironically, this kind of system is stable only as long as the participants are sure that it will continue. As long as the system is closed and the cycle secure, young people perceive their service as a tolerable burden, knowing that one day they will, in their turn, command the service of others.
>
> The cycle of *tautua* has been broken in the minds of many young people today. *New technology and a market economy make individual production, profit, and accumulation of wealth possible*. Many young people seek their futures in wage labour outside the village or even overseas, and they doubt that their own service will ever be repaid by a younger generation. In these circumstances, they no longer serve so gladly. (p. 162, italics added)

One attempt to augment the sense of meaning and identity among young males was to increase the number of *matai* titles granted. According to O'Meara (1990), the ''number of *matai* has been growing rapidly over the last three decades, so that now most adult men hold titles. In rural areas such as Savai'i, 75 percent of all men 21 years and older are matai.[4] That is more than double the percentage of thirty years ago" (p. 151). But apparently this "oversupply" has had the effect of diminishing the importance of, and respect for, these titles. For example, many young men have been given titles without the traditional "apprenticeship" and therefore lack many of the skills necessary to exercise their power wisely. Evidently, some of these less qualified *matai* are involved in more conflicts with both elder *matai* and younger untitled men, in part because some of these young *matai* apparently do not conform to the consensus-building conventions of *fa'a Samoa* (cf. Leacock, 1987).

So, where does this leave the young person who is coming of age and looking to develop a sense of identity as an adult?

Freeman would have us believe that young people in Samoa have always had problems with their adolescence because of the nature of traditional Samoan society, but many observers disagree with him (Leacock, 1987). In her analysis of the problems facing young people in contemporary Samoa, Leacock argued that Freeman has been remiss in his "failure to deal seriously with the complexities of recent socio-historical change" (p. 177). In addition, she contended that "it is a serious misrepresentation of the situation to say that youth difficulties simply follow from the authoritarianism of the Samoan past. *Instead they follow from the fact that the nature of youth as a life period has been transformed in many ways*" (p. 186, italics added). Similarly, in response to Freeman's citation of suicide statistics, Shankman (1983) argued that a "more plausible explanation might lie in the modernization of Western Samoa and its interaction with traditional Samoan culture, since there are different rates of suicide for Western Samoa and American Samoa, where the suicide rate is considerably lower" (p. 52).

The issue of suicide and its recent rise in Western Samoa strikes at the heart of the dilemma facing those now coming of age in Samoa. Moreover, when we examine the nature of the suicide problem, we see more clearly a principal flaw in Freeman's critique of Mead's coming-of-age thesis.

The most comprehensive analyses of suicide in Western Samoa were conducted by Bowles (1985) and MacPherson and MacPherson (1985). According to Bowles, the suicide rate was low in the early 1960s (about 2 per 100,000) and it rose slowly until the mid-1970s (about 10 per 100,000). After this, it rose dramatically in the early 1980s and began a decline again by the mid-1980s. Averaged between 1981 and 1983, Bowles reported a rate of 22.6 for the entire population, with the following breakdown based on age and gender: For males, the total rate was 31.3, but for males 15 to 24 years of age it was 71.0 and for males 25 to 34 it was 75.6; for females the total rate was 13.3, but for females 15 to 24 years

[4]According to O'Meara (1990) "less than 0.02% of all *matai* are women" (p. 33).

of age it was 35.8 and for females 25 to 34, it was 20.4 (note that the actual total number suicides is 106 for 3 years). More recent figures reveal that in spite of a prevention program and an apparent decline, the problem persists. In 1990, there were 27 confirmed suicides, constituting a rate of 16.9 for a population of 160,000 (Aiavao, 1991).

Based on their sociohistorical analysis of Samoan culture, MacPherson and MacPherson (1985) concluded that although forms of suicide have probably existed throughout the history of Samoan culture, "suicide . . . does not seem to have been an institutionalized response" (p. 37) to problems. They also concluded that the recent suicides constitute forms of "anomic" suicide. In a similar vein to the analyses presented here, MacPherson and MacPherson developed a "blocked opportunity model" that argues that suicides since the mid-1970s can be explained in terms of rising expectations regarding affluence and personal freedom produced by mass education, the media, the wage economy, and emigration prospects. These expectations have been unmet for large numbers of youth who face limited opportunity for paid employment, and who in the mid-1970s had their emigration possibilities severely limited. But, instilled psychologically with alternative conceptions of what life could be like, many are now forced to live in villages with limited economic prospects as well as with families demanding a blind obedience to traditional customs. Accordingly, many of the cases that MacPherson and MacPherson examined involved a thwarted attempt by a young person to exercise some type of autonomy disapproved of by a parent or a *matai*. Hence, many of the suicides and attempted suicides appear to constitute a "statement" by a frustrated individual against what is perceived as an intransigent traditional authority figure. Evidently, much of this desire to exert independence has been stimulated by exposure to Western influence, especially education and the mass media. It is of interest to note Mead's predictions regarding the problems that would emerge in Samoa when individual choice was demanded by the young (e.g., 1928, pp. 169–171).

O'Meara provided a similar explanation for the recent rise in suicide:

> The correlation of the suicide epidemic with the rapid modernization of the post-independence era in Western Samoa is no accident. The desires and expectations of young people are changing very fast. Radios, movies, television, videos, and New Zealand-style education all give people new ideas and new dreams. . . . The closeness of that other world sometimes makes patience difficult, yet the actual pace of social and economic change makes the fulfilment of these expectations very unlikely. Rapid change alone is not the problem. Suicide is uncommon in American Samoa, where change has been far more rapid and dramatic than in Western Samoa, and where half the population is made up of migrants from Western Samoa. The real

> problem appears to be *uneven* change, specifically the lag between young people's growing expectations and the social and economic realities in which they live. (p. 111)

Given the no-win situation that many young Samoans face, in a sense it is surprising that there have not been more suicides. It is also estimated, however, that about twice as many *unsuccessful* suicide attempts take place (Bowles, 1985, p. 17). More recent reports suggest that the frustration among the young is being manifested in other ways. For example, marijuana smoking has become "a problem in Western Samoan schools, especially in rural areas . . . Some schools [report that] drug abuse has replaced cigarette smoking and beer drinking as the main offence leading to expulsion" ("Drug Abuse Hits Schools," 1991). Foreboding a more serious problem, it has been reported that "Western Samoa's Police Commissioner . . . has called for the establishment of a special jail for young people" ("Special Youth Jail?," 1992).

We can put the problem of suicide in Samoa into perspective in two other ways.

First, it appears to have the qualities of an epidemic, which means that potentially there is a "cure." The peak of this epidemic in the early 1980s appeared to represent a "contagion" of collective behavior from which it became "fashionable" to drink the weedkiller "paraquat."[5] The death from this poison is agonizing and prolonged (sometimes more than a week), thereby ensuring that the authority figures "responsible" are made to suffer also. Of the 49 known suicides in 1981, 39 were from paraquat poisoning; in 1990, 19 of the 27 suicides were from paraquat (Aiavao, 1991). It is believed that many of the attempts are not genuine suicide attempts, but simply either a means of challenging authority or a passive–aggressive attempt to hurt someone. Apparently, some suicide victims take only a small amount, thinking that they will just get sick, but even a small amount of paraquat can result in death. Access to paraquat has still not been restricted, despite 277 known deaths from it since 1973 (Aiavao, 1991).

Second, we can compare Samoan suicide rates with those from other countries, and take lessons from this comparison. It is often said that Western Samoa has the highest rate in the world; in fact, even some guidebooks now make reference to it (e.g., Swaney, 1990). But, Samoa should not be singled out so readily. In point of fact, the suicide rate for young people increased in many countries around the world between the 1960s

[5]There is considerable evidence from U.S. studies that when a suicide is publicized by the media, the rate of suicide increases among people with similar characteristics to the person who committed suicide (Phillips, 1979; Stack, 1987).

and the 1980s, including major industrialized nations. In Canada, for example, it rose from 5.3 per 100,000 for 15- to 19-year-olds in 1960 to 20.2 in 1986, and from 12.3 for 20- to 24-year-olds in 1960 to 32.8 in 1986 (Beneteau, 1988). Moreover, if we look at Canada's indigenous population, we find a rate of 100 per 100,000 among Native Canadian men ages 15 to 19. This rate is stable and is clearly above the rate for Samoan men of the same age. No doubt, similarly high rates can be found among groups that have been disenfranchised in some way. But the rates should also be particularly high among those who have been culturally disenfranchised and who are attempting to come of age, as is the case with both Samoan and Native Canadian young people (cf. Rubinstein, 1985, on suicide in Micronesia).

From these two perspectives we can see that Samoa is not alone with its suicide problem, and that the remedy to this epidemic somehow lies with a lack of a "franchise." To effect a "cure," the questions that must be answered pertain to the exact nature of the relationship between suicide and the lack of a franchise, including how to "re-enfranchise" the young, given that without a franchise the young have no representatives of their own to speak for them on policy matters. I return to this issue later in this chapter.

These suicide statistics likely represent the "tip of the iceberg" with respect to the lack of personal meaning and sense of alienation experienced by many of the young. The alienation associated with this lack of meaning has been expressed by a number of Samoa's poets (Malifa, 1975; Petaia, 1980; A. Wendt, 1974). A. Wendt's (1973, 1977, 1979) novels capture some of this alienation and despair, as does a recent movie based on one of his novels (*Flying Fox and the Freedom Tree*; see Robie, 1991, for a review). The poem "Kidnapped" especially captures some of the feelings produced by an "alien" and alienating educational system (Petaia, cited in A. Wendt, 1974):

I was six when
Mama was careless
she sent me to school
alone
five days a week

One day I was
kidnapped by a band
of Western philosophers
armed with glossy-pictured
textbooks and
registered reputations
"Holder of B.A.
and M.A. degrees"

I was held
in a classroom
guarded by Churchill and Garibaldi
pinned-up on one wall
and
Hitler and Mao dictating
from the other
Guevara pointed a revolution
at my brains
from his "Guerilla Warfare"

Each three month term
they sent threats to
my Mama and Papa

Mama and Papa loved
their son and
paid ransom fees
each time

Each time
Mama and Papa grew
poorer and poorer
and my kidnappers grew
richer and richer
I grew whiter and
whiter

On my release
fifteen years after
I was handed
(among loud applause
from fellow victims)
a piece of paper
to decorate my walls
certifying my release

As just mentioned, one way in which many young people once "escaped" the frustrations of living in contemporary Western Samoa was to emigrate. Emigration from Western Samoa has been primarily to New Zealand, its colonial "ruler" since 1914. The Samoan community in New Zealand now numbers some 100,000 (Meleisea, 1987a, p. 161). For some time, the young could freely move to New Zealand to work temporarily, but in the mid-1970s the New Zealand government became concerned about "overstayers," and have since restricted work permits. Since then, immigration has been restricted to those who "have a guarantee of a job in New Zealand," or who qualify under a special quota system that allows 1,100 Western Samoans per year on family or humanitarian grounds

(Immigration Division, New Zealand, 1982). The resulting work scheme has led to a trickle of persons being admitted for temporary employment: 11 permits in the first year of the program (1977), none in 1983, and 3 in 1984 (Labour Department, Western Samoa, 1984). According to MacPherson and MacPherson (1985), this move by New Zealand has constituted a serious blow for many young people in terms of their plans and expectations, particularly because this period in New Zealand had come to constitute something of what E. Erikson (1968) called an "institutionalized moratorium," in this case a *Wanderschaft*, in much the same fashion that traveling to Europe constitutes one for young North Americans (cf. Norton, 1984).

This chapter began with the assertion that young people have been largely forgotten in the furor among social scientists over the Mead–Freeman controversy. But, of the limited attention given young people, young women have been given even shorter shrift. Indeed, there is an irony in the fact that Mead's study of a few female adolescents in the 1920s has led to so much attention being paid to the reputations of social scientists and so little attention being paid to young women struggling to come of age under the conditions just described. Moreover, in relation to young men, young women appear to have lost even more.

As was seen in chapters 4 and 5, young women have lost the organization—the *aualuma*—that, in precontact Samoan culture, gave them solidarity and semi-autonomous sexuality. In what appears to have been an attempt by missionaries to establish a patriarchal nuclear family structure with its associated morality, the role of women in Samoa was targeted for dramatic change. By the time of Mead's study, the chosen few who maintained their chastity were trained to be pastors' wives in the boarding schools, whereas the remainder were left mainly on their own, forced to face an adult world that evidently was increasingly hostile to expressions of their autonomy and individuality. According to O'Meara (1990):

> contemporary Samoans apply a familiar 'double standard' toward unmarried males and females. Young, unmarried men are allowed (or even encouraged by each other) to have affairs (though only with unmarried women). The same activity is forbidden of girls, whose virginity and reputations are social assets as well as moral virtues. (pp. 107–108)

Young women also seem to have lost much of the moratorium period that Mead described, where they could enjoy themselves with a "time out" before taking on adult responsibilities and family commitments. O'Meara (1990) wrote that in the religiously conservative village he studied "young women are . . . closely guarded by other family members"

(p. 104) and that "women's daily activities are delineated partly with an eye on keeping [them] close to home" (p. 101). He also noted that most "families go to great lengths to guard and restrain their young girls. In the face of such constant chaperoning, most girls have to actively conspire in order to meet privately with a lover or a suitor" (p. 108). However, he also noted instances of premarital affairs and births, and he speculated that much of this constitutes a form of rebellion against parental authority and an attempt to hurt parents in a passive–aggressive manner, similar to the suicide attempts discussed earlier. His sources in that village told him that "sexual escapades of this kind are an increasing problem" (pp. 108–109).

O'Meara also gave us a glimpse of what daily life is now like for women living in Western Samoan villages in terms of the division of labor that has evolved:

> Males of all ages find more time to play or rest than females. In the late afternoons the young men and boys can usually be found relaxing or playing cricket on the village green, playing rugby on a sand flat exposed by the tide near the lagoon shore, or playing volley ball at the school grounds. A few young women join in the volleyball, but most remain at home, cooking and tending to the many children or countless household chores. Even into advanced middle age, women are expected to keep busy (though not all do). Meanwhile, their husbands often sleep, play dominoes, or discuss the intricacies of the latest social or political manoeuvre, leaving their own household duties half-completed. Women sometimes express resentment towards men for this unequal division of labor. (p. 70)

We can see evidence that as power shifted in social relations over this century, at the microlevel of domestic roles, men appear to have gained at the expense of women. Furthermore, at the more macrolevel of political participation and power, women appear to have gained little from recent cultural change. Again, O'Meara gave us a glimpse of this:

> Like men, women gain more control over their lives as they grow older. Even if a woman outlives her parents, however, she still may not fully control her own life until she is an elderly widow. There are exceptions, of course, when a woman rises to authority in her own household, her extended family, or even in village affairs. I know of no such cases in Vaega, however [the village he studied]. A very few women ever rise to national political prominence, but even though these women are exceptionally talented, they usually gain their initial opportunities through genealogical or marital relationships with powerful men. (p. 70)

With few women in positions of formal power to speak for them, it is unlikely that the rights—the franchise—of young women coming of age will improve. Thus, we can identify a "crisis" in gender roles, whereby the gulf or disparity between the status of women and men in Samoa has widened, with women experiencing a sharp decline in status. This crisis seems to be contributing to the growing social malaise there, particularly among young women.

DEALING WITH AN UNFOLDING TRAGEDY FACING WESTERN SAMOAN YOUTH

Leacock (1987) is one of the few social scientists to have focused on the problems facing contemporary young Samoans. She concluded that "all indications are that adolescence has indeed changed from being a period of relatively little stress . . . to being highly charged with stress manifested by delinquency and suicide" (p. 181). Freeman somehow missed this in his critique of Mead's work. But, as has been seen throughout this book, his critique is flawed because he misrepresented crucial elements of both her position and Samoan cultural history. Inevitably, then, the "mission" he set for himself will fail.

In spite of these misspent efforts, there is at least one positive consequence of the worldwide attention that Freeman has drawn to Samoa; namely, awareness of the desperate situation facing many young Western Samoans attempting to come of age in a culture that has been inundated with Western influences. In the first part of this chapter, we examined this serious situation. In this last part of the chapter, I make recommendations regarding what might be done to alleviate it.

As is the case in many Third World nations, young people have been culturally disenfranchised because of the "imperialism" of Western religious and economic practices. In this light, perhaps the best that may come of the Mead–Freeman controversy is an awareness of the trends that have robbed young Samoans of much of their cultural heritage. Then, perchance, the attention paid to Freeman (and his attack on Mead and American anthropology) can be diverted to finding solutions for the very real problems facing those now "coming of age in Samoa."

Policy Recommendations

Leacock (1987) noted that the problems facing young Samoans are shared by young people in many countries where "traditional cultures" have been seriously distorted by the imposition of international capitalism: "Elsewhere in the world, delinquency, suicide, and other escalating problems of Third World youth are seen as arising from new social and economic conflicts, and from the malaise and hopelessness associated with such difficulties as school failure, unemployment, and loss of cultural identity'' (p. 178).

Simply stated, the introduction of capitalism into ''traditional cultures'' often culturally disenfranchises the young because it breeds individualism and selfishness. With a decline in community orientation among adults, the young are left with less guidance, and fewer of the fruits of collective labor are shared with them.

In order to avoid the problems engendered by Western economic and cultural imperialism, ideas for the solutions to many of the problems discussed here should come from within Western Samoa, so it is perhaps presumptuous for a Westerner such as myself to ''interfere'' in this respect. On the other hand, with due respect I offer some of my thoughts on this matter, accumulated as I investigated the Mead–Freeman controversy. Accordingly, I discuss what I think might be done in rectifying the transformations that have taken place in Western Samoa over the past 150 years in the areas of religion, education, and the economy.

Religion

The missionaries were obviously well intentioned, but it is clear from what we saw previously that their influence is partly responsible for the situation now confronting many young Samoans. In this light, the responsibility falls to some extent upon the clergy now in Samoa to address the cultural disenfranchisement of young Samoans in whatever ways they can. For example, given their integration deep into the life of most villages in Samoa, it can be argued that the onus is on pastors and religious authorities to restore the dignity previously accorded to coming of age, and to re-institutionalize structures such as the *'aumaga* and *aualuma*. Energy and resources could be directed toward providing more guidance and structure to those coming of age, thereby enhancing the sense of meaning and purpose in life of young people. These leaders should take heed of their reputation, as described by Crocombe (1989): ''Christians have not necessarily practised all they preached, and allegations of public exploitation by ultraconservative churches in Samoa . . . contain elements of truth. The average stomach girth of religious ministers . . . is sufficient indication'' (p. 74).

My recommendation is for contemporary religious leaders in Samoa, who owe their callings to the efforts of missionaries with a ''vision,'' to embark upon a new ''mission'' with a new ''vision'' —to save the young from the cultural disenfranchisement engendered by the international economy. In view of the evidence presented in this book, the ''new missionaries'' could set out to re-institutionalize benign and meaningful passages to adulthood, replacing the institutions ravaged by the "old mission."

Education

Most contemporary institutions in Western Samoa are based on the British model, by way of New Zealand's influence. This is certainly the case with the educational system,[6] which has been criticized because of its irrelevance to Samoan culture. Writing in the 1970s, Pitt and MacPherson (1974) said the following about that system:

> While Western Samoa was a Trust Territory administered by New Zealand, the philosophy behind the education system did not promote maximum teaching efficiency. It was primarily concerned with giving Samoans a European-style, basically humanistic education. The Samoan context was not taken into account nearly enough. For example, children used cultural materials based on meaningless foreign examples—like the readers which told of robins in the snow or train trips to London. Undue emphasis was placed on the use of English which even the teachers did not fully understand. (pp. 99–100)

Efforts have been made recently to correct this inadequacy. For instance, with respect to relevance of curriculum, currently under way is a "Samoanization of assessment procedures and more comprehensive curricula at Junior Secondary and Senior Secondary Levels" (Department of Economic Development, Western Samoa, 1987, p. 173). One of the five explicitly stated objectives and goals of educational policy is "to prepare Samoans particularly the youth to handle and appreciate the challenges and pressures of an increasingly modern society" (Department of Economic Development, Western Samoa, 1987, p. 180). At the primary level, an objective is "to cater to [students'] personal and moral development so that they are induced to think rather than by rote as previously done," while at the secondary level an objective is to facilitate the pursual of "a 'student's own' respective area of choice" (p. 181).

More recently, a system has been adopted whereby students are graded on a 9-point scale in each subject. This system eliminates the conception of pass–fail, and introduces the notions of satisfactory–unsatisfactory ("Education Director," 1991). The intention is to stop the practice of label-

[6]Education in Western Samoa is not compulsory. As of 1981, 81.8% of the 5 to 19 age group were in school, up from 72.1% 10 years earlier. In terms of an age breakdown, 81.1% of 5- to 9-year-olds were in school in 1981, as were 97.5% 10- to 14-year-olds and 64.9% of 15- to 19-year-olds. The largest increase in enrollment by age group was the 15- to 19-year-old group, 43.8% of whom were in school in 1971. In addition, many Samoans have been educated in New Zealand, particularly at the secondary and tertiary levels.

ling a student as a failure. The label of "failure" has serious consequences in any culture, but it is especially deleterious in a shame-oriented culture.

Several projects have been launched to deal with the problem of delivering a useful education to young Samoans. One such project, the "Intensification of Vocational and Skills Training Programme," has as its priority out-of-school youth who have high employment and skills potential. It also has the mandate to conduct market studies to assess the employability of youth. These apprenticeship plans, however, have been hampered by a lack of funds and a lack of skilled personnel who are willing to manage the program for the wages offered or to teach for the meagre remuneration the government can afford. One program had 83 apprentices in 1983 but only 60 by 1987 (Department of Economic Development, Western Samoa, 1987, p. 178); another, created by the Apprentice Act of 1972, had only two positions in 1984 (Labour Department, Western Samoa, 1984).

Thus, inadequate finances set up a "loop" whereby a problem feeds itself.[7] In fact, in 1985 the entire education budget was only 7.7665 million Western Samoan *tala* (about $4 million U.S.) and this constituted about 25% of the government expenditures for that year (Department of Economic Development, Western Samoa, 1987, p. 229). In Western societies, one school alone might operate on such a budget! Besides mission schools, the only major form of relief comes from the Peace Corps volunteers who make up a proportion of the 1,500 teachers who teach some 50,000 students (Douglas & Douglas, 1986, p. 510).

In 1984, the National University of Samoa was founded, but it has experienced difficulties getting on track as a degree-granting institution. As of 1987, it still provided only a University Preparatory Year to prepare students for undergraduate studies overseas, mainly in New Zealand, Australia, and Fiji (Department of Economic Development, Western Samoa, 1987, p. 129). By 1987, 201 students had graduated, with 126 moving on to university programs. Plans are in place to establish degree programs in education, commerce, accounting, arts, and science.[8] The University

[7]The bottom line of the problem facing the government in attempting to implement many policies is, of course, a lack of finances. For example, the Ministry of Youth, Sport, and Culture must function with little money beyond its own operating budget. Recently, two new programs were added, but they had meager budgets: the Sports and Cultural Development Programme for Youth was to receive 11,000 *tala* per year (about $5,000 U.S.), whereas the Youth Training program was to receive 77,000 *tala* in the first year and 27,000 in the second year (Department of Economic Development, Western Samoa, 1987, p. 195).

[8]If the National University of Samoa could expand to provide undergraduate and graduate degrees, Western Samoa would perhaps become a more vibrant intellectual and cultural centre. This could be accomplished with the assistance of some the hundreds of thousands of academics around the world, in the form of sponsorships, exchanges and visiting professorships. Consequently, the National University of Samoa could not only educate many its own citizens for the more highly skilled business, professional, and administrative positions, but it could address its serious brain drain problem.

of the South Pacific also has a small campus near Apia that provides courses in agriculture.

Although the official objectives of the educational policy cited here are reasonable, several problems are evident. First, although it is difficult to be too critical of efforts to raise the level of educational attainment of a nation, mass education should not be viewed as a panacea for dealing with social and economic problems. The model for this educational system comes from Western societies, which themselves have enormous problems in terms of their own educational systems (e.g., Collins, 1979). Wanting to "blindly" educate everyone through secondary school (and university) may be well intentioned, but the side effects of such social engineering must be recognized and addressed. Again, this is not to say that education itself should be discouraged; rather, education without clearly articulated and integrated goals has not been an effective mechanism for economic development anywhere in the world.

To reiterate, although mass, Western-style education undoubtedly has certain benefits, it may also have some deleterious effects. These negative side effects include an alienation associated with the creation of expectations that cannot be met, and the cultural disruption that results when values are inculcated that conflict with the circumstance students face in their home life and when they leave the school. Certainly, the intention to create a heightened sense of awareness and cognitive functioning is a laudable one. But, if the cultural setting is not appropriate for the forms of cognitive and personal development stimulated by Western-style, mass educational experiences, policymakers must be certain that they also inculcate the psychological qualities that enable individuals to deal and live with these conflicts. From the point of view of social engineering, there is a serious problem with the lack of knowledge regarding how to systematically inculcate the psychological qualities that "immunize" people from the alienation often created by mass education (cf. Côté & Levine, 1987).

Human capital theory, developed by economists, advances the view that "individuals are like a piece of machinery, a capital good, and can increase their value in the labor market by increasing their education, especially training in occupational skills" (Ballantine, 1989, p. 301). Although human capital theory has informed the educational policy behind the expansion of educational systems in industrialized countries since the 1950s, it has been exposed as being of limited validity. This is especially the case beyond the point of achieving functional literacy among the population, so that basic commerce takes place, and beyond producing a *small number* of highly trained workers, so that specialized functions are performed (cf. Lockhart, 1971, 1975; Porter, 1984). Although a literate population is beneficial to an economy, much of the learning that takes place beyond the point of basic literacy is not applicable to most jobs in the industrial and service sectors of the labor force (Berg, 1970; Collins, 1979). Instead, what results is an inflation of educational credentials—credentialism—that simply sets expensive and arbitrary standards for access to jobs. Students are often merely kept "busy" for a requisite number of years, and "warehoused" in schools until they are certified as "properly educated."

Policymakers must deal with the fact that modern Western education—which emphasizes individualism, careerism, and consumerism—does not correspond with the values of *fa'a Samoa*. Moreover, there is no absolute reason for Samoa to participate fully in the international economy; in fact, by doing so it appears that much will be lost and given away, as has been the history of Samoa's contact with the *palagi*. The contradictions imposed upon Samoan youth are illustrated in the following statement of official policy, from which some programs discussed earlier were fashioned:

> Such programmes shall aim to develop and transform the youth into creative, productive, and socially responsible citizens and prepare them for the task of nation building. In recent years Samoans want wider opportunities for self-expression and individual achievement. Youth counselling and guidance programmes shall be geared toward value orientation and moral transformation and address such issues and problems on adolescence and reluctance to accept traditional roles by a growing number of young Samoans. (Department of Economic Development, Western Samoa, 1987, p. 191)

Within this policy statement are the contradictory goals of instilling individualism while coaxing young people to accept traditional community roles. Although the need for such programs exists, their goals must be carefully considered. For example, to deal with the need of combining Western values with Samoan traditions, thought might be given to establishing new customs, such as a synthesis of the *'aumaga* and *aualuma* with secondary education. Accordingly, young people primarily would learn the values and skills of their ancestral culture, but secondarily they could develop non-Samoan knowledge. This would potentially revitalize the village economy and make wage labor less necessary, as these youth groups return to carrying out collective projects. In addition, the need to leave the village in search of wage labor could be reduced if these new youth structures taught craft skills and fed local self-sustaining industries. The consequences of re-mobilizing youth labor include reinstating local village autonomy, restoring the dignity to being responsible for one's community, and returning a sense of meaning to those coming of age. The Western Samoan government can contribute to this by undertaking more initiatives like the "Rural Development Programme." This program has benefited women (cf. Muse, 1991; Natarajan, 1983), and similar programs can be directed to explicitly meet the needs of young people.

This is not to say that Samoans should abandon the world educational/economic system, or that the world educational/economic system should abandon Samoans. Rather, given the uniqueness and potential of the Samoan situation, one could hope that new models could be developed to help Samoa and other developing countries avoid the traps that the educational/economic morass creates. Salmi (1992) discussed strategies for dealing with such problems as they apply to higher education.

The Economy

As noted previously, around the world it is generally assumed that formal education constitutes a period of preparation for the labor force. On the basis of human capital theory, it is further assumed that an "investment" in education by the state and the individual will lead to some tangible return for both (cf. Pitt, 1970). As also noted previously, these expectations have been found to be unrealistic as the solution to economic problems, particularly in an "undeveloped" country like Western Samoa. It is openly admitted by the Western Samoan government that "at present, there is no coordinated framework for national manpower planning. . . . Overall the training of personnel for manpower requirements for the public and private sector remains an ad-hoc exercise" (Department of Economic Development, Western Samoa, 1987, p. 22). This statement characterizes the "patchwork" economic system in Western Samoa. Nearly all observers agree that there are significant problems with planning and coordinating efforts in several sectors of the Western Samoan economy. By the same token, this is an area in which local solutions can be attempted.

The employment that is available, is generally of low wage. The minimum wage was 55 *sene* per hour (about 25¢ U.S.) in 1984, and the average salary for those in paid employment was about 2,300 *tala* per annum (Labour Department, Western Samoa, 1984). There appears not to be much variation in salaries, primarily because there is not much variation in the type of employment available—it is largely clerical and service, with some light manufacturing (cf. Meleisea & Meleisea, 1980; "Western Samoa Push For Investment," 1992). Of the 21,400 known to be in paid employment in 1983, one third were public servants (Labour Department, Western Samoa, 1984). Moreover, there is some question regarding the appropriateness of the training of public servants:

> Western Samoa's labour market is characterized by some serious imbalances. First and foremost, while there is a growing number of General Arts & Science graduates employed in the service, there is a lack of specialists particularly in the scientific field (Department of Economic Development, Western Samoa, 1987, p. 22)

As for unemployment, it is difficult to get accurate statistics because there are no unemployment insurance or welfare systems. Leacock (1987) pointed out that youth unemployment has "no counterpart in societies based on subsistence farming, where the economic future of young people [is] assured." But around the world, in countries forced into the international economy, "youth unemployment is on the increase, and everywhere with deleterious psychological effects" (p. 178). The Western Samoa government does not keep track of unemployment statistics, partially for the following reasons:

> Employment here is not gauged in terms of formal labour requisites. And the figures do not denote full time employment. In fact, there is considerable part-time employment. Employment in the Western Samoan sense, is employment of virtually any sort, from working as a teller in a commercial bank to growing bananas in the backyard. (Treasury Department, Western Samoa, 1988, p. 10)

This report, compiled to attract foreign investment to Western Samoa, goes on, however, to admit that "in other words, there is gross underutilization of the country's resources, especially where labour is concerned" (p. 10). But it goes on to argue that the massive "underemployment" is an asset because of the labor force awaiting the development of capital enterprises. Apparently, however, these efforts to entice multinationals are meeting with some success (e.g., McCabe, 1992). On the other hand, multinationals will only be attracted by very low wages and will offer jobs requiring low levels of skill. For example, the automotive manufacturer Yazaki recently opened a branch plant in Apia, employing some 1,500 people. This operation assembles electrical components. The managing director of the Yazaki Australia, who set up the project, is quoted as saying the following about Samoan workers:

> We have recruited, selected, inducted, trained and now promoted many people, and find them to be excellent. . . . In some sense, our assembly operations are akin to handcrafting. It therefore follows that a nation with a heritage of basket-weaving and thatching will be very adept. Attributes such as dexterity, suppleness of limbs, basic body strength, good eyesight, superior binocular vision, superior acuity, accurate colour recognition, good co-ordination and motor actions are important. (McCabe, 1992, p. 39)

Note that there is nothing in these attributes that reflect the need for a secondary education. Note further the "psychosocial attributes" that are identified as making Samoans "good workers":

> He said Samoans had a pride in achievement, accepted authority, were aware of the need to safely preserve materials, produce error-free outcomes, report suspected faults, practice error containment and self-inspection functions, and to cooperate through "buddy checking" systems—for all this was readily facilitated by people "whose racial upbringing is based on harmonisation." (McCabe, 1992, p. 39)

In spite of what has to be a patronizing relationship with these multinationals, the government of Western Samoa faces a very serious economic problem as a member of the international community. According to Labour Department statistics, in 1981, 87,110 citizens were over the legal working age of 15, constituting 55.8% of the population. Of these, 41,506 were "economically active" (85% of the "economically active" were men). As the earlier statistics indicate, however, only about one half these would be in "paid employment," the rest presumably working in their *aiga* plantations and related activities (Labour Department, Western Samoa, 1984). These figures presumably include those driving the estimated 500 taxis in Apia ("Taxi License," 1991), a city of only 45,000 inhabitants (O'Meara, 1990). In any event, putting these figures together means that only about 25% of the adult population are in the wage economy labor force.

As for youth unemployment, if the general level of "unemployment" is about 75%, we can be sure that it is significantly higher for the young because this is consistently the case in other countries. In terms of dealing with the problem of youth unemployment, the government appears to be counting on the impact of foreign investment: "obviously we have to further develop industry and service sectors which will eventually utilize the talents of our youth" (Treasury Department, Western Samoa, 1988, p. 10). Unfortunately, as we have just seen, most foreign investment will be exploitative. A recent wildcat strike at the Yazaki plant signals that the promise of economic salvation through cooperation with multinationals is probably illusory (North, 1993).

Granted, the young can work at "unpaid labor" for their *aiga*, but as we have seen, it is questionable how satisfactory this is for the increasing number of high school graduates. Even many of those who do not aspire to work in the wage economy, and instead work within the traditional *aiga* system, seem to develop an appetite for consumer goods—especially "identity" items like running shoes, ghetto blasters, and the latest Western fashions—that they view in the media or see on trips to

Apia or American Samoa. Obviously, however, unemployment and low wages provide little cash with which to buy such goods. Concern has been expressed about this problem from many sources, and locally there is an impatience with the inaction in dealing with it, as this recent newspaper commentary indicates:

> while so many people are thinking about getting a job and earning money for the family one cannot help but wonder just what the rest, or should one say the huge majority, of school leavers without jobs are going to be doing. It looks like there will be a whole lot more young people around here with nothing to do and the increase in juvenile crime is about to take off. . . . Such a pity that with all the talk we keep hearing of how we look after our own no one really wants to look at this problem any longer. . . . ("Column Seven," 1991)

Clearly, it is wrong to say that the government, or Samoans in general, do not care about what is happening to their young. Official government policy is informed by *fa'a Samoa*, which includes the principle of care for everyone. As we have seen throughout this book, however, the problem is that the entire society is being swept by the currents of change, so it is difficult to focus attention on what to do about the problems affecting those coming of age. MacPherson (1988) provided a detailed analysis of the economic problems in Western Samoa brought on by this change and how these problems can be dealt with by harnessing traditions, rather than rejecting them.

THE CULTURAL HERITAGE OF THE YOUNG: INDEPENDENCE OR DEPENDENCE?

Western Samoans are proud of their political independence and the fact that they were the first nation of the South Pacific islands to break its colonial dependence. Ironically, it may be economics, not politics, that returns Western Samoa to a colonylike dependence. This may happen if multinational corporations are allowed to exploit Samoa's "cheap labor." We can hope that Western Samoa may also be the first to resist this form of dependency. To do so, however, will require explicit policies designed to instill local autonomy.

As argued previously, it appears that the assumptions driving many current policies in Western Samoa are based on "human capital theory" and "modernization theory" (cf. Pitt, 1970). Human capital theory predicts that economic activity is stimulated in direct proportion to the amount of education obtained by workers in the labor force—that "investments" in education yield dividends for the economy. Similarly, modernization theory predicts that economic activity is stimulated when certain "beliefs, values, and behaviors" are adopted by a population; namely, "diligence, rational calculation, orderliness, frugality, punctuality, and achievement motivation—and new social values such as meritocracy, getting ahead on one's own ability" (Ballantine, 1989, p. 301).

Although both theories appear reasonable at a common sense level, both have been questioned because of their limited applicability. For example, meritocratic principles remain an ideal rather than a reality in most advanced industrial nations, especially capitalist ones (Krauze & Slomczynski, 1985). In addition, investments made in education in many Third World countries are often lost through "brain drain," as those with higher levels of education leave the country because of low wages and unemployment (Ballantine, 1989). Western Samoa currently has a serious brain drain problem (e.g., Crocombe, 1989). Finally, knowledge on its own does not stimulate economic activity. Rather, only specific forms of knowledge that are directly relevant to fiscal realities stimulate economic activities. For the majority of jobs in most countries, this level of knowledge is reached with a grade nine education and functional literacy (cf. Porter, 1984). Being well read and worldly—having Western-style "cultural capital"—may be personally gratifying, but on their own these attributes do little in terms of the day-to-day realities in the wage labor force, especially in countries like Western Samoa where most jobs involve service, clerical, or manual labor.

Samoans were promised 150 years ago that if they embraced Christianity, they would inherit the material comforts of the *palagi*. They were assured in this century that if they embraced capitalism they would inherit the affluence of *palagi* societies like New Zealand and Australia. Like most other countries touched by Western values, Samoa has been caught up in the "myth of progress," based on the assumption that "growth is good for society and the individual" (Ballantine, 1989, p. 308). Unfortunately, in believing the myth, countries like Western Samoa simply become "small fish" in a big "economic pond." They are useful to the "big fish" in that pond, but only as consumers, sources of cheap labor, and a source of natural resources. On the other hand, in a sense Western Samoa has been fortunate because it does not have many natural resources to attract the attention of these "big fish" (except its hardwood lumber, but most of the pristine stands have already been cut; see Cox & Elmqvist, 1991). Consequently, it has been left largely alone. If it were resource rich, I doubt if it would now be an independent nation—New Zealand would not likely have so easily consented to its independence.

A perspective that sheds light on this discussion is "dependency theory" (see Allahar, 1989, for a review). This theory takes a global perspective and examines the history of contact among nations. When viewed from this perspective, investments in mass education made with the intention of fostering "modern values" pale in comparison to the role played by such things as "a nation's structural position in the world economy, trade flow, dependence on primary product exports, state strength, degree of foreign investment, and the presence of multinational corporations" (Benavot, cited in Ballantine, 1989, pp. 301–302). Moreover, the role played by education in economically dependent countries is not so much the direct stimulation of the local economy as it is the inculcation of attitudes that nurture an acceptance of the world economic order, particularly among the political elite (cf. Crocombe, 1989). As Ballantine (1989) explained:

> A chain of exploitation exists at several levels: metropolitan (developed) countries over peripheral (developing) countries; centers of power in third world countries over peripheral rural areas; and so on down to the village level. In this system, the peripheral areas may gain by getting needed resources, but *the price is domination (by the metropolitan or center areas) over local affairs—curricula, texts, and reforms*, for example. (pp. 308–309, italics added)

Although not writing specifically about Samoa, Allahar's (1989) reference to the Third World in general, aptly applies to the history of Samoa and its current position in the international economy:

> beginning with the voyages of so-called "discovery" and the capture of colonial territory and continuing to the present time, the economic and political structures of the colonial and ex-colonial territories have been *distorted* to meet the needs of metropolitan capitalism. (p. 89)

In addition, Allahar's characterization of Third World economies that have become fully intertwined with the international capitalist economy provides a warning of where Western Samoa may find itself if it continues to entice multinational corporations:

> By tailoring their economies to meeting the needs of advanced ones, peripheral countries become dependent on the advanced for supplies of capital, credit, technology, expertise, and the very market demand that makes possible continued production. Hence local needs and local markets tend to be neglected, for the better part of all economic activity is directed toward external markets and consumers. (p. 90)

But, Western Samoa has the potential to turn the tide away from economic dependency in the world economic system. After all, Samoans thrived for several millennia before contact with the *palagi*. Moreover, their geographical isolation becomes an asset in resisting this dependency because Samoans have the political franchise to pick and choose which influences they accept onto their shores. We can hope that Samoan pride and independence will provide the strength necessary to resist economic domination. Perhaps Samoans can pioneer new models of local autonomy that can be used to help themselves and other countries avoid the cycle of economic dependency and poverty. The future of young Samoans depends on it.

CHAPTER EIGHT

Conclusion: Mead's Samoa in Sociological Perspective

To complete this interdisciplinary examination of the validity of Mead's account, in this concluding chapter I place Mead's Samoa in sociological perspective. With this perspective I round out the assessment as to whether the social structures Mead described in 1920s Ta'u would plausibly have been conducive to a coming of age that was "not a specially difficult" one (Mead, 1928, p. 197). In doing so, I specifically focus on Mead's claim that, with few exceptions, for her informants "adolescence represented no period of crisis or stress, but was instead an orderly developing of a set of slowly maturing interests and activities" (p. 157).

I begin this sociological analysis by backtracking to clarify several concepts bandied about during the Mead–Freeman controversy. Throughout the controversy, references have been made to notions such as "adolescence" as if their definitions and applications were well established. In reality, this notion remains quite controversial in the human development literature. Therefore, to move the Mead–Freeman debate toward a resolution, a thorough analysis of several concepts needs to be undertaken.

ADOLESCENCE AS A STAGE OF LIFE

Any discussion of the concept of adolescence must begin with the recognition that the very notion of "adolescence" is not a culturally universal concept—in some cultures there is no period of "adolescence," as Westerners know it, and there are no words to describe it. Moreover, in cultures where a prolonged period between childhood and adulthood does exist, "adolescence" takes different forms depending on socioeconomic conditions. In short, adolescence is not a universally recognized or institutionalized stage of life; rather, conceptions of it emerge under particular socioeconomic circumstances where a prolonged period between childhood and adulthood can be sustained.

With respect to the idea that a culture may not have a conception of "adolescence" at all, Sprinthall and Collins (1984) stated the following:

> can an adult society ignore something as real as adolescence? That idea may strike you as odd, but such has been the case for adolescence—and for other developmental periods as well. For example, until adults recognized and allowed childhood to emerge, it hardly existed. For long centuries it was thought that as soon as a child reached the age of six or seven, the child was ready to be trained as an adult. Children were considered as little more than midget-sized adults. Except for a tiny proportion of the rich and well-born, they worked alongside adults in the fields, they fought adult wars, they worked in the mines, and with the coming of industrialization they worked from dusk to dawn in the factories. (p. 2)

From this passage, we can see that childhood in preindustrial *Western* culture was closer to the childhood in precontact Samoa as described in chapter 4, than it is to childhood in contemporary Western culture. Thus, childhood has changed in both Western and Samoan culture. Of importance to the Mead–Freeman controversy is the fact that childhood and adolescence can be structured in a variety of ways, and that Western models are neither the only nor the best models to emulate. Moreover, since Mead carried out her study, we have accumulated a considerable amount of knowledge regarding how Western adolescence evolved. For example, as noted by Sprinthall and Collins, the contemporary Western life cycle began to take its present form with the onset of industrialization:

> only in the past 150 years or so have adult Western societies even recognized childhood, the juvenile years from 6 or 7 to 12 or 13, as a special stage of growth. . . . Once childhood was discovered, a whole series of changes followed. . . . What was true for the discovery of childhood in the last century has been the case for adolescence in this century. Only recently have adults in industrialized nations and cultures begun to perceive adolescents' physiological and psychological needs and capabilities as unique, and this perception has created the opportunity to recognize a stage of human growth. . . . In the last half of the twentieth century we are beginning to witness some changes in how adolescents are treated by adult society, similar to the changes experienced by juveniles in the nineteenth century. (p. 3)

Sprinthall and Collins attributed the emergence of adolescence largely to the perceived need to educate the young, as do many other social scientists (see Klein, 1990). Reminiscent of the efforts of missionaries in Samoa described in chapter 4, primary schools were established usually on the initiative of reformers intent on protecting the young from various "evils" associated with urban-industrial influences (cf. Collins, 1979). With primary schools established, the conception of childhood became cemented in peoples' minds. More recently, secondary schools were established, institutionalizing adolescence and cementing peoples' conception of this age period as well.

Although mass education and various laws have had a dramatic impact on the conception of adolescence, there is evidence that the "cement" demarcating adolescence has not yet fully hardened. In fact, it is difficult to firmly define the boundaries of adolescence in contemporary Western societies. For many people, including many social scientists, "adolescence" is taken to correspond to the "teen" years, at least until age 18. According to Montemayor, Adams, and Gullotta (1990), however, in the United States the U.S. legal establishment specifies that adolescence "begins at 16 years of age and ends at 21" (p. 10). In fact, Montemayor et al. devoted their entire volume to trying to understand the transition from childhood to adulthood in contemporary Western societies. Thus, although well institutionalized in Western societies, the demarcation of adolescence is variable, with different observers defining its boundaries in different ways (cf. Gold & Petronio, 1980).

Numerous accounts of the evolution of childhood and the "invention" of adolescence in Western culture are available (e.g., Aries, 1962; Coleman, 1974; Demos & Demos, 1969), so I leave it to the reader to consult these if desired. The point to be taken here, however, is that in light of cultural variation, there are no hard biological "facts" defining adolescence, as there are of puberty.

In spite of these difficulties, the term *adolescence* is used by most social scientists to designate the period between the "biological maturity" produced by puberty and the "social maturity" recognized by an individual's adult culture. Social maturity, however, is not accomplished in some cultures—mainly more affluent cultures—until long after biological maturity has been reached. Under such conditions, the stage of life we call adolescence emerges, and social institutions usually develop to supervise the behavior of those passing through it. Thus, when attempting to discover the primary causes of the behavior of adolescents, we must first gain an understanding of the nature and impact of these social institutions. In addition, what must be emphasized is that biology cannot logically be considered the primary cause of a life stage that is social in origin.

A few words on the expression "coming of age" are also appropriate before proceeding. To come of age in a society is to "qualify" for adulthood because of one's attributes. These attributes may be defined biologically, psychologically, socially, or legally by a society. As was seen earlier, there is no culturally universal standard for the end of adolescence, and hence for coming of age. The term *coming of age* was used by Mead to convey this notion of the transition to adulthood, but she also did not explicitly define the term. Rather, her usage is metaphorical, as is its general usage. The term is primarily heuristic, however, because it draws our attention to the processes of development, rather than to the state of being "adolescent" as opposed to "adult." It also directs us to examine the social institutions that ostensibly *guide* individuals into adulthood.

To conclude this examination of the nature of adolescence, there is no one way for a culture to induct children into adulthood. Equally important is the idea that because adolescence is a cultural phenomenon, we should not expect to discover "instincts" that might guide behavior during this passage. To the contrary, we should expect to find in all well-functioning cultures provisions by which adult generations guide succeeding generations into adulthood. In sociological terms, these provisions are called "institutionalized moratoria" (E. Erikson, 1968). The key feature to be examined is the effectiveness of these institutionalized moratoria in producing social maturity among new members. Accordingly, we now turn to a consideration of adolescence as a social institution. In doing so, we ask questions about the adequacy of that institution in terms of its ability to guide young people through the stage in a relatively stress-free manner. Thus, we have returned to the basic question posed by Mead in *Coming of Age*. Now, however, we have an additional 65 years of theory and research upon which to rely.

INSTITUTIONALIZED MORATORIA AND MEAD'S SAMOA

In reference to the social structures that can emerge to define adolescence, E. Erikson (1980) argued that most cultures provide their new members with some sort of "time out" between childhood and adulthood. This usually involves a moratorium from adult responsibilities, during which they can take time to develop their adult identity. In his words: "Societies offer, as individuals require, a more or less sanctioned intermediary period between childhood and adulthood, institutionalized psychosocial moratoria, during which a lasting pattern of 'inner identity' is scheduled for relative completion" (p. 119).

There is also usually some form of structure or guidance given the young person (hence the term *institutionalized*). Together with a freedom to experiment with various roles (hence the term *moratorium*), young people can explore themselves and their world without being expected to carry permanent responsibilities and commitments. In E. Erikson's (1968) words, "these moratoria coincide with apprenticeships and adventures that are in line with society's values" (p. 157). Apprenticeships include schooling and forms of "service" (military or voluntary, like the Peace Corps), whereas adventures can take various forms, including travel (the *Wanderschaft*), or just "dropping out." In societies that institutionalize them, all of these forms of activity are socially recognized as legitimate for young people, as opposed to, say, children or the elderly.

Mead's description of the period granted to both males and females on Ta'u corresponds in several ways to this description. For males, as we saw earlier, "service" (*tautua*) in the *'aumaga* was well institutionalized. This experience provided some opportunity for the type of role experimentation that would contribute to the "lasting pattern of 'inner identity' " about which Erikson writes. Moreover, the *'aumaga* constituted a form of apprenticeship (as did the *aualuma* in precontact culture) that would have provided "a moratorium characterized by defined duties and sanctioned competitions as well as special license" (E. Erikson, 1968, p. 185). In precontact Samoa, these apprenticeships would have been complemented with elaborate initiations and welcoming ceremonies (see chapter 4).

Evidence of the "special license" of the moratorium (temporary freedoms not granted adults or children) can be found throughout Mead's account. For example, as was seen earlier, she described how many of her informants were permitted to forestall full adult responsibilities with the defensive statement, "I am but young." She also described the "selective playfulness" among the young that was socially recognized (implicitly endorsed) by many adults with respect to sexual experimentation. In addition, both males and females participated in the *malaga* (visiting parties to other islands and villages), as well as in expeditions to gather food and craft supplies, so something equivalent to a *Wanderschaft* was available.

Characteristics of Effective Institutionalized Moratoria

With the concepts of adolescence and institutionalized moratoria clarified, I now specify four social conditions that should be present to minimize the possibility that young people will experience difficulties as they pass from childhood to adulthood in a given society. For each of these four conditions, I then examine Mead's Samoa to determine whether these would have been met.

Social Organization

For adolescence to be relatively stress free, a society should be adequately organized so that this transitional stage is marked by a *continuity* between childhood and adulthood (cf. Benedict, 1938). Thus, a learning of the basis of adult roles should be accomplished during this stage, and this learning should be a logical extension of what was learned as a child. Similarly, the acquisition of adult responsibilities should take place in a fashion that does not tax the individual's capacity to exercise those responsibilities. In cultures where these conditions are not met, we should expect to find adolescents encountering difficulties both in terms of their day-to-day behavior as "adolescents" and in terms of their ability to project themselves into the future. Cultures that are *socially disorganized* lack integration among their institutions. For example, there may be a lack of coordination between the family and the educational system, or between the educational system and the adult world of work. Under these circumstances, adolescents are left to deal individually with conflicting expectations when moving from one institutional setting to another. The experience of this type of conflict can create psychological confusion and interfere with the development of attributes defined as appropriate to adulthood in a given culture. Ideally, institutions work in unison so that as individuals move from one setting to another, they do not encounter serious disjunctures of experience: Thought and behavior patterns that prevail in one setting should be more or less appropriate in another setting, especially if one setting is supposed to constitute a preparation for another (as adolescence ostensibly is to adulthood).

Social Organization in Mead's Samoa. From Mead's descriptions of the structural arrangements governing adolescence and the transition to adulthood, there is little doubt that they provided adequate guidance for most young Samoans. Several factors should have ensured this.

First, for both males and females, learning took place gradually, and young people moved on to more complex tasks as they were able. There was apparently little pressure to take on tasks for which the person was not prepared.

Second, there was evidently no shame in being "slow" at something because of the cultural norm that set group activities at the pace of the slowest person. Moreover, undue "precocity" was negatively sanctioned, especially among the young, so there was little point in someone trying to outdo someone else. Mead (1928) noted, however, that when she conducted her study the norms regarding precocity were diminishing in importance, primarily because of the influence of the educational system. In her words: "Even the stern attitude formerly taken by the adults towards precocity has now been subdued, for what is a sin at home becomes a virtue at school" (p. 276).

Third, individuals of all ages would have felt few ambiguities regarding what was expected of them because of the stable and explicit definition of roles.

These factors would have combined to not only reduce competition, but also to minimize the extent to which individuals compared themselves to some ideal standard of accomplishment (the exception to this was the individual aspiring to a *matai* title). Thus, each individual would have known where they stood in relation to community roles, and membership in village groups was well defined.

It is worth arguing that these cultural arrangements make great sense in an island-bound culture where there are limited resources and quite literally no where else to go. In other words, there is little point in encouraging innovation when everyone has enough to eat and where there are few material resources to be accumulated. Moreover, the discouragement of innovation and precocity would ensure cultural stability—a "resource" apparently much more important to an island-bound culture than would be any material comforts accruing from innovation. The Western obsession with "achievement" and "striving" has led to world domination, but Westerners are not necessarily any more fulfilled than were Samoans before Western contact. Indeed, it appears that the Western middle-class "future orientation" has now been internalized by many Samoans, convincing them that they must be dissatisfied with their present circumstances in order to be happy in the future.

These features of Samoan social organization would account in part for the "casual attitude" reported by Mead. Apparently there was simply little pressure on most young people to hurry, to be extremely productive, or to "prove themselves" through innovation.

Role Induction

Effective institutionalized moratoria should provide some sort of role induction. By this I mean that *role learning* in adolescence should constitute a preparation for adult roles and a basis on which the young recruit is *welcomed* into an adult community. To the extent that roles played in adolescence are irrelevant to, or in conflict with, adult roles, the transition to adulthood can become problematic. This may be manifested either as part of a lack of welcoming from the adult community or a "refusal" of the recruit.

In Western culture it can be argued that much of the role learning and behavior of adolescence is irrelevant to adulthood. Many adolescents have few work or family responsibilities, they must function with the low status associated with the student role, and they have few practicable choices about their present lifestyle. Accordingly, the youth cultures and subcultures now common in many Western societies can be seen to have emerged to fill the "voids" of adolescence—particularly as they represent resentment about these voids and a diffuse rebellion against "adult authority" (cf. Brake, 1985). Adults, when reacting to these subcultures (particularly gangs), often exhibit fear or contempt, driving a further wedge between the adolescent and the adult community. This cycle of resentment appears to be a product of the force prolonging the period of youth and increasing the disenfranchisement of young people. In more regulated societies, the differences between the adolescent world and the adult world are minimized.

Role Induction in Mead's Samoa. By the time Mead did her study in the 1920s, many structures associated with the induction into adult roles had been altered or eliminated by the missionaries. For example, the requirement of tattooing for membership in the *'aumaga* had apparently been taboo for two generations (Mead, 1928, p. 267) and ceremonies seldom marked induction into the *aualuma* (p. 275). Nevertheless, it does not appear that the general "role induction ethos" of Samoan culture had yet been fully compromised by missionary influences.

For young males, preparation for adult roles was still evident. By their early teens they were skilled in the basics of adult work activities and during their "youth" they worked alongside adults in the *'aumaga*, which would eventually introduce them to full adult status. In addition, the license to remain single enabled those who did so to take life more casually than did those who married early, especially in comparison to those married men aspiring to a *matai* title.

Young females encountered less structure, but they too learned most of the skills of adulthood during their childhood. The period between puberty and their early 20s permitted them the time to hone these skills and to prepare psychologically for their adult roles, apparently at a relatively leisurely pace. In particular, fine mat weaving and other craft skills were developed during this period. Upon marriage, females were considered "adults" and were apparently well prepared for this status. Thus, because of their skills preparation, and the recognition of this by their community, the moratorium they experienced before marriage was more "socioemotional" than "instrumental" in terms of preparation for adulthood.

Social Control Mechanisms

The logical extension of the first condition and the requisite of the second condition, is that social control mechanisms must be in place to ensure that behavior is regulated. These mechanisms should be structured to ensure that roles are meaningfully integrated into a social order and division of labor. Social control mechanisms can be defined as patterns of reward and punishment that direct behavior in certain ways. These contingency patterns make clear what behavior is appropriate or desirable, as defined by cultural norms and values.

When these mechanisms do not exist, it is unclear to individuals, particularly new individuals attempting to learn the requirements of the culture, what they should do to act appropriately. In other words, individuals can become confused without a well-regulated social environment. Moreover, it is not enough that norms simply *exist* regarding what is right and wrong; these norms must also be *enforced* by human agents. If they are not enforced, the norms become meaningless over time as fewer individuals internalize or respect them. When adolescents are confronted with poorly constructed and ineffectively executed social control mechanisms, they can experience, among other things: (a) confusion regarding how to behave; (b) a lack of attachment to, and resentment toward, individuals subjecting them to these mechanisms; (c) an absence of moral conviction; (d) a lack of meaning in their lives; and (e) a sense of confusion about whom they are and where they are headed as individuals. All these have become central "symptoms" of the turbulent and stressful forms of adolescence found in Western societies. Indeed, these symptoms are so commonplace that they are now considered "normal" characteristics of adolescence in many Western societies. Yet, for the young, they can be painful and can stimulate adolescents to organize themselves into subcultures (especially gangs) in an attempt to give their lives meaning and structure.

Social Control Mechanisms in Mead's Samoa. The institutions confronting Samoan youth were well-structured and well-maintained, partly because of the effectiveness of social control mechanisms. As discussed earlier, these social control mechanisms included the day-to-day interpersonal normative pressures associated with living in a small community where very little takes place in private; the nature of the Samoan *aiga* and the requirement of loyalty and duty to it from its members; the *ifoga* (forgiveness ceremony); the *tautua* (service to the *matai*); the allotment of fines and punishments by the *fono* to the offender *as well as* his or her *aiga* and *matai*; and banishment or execution if the offense were severe enough. Apparently, punishments were immediate (cf. Gerber, 1975), and were perceived by most violators to be justified (cf. Holmes, 1987, p. 106). Moreover, the apprehension regarding shaming oneself—and by implication one's *aiga*—would have been an effective approach/avoidance motivator, particularly because of the lack of privacy. A "shame-oriented" culture can be much more orderly than a "guilt-oriented" one, because shame is an overt, collective phenomenon, whereas guilt is a covert, personal one (cf. Gerber, 1975).

Deviance

Finally, stemming from Condition 3, social control mechanisms must be effective in dealing with various types of deviant behavior. One type of deviant behavior can be seen as a "normal" by-product of social organization. This type of behavior is normal because it stems from the fact that when rules (norms) exist, violations will eventually ensue. In other words, if there is no rule with respect to a behavior, there can be no violation. For example, if there is no rule prohibiting premarital sexual behavior, there will be no deviance in this regard, and no one will be labelled as this type of "deviant" (cf. K. Erikson, 1966). A second type of deviance constitutes a by-product of particular types of culture. In this view, "culturally endemic" deviance results from poorly integrated reinforcement patterns that cater to our base capacities as "human animals," such as selfishness and egocentrism. When a culture rewards these animal capacities, they may take prominence over other human capacities such as loyalty, sharing, and duty. Yet another type of deviance is the result of a cultural incapacity to impose its normative pattern on members with idiosyncratic "temperaments" (e.g., as described by Mead concerning some of her "deviants"). Each of these sources of deviance constitute challenges for all cultures to establish mechanisms that ensure relatively harmonious day-to-day community functioning.

Deviance in Mead's Samoa. The previously mentioned social control mechanisms should have discouraged deviant behavior in the first instance, and remedied any deviance-related damage to community relations in the second instance. With respect to the incidence of deviance in precontact culture, it was noted earlier that the missionaries were very thorough in documenting the "evils" they perceived. Accordingly, had serious problems existed among the young, such as suicide and delinquency, the missionaries most certainly would have mentioned them and set out a strategy to deal with them. No mention was made of a serious problem of deviance among the young, however.

As a thorough researcher, Mead extensively documented the deviance in the three villages she studied. In fact, Mead's Appendix IV deals specifically with the topic of "The Mentally Defective and the Mentally Diseased," and her chapter XI deals with the question of "The Girl in Conflict." Moreover, references are made throughout the book to the concerns associated with "deviance and social control" issues. For example, in reference to the issue of "crime" and the impact of Western justice on precontact Samoan justice, Mead wrote that

> the Samoan is not in the habit of committing many of the crimes listed in our legal code. He steals and is fined by the government as he was formerly fined by the village. But he comes into very slight conflict with the central authorities. He is too accustomed to taboos to mind a quarantine prohibition which parades under the same guise; too accustomed to the exactions of his relations to fret under the small taxation demands of the government. (p. 276)

In other words, most Samoans were still influenced by their socialization into precontact culture, and were motivated by conditioning from that culture rather than from a fear of legal action from government officials.

The deviance that Mead detailed in her chapter entitled "The Girl in Conflict," has been the object of criticism by Freeman. As noted in chapter 2, most of the deviance discussed by Mead was minor, and would not likely have resulted in criminal indictment in Western societies. Rather, this deviance constituted either "serious conflict" or "serious deviation from group standards." Readers will recall that two cases of serious conflict were recorded, both of which had begun before puberty. In addition, three cases of "serious deviation from group standards" were noted, having been precipitated by an awareness of alternative adult roles stemming from missionary/Western influence; and two additional cases of minor or potential deviance were recorded: one potential delinquent, and one "delinquent in the making" (p.182). In Mead's estimation, however, this deviance "in temperament or in conduct . . . [was] . . . in many cases . . . only charged with possibilities of conflict and actually had no painful results" (p. 158). The remainder of her informants, "showed a surprising uniformity of knowledge, skill and attitude, and presented a picture of orderly, regular development in a flexible, but strictly delimited, environment" (p. 184).

With respect to the storm and stress issue, if we interpret the aforementioned conflicts to represent symptoms of storm and stress, then the following comparisons can be made with recent North American research. Of the 25 postpuberty informants, three could be said to have experienced some minor difficulties in what is now called "identity formation" by human development researchers (establishing "a lasting pattern of 'inner identity'," as quoted from Erikson), although two experienced more serious and chronic "delinquency." Thus, 12% (3 out of 25) of Mead's informants might have experienced difficulties in identity formation, compared with 50% to 70 % of contemporary Canadian and U.S. young people (e.g., Côté, 1986; Marcia, 1980). An additional 8% (2 out of 25) engaged in some form of "delinquent behavior," compared with up to 80% for U.S. young people (Gold & Petronia, 1980). Thus, even with this generous stretch of the notion of storm and stress, it appears that Mead was reasonable in her conclusion that most of her informants experienced a coming of age that was "not a specially difficult" period and that adolescence itself did not represent an inevitable "period of crisis or stress."

If the four sociological conditions just listed are met, the young person should find some sort of order in roles, a predictability in outcome, and a sufficient reward for adhering to social conventions. From this account, there are ample grounds to conclude sociologically that coming of age in "Mead's Samoa" occurred as part of a relatively smooth passage from childhood to adulthood for the majority of her informants, and that any symptoms of adolescent storm and stress would have been less common than is now the case in Western culture. The charge has been made, however, that coming of age was *experienced* as stressful by many young Samoans (see Freeman, 1983, chapter 17). One way to assess the experiential aspect of this issue is to focus on one of the primary differences between adolescence in Mead's Samoa and adolescence in Western cultures, namely, the amount of choice available to the young person.

THE ISSUE OF CHOICE

One final issue involves something that might have troubled those readers who began this book skeptical that social conditions in Mead's Samoa would have been experienced by most young people as benign. The issue in question is having the "right" to choose one's destiny.

In comparison to Western societies, in Mead's Samoa young people had far less choice regarding the specific content of their future adult identities. Mead noted that this had the effect of eliminating much conflict from their lives: They did not have to choose among competing religions; they did not have to choose among competing political philosophies; and they did not have to choose from among a bewildering array of adult occupations. In contrast, Mead noted there was a virtual requirement in the United States that young people choose for themselves among the myriad of religious, political, and occupational options. In Mead's (1928) words: "The principal causes of our adolescents' difficulty are the presence of conflicting standards and the belief that every individual should make his or her own choices, coupled with a feeling that choice is an important matter" (pp. 234–235).

In contrast, in Mead's Samoa:

> The growing child is faced by a smaller dilemma than that which confronts the American-born child of European parentage. The gap between parents and children is narrow and painless, showing few of the unfortunate aspects usually present in a period of transition. . . . essentially the children are still growing up in a homogeneous community with a uniform set of ideals and aspirations. (p. 273)

Aptly noting that "the need for choice [is] the forerunner of conflict" (p. 202), Mead predicted that the introduction of choice into the lives of Samoans coming of age was going to have dramatic implications. As we have seen, Mead appears to have been right. One reason why the issue of choice had not yet affected most of her informants was the lack of exposure to many Western institutions. Even the pastors' village boarding schools were not yet affecting the world view of most of Mead's young informants, and they were "likely to pass through the school essentially unchanged [in their] fundamental view of life" (p. 170). In contrast, those "who left their village and spent several years in the boarding school under the tutelage of white teachers were enormously influenced" (p. 170), largely in terms of adopting nontraditional adult identities based on a career as a nurse or a pastor's wife. Mead saw an end to this conflict-free situation, however, as is evident in the following passage:

> while religion itself offered little field for conflict, the institutions promoted by religion might act as stimuli to new choices and when sufficiently reinforced by other conditions might produce a type of girl who deviated markedly from her companions. That the majority of Samoan girls are still unaffected by these influences and pursue uncritically the traditional mode of life is simply a testimony to the resistance of the native culture, which in its present slightly Europeanized state, is replete with easy solutions for all conflicts; and to the apparent fact that adolescent girls in Samoa do not generate their own conflicts, but require a vigorous stimulus to produce them. (pp. 170–171)

The exceptions were the "upward deviants," who had been stimulated to "deviate" by their exposure to Western education. They wished

> to exercise more choice than is traditionally permissible, and . . . in making their choices, come to unconventional and bizarre solutions. The un-

> traditional choices which are encouraged by the educational system inaugurated by the missionaries are education and the pursuit of a career and marriage outside of the local group . . . a self-conscious evaluation of existence, and the consequent making of self-conscious choices. All of these make for increased specialization, increased sophistication, greater emphasis upon individuality, where an individual makes a conscious choice between alternate or opposing lines of conduct. (p. 171)

Mead argued that the lack of choice was not experienced as oppressive or as a misfortune by most of her informants, except for the few who were "temperamentally" unsuited for such circumstances. Rather, she saw several mechanisms in Samoan culture that socialized people to accept this situation and to not view it as negative. For example, *children* were "urged to learn, urged to behave, urged to work, but they [were] not urged to hasten in choices which they make themselves" (p. 231), and *adolescents* were not "pressed to make momentous decisions which would spoil part of their fun in life" (p. 232). In addition, by "the time she reaches puberty the Samoan girl has ***learned to subordinate choice*** in the selection of friends or lovers to an observance of certain categories" (p. 210, italics added). Many Westerners balk at the idea of restrictions of choice, reflexively viewing such circumstances with disdain. It is worth examining this issue further, however, because of the implications of the insights yielded from such an examination. For example, even at the level of common sense, it is easy to realize that an unbridled freedom of choice does not necessarily lead to happiness and fulfillment. As Mead pointed out, too much choice can be a source of unhappiness and confusion, especially when there is little guidance in choice making or when the choices are illusory.

I believe that when we are sensitive to the cultural requirements of Mead's Samoa, it would be the presence of choice, not the absence of choice, that would be incongruent with cultural identities. Further, the presence of choice is likely responsible for much of the identity confusion and stress and storm that can now be witnessed in contemporary Samoa. Indeed, this preoccupation with choice seems to be very much a Western, Protestant, and 20th-century phenomenon (cf. Baumeister, 1986; Mead, 1928, pp. 232–233, located the Western concern over individual choice with the Reformation and the rise to prominence of Protestantism). There is ample evidence from North American studies that excessive occupational and ideological choice among those moving from childhood to adulthood can itself be stressful. This is partially because choice is often an illusion for many people—they simply cannot "be" or do many of the things to which they have aspired because of a lack of opportunity.

In other words, identity confusion often stems from "over-choice" in a situation where the actual range of choice and control over choices is quite limited, especially for those from the less privileged groups of a society (Côté & Levine, 1987). Indeed, the introduction of choice and the competition that goes along with it has been found to be very stressful for many contemporary young Samoans, especially those raised under more traditional circumstances (cf. Baldauf & Ayabe, 1977).

Obviously, this book is not the place to exhaust the monumental issue of "freedom of choice." It is an issue over which revolutions erupt and civil wars are waged. What can be said in the context of the coming-of-age issue, however, is that in our desire for absolute freedom of choice in the West, we have forgotten that humans are not genetically programmed for making specific choices during their lives. Rather, exercising choice is a capacity to be acquired on the basis of experiences within social institutions. What we have forgotten in Western culture is that young people need guidance in developing the capacity to make choices that are personally and socially responsible. This guidance should be present in the institutions that ostensibly prepare the young for adulthood. In the West, we have failed many young people in this regard; in imitating Western culture, contemporary Samoan culture is making the same mistake.

The significance of this problem can be put into context when we examine the relationship between mental health and social organization. Seligman (1988), for example, argued that the "rampant individualism" of U.S. society, along with a decline in commitment to common social institutions, has led to high rates of emotional depression in the span of the last two generations. In fact, it is estimated that "today's young [American] people [are] about 10 times as likely to be depressed as were their parents and grandparents" (pp. 50–52). Seligman attributed this "epidemic of depression" to the tremendous expectations placed on the "self" to be both the source and the "architect" of most forms of gratification—to "decide, prefer, plan, and choose [its] own course of action" (p. 52). However, this selfishness "need not lead to depression as long as we can fall back on large institutions" (p. 55). I would add, following Mead's conclusion, that mental health problems can be averted if "coming-of-age institutions" are properly and benignly structured in the first place to give the individual the capacity to function in an autonomous, yet "socially responsible," manner (cf. Côté & Levine, 1987). With "democracy" breaking out globally during the 1990s, we must be careful to balance the benefits associated with the right to choose, against possible liabilities. These liabilities are created when people do not have the psychological capacities to make complex choices, or when the opportunities are actually illusory, and no amount of effort or capability will produce the desired goal.

LIMITATIONS OF THE PRESENT STUDY

Before concluding, it is appropriate for me to reflect upon the limitations of the study described in this book. The primary limitation of this study of Mead's coming-of-age thesis and the Mead–Freeman controversy is that direct data pertaining to Samoan youth are sparse, particularly information pertaining to precontact Samoa. The social history constructed in chapters 4 and 5, therefore, was reliant on secondary sources and much of the information was descriptive, so it was often left to the investigator and reader to draw their own conclusions regarding coming-of-age issues. These secondary sources were often European observers who may not have appreciated the fullness and richness of Samoan culture. Moreover, as male observers they may not have appreciated the role of females in Samoan culture, so a number of important details may have been lost. With these problems in mind, as much as possible I used information that was verified by other sources, especially scholars from Samoa (e.g., Meleisea) and women scholars (e.g., Schoeffel). Fortunately, some records were kept and many of the practices survived well into this century.

The same limitation of sparse data applies to information examined in chapters 2 and 3. Much of the information examined was not collected with the primary purpose of studying coming-of-age processes, and it is not possible to go back and repeat Mead's study of the 1920s (although Holmes' restudy during the 1950s supported Mead's thesis). Consequently, it was necessary to rely on inference, and to piece the information together much like is done in a legal investigation. The comparisons made of Freeman's evidence with evidence from other parts of Samoa and from other countries were enlightening, but one is still dealing with inferences and issues of plausibility rather than definitive conclusions that might be drawn from controlled experiments. However, to compensate for these limitations, evidence was examined in light of state-of-the-art theory and research that was not available to Mead, and that Freeman has not used.

These are the approaches taken when dealing with legal issues, so early in this book I asked readers to take the role of "jurists" in evaluating the evidence and arguments. Only when enough evidence had been compiled on which to base a sound judgment, could a verdict on the matter be made. Of course, as with legal decisions, the verdict passed in this case only stands as valid in terms of "reasonable doubt." But, as I argued, there is reasonable doubt with all of Freeman's evidence and arguments with respect to Mead's coming-of-age thesis, regardless of which disciplinary perspective is taken. As demonstrated, each piece of evidence examined was either discounted as misleading or interpreted in ways that do not refute Mead's thesis.

FUTURE RESEARCH

It was just noted that a limitation of this study is that it had to deal with a paucity of data about Samoan youth. Although more information is now available about youth in contemporary Samoa, researchers should take up the task of providing effective documentation of current circumstances so that another controversy does not arise that presents as many ambiguities as does the Mead–Freeman controversy (see Baker, Hanna, & Baker, 1986, for such efforts). These research efforts should also be directed at cataloguing youth problems and making recommendations to help rectify them. Thus, aside from descriptive documentation, there is some urgency that research efforts be directed at identifying what can be done to buffer Samoan youth from the impact of Western culture and from international capitalism. In doing so, this research should look to the strengths of Samoan culture and character, as well as to weaknesses created by social change that leaves young Samoans vulnerable as they struggle to come of age. For a model, see Reid's (1990) study of moral reasoning. Note her identification of the sociocentrism institutionalized in the Samoan *fono* and the postconventional reasoning associated with methods of dispute resolution. Researchers should also consult Flay, Bull, and Tamahori (1976) for a treatment of how to develop questionnaires appropriate for Polynesian respondents.

In terms of a major research thrust, one particularly promising line of study has been developed by North American researchers, but before that line of study can realize its potential, the issue of cross-cultural validity must be confronted, as I explain later. This line of research focuses on "identity formation" as a central issue in adolescent development. Its promise lies with its "psychosocial" perspective, namely, the potential to incorporate psychological concepts with sociocultural ones (cf. Côté, 1993).

The line of research in question is referred to as the "identity status paradigm" (e.g., Marcia, 1964, 1976, 1980) and is based on Erik Erikson's (e.g., 1956, 1958, 1963) theory of ego development. Central to this paradigm is the issue of conscious choice made by individuals regarding life plans and belief systems. The period during which individuals choose among career and belief options is postulated by identity status researchers to constitute a form of identity crisis. This identity crisis, or period of conscious decision making, can last for years. Even so, it is postulated that experiencing a period of conscious decision making is in general psychologically beneficial for the individual. Evidence to support this claim links the crisis with certain personality characteristics like autonomy, internal control, cultural sophistication, and the need for achievement (cf. Côté & Levine, 1988a). Moreover, on the basis of the belief that experiencing this identity crisis is good for the individual, these researchers also recommend that everyone be encouraged to experience it, and therefore "achieve" an identity.

Those who do not go through this period of conscious decision making are said by identity status researchers to have avoided the identity crisis and "foreclosed" on their adult identity formation. That is, they do not experience this identity crisis and they uncritically accept family- or community-conferred roles. It is further assumed that people who foreclose on their identity formation suffer certain deficits, including a more limited sense of "ego identity" (a sense of temporal-spatial continuity).

Applying this paradigm to Mead's informants, it follows that nearly all would be classified as "identity foreclosed." Accordingly, they would be viewed by identity status researchers as less "advanced" in terms of ego development than American youths. A problem with this form of analysis, then, is that it is based on the assumption that ego development is greater if an individual experiences a Western-style "identity crisis," defined in terms of the activity of consciously exploring options regarding work roles and beliefs. But, the ability to engage in choice behavior was limited by Samoan culture, as it is by most non-Western cultures. Moreover, Mead's "deviants" would likely be classified as "identity moratorium" in the case of the upward delinquents, and as "identity diffusions" in the case of the downward delinquents. ("Identity moratorium" describes the process of deciding about which adult commitments to make, while "identity diffusion" involves avoiding both the decision making and commitments.)

With respect to the cross-cultural relevance of the identity status paradigm, Marcia (1976) argued that "when the statuses are applied in other cultures they will take on different significance, according to a particular culture. For example, Foreclosure will have a different meaning . . . in a society where roles are prescribed and an 'identity crisis' is not the norm" (p. 117). Marcia referred to this type of identity formation as "developmental Foreclosure" because such individuals have not "been exposed to an identity-challenging environment" (p. 118). In spite of this declaration, very little research or theory has dealt with the ego development that takes place for "developmental foreclosures."

Thus, it can be argued that the issue of the cross-cultural implications of the identity statuses is undertheorized and underresearched with this paradigm. Although it highlights the cultural relativity of the issue of choice, the identity status paradigm does not provide the theoretical concepts with which to understand the types of ego development that might be accomplished by people in cultures that are not choice- and self-oriented. In contrast, in Erikson's general theory, people of all cultures can develop a strong sense of ego identity based on role validation and community integration, especially when there is a lack of ambiguity regarding beliefs (cf. Côté & Levine, 1988b). In speaking to this general issue, E. Erikson (1963) wrote that

> even the most 'savage' culture must strive for what we . . . call a 'strong ego' in its majority or at least in its dominant minority—i.e., an individual core firm and flexible enough to reconcile the necessary contradictions in any human organization, . . . and above all to emerge from . . . infancy with a sense of identity and an idea of integrity. (pp. 185–186)

On the question of cross-cultural applications of the identity status paradigm, precontact Samoan culture would be called a "foreclosed society" (Marcia, 1976). As just argued, however, individuals in all societies should have a generally good sense of ego identity if they are effectively supported by their community. In foreclosed societies they may not have the autonomous form of identity referred to by identity status researchers, but it would be culturally inappropriate for them to have such an autonomous identity. So, herein lies the challenge to identity status researchers—to adapt the paradigm to be sensitive to forms of psychosocial development that occur in other cultures.

Instead of a form of ego development that helps people function in middle-class urban environments, individuals in foreclosed societies likely have other strengths that help them function and continue to mature in those environments (see Mageo, 1989, for a linguistic-anthropological study of the structure self and identity in Samoa). For example, one would expect advanced forms of ego development to be stimulated as Samoans passed through Erikson's last three psychosocial stages of intimacy, generativity, and integrity. All three of these stages appear to have been well-institutionalized in precontact culture, and in Erikson's view, the better institutionalized a stage, the more it nurtures ego development.

In fact, an argument can be made that these stages—particularly generativity and integrity—were more thoroughly institutionalized in precontact Samoan culture than in contemporary Western culture, where the glorification of choice has led to a "selfishness," as opposed to Samoan "otherness." In Erikson's stage hierarchy, fulfilment is derived by becoming less selfish, rather than more selfish, as one encounters the stages of intimacy, generativity, and integrity. Because they were well-institutionalized, one would expect people to enter these stages earlier and to move through them more quickly, thereby accruing and using their associated strengths for a greater portion of their lives. In terms of specific institutions, the *'aumaga* and the *fono*, for example, unquestionably stimulated various skills associated with ego mastery (cf. Reid, 1990).

Nevertheless, some Western readers may still feel that the relative lack of choice may be stress-producing and an impediment to development for many adolescents in any culture. This may be so for some individuals, but if we use Mead's study as a reference point it is unlikely that more than a handful of her informants were bothered by it (i.e., the three "upward deviants"). Certainly, there is ample evidence that Samoan childrearing techniques and cultural conditioning prepared those coming of age for this, by effecting a high degree of conformity-oriented behavior and a low degree of individuated or "creative" behavior (e.g., Holmes, 1987). Indeed, similar childrearing techniques prevail in other South Pacific cultures. As Crocombe (1989) argued, in many South Pacific cultures, typical socialization is such that individuals "have been conditioned by their cultures not to 'push' themselves . . . much of their cultural conditioning has taught them not to innovate, not to work out their own destiny, not to strive to improve their position" (p. 40).

The implications of this cultural conditioning for the identity status paradigm emerge from one of the few cross-cultural studies conducted using that paradigm. In New Zealand, Chapman and Nichols (1976) assessed *occupational* identity status among Maori (Polynesian) and Pakeha (European descent) high school students. They found that more Maori youth were "identity diffused" ("not committed to an occupation and had not seriously contemplated possible occupations"), although more Pakeha youth were "identity achieved" (p. 61). These findings were interpreted with the assertion that "Maoris typically see occupation as a means of providing the necessities of life and of making it possible to extend hospitality while Pakeha more commonly see occupations as a vehicle to and index of success" (p. 65). Noting differing cultural meanings regarding choice and commitment around occupation, Chapman and Nichols argued that the "greater frequency of identity diffusion among Maoris may indicate that this is an adaptive, role-appropriate status for Maoris" (p. 69).

The Chapman and Nichols study suggests that several questions need to be addressed by future research. For example, just why might something like "identity diffusion" be adaptive for one group and not another? And, how might individuals from such groups develop strengths independent of, or in spite of, such conditions. In addition, a specific research question that can be pursued in New Zealand (and other Western countries with indigenous populations) is to identify what replaces *conscious decision making* as a source of ego development in Maori culture. One avenue to explore in this regard is the *guidance* the culture may provide the young that makes conscious decision making unnecessary as a stimulus to development. Interestingly, this brings us back to Mead's concern over conflict and choice, discussed earlier.

A challenge for future research is to adapt theories developed by

Western researchers to other cultures in the sense of determining the psychosocial strengths associated with various forms of cultural conditioning. The past undertheorizing about cultural differences in socialization and human development is an impediment to this task. One starting point is to recognize macro, political-economy perspectives, such as those discussed in the last chapter, and to link them with micro, sociopsychological, and developmental concerns discussed in this chapter.

An issue for this research to deal with pertains to the problem of identity in a world in which there is a declining respect for authority and tradition. This decline of authority has been ongoing in Western societies for some time, but as it has taken root in places like Samoa, its repercussions have been sudden and dramatic. Accordingly, societies like Western Samoa provide a site in which to study change that has accelerated in a very short time, in relation to the less rapid change in Western societies. Comparisons of these changes should shed light on problems faced in both types of societies. For example, it is clear from the study just presented that as a culture grapples with its identity, those attempting to come of age in that culture also grapple with their identity. Thus, change that is too rapid and unregulated is detrimental to identity formation processes. Without a clear sense of identity, humans have a very difficult time functioning as social beings. The dawning global civilization engendered by international capitalism must deal with this, but to do so a sound understanding is needed of the relationship between culture and identity.

These are the types of challenges and issues that inspired Margaret Mead.

References

Adams, G. R., Montemayor, R., & Gullotta, T. P. (1990). *Biology of adolescent behavior and development*. Newbury Park, CA: Sage.

Aiavao, U. (1991, July). Slow suicides in Samoa. *Pacific Islands Monthly*, p. 37.

Ala'ailima, F. (1984). Review of *Margaret Mead and Samoa. Pacific Studies*, 7, 91–92.

Allahar, A. L. (1989). *Sociology and the periphery: Theories & issues*. Toronto: Garamond Press.

Appell, G. N. (1984). Freeman's refutation of Mead's *Coming of Age in Samoa*: The implications for anthropological inquiry. *The Eastern Anthropologist, 37*, 183–214.

Appell, G. N., & Madan, T. N. (1988). *Choice and morality in anthropological perspective: Essays in honor of Derek Freeman*. Albany, NY: State University of New York Press.

Aries, P. (1962). *Centuries of childhood: A social history of the family*. New York: Random House.

Badock, C. R. (1983). *Margaret Mead and Samoa: The making and unmaking of an anthropological myth* [review]. *British Journal of Sociology, 34*, 606–607.

Baker, P. T, Hanna, J. M., & Baker, T. S. (1986). *The changing Samoans: Behavior and health in transition*. New York: Oxford University Press.

Baker, T. S. (1984). *Margaret Mead and Samoa: The making and unmaking of an anthropological myth* [review]. *Human Biology, 56*(2), 402–404.

Baldauf, R. B., Jr., & Ayabe, H. I. (1977). Acculturation and educational achievement in American Samoan adolescence. *Journal of Cross-Cultural Psychology, 8*, 241–255.

Ballantine, J. H. (1989). *The sociology of education: A systematic analysis* (2nd ed.). Englewood Cliffs, NJ: Prentice-Hall.

Barnouw, V. (1983). Coming to print in Samoa: Mead and Freeman. *The Journal of Psychoanalytic Anthropology, 6*, 425–433.

Baumeister, R. F. (1986). *Identity: Cultural change and the struggle for self*. New York: Oxford University Press.

Benedict, R. (1938). Continuities and discontinuities in cultural conditioning. *Psychiatry, 1*, 161–167.

Beneteau, R. (1988, Winter). Trends in suicide. *Canadian Social Trends*, 22–24.

Berg, I. (1970). *Education and jobs: The great training robbery*. New York: Praeger.

Bernard, R. H. (1988). *Research methods in cultural anthropology*. Newbury Park, CA: Sage.

Bock, P. K. (1983). The Samoan puberty blues. *Journal of Anthropological Research, 39*, 336–340.

Bowles, J. R. (1985). Suicide and attempted suicide in contemporary Western Samoa. In F. X. Hezel, D. H. Rubenstein, & G. H. White (Eds.), *Culture, youth and suicide in the Pacific: Papers from an East-West Center Conference* (pp. 15–35). Honolulu: Center for Asian and Pacific Studies, University of Hawaii at Manoa.

Brady, I. (Ed.). (1983). Special section: Speaking in the name of the real: Freeman and Mead on Samoa. *American Anthropologist, 85*, 908–947.

Brady, I. (1991). The Samoan reader: Last word or lost horizon? *Current Anthropology, 32*, 497–500.

Brake, M. (1985). *Comparative youth culture: The sociology of youth cultures and youth subcultures in America, Britain and Canada*. London: Routledge & Kegan Paul.

Brewer, W. K. (1975). *Armed with the spirit: Missionary experiences in Samoa*. Provo, UT: Young House. (Original work published 1930)

Broad, W., & Wade, N. (1982). *Betrayers of the truth: Fraud and deceit in the halls of science*. New York: Simon & Schuster.

Brooks-Gunn, J., & Reiter, E. O. (1990). The role of pubertal processes. In S. S. Feldman & G. R. Elliott (Eds.), *At the threshold: The developing adolescent* (pp. 16–53). Cambridge, MA: Harvard University Press.

Brooks-Gunn, J., & Warren, M. P. (1989). Biological and social contributions to negative affect in young adolescent girls. *Child Development, 60*, 40–55.

Buchholz, T. G. (1984). *Margaret Mead and Samoa: The making and unmaking of an anthropological myth* [review]. *Commentary*, 77, 78–80.

Calkins, F. G. (1962). *My Samoan chief*. Honolulu: University of Hawaii Press.

Cassidy, R. (1982). *Margaret Mead: A voice for the century*. New York: Universe Books.

Caton, H. (1984, March). Margaret Mead and Samoa: In support of Freeman's critique. *Quadrant*, 28–32.

Caton, H. (Ed.). (1990). *The Samoa reader: Anthropologists take stock*. Lanham, MD: University Press of America.

Chapman, J. W., & Nichols, J. G. (1976). Occupational identity status, occupational preference, and field dependence in Maori and Pakeha boys. *Journal of Cross-Cultural Psychology*, 7, 61–72.

Coleman, J. S. (1974). *Youth: Transition to adulthood*. Chicago: University of Chicago Press.

Collins, R. (1979). *The credential society: A historical sociology of education and stratification*. New York: Academic Press.

Column Seven. (1991, January 11). *Samoa Times*, p. 2.

Côté, J. E. (1986). Identity crisis modality: A technique for measuring the structure of the identity crisis. *Journal of Adolescence, 9*, 321–325.

Côté, J. E. (1992). Was Mead wrong about coming of age in Samoa? An analysis of the Mead/Freeman controversy for scholars of adolescence and human development. *Journal of Youth and Adolescence, 21*, 499–527.

Côté, J. E. (1993). Foundations of a psychoanalytic social psychology: Neo-Eriksonian propositions regarding the relationship between psychic structure and cultural institutions. *Developmental Review, 13*, 31–53.

Côté, J. E., & Levine, C. (1987). A formulation of Erikson's theory of ego identity formation. *Developmental Review, 9*, 273–325.

Côté, J. E., & Levine, C. (1988a). A critical examination of the ego identity status paradigm. *Developmental Review, 9*, 147–184.

Côté, J. E., & Levine, C. (1988b). The relationship between ego identity status and Erikson's notions of institutionalized moratoria, value orientation state, and ego dominance. *Journal of Youth and Adolescence*, *17*, 81–99.

Cox, P. A., & Elmqvist, T. (1991). Indigenous control of tropical rainforest reserves: An alternative strategy for conservation. *Ambio*, *20*, 317–321.

Cranberg, L. (1983a). Ta'u revisited. *Human Organization*, *42*, 182.

Cranberg, L. (1983b, July). Samoa [Letter to the editor]. *Life*, p. 19.

Crocombe, R. (1989). *The South Pacific: An introduction* (5th ed.). Suva, Fiji: University of the South Pacific.

Demos, J., & Demos, V. (1969, November). Adolescence in historical perspective. *Journal of Marriage and The Family*, 632–638.

Department of Economic Development, Western Samoa. (1987). *Western Samoa's Sixth Development Plan: 1988–1990*. Apia, Western Samoa: Author.

Department of Statistics, Western Samoa. (1989). *Annual Statistical Abstract 1989*. Apia, Western Samoa: Author.

Douglas, N., & Douglas, N. G. (1986). *Pacific Islands yearbook* (15th ed.). North Ryde, NSW, Australia: Angus & Robertson.

Drug abuse hits schools. (1991, November). *Pacific Island Monthly*, p. 23.

Education Director backs new exam system. (1991, January 30). *Samoa Observer*, p. 1.

Ember, M. (1985). Evidence and science in ethnography: Reflections on the Mead-Freeman controversy. *American Anthropologist*, *87*, 906–910.

Erikson, E. H. (1956). The problem of ego identity. *Journal of the American Psychoanalytic Association*, *4*, 56–122.

Erikson, E. H. (1958). *Young man Luther*. New York: Norton.

Erikson, E. H. (1963). *Childhood and society* (2nd ed.). New York: Norton.

Erikson, E. H. (1968). *Identity: Youth and crisis*. New York: Norton.

Erikson, E. H. (1980). *Identity and the life cycle: A reissue*. New York: Norton.

Erikson, K. (1966). *Wayward puritans: A study in the sociology of deviance*. New York: Wiley.

Feinberg, R. (1988). Margaret Mead and Samoa: *Coming of Age* in fact and fiction. *American Anthropologist*, *90*, 656–663.

Festinger, L. (1957). *A theory of cognitive dissonance*. New York: Harper & Row.

Filoiali'i, L. A., & Knowles, K. (1982). The ifoga: The Samoan practice of seeking forgiveness for criminal behaviour. *Oceania*, *53*, 384–388.

Flay, B. R., Bull, P. E., & Tamahori, J. (1976). Designing a questionnaire for Polynesian and Pakeha car assembly workers. *Journal of Cross-Cultural Psychology*, 7, 235–241.

Freeman, D. (1983). *Margaret Mead and Samoa: The making and unmaking of an anthropological myth*. Cambridge, MA: Harvard University Press.

Freeman, D. (1985). A reply to Ember's reflections on the Freeman-Mead controversy. *American Anthropologist*, *87*, 910–917.

Freeman, D. (1987a). Comment on Holmes's quest for the real Samoa. *American Anthropologist*, *89*, 930–935.

Freeman, D. (1987b). Holmes, Lowell D.: *Quest for the real Samoa: The Mead/Freeman controversy and beyond* [review]. *Journal of the Polynesian Society*, *96*(3), 392–395.

Freeman, D. (1987c). Towards an anthropology both scientific and humanistic. *Canberra Anthropology*, 44–69.

Freeman, D. (1989a). Fa'apua'a Fa'amu and Margaret Mead. *American Anthropologist*, *91*, 1017–1022.

Freeman, D. (1989b). Holmes, Mead, and Samoa. *American Anthropologist*, *91*, 758–762.

Freeman, D. (1991). There's tricks i' th' world: An historical analysis of the Samoan researches of Margaret Mead. *Visual Anthropology Review*, 7, 103–128.

Freeman, D. (1992). Paradigms in collision: The far-reaching controversy over the Samoan researches of Margaret Mead and its significance for the human sciences. *Academic Questions, 5*(3), 23–33.

Gailey, C. W. (1987). *Kinship to kingship: Gender hierarchy and state formation in the Tongan Islands.* Austin: University of Texas Press.

Gerber, E. R. (1975). *The cultural patterning of emotions in Samoa.* Unpublished doctoral dissertation, University of California, San Diego.

Gilson, R. P. (1970). *Samoa 1830 to 1900.* London: Oxford University Press.

Gold, M. G., & Petronio, R. J. (1980). Delinquent behavior in adolescence. In J. Adelson (Ed.), *Handbook of adolescent psychology* (pp. 495–535). New York: Wiley.

Goodale, J. (1984). *Margaret Mead and Samoa: The making and unmaking of an anthropological myth* [review]. *Pacific Affairs, 57,* 180–182.

Goodman, R. A. (1983). *Mead's Coming of Age in Samoa: A dissenting view.* Oakland, CA: Pipperline Press.

Gould, S. J. (1981). *The mismeasure of man.* New York: Norton.

Grattan, F. J. H. (1948). *An introduction to Samoan culture.* Papakura, New Zealand: R. McMillan.

Greksa, L. P., Pelletier, D. L., & Gage, T. B. (1986). Work in contemporary and traditional Samoa. In P. T. Baker, J. M. Hanna, & T. S. Baker (Eds.), *The changing Samoans: Behavior and health in transition* (pp. 297–326). New York: Oxford University Press.

Handler, R. (1984). Review essay/Ruth Benedict, Margaret Mead, and the growth of American anthropology. *The Journal of American History, 71,* 364–368.

Hanson, F. A. (1973). Political change in Tahiti and Samoa: An exercise in experimental anthropology. *Ethos, 12,* 1–12.

Harris, M. (1983). Margaret and the giant-killer: It doesn't matter a whit who's right. *The Sciences, 23*(4), 18–21.

Heimans, F. (producer). (1988). *Margaret Mead and Samoa* [film]. New York: Brighton Video.

Holmes, L. D. (1957a). *A restudy of Manu'a culture: A problem of methodology.* Unpublished doctoral dissertation, Northwestern University, Chicago, IL.

Holmes, L. D. (1957b). Ta'u: Stability and change in a Samoan village. *Polynesian Society Journal, 66,* 301–338, 398–435.

Holmes, L. D. (1974). *Samoan village.* New York: Holt, Rinehart & Winston.

Holmes, L. D. (1980a). Factors contributing to the cultural stability of Samoa. *Anthropological Quarterly, 53,* 188–197.

Holmes, L. D. (1980b). Cults, cargo and Christianity: Samoan responses to Western religion. *Missiology: An International Review, 8,* 471–487.

Holmes, L. D. (1983a). Margaret Mead's Samoa: Views and reviews. *The Quarterly Review of Biology, 58,* 539–544.

Holmes, L. D. (1983b). South seas squall: Derek Freeman's long-nurtured, ill-natured attack on Margaret Mead. *The Sciences, 23,* 14–18.

Holmes, L. D. (1983c). On the questioning of as many as six impossible things about Freeman's Samoa before breakfast. *Canberra Anthropology, 6,* 1–16.

Holmes, L. D. (1987). *Quest for the real Samoa: The Mead/Freeman controversy and beyond.* South Hadley, MA: Bergin & Garvey.

Holmes, L. D., & Holmes, E. R. (1992). *Samoan village then and now* (2nd ed.). Fort Worth: Harcourt Brace Jovanovich.

Hooper, A. (1984). *Margaret Mead and Samoa: The making and unmaking of an anthropological myth* [review]. *Oceania, 55,* 224–225.

Howard, A., & Kirkpatrick, J. (1989). Social organization. In A. Howard & R. Borofsky (Eds.), *Developments in Polynesian ethnology* (pp. 47–93). Honolulu: University of Hawaii Press.

Hunt, T. L., & Kirch, P. V. (1988). An archaeological survey of the Manu'a Islands, American Samoa. *Polynesian Society Journal, 97*, 153–183.

Immigration Division, Department of Labour, New Zealand. (1982). *Samoan Guide to Permanent Entry into New Zealand*. New Zealand: Author.

Irwin, G. (1965). *Samoa: A teacher's tale*. London: Cassell.

Karlsen, C. F. (1987). *The devil in the shape of a woman: Witchcraft in colonial New England*. New York: Norton.

Katchadourian, H. (1977). *The biology of adolescence*. San Francisco: Freeman.

Keesing, F. (1934). *Modern Samoa*. London: Allen & Unwin.

King, J. (1981, July/August). The myth of suicide in American Samoa. *The New Pacific Magazine*, pp. 15–18.

Klein, H. (1990). Adolescence, youth, and young adulthood: Rethinking current conceptualizations of life stage. *Youth & Society, 21*, 446–471.

Krauze, T., & Slomczynski, K. M. (1985). How far to meritocracy? Empirical tests of a controversial thesis. *Social Forces, 63*, 623–642.

Kuklick, H. (1984). *Margaret Mead and Samoa: The making and unmaking of an anthropological myth* [review]. *Contemporary Sociology, 13*, 558–562.

Labour Department, Western Samoa. (1984). *Labour Department Annual Report: 1984*. Apia, Western Samoa: Author.

Laing, P. K. (1987). Holmes, Lowell D.: *Quest for the real Samoa: The Mead/Freeman controversy and beyond* [review]. *Journal of the Polynesian Society, 96*, 395–399.

Leach, E. (1983). The Shangri-la that never was. *New Society, 63*, 477–478.

Leacock, E. (1987). Postscript: The problems of youth in contemporary Samoa. In L. D. Holmes (Ed.), *Quest for the real Samoa: The Mead/Freeman controversy and beyond* (pp. 177–188). South Hadley, MA: Bergin & Garvey.

Leacock, E. (1988). Anthropologists in search of a culture: Margaret Mead, Derek Freeman, and all the rest of us. *Central Issues in Anthropology, 8*, 3–23.

Levy, R. I. (1984). Mead, Freeman, and Samoa: The problem of seeing things as they are. *Ethos, 12*, 85–92.

Linnekin, J. (1991). Fine mats and money: Contending exchange paradigms in colonial Samoa. *Anthropological Quarterly, 64*, 1–12.

Lockhart, A. (1971). Graduate unemployment and the myth of human capital. In D. T Davies & K. Herman (Eds.), *Social space: Canadian perspective*. Toronto: New Press.

Lockhart, A. (1975). Future failure: The unanticipated consequences of educational planning. In R. M. Pike & E. Zureik (Eds.), *Socialization and values in Canadian society* (pp. 196–215). Toronto: McClelland-Stewart.

Lockwood, B. (1971). *Samoan village economy*. Melbourne: Oxford University Press.

Lockwood, V. S. (1993). *Tahitian transformations: Gender & capitalist development in a rural society*. Boulder, CO: Lynne Rienner.

MacPherson, C. (1988). The road to power is a chainsaw: Villages and innovation in Western Samoa. *Pacific Studies, 11*, 1–24.

MacPherson, C., & MacPherson, L. (1985). Suicide in Western Samoa: A sociological perspective. In F. X. Hezel, D. H. Rubenstein, & G. M. White (Eds.), *Culture, youth and suicide in the Pacific: Papers from the East-West Center Conference* (pp. 36–73). Honolulu: East-West Center.

Mageo, J. M. (1988). Malosi: A psychological exploration of Mead's and Freeman's work and of Samoan agression. *Pacific Studies, 11*, 25–65.

Mageo, J. M. (1989). Aga, Amio and Loto: Perspectives on the structure of the self in Samoa. *Oceania, 59*, 181–199.

Malifa, S. (1975). *Looking down at waves: A collection of poems*. Suva, Fiji: Mana Publications.

Marcia, J. E. (1964). *Determination and construct validation of ego identity status*. Unpublished doctoral dissertation, Ohio State University, Columbus.

Marcia, J. E. (1976). *Studies in ego identity*. Unpublished manuscript.

Marcia, J. E. (1980). Identity in adolescence. In J. Adelson (Ed.), *Handbook of adolescent psychology* (pp. 159–187). New York: Wiley.

Marquardt, C. (1984). *The tattooing of both sexes in Samoa* (S. Ferner, Trans.). Papakura, New Zealand: R. McMillan. (Original work published 1899)

Maugham, W. S. (1985). *The trembling of a leaf*. Honolulu, HI: Mutual Publishing.

McCabe, B. (1992, April). Samoan sights on new business. *Pacific Islands Monthly*, p. 39.

McDowell, N. (1984). Review of *Margaret Mead and Samoa*. *Pacific Studies*, *4*, 99–140.

McGovern, B. (1988). *Western Samoa*. Sydney, Australia: South Pacific Trade Commission.

Mead, M. (1928). *Coming of age in Samoa: A psychological study of primitive youth for Western Civilization*. New York: Morrow Quill Paperbacks.

Mead, M. (1931). The role of the individual in Samoan culture. In A. L. Kroeber & T. T. Waterman (Eds.), *Source book in Anthropology* (pp. 545–561). New York: Harcourt, Brace & World.

Mead, M. (1937). A reply to a review of "sex and temperament in three primitive societies." *American Anthropologist*, *39*, 558–561.

Mead, M. (1961). [Review of] *Ta'u: Stability and change in a Samoan village*, by Lowell D. Holmes. *American Anthropologist*, *63*, 428–430.

Mead, M. (1969). *Social organization of Manu'a* (2nd ed.). Honolulu: Bernice P. Bishop Museum. (Original work published 1930)

Mead, M. (1972). *Blackberry winter: My earlier years*. New York: Morrow.

Mead, M. (1977). *Letters from the field, 1925–1975*. New York: Harper & Row.

Meleisea, M. (1987a). *Lagaga: A short history of Western Samoa*. Suva, Fiji: University of South Pacific.

Meleisea, M. (1987b). *The making of modern Samoa: Traditional authority and colonial administration in the modern history of Western Samoa*. Suva, Fiji: Institute of Pacific Studies of the University of the South Pacific.

Meleisea, M., & Meleisea, P. (1980). "The best kept secret": Tourism in Western Samoa. In Institute of Pacific Studies (Eds.), *Pacific tourism: As islanders see it*. Suva, Fiji: University of the South Pacific.

Montemayor, R., Adams, G. R., & Gullotta, T. P. (1990). *From childhood to adolescence: A transitional period?* Newbury Park, CA: Sage.

Montemayor, R., & Flannery, D. J. (1990). Making the transition from childhood to early adolescence. In R. Montemayor, G. R. Adams, & T. P. Gullotta (Eds.), *From childhood to adolescence: A transitional period?* (pp.). Newbury Park, CA: Sage.

Moyle, R. (Ed.). (1984). *The Samoan journals of John Williams 1830–1832*. Canberra: Australian National University Press.

Muensterberger, W. (1985). *Margaret Mead and Samoa: The making and unmaking of an anthropological myth* [review]. *Psychoanalytic Quarterly*, *54*, 101–105.

Murray, S. O. (1990). Problematic aspects of Freeman's account of Boasian culture. *Current Anthropology*, *31*, 401–407.

Murray, S. O. (1991). On Boasians and Margaret Mead: Reply to Freeman. *Current Anthropology*, *32*, 448–452.

Muse, C. J. (1991). Women in Western Samoa. In L. A. Adler (Ed.), *Women in cross-cultural perspective* (pp. 221–240). New York: Praeger.

Muuss, R. E. (1988). *Theories of adolescence* (5th ed.). New York: Random House.

Nardi, B. A. (1984). The height of her powers: Margaret Mead's Samoa. *Feminist Studies*, *10*, 323–337.

Natarajan, N. (1983). *Rural development projects and women in Western Samoa. ILO study*. Apia, Western Samoa: University of South Pacific.

Ngan-Woo, F. E. (1985). *FaaSamoa: The world of Samoans*. Auckland, New Zealand: Office of the Race Relations Conciliator.

North, D. (1991, February). American Samoans doing the most. *Pacific Islands Monthly*, p. 25.

North, D. (1993, April). Sputtering unions. *Pacific Islands Monthly*, p. 12.

Norton, R. (1984). Titles, wealth and faction: Electoral politics in a Samoan village. *Oceania*, *55*, 100–117.

O'Meara, T. (1990). *Samoan planters: Tradition and economic development in Polynesia*. Fort Worth, TX: Holt, Rinehart & Winston.

Offer, D., & Offer, J. B. (1975). *From teenage to young manhood: A psychological study*. New York: Basic Books.

Oliver, D. (1961). *The Pacific Islands*. New York: Doubleday.

Paikoff, R. L., & Brooks-Gunn, J. (1991). Do parent–child relationships change during puberty? *Psychological Bulletin*, *110*, 47–66.

Park, C. B. (1980). *The population of American Samoa*. Honolulu: University of Hawaii School of Public Health and East-West Population Institute.

Patience, A., & Smith, J. W. (1986). Derek Freeman and Samoa: The making and unmaking of a biobehavioral myth. *American Anthropologist*, *88*, 157–162.

Paxman, D. B. (1988). Freeman, Mead, and the eighteenth-century controversy over Polynesian society. *Pacific Studies*, *11*, 1–19.

Petaia, R. (1980). *Blue rain*. Apia, Samoa: U.S.P Centre, Western Samoa.

Pfieffer, M., & Côté, J. E. (1991). Inglehart's silent revolution thesis: An examination of life-cycle effects in the acquisition of postmaterialist values. *Social Behavior and Personality*, *19*, 223–235.

Phillips, D. P. (1979). Suicide, motor vehicle fatalities and the mass media: Evidence toward a theory of suggestion. *Sociological Review*, *84*, 1150–1174.

Pitt, D. (1970). *Tradition and economic progress in Samoa: A case study of the role of traditional social institutions in economic development*. Oxford: Clarendon Press.

Pitt, D., & MacPherson, C. (1974). *Emerging pluralism: The Samoan community in New Zealand*. Auckland, New Zealand: Longman Paul.

Police & Prisons Department, Western Samoa (1965). *Annual Report of the Police & Prisons Department—1965*. Apia, Western Samoa: Author.

Popper, K. (1968). *The logic of scientific discovery*. New York: Harper & Row.

Porter, J. (1984). Education and the just society. In A. Himelfarb & C. J. Richardson (Eds.), *Sociology for Canadians: A reader* (pp. 460–473). Toronto: McGraw-Hill Ryerson.

Rappaport, R. A. (1986). Desecrating the holy woman: Derek Freeman's attack on Margaret Mead. *American Scholar*, *55*(3), 313–347.

Rappaport, R. A. (1987a). Reply to Freeman. *American Scholar, 56*(2), 304.

Rappaport, R. A. (1987b). Reply to Freeman. *Scientific American*, *256*, 6–7.

Reid, B. V. (1990). Weighing up the factors: Moral reasoning and culture change in a Samoan community. *Ethos*, *18*, 48–70.

Reyman, J. E. (1985). Some comments on the Freeman-Mead controversy. *American Anthropologist*, *87*, 393–394.

Robie, D. (1991, January). Troubled times reflected in Samoans' inner search [film review]. *Pacific Islands Monthly*, pp. 45–46.

Rokeach, M. (1960). *The open and closed mind*. New York: Basic.

Rowe, N. A. (1930). *Samoa under the sailing gods*. London: Putnam.

Rubinstein, D. H. (1985). Suicide in Micronesia. In F. K. Hezel, D. H. Rubenstein, & G. H. White (Eds.), *Culture, youth and suicide in the Pacific: Papers from an East-West Center Conference* (pp. 88–111). Honolulu: Center for Asian and Pacific Studies, University of Hawaii at Manoa.

Salmi, J. (1992). The higher education crisis in developing countries: Issues, problems, constraints and reforms. *International Review of Education*, *38*, 19–33.

Scheper-Hughes, N. (1984). The Margaret Mead controversy: Culture, biology, and anthropological inquiry. *Human Organization, 43*, 85–93.

Schoeffel, P. (1979). *Daughters of Sina: A study of gender, status and power in Western Samoa*. Unpublished doctoral dissertation, Australian National University, Canberra.

Schoeffel, P. (1986). *The Samoan journals of John Williams 1830–1832* [review]. *Oceania, 57*, 63–64.

Schoeffel, P., & Meleisea, M. (1983). Margaret Mead, Derek Freeman and Samoa: The making, unmaking and remaking of an anthropolical myth. *Canberra Anthropology, 6*, 58–69.

Seligman, M. E. P. (1988, October). Boomer blues. *Psychology Today*, pp. 50–55.

Shankman, P. (1983). The Samoan conundrum. *Canberra Anthropology, 6*(1), 38–57.

Shore, B. (1982). *Sala'ilua: A Samoan mystery*. New York: Columbia University Press.

Shore, B. (1983). Paradox regained: Freeman's Margaret Mead and Samoa. *American Anthropologist, 85*, 935–944.

Special youth jail? (1992, April). *Pacific Island Monthly*, p. 16.

Spindler, G., & Spindler, L. (1990). *Foreword*. In T. O'Meara, *Samoan planters: Tradition and economic development in Polynesia*. Fort Worth, TX: Holt, Rinehart & Winston.

Sprinthall, N. A., & Collins, W. A. (1984). *Adolescent psychology: A developmental view*. Reading, MA: Addison-Wesley.

Stack, S. (1987). Celebrities and suicide: A taxonomy and analysis. *American Sociological Review, 52*, 401–412.

Stair, J. B. (1983). *Old Samoa or flotsam and jetsam from the Pacific Ocean*. Papakura, New Zealand: R. McMillan. (Original work published 1897)

Stanner, W. E. H. (1953). *The south seas in transition*. Sydney: Australasian Publishing Co.

Swaney, D. (1990). *Samoa: Western & American Samoa*. Hawthorn, Victoria, Australia: Lonely Planet Publications.

Taxi license deadline extended. (1991, January 11). *Samoa Observer*, p. 1.

Tepperman, L. (1977). *Crime control: The urge toward authority*. Toronto: McGraw-Hill Ryerson.

Treasury Department of the Government of Western Samoa. (1988). *Western Samoa: Setting a new course for growth*. Institutional Investor.

Tribe, K. (1984). *Margaret Mead and Samoa: The making and unmaking of an anthropological myth* [review]. *Sociological Review, 32*, 398–401.

Turnbull, C. M. (1983, March 28). *Margaret Mead and Samoa: The making and unmaking of an anthropological myth* [review]. *The New Republic*, 32–34.

Turner, G. (1986). *Samoa: Nineteen years in Polynesia*. Apia, Samoa: Western Samoa Historical and Cultural Trust. (Original work published 1861)

Twain, M. (1924). Autobiography. New York: Harper & Brothers.

Ward, R. G. (1967). *American activities in the central Pacific 1790–1870 Vol. 6*. Ridgewood, NJ: The Gregg Press.

Wendt, A. (1973). *Sons for the return home*. London: Penguin.

Wendt, A. (1974). *Some poetry from Western Samoa*. Suva, Fiji: Mana Publications.

Wendt, A. (1977). *Pouliuli*. London: Penguin.

Wendt, A. (1979). *Leaves of the banyon tree*. London: Penguin.

Wendt, A. (1983, April). Three faces of Samoa: Mead's, Freeman's and Wendt's. *Pacific Islands Monthly*, pp. 10–14, 69.

Wendt, F. (1984). Review of Margaret Mead and Samoa. *Pacific Studies, 40*, 92–99.

Western Samoa push for investment. (1992, April). *Pacific Island Monthly*, p. 31.

Williamson, R. W. (1975). *Essays in Polynesian ethnology*. Cambridge: Cambridge University Press. (Original work published 1939)

Young, R. E., & Juan, S. (1985). Freeman's Margaret Mead myth: The ideological virginity of anthropologists. *Australia and New Zealand Journal of Sociology, 21*, 64–81.

Yusuf, S., & Peters, R. K. (1985). *Western Samoa: The Experience of Slow Growth and Resource Imbalance (World Bank Staff Working Papers)*. Washington: The World Bank.

Author Index

W

Y

Subject Index

N

P

R

S

T

For Product Safety Concerns and Information please contact our EU representative GPSR@taylorandfrancis.com
Taylor & Francis Verlag GmbH, Kaufingerstraße 24, 80331 München, Germany

www.ingramcontent.com/pod-product-compliance
Ingram Content Group UK Ltd.
Pitfield, Milton Keynes, MK11 3LW, UK
UKHW021959180926
475701UK00003B/97

* 9 7 8 1 1 3 8 8 7 3 3 1 5 *